BLACKPOOL

THE COMPLETE RECORD

1887-2011

BLACKPOOL

THE COMPLETE RECORD

1887-2011

ROY CALLEY

DB PUBLISHING

First published in Great Britain in 2011 by The Derby Books Publishing Company Limited,
3 The Parker Centre, Derby, DE21 4SZ.

This paperback edition published in Great Britain in 2014 by DB Publishing, an imprint of JMD Media Ltd

ISBN 978-178091-380-3

Printed and bound in the UK by Copytech (UK) Ltd Peterborough

CONTENTS

Foreword	6
Introduction	9
The History of Blackpool	10
The Bloomfield Road Story	88
Matches to Remember	96
Blackpool stars	138
Blackpool Managers	230
League Seasons	258
Blackpool FC Statistics	486
Internationals	487
Player Records	489
Roll of Honour	509

Foreword

Blackpool Football Club's souvenir shop has among its merchandise a birthday card, which on the front has the words 'Happy Birthday to the Seasiders number-one fan.'

Roy Calley could well have received one of those cards, as I expect all who have known him will vouch for the fact that, despite his living in the South, he still eats, lives and breathes Blackpool FC. Not bad for someone who grew up supporting the team through some of the more difficult days. Whatever, he has stuck with them through thick and thin, and now he feels the time has come to put into words what it has been like for someone like him supporting the Pool, quite often from a distance, in this new and updated version of the *Complete Record.*

I first met Roy when he became a football producer with BBC Radio, and we would talk about the fortunes of our team long before we ever got round to discussing the live commentary the next day. Roy always had his priorities in place, Blackpool FC first, second, third…

I have always had the same passion for my only club, and I feel sure that Roy, through the statistics, reports, and biographies in this book, will relate the agonies and ecstasies that follow when you support a club like ours.

My good wishes...

Jim Armfield

FOREWORD

Blackpool FC grabbed my attention early in life. How could it have been otherwise? Brought up within a mile of the ground in South Shore, I was taken to my first game at Bloomfield Road at the age of seven. At that time (the very end of the 1960s and start of the 1970s), whether in the concrete playground at Thames Road Junior School or the perfectly-manicured fields(!) at Hampton Road or Fisher's Field, I dreamt of being Alan Suddick, Tony Green or Tommy Hutchison. Later on, my heroes became Micky Walsh and Bob Hatton, then Colin Morris and Dave Bamber.

But players come and go; that's the nature of football. And it's why the supporters are the lifeblood of any club. Blackpool began their lengthy downward spiral by suffering relegation to the Third Division in 1978 (on the night before my first 'O' Level!). The next 29 years in the bottom two tiers were largely grim ones, though not without some fun along the way. As I often joked then, supporting Blackpool was akin to a life sentence with no opportunity for parole!

Yet looking back, I wouldn't have it any other way. There is something special about fans who support their local club and there is something very special about Blackpool, both as a town and as a football club. Like many others, I have had to move away to seek fame and fortune (or at least to find a job which pays the mortgage!). But even now, I still love the buzz of leaving Euston to get to a home match and hopping on the 'rattler' to Blackpool South, to the sun and the sea and the sand and, of course, Bloomfield Road.

Roy Calley has had a similar journey, supporting the Pool since boyhood. His original book, *Blackpool: A Complete Record*, published in 1992, has pride of place on my bookshelves. I am delighted Roy has decided to update the book. I know how hard he has worked on it and I recommend it to all those who love Blackpool FC.

It is fitting that this new book coincides with an upturn in Blackpool's fortunes and it would be remiss of me not to thank the players and managers, especially Simon Grayson, Tony Parkes and particularly Ian Holloway for making our dreams come true. Despite our heartbreaking relegation from the Premier League, we've just witnessed a wonderful season.

We've played football as it's meant to be played and hopefully encouraged a new generation of Seasiders who will be proud of their town and proud of their team.

The future is still bright, the future is tangerine!

David Oates
BBC Radio Sport Football Commentator
27.05.11

Introduction

When Blackpool FC were promoted to the Premier League in May 2010, I felt it was the best time to update the book I had worked on as a labour of love 19 years previously. In those days there was no internet, and research was a tedious affair, with long hours spent looking at old micro-films of aged newspapers. When the publishers kindly agreed to update the book, I remembered how difficult the original was to work on and whether I would be able to do the justice the club's history deserves. As it was, after reading the 1992 version, I decided a complete re-write was needed. This is the book that you have now.

As with all statistical records, they can be open to conjecture and are almost impossible to be totally accurate. The main criticism of the early book was that there were questions concerning team line-ups in the late 19th and early 20th centuries, but as the records were taken from the contemporary local newspapers, their mistakes become my mistakes. The problem is that when football was a fledgling sport, it was anything but professional. Players would wear shirts without numbers, and many would literally drift in and out of the game, sometimes to be replaced by another without any acknowledgement. Also attendances were quite often a casual affair with the local reporter either guessing the number, or the club rounding up the figure to the next thousand. The two World Wars were especially haphazard unsurprisingly, especially as Blackpool in particular had many 'guest' players. Thankfully, the Football League started compiling records from 1925, which made the research a lot easier – but there will still be mistakes which someone will point out, I'm sure.

I hope I have been true to the club with its history, and the biographies of the managers and the top players will hopefully be self-explanatory. As for the 'matches to remember', they were chosen as defining moments for the club, although I'm aware that certain games will be missing, such as the FA Cup victory over Arsenal in 1970 and the win at Kidderminster in September 2000, these matches were omitted due to the fact that more important games took place in that period.

I don't deny that this has been another labour-of-love, but also far more difficult than I expected, and I thank the fans who have helped along the way. I hope you enjoy reading it, and hopefully it will sit comfortably alongside the other excellent books written about our beloved football club. Here's to the next one.

Roy Calley
Summer 2011

The History of Blackpool

At 4.52pm on Saturday 22 May 2010 referee Andre Marriner looked at his watch, glanced at his two linesmen and then blew his whistle to bring one of the most entertaining Championship Play-off Finals in history to an end. In so doing, he delighted the hearts of 37,000 Blackpool fans bedecked in tangerine, plus many more up and down the country, who had willed the famous old club to victory. It was the conclusion to a fairytale that played out its last act at a sweltering Wembley stadium as Blackpool Football Club returned to the top flight of English football for the first time since 1971.

The celebrations that followed were rapturous, both on and off the field, as the enormity of the achievement hit home, and the words that were broadcast by the stadium PA announcer, 'Blackpool are in the Premier League,' will live long in the memory of those who heard them. As fans, players, management and officials hugged, danced, cried and cheered in an outpouring of emotion not seen at the stadium for some time, there was a sense of disbelief too. They had witnessed an extraordinary 90 minutes of football that had summed up the 2009–10 season for Blackpool. Brash, attacking football mixed with flair and colour, mirroring the town and its image – a fitting tribute to the many names and images that have defined the club down its long and illustrious history.

Blackpool as a town has always had both good and bad times. The heyday, when thousands of visitors embarked on its famous promenade to take in the many miles of golden sand, tease themselves with the arcades and the attractions of the Pleasure Beach and the required trip to the top of the Tower, occurred after the war and continued reasonably unabated until the mid–1970s. However, with the advent of cheaper air travel and the desire to explore beyond our shores, Blackpool fell from grace, and its appeal became like that of an older and former lover – once elegant and desirable but now a sad reminder of days past. The attraction of the resort now lay in cheap weekends of hedonistic pleasures, of stag and hen weekends supported by numerous drinking establishments. The weekend away in Blackpool became a by-word for raunchy behaviour and unsolicited extravagances. Only now, in the 21st century, are we seeing the town's return to its former grandeur with extensive regeneration of the most popular attractions.

Unsurprisingly, the football club has ebbed and flowed in almost exact unison with the town. The Seasiders were one of the country's biggest draws both before and after World War Two, and it is one of the great domestic sporting mysteries that they were not far more successful. Players of such note and talent as Stanley Matthews, Stan Mortenson, Alan Ball, Jimmy Armfield and Tony Green, added to earlier stars like Jimmy Hampson, have left their indelible mark on the club and indeed the footballing world in general. It was only in the last two decades of the 20th century that the club completely fell from grace, and as the town struggled to retain the respect of the people, so did the football club struggle to retain the stature it had gained in previous times. Fortunately, the players and the teams of that era ensured that the Bloomfield Road club remained one of the most famous and well-loved in the country, and with the return of success that outpouring of affection should continue for quite some time.

Blackpool Football Club is still best remembered for its great team of the 1950s and especially for the famous 'Matthews Cup Final' of 1953, when they came back from a 3–1 deficit with 20 minutes remaining to snatch a 4–3 victory over Bolton Wanderers in the dying seconds to win the FA Cup for the first and only time to date. During that post-war period, the Seasiders made three Wembley FA Cup appearances in six years and flirted with the League Championship on more than one occasion. They also supplied the national teams with many players, notably in 1953 when four Blackpool men lined up for England at Wembley, causing the *Daily Mirror* to pen the headline 'Blackpool FC are playing Hungary today,' albeit on a day that English football would later want to forget. Yet the story of Blackpool Football Club is not just about the great team of that era. Two decades earlier the town had a team of which it could also be proud, with players such as Hampson and Peter Doherty delighting both home and opposing supporters alike, and later the mini-European triumphs in the early 1970s gave a reminder of what could have been if such competition had been introduced at an earlier date.

There have, of course, been many frustrations and failures over the years. Long-standing supporters will remember the ignominy of applying for Football League re-election in the early 1980s and the depressing football played in that time in front of sparse attendances in a dilapidated ground that only seemed to exist through sheer willpower. Those days, thankfully, seem to be behind the club, and with top-flight football back at the new-and-improved Bloomfield Road the future is bright – the future is Tangerine.

The Beginning

It is generally believed that Blackpool Football Club was formed on 26 July 1887 and came about through a breakaway group from St John's FC. This is open to conjecture, though, as there does appear to be documentary proof of a Blackpool club existing 10 years previously, and in a published history of Blackburn Rovers FC there is a reference to a game against Blackpool in December 1880, but whether this was the early incarnation of the club we know today is not clear. It is possible that it was referring to Victoria FC, who played their games on Manchester's Field, off Caunce Street, but without further details we have no choice but to go with the generally accepted version of how the club was formed.

The St John's club had been in existence for about 10 years and had risen, phoenix-like, from the ashes of the disbanded Victoria Club. Five members of St John's – Revd N.S. Jeffrey, Sam Bancroft, Dick Swanbrick, Dick Worthington and W.J Brown – felt the town of Blackpool should have a football club bearing its name, and after a healthy disagreement with the other members they left the club and went next door to the Stanley Arms Hotel, where they immediately founded Blackpool Football Club. The new organisation appeared

Blackpool 1887–88.

to be of more interest than the old as gradually the players switched from one to the other, and this new team entered their first competitive game against Chorley at Dole Lane. They recorded a 2–1 victory, and Hargreaves will be the man forever listed as the scorer of Blackpool's first-ever goal, 'a ponderous kick half the length of the field'. Corry added a second before the hosts scored a late consolation. The debut season was reasonably successful for the fledgling club as they went on to win the Fylde Cup and the Lancashire Junior Cup. The victory in the latter competition was gained at the expense of Preston St Joseph's in a game that was played at Preston North End's Deepdale ground, a venue Blackpool were displeased with as they rightly argued its lack of neutrality. It was played on 24 March 1888, and the Seasiders won 2–1 courtesy of goals from Nelson and Parr, who scored the winner in the last minute.

The club also managed to announce a profit of some £20 at the end of the campaign, with £66 being contributed in membership and subscription fees. It is fair to say that the club started the way they meant to go on, as debts have rarely played a major part in Blackpool's history. The profit was almost trebled by the end of the following season, when Blackpool became one of the founder members of the Lancashire League. Their home, Raikes Hall Gardens (or the Royal Palace Gardens, as it was commonly known), was part of a vast entertainment complex that included a theatre, boating lake, scenic railway and a racecourse. It was a huge success at the time, but at the turn of the century, with the piers, promenade and Winter Gardens becoming a much bigger attraction, it was sold in an almost derelict state. Today there is little, if anything, to remind the locals of either the football ground or the complex because it was redeveloped as housing and now is part of the suburbia of the town. Attendances at the Gardens for Blackpool's games averaged around the 2,000 figure, so those early years were certainly a financial success for the club.

The fact that the club existed at all was in no small part to the vision of the men that night in the Stanley Arms Hotel and also to the rivalry that quickly built up between Blackpool and their neighbours, South Shore Football Club. Games between the two were fiercely contested, and when the two amalgamated some years later it caused a certain amount of anguish among long-standing supporters. After a particularly one-sided 4–0 victory for Blackpool, it was reported in the *Blackpool Gazette and News* that 'He must be a hot-headed supporter of either South Shore or Fleetwood Rangers who will not admit that the Blackpool team is the strongest in the Fylde. To our mind, the sooner the South Shore and Blackpool clubs are fused into one, the better it will be.' However, the members of South Shore stood firm, and it was not until some time later that the merger took place. Incidentally, the last game between the clubs ended in a 1–0 victory for South Shore.

It was Blackpool, though, who made headway in the Lancashire League, and at the end of their first season they had won more games than they had lost and finished fifth out of 13 clubs. The following three seasons saw them finish runners-up to Bury in 1890–91 and 1891–92, and to Liverpool on goal average in 1892–93. One year later they were champions, having won 15 of 22 games, and they finished three points clear of their nearest rivals. The following season they again were runners-up, but then they struggled near the foot of the table, and the board wisely decided they could no longer make any further progress in local football. On 13 May 1896 Blackpool Football Club became a limited company and after one rejection were subsequently elected to the Football League. They joined the Second Division along with Gainsborough Trinity and Walsall, the newcomers replacing Crewe Alexandra, Burslem Port Vale and Rotherham County.

In the 1891–92 season Blackpool competed in the FA Cup first round proper for the first time, but they were easily beaten 3–0 at Raikes Hall by Sheffield United, who then repeated the feat the following season but this time by three goals to one. It was four years later that they won their first FA Cup tie, beating Burton Swifts in the first round, only to go out three weeks later at the hands of Bolton Wanderers. It was reported that the players were on a win bonus of 10 shillings (50p); their opposition were due to paid an extra 45 shillings (£2.25) if they were successful.

When the Football League arrived in Blackpool in 1896, it was an ambition realised for one man in particular. Mr Leonard Seed was one of the first to be elected to the Board of Directors, and it was his vision and belief that kept the club moving forward in those early years. It is certainly worth mentioning the Seed and later the Parkinson families have, over the years, been instrumental in preserving Blackpool Football Club's existence and ensuring the club's future.

What of the players who lined up on that historic day in September 1896 for Blackpool's first-ever Football League match? Among them was Jack Parkinson, a tall, strong forward who was to give sterling service to his club for many years to come and who was one of the few professional players that Blackpool had on their books. In that first season he was the top scorer, and he proceeded to score regularly until he moved to centre-half. Then there was Charlie Mount, a fast outside-left who had the honour of scoring Blackpool's first

League goal, against Lincoln City. Despite his success, however, he was sold during the summer of 1897, a move which did not go down well with fans.

That first game against Lincoln resulted in a 3–1 defeat, though the Imps would finish bottom of the Division at the end of the season, whereas Blackpool attained a comfortable mid-table position. They also managed to attract reasonable attendances to Raikes Hall, but within a year the optimism had changed as the club announced a loss of £1,183. They had started with capital of £2,000, but the players' wages had accounted for £1,470 and, with attendances falling to the 2,000 mark, the financial position was not as healthy as it had been. On the pitch they had failed to progress and could only finish in 11th place, and they were also unsuccessful in their progress to the first round of the FA Cup. There had been calls from members for the directors to take the club out of the Football League, with all of its expense, and consolidate for a few more seasons in local football once more, but this idea was rejected and Blackpool struggled on.

The club was also forced to relocate to a new home, the Athletic Grounds on the site of the current Stanley Park, due to the forthcoming closure of Raikes Hall. It seemed to ease the financial burden slightly as a loss of £441 2s 5d was announced, despite a reduction in admission prices. Curiously, they played their first seven home games at their new ground and then the other 10 at Raikes Hall before eventually settling on the Athletics Ground.

Unfortunately, on the field things became progressively worse as the team finished in 16th place, two points clear of Loughborough Town, and failed to gain re-election. The Seasiders dropped out of the Football League with another Lancashire club, Darwen, who had finished bottom. They were replaced by Chesterfield and Middlesbrough, while Loughborough survived for another season. The FA Cup offered little as they failed to reach the first round proper once more, and a new record for consecutive defeats was set when they lost eight in a row between November and January. Maybe this was the reason why their neighbours, South Shore, still enjoyed better attendances than Blackpool? When the amalgamation came about, it was believed that the combined support would make a stronger club. There had been much resistance from South Shore about a possible merger, despite the vote of approval from their president, Thomas Carter. They had enjoyed their own success and had one historic moment on 14 January 1885, when they had beaten the mighty Notts County in the FA Cup at Waterloo Road, a first taste of Cup giant killing, and had spread their name across the footballing country. On 12 December the merger was formalised, with most of the South Shore players joining Blackpool, and the 'new' club set up home at South Shore's home, Bloomfield Road, which had become their ground after they had moved from Waterloo Road, known at the time as 'Gamble's Field'. From that moment on, excluding another brief return to Raikes Hall, Bloomfield Road has remained the spiritual home of Blackpool Football Club.

During the close season Frank Wilson, a centre-forward signed from Gravesend United two years earlier, died at the age of 22 from 'maniacal exhaustion caused by football and excitement'. On the day he died, he should have been transferred to either Aston Villa or Sunderland.

The one season out of the Football League was a success for Blackpool as they finished third in the Lancashire League and were duly re-elected to the Football League on 25 May 1900, along with Stockport County, this time at the expense of Loughborough and Luton Town.

Blackpool c.1900.

EARLY TWENTIETH CENTURY

For the new campaign, the team was rebuilt in an attempt to cope with League football again. Notable signings came in the form of Joe Dorrington, a goalkeeper from Blackburn Rovers, Harold Hardman, a local schoolboy who played at outside-left and who went on to greater things at Everton and eventually became a director at Manchester United, and the return of the great Jack Parkinson, who had enjoyed a brief taste of First Division football with Liverpool. Going in the opposite direction was Jack Cox, who was sold to Liverpool for the grand sum of £150.

The first season back saw a mid-table finish of 12th, although they did suffer a 10–1 defeat at the hands of Small Heath. In that game the referee had actually blown for full-time

The 1901–02 team.

Blackpool 1903–04. First row (left to right): Mr H. Cookson, Mr. H.E. Leivers (Assistant Secretary), Hull, Scott, Jones. Second row: Booth (trainer), Threlfall, Birket, Rooke, Anderson, Wolstenholme, Mr T.A. Barcroft (Honorary Secretary). Third row: Anderton, Pentland, Bennett.

four minutes early, with score at 9–1, but after he realised his mistake and the players had left the pitch he called them back on to play the remainder and Small Heath duly scored again. The 1901–02 campaign saw little change, with another mid-table finish, but by this time the club was surviving on the meagre gate receipts and the generosity of the subscribers and members. They were difficult times financially for the club, who by this time had moved to their now-permanent home of Bloomfield Road.

In 1903 Mr R.B. Middleton moved to Blackburn Rovers to become their secretary, and Tom Barcroft took over the duties at Blackpool. It was, at first, a temporary appointment, yet he stayed in the position for over 30 years and firmly established the club as it steered its way through the rough waters of the early years. There have been many personalities involved with Blackpool Football Club down the years who have rightly been lauded for their contributions both on and off the pitch, but some are seldom heard of or remembered. Tom Barcroft deserves the plaudits for his immense contribution at the turn of the 20th century.

Between 1901–02 and 1904–05 Blackpool enjoyed little success, with only 14th and 15th positions attained in the League, although there were a few good signings. The eccentric goalkeeper 'Tishy' Hull was one of the best, never without his flat cap and performances that could veer from the brilliant to the bizarre. There was also an improvement in attendances, with as many as 7,000 turning up for a game with Bolton Wanderers, although it was reported this was boosted by at least 3,000 travelling supporters. However, finances were still in a precarious position, and a new board of directors was installed for the start of the 1905–06 season, with Charlie Ramsden as chairman and Tom Barcroft remaining as secretary, despite a move to vote him off the board.

In January of that season Blackpool reached the first round of the FA Cup for the first time in nine years. A 2–1 defeat at Bristol City followed, but one year later the club had their finest moment to date. After beating Crystal Palace over three games, they were drawn at home to the powerful Sheffield United side. The board, always mindful of financial restrictions, 'sold' the ground rights and agreed to play the tie at Bramall Lane. Despite the protest from supporters, the game went ahead in South Yorkshire on 2 February, and remarkably Blackpool won 2–1. What made the victory even sweeter was that the club came away with a £300 profit from the game. It was an outstanding result, and for the first time Blackpool Football Club earned nationwide recognition. They then netted £650 from the next tie at Newcastle United, but they were overwhelmed 5–0 in front of over 35,000 fans. It was, however, Blackpool's first flirtation with the attraction of the FA Cup, something that, half a century later, would be the glittering prize that would bring the Seasiders to the world's attention.

During this time, the transfers of players in and out of the club gathered apace. Arrivals included Duckworth, Jimmy Connor and a talented Liverpool junior called Gow. In the meantime, the tricky outside-left Marshall McEwan left for Bolton Wanderers, inside-forward Harry Hancock joined Oldham Athletic and regulars Morgan, Kearns, Hogg and Chadwick also departed.

It was also during the 1905–06 season that the club had their first serious brush with the football authorities over crowd behaviour. It came after the 3–0 home defeat by West

Blackpool 1904–05.

Bromwich Albion, when referee W. Gilgryst was escorted from the field by two police officers. He had made some rather controversial decisions, including the 'sending-off' of a spectator for abusive language, and at the final whistle nearly 200 fans invaded the pitch. The club was severely censured by the Football League and told to ensure that such scenes would never happen again. Although Blackpool has never been known for its unruly element among the supporters, there was a time in the early 1980s when the activities of its fans far outweighed anything that was happening on the pitch.

In that same season a reporter from the local newspaper, *The Scribe*, requested that Blackpool invest a 'five pound note' to build a press box because he had spent the whole of the game against Championship challengers Manchester United outside the gates trying in vain to gain admittance, the ground already having reached its 7,500 capacity.

One year on from the Sheffield United success, the directors again sold the ground rights of an FA Cup tie. This time it was the first round against West Ham United, and as the recently opened Upton Park attracted 13,000 on that January afternoon, the club's coffers were boosted to the tune of £300. It had been announced that Blackpool were losing around £50 per week, with expenditure of £80 per week far outweighing any monies coming through the turnstiles. Unfortunately, the FA Cup was not to provide any further financial interest as the Hammers won 2–1. The season in Division Two ended with an underwhelming 13th position.

For the start of 1907–08 a new board had been introduced again, with the promise of more money being made available. Fred Seed succeeded Charles Ramsden as chairman, and the club invested in the transfer market. Birch was signed from Atherton, and the effective Owers went to West Brom for a large fee – starting a sad trend down the years of selling to survive – although he only made four appearances for the Throstles, as they were then known, before moving to Chesterfield two years later. Unfortunately, some bad injuries at

The 1910–11 Blackpool squad.

the start of the season, including a broken leg suffered by inside-forward King, left Blackpool weakened, and they struggled in the League once again and made an early exit in the FA Cup at the hands of Manchester United. That game saw over 3,000 fans travel to watch their team and, in a crowd of 12,000 at Bank Street, Clayton, make most of the noise – something that the current generation of Blackpool fans have become well known for.

The summer of 1908 saw the arrival of 22-year-old centre-forward George Beare, who had been scoring regularly for Southampton reserves. Beare had a reasonable amount of success with Blackpool before going on to better things with Everton, and a journalist later wrote of him, 'If he did not enjoy playing football, he would probably have been one of our leading music hall comedians, as he is an expert card manipulator, a trick cyclist of no little repute and an expert billiards player.'

Of more mundane talents was a young miner called Whalley, who joined Blackpool from Dinnington Colliery in Sheffield, while the hugely talented and popular Bob Whittingham signed for Bradford City in January 1909 before moving to Chelsea for £1,300 a few months later. Whittingham had a powerful shot, and one goalkeeper commented, 'I'd rather face his satanic majesty than Whittingham'. Although he left midway through the season, he was still Blackpool's top scorer, and his departure left a huge gap in the forward line. The team struggled and finished bottom, having to apply for re-election once more. Thankfully, another trip to Newcastle in the Cup provided much-needed financial revenue, where more than 30,000 fans saw the Seasiders lose 2–1.

Jack Cox returned to Blackpool at the start of the 1909–10 season, this time as an unofficial player-manager, and it was his guidance and experience that helped a recovery on the pitch. The team finished in a comfortable mid-table position. There had been one or two changes in playing personnel, with the amateur centre-forward W.L. Grundy turning his hand to hockey after not being invited back to Blackpool at the end of the previous season. The veteran Jack Parkinson moved to Barrow on a free transfer after giving the club many years of service. A year later he would be killed in a tragic accident at a local swimming baths.

As the club's finances continued to give cause for concern, they were once again obliged to sell ground rights to another FA Cup game. This time the match, which was against Manchester United, realised takings of £680, with 20,000 spectators seeing the home side win 2–1 at the new Old Trafford.

There had been vast improvements in Blackpool's fortunes in the Second Division, with the seventh-place finish their most successful to date. They played to a crowd of 15,000 in the penultimate home match, against Burnley, giving cause for optimism that the club could survive without having to constantly sell its best players. As it was, Joe Clennell, Blackpool's star inside-forward, went to Blackburn Rovers and was later sold to Everton for £1,500. He had contributed 18 goals that season, with only centre-forward Morley also reaching double figures.

The next two seasons of 1911–12 and 1912–13 were huge disappointments, as 14th place was followed by a near disastrous 20th place, rock bottom of the Second Division. This meant another application for re-election, but happily they survived. It was quite obvious where the problems lay on the pitch, as not one player was able to score more than 10 goals in either campaign. Again, and predictably, the FA Cup provided little cheer. A marathon tie against Crewe Alexandra in 1912 was followed by yet another decision to sell ground rights in 1913. This time the opponents were Tottenham Hotspur, who showed scant regard for Blackpool's previous giant-killing reputation by putting six past them in the replay at White Hart Lane. Unfortunately, there was no financial bonanza this time, as an aggregate of only 15,000 fans watched the two games, realising around £750 in gate receipts.

The 1913–14 season was again disappointing, though the League position did show a slight improvement as Blackpool finished in 16th place, but there was an early exit in the FA Cup as Southern League Gillingham ended the Seasiders' interest. One of the most notable signings of the season was Joe Lane from Sunderland. Lane, who had been playing Hungarian football before joining the north-east club, cost Blackpool £400 and proceeded to repay that immediately. He netted 11 times in his first season and continued to be a regular goalscorer in his time with Blackpool, including 28 the following season. In all he scored 67 goals in 99 appearances over three seasons – certainly worth the small sum paid for him.

Another strong forward, Charlton, was seriously injured during the home game with Leicester Fosse in April, suffering a fractured skull after a collision with a defender. For quite some time his life was in danger, but fortunately he made a full recovery. At the next home match a collection was made among the fans, and £211 was raised for Charlton and his family.

At the start of the 1914–15 campaign Albert Hargreaves, a director and a former referee, suggested to the Football League that they should consider extending the season for financial reasons, but the suggestion was voted down. It proved rather unfortunate for Blackpool, as they enjoyed their best form towards the end of the season and a late surge,

A postcard showing the Blackpool squad at the start of World War One, 1914.

in which they won eight of their last 10 games, saw them finish in a respectable 10th position. They were helped enormously by Joe Lane, with his 28 goals, especially as no other player managed to reach double figures. Interest in the FA Cup ended quickly again with a first-round home defeat to Sheffield United. On this occasion the ground rights were not sold, and a healthy crowd of 7,500 turned up at Bloomfield Road.

In August 1914 war had been declared and football, like other professional sports, was suspended at the end of the season. The club had made a couple of important signings in Billy Rooks and Len Appleton, but as the spectre of one of the bloodiest conflicts in human history became apparent, people's attentions turned from pastimes to more pressing matters.

The game did eventually restart with unfamiliar regional leagues due to the ban on travel, and Blackpool fielded a side during those war years. In the first season, 1915–16, they finished third in the Lancashire section's principal competition, followed by second in the subsidiary competition. It was competitive football in name, but it paled into comparison to the pre-war years of League football.

Blackpool were not as successful again until 1918–19, when they won the subsidiary competition's Section A, which comprised of Blackpool, Preston, Burnley and Blackburn. The leaders of the four sections qualified for the semi-finals of the Lancashire Senior Cup, in which Blackpool lost 1–0 at home to Liverpool in front of an estimated 10,000 fans. That game had seen an impressive Blackpool display, as they had out-played their better opponents, but they were denied by a last-minute goal.

They were helped, especially in the first wartime season, by many 'guest' players who found themselves stationed in the town. Among them were four famous players from Blackburn Rovers – the great Bob Crompton, Eddie Latheron, George Chapman and Joe Hodkinson. They played regularly for the Seasiders and earned the club the new nickname of Blackpool Rovers. There were times during the war when the club struggled to raise a team, and on occasions they had to rely almost entirely on soldiers who were in the town, mostly stationed at Squires Gate. They excelled, though, and even managed to record a 9–0 victory over Oldham Athletic, helped somewhat by England international Harry Hampton, who scored four.

By the time the war ended in August 1919 and football resumed competitively, Blackpool had joined the growing band of football clubs who employed a full-time manager. Bill Norman had taken over the position 12 months previously after leaving Huddersfield Town, the club he had joined after masterminding Barnsley's 1912 FA Cup success. Norman was a fitness fanatic and organised strict training regimes in a bid to make his players the fittest in the land. It worked, and the club enjoyed their best season by finishing fourth in Division Two and winning the Central League Championship, although interest in the FA Cup came to an early end at neighbours Preston. After four wartime seasons there had been many changes in the playing staff, with regulars George Wilson moving to Sheffield Wednesday, Peter Quinn to Preston, Jimmy Jones to Bolton Wanderers and Bobby Booth to Birmingham.

The biggest change, though, came in March 1920, when Joe Lane was also sold to Birmingham, for a record fee of £3,600. This caused uproar in the town, and many fans questioned the ambition of the board of directors, with the team seemingly in its strongest-ever position. They could not, however, question the financial position that the club now found itself in, as incoming transfer fees plus record gate receipts had realised a profit £2,383, as opposed to a loss of £1,337 the previous year. It was not all good news, though, as a fire had all but destroyed the West Stand and a large amount was paid for rebuilding.

The start of the 1920–21 season saw optimism around the club and another serious push for promotion. It was clear that the sport was now reaching further than before as the Third Division was introduced, effectively extending the Football League by another 22 clubs. Blackpool were well-established in the now-middle tier, though ambitions were for greater things. However, despite the help of goals from forward Jimmy Heathcote – 18 in total – promotion was missed after a poor run-in at the end of the season. Blackpool only won one of their last eight games and, for the second season running, they finished fourth. It was a huge disappointment to the fans, especially as the team had been top of the table for a large part of the season. They were also embarrassed by Third Division Southend United in the FA Cup second round, a now-familiar story.

On the playing front, a significant appearance during the season was that of winger Georgie Mee. He made his debut in December 1920 and proceeded to play in every one of Blackpool's League games until September 1925 – well over 190 consecutive games – a marvellous achievement, and one which still stands today as a club record. Sadly, full-back Horace Fairhurst died after receiving a knock on the head during a game at Barnsley. He was a young player who seemed to have a great future ahead of him. At the end of the season Blackpool played a benefit match against Preston, with the proceeds split between Fairhurst's widow and the children of team member Bert Tulloch, whose wife had died on the same weekend.

The following season was dreadful for Blackpool as they fought relegation to the Third Division North (a new League had been added – Third Division South – bringing the total of Football League clubs to 86). They actually approached the final two games of the season, both against West Ham United, knowing that nothing short of maximum points would be enough to ensure safety for one more season. With the Londoners aiming for promotion, it seemed an unlikely prospect, yet remarkably Blackpool won both, 2–0 at Upton Park followed by 3–1 at Bloomfield Road seven days later. Blackpool stayed up, and West Ham stayed down. It was a mystery as to why the team struggled so badly, especially when players of such calibre as Harry Bedford, signed from Nottingham Forest, joined the club. Bedford was to emulate Joe Lane with his prolific goalscoring talents for the Seasiders. Also joining was Bert Baverstock from Bolton Wanderers, who was quickly made captain. Baverstock was a fine player, but injuries reduced his appearances for the club.

Predictably the FA Cup provided no success, and at the end of the season the directors announced another financial loss, this time of £2,994. The Bloomfield Road ground continued to expand, though, and with extra capacity on the Spion Kop – now the South Stand – some 18,000 spectators could watch the team play, a figure that the current generation of fans could only dream of until promotion to the Premier League.

At the end of 1922–23 – which had seen the team pushing for promotion throughout, only to finish fifth – manager Bill Norman and his assistant Allan Ure both moved to Leeds United, though Ure, Norman's son-in-law, returned to Bloomfield Road a few years later. It was another disappointing outcome to what had at first seemed to be a successful campaign, and with Harry Bedford scoring 32 goals, expectations were understandably high. Unfortunately, the team only won three of their last 10 games and so slipped out of contention. With criticism from the supporters, Norman felt it best to leave. Again, though, he had been hampered by lack of funds to bring in new players, with the only real exception being Harry White from Arsenal for £1,125. White, who was also a Warwickshire county cricketer, had played in an England trial in 1919 and had scored 40 times in 101 appearances for the Arsenal. That Norman could sign anyone was a surprise, given the serious financial difficulties the club faced. The overall loss for the season had increased to around £4,000, and desperate measures were now required to rectify it. One pleasing aspect, though, was the increase in attendances at Bloomfield Road, with some 20,000 reported for the game with Barnsley. With the official capacity at 18,000, it must have made for an uncomfortable experience for many, not helped by a 1–0 defeat.

For the new season there was a new manager. Major Frank Buckley joined the club after previously managing Norwich City, although he had been out of the game and was working as a commercial traveller when Blackpool signed him up. A tactical visionary, Buckley revolutionised the way the team played. He was a controversial figure and also one of the highest-paid managers in the Football League – certainly a gamble for the cash-strapped club.

The campaign started badly as Blackpool failed to win any of their first seven games, but gradually it all came together and, with the help of another incredible 32 goals from Bedford, the team eventually finished fourth, missing promotion by two points.

It was also during this season that the club first adopted the now-famous tangerine colours so recognised in the footballing world. Albert Hargreaves, still a director and again a referee, had officiated at a Holland-Belgium international and was so impressed with the Dutchmen's orange colours that he suggested that Blackpool wore them the following season. No club had worn that colour as a plain shirt before, so this was a radical change. The colours were received well by fans, although the combination of orange shirts with black collars, cuffs and shorts gave the kit an 'uneven' look. After an FA Cup defeat at Blackburn in 1925, the black shorts were replaced with white when it was suggested that Blackpool lost the game due to the players not being able to see each other in the murky atmosphere, an excuse used by many down the years.

Before this change the team had worn a variety of kits, from the original red shirts and white shorts, to blue and white stripes, and then red, yellow and black hoops during World War One (in deference to the many Belgian refugees who were in the town) before adopting white shirts and blue shorts. The list seems endless, but it was the orange that became the most popular, although that did not stop the board introducing another change in 1934, when the team appeared in alternating dark and light blue stripes, but thankfully they bowed to public pressure in 1939 and introduced the colour we all now know as tangerine. It is now inconceivable that Blackpool Football Club should be associated with any other colour than tangerine.

There were more off-field problems for 1924–25, nearly all financial. A writ had been presented to the club for £3,618 from the builders of the rebuilt stand. It had cost £4,618, but only £1,000 of that had been paid. After a lengthy and drawn-out meeting, it was decided to double the share capital, bringing it up to £10,000 to pay off the outstanding debt. The board underwent quite a few changes, with new members being added in the hope of providing much-needed cash to alleviate the desperate position. Sir Lindsay Parkinson resigned as president to be replaced by Alderman John Bickerstaffe, and the new Blackpool Supporters' Club was formed. In its infancy it could boast around 300 members.

On the field, without new blood, the team struggled badly and spent the season fighting relegation, although once again Harry Bedford scored 24 goals, but only the consistent Malcolm Barrass also reached double figures. There was, for once, more than a passing interest in the FA Cup, with the previously mentioned fourth-round exit at Blackburn Rovers, where Blackpool lost 1–0 in front of over 60,000 fans. Two of the club's top players left Blackpool during the next season, both for large fees. Herbert Jones went to Blackburn Rovers for £3,850 – one of the highest fees paid for a full-back at that time – and goalscorer Harry Bedford was sold to Derby County for £3,500. These transfers were a huge loss to the team but a huge financial gain. Despite this, Blackpool finished sixth. The board spent a large part of the income on the new South Stand, although the final cost of £13,146 was certainly more than budgeted for. Nevertheless, it had increased the capacity at Bloomfield Toad to well over 20,000.

The 1926–27 season saw Teddy Rosebroom and Stanley Streets move to Chesterfield and Clapton Orient respectively, while centre-forward Tom Browell was bought from Manchester City for £1,100. Browell, now well into the veteran stage, had played in the previous season's FA Cup Final and was brought in to add experience to the team. Unfortunately, Blackpool made little progress and could only finish ninth, with only a passing interest in the FA Cup. The big success of the season was the form of centre-forward Billy Tremeling, who scored 31 League and Cup goals. Later he moved to centre-half to accommodate an even richer goalscoring talent in Jimmy Hampson.

Hampson was signed from Nelson for £1,000 in October 1927 and proved to be one of the club's greatest buys. In his first season, he scored 31 goals in 32 League appearances, including four in a home win over Nottingham Forest. His contribution to the team over the next decade was beyond equal, and he can still to this day be rightly considered one of Blackpool's greatest players.

There were many other new faces to arrive at Bloomfield Road for that season. Johnny McIntrye came from Bristol Rovers, Horace Williams from New Brighton, William Grant from East Stirling, Syd Brooks from Scunthorpe and a twin signing for £4,500 of Jack Oxberry and Stan Ramsay from the North East. There was also a new manager in the shape of Sydney Beaumont, a former Preston player, who came in to replace Frank Buckley, who had moved to Wolves. Beaumont only lasted a year though, as the Seasiders struggled to 19th, avoiding relegation by just one point. He departed shortly after.

In a bid to cut costs, the board decided not to appoint another full-time manager, instead giving the honorary title to director Harry Evans. He went on the hold the position for five years, with no little success. His first season, though, did not see the club perform well, and they finished eighth and were severely embarrassed at Third Division Plymouth in the FA Cup. All of this was despite an incredible 40 goals from Jimmy Hampson, but the team's inconsistency was starkly exposed in October and November when they recorded successive results of 1–4, 4–0, 2–8 and 7–0! The last game, against Reading, saw Hampson score five times.

There had been a few additions to the squad, with only the tough-tackling Jimmy Hamilton joining from St Mirren and goalkeeper Bill Mercer coming in from Huddersfield Town. Sadly, though, it was yet another disappointing campaign, and the pressure on the team to finally accomplish something was growing. It was said among the fans that 1929–30 was a make-or-break season for the club. Success had to be achieved after so many seasons of disappointment.

Success at Last

Success was achieved, and in dramatic fashion. The team, under the guidance of Harry Evans, were finally promoted to the First Division. Blackpool were challenging throughout the season and eventually gained promotion at fellow challengers Oldham Athletic in front of more than 45,000 fans. They claimed the title on the last day of the season with a goalless draw away to Nottingham Forest, pipping Chelsea, who had lost at Bury, to the post. To date, it is the only League Title the club has ever won.

Jimmy Hampson's 45 League goals in a single season was a Blackpool record, and it still stands today. In fact, Hampson was the top scorer throughout the country that season, but, in typical shy fashion, he sneaked off the train at Kirkham on the way back from

1929–30 team group.

The Blackpool team meeting Edward VIII at Newcastle, 1932.

Nottingham to avoid the hundreds of fans who were ready to greet the team at Blackpool North station. It was also encouraging to see the attendances rise at Bloomfield Road, with over 24,000 for the visit of Oldham and the same number outside the Town Hall to celebrate the team's promotion. To add to the statistics, Hampson scored his 100th goal in only his 97th game, and the points tally of 58 was equalled only once more by the club before the advent of three-for-a-win. It would equate to 85 points from 42 matches today.

The feat was even more remarkable for the relatively few additions to the squad, with only Charles Broadhurst and Perry Downes joining. It had been a truly memorable season, though, and the players and backroom staff enjoyed their summer, which was filled with many civic receptions and dinners held in their honour.

Before the start of the new season in the First Division, there were many changes, not least to the ground itself. During the close season a vast new terrace was erected on the north side of Bloomfield Road, the Spion Kop, which at its peak could hold 12,000 people. It was not concreted for quite some time, but it did increase the capacity to around 30,000.

The playing staff was strengthened by the arrivals of J. McLelland, Eric Longden, Jack O' Donnell and Jackie Carr from Middlesbrough, yet the 1930–31 season turned out to be a near-disaster for Blackpool. The team, which had done so much to gain promotion, found itself completely out of its depth and proceeded to capitulate almost on a weekly basis. The scene was set with the first game of the campaign, at home to Arsenal, when the visitors won, almost contemptuously, 4–1 in front of 29,000 fans. Four days later Blackpool recorded a 4–2 win at Manchester City, but that was an early respite to a nightmare season.

Programme cover from 1932.

Four goals were conceded on five separate occasions, five goals four times, six goals twice, seven goals on three occasions and finally 10 were conceded on one humiliating afternoon at Huddersfield Town. In total, the defence leaked a First Division record of 125 goals as the Seasiders lost 21 games.

Somehow the club escaped relegation, with 32 goals from Jimmy Hampson enough to secure First Division football for another year. A '£10,000' goal from Albert Watson in the final match at home to Manchester City became legendary. The equaliser by the full-back was said to be worth at least that amount as it secured the club's immediate future with the promise of yet more large attendances for the next season. Finances were still causing concern, though, as the club now had a bank overdraft of over £17,000. For the record, Blackpool finished 20th, a point clear of Leeds United, while Manchester United finished bottom.

There was an improvement for the following season, with only 102 goals conceded, including another seven at Manchester City and a further five occasions when five were let in. Blackpool had bought heavily in the close season, with the top signing being Phil Watson from Hamilton Academical for £3,000. Watson took the place of the departed Billy Tremeling, who moved to neighbours Preston. Walter Lax was bought from Lincoln City, for whom he had scored 26 goals the previous season, and Jack Everest from Rochdale and a new goalkeeper, Alec Roxburgh, also joined. Attendances were significantly down, however, which was hardly surprising bearing in mind they were facing another dismal season battling relegation. They avoided it by winning their final two games of the season, against Huddersfield Town and Sheffield United, with Jimmy Hampson again top-scorer with 23 goals. Once more, the FA Cup was a depressing tale and their run came to an early end.

Inevitably, after two seasons of struggle, Blackpool were finally relegated to Division Two. Jimmy Hampson, for so long the great favourite who could do no wrong, only scored 18 times and now came under criticism from the fans and local newspapers. There were also reports of discontent within the club. Eric Longden returned to Hull City for a nominal fee, but the tricky outside-right Alec Reid agreed to come to Bloomfield Road from Preston North End. With the Seasiders finishing at the bottom of the table, there were calls for a full-time manager to be appointed once more. During the summer months that followed, there was also a major boardroom reshuffle, with no fewer than six long-standing directors resigning. Only Sam Butterworth and Harry Evans remained, with Butterfield becoming life president and Evans relinquishing the manager's position to become chairman.

Eventually a new manager was appointed, and Alex 'Sandy' McFarlane, a former Scottish international player with 13 years of managerial experience, took over. McFarlane was a strict disciplinarian and perfectionist, who showed his ruthlessness at the end of his first season by a mass clear-out of established players. Out went Frank McDonough, Bobby Crawford, Bertie Thomson, Charlie Rattray, Walter Bussey, Albert Butterworth, Sammy Armes and Sidney Tufnell – all regulars who had contributed greatly to the team down the years.

The exodus was almost certainly brought about due to a poor season in the lower division. The team finished 11th and, of course, only had a brief interest in the Cup. Matters were not helped by a series of injuries to Jimmy Hampson, who was at his least effective since joining the club and managed to score just 13 times.

The following season a concerted push for promotion was made with the signing of Richard Watmough from Bradford City for £3,000 and the acquisition of John Middleton from Darlington. The Seasiders actually only missed going up by three points, finishing in fourth place, simply due to an inability to win any of their three remaining games. They played a lone FA Cup game. Jimmy Hampson was returning to his old form, topping the scoring chart with 20, and he was joined by an exciting newcomer in Peter Doherty, a player who went on to become one of the country's greatest-ever footballers. Doherty signed from Glentoran for £1,000, and the regular partnership of Hampson, Doherty and Bobby Finan, who had joined the club from non-League football, would have been a mouth-watering prospect, but sadly injuries to one or the other meant the dream was never fully realised. Surprisingly, with the team on the up, Alex McFarlane was released by the club.

The Joe Smith Years

If Jimmy Hampson had been one of the best players the club had signed up to that point, then surely Joe Smith was the best manager they employed. In August 1935 he joined from Reading and remained at Bloomfield Road for 23 years, and he eventually transformed Blackpool into one of the most powerful football teams in the country.

Smith was a relaxed man who thoroughly enjoyed the game, and it showed with the teams he produced at Bloomfield Road down the years. One of his first signings was Fred Chandler, from his old club, but essentially he stayed true to the team that had done so well the previous season. Although only 10th place was attained in his first campaign, the huge success of Bobby Finan at centre-forward, where he scored 34 goals, gave an optimistic indicator of the future.

Division Two runners-up, 1936–37.

A footnote to that season was that the FA Cup tie at home to Margate was the first game captured on film at Bloomfield Road. It was filmed by the Tower Company and later shown at the Grand Theatre and Winter Gardens. Blackpool won 3–1.

One year on and Blackpool were promoted once more, finishing second to Leicester City. First Division football was attained with minimal outlay on new players, with only Alec Munro costing a substantial fee. He came from Hearts for £3,500, while other signings included Danny Blair from Aston Villa, Frank Hill from Arsenal and Willie Cook from Bolton Wanderers. The twin strike force of Hampson and Finan contributed 44 goals between them, and with Dickie Watmough and Sammy Jones also notching up double figures, the team looked a safe bet for the following season. Sadly, the old problem of finances continued to cloud the club's ambitions, and Peter Doherty was sold to Manchester City for the large fee of £10,000.

In Blackpool Football Club's history, the season of 1937–38 will forever be overshadowed by the death of the great Jimmy Hampson. He was on a fishing expedition off the coast of Fleetwood on 10 January when his boat collided with a trawler and sank. His body was never recovered. The whole of Blackpool, and indeed the footballing world, mourned his loss. His record of 252 goals is, unsurprisingly, still a club record.

On the field, the team did well and finished in a respectable mid-table position, although a heavy FA Cup defeat at Aston Villa in front of 70,000 fans was true to form. Among the players who were emerging at that time were George Farrow, a right-back from Bournemouth, and Jock Wallace, who was challenging Roxburgh for the goalkeeping position. New signings Frank O'Donnell and Willie Buchan, both from Celtic, each cost £10,000; Eric Sibley and Malcolm Butler were cheaper imports.

For 1938–39, Blackpool spent over £60,000 on new players, a huge amount for the day. The club paid Bolton and Sheffield United £5,000 and £10,500 for George Eastham and the mighty 'Jock' Dodds respectively, and Frank O'Donnell's brother, Hugh, cost a further £2,500. Frank himself only stayed at Bloomfield Road for a year before joining Aston Villa for £10,500. Tom Lewis joined from Bradford, while Richard Watmough went to neighbours Preston.

The spending was a huge gamble, but one which was to secure success for the club for many years to come. They achieved 15th place and another early exit in the Cup, but the signs of success were already there. The fans turned out in greater numbers than before, and the team had even reverted to their now-famous tangerine shirts. The omens were good.

At the outbreak of war in September 1939 Blackpool stood proudly at the top of the First Division after winning their opening three games, and although it was far too early to predict the outcome, many fans thought the team was the best they had seen and were capable of lifting the title. As it was, with competitive League football suspended for the duration of the war, Blackpool became – with the help of many 'guest' players – one of the country's top teams throughout the wartime period.

In that first wartime season's regional league, the Seasiders finished third and reached the quarter-finals of the War Cup, helped by the remarkable scoring feats of Jock Dodds. Not since Jimmy Hampson had Blackpool possessed a player with such goalscoring talents. He netted 30 in 18 appearances, including seven in an 11–2 destruction of Oldham Athletic.

The 1941 War Cup against Aston Villa. Blackpool won 2–1.

Over the next few seasons, Dodds scored at will – eight times against Stockport County, seven against Tranmere Rovers, and altogether he scored 208 goals during the war years and 66 alone in 1941–42.

Blackpool were sweeping all before them, winning the Northern Section's first competition on three occasions, lifting the Lancashire Cup once and reaching the War Cup Final twice, winning it in 1943. They also played a famous challenge match at Chelsea's Stamford Bridge stadium against the mighty Arsenal, who were the winners of the Southern War Cup. In what was described at the time as one of the best footballing performances ever, Blackpool came from 2–0 down to win 4–2. All of this was achieved with the help of many guest players, who, like in World War One, found themselves stationed in the town, including Dix (Tottenham), Stevenson (Everton), Paterson (Celtic), Pope (Hearts and Leeds), Savage (Leeds), Hubbick (Bolton) and Gardner (Aston Villa).

Another guest player was an outside-right who played for Stoke

Jock Dodds Captain receiving the Cup.

A wartime team from 1942–43.

City during peacetime and made international appearances. Stanley Matthews made habitual appearances in Blackpool's tangerine shirt during the war years, teaming up with a promising youngster, Stan Mortensen. Though unaware at the time, this was a tantalising glimpse of what was to come for the Blackpool supporters.

One positive aspect of the war for the club – if anything positive could be gained from the conflict – was the wiping out of the bank overdraft, which stood at £33,704. With the Armed Forces requiring Bloomfield Road for various reasons, the rent paid by the War Office helped the club become solvent once more.

When peace returned to Europe, Blackpool found themselves in a stronger position than before. Despite the sale of Jock Dodds to Shamrock Rovers and the departure of Hugh O'Donnell, manager Joe Smith started to gather around him some of the most talented footballers in the country, and, with the help of Stan Mortensen's 28 goals, the team finished in fifth position, by far the highest final position attained by the club to date.

Attendances everywhere were booming, and Blackpool's attractive football certainly appealed to the fans as they flocked to Bloomfield Road in their thousands. The game against Blackburn Rovers on Boxing Day 1946 was the ground's very first all-ticket affair. The FA Cup continued to be of little interest, although that was to change in the coming years.

During the summer of 1947 Blackpool made probably their greatest signing when Joe Smith persuaded Stoke City to release Stanley Matthews for £11,500. Matthews had fallen in love with the town and the club after his stay during the war and was more than eager to don the tangerine shirt once more. It was to prove a remarkable partnership for the club and player as Blackpool FC entered the most successful era in its long history, and the famous 'M' plan became legendary. Matthews, Mortensen, Munro, McIntosh, McCall and Mudie appeared in the forward line and struck fear into opposing defences, and with the help of such players like George Farrow, Harry Johnston and Eddie Shimwell at the back, the team were at times irresistible. This was truly a golden era.

Other new names for 1947–48 included Joe Robinson, Albert Hobson and Walter Rickett, but the club released Jimmy Blair to Bournemouth and, sadly, one of Blackpool's best goalkeepers, Jock Wallace, to Derby County for just £500.

In the League the club finished a disappointing ninth, but 1948 saw Blackpool's first-ever trip to Wembley for an FA Cup Final. In a competition that hadn't exactly been embraced by the club previously, their route to the semi-finals was admittedly rather easy, but the 3–1 victory over Tottenham Hotspur at Villa Park was a true test, with the 'Pool 1–0 down with only four minutes to go. Stan Mortensen's equaliser and then two further goals in extra-time ensured a trip to the Empire Stadium, where they met Manchester United, who had endured a much harder route to the Final as they had to play every one of their ties away from home; Old Trafford was still being rebuilt after extensive damage during the war.

The 1948 FA Cup Final at Wembley was probably one of the best games of football ever seen at the old stadium, but it ended with a 4–2 defeat for Blackpool. It was certainly a harsh scoreline, as the Seasiders had certainly contributed greatly to the spectacle, but United's superior class won the day. Stan Mortensen's goal meant he had scored in every round, a feat rarely achieved. Four days later the teams met again in a League game at Bloomfield Road, with Blackpool winning 1–0, although the score did not reflect their dominance. It

The Blackpool squad from 1947–48.

Blackpool in action in the 1948 FA Cup semi-final against Tottenham Hotspur.

was shallow recompense for the team, but at the end of the season Blackpool bowed out with an incredible 7–0 thrashing of neighbours Preston North End at Deepdale. Jimmy McIntosh, who had been dropped for the Final seven days previously, scored five.

As a footnote, it was in the late 1940s to the early 1950s that Preston became regarded as Blackpool's main rivals. Up to that point, rivalries between clubs were a tepid affair, but after the war both Blackpool and Preston looked to each other in a more competitive way. It had started as light-hearted arguments between fans as to who was the better player, Tom Finney at Preston or Stanley Matthews at Blackpool, then as the years went by it became more serious. Now the rivalry between the clubs, and especially the fans, is as intense as anything seen in the country, and sadly a certain amount of unpleasantness follows such a fixture at times. There will be more of this as our history unfolds.

The 1948–49 season was something of an anticlimax as the team finished in a distant mid-table position. It was not helped by injuries to both Mortensen and Matthews, severely curtailing any firepower up front. Many players left the club – Jim McIntosh to Everton, George Dick to West Ham and Murdoch McCormack, George Farrow and Tommy Lewis also departed. They were replaced by Rex Adams from amateurs Oxford City, Willie Wardle from Grimsby Town, Ewan Fenton and Jackie Wright, and a giant of a goalkeeper, George Farm from Hibernian. Farm was only playing third-team football for the Scottish club when Blackpool signed him, yet he went on to become one of the country's greatest 'keepers.

The following season saw an improvement with a final position of seventh in the League, Mortensen's 22 goals contributing greatly. A quarter-final defeat at Liverpool ended any further FA Cup involvement, but the reserve side won the Central League Championship, scoring 82 goals in the process. They were helped significantly by Jackie Mudie, who was on the verge of a breakthrough to the first team.

Other new faces included the amateur W.J. Slater and the talented Bill Perry. Out went Joe Robinson – a goalkeeper unable to oust George Farm – Alec Munro and Ron Suart, who joined Blackburn Rovers.

Blackpool's success was certainly reflected by the crowds they were attracting all over the country, with over 70,000 turning up at Goodison Park, although the man they had come to see, Stanley Matthews, was injured and did not play. At home, too, attendances had improved dramatically, with over 12,000 turning up to watch the reserves beat Burnley. Financially, after years of struggle, Blackpool Football Club had never had it so good.

The Atomic Boys

It was around this time that the famous Atomic Boys were in their prime. This was a group of Blackpool supporters, led by Syd Bevers, who travelled the country in weird and wonderful costumes, and during the early part of the 1950s they seemed to be as well-known as the team itself. As well as travelling in some numbers, their antics provided amusement and entertainment before and during the game.

The idea came about just after the war, on 4 February 1946, at Elland Road, Leeds. As Syd Bevers said many years later, it was out of necessity that the group came together. 'It was a marathon match with Middlesbrough. We had drawn the two-legged FA Cup tie 5–5 on aggregate and had to play a deciding game at a neutral ground, and Leeds was selected. At the game I particularly noticed there as something missing in an England that was recovering from World War Two and needed something to brighten up spirits generally – and that was colour. I don't think you would have known who was supporting who – there was definitely a distinct lack of colour.'

After the 1–0 defeat, Bevers spoke to fellow supporters, and the seed was planted. They decided to call themselves the 'Atomic Boys', simply because the atomic bomb was on most people's minds at the time, and 'they went down a storm wherever they went!' At first they all dressed in tangerine coats, white trousers and a straw hat, but Syd wanted the group to stand out as much as possible, so other members were encouraged to wear all manner of fancy dress and costumes, while Syd – as the leader – continued to wear the traditional colours. They quickly became a draw at away grounds and, for reasons unfathomable today, they also took along a live duck as mascot, even somehow smuggling it into Wembley for the 1953 FA Cup Final. It was naturally white, but on one occasion they attempted to dye it tangerine without too much success. The thought of such a thing today would have the combined forces of the RSPCA and Health and Safety having a collective heart attack. The usual pre-match routine would be for Syd Bevers to parade the duck on the centre circle before kneeling down in an extravagant gesture and kissing the same spot.

The Atomic Boys continued to follow Blackpool from the late 1940s until the early 1960s, their fame actually transcending football as they were asked to attend many charity functions. Before the 1953 Cup Final, Syd Bevers somehow managed to get into 10 Downing Street to present the Prime Minister, Sir Winston Churchill, with a stick of Blackpool rock. Sadly, the PM was not there to receive it.

Eventually the group faded away, although they continued to support Blackpool. In the 1980–81 season, manager Alan Ball actually asked for the Atomic Boys to reform and bring along a duck as mascot, but in those hooligan-blighted years it was doomed to failure. Their time had gone. The legacy has lived on, though, and at many games, especially important ones, the Tangerine fans can be seen wearing crazy fancy dress. Among the 37,000 at Wembley in 2010, there were Tangerine nuns, stilt walkers and ostriches. Syd died in February 2007, but if he were still alive today he and his group of friends would have been proud.

Syd Bevers returned in the 1980–81 season.

1950s – The Golden Era

For the second time in four years Blackpool made it to the FA Cup Final against Newcastle United, although it was a shame that their appearance in 1951 seemed to overshadow what had been an excellent League campaign, where they finished in their highest position of third. There had been few additions to the squad, with the exception of Allan Brown. He was signed from East Fife for £26,500, a record amount paid to a Scottish club which was certainly repaid down the years. Ian McCall was sold to West Brom for £10,500, but essentially the team remained the same as the previous season. The successful League campaign was helped by 47 goals from Mortensen and Mudie, with the genius of Matthews on the wing. They were at times a stunning team to watch, and it has never failed to amaze fans and football historians how such a team failed to lift the greatest honour in the domestic game – the League Championship.

The Cup run was a far more difficult proposition than the 1948 competition, none more so than the semi-final match against Birmingham City, which was eventually decided after a replay. For the Final, the Seasiders were missing the influential Allan Brown, who had

Stanley Matthews in action from the 1951 FA Cup Final against Newcastle.

Stan Mortensen shields the ball from a Fulham player, 1951.

sustained a serious injury the previous week at Huddersfield. His absence sadly showed as Blackpool tried an unfamiliar offside game, and they paid the price by losing 2–0. It could have been worse if Newcastle's Jackie Milburn been a little more ruthless in front of goal, though his two efforts were enough to sink Blackpool. It was probably one of the few tactical mistakes made by manager Joe Smith, and it left fans wondering whether the veteran Stanley Matthews would ever get his winners' medal.

At the end of the season Blackpool played in a mini-series of challenge matches as part of the Festival of Britain. On 12 and 14 May they hosted Belgians Anderlecht and French club Rennes, and they ran out 2–0 and 3–0 winners respectively.

Predictably, the 1951–52 season was something of a let-down. Ninth place was the final finishing position in the League, and there was an embarrassing exit at West Ham in the FA

The captains shake hands at the start of the 1951 FA Cup Final.

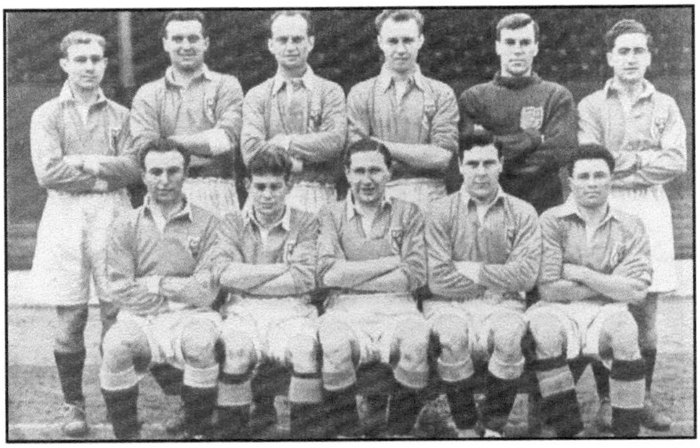

1951–52 team photograph.

Cup. Ernie Taylor, who had so impressed in the Cup Final, was signed from Newcastle for £25,000, but Willie McIntosh left for Stoke, while Bill Slaters was bought by Brentford. 'Morty' scored a total of 26 goals, but Matthews could manage only 19 appearances due to injury, which went some way to explanation of the team's lack of success that season. The crowds were still flocking to Bloomfield Road, however, as over 32,000 saw a goalless draw with Arsenal during the Easter holiday.

The 1952–53 season will always be remembered for the FA Cup Final, although Blackpool did remarkably well in the League once more. The opening game of the season saw 36,000 at Bloomfield Road for the draw with Preston, and a consistent campaign ended with a seventh-place finish. New names emerging were Dave Durie, David Frith and the

Blackpool faced Southampton in the fifth round of the 1953 FA Cup.

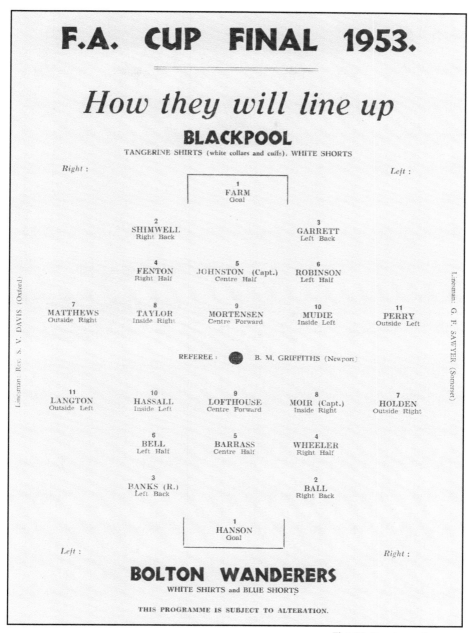

F.A. CUP FINAL 1953.

How they will line up

BLACKPOOL

TANGERINE SHIRTS (white collars and cuffs), WHITE SHORTS

Right : *Left :*

1 FARM Goal

2 SHIMWELL Right Back — 3 GARRETT Left Back

4 FENTON Right Half — 5 JOHNSTON (Capt.) Centre Half — 6 ROBINSON Left Half

7 MATTHEWS Outside Right — 8 TAYLOR Inside Right — 9 MORTENSEN Centre Forward — 10 MUDIE Inside Left — 11 PERRY Outside Left

Linesman: Rev. S. V. DAVIS (Oxford)

REFEREE : B. M. GRIFFITHS (Newport)

Linesman: G. F. SAWYER (Somerset)

11 LANGTON Outside Left — 10 HASSALL Inside Left — 9 LOFTHOUSE Centre Forward — 8 MOIR (Capt.) Inside Right — 7 HOLDEN Outside Right

6 BELL Left Half — 5 BARRASS Centre Half — 4 WHEELER Right Half

3 BANKS (R.) Left Back — 2 BALL Right Back

1 HANSON Goal

Left : *Right :*

BOLTON WANDERERS

WHITE SHIRTS and BLUE SHORTS

THIS PROGRAMME IS SUBJECT TO ALTERATION.

The FA Cup team line ups.

giant Roy Gratrix, but leaving the club were Len Stephenson and Jackie Wright. The forward line of Taylor, Mortensen, Brown and Perry provided most of the goals. Matthews was still suffering from niggling injuries, which meant he could only play in half of the first-team fixtures that season.

Matthews in action during the FA Cup Final.

Mortensen scores in Blackpool's FA Cup win.

The FA Cup Final against Bolton Wanderers will always be remembered as the greatest of them all – the day Stanley Matthews finally achieved his winners' medal and the team came back from a seemingly hopeless position. The Seasiders were 3–1 down with 20 minutes to go and 3–2 down in the final minute, but they triumphed 4–3. Mortensen's hat-trick was the first ever scored in an FA Cup Final at Wembley, and that glorious May afternoon ensured Blackpool Football Club's fame for evermore.

The Final was not just about Matthews, Mortensen, Blackpool and football. In a way it typified the new era that the country was heading into. The newly crowned Queen Elizabeth II was present at the game, television beamed the excitement into thousands of living-rooms up and down the country and, in the year when Everest was officially conquered, the match became a defining moment in the sporting psyche of a sporting nation. It has been said that, along with the 1966 World Cup Final and Roger Bannister's four-minute mile, the game was 'one of the most mythologized in British sporting history'.

The fact that the match was transmitted to a record television audience only enabled the sense of occasion to be enhanced among the people of the nation, who would crowd round their black-and-white sets to watch the grainy pictures. Today, in an age where televised football can now be seen at any time on virtually any channel, the appeal of watching one match, albeit the biggest of the season, in those days of austerity, cannot be underestimated. In fact, both the Football Association and the Football League looked upon television as an irritation and almost an irrelevance, such was the minimal impact it had on attendances, but the BBC stood by their decision to continue to show Finals live, paid their £1,000 fee and televised history.

Blackpool's route to the Final had been difficult, having overcome Sheffield Wednesday, Arsenal and Tottenham Hotspur on the way, and only a last-minute error by Spurs and

HRH Queen Elizabeth II meets the players as they collect their medals.

The Blackpool players celebrate with the trophy at Wembley.

The Blackpool players receive their medals from the Queen Mother.

The Blackpool players parade the trophy along the promenade.

The 1952–53 FA Cup winners.

England full-back Alf Ramsay gave Blackpool their semi-final victory. Their return from the Final made it all worthwhile, as thousands of fans greeted them at Blackpool North train station. When their train stopped at Warrington, Wigan and Preston, crowds stood on the platforms to cheer them on. On the promenade, fans had started to gather six hours before their arrival. Estimates vary on the number there to greet the team, but figures of around 100,000 were not exaggerated.

Among this celebration, a thought must have been spared for poor Allan Brown. He had missed the 1951 Final and now missed the game against Bolton after breaking his leg when he scored the winner against Arsenal in the quarter-final. He also missed the Charity Shield game against the same opponents in October, a game the Seasiders lost 3–1 at Highbury.

The Blackpool players on a ship at Dundee, October 1953.

The following season saw another concerted push for the elusive League Championship, but a particularly unfruitful Christmas period, where only five points were gained from 10 matches, contributed to a final position of sixth. New players had been added, with Jim Kelly being signed from Watford for around £15,000 and Johnny McKenna, an Irish international, from Huddersfield Town. Johnny Crossland left for Bournemouth, George McKnight moved to Chesterfield and John Ainscough went into non-League football. Allan Brown continued his long recovery from a broken leg and cartilage injury, and Mortensen managed another 21 League goals.

The most amazing result of the whole season came in the FA Cup. Despite being defending champions, Blackpool took four matches to dispose of Luton Town, then two games with West Ham United before losing 2–0 against Third Division Port Vale in front of 40,000 fans. It was one of the biggest shocks in FA Cup history, but it paled into insignificance when compared to what happened one year later.

In January 1955 Blackpool went down by the same scoreline to Third Division York City at Bloomfield Road in the FA Cup third round. It was, in footballing terms, an absolute disaster for the club, and without the exploits of 'keeper George Farm it could have been more humiliating. The 26,000 fans present could only watch in despair and sheer incredulity as their heroes blustered and blundered their way through the 90 minutes, as little York cut through the threadbare Blackpool defence at will.

The League offered little better for the club, with a desperate fight against relegation. After so many seasons of success, this came as a shock to both players and fans alike, and it was certainly a test of character. It looked like their fate was decided with only three games remaining, but an incredible 6–1 victory at Manchester City – with three goals from Perry – saved them. Why the team that had seen and provided so much success in recent years should struggle so badly was a mystery, but fortunately First Division football had been ensured for another season.

The 1955–56 season was significant for many reasons. First, two of the club's greatest servants, Harry Johnston and Stan Mortensen, departed to face new challenges. Johnston became manager of Reading, and Morty went to Hull City. Their places were filled by Roy Gratrix and Jackie Mudie, who switched to centre-forward, allowing Dave Durie to take over the inside-left position. Second, the highest-ever attendance was recorded at Bloomfield Road, when 38,098 crammed into the ground on 17 September to see Blackpool beat Wolves 2–1. However, the most significant event of the campaign was the team's final position in the runners'-up position at the end of the season, 11 points behind champions Manchester United and just above Wolves on goal average. It was, and still is, the highest that Blackpool Football Club has ever finished in a top-flight League campaign. The fact that this was achieved with a team that was gradually changing, with a lot of new faces breaking through, speaks volumes for the wealth of talent that could be seen wearing the tangerine shirts during those golden years.

There were two other interesting facts from that season. Firstly, the fastest goal by a Blackpool player was scored by Ernie Taylor in the FA Cup at Manchester City after 13 seconds – although that was beaten in 1995 by James Quinn at Bristol City with a strike after 11 seconds – and unfortunately for Taylor the game was abandoned due to fog, and Blackpool predictably lost the rearranged game. Secondly, goalkeeper George Farm got his name on the score sheet when he took over the centre-forward position after an injury during the home game with Preston. Unfortunately, Blackpool were trounced 6–2.

The Cup-winning squad of 1953 was gradually breaking up, but it was encouraging to

Blackpool FC 1956–57.

see the new talent taking their places. A young defender, Jimmy Armfield, was showing his talent, with Jim and Hugh Kelly in the half-back line. Jackie Mudie had taken over the goalscoring duties from Mortensen and managed 32 goals during the 1956–57 season. He was helped by Dave Durie, who scored 20.

That season saw Blackpool slip to fourth, despite scoring a total of 93 goals. Their interest in the FA Cup ended at the fifth-round stage, despite their earlier 6–2 mauling of Fulham, when Mudie scored four. Attendances were down significantly, with only four games at Bloomfield Road attracting over 30,000 and the last match of the season, at home to Burnley, attracting fewer than 14,000. This prompted the local newspaper to declare that the Blackpool public did not deserve First Division football, and unless a new, comfortable stadium was built, it could not see football being played in the town for much longer. Long-suffering Blackpool fans waited a long time for the new ground – approximately half a century, in fact – and thankfully the prophesies were never realised as Bloomfield Road has continued to be the home of Blackpool Football Club, despite some scares in the 1980s.

That season saw the departures of Allan Brown, who joined Luton Town for £10,000, and Jim Kelly, who retired at the end of the season. In a footnote for that season, Blackpool became the first club to fly to a match on the 19 April 1957. The game was against Arsenal at Highbury, and it ended 1–1. At the end of the campaign Blackpool played Barcelona in a friendly in Spain. They drew 3–3.

THE DECLINE

Seventh place at the end of the 1957–58 season was evidence for the fans that the team's best days were now behind them, and with no player able to achieve the 20-goal mark, Blackpool's challenge was fast fading. The FA Cup was again now no more than a temporary diversion, and a heavy defeat at West Ham United ended interest for another season. There was hope, though, with the emergence of a new scorer in Ray Charnley, a centre-forward, but it was clear that the maestro himself, Stanley Matthews, was now bowing to the passing years. It was believed that he would soon return to Stoke City, but by the end of the campaign he was still registered with Blackpool.

Sadly, 1958 saw the retirement of arguably the greatest Blackpool manager ever, Joe Smith. After 23 years he finally gave in to his ill health and stood down, proud in the knowledge that he had transformed the club into one of the great powerhouses of the

Durie's goal against West Bromwich Albion, December 1957.

English domestic game and raised their profile above and beyond anything imagined when he joined in 1935. There are few personalities who stay loyal to one club, and even fewer who leave such an ingrained mark in the consciousness of the people who surround it. Joe Smith will forever be linked with greatness, and his achievements at Bloomfield Road could never be demeaned. It is unlikely that Blackpool Football Club will be fortunate enough to see his like again.

Smith was succeeded – certainly not replaced, as that was almost impossible – by one of the club's 'old boys', Ron Suart. A quietly spoken, deep-thinking man, he had the unenviable task of rejuvenating a tired squad and injecting new blood into a fading challenger. Suart's first task was to oversee a post-season tour of America, Australia and Hong Kong, where Blackpool won all 14 matches, including five Test games against Australia, and scored 87 goals in the process. If only English League football could be as easy and satisfying.

As it was, the first season in the new era was reasonably successful, with an eighth-place finish. Charnley managed to score 20 goals, with Mudie and Perry also breaking into double figures. The Seasiders even managed to reach the sixth round of the FA Cup, but a one-goal defeat to Luton Town in the replay, courtesy of ex-'Pool man Allan Brown, was a disappointment as many fans had felt that Wembley was beckoning once more. The great Ernie Taylor departed Bloomfield Road for Old Trafford to join a severely depleted Manchester United squad following the terrible Munich disaster.

The following season inevitably saw many changes in team personnel, with Ewan Fenton, Jackie Wright and George Farm all leaving. Joining were Bruce Crawford, a junior, Arthur Kaye from Barnsley, 'Mandy' Hill, a local schoolboy, and goalkeeper Tony Waiters

Stanley Matthews is tackled by a Spurs player, 1958.

from Macclesfield Town, who later went on to play for England. Charnley kept on scoring, netting another 18 that season, and Matthews kept on defying both the odds and the fans, who were convinced he was on the verge of leaving, by turning out regularly and actually starting a partnership with Charnley. The team, however, failed to make an impact and finished in 11th place. It was to be the last time, up to the present day, that Blackpool were able to finish in the top half of the upper tier of English football. The team's demise was brutally emphasised in February when a rampant Manchester United won 6–0 at

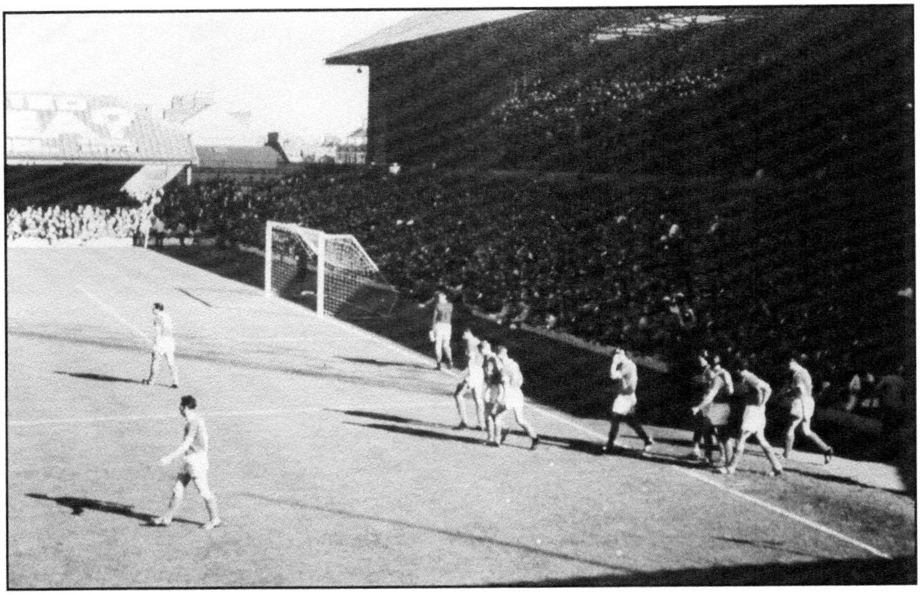

Running out against Nottingham Forest, 1961.

A smart save is made in the Wolves match, 1961.

Bloomfield Road, a scoreline that flattered Blackpool more than their visitors. The FA Cup interest ended in a fourth-round replay to eventual winners Blackburn Rovers. There was a tour of Nigeria and Rhodesia in the summer, where Blackpool won seven of their eight games, but there were few associated with the club who did not believe that the future was now anything but rosy.

The pessimism seemed justified as the club entered the 1960s. The start of the 1960–61 season saw the team win just one of their first 13 games, and they spent the entire campaign looking to avoid the trapdoor out of the First Division. They did it by winning six points from their last four games, pushing rivals Preston and also Newcastle down, but it was of scant consolation. Suart was now under intense pressure as manager, and certainly his cause was not helped by a 6–2 thrashing by Scunthorpe United of the Second Division in the FA Cup. Even the new League Cup was to prove of little pleasure as Blackpool were beaten by Leeds United in a second-round replay – they had been given a bye in the first – where Don Revie scored for the visitors.

The playing personnel was again changing, with Hugh Kelly, Brian Snowdon and Peter Smethurst, a South African import who did not make the grade, all leaving, and no fewer than eight players making their debuts for the club that season. Among them was Glyn James, a future Welsh international who was to play for many years for Blackpool, Gordon West, who shared the goalkeeping duties with Waiters, Ray Parry and Leslie Lea. The latter soon became a favourite with the fans.

The supporters, however, were deserting the club in their droves. For the first time in 15 years a home attendance of under 10,000 was recorded for the visit of Leicester City. Just 8,752 saw the Seasiders crush their opponents 5–1, followed a few weeks later by a turn-out of 9,947 for the visit of West Ham United, where the Hammers were hammered 3–0. Both were encouraging results, but off the field it was a depressing glimpse of an uncertain future.

The final proof that the golden days had ended for Blackpool Football Club came during the 1961–62 season, when the great Stanley Matthews returned to Stoke City. All the stars, with the exception of Bill Perry, had now gone, and Matthews's departure brought down the final curtain on a great era for the club. It seems inconceivable now that the club could ever boast that level of talent ever again. The 1950s truly were the time of Blackpool FC, and the following decade was but a shadow.

It is now obvious why Blackpool, and indeed so many clubs of similar size, fell from grace at the start of the 1960s. The maximum wage for players, strictly enforced since the start of professional football, was finally abolished after a threatened player's strike on 14 January 1961. Johnny Haynes, an England international, became the first player to earn £100 per week, and from that moment on the die was cast for the haves and have-nots. Sadly, Blackpool were very much in the latter group.

As a seaside town, very much relying on the tourist industry for income, Blackpool plays host to a cosmopolitan population. Without an industry to speak of, locals leave for work and prosperity, while people coming into town do not have prior connections with the area. Inevitably, that trickles down to the football club, and so the poor attendances down the years can be easily explained by the support moving away. While Blackpool FC has always had a healthy following, especially at away fixtures, the home attendances have been lacking

Blackpool v Manchester United, 1964.

at times. With the likes of Manchester United, Everton, Liverpool, Tottenham Hotspur, Leeds United and others all able to call on large support, Blackpool, and many clubs like them, struggled to attract the top players. Poor attendances meant smaller revenue and, in turn, limited resources to entice. It is a depressing story that continues to be told until this day, unless – like Blackpool in the first decade of the 21st century – a wealthy benefactor can be found.

For the 1961–62 season there was actually an improvement, with the club reaching 13th place in the First Division and an excellent run in the League Cup that saw Blackpool reach the semi-finals. They were beaten by Norwich City over two legs, but the competition was very much in its infancy and there was no Wembley Final to aim for. Even so, it had been the best Cup run for many years as the FA Cup had again offered little distraction. Ray Charnley added another 30 goals to his tally, and Graham Oates made his debut, but overall it was an undramatic campaign.

Another 13th-place finish the next season, early defeat to Norwich City in the FA Cup and just three games before losing to Manchester City in the League Cup just about summed up 1962–63. Charnley scored 22 goals, and a hard-tackling defender, John McPhee, made his debut. Overshadowing that, though, was the first showing of the brilliant Alan Ball. He burst on to the scene and made a huge impact at the club for the next four years. The final chapter of the 1950s was written with the departure of Bill Perry. He had been transfer-listed and eventually ended up at Southport after 13 years' service for Blackpool.

There was a pre-season tournament in Malaga before the 1963–64 campaign, where Blackpool were hammered by Real Madrid 4–1 before they beat Monaco 2–1, but the League season was a depressing fight against relegation. The Seasiders finished 18th and, with early exits from both Cup competitions, the critics turned against manager Ron Suart. The fans' anger was reflected in the attendances, as they had now dropped to an average of 16,000 – the lowest in Division One. Alan Ball was top scorer with 13, although Ray Charnley did score four against Charlton Athletic in a 7–1 League Cup thrashing. It was about the only bright spot of a dark and depressing season.

There was little improvement the following year. A mid-season run that saw 14 games without a victory and seven consecutive defeats resulted in a 17th-place finish. Charnley was top scorer with 21, but the interest around Ball was now growing and it seemed just a matter of time before he went on to greater things. Newcomers included Ian Moir and Jimmy Robson, but the highly dependable Roy Gratrix left after 12 years, and the excellent goalkeeper Gordon West moved to Everton. In a bizarre footnote to the season, Blackpool and Sheffield United played a 10-game competition between themselves in New Zealand in May and June. United won it by six games to four before Blackpool travelled to Hong Kong to hammer the national side 7–2.

To say the team at that time were uninspiring is a huge understatement. In 1965–66 they finished mid-table again and left both Cup competitions at conveniently early stages. There were new names with Hugh Fisher, Ronnie Brown and goalkeeper Alan Taylor, and Emlyn Hughes made his debut in the last game of the season. He actually only made 33 appearances for the club before Liverpool manager Bill Shankly paid £65,000 for his services, but the big loss was inevitably Alan Ball. He was eventually sold to Everton for a British record fee of £112,000 and started a trend that was to become depressingly familiar at the club in the following years. Ball had shared the top goalscoring duties with Charnley but, being a full England international, there was little hope of Ball remaining at Blackpool. His transfer was not completed until after the 1966 World Cup, however, so he was a Blackpool player when he played in the magical Final against West Germany. Spare a thought for Jimmy Armfield, though. After playing for England 43 times, including 15 as captain, and appearing in the 1962 World Cup, he missed the 1966 tournament through injury, despite being part of the squad. As ever, he was modest and humble and publicly stated that he was proud that the club's colours were kept flying by the appearance of Alan Ball, especially in the Final.

Relegation

After so many years of just avoiding relegation, there was a certain inevitability about the 1966–67 season. While the country was basking in the glory of World Cup victory, Blackpool fans faced the new campaign in the knowledge that they had one of the weakest squads in the division, and it came as no surprise to anyone that the team were relegated at the end of the season. As might be expected, though, their route to the Second Division was hardly straightforward. They only managed to gain seven points at home, with one victory,

The 1966–67 team.

The players watch a Blackpool penalty scored by Alan Skirton against Middlesbrough, 1967.

although that was against fellow strugglers Newcastle United 6–0. They also created the odd record of winning more games in Liverpool than in Blackpool, as they beat both Liverpool and Everton at their grounds. To add to the bizarre nature of their season, another of their away victories was at Southampton by five goals to one. There were positives, with the signings of Alan Skirton from Arsenal and Alan Suddick, who came to Blackpool from Newcastle United for a club record fee of £60,000.

Predictably, Ron Suart could not hope to survive such a dreadful season, and at the turn of the year he resigned after nine years in charge. He was replaced by the great Stan Mortensen, surely the most popular appointment the board of directors could have made. Morty immediately began to dismantle the old team. He was not afraid to make unpopular decisions, notably selling Ray Charnley to Preston after a heavy defeat at home to Millwall – although Charnley had scored the only goal. There were some good acquisitions, though, with Gerry Ingram coming from Mortensen's old club, Hull City; Tom White, a big centre-forward from Crystal Palace; Tommy Hutchison from Alloa Athletic, and the discovery of them all, Tony Green from Albion Rovers. He was one of the most exciting players ever to be seen at Bloomfield Road, and certainly made up for the departure of Alan Ball one year previously.

Blackpool spent the season pushing hard for promotion back to the top tier, and after six consecutive victories, they went into the final game at Huddersfield Town knowing that a win would probably secure an immediate return. They won 3–1, but after the premature celebrations had died down there was absolute despair in the knowledge that their nearest rivals, Queen's Park Rangers, had won at Aston Villa by virtue of a last-minute own-goal. QPR had deprived Blackpool of promotion due to a better goal average – 0.86 to 'Pool's 0.65. It was unbelievably cruel, made even worse by the knowledge that the 58 points was a record for a club to achieve and still not gain promotion. Blackpool had been consigned to another season of Second Division football.

Mortensen continued his rebuilding for the 1968–69 season. Leslie Lea was transferred to Cardiff City, Ian Moir to Chester City, Gerry Ingram to Preston, Graham Oates to Grimsby Town and, surprisingly, Alan Skirton to Bristol City. As well as changing the squad, it also helped the rather shaky financial situation at the club – something that had reappeared and was to stay for many more years.

Bill Bentley was signed from Stoke City and took over as left-back, while Terry Alcock, signed one year previously from Port Vale, now broke into the first team. Unfortunately, the season was one of disappointment, with the Seasiders ending it in eighth position. Despite a good run in the League Cup, where they went out heavily to Arsenal, the campaign was a let-down. The board, perhaps panicked into action by a lack of success and disturbed by rumours of players' lack of discipline, made a most regrettable decision – they sacked Stan Mortensen. It was greeted by the fans with a mixture of shock and anger, as Morty was as popular a manager as he had been a player. Worryingly, it started a depressing trend at Bloomfield Road where managers came and went with alarming frequency, so much so that the common joke was that their names were chalked on the manager's office door to save paint.

Les Shannon was appointed at the beginning of May and set about putting a team together that would eventually gain promotion in his first season in charge. Shannon added

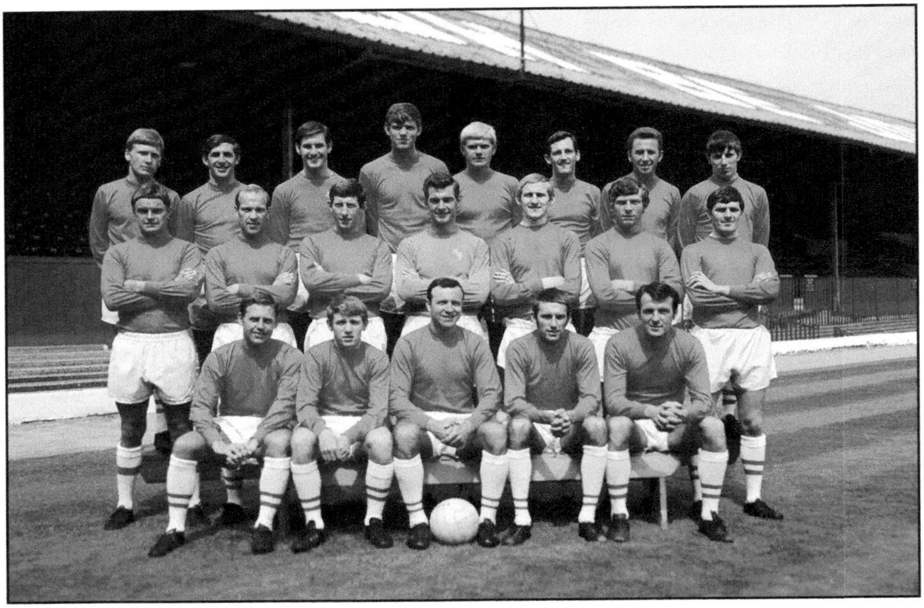

Blackpool team, 1968–69.

players such as Mickey Burns from non-League Skelmersdale United, David Hatton, Fred Pickering and Harry Thompson – another in the long line of Scottish goalkeepers who came to the club. Promotion was gained at Deepdale, of all places, against arch-rivals Preston North End. On an emotional Monday night, Pickering scored a hat-trick that gave Blackpool a 3–0 victory, putting them back in the First Division, and incredibly pushed Preston to the Third Division. The capacity attendance of 35,400 was supplemented by around 20,000 Blackpool fans who had made the short journey, and full-back Jimmy Armfield later said, 'The real rivalry started that night. It was such a significant result for both teams. Many Blackpool fans walked back to Blackpool that night and our bus passed them on the way home, dancing and singing by the road.'

The two Cup competitions did not divert Blackpool from their ultimate goal, but the FA Cup saw a remarkable game against Arsenal in the third-round replay, with Blackpool winning 3–2 after being two goals down. It had been a hugely successful season, and the fans, players and management looked forward to the return to the First Division, a place where Blackpool seemed to belong. Somebody once said 'the First Division without Blackpool is like strawberries without cream.'

Sadly, the strawberries and cream went off very quickly, as Blackpool found life in the First Division as unforgiving as the last time they had graced it. From the opening match, where they lost 3–0 to fellow promotion achievers Huddersfield Town, they struggled. There had been only two victories recorded by the time Championship challengers Chelsea came to town in October, and that game was to herald the end for manager Les Shannon. The FA Cup holders were completely overrun in the first half and Blackpool held an incredible 3–0 lead, yet somehow, after a complete capitulation in the second period,

Chelsea ran out 4–3 winners. If the result was not bad enough, the decision by Shannon to substitute two-goal hero Fred Pickering brought howls of protest from the Blackpool fans, and that effectively sealed his fate. With apparent dressing-room discontent, he resigned a few days later with Blackpool firmly embedded in the relegation zone.

Shannon was quickly replaced by Bob Stokoe, a man the club had tried to lure away from Carlisle United a year or so previously, but there was little he could do to change the team's fortunes. Even the return of Tony Green, after a lengthy lay-off through injury, failed to stop the rot, although a famous 4–0 FA Cup victory in January against West Ham United will go down as one of Green's best games in a tangerine shirt. The fact that Blackpool used a total of 28 players that season goes some way to explaining the mere four wins and eventual relegation alongside Lancashire neighbours Burnley.

During the summer of 1971 Blackpool entered the Anglo-Italian Cup. It was a chance for the club to regain a little pride following their disastrous season – something they did quite successfully. The competition consisted of 12 teams, six from each country, with the winners of each group meeting in the Final. Blackpool topped the English group by winning two, drawing one, losing one and scoring 10 goals in the process. That gave them 15 points, and they met Bologna in the Final at the Stadio Comunale. A total of 26,000 fans saw a 2–1 victory for the Seasiders after extra-time, and so the first piece of silverware for 18 years could be displayed at Bloomfield Road. It was a superb performance against a talented side and a tremendous boost for the season ahead. The next day thousands of fans lined the promenade to welcome back their returning heroes.

The Blackpool players receive instructions with the help of Subbuteo in 1971.

Winning the Anglo-Italian Cup, 1971.

For the start of the 1971–72 season Stokoe began a massive clear-out of players in an attempt to trim the huge squad. Out went Fred Pickering, Fred Kemp, Alan Taylor, Graham Rowe and Jimmy Armfield. The latter had actually retired at the end of the previous season, playing his last match in the 1–1 draw with Manchester United. He had played for 17 years and amassed 569 Football League appearances – still a club record for Blackpool.

New players to arrive included goalkeepers John Burridge and George Wood, Chris Simpkin, Dave Lennard and Keith Dyson. Dyson came in an exchange deal that took Tony Green to Newcastle United and also boosted the finances by around £150,000. On the field a creditable sixth place was achieved, and an excellent run in the League Cup saw Blackpool beaten in the quarter-finals by eventual winners Tottenham Hotspur. It had been an encouraging debut season for Stokoe.

1971–72 Blackpool team group.

Blackpool team 1973–74.

During the summer Blackpool defended their Anglo-Italian Trophy and again made it to the Final. This was helped by their final group game, which saw a remarkable 10–0 home victory over Lanerossi, but the Final itself was a different proposition. In front of 70,000 fans in the Olympic stadium, A.S. Roma easily overcame a stubborn Blackpool side and ran out comfortable 3–1 winners.

1972–73 was a disappointing season as only seventh place was achieved, but again the team made it through to the quarter-finals of the League Cup, losing to Wolves by a late goal in the replay. The main transfer action involved Tommy Hutchsion. He moved to Coventry City, with Billy Rafferty coming the other way, but the biggest change was again involving the manager. Bob Stokoe was lured away to his native North East and joined Sunderland, wanting the challenge of a bigger club. It angered fans, as he had previously stated his desire to stay at Bloomfield Road for a minimum of five years. For him, the move was a good one, as he took Second Division Sunderland to a famous FA Cup Final victory over mighty Leeds United. Blackpool, meanwhile, faded away from any possible League challenge.

The summer of 1973 saw another Anglo-Italian journey, but this time it did not end in the Final. A new manager had been appointed in Harry Potts, a deep thinker and certainly a football tactician. He had been pursued by the club in the 1950s as a player, so there were high expectations. His first season in charge could, and indeed should, have resulted in promotion back to the top flight, but in the final game of the season, away at Sunderland, they let slip a 1–0 lead with seven minutes to go, only to lose 2–1. If Blackpool had won they would have edged out Carlisle United on goal average, a team that they had hammered 4–0 at Bloomfield Road one week previously. It was another sickening disappointment for Blackpool fans. The squad had been strengthened with the additions of veteran Wyn Davies and a future prolific scorer in Mickey Walsh. Also joining was a promising defender, Paul Hart, but the 1973–74 season was looked upon a as missed opportunity.

The next two seasons saw the team take a step backwards, with seventh and 10th-place finishes respectively. Goals were the main problem, as only 38 were scored in the 1974–75 season and just two more the following season. It was hardly surprising that in May 1976 Potts, never hugely popular with the fans, left the club. Although there had been little success on the field and the football adopted was unnecessarily negative, Potts had performed well in the transfer market. He had bought sparingly but effectively and had sold players on for large profits. Mickey Burns had gone to Newcastle United for £175, 000 and John Burridge had signed for Aston Villa for £75,000.

The club then turned to a former great player in Allan Brown for their next managerial appointment. He took over for the 1976–77 season on the back of successful spells with numerous other clubs and immediately made some shrewd signings, notably that of Bob Hatton. He went on to a prolific goalscoring partnership with Mickey Walsh, one of the most potent the club had seen for many years. Also joining was Iain Hesford, another young and talented goalkeeper who was to make his name at Bloomfield Road. The season was successful, with a fifth-place finish, although they missed out on promotion to Nottingham Forest by just two points. Within 12 months Brian Clough's men had gone on to a League Championship, while Blackpool reached new depths. For that campaign, though, goalscoring no longer seemed to be a problem, with Mickey Walsh scoring 28 and Bob Hatton 11. It seemed that the future was bright once more for Blackpool. How things were about to change.

Blackpool team, 1976–77.

The Decline

It is difficult to explain, or indeed understand, the events that transpired during the 1977–78 season. Suffice to say, it was the most disastrous in the club's history. Admittedly, the promotion push seemed half-hearted, but in early February, the team had won their last two home games against Charlton Athletic and Blackburn Rovers respectively and put five past both of them. They were on the verge of the promotion race when, inexplicably, Allan Brown was sacked. It seemed that an argument between him and chairman Bill Cartmell had spilled over into the local newspapers, and just a couple of days after the 5–2 victory against Blackburn Brown was dismissed. It was, arguably, one of the worst decisions ever taken at Bloomfield Road (even matching the astonishing dismissal of Stan Mortensen in 1969) and was the catalyst for a fall from grace that hardly seems possible. The team, who were comfortably mid-table in March, only won one of their last 16 League games and plummeted into the relegation zone. They had finished their season and were on a tour of America when they heard the news. Orient, who had to win at Cardiff to avoid the drop, did just that by a goal to nil, and Blackpool were relegated to the Third Division for the first time in their history. To compound their hurt, Preston were promoted the other way.

Even today, the reasons for the manager's departure are unclear, but that, coupled with an injury to Bob Hatton, somehow weakened the spine of the team and, frankly, they capitulated. It was no comfort that their goal difference was minus one, significantly better than other teams around, or that just one more point would have left them in 14th. Blackpool were down and set to stay that way for 29 more years.

Predictably the mass exodus of players who had contributed to the downfall started, and it continued unabated as third-tier football was realised. George Wood, Mickey Walsh and Bob Hatton were the three main stars to leave, although Walsh and Hatton had scored 36 goals between them the previous campaign, and Wood was as reliable as ever. Jimmy Meadows had been given temporary charge of the team, but he was replaced by the returning Bob Stokoe for his second spell at the club.

The first season in the Third Division was hardly spectacular, with a 12th-place finish, helped by 16 League goals from Derek Spence. Attendances were at an all-time low, without a single League game played in front of a five-figure crowd. The only bright spot was a 2–0 League Cup victory over First Division Ipswich Town, but it was a glimmer in a fog of despair. Stokoe did not stay long. He walked out of the club at the end of the season and never returned.

Stan Ternent was installed in the merry-go-round that was now the Blackpool manager's position. He had worked alongside Stokoe so was seen as the obvious replacement. He managed to stabilise the side, and with Tony Kellow and Derek Spence building up a budding striking partnership he looked as if he was moving the team in the right direction. Unfortunately, he was never given the time to see the final outcome. After only five months in charge, he was replaced by former playing great Alan Ball. The club had been pursuing Ball for some time, and when he agreed to begin his managerial career at Bloomfield Road he was greeted ecstatically by the fans. His arrival was seen as heralding a return to former greatness for the club, but sadly it turned out to be anything but. Blackpool only avoided relegation on the final day of the season, winning 2–0 at Rotherham United, and finished 18th.

Ball proceeded to spend large amounts of money on players who had seen their best days, and he introduced many youngsters who seemed unready for League football. None of it worked and, despite his enthusiasm, it was clear that Alan Ball was learning on the job as a manager. By the end of the 1980–81 season Blackpool were in the Fourth Division. It had been an awful season, with only nine League victories, and even the 4–0 FA Cup home win over neighbours Fleetwood Town was tainted by Ball's remarks that the fans – over 10,000 of them – had turned up to see Blackpool lose. Alan Ball departed in February, sacked after a defeat at Brentford, his glittering reputation at Bloomfield Road tarnished by his managerial failure.

As the team's fortunes continued to wane, the reputation of a small minority of Blackpool fans became of national interest. The club has always had a vociferous and passionate following, even if at times in smaller numbers, but there have been occasions in the history of Blackpool Football Club when its fans have tarnished the image of its past. The Atomic Boys of the 1950s had caused a sensation at visiting grounds with their happy band of followers, but the 'fans' of the 1980s caused something entirely opposite.

In 1974 a Blackpool fan, Kevin Olsson, was murdered at a game with Bolton Wanderers at Bloomfield Road – reported as the first death from football hooliganism at an English ground. The authorities brought in sweeping measures to try to combat the rise of hooligan-related incidents, but by the start of the 1980s it was rife throughout the game. Blackpool, now a 'big' club in the small Fourth Division, were always an attraction and brought large number of supporters to away games. Unfortunately, a lot of the grounds were unprepared for such a following, and segregation and police cover were at times totally inadequate. It was this cocktail that combined to make the explosive reaction that was the Blackpool hooligan.

Games at Rochdale and Bury in 1984 and 1985 were particularly unpleasant after fans had caused mayhem inside and out of the ground. A match with Chester in 1985 was held up to clear Blackpool fans from the pitch, and in May 1984 the club made national headline news when Blackpool fans created chaos in Torquay ahead of the match at Plainmoor. There was even a report on the *Six O'Clock News* on the BBC highlighting the problems the club had with its followers, something that only contrived to make the situation worse. The Football Association had launched numerous investigations, but nothing was done, and it is fair to say that Blackpool themselves seemed to do little to combat the rise of unsavoury behaviour. Thankfully, hooliganism virtually died away following the twin Heysel and Hillsborough disasters. Now most supporters up and down the country can attend a football game in relative safety, although there will always be outbreaks of disorder on occasions. Blackpool is quite a safe environment to watch football, but the decade of the 1980s is one that has stained the image of the club. Hopefully that stain will fade away as the years pass.

Back to matters on the field, and following Alan Ball's departure the club found itself in serious financial difficulty. They had paid a club record £116,000 for Jack Ashurst two years previously and had not recouped any of that sum. Not only that, but attendances were at an all-time low. There were reports of the local council being ready to step in and help and also of a supermarket chain willing to buy Bloomfield Road and relocate the club. These were worrying times for the fans.

On the field, the team finished 12th in its first season in Division Four, despite leading the table at an early stage of the season. This was done under the managership of Allan Brown once more. He had been brought in to pick up the pieces following the Alan Ball reign and, with the help of a new striker in Dave Bamber, it looked quite promising. Tony Kellow and Derek Spence had moved on, but a good FA Cup run that ended in a fourth-round replay defeat at Queen's Park Rangers helped the finances. All too predictably, though, the manager found the job almost impossible and, after yet more boardroom pressures, Brown resigned in April, just over a year into his second stint at Bloomfield Road.

During the summer months there were changes at boardroom level, with a new set of directors promising greater stability and certainly a more positive outlook. They searched for an ambitious young manager capable of revitalising the team, and they found him in Sam Ellis.

Ellis, a Lancastrian, had been a successful player and was learning about football management under Graham Taylor at Watford. It was an excellent appointment as he brought a new sense of pride to the club and a instilled a winning attitude into the players. It took time, though, and if there was ever a test of the new board's attitude then the 1982–83 season was certainly that. Blackpool finished in 21st place and were forced to seek re-election. They lost to neighbours Preston in the FA Cup and played in front of just over 1,700 against Colchester United – a new low for the club in the League.

There had been no money to spend, so Ellis had scoured the youth and free-transfer markets for his purchases. He made some money by selling Dave Bamber and Colin Morris for reasonably large fees, and he brought in Paul Stewart, a ready-made replacement for Bamber. It had been a difficult first season for the new manager; whereas in the past he would have almost certainly have been sacked, now it was clear that this was part of a huge rebuilding process. Re-election was granted, and Blackpool were never to finish that low again.

The following campaign saw the fruits of Ellis's labours blossom with a concerted promotion push. The fact that it was missed, with an eventual sixth-place finish, was of no consequence as the team were now playing with more passion and cohesion than before, and they believed they could win. They had even enjoyed a decent FA Cup run, highlighted by a 2–1 win over Manchester City at Bloomfield Road in front of 15,000 fans – although that was overshadowed in the

Sam Ellis and his team in the 1980s.

The team celebrate promotion back to the Third Division.

national limelight by Bournemouth beating Manchester United 2–0 the same weekend. The club seemed to be back on the upwards slope.

For 1984–85 there were notable new signings. Ian Britton from Dundee United, Eamonn O'Keefe from Port Vale and Mike Walsh from Manchester City were the highlights, and the team never looked back. A successful campaign saw them finish second to Chesterfield after a superb 4–0 victory at fellow chasers Darlington, and Blackpool were back in the Third Division. It had been a great achievement, and after so many years of despair and failure it was a wonderful boost to not only the club but to the town, and it was celebrated in some style. Sam Ellis was a hero at Bloomfield Road, and it was hardly surprising that many top clubs were keeping an eye on him. There had been a low spot in the season, though, when non-League Altrincham beat Blackpool at Bloomfield Road in the FA Cup first round. Amazingly they repeated the feat one year later. Despite this, Blackpool were back, as their fans never failed to sing as the campaign came to its denouement.

Back in the Third Division the club did quite well, staying in the top four right through to Christmas, but then a serious injury to O'Keefe kept him out of the first team and took away much of the Seasiders' fire-power. It was a disaster for O'Keefe as the injury all but ended his playing career.

A 12th-place finish was reward enough for a steady season, although the team had lost twice to rivals Preston in the League Cup, but there were more worrying signs off the field. The club was facing hefty bills for the upkeep of the now dilapidated Bloomfield Road, and the Manchester supermarket chain was looming menacingly. At one stage it looked like the final home game of the season, against Newport County, could be the last at the famous old ground with rumours of a share at Deepdale, home of Preston.

It was with the financial situation in mind that steps were taken in 1986 to try and ensure the future of the club, whether in the town or not. The club's assets were converted into a property company, with its shareholding transferred, while the board began negotiations with a Manchester group of developers. They wanted to buy Bloomfield Road for their supermarket chain and relocate both the football club and Blackpool Rugby League club a few hundred yards away. The clubs would then share an all-seater stadium that would form a vast entertainment complex.

Unfortunately, the plans were frustrated by the council who refused to give planning permission to the idea. This meant that the rugby club ended up playing its fixture at Bloomfield Road to save costs and eventually left the town altogether. The football club, meanwhile, had arranged a loan of £150,000 in stages to guarantee its future, following many appeals and a supporters' march through the town. In fact, it was the loyalty and passion of the fans that effectively kept the club afloat during that time. There were promenade 'fun runs' and other cash-raising schemes, one of which actually paid the transfer fee of Colin Methven from Wigan Athletic. Eventually, another power struggle in the boardroom saw the club soldier on, albeit badly wounded.

For 1986–87 there were many player changes. Paul Stewart was sold to Manchester City in March for £200,000, while earlier both Mike Conroy and Ian Britton had departed. Alex Dyer went to Hull City, but a new defender in Steve Morgan was emerging. Also, the once-prolific scorer, Craig Madden, joined from West Brom. The season started well enough once more, and indeed by February the team were still handily placed for promotion, but following the necessary sale of Stewart, they faded and finished ninth. Stewart was still top scorer with 21 goals. Sadly, attendances were falling again, and fewer than 2,000 turned up for the game with Fulham in April. As a footnote, Blackpool were, for the second successive season, knocked out of the League Cup over two legs by Preston. Despite the gradual progress on the pitch under Sam Ellis, he was now under pressure from the fans unhappy at the style of play deployed by the men in tangerine.

Tenth place was attained the following season, with Blackpool even having an outside chance of making the new Play-off system, but four defeats in their last eight games saw them fade away. There was a new striking discovery in Mark Taylor, who scored 21 League goals and became an immediate favourite with the fans. Unfortunately, he was to suffer serious injury shortly after, which kept him out of the game for some time. There was even success in both Cup competitions. An unlucky away defeat to Manchester City in the FA Cup and a deserved win over Newcastle United at home in the League Cup were the highlights. The club also celebrated its centenary with a champagne reception and seven-course dinner. The biggest change came at boardroom level, though, with local entrepreneur Owen Oyston gaining a larger financial stake in the club and replacing Ken Chadwick as chairman. The Oyston family have kept a firm hold on the club ever since, and were responsible for ensuring its survival in their early days of control.

New players arrived for 1988–89, including Andy Garner from Derby County, and the emergence of Tony Cunningham up front should have resulted in a successful season. Unfortunately, it was not to be, and after a home FA Cup defeat by Bournemouth there were fan demonstrations aimed at the manager. Sam Ellis could not hope to survive, and he left the club by 'mutual consent' after a 4–2 loss to Reading. By winning four of their last five games, Blackpool avoided relegation, but it had been too close. The chairman publicly stated that the team would not find themselves in that position again, so whoever the new manager was to be had pressure already. If there was one bright spot from the sorry campaign, it was a League Cup two-legged victory over Sheffield Wednesday.

Helping Blackpool avoid the drop was Jimmy Mullen, who had been asked to take the manager's job on a temporary basis following Ellis's departure. With Len Ashurst, he had steadied things and ensured Third Division football for another season, so it was no surprise that former Newport County player-manager was given the job on a permanent basis – a popular decision with the fans. He barely lasted a year.

The writing was on the wall during the opening League fixture with Wigan Athletic at Bloomfield Road. A turgid goalless draw that did not see a Blackpool shot on goal until the 89th minute. The fans were not happy, and it was clear that it was going to be another season of struggle. Players had come in, notably goalkeeper Steve McIlhargey, plus strikers Gordon Owen and Gary Brook. Carl Richards was another useful addition, but the team never looked a cohesive unit, and they struggled in the bottom four all season. The one bright spot was a particularly successful FA Cup run that saw them eventually beaten in the fifth-round second replay by Queen's Park Rangers, but the season was a disaster and Blackpool were relegated back to the Fourth Division for the second time in their history. Mullen was predictably sacked, and the new decade saw yet another team rebuilding process. To cap it all, the penultimate home fixture, against Swansea City, was played in front of fewer than 1,900. The bad days were back.

It needed an experienced manager to turn things round, so the board looked to Graham Carr. He had been successful with Northampton Town and, with assistant Billy Ayre, there was a belief that promotion could be gained immediately. Carr made a surprising and unpopular decision in selling fans' favourite Colin Methven to Walsall, and his cause was not helped with a truly astonishing defeat to Halifax Town at the Shay. The home side were bottom of the Football League, had not won at home and had conceded four to 91st team Hereford United the week before. They beat Blackpool 5–3 after being 3–1 down within 12 minutes. A few weeks later, with the team going nowhere but down, Carr was dismissed. He was in position for just five months, and so holds the unenviable record as Blackpool's shortest-serving manager.

David Bamber in action during a match against Hereford from the 1990–91 season.

A signed team photograph from 1991–92.

His place was taken by Billy Ayre, and so there followed an incredible transformation of the club's fortunes – one that was as unexpected as remarkable. With only one true signing, the return of striker Dave Bamber, the team lost only five of their remaining 30 League games and created records along the way. They won 15 consecutive home League matches during that campaign and the early part of the next, and went into the last match of the season, away at Walsall, in second place and needing just a point for automatic promotion. Sadly, in front of a large Blackpool following, the team froze and were beaten 2–0. It was first venture into the Play-offs and Blackpool did not disappoint in the semi-finals, easily overcoming Scunthorpe United. So now for a return to Wembley.

Sadly, on the day the team qualified for the Play-off Final, it was announced that Stan Mortensen had died, at the age of 69.

The Final, against Torquay United, was typical of Blackpool's roller-coaster way of doing things. 15,000 had travelled down to London on a bitterly cold May evening for Blackpool's first appearance at the old stadium for 38 years and fully expected to return victorious. Torquay had finished seven points adrift of the Seasiders, yet on the evening had matched Blackpool in every department. It was an open and entertaining game that finished 2–2 after extra-time. A penalty shoot-out followed, and as the clock ticked toward 11pm, a season's endeavour was subject to sudden death penalties after both teams scored four each. Sadly for Blackpool, and Dave Bamber in particular, he missed and Torquay were promoted. It was cruel, especially for Bamber who had scored 17 League goals that season, but it meant another season of lower tier football for Blackpool.

The board kept faith with Ayre and he was rewarded with another contract. Blackpool were one of the firm favourites for the title and went into the season with renewed optimism, although little money was made available to strengthen the squad. Alan Wright was sold to Blackburn Rovers for £400,000 in the early part of the campaign, which was frustrating, but Kenny Dalglish's side were one of the power houses of English football, so it was hardly surprising that Ewood Park was such a lure.

Again the promotion push was sustained, and by the end of the season they had won 31 of their last 35 home League fixtures, stretching back to the previous season, but in a case of

Action from the 1992 season against Scunthorpe at Wembley in the Play-off Final.

déjà vu they went into their last game of the season, away at Lincoln City, needing a point to go up. Again, with a huge tangerine following, they lost 2–0 and the Play-offs beckoned once more. Barnet were despatched in the semi-finals, and on a hot and sultry May afternoon Blackpool appeared at Wembley for the second successive season. 13,000 Blackpool fans baked in the hot sunshine as they took on Scunthorpe United, who had finished four points adrift of them. The game was hardly a classic, and after extra-time the scoreline was 1–1. Yet another penalty shoot-out, but this time Blackpool were victorious and were promoted at the second time of asking. Dave Bamber, who had endured his own personal nightmare 12

Celebrating the Play-off win, 1992.

months previously, was instrumental in the team's success after contributing 28 League goals. It was a day of celebration, and with the introduction of the new Premier League it meant that they would take their place in the Second Division for 1992–93.

The inaugural season for the new Division Two should have seen Blackpool continue to make progress, but sadly that turned out not to be the case. The board, ever mindful of financial restrictions, did not back Billy Ayre with a transfer budget, and in fact at the start of the campaign influential midfielder Paul Groves was sold to Grimsby Town for £150,000. Yes, Grimsby were in Division One at the time, but it was hardly a positive statement of intent from the board. The situation became so concerning that in January the game with Rotherham United was dubbed 'Buy A Player', as the proceeds from the gate receipts – from a larger than usual crowd of over 6,000 – would all go to funding the purchase of a new signing. That player was Andy Watson, who was bought for £55,000, and he repaid the fans quickly by scoring two of the goals in the 3–3 draw with Preston North End at Deepdale.

The team struggled, unsurprisingly, in the higher division, only winning two of their first 21 League games, but the combination of 16 goals from fan favourite David Eyres, and the sheer passion of Ayre himself, somehow secured Second Division football for another season. Blackpool finished in 18th place, four points clear of Preston, who were relegated.

The situation continued during the summer of 1993 with both Eyres and Trevor Sinclair leaving the club. Eyres joined Burnley, something the fans never forgave, and in fact later went on to play for Preston too, while Sinclair was sold to Queen's Park Rangers for £600,000. Sinclair had made his debut in August 1989 at the age of just 16, and was clearly destined for great things. He played 112 times for Blackpool, and later in his career was to make 12 England appearances.

The Blackpool squad from 1993–94.

It meant a weaker squad than the one that had won promotion two years ago, but Andy Watson's 20 League goals went some way to keeping Blackpool up for another season. As it was, safety was secured on the final day of the season when the Seasiders beat Leyton Orient 4–1 at home, while Fulham were slipping up. The celebrations at the end of the game were similar to the ones that greeted promotion two years previous, but it had been another close call. To give some indication of how poor the team had been, in January, on the back of seven consecutive League defeats, Blackpool fans were given free admission to Bloomfield Road for the game with Swansea City in the hope of boosting the side. Over 7,000 turned up, and Blackpool drew 1–1.

In June 1994, Billy Ayre was sacked by chairman Owen Oyston. It was a hugely unpopular decision and seemed scant reward for the man who had turned the club's fortunes around with little cash made available. The fans protested, but to no avail, and their anger hardly subsided when it was announced that Sam Allardyce would be his replacement. Allardyce was starting his managerial career, but as he had been brought from Preston he was hardly going to win over the fans easily. The unrest among the Bloomfield Road faithful stayed for many months, and one notable example was in a League Cup tie with Chesterfield at Bloomfield Road, a chant of 'Billy Ayre's Tangerine Army' rang around the ground. Hardly welcoming.

If Allardyce's arrival was greeted in a muted fashion, then the opposite could be said of another who travelled the short journey up the M55 from Preston to Blackpool. Tony Ellis was signed for £165,000 after a spectacular fall out with Preston boss Gary Beck. He instantly became a favourite with Blackpool fans, for obvious reasons, but also contributed 17 League goals that season. Sadly, one transfer that was not successful was that of goalkeeper Les Sealey. He came from Manchester United, but after schooling problems for his children he left in November for West Ham United.

In his first season in charge, Allardyce took Blackpool to a mid-table 12th position, their highest for years, but he continued to struggle to win over the fans. The style of football was not pretty, but it was clear he was a manager of immense talent. Sadly there were many low points during the season. The opening game, and Allardyce's first, saw Huddersfield Town romp to a 4–1 win at Bloomfield Road. Then there was the 7–1 thrashing at Birmingham City, plus York City completing the double with 4–0 and 5–0 victories (although York had won 5–0 at Bloomfield Road the previous season) and of course the 1–0 loss to Preston in the FA Cup. Despite all of that, the season was a success and the fans could look to the next with optimism.

Allardyce continued to strengthen the side and was given funds to do so as well. In the summer of 1995, he bought striker Andy Preece from Crystal Palace for £200,000, and it was felt that the team was strong enough to push for promotion. The promotion push took place, but the season was to go down in Blackpool history as one of the most depressing since 1977–78.

It was going so well. Blackpool were clearly one of the strongest sides in the Division and were in touch with the promotion race all season. In March, after a home victory over Burnley, they topped the League – the first time since 1978, and by the end of that month still sat atop the standings. They led Swindon Town by five points (albeit they had three

Sam Allardyce's squad from 1995–96.

games in hand), Crewe Alexandra by 10 points, Notts County 11 and Oxford United were 14 points adrift. With only seven League games left to play, it seemed impossible that promotion would not be won. Somehow Blackpool managed the impossible. They lost four of their remaining seven games, drew two and won the last one – at York City. Meanwhile, Oxford United won six of their last eight games (including a 1–0 win over the Tangerines) and drew two. Even on the last day of the season, Blackpool were 45 minutes from promotion as they led York 1–0 at half-time, while Oxford were being held by Peterborough United. It was not to be, as Oxford scored four second-half goals. Blackpool missed out by a point and were consigned to the Play-offs – something that seemed inconceivable six weeks previously.

The torment continued. They met Bradford City at Valley Parade in the semi-final first leg – a team who had finished a full 11 points behind Blackpool – and won comfortably 2–0. In the return leg, somehow Blackpool were beaten 3–0. The game has gone down in local folklore, and there are still mumblings and conspiracy theories, none of them proved, but it is fair to say that those two games summed up the entire campaign for Blackpool. The win was the team that had so taken the Division by storm, whereas the defeat was the team that had capitulated so badly at the end of the season when it mattered. Something or someone had to be blamed, and again it was the manager.

Just two weeks after the Bradford debacle, Allardyce was sacked by Owen Oyston from his prison cell. Oyston had been imprisoned for six years after being found guilty of rape just one week previously and had taken the decision alone. It is difficult to understand such an action as Allardyce had given Blackpool their most successful season since 1969–70, and if the team had been kept together, there was no doubt they would have had an extremely strong chance of promotion the following season. Such decisions make different futures. It is fair to say it took the club over a decade to recover.

Gary Megson was brought in as the new manager for the 1996–97 season. Again, another unpopular choice as at that time he had little management pedigree. One of the first things he did was to break the club's transfer record by signing Chris Malkin from Millwall for £275,000, but ultimately that turned out to be a poor buy. Malkin suffered from a variety of injuries, only appeared 65 times in a three-year period for Blackpool, scoring just six goals, and was eventually given a free transfer in 1999 to non-League Telford United.

The season, which should have promised so much, delivered so little. Megson splashed out again, with the £200,000 signing of Ian Hughes from Bury, but they were mid-table for most of the campaign, and the manager had clearly failed to endear himself to the demanding fans. Tony Ellis was top scorer for a third successive season, with 15 League goals, and only a late run of eight wins in their last 11 League games got them close to the Play-off positions. As it was, Blackpool finished seventh, four points adrift of Crewe Alexandra. An equally low spot was a 1–0 home defeat to Hednesford Town in the FA Cup, but in the League Cup they came close to a shock victory over Chelsea. 4–1 down from the first leg, they went to Stamford Bridge and won 3–1 with goals from Tony Ellis and James Quinn, very nearly taking the game into extra-time. It was a poor season though, and at the end Megson decided to leave and join Stockport County, who had just been promoted to Division One. It left a bitter taste for the fans and Vicky Oyston, who had taken over the running of the club since her husband had been sentenced. There were many legal wrangling between the two clubs, which took some time to resolve. Again, though, Blackpool were on the hunt for a new manager.

That new man was Nigel Worthington, a former Northern Ireland international, who had never managed before. He arrived at Bloomfield Road initially as a player-manager, but after only nine appearances he hung up his boots to concentrate full-time on managing. His appointment was greeted in an underwhelming fashion by the fans once more, and the omens for the season did not look good. During the 1997–98 season, he sold both strikers Tony Ellis and Andy Preece to Bury, and so breaking up what was a rich partnership at the club. Ellis was sold for £70,000 after scoring 65 goals, while Preece went for nothing after scoring 35. Phil Clarkson was to become the club's top scorer that season with 13 League goals, but a 12th-place finish confirmed that the team were now sliding downwards. There were few bright spots, but a two-legged League Cup victory over Manchester City and a dogged defeat at Coventry City in the next round stood out.

The demise continued the following season, with a 14th-place finish and few, if any, bright spots. Nigel Worthington had hardly galvanised the side, and the discontent spread among the supporters. Martin Aldridge was the team's top scorer with 10 in all competitions, after joining the club at the beginning of the season following his release by Oxford United, but he was to be transferred to Port Vale at the beginning of the next season. Tragically, in January 2000 he was killed in a car crash at the age of 25.

Off the field, there were yet more problems. Supporters had become disillusioned with the Oyston family, and there were numerous demonstrations against them, including a pitch invasion and coffin-carrying march to Bloomfield Road. Vicky Oyston, who was now running the club in the absence of her husband, had opened negotiations with a Midlands-based consortium for an £18 million takeover, but it came to nothing. There was also a strong suggestion that the club would re-locate to a Greenfield site on the edge of town called Whyndyke Farm with input from local businessman David Haythornthwaite, but again this came and went. Eventually, on 3 April 1999 Vicky Oyston relinquished control of the club, and her son Karl took over. The Oyston family continued their ownership of Blackpool Football Club. A final footnote to a pretty depressing season was that for the last match of the campaign, at home to Colchester United, home fans were allowed to stand on the Kop for the first time in years. It was largely a sentimental gesture, but one that was appreciated by older supporters who had spent their youth cheering on the team from the vast expanse of the North Stand terracing.

Striker John Murphy was bought at the start of the 1999–2000 season from Chester City as Nigel Worthington attempted to bring some much-needed power to the forward line. Blackpool were regarded as one of the season's favourites for relegation, and the first half of the season did nothing to dispel that. They only won one of their first 13 League games, and had twice conceded five goals, one a 5–0 home defeat to Bury. Their cause was not helped at all by striker Brett Ormerod suffering a broken leg, which kept him out for the season. The only saving grace was an FA Cup run that took them to Arsenal in January for a third-round tie. The team played above themselves that Monday evening and were unlucky to lose 3–1, but just five days later they were embarrassed 3–0 at Preston, and so Worthington's disappointing reign came to an end. He resigned a few days later with the fans jeers ringing in his ears, saying he could not take the team any further. They were deep in relegation trouble, and only a footballing miracle could save them it seemed.

The Revival

The arrival of former Liverpool and England midfielder Steve McMahon was greeted with enthusiasm by the fans. McMahon had previously managed Swindon Town with a limited amount of success but was seen as someone who had the drive and personality to transform the club's fortunes. He agreed to become the new Blackpool manager in January 2000, and it is fair to say that the seeds for the club's incredible rise up the footballing ladder in the next decade were sown with his arrival. He came too late to save the inevitable relegation to the bottom tier, though. That was confirmed in the last away game of the season, at Oldham Athletic, when an injury-time equaliser – celebrated by the Oldham players and fans as if they had won the Cup Final – consigned Blackpool to Division Three. To rub salt in the wounds of the long-suffering tangerine fans, Preston were crowned champions of Division Two on that day. John Murphy was the top scorer with 10 goals, but it was clear that the team needed a complete re-build to have any hope of a quick return. Finances were, as ever, tight and the club played host to two 'Break the Gate' games where the revenue from anything above the hardcore 3,500 fans would be given to the manager for team strengthening. Some of that money was spent on the acquisition of a hard-tackling midfielder in Richie Wellens from Manchester United. One further footnote, was that the home 'derby' fixture against Preston North End saw a 10,000-plus crowd – the last time five figures was attained at Bloomfield Road for 10 years.

A pre-season tour of the Caribbean seemed a little extravagant for the club, but it was an ideal way for the players to bond – many of them who had arrived on loan once McMahon had identified where the weaknesses were. One of the most influential was Paul Simpson, who signed on a free transfer from Wolves, and with Ormerod back to fitness the team looked to be strong enough for promotion. The early part of the campaign was worrying, though, as the team plummeted down. By the end of September, Blackpool were 91st in the English Football League, and there were rumours that McMahon had little time left. A victory at Kidderminster Harriers by 4–1 on a Friday evening seemed to be the tonic the team and the fans required, but even then the rest of the season was not exactly straightforward. There was a heavy home defeat to Norwich City in the League Cup and an embarrassing 7–0 loss at Barnet in the League, but gradually the team got into their stride. John Murphy scored regularly – 18 in the League alone – and with big wins over Torquay United, Scunthorpe United and Kidderminster Harriers, Blackpool sneaked into seventh place at the end of the season, and the Play-offs.

Hartlepool United were dispatched in the semi-finals, and on 26 May 2001 Blackpool met Leyton Orient at Cardiff's Millennium Stadium in the Final. 15,000 Blackpool fans saw the predictable roller coaster 90 minutes, with Blackpool a goal down within a minute, but at half-time the score was tied at 2–2 with goals from Ian Hughes and Brian Reid, a £20,000 buy

The Blackpool squad, 2000–01.

from Dunfermline Athletic. The second half saw Blackpool overwhelm their opponents as they were clearly fitter and better prepared for the big-match atmosphere, and with goals from Simpson and Ormerod they won 4–2 and were promoted back to the Second Division.

Off the pitch, things were changing rapidly with the re-building of the now ramshackle Bloomfield Road. The old Spion Kop and the West Stand had been demolished, and rising up in their place was a new combined stand that was gradually bringing the club and its facilities into the 21st century. The two combined stands held around 7,800 seated fans and boasted executive boxes and concourse with new refreshment facilities. It looked as if

The big screen showing the final score at Cardiff. (Courtesy of Danny Roper)

Bloomfield Road was finally going to become the stadium that the Oyston family had promised for so many years.

On the pitch, the new season in a higher division was reasonably successful with a comfortable 16th-place finish. John Murphy and Brett Ormerod were joint top scorers with 13 League goals each, but on 7 December 2001 Ormerod was sold to Southampton for £1.75 million. The club had rejected an earlier offer from Wigan Athletic, but it was clear that Ormerod was destined for better things – it was, at that time, the highest fee paid for a Blackpool player. In the New Year, McMahon added to the team with the signings of Chris Clarke from Halifax Town for £120,000 and striker Scott Taylor from Stockport County on a free transfer.

The highlight of the season was another trip to the Millennium Stadium, this time for the Final of the Football League Trophy. It was a competition that few clubs took seriously unless they reached the final stages, and Blackpool's only flirtation with that had been in 1989 when they had been beaten over two legs in the Northern Final by Bolton Wanderers. Now they met Cambridge United, and the Blackpool fans, who made up the majority of the rather small crowd, saw a comfortable 4–1 victory with goals from Murphy, Clarke, Hills and Taylor. It was Blackpool's first silverware for 31 years.

The 2002–03 season was pretty unremarkable, but there had been some useful additions to the squad. Simon Grayson, an experienced defender, Peter Clarke came on loan from Everton and then two years later joined on a permanent deal, Martin Bullock became established in midfield, Keith Southern joined from Everton and Kenny Dalglish's son Paul joined in August to strengthen the forward line. The season ended with a 13th-place finish,

The players go up to collect the trophy, 2002. (Courtesy of Danny Roper)

John Murphy top scoring with 16 League goals, but there were now criticisms of the inconsistency the side was showing. It was never more obvious when after a particularly impressive 3–1 win at Luton Town, followed by a home victory over Brentford, the team lay in 6th and a Play-off place. They only won one of their last 14 games to slip away. The football was pretty, but the spine of the side at times seemed to be weak, and defeat arrived far too easily – odd, bearing in mind the character of the manager. Finally, in 2003, the old South Stand was demolished giving the ground a curious lop-sided feel, as the East Stand had gone by this time too.

The following season saw more players, mostly on loan, arrive as McMahon attempted to bolster what was a weak squad. The likes of Mike Sheron and Mike Flynn from Barnsley and Neil Danns from Blackburn Rovers arrived, but the writing was on the wall after the opening game. A 5–0 defeat at Queen's Park Rangers – with Blackpool unfathomably playing in black despite it being the hottest day of the year – and McMahon was under pressure. There were mutterings of discontent between chairman and manager, and it had become obvious that the relationship between McMahon and the local media was now at breaking point. There was a high spot with a home League Cup win over Birmingham City, but the team struggled to a 14th-place finish with neither promotion nor relegation occupying the minds of fans. Scott Taylor replaced Murphy at the top of the scoring charts, with 16 League goals, but the campaign was remembered for two reasons. The first was yet another trip to Cardiff for the Final of the Football League Trophy. This time Blackpool met Southend United, making their first-ever trip to a Final, and for once the Blackpool fans were outnumbered by their opponents as only 16,000 had made the trip, but on the field Blackpool were dominant and goals from Murphy and Danny Coid got back the trophy they won two years previous.

The second was of course the position of the manager. McMahon had become increasingly frustrated at the lack of funds for team strengthening and had also polarised opinion among the supporters with some of his comments and media appearances. In January he resigned, only to burst into the press conference midway through to announce he had changed his mind! It was shown live on television and was poor comic book farce – something that did not do him or the club any favours. An uneasy truce continued for the rest of the season, although by this point he had lost the support of the fans, and after another disagreement with Karl Oyston he resigned again after the penultimate match of the season. Simon Grayson was given the task of picking the side for the final match at Bristol City. It was an ignominious end to the Steve McMahon chapter. He had brought enthusiasm and passion, and it is fair to say that without his input the re-building of Bloomfield Road may never have been started, but the expectations that he set were sadly never realised.

The new man in charge was former Scotland international Colin Hendry. He had been hugely successful in his playing career and had ended it by appearing 14 times in 2002–03 in a tangerine shirt. Much was expected of him, especially with his reputation as a hard-tackling Scotsman who had proved to be a real winner. Unfortunately, his time in charge was an unmitigated disaster.

He was appointed in June 2004 and made an early signing in striker Keigan Parker from St Johnstone, plus brought in veteran 'keeper Sasa Ilic from Sheffield United. The former was an excellent purchase and contributed greatly to the success of the side in years to come, whereas Ilic played just three games before moving on. The first of those was the opening League fixture at Doncaster Rovers. Again, for reasons only known to the club, the team appeared in black on another sweltering day and were comfortably beaten 2–0. Within a week they had lost their opening three League games, including a 4–0 home defeat to Stockport County, and were looking early relegation favourites. It did not look good, and after only one victory in their first nine League games there was pressure on the manager. Somehow, a string of results dragged them away from the drop-zone, but the sale of Scott Taylor to Plymouth Argyle in December for £100,000 hardly helped matters. Despite his departure, he was still the club's top scorer with 12 League goals. The Cup competitions played little interest and the team finished an uninspiring 16th, but after one season of Hendry's management, there was little hope from the fans of the team moving forward. Despite this, the sentiment aimed toward him was always positive, mostly due to the tragic circumstances in his personal life, but there were many who doubted his ability to transfer his playing success to management.

During the close season, Scott Vernon was signed from Oldham Athletic after appearing on loan the previous season. He was an excellent acquisition, and his goalscoring certainly proved that Hendry could seek out a decent player, but the 2005–06 season started the way the previous had ended, with the team struggling badly. Just three wins in their opening 16 League games, followed by a humiliating defeat at Doncaster Rovers in the FA Cup, and Hendry's reign was over. Chairman Karl Oyston announced that the manager was now on 'gardening leave' while a financial settlement was agreed. It was sad, but entirely inevitable. Colin Hendry, one of the nicest men in the game, had proved yet again that good footballers do not always make good managers.

The chairman said publicly that he would take his time with a new appointment, but Simon Grayson was promoted to temporary manager for the next home match with Scunthorpe United, won it 5–2 and never looked back. He successfully steered the team away from the relegation zone, with the help of 13 League goals from Keigan Parker and players such as Jason Wilcox coming on loan. He also promoted youngster Matthew Blinkhorn to the first team, and so a 19th-place finish was regarded as hugely successful. On the back of that, Grayson was given the position on a full-time basis. It was fortuitous for both club and the individual as Grayson has proved down the years how good a manager he is. In fact, despite his later success at Blackpool and subsequently Leeds United, he has said publicly that keeping the Tangerines in League One that season was one of his greatest achievements.

There were developments off the field, too, during that season, as in December 2005 the Oyston family announced that they were considering bids from three possible investors. Eventually, Latvian businessman Valeri Belokon agreed in May 2006 to invest £5 million in the playing side and then extended his shareholding to 20 per cent. He was made president of the club and made the remark that he wanted to see Blackpool in the Premier League 'within five years'. No-one took it seriously. To prove their commitment to the new-found relationship, the team enjoyed a pre-season tour of Latvia in 2006.

The start of the 2006–07 season did not seem to offer too much hope of success for the fans, as the first three League games were all lost, but a 4–2 victory at Bristol City suddenly

Simon Grayson and the 2006–07 squad.

suggested a hint of what was to come. The team continued to find their feet in the early part of the season, and with few new faces – notably Andy Morrell from Coventry City, Michael Jackson from Tranmere Rovers, and Wes Hoolahan on loan from Scottish club Livingston – it was obvious that the football that was being played was far more attractive than anything seen for years. Clearly, Simon Grayson had galvanised the team. Oddly, it was a 2–0 defeat away to Carlisle United in midweek that convinced supporters and players alike that the team was good enough to sustain a promotion challenge. Despite the scoreline, they had completely overwhelmed the home side. They then went on a seven-match unbeaten run, which resulted in Grayson being named Manager of the Month for December. Even the FA Cup was giving pleasure as they made it to the fourth round for the first time in 17 years, only to lose 3–2 in a replay at Norwich City.

As the season entered its last third, Blackpool embarked on a quite remarkable run. Always in touch with the promotion race, despite a temporary blip at the beginning of the year, they won 14 of their last 17 League games (including the Play-offs) and an amazing 10 in a row. In fact, if they had started their unbelievable form just a little earlier, they would almost certainly have been promoted automatically. As it was, they went into the final game of the season, away at Swansea City, still in with a chance, but despite an incredible 6–3 victory, with Andy Morrell scoring four (he was the season's top scorer on 16), they were pipped by Bristol City. Again Grayson was named Manager of the Month.

The Play-offs beckoned and a chance to banish the demons of 11 years previously. Oldham Athletic were the opponents, and the 2–1 and 3–1 scorelines give no hint to the complete dominance that Blackpool had shown over the two legs. In the Oldham side was Richie Wellens, a great servant to Blackpool, but he had moved away from Bloomfield Road 18 months earlier to seek success. He must have looked at what was happening at Blackpool and questioned his decision.

The Final at Wembley against Yeovil Town must surely go down as one of the most one-sided domestic games in the stadium's history. Around 31,000 Blackpool fans travelled on a soggy and miserable day in London, but they were rewarded with a performance of such complete and total dominance that the score of 2–0 again gives scant credit to the players. Goals from Michael Jackson and a stunner from Keigan Parker gave the Tangerines victory, and such was the nature of the game that their opponents had only one decent chance on goal – and that came with six minutes remaining. Blackpool were promoted to the Championship, the first time they would grace the top half of English domestic football since 1978. Manager Simon Grayson deserves all the credit for transforming a side, that 12 months previously had just avoided relegation, to one that played attractive and winning football. It was a celebration that went on long and hard as the Blackpool fans looked forward to a season with some of the bigger clubs, plus the revival of the 'derby' days with Preston North End.

Off the field, sadly progress seemed to have stalled. Bloomfield Road was clearly un-equipped for Championship football, with the two new stands already showing their age and the East Stand now a temporary 1,800 open-air all-seater. It was given the amusing nickname of the 'Gene Kelly stand' by home fans, due to visitors regularly getting a soaking. There was no stand behind the South goal, and so the fans naturally expected the chairman to start building with immediate effect. That did not happen, and Blackpool went into the new season still with a capacity of 9,800. The relationship between supporters and chairman, hardly amiable at the best of times, was not helped when Oyston publicly stated that only '50 to 100 fans were being locked out'. As a balance, it has to be said that the club has always been financially solvent under the Oyston regime, something that cannot be said for numerous clubs up and down the country.

To compete at a higher level, the team naturally had to be strengthened, but with little money made available Grayson brought in players through the loan system – something which he used extensively. There were useful additions, with loan players Wes Hoolahan and Ian Evatt being signed permanently from Livingston and Queen's Park Rangers respectively, but effectively the squad that performed so well in League One were now asked to compete in the Championship. The season started well, with the 10 straight victories from the previous season being extended to 12 with a League win at Leicester City and a League Cup win over Huddersfield Town. Gradually, though, Blackpool fell down the table and were destined to spend the campaign looking at the drop zone. Highlights of the season were a 1–0 victory at Preston North End, courtesy of a cheeky penalty from Hoolahan, and a League Cup fourth-round tie at Tottenham Hotspur – the first time they had got that far for 35 years. They were beaten 2–0 at White Hart Lane, with most of the media attention surrounding new Spurs boss Juande Ramos. Earlier in the competition they had knocked out Derby County on penalties at Pride Park. All in all, it was a nervy season at second-tier level, and big victories at home against Burnley on New Year's Day, Coventry City and Charlton Athletic ensured they were not in the bottom three. In fact, safety was guaranteed on the last day of the season with a home draw with Watford, although the last 15 minutes were played like a friendly fixture as the result suited both teams – Watford qualifying for the Play-offs. Blackpool finished two points clear of Ian Holloway's Leicester City who were relegated, quite ironic as history was to prove. Ben Burgess had been top scorer with nine goals in the League, with loan signing Paul Dickov second on six, and he only played 11 times in the tangerine shirt.

During the season, Scott Vernon was released to Colchester United, and in May Keigan Parker joined Huddersfield Town, Michael Jackson was released (so both Wembley scorers had left the club within 12 months) and Wes Hoolahan and Kaspers Gorks went to Norwich City and Queen's Park Rangers respectively for £250,000 each. Coming in was Welsh international David Vaughan for £200,000 from Real Sociedad, as Grayson attempted to strengthen for another tough season.

The new season saw little else in the transfer market, with Grayson continuing to utilise the loan market, and unsurprisingly the campaign started in an underwhelming fashion. An early defeat to Macclesfield Town in the League Cup, plus struggling performances in the League, had evaporated the optimism from two years ago. Also, off the field there was no news on the development of the ground, much to the fans' dismay. A home humiliation by Preston North End led the supporters to openly question Grayson, something that had not happened before, and it was clear the love affair that he had with the club was unravelling. He had earlier been linked with the vacant Leicester City manager's job but had continued to stay loyal to Blackpool, but when Leeds United offered him their position he immediately resigned.

It was not really a surprise that Grayson would end up at Elland Road, even though they were a League below Blackpool. He lived near the ground and had supported them as a boy, and even the most rabid Blackpool fan would agree that the size of the clubs just could not compare. Most fans wished him well, as he had produced something that no Blackpool supporter could dream of a few years ago – a Championship team.

The problem that chairman Karl Oyston had, as well as taking legal action against Leeds, was to find a new manager over the Christmas period. That fell to assistant Tony Parkes, who for the seventh time in his career took over in a temporary capacity following the departure of the full-time manager. Parkes, a footballing man through and through, was the ideal person to steady the rocky ship that was the Blackpool team. His first game, away at Sheffield Wednesday, resulted in a draw, but as the New Year turned he had to contend with a whole host of loan players returning to their parent clubs. Not surprisingly, Blackpool were beaten by non-League Torquay United in the FA Cup a few days later, but slowly though he steered them in the right direction, with the return of an old hero, Brett Ormerod, signing again from Preston. The highlight of the second half of the season was another 1–0 victory at Deepdale, courtesy of a Charlie Adam goal. Adam had come to Bloomfield Road on loan from Rangers and had made an immediate impact. That result effectively ensured Blackpool's safety, and Parkes eventually steered the team to 16th place, 10 points clear of relegation.

It seemed almost certain that Parkes, and his assistant Steve Thompson, would get the positions permanently, yet Karl Oyston clearly had other ideas. In May, Parkes met the chairman and left the meeting later without a job. There are varying stories told as to why he was not appointed, but Parkes maintains that the financial offer he was made to continue was not sufficient and so he left with immediate effect. Whatever the truth, it seemed a

The author and the Blackpool team ahead of the 2009–10 season.

harsh way to say goodbye to a genuinely nice and talented man who had stepped into the breach at quick notice and conducted his affairs with success. Blackpool owed their Championship status to him.

Three days later, on 21 May 2009, the remarkable appointment of Ian Holloway was announced. It was remarkable due to the fact that no one has ever understood how it came about. Again, stories abound of Holloway actively pursuing Oyston to be given an interview, or the interview nearly not taking place due to late arrivals. Whatever, the fact is that Blackpool had as their new manager one of the most charismatic and talented managers in the country. Holloway's stock had fallen dramatically since he had been sacked by Leicester City after relegation a year previously, and in that time out of the game he had reflected on his football principles. When he was given the chance to manage again he said he would change and play a more attacking game. He got that chance at Bloomfield Road.

There are some things that automatically go together: strawberries and cream, Morecambe and Wise, fish and chips – and now, Blackpool and 'Ollie'. The two were drawn together, and the fit was that of a leather glove. They complimented each other. The brashness of the town, the history and the culture of the club and the quirkiness of the manager. Every season in Blackpool's history is said to be a 'roller coaster', and this was one that would be described, in advance, as just that. The 2009–10 season would go down as the most dramatic in the club's long and illustrious history.

The first thing that Holloway did was to make the signing of Charlie Adam permanent. He paid £500,000 – a new club record – to Rangers, and it is fair to say that it was the best half a million pounds spent by the club in its history. Neil Eardley was brought from Oldham Athletic for £350,000, plus numerous free and loan signings that significantly strengthened the squad. Money was recouped, however, with the transfer of Shaun Barker to Derby County for around £900,000.

Holloway was true to his word when he said he would attack the Championship. It took the players a little time to adjust to the new style of play, hence the opening four games resulting in draws, but it became quickly obvious that the team were far from the relegation candidates that the media had labelled them at the start of the season. Early-season victories against Newcastle United and a hammering of Wigan Athletic in the League Cup gave reason for optimism, and with the exception of a two-week period Blackpool were never out of the top 10. Despite this, they were never on 'the promotion radar' as far as the experts were concerned, but the results kept coming. Dominant wins at home to Sheffield United and at Middlesbrough proved their pedigree, and it was noticeable that a bad run was almost immediately followed by a complete return to form. What took place on the pitch was matched off it, with the building of the new South Stand, named after Jimmy Armfield, so finally Bloomfield Road could play host to a five-figure attendance once more. Three days after the opening of the stand, Blackpool outplayed fellow promotion candidates Swansea City, beating them 5–1 at home, and so continued a run similar to the promotion season of three years previous. They won six of their last eight League games, moving in to the Play-offs with a victory at Peterborough United and then confirming their position in the final game at home to Bristol City. This was done with the help of DJ Campbell, who had come to the club on loan from Leicester City for the second successive season, plus the arrival of Seamus Coleman from Everton and Stephen Dobbie from Swansea City, both on loan. Again, Blackpool were in the Play-offs, but this time it seemed more of a celebration being there, as opposed to the necessity from a long season's final frustration.

Nottingham Forest stood between themselves and another Wembley appearance, and a nervy first leg saw Blackpool lead 2–1, but the second will go down in Blackpool footballing folklore. Blackpool had beaten Forest three times already, and the last time Billy Davies's side had lost at the City Ground had been to Blackpool, and they had gone 19 home League games without defeat, with the last eight not conceding a goal. It was a tall order, yet none of this fazed Blackpool, and a second-half performance of complete and total dominance saw them win 4–3 on the night and 6–4 on aggregate. The scoreline from the second leg gives no hint to the level of performance that the players of Blackpool Football Club produced that evening, and their reward was another Play-off Final at Wembley in the knowledge that they were just 90 minutes from the Premier League.

Again, Blackpool were the underdogs against a Cardiff City side that were desperate for success due to their on-going financial problems, yet 37,000 tangerine-clad fans made a sunny Wembley a riot of colour. In some of the hottest temperatures imaginable – 105 degrees Fahrenheit at pitch level – the two sides played out one of the most entertaining and compelling first 45 minutes of football seen at that level. Twice Cardiff took the lead, and twice Blackpool responded immediately, with a peach of a free-kick from Charlie Adam and then a bundled goal from Gary Taylor-Fletcher. It was fitting that the winner, scored just before half-time, was from Brett Ormerod, who had scored in the Third Division Play-Off Final at the turn of the century. The second half could not attempt to live up to the first, and Blackpool were content to sit back and allow

The teams line up before the start of the Play-off Final at Wembley.
(Courtesy of Steve Higginbottom)

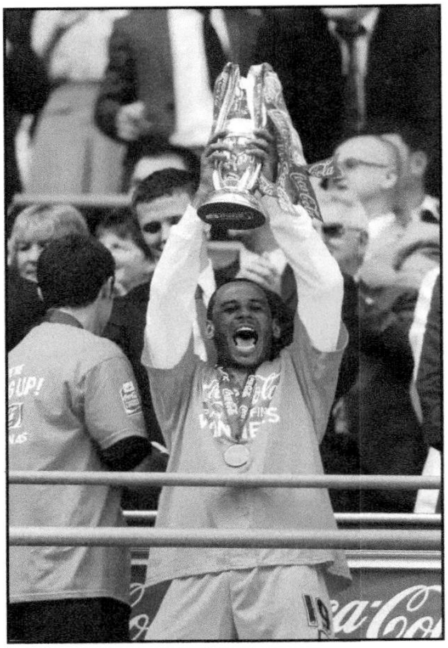
DJ Campbell lifts the Play-off trophy to the fans.

their opponents to attack, yet never found themselves under threat. The final whistle went, and Blackpool had made it. They had created a curious record of promotion via the Play-offs at three different levels, but far more importantly they had returned to the top tier of English domestic football for the first time in 39 years. They were the perennial underdogs, unfancied, unfashionable in the eyes of many and a club who had lived on past glories for too long, yet on that stifling May day they had given hope to the dreams of many supporters of equal clubs that the fairytale can come true.

Two days later, the victorious side, led by the already-legendary manager Ian Holloway, was greeted by a crowd of around 80,000 along Blackpool promenade. The town had not seen scenes like that since the 1953 Cup-winning side, and Holloway, always ready with a witty remark and a soundbite, jokingly asked where they had all been all season. He also promised that he would attack the Premier League too and would not change his style of play. It was manna from heaven for the supporters who had played their part in the remarkable rise of the club over the previous 10 years. 'Rising like a phoenix' is a well-used cliché, but this was never more true of Blackpool. As the summer of 2010 approached, the feeling was that the future was bright, the future was Tangerine.

As their first season in the Premier League approached, it was clear the club were no where near prepared for the most expensive and glamorous League in the world. Off the field, major upgrades were needed to Bloomfield Road. A new 'temporary' stand was erected on the East Side, bringing the capacity up to a more respectable 16,200, but it was not ready in time for the opening game, meaning the fixture with Wigan Athletic was switched to the DW stadium. Also new press facilities, floodlights, medical centre and commercial shop were hastily built in line with Premier League rules. It was simply a race against time.

On the field, manager Holloway spent most of the summer trying desperately to attract new players to the club, with little success. It was only with two days to go before the start of the season that he was able to announce a handful of new players (including the experienced Marlon Harewood) to the press and fans, yet amazingly after the first match of the season, Blackpool sat atop the PL for two crazy hours after a stunning 4–0 win at Wigan. They dropped to second at 7pm after Chelsea humiliated West Brom at Stamford Bridge.

Soon after, DJ Campbell joined the club permanently for £1.25 million, a new club record, and the team was now resembling one that would be able to compete at the top level.

From thereon, Blackpool entertained like no other promoted team before them. Holloway's promise to attack in every game brought praise from pundits, and the term 'breath of fresh air' was used constantly about the team, as they played their open and expansive football against any type of opposition. It seemed to be working as by the end of the year, Blackpool sat comfortably in the top half of the League after recording five away victories (the same as eventual champions Manchester United), including an incredible 2–1 win at Liverpool. That victory brought the national sporting press to meltdown as they picked over the bones of the crisis club that was Liverpool. Blackpool looked set to avoid relegation and had certainly passed the 10-point mark that everyone had predicted would be almost impossible to gain. In fact, most experts suggested that they would not even win a corner in 2010–11, never mind a game!

Sadly, the New Year saw the team simply run out of steam. January was a let down. Charlie Adam, who had already won a court case against Karl Oyston for non-payment of a bonus from the previous season, was expected to leave the club and join one of Liverpool, Manchester United or Tottenham. As it was, every approach was turned down, and he continued to play in the tangerine shirt.

Also the transfer window brought little cheer with the only notable signings being that of James Beattie on loan from Rangers and Andy Reid from Sunderland for £1 million. Only three more games were won in 2011, including a second against Liverpool, and so despite picking up 39 points and winning 10 times, the 4–2 last-day defeat at Manchester United meant that Blackpool were making a hasty return to the Championship. It mattered not that the club had only dropped into the relegation zone a few weeks previous, or that they had been on the receiving end of some rather harsh and bad decisions, or that they had thrown away too many points with late goals, the fact was that on 22 May 2011, one year to the date of promotion, referee Mike Dean blew his whistle just before 6pm and ended the 'roller coaster/fairy-tale' that had been Blackpool's first foray into the Premier League. Only time will tell whether the club is strong enough to recover and return to entertain with their colour and vitality.

The Bloomfield Road Story

Bloomfield Road has been Blackpool Football Club's home ground for over 110 years and has seen its share of highs and lows, but the ground of the present era bears no resemblance to one of the past that hosted the talents of Matthews, Mortensen, Hampson and Green. It has undergone one of the longest rebuilds in history, but it is slowly becoming the comfortable all-seater stadium so demanded by present-day football fans. It may still have a capacity of only 16,000 (at the time of writing) but, with the club enjoying more success now than for over 50 years, there is no reason not to believe that the ground will be expanded and become a home that the club is truly proud of.

The story of Blackpool FC's grounds goes well back beyond the existence of Bloomfield Road, though, as the club had two homes before settling on their current one. The first, at the time of the club's formation, was in the Royal Palace Gardens, or Raikes Hall as it was more commonly known. The gardens were part of a vast entertainment complex which included attractions such as a theatre, boating lake, a skating rink and sporting facilities for tennis, cricket and bowling. It was the cricket field that was made available during the winter months, although not without opposition from cricket lovers as the fledgling football club took to its green pastures.

The shape of the field was, for obvious reasons, unusual for football, but at least it offered covered accommodation for the spectators. On the northern side of the ground, and immediately adjacent to the popular boating lake, there ran a large all-seater stand that could comfortably accommodate around 1,000 people, although the rest of the ground was cordoned off by little more than a single length of rope. The entrance fee was fixed at 3s 6d, and the first home game for Blackpool was against Leek. They won easily 4–1.

Raikes Hall remained the club's home until August 1897, when they were forced to move out after it had been decided to earmark the whole complex for housing development. Blackpool then moved to the Athletic Grounds – now the site of the vast Stanley Park – situated near to where the cricket ground is today, although not on the site of the athletic track deep in the park complex.

It seemed a popular move as the first home match against Burnley in the League attracted a crowd of 4,000, the Mayor of Blackpool 'ceremoniously' kicking-off the game. It seemed a fine alternative and was quite comfortable by the standards of the day. On the west side, there was a covered stand, with a short length of uncovered seating opposite, plus a full racecourse ran the full length of the 24-acre perimeter. Unfortunately, its remoteness from the town meant that attendances started to suffer, with the game against Small Heath in 1899 realising only £27 in gate receipts. Also, there had been many complaints from local residents who were unhappy with the unruly elements that were attracted to the club. Bad language seemed to be the main problem, so the club were under pressure to move again.

The final game played there, against local rivals South Shore, attracted only 300 spectators, so it was decided to leave after just two years, despite signing a five-year lease with the landlords. Blackpool moved back to Raikes Hall for a short time, as up to that point only 71 housing plots had been sold, but in December 1899, the club finally arrived at the place it was to call home for evermore – Bloomfield Road.

It was the new home of South Shore FC, who had recently moved from their old ground on Waterloo Road, and at the time was quaintly called 'Gamble's Field' after the local farmer who owned the land. It was surrounded by allotments and offered little in the way of accommodation, with only a small stand on the west side seating around 300. The rest of the ground was completely open, with a white fence marking the boundaries. After the amalgamation of the two clubs, it was renamed Bloomfield Road and Blackpool played their first match there – beating Horwich 3–0 in a friendly.

It was many years before the ground saw any noticeable improvements, and by 1906 the local press were pleading with the club to provide a decent press box as they found it difficult to report on a match from the touchlines. In 1907, a paddock was built in front of the stand to increase the capacity, but 10 years later a serious fire all but destroyed it and necessitated a complete rebuild.

Two years later, the Spion Kop – now the South Stand – was erected and could hold 1,000 spectators, and with the building of the concrete East Paddock the capacity was raised to 18,000, although the cost of around £3,000 nearly bankrupted the club. In fact, a writ was issued against the directors for non-payment of £3,618, with only £1,000 of the bill settled

An early photograph of workers preparing to lay a new pitch at Bloomfield Road.

An aerial photograph showing the massive North End terrace at Bloomfield Road.

at that point. It needed a hastily convened meeting and a decision to double the share capital to £10,000 before the debt could be repaid.

On the north side of the ground, a curious stand had been erected. Called the Motor Stand, holding 2,000 people, it was purchased from Blackpool council in 1908 for £100 after numerous money-raising schemes. It did mean that Blackpool were one of the few clubs in the country to have stands on all four sides of their ground – something they were not able to boast during the early years of the 21st century.

A fire in the West Stand in January 1917 saw it become an inferno, and many of the club's momentos – such as Cups, records and programmes – were destroyed, meaning a complete rebuild once more. It was completed for the start of the 1929–30 season, and at that time the pitch was moved to accommodate a paddock in front of the South Stand.

Earlier, in 1925, a new construction had been erected on the south side of the ground, costing around £13,000 and eventually holding 4,000 fans. It also housed a new boardroom, offices, dressing rooms, baths and refreshment bars and was looked upon as one of the most modern in the Football League.

It was in the summer of 1930, after promotion to the First Division, that a massive new terrace was built at the north end which, after being concreted, could hold 12,000 spectators and so increased the capacity to 30,000. It was originally made out of cinders and railway sleepers, but locals helped raise money to bring it into the modern age with a concrete base. The Motor Stand, which had stood on that spot, was then moved to a position between the new structure and the West Stand, and so Bloomfield Road was complete. For the next 70 years the changes were almost entirely cosmetic, as the ground looked essentially the same from 1930 until 2000, with seemingly little heed or interest paid to either modernisation or aesthetics.

Representative games had become commonplace at Bloomfield Road, with the first being a women's international game in 1920 involving England and Ireland, but the only time a full international game was played was on 17 October 1932 when England met Ireland in front of 23,000. The Football League played five games there, the first being in 1931 and the last as late as 1960. There were also two Amateur internationals involving England in 1927 and 1936.

At the end of World War Two, massive repairs were needed, not because of bomb damage, but due to the fact that the Armed Forces had used it extensively. The club did not complain, as the rent they had received had more than paid off their bank overdraft.

A roof was added to the Kop in 1954, and with the extension of the East Paddock the capacity was raised to its all time high of 38,000. Floodlights were installed three years later, and with extra seats in the West Stand the club had a ground it could be proud of.

Attendances had gradually risen as the team progressed, peaking on 17 September 1955, when 38,098 turned up to see a victory over Wolves in Division One. Gradually, as the team's fortunes declined following their 'glory years' the attendances tailed away. In fact, the capacity was reduced to 30,000 in the late 1960s, with the addition of new seats, but that figure was smashed with the visit of champions Everton in 1970 when officially 30,705 paid to see a 2–0 defeat. With fans on the touch lines and climbing the floodlight pylons, it seemed closer to 33,000, though.

Bloomfield Road in 1961.

During the 1970s, the board introduced a radical measure of putting seats in the East Paddock, but this proved so unpopular that it was scrapped within 12 months. Also one of the most regrettable decisions taken by the board – among the many that have been taken down the years – was the removal of the Kop roof in the early 1980s. Safety reasons had been given, but it was later revealed that it cost nearly as much to dismantle it as it would have to repair it.

Sadly, Bloomfield Road then became a shadow of its former glories and became pitiable venue at which to play football. The capacity, now down to 18,000, was then reduced to 12,000 as new safety measures were introduced, and then down to 9,600. That capacity was to remain, despite the ground changing, right up until 2010. The North West stand was finally pulled down, and the Kop only half used – and that for away fans only – as Bloomfield Road became a laughing stock in the football world.

In March 1986, the directors had announced they were ready to sell the ground to a Manchester development company and share firstly with the Rugby League club (and possibly Preston North End), but thankfully the council rejected the proposal, and Bloomfield Road continued as the less-than-luxurious home of Blackpool Football Club.

As the 1990s arrived, chairman Owen Oyston unveiled numerous ambitious plans to transform the ground. Anything from 25,000 to a 40,000 capacity all-seater stadium which would be part of a huge entertainment complex, sliding roof, floating pitch (and maybe even an ornamental pond in the corner!) that could host the Euro '96 Championship was suggested, but predictably none of it came to fruition. Critics could argue that they had heard it all before, as back in 1971 the club had planned a new stadium – the 'Wembley of the North' – at Stanley Park, which eventually became a zoo!

Bloomfield Road during the 1990s.

Bloomfield Road during the construction of the new North and West Stands in 2001.

At one stage there was a serious possibility of the club moving to a green-belt area of land called Whyndyke Farm, but a disagreement between the owner and the new chairman, Vicki Oyston, ended any further progress. Finally, though, in 2000 the old ground started to be transformed. Blackpool council gave the go-ahead for redevelopment, and in 2000 and 2001 the Kop and the West Stand were demolished, and within a year a new, gleaming stand that encompassed the North and West of the ground was built and opened. The East Paddock –or 'Scratching Sheds', as had been affectionately known by the fans – was demolished, and that was followed by the old South Stand.

It was ripe for the complete redevelopment of Bloomfield Road, especially as two matches of the 2005 Women's UEFA Championship had been played there, but it was not until 2010 that the stand was extended to cover the South part of the ground. Chairman Karl Oyston decided it would be him, and not the fans, who dictated when the building would take place and the capacity increased. This was despite the fact that Blackpool had been promoted to the Championship and were playing in front of bigger crowds. His comment that only '50 to 100 people' were missing out on matchdays was not appreciated.

By the end of the 2009–10 season – when Blackpool were promoted to the Premier League – Bloomfield Road's capacity had risen to just under 13,000. In fact, Bloomfield Road was now able to play host to a five-figure attendance for the first time in over a decade.

Obviously, Bloomfield Road came nowhere near meeting the strict standards of the Premier League, not least in its small capacity. That meant a temporary stand was erected on the eastern side of the ground, replacing the old 'Gene Kelly' stand (for away fans who would be singing in the rain, as it had no roof) with a capacity of around 5,000. It had new press facilities, plus refreshment areas and brought the capacity up to a more respectable 16,000. It was not ready in time for the start of the season, and so the opening fixture with Wigan Athletic was switched to the DW stadium. There were also other requirements to be met before any top-tier football could be played, such as new floodlights, television camera positions, a new large screen for television images and scoreboard etc, plus the outside of the ground was spruced up to make it a more appealing proposition than old.

Now Bloomfield Road is a pleasant, welcoming place, not out of place in modern-day football. The capacity is still the smallest in the Premier League – which could, and probably will, be increased – but the fans have a four-sided stadium for the first time since the late 1990s, and even then a large part of it was closed down. The fans have made it into an intimidating arena, as they have now been recognised as some of the most passionate in the country.

Bloomfield Road has undergone changes. Some have been painfully slow, but the ground is now one to be proud of.

Blackpool Matches to Remember

Lincoln City 3 Blackpool 1

Second Division – 5 September 1896

Blackpool's first-ever Football League game was in the Second Division against Lincoln City and ended in defeat. That the game took place at all is quite remarkable, with the team taking six hours to travel from the Fylde Coast to Lincoln, where they found the conditions atrocious.

The players, directors and club doctor caught the 7am train from Blackpool North Station and then had to endure a journey via Manchester and Birmingham. They had to change trains twice and, with their only exercise a quick run up and down the platform, it was hardly surprising that they were not in the best condition to take on their opponents.

The game was due to kick-off at 2pm but, due to the fact that it had been raining incessantly and the pitch now resembled a swamp, the referee delayed the start by 15 minutes while the players acclimatised themselves.

When the match finally got under way, Blackpool, playing in their blue-and-white-striped shirts, mounted many early attacks, forcing Lincoln's French goalkeeper, Boullemier, into action. After only five minutes though, they were caught at the back when Lynes broke away, beat two defenders and hit a ferocious shot. 'Keeper William Douglas had no chance and Lincoln were 1–0 ahead.

Undeterred, Blackpool continued to push forward at every opportunity, and so it was a devastating blow when they conceded again a minute before half-time. Lynes once again found the Blackpool defence in disarray and broke through. He pushed the ball to the unmarked Kirton on the right, and the Lincoln outside-left made sure, with Douglas helpless.

The players came out reluctantly for the second half as conditions had worsened and the majority of the 1,500 spectators had decided that a warm fireplace was preferable to standing around in a muddy field. Blackpool showed a little more commitment though, and after 10 minutes of the second period they scored their first-ever Football League goal.

It came about after a Lincoln defender had handled the ball on the edge of the penalty area. Charlie Mount stepped up and hit a 20-yard free-kick straight past Boullemier. Much jubilation and handshaking followed among the 'Pool players, who fired with new optimism and continued to press forward.

Sadly, they could not draw level, and indeed with five minutes left they went 3–1 down when their shaky defence allowed Kirton to once again find room and lob the ball over 'keeper Douglas.

The *Athletic News* reported that Blackpool had a weakness in front of goal, plus a rather poor defence. It was surprising then that the team acquitted themselves rather well in their debut season. They finished in eighth position, their highest until 1911, whereas their opponents actually finished bottom.

Lincoln City: Boullemier, Wilson, Byres, Hannah, Timmis, Smith, Lynes, Fraser, W. Gillespie, M. Gillespie, Kirton.
Blackpool: Douglas, Parr, Bowman, Stuart, Stirzaker, Norris, Clarkin, Donnelly, J. Parkinson, R. Parkinson, Mount.
Attendance: 1,500

Sheffield United 1 Blackpool 2

FA Cup Second Round – 3 February 1906

When the draw was made for the second round of the FA Cup, the Blackpool directors must have rubbed their hands with glee. After seeing their team struggle through a three-match-marathon first-round tie against non-Leaguers Crystal Palace, the 'Pool had been given a lucrative home draw against the mighty Sheffield United.

Blackpool were, as always at that stage of their history, in financial difficulties, with attendances averaging around 3,500 – barely enough to pay the club's weekly expenses – so the promise of First Division opposition at Bloomfield Road was very welcome.

Sheffield United were one of the giants of the Football League and could boast players of immense skill and ability, such as Lipsham, Donnelly and Drake. The chances of struggling Blackpool getting the better of them were remote to say the least, particularly as the Seasiders had notched up only five League victories up to that point.

The Blackpool team from 1905–06.

About a week or so before the tie, the Sheffield directors, mindful of Blackpool's financial problems, offered to switch the game to Bramall Lane, where a much larger crowd could be expected. At first Blackpool refused, then agreed, only to quote an over-inflated fee for the privilege. It seemed that negotiations had broken down, but eventually a compromise was reached and the game went ahead in Sheffield.

Many Blackpool supporters criticised the move, but it was pointed out that if the game had taken place at Bloomfield Road, the club would make £150. Now they would be guaranteed at least £300, a much-needed windfall for a club in such severe financial straits. To prove the point, it was also noted that the entire Sheffield team could afford to spend the preceding week relaxing in Skegness, a 'luxury' that the Blackpool club could only dream about.

Sheffield started the game in a confident mood and immediately laid siege to the Blackpool goal. 'Pool's defenders tried valiantly to keep out the forwards with some desperate defending, and only the brilliant goalkeeping of 'Tishy' Hull stopped the Yorkshiremen from scoring. Eventually though, they succumbed when England's Bert Lipsham scored a fine goal. A corner from the right had not been cleared properly, and from the ensuing cross the former Crewe left-winger smashed the ball past the fully stretched Hull.

After only 15 minutes Blackpool were one down and seemingly heading for a hiding. Their cause was not helped a few minutes later when Jack Scott was carried off with a serious injury, leaving Blackpool down to 10 men. Thankfully, the defender was made of sturdy stuff and 20 minutes later he rejoined the fray.

As the game progressed, the Seasiders settled and started to look dangerous on the breakaway, although Sheffield's 'custodian', Leivesley, was not really troubled and at half-time Sheffield United held the slender lead.

The second half saw a resurgent Blackpool side moving forward in numbers and pressing the Sheffield goal. It paid off, as after just two minutes of the restart, Harry Hancock equalised. A Sheffield attack had broken down and Sam Johnson sent a long ball up to forward Bate, who dribbled it to the corner flag before being fouled. From the free-kick, taken by Johnson, Blackpool's inside-right headed home. Blackpool were level and the 250 supporters who had made the journey were overjoyed.

A couple of minutes later the inconceivable happened as Blackpool took the lead. The Sheffield United defender Groves was robbed by Jimmy Connor on the halfway line and he sent a through ball to Bates, who in turn found Hancock. A stunning 20-yard shot into the corner of the goal and Blackpool were 2–1 up. They were now poised to produce an incredible upset.

Sheffield United were now in a state of panic, under severe criticism from their supporters, and it seemed that they completely fell apart. After 55 minutes, Teddy Duckworth missed an open goal, and with just five minutes left, Hancock nearly completed his hat-trick when he headed against a post.

As the final whistle blew, the players embraced each other, some in tears. They had overcome all the odds and deservedly beaten their illustrious opponents. The result caused shockwaves around the country, with newspapers highlighting the game. Even the local gazette devoted five full-length columns to the team in their match report, the club receiving more publicity than ever before.

Back in the town, it was around 10pm when people heard the incredible news, and when the train carrying the team pulled into the station in the early hours of the following morning, there were around 2,000 supporters to greet them. Even veteran defender Jack Parkinson was overcome, commenting that he felt as if someone had walked up and given him a £10 note!

Unfortunately, in the third round Blackpool faced Newcastle United away and were soundly beaten 5–0. Nevertheless, Blackpool had made headlines in a Cup competition they were to grace in later years.

Sheffield United: Leivesley, Groves, Benton, McCormack, B. Wilson, Parker, Donnelly, Bluff, Brown, Drake, Lipsham.
Blackpool: Hull, Crewdson, Scott, Threlfall, Parkinson, Johnson, Duckworth, Hancock, Francis, Connor, Bate.
Attendance: 10,219

Oldham Athletic 1 Blackpool 2

Second Division – 21 April 1930

As the 1929–30 season came to a close, three teams were in with a chance of promotion to the First Division. Blackpool were the leaders, and had been for most of the season. Chelsea were in second place with Oldham Athletic in third, one point behind.

As luck would have it, the fixture list had thrown up a meeting between the two Lancashire sides on Easter Monday. It was simple really; Oldham had to win to keep in touch with Chelsea, while Blackpool could effectively clinch promotion if they came away from Boundary Park with the two points.

Interest in the game was incredible, with the ground packed to capacity and the gates closed some 30 minutes before kick-off. Blackpool were the team in form, winning five of their previous six games, and they had brought with them a large and noisy following, although the roar that greeted the home side as they took to the pitch was heard for miles around.

It was Blackpool who were the more settled side from the kick-off, and they came close to scoring in one of the first attacks of the game when Jack Oxberry finished off a move he had started, only to see his powerful shot hit the bar. Gradually though, the Latics, roared on by their supporters, became more and more confident and started to give the 'Pool defence some worrying moments, with former Blackpool man Joe Taylor coming close on numerous occasions.

Moments before half-time, Oldham outside-right Worrall was allowed to run almost the full length of the field before a timely tackle by Sid Tufnell saved the day. It had been a frantic first 45 minutes, yet surprisingly the teams went in at half-time goalless.

In the second half, Blackpool stepped up a gear and completely dominated. Within a minute of the restart, Charlie Rattray found Jimmy Hampson free, yet somehow the great scorer put the ball over the bar. Ten minutes later, Hampson was brought down in the area after beating two men, and referee Mr Watson had no hesitation in awarding a penalty. Up stepped Hampson and shot well wide of the post. The Blackpool supporters groaned in despair as it seemed that it was not to be their day.

Within 10 minutes, however, Hampson had made amends when he took a pass through the middle of the field, shimmied past two defenders, and hit a fierce shot into the net. It was his 45th League goal of the season, and surely the most important. Within three minutes, the travelling fans had even more to cheer about as Blackpool went 2–0 up. Rattray picked up a loose ball on the right, crossed it to Hampson and watched as he unselfishly drew the defenders towards him before leaving Oxberry in the clear. The pass to the inside-left was perfectly timed, and from an acute angle Oxberry slammed it into the net.

The game was effectively over, although with eight minutes remaining Oldham did score. Blackpool's defence was caught unawares, leaving 'keeper Horace Pearson alone to deal with a difficult cross. He misjudged the flight and Worrall beat him to it, planting the ball into the empty goal.

Oldham pushed for an equaliser, but Blackpool held firm. The final whistle was greeted with an enormous cheer from the travelling supporters, as promotion had now been assured. For Oldham it was a sad end to their season, as they were beaten to the other spot by Chelsea the following Saturday.

Later that evening, the Blackpool players were met by thousands of fans at the train station, celebrating promotion to the First Division for the first time in the club's history. There was one player above all who they had come to acclaim – Jimmy Hampson. Sadly for them, he had got off at an earlier station to avoid any fuss, but a few days later they cheered as he appeared on the town hall steps and would not let him go until he had made a speech. The mild-mannered and shy man was later heard to say that it was more difficult addressing a crowd of 30,000 than scoring a goal in front of them! His goals had earned the team a place in the top tier of English football, and the fans would not let him forget it.

Oldham Athletic: Moss, Ivill, Porter, Adlam, King, Goodier, Worrall, Dyson, Taylor, Hargreaves, Watson.
Blackpool: Pearson, Grant, Watson, Wilson, Tremelling, Tufnell, Rattray, Broadhurst, Hampson, Oxberry, Neal.
Attendance: 45,304

Blackpool 1 Arsenal 4

First Division – 30 August 1930

The last Saturday of August 1930 saw the realisation of a dream for Blackpool Football Club, as they started their first ever season in Division One. After the success of the previous campaign, the whole town had been buzzing, and when the fixture list paired the 'Pool with mighty Arsenal on the opening day, the excitement was heightened even more.

In the summer months immediately following promotion, the directors brought Bloomfield Road up to First Division standard, and this involved building the massive 'Spion

Kop'. The enormous terrace was capable of holding 12,000 spectators, and on this great day it was packed to capacity. The attendance was given as nearly 29,000 – the highest figure to date to watch a game at Bloomfield Road.

The match was of such importance to the town that the mayor and mayoress, complete with official regalia, opened the new stand before the game. In his speech, Mayor Gath promised that Blackpool would be a force to be reckoned with in the First Division, and Arsenal were on to a hiding to nothing! In return, Arsenal paraded their recently won FA Cup around the ground to show the expectant Blackpool fans.

What followed in the next 90 minutes though, proved a severe and harsh lesson for everyone involved with Blackpool FC. Arsenal dismantled the home defence with consummate ease and showed that there was a huge gap between themselves and the newly promoted side.

Their first goal came midway through the first half when Lambert converted a penalty after Jack had been brought down in the box. It was the only goal in the first period, but it was clear that the Gunners had more to come. The second came from a free-kick just outside the area, when Jones's powerful shot was only parried by 'keeper Pearson, and inside-right Jack snapped up the rebound.

A brilliant individual goal from Bastin followed to make it 3–0, before a second from Jack, with the help of centre-forward Lambert, completed the rout. Blackpool did manage a solitary goal from Jimmy Hampson – it was almost inevitable that the first goal they scored in the top tier would come from him – and also had a seemingly good goal disallowed, but as Arsenal had also been denied by the referee there were few complaints.

It was a fiery baptism for Blackpool and their disconsolate players, but amazingly they recovered sufficiently four days later to record a remarkable 4–2 victory at Maine Road against Manchester City. Their defensive frailties had been exposed though, and in that debut season in the First Division Blackpool conceded 125 goals, and yet somehow avoided relegation!

Blackpool: Pearson, Grant, Watson, McMahon, Tremelling, Tufnell, Neal, Carr, Hampson, Oxberry, Downes.
Arsenal: Preedy, Parker, Hapgood, Jones, Roberts, John, Hulme, Jack, Lambert, James, Bastin.
Attendance: 28,723

Blackpool 4 Chelsea 0

First Division – 29 October 1932

This game between Blackpool and Chelsea promised to be nothing more than an ordinary League clash, yet at the end of the 90 minutes, the few hardy souls who had braved the elements that October day realised that they had witnessed one of the most remarkable football matches in Blackpool's history.

It was not the emphatic scoreline that made the match so exceptional, although that was unusual in itself, but the fact that by the end of the game Chelsea had only six players left on the pitch.

For two weeks previously it had rained incessantly on the Fylde coast, and most of Blackpool was flooded, with the promenade closed to traffic and pedestrians. Bloomfield Road had not escaped the deluge of course, and despite excellent drainage, by the morning of the game there was over two inches of water on the pitch.

Incredibly, the match was given the go ahead, despite fierce protests from the Chelsea management, who quite rightly argued that there was no way that a game of football could be played on that surface. In fact, when the players stepped out on to the pitch, the rain was still falling in bucketloads; water polo seemed a better option!

Whether it was because of Blackpool's northern grit or the archetypal 'soft' southerners is not clear, but it was the Seasiders who adapted to the conditions, while their opponents had no appetite for the game whatsoever. They complained constantly to the referee, and that was despite the fact that in the first half Blackpool were kicking against the howling and driving rain.

By half-time 'Pool were 3–0 up, coming from Hampson (two) and Wilkinson. The Pensioners were just not up for the game, and throughout had pleaded with the referee to abandon. Mr Jones ignored their pleas, mindful that the home side had adapted so well and had moved into a three-goal lead. During the interval, the Chelsea officials approached the referee with more requests to call a halt to the proceedings, but again they fell on deaf ears.

As the teams returned for the second period, the rain was still falling and the pitch was now a sea of water. It was also noticeable that only eight Chelsea players had returned, their centre-half retiring with cramp and two others refusing point-blank to continue. Eventually they were persuaded to return, and after 60 minutes Chelsea were back to 10 men. It did not last long though, as they very quickly became disillusioned and walked off again!

Mr Jones, after consulting with a linesman, just shrugged his shoulders and dropped the ball, continuing play. The remaining Chelsea players were totally disenchanted with the situation and Blackpool dominated even more. After 75 minutes Hampson completed his hat-trick, scoring a brilliant individual goal in worsening conditions.

The game was won, and it came as no surprise to see two more Chelsea players walk off the field arm in arm. There were only six blue shirts left in play, but to be fair, those remaining Chelsea players did themselves proud by defending valiantly and not conceding again. When the final whistle blew, it was the Blackpool team who received the standing ovation – not for the victory, although it was most welcome in what was already a desperate season, but because no 'Pool player had needed any treatment or had complained about the conditions.

After the game, the referee reported the incident to the Football League, and in turn the Chelsea officials reported Mr Jones for his handling of the whole affair. It did not matter, however, as the result was allowed to stand and Blackpool had picked up two very valuable points.

It is unlikely that a game like that would be played in the modern era, as health and safety is now paramount, but the 7,000 spectators saw something special that October day.

Blackpool: McDonough, Wassell, Everest, A. Watson, P. Watson, Rattray, Wilkinson, Butterworth, Hampson, McLelland, Smalley.
Chelsea: Woodley, Odell, Law, Allum, O'Dowd, Ferguson, Oakton, Rankin, Mills, Miller, Pearson.
Attendance: 7,311

Arsenal 2 Blackpool 4

War Cup Final – 15 May 1943

During the years of World War Two, Blackpool had one of the finest teams in the country. With the help of many 'guest' players who found themselves stationed in the town, the Seasiders all but dominated their regional Leagues and also found success in the Cup.

During 1942–43 they completed the double of winning the Northern Regional League and the Northern Wartime Cup – the latter by beating Sheffield Wednesday over two legs. They were then invited to compete in a game at Stamford Bridge against the Southern Cup winners, Arsenal, in a game billed as the 'Championship of England'.

The Gunners, who had won their Final by beating Charlton Athletic over two legs, were apparently so confident of success that they had a photograph taken of their team with the trophy before the game! It is also interesting to note that after Blackpool had beaten them, the Cup was never released and was not seen again.

The game was played in front of a near full house, most of them cheering on the Londoners and creating an intimidating atmosphere for Blackpool. Arsenal's pre-match confidence seemed well placed when after only seven minutes they were two goals up. Ray Lewis had given them the lead after four minutes with a shot from the edge of the penalty area, and three minutes later Dennis Compton made it two.

Many Blackpool players said after the game that at that time they felt as if they would be on the receiving end of a hammering, as they were defending desperately. Slowly,

The Blackpool team before the 1943 War Cup Final against Arsenal.

though, they began to play as a unit, and after 20 minutes Ronnie Dix reduced the arrears with a fine goal. It was a perfect time for Blackpool and soon they were playing the flowing, attractive football that they had become reknowned for.

For their part, Arsenal kept up their attacking policy and came close to increasing their lead on a number of occasions, but 'keeper Savage was their equal. It was no surprise though, when, with about 60 seconds of the first half remaining, Blackpool equalised through Burbanks. It made the score 2–2 and set up an exciting second half.

The game was being broadcast live on radio throughout the country, and it was reported that the streets of Blackpool were deserted on a traditionally very busy May day. With wartime travel severely restricted, the wireless was the only way in which supporters could keep up to date with their team's progress.

The second half was just as exciting, with Blackpool gradually beginning to take control. A tactical switch at the interval, involving Dix and Dodds, seemed to catch the Arsenal defence, and after 75 minutes 'Jock' Dodds scored one of his trademark goals from outside the area to make it 3–2.

Now it was the Gunners who were defending desperately, and only some superb goalkeeping by Marks kept the scoreline down. After 82 minutes though, Bobby Finan made it 4–2 after a mêlée of players had failed to clear the Arsenal goalmouth.

The victory was complete and Blackpool had confirmed their status as the finest team in the country. The newspapers were full of praise for the victors, with the *Daily Mail* going as far to say that Blackpool's performance was one of the 'greatest by a football team since the game was invented.' High praise indeed, but by all accounts it was certainly justified.

It was something of a swansong, though, for within a year, with the war coming to an end, the players who turned out for Blackpool that day began to drift back to their old clubs, although the nucleus of an even greater Blackpool team was now in place.

Arsenal: Marks, Scott, L. Compton, Crayston, Joy, Hale, Kirchen, Drake, Lewis, Bastin, D. Compton.
Blackpool: Savage, Pope, S. Jones, Farrow, Hayward, Johnson, Matthews, Dix, Dodds, Finan, Burbanks.
Attendance: 55,195

Blackpool 2 Manchester United 4

FA Cup Final – 24 April 1948

The 1948 FA Cup Final has been described as the best Wembley Final ever in terms of skill and ability. The teams had a combined reputation for fast, skillful and always entertaining football, so when Blackpool and Manchester United made it to the FA Cup Final in 1948, the whole country looked forward to the encounter.

Both sides took to the pitch wearing unfamiliar colours: Blackpool in white shirts with black shorts, and Manchester (as they were always referred to) in blue shirts with white

Programme cover from the 1948 Final.

shorts. The colour clash of tangerine and red had forced the Football Association to demand a change of strip.

Blackpool had come to the Final seriously understrength, with Ron Suart and Jim McIntosh both missing from the side that had performed so well in the previous rounds. It was the Seasiders, though, who had the first chance of the match, and they squandered it badly. Alec

Munro, receiving a pass from Stanley Matthews, incredibly mishit a shot from only a couple of yards out. Just two minutes on the clock and Blackpool could have been ahead.

After 14 minutes though, they took the lead. Stan Mortensen was brought down on the edge of the area by Allenby Chilton and referee Mr Barrick pointed to the spot. There was controversy over the decision, as there was a suggestion that the incident took place outside of the area, but there was no question as to the way Eddie Shimwell took the penalty. It was slammed into the net and Blackpool were 1–0 up, Shimwell becoming the first full-back to score in a Wembley Final.

The goal seemed to inspire Manchester United, though, and constant forays into the Blackpool area followed. The subsequent equaliser on 30 minutes was no surprise, with a harmless cross from Delaney not cleared by Joe Robinson or defender Eric Hayward, and in their confusion they allowed Jack Rowley to nip in and score. It was a bad defensive mix-up for which Robinson afterwards took the blame.

Seven minutes later, though, Blackpool were back in front. Stan Mortensen, who had scored in every round of that season's competition, converted a Matthews free-kick, helped by a touch from Hugh Kelly, and the Seasiders went in at half-time 2–1 ahead. The thousands of Blackpool fans in the stadium and back home listening on their radios must have felt that the Cup was on its way to the seaside.

The second half saw Blackpool looking to extend their lead, with Matthews becoming more and more influential on the right wing. In the centre of the field was the colossus that was Harry Johnston, marshalling his players. The football played was some of the most entertaining the stadium had ever witnessed, and already the game was living up to its 'classic' billing.

Manchester's equaliser came completely unexpectedly, and quite controversially too. On 70 minutes Kelly had been penalised for handball, something which he argued was accidental.

Action from the 1948 FA Cup Final against Manchester United.

While the referee was explaining his decision, Johnny Morris took the free-kick for Rowley to once again take advantage of a mix-up between Robinson and Hayward. It was 2–2, and the momentum was now with the team in blue.

After 80 minutes, following a Blackpool attack, John Anderson made a long and accurate pass to Stan Pearson, deep in the Seasiders' half. Pearson turned and then fired a 25-yard shot into the goal past Robinson. For the first time, Blackpool were behind.

Shortly afterwards the fourth goal was scored, again by Pearson, and again it was another rasping shot that helped on its way by Kelly. It was 4–2 and the FA Cup went to Manchester United, but Blackpool had played their part in a superb exhibition of football. In his report on the game, writer David Prole said, 'If United's display was as close to perfection as any team could hope to go, Blackpool's was not far behind.'

Strangely, as these things tend to happen, a few days later the two teams met again in a rearranged League match at Bloomfield Road, and Blackpool won 1–0 with a Mortensen goal. The score did not reflect the level of dominance that Blackpool had that day, but United had already won their coveted trophy. Blackpool would be back at Wembley very soon.

Blackpool: Robinson, Shimwell, Crosland, Johnston, Hayward, Kelly, Matthews, Munro, Mortensen, Dick, Rickett.
Manchester United: Crompton, Carey, Aston, Anderson, Chilton, Cockburn, Delaney, Morris, Rowley, Pearson, Mitten.
Attendance: 99,842

Blackpool 0 Newcastle United 2

FA Cup Final – 28 April 1951

Blackpool's second appearance in an FA Cup Final was a huge disappointment and certainly an anti-climax for all of their supporters. The team was at the height of its power and had just finished third in the First Division – the highest place to date.

Newcastle United were worthy opponents, but most experts were of the opinion that Blackpool, at full strength, were capable of lifting the trophy for the first time in the club's history. The only casualty was Allan Brown, who had suffered a serious knee injury and was replaced by the amateur Bill Slater. Ironically, Brown was also to miss the 1953 Final through injury.

It has been said since that Blackpool lost the game before a ball was kicked due to a tactical error. Manager Joe Smith had decided that Newcastle centre-forward Jackie Milburn would be too fast for Eric Hayward, so he deployed an unfamiliar offside game. It was something that the Blackpool defenders were not comfortable with, and it ultimately led to the team's defeat that cold April day.

The early pressure had come from Blackpool – wearing their traditional tangerine shirts, as opposed to three years previous – with Bill Slater and Stan Mortensen coming close in the opening 10 minutes, and the Newcastle 'keeper, Fairbrother, making a superb save to deny 'Morty'. Newcastle were biding their time, though, and as soon as they saw the Blackpool defence's unease with the offside trap, they exploited it as often as possible.

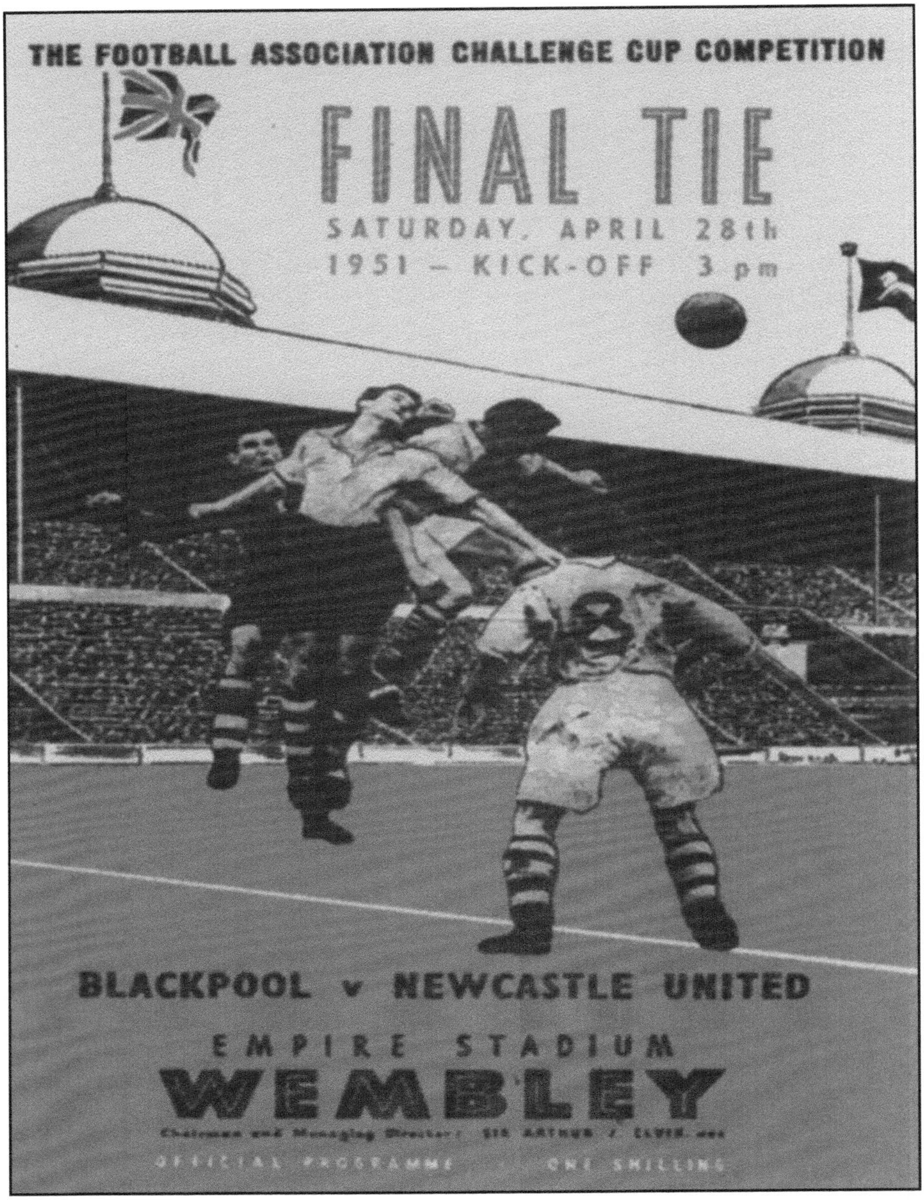

Programme cover from the 1951 Final.

On four occasions Milburn managed to evade the fragile defence, only to be denied by George Farm in the Blackpool goal. At one point Milburn did have the ball in the net, but was overruled by the referee. Blackpool did continue to push forward, but Mortensen was subdued, while Matthews was running relentlessly without any final product and struggling against the marking of Corbett.

Newcastle take the lead in the 1951 FA Cup Final.

At half-time it was goalless, but it was the Newcastle supporters in the Wembley crowd were the more positive of the two. Blackpool were floundering, and a second-half change seemed to be the answer if they were to lift the Cup.

But the change did not come, as the offside trap continued, and within five minutes the inevitable happened. George Robledo intercepted a pass from Matthews and quickly found Milburn. 'Wor Jackie' took advantage of the backline's hesitation in waiting for the whistle, raced through and shot hard past the helpless Farm. Five minutes later it was 2–0, with Milburn the scorer again. The Blackpool defence, now in something close to disarray, allowed Walker to take the ball down the right wing, pass to Ernie Taylor (soon to become a Blackpool player), who in turn saw Milburn and left him with a delicate back pass. Milburn's shot was too powerful for Farm, and effectively the game was over.

Blackpool pushed forward once more, but their efforts were in vain, and in fact Milburn came close to a hat-trick with a bullet header, but that would have been an unfair scoreline on a valiant Blackpool side.

As the teams left the pitch, with Newcastle celebrating and Blackpool disconsolate, the question remained: would Stanley Matthews ever realise his dream and win the FA Cup?

Blackpool: Farm, Shimwell, Garret, Johnston, Hayward, Kelly, Matthews, Mudie, Mortensen, Slater, Perry.
Newcastle United: Fairbrother, Cowell, Corbett, Harvey, Brennan, Crowe, Walker, Taylor, Milburn, Robledo, Mitchell.
Attendance: 100,000 (approx.)

Blackpool 4 Bolton Wanderers 3

FA Cup Final – 2 May 1953

So much has been said and written about the 1953 FA Cup Final that it is almost impossible to do it justice in a few short paragraphs. Although it was not a classic match in the footballing sense, the game has come to be regarded as the most famous FA Cup Final of all time.

1953 Cup Final programme cover.

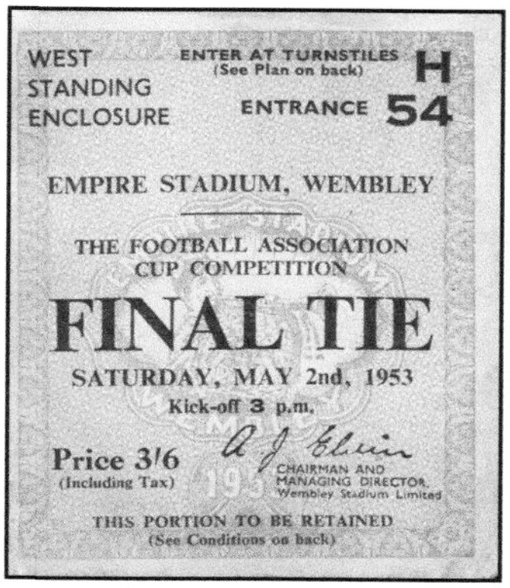
WEST STANDING ENCLOSURE
ENTER AT TURNSTILES (See Plan on back) H
ENTRANCE 54
EMPIRE STADIUM, WEMBLEY
THE FOOTBALL ASSOCIATION CUP COMPETITION
FINAL TIE
SATURDAY, MAY 2nd, 1953
Kick-off 3 p.m.
Price 3/6 (Including Tax)
CHAIRMAN AND MANAGING DIRECTOR, Wembley Stadium Limited
THIS PORTION TO BE RETAINED (See Conditions on back)

1953 FA Cup Final ticket.

Inevitably dubbed the 'Matthews Final', it was a game that included the first hat-trick scored in a Wembley FA Cup Final, and a quite remarkable fightback by Blackpool from 3–1 down to win the trophy after scoring twice in the final minute.

When Blackpool reached Wembley for the third time in six years, the whole nation celebrated. It was mainly due to the love that people had for the great Stanley Matthews, and his desire for a Cup-winners' medal. Within 90 minutes of kick-off, the 1953 FA Cup Final had transcended just mere sport and had almost become a pivotal moment in an era. It became more than just a game of football.

After the disappointments of 1948 and 1951, it seemed that there was no one – except those of the Bolton persuasion – who did not want to see Blackpool, and of course Matthews, win. After two minutes though, it looked like that dream was to be shattered already.

Nat Lofthouse had given Wanderers the lead with a goal that had 'Pool 'keeper Farm squirming. The centre-forward had unleashed a 20-yard shot, and Farm – usually the most reliable of 'keepers – somehow allowed the ball to slip through his hands and roll into the net. Blackpool were losing already.

The goal continued Lofthouse's record of scoring in every round, but it also served to unnerve Farm and his teammates. The Bolton forwards were attacking constantly, taking advantage of a rather statuesque tangerine defence, and just four minutes later it should have been 2–0; Lofthouse, again from a pass from Holden, missed a golden opportunity.

These were worrying moments for Blackpool fans. Their team had frozen two years ago against Newcastle United and were not looking confident in these early minutes. Then there was a serious injury to Bolton's Eric Bell, and the Wanderers were forced to reorganise. Bell was put out on to the left wing, where he spent the rest of the game hobbling and in some pain. There were no substitutes, of course, so Bolton were effectively reduced to 10 men for 70 minutes.

This inspired Blackpool, and they pushed forward looking for an equaliser. Ernie Taylor and Bill Perry were both looking dangerous and both had chances to score. Poor finishing kept the score at 1–0, though. When the equalising goal came, it was a classic worthy of such an occasion. Mortensen ran 30 yards with the ball, shaking off the attentions of two defenders, and then unleashed a powerful shot that gave Bolton 'keeper Hanson little chance. The ball had deflected off Hassall, but it was rightly credited to Morty.

Blackpool had drawn level and now started to play the type of football that had made them so popular, yet it was Bolton who came close to scoring within a couple of minutes. Lofthouse found himself free and in a one-on-one with Farm, only to blast over the bar. But after 40 minutes, Bolton did go ahead once more. Again, George Farm was indecisive as Langton floated the ball into the area, and he hesitated as Moir glanced it into the net. Five minutes later, the half-time whistle blew and Blackpool were trailing 2–1.

Stanley Matthews challenges for the ball in the 1953 Cup Final.

At half-time, manager Joe Smith told his players to carry on the way they were playing and they would get their reward. He was happy with what he had seen and decided against any tactical changes. The lack of change seemed to be working as Ernie Taylor nearly scored from the obvious Matthews cross within a couple of minutes of the restart. Then there was yet another blow as Bolton increased their lead, totally against the run of play. The ball was floated into the area, and somehow the injured Bell had risen above the defence and headed past Farm. It was 3–1 and the hopes and dreams of Matthews, Blackpool and seemingly most of the country were evaporating.

The goal actually seemed to galvanise Blackpool. Players afterwards have said that they knew they were the better team. They certainly knew that they were the fitter team, especially as so many Bolton players were beginning to show signs of cramp, and it seems that they knew they would win! From that moment on it was a wave of Blackpool attacks.

One of those relentless waves came in the form of Matthews, who outpaced Banks on the right, crossed the ball perfectly, 'keeper Hanson failing to connect, and Mortensen scoring his second under intense pressure. The fightback had begun.

A succession of Bolton players suffered cramp, disrupting the game, and that gave Blackpool more and more confidence. A tactical switch was made between Perry and Jackie Mudie and, after a defensive mix-up, it nearly paid immediate dividends as Mortensen's shot was saved for a corner by Hanson. Blackpool were dominant, yet time was running out and the looks of desperation on the 'Pool fans' faces were etched strongly as they all wished and prayed for Matthews to win his long-desired medal.

With just two minutes remaining, Mudie was sandwiched between two defenders as he charged toward goal. A free-kick was awarded just outside the area, and Mortensen stepped up. Legend has it that Morty saw a gap in the wall and shouted to a teammate that he was going to 'have a go'. With that, he unleashed an unstoppable shot that nearly burst the net. Blackpool were level.

It was the first hat-trick at a Wembley Cup Final and his teammates mobbed him with delight, but there was one last act to be played out in this theatrical extravaganza. Straight from the kick-off, the tangerine shirts surged forward once more. Matthews tormented on the right, produced an inch-perfect cross, only for Mudie to shoot wide. The seconds ticked away. Taylor slid another pass to Matthews and, as Banks came to tackle, Matthews went to the byline and

The players celebrate with the fans during a open-top bus parade on Blackpool promenade.

cut back a hard and accurate ground pass behind the retreating defenders. It was Bill Perry who met it, and within an instant it was 4–3 to Blackpool and the FA Cup was theirs.

A remarkable end to a remarkable match, and many of the Blackpool players were left in tears as the whistle blew.

For Matthews there was a winners' medal at the age of 38, gratefully received from Queen Elizabeth II. Mortensen achieved the first ever hat-trick at Wembley, and he showed no hint of envy or jealousy down the years as each time the Final was referred to as the 'Matthews Final'. For Blackpool it was the greatest day in their history, something still to be repeated, and a fitting testament to Joe Smith's vision as a manager.

The 1953 FA Cup Final became more than a game, as history retold it over and over again. If you watch the grainy black-and-white footage today, it seems slow and pedestrian, but it captured the hearts of a nation like few sporting encounters before or since.

Blackpool: Farm, Shimwell, Garrett, Fenton, Johnston, Robinson, Matthews, Taylor, Mortensen, Mudie, Perry.
Bolton Wanderers: Hanson, Ball, Banks, Wheeler, Barrass, Bell, Holden, Moir, Lofthouse, Hassall, Longham.
Attendance: 100,000 (approx.)

Blackpool 7 Sunderland 0

First Division – 5 October 1957

Games between Blackpool and Sunderland in the 1950s were always keenly contested affairs, and more often than not they would result in high-scoring results; this match would be no different.

Before the game, most 'Pool fans thought that their team had 'nowt to beat', and within only 45 seconds they appeared to be right. Dave Durie rose above the defence to nod in from a corner and Blackpool were ahead. The Sunderland backline that day was decidedly shaky, and within 10 minutes had conceded two more goals. Durie again and Ray Charnley taking advantage of goalkeeping errors to give the Seasiders a 3–0 lead with barely 12 minutes gone.

A near-capacity crowd roared on Blackpool and, with Stanley Matthews in superb form, the Sunderland players could be forgiven for wishing they were anywhere else but Bloomfield Road. Blackpool's defence, marshalled by the excellent Jimmy Armfield, had little to do, and indeed Armfield nearly got on the score sheet himself.

Just before half-time, though, Charnley got his second and Blackpool's fourth. It was a superb solo effort and rounded off an amazing first 45 minutes for the tall centre-forward, as he had tormented the Sunderland defence throughout. The players left the pitch to a huge ovation, the biggest cheer reserved for Charnley.

In the second half, knowing that the game was effectively lost, the visitors started to play more composed football. They were encouraged by the sight of Bill Perry out on the wing alone and now no more than a spectator due to an injury. Then on the hour Charnley himself went off with a bad head injury and did not return until the final few minutes.

Blackpool were too good though, and two more goals from Ernie Taylor (although there was a suspicion that one of them was an own-goal from Charlie Hurley) and one from the limping Perry gave the Seasiders a 7–0 victory. It was all the more remarkable bearing in mind that in the second half they were playing with only nine-and-a-half fit men!

Incredibly, two weeks later in the next home game, virtually the same team, but without the injured Charnley, were overwhelmed by a powerful Manchester United team and lost 5–2. In the return fixture with Sunderland the following February, Blackpool won 4–1, and so the entertainment continued.

The victory remains Blackpool's biggest ever at home in the Football League, only matched by the 7–0 win at rivals Preston North End (who were much weakened) at Deepdale in 1948.

Blackpool: Farm, Armfield, Garrett, J. Kelly, Gratrix, H. Kelly, Matthews, Taylor, Charnley, Durie, Perry.
Sunderland: Fraser, Hedley, McDonald, Anderson, Hurley, Elliott, Hannigan, Revie, Spencer, O'Neill, Grainger.
Attendance: 33,172

Blackpool 6 Newcastle United 0

First Division – 22 October 1966

During the disastrous campaign of 1966–67, Blackpool managed only one home League victory, and it came in late October, just seven days after their first victory of the season.

Their opponents, Newcastle United, were expected to provide tough opposition, as indeed did most visitors to Bloomfield Road that season, yet on that incredible day everything went perfectly for a Blackpool side playing with unusual passion and commitment.

The facts do not really tell the full story. Ian Moir's goals had given Blackpool a 2–0 lead within 16 minutes, and Alan Skirton and Ray Charnley had made it four by half-time.

In the second half, Jimmy Robson's goal and another by new signing Skirton brought the score to 6–0, and even Leslie Lea was allowed the luxury of a disallowed goal. Yet the home side did not have it all their own way. Newcastle were determined, and even at 6–0 down, they fought and produced two world-class saves from Tony Waiters in the final 10 minutes. The game was open and entertaining, and it was only Blackpool's finishing that provided the difference between the two teams.

Skirton, who had signed from Arsenal the previous month, was Man of the Match and came close to adding to his two goals, only to be denied by the brilliance of 'keeper Hollins. On the opposite side, a young Alan Suddick shone and tried time and time again to take on the whole of Blackpool's defence. With a midfield line up comprising Fisher, Rowe and McPhee, it was hardly surprising that he impressed all those at Bloomfield Road – so much so that six weeks later Blackpool signed him for a then-record fee.

The side that had played so well that day only went on to win two more games all season – away at Liverpool and Everton – and so boasted the curious record of winning more games in Merseyside than the Fylde coast! They were, of course, relegated at the end of the season.

The result did not really register with the rest of the country, as tragically on that weekend the terrible disaster befell the mining village of Aberfan and football did not matter.

Blackpool: Waiters, Thompson, Hughes, Fisher, McPhee, Rowe, Skirton, Robson, Charnley, Moir, Lea.
Sunderland: Hollins, Cragg, Clark, Moncur, Thompson, Hey, Robson, Bennett, McGarry, Suddick, Knox.
Attendance: 21,202

Huddersfield Town 1 Blackpool 3

Second Division – 11 May 1968

Despite winning their previous six games, Blackpool came to this last match of the season knowing that even if they won, they could still be denied promotion to Division One if their nearest rivals, Queen's Park Rangers, won at Aston Villa.

Expectations were high, and over 4,000 Blackpool fans made their way over the Pennines – their bodies in Huddersfield, but their thoughts also in Birmingham. The game was only given the go-ahead 15 minutes before kick-off, after a torrential downpour the previous day and that morning had made the pitch a sea of mud. It would have been difficult to have called it off, bearing in mind the importance of the occasion.

Blackpool began tentatively, mindful of the pressures, and also in the knowledge that they could not afford to lose. The pitch stopped any decent football being played, and the rain continued to pour throughout the 90 minutes. It became so bad that at one stage the referee ordered Tony Green back to the dressing room to change his shirt, as he could not distinguish between the teams due to the filthy conditions.

The first half was a battle; Huddersfield, under no pressure, created the best chances, but Blackpool defended admirably. Two saves by Alan Taylor from Worthington kept the score goalless. Inevitably, the opening goal did come though, on 40 minutes from Town's left-back Legg. The tension rose for the travelling fans, but the electronic scoreboard showed that Queen's Park Rangers were also a goal down at Aston Villa. Even that was fraught with high anxiety, as whoever was manning the board had a black sense of humour and changed the QPR score from one right through to 10, before resting on nil. With 45 minutes of the season left, Blackpool were in Division One.

The restart saw a more determined Blackpool effort, and soon the equaliser came through Alan Suddick. That was followed by comical defending from the home side that saw McGill put through his own goal, and so Blackpool were ahead 2–1. At Villa Park, Queen's Park Rangers had equalised, but if the scores stayed the same then the 'Pool were up.

Alan Skirton produced a terrific shot that made it 3–1, and promotion was surely theirs. The Blackpool fans celebrated, making Leeds Road a mini Bloomfield Road with a mass of tangerine scarves. Blackpool pressed for a fourth, with Green and Tommy Hutchison now breaking through the home defence at will, but there was no need as victory was assured.

When the final whistle blew, the Blackpool fans ran on to the pitch to embrace their heroes, also chanting manager Stan Mortensen's name. He had been there for just one year, and it looked as if he had led his beloved club back to the top tier of football again. Sadly, it all ended in tears.

Morty appeared, looking shaken. Blackpool had been cruelly denied, as in the dying seconds at Villa Park a home defender had scored an own-goal and QPR had won 2–1 and so pipped Blackpool for promotion. They had won it by virtue of a better goal average – 1.86, as opposed to Blackpool's 1.65 – and so 'Pool had another season of Second Division football ahead of them. To rub salt into the open wound, Blackpool had achieved 58 points, the highest for a team that failed to gain promotion.

The fans left the ground in tears. It had been a cruel end to the season. Blackpool had to wait two years before they finally returned to the First Division, but by then Mortensen had been sacked by an impatient board.

Huddersfield Town: Oldfield, McGill, Legg, Smith, Nicholson, Cherry, Harper, Worthington, Aimson, Shaw, Dobson.
Blackpool: Taylor, Armfield, Mowbray, Craven, James, McPhee, Skirton, Green, White, Suddick, Hutchison.
Attendance: 11,603

Preston North End 0 Blackpool 3

Second Division – 13 April 1970

Two years after the Huddersfield disappointment, Blackpool found themselves in a similar position when they travelled to rivals Preston North End for the penultimate match of the season. This time, though, they knew that victory would not only guarantee a return to the First Division, but would almost certainly consign their neighbours to the Third Division for the first time in their history.

The game was played on a Monday evening in front of a capacity crowd of 34,000, of which over half were made up of Blackpool fans, with another 3,000 locked out. Predictably, the atmosphere was tense, with so much depending on the outcome for both teams. It was Blackpool, who six days earlier had gained an excellent draw at fellow promotion candidates Swindon Town, who played the more relaxed football.

Preston were short of confidence and were overwhelmed almost from the start, and so it was no surprise that the visitors took the lead on 16 minutes. A right-wing cross from Mickey Burns was met by Fred Pickering to nod in at the far post, and Blackpool were 1–0 up.

The celebrations from the tangerine following started early as Blackpool piled on the pressure, and it was only some first-class saves from North End 'keeper Kelly that kept the score down. They did test Harry Thompson on a couple of occasions from Archie Gemmill, but it was Blackpool who always looked likeliest to add to the scoreline.

The second goal came on 40 minutes, and was again from Pickering. Tommy Hutchison had sent Bill Bentley clear on the wing, and his perfectly aimed cross was met by Pickering's head, and at half-time promotion was virtually assured at 2–0.

Fred Pickering leaps into the net after scoring one of his hat-trick goals against Preston at Deepdale.

The second period carried on the way the first had ended, with wave after wave of Blackpool attacks, and on 58 minutes Pickering got his and Blackpool's third goal. A shot from Hutchison rebounded off the legs of Kelly, and Pickering tapped in the rebound. The game was one-sided, and the Deepdale ground was a mass of celebrating Blackpool fans.

Blackpool toyed with Preston until the final whistle, and the home side were indebted to their 'keeper who was playing the game of his life, and with five minutes remaining the Blackpool players passed the ball to each other at will, without a white shirt getting close. The chant of 'Blackpool, Blackpool!' could be heard for miles around as the fans ecstatically embraced the remarkable events that were transpiring in front of them.

As the game ended, thousands of Blackpool fans invaded the pitch in celebration and chaired their heroes off. The Preston fans trudged disconsolately away, as it was clear that Third Division football was an inevitability, and at the hands of their bitter rivals too.

Battles between Blackpool and Preston North End have always been exciting and frantic, but none before, or indeed since, have been as dramatic as this. Preston were relegated the following weekend, and Blackpool enjoyed their return to the top tier, despite actually losing their final match of the season at Bloomfield Road.

Preston North End: Kelly, Patrick, McNab, Hawkins, Cranston, Heppolette, Lee, Spavin, Lloyd, Gemmill, Temple.
Blackpool: Thompson, Armfield, Bentley, McPhee, James, Hatton, Burns, Craven, Pickering, Suddick, Hutchison.
Attendance: 34,000

Blackpool 3 Chelsea 4

First Division – 24 October 1970

Of all the football matches staged at Bloomfield Road down the years, this game played on the 24 October 1970 between struggling Blackpool and 'aristocrats' Chelsea must surely be one of the oddest and most bizarre.

Chelsea arrived at the seaside as FA Cup holders and challengers for the League title, while Blackpool were rooted to the foot of the table after an already disastrous campaign, yet at half-time Blackpool were leading comfortably 3–0!

The story of that first period was one of complete and total dominance from the home side. Goals from Alan Suddick, who was carving open the Chelsea defence at will, and two from Fred Pickering – the last and Blackpool's third being the pick – saw the Tangerines leave the field after 45 minutes to an ovation not heard at Bloomfield Road for some time. Chelsea were shell-shocked. Home fans were even contemplating a record scoreline, such was their dominance. But it was not to be.

Chelsea's Phillips grabs the ball as Pickering and Suddick wait to pounce.

If the first half was incredible, the second was unbelievable. Chelsea, with nothing to lose, came out and played their expansive brand of football, while Blackpool seemed content to sit back and protect their lead. Even when Keith Weller pulled a goal back, there were no alarm bells. Blackpool sat back, much to the frustration of their increasingly anxious fans.

On the hour mark, Chelsea boss Dave Sexton replaced Tommy Baldwin with Charlie Cooke, and he immediately changed the game. His forays down the left caused the home defence problems, yet with 15 minutes to go it was still 3–1 and the points were beginning to look safe.

Then one decision changed the whole complexion of the game. Blackpool manager Les Shannon inexplicably took off Fred Pickering, replacing him with John Craven. It was extraordinary as Pickering had been superb, and the decision was greeted badly by the fans. It was said that according to Shannon, Pickering was carrying an injury, but the player always denied it. Whatever the reason, it changed the game completely, and within minutes Peter Osgood had scored Chelsea's second, converting a Webb cross.

Not long after they were level. Harry Thompson, now unnerved, dropped a cross and, Weller nipped in to score. It was 3–3 with a minute to go and Blackpool were now defending valiantly for a draw, but fate was cruel that day. The normally dependable defender Dave Hatton attempted a back pass to 'keeper Thompson from some way out, and incredibly fe sliced it past the 'keeper into the net. It was stunning; the Chelsea fans and players celebrated, while the Blackpool contingent stood and stared in disbelief. Somehow Blackpool had literally snatched defeat from the jaws of certain victory.

Three days later, following intense criticism, manager Shannon resigned. He was replaced by Bob Stokoe, but the downward slide could not be halted and Blackpool were relegated after just one season in the First Division. This game summed up their season.

Blackpool: Thompson, Armfield, Mowbray, Hatton, James, Bentley, Burns, Green, Pickering, Suddick, Hutchison.
Chelsea: Phillips, Mulligan, Harris, Hollins, Hinton, Webb, Weller, Hudson, Osgood, Baldwin, Houseman.
Attendance: 24,940

Bologna 1 Blackpool 2 (after extra-time)

Anglo-Italian Cup Final – 12 June 1971

The Anglo-Italian tournament of 1971 restored pride to Blackpool Football Club after their disastrous relegation campaign from Division One. The Seasiders began the competition with morale low, yet after four qualifying matches they had scored enough goals and points to win themselves a place in the Final at the Stadio Comunale in Bologna. Their opponents were regarded highly in Italy, and were at the time one of the country's top teams.

A crowd of around 40,000 turned up, fully expecting a home victory. The game kicked off at 5pm local time and was shown live on television back in Britain, although, strangely, extra-time was not shown due to scheduling commitments; live football on the television was in its infancy then.

It was hot, but not oppressive, and that may be the reason for the stale opening of the first half. Bologna were predictably cautious, and Blackpool were getting used to playing in rather warmer conditions than they were used to. Despite a few breakaways from the Blackpool attack, it was the home side who took the lead on 32 minutes when number 11, Pace, finished off a fine move that left John Burridge floundering.

It remained that way until half-time, but after a stirring team talk from manager Bob Stokoe, Blackpool came out committed for the second period. Alan Suddick took control of

The Blackpool players celebrate winning the 1971 Anglo-Italian Cup.

the midfield, and Bill Bentley fed the attack. The equaliser came on 62 minutes after an inch-perfect through pass from Bentley was met by John Craven, who smashed it beyond the 'keeper.

The goal galvanised the team and the small band of Blackpool fans who had made the trip. Mickey Burns came close to getting the second, but produced a fine save from veteran 'keeper Vavassori late in the match, and Craven too nearly snatched the winner in the final few minutes. Stokoe made two substitutions, with Wann and Johnstone replacing Ainscow and Craven, both players suffering from exhaustion from the unaccustomed heat.

Extra-time came with the home fans strangely muted. Their team was now being outplayed by a side that was free flowing in its passing and was looking more and more likely to snatch the win. The blue-and-red scarves were still waving, but more in hope than expectation.

The winner came on 99 minutes when Mickey Burns scored an absolutely superb goal. He took the ball from his own half, following a lovely 30-yard pass from Dennis Wann, shrugged off a couple of defenders and volleyed it into the net. Blackpool were ahead, and at that point Bologna were a beaten side and effectively gave up. In fact, Blackpool then spent the next 10 minutes passing to each other with ease, something which was appreciated and jeered by the Italian fans in equal measure.

Blackpool won the Cup that day – their first silverware since the 1953 FA Cup Final – and the fans celebrated all night in the lovely city of Bologna. The Italian supporters showed grace and sportsmanship by applauding the white-shirted English players off the pitch. The next day when the team returned home, they were greeted by as many as 50,000 fans on the promenade. Pride had been restored to Blackpool Football Club.

Bologna: Vavassori, Roversi, Fedele, Perani, Janich, Gregori, Cresci, Rizzo, Salvodi, Scala, Pace.
Blackpool: Burridge, Bentley, Hatton, Ainscow, Alcock, Suddaby, Burns, Green, Craven, Suddick, Hutchison.
Attendance: 40,000 (approx.)

AS Roma 3 Blackpool 1

Anglo-Italian Cup Final – 24 June 1972

One year later, Blackpool returned to Italy to defend their trophy, but this time against a far more able and organised side in Roma. Their opponents were odds-on to win the game, and in temperatures of nearly 100 degrees Fahrenheit, Blackpool struggled.

The Olympic Stadium was about three quarters full with a crowd of 75,000, and the noise and spectacle at kick-off went some way to unnerving the Tangerine players. The first half was evenly matched, with both sides coming close to scoring and Roma employing the usual Italian tactic of the breakaway. They should have been ahead within 10 minutes as Rigani's header went over the bar from close range, and then shortly after Spadani's effort was well saved by John Burridge in goal.

Substitute Terry Alcock scores a consolation goal for Blackpool in Rome's Olympic Stadium.

Blackpool were never really positive in the game, especially in front of goal, and twice they spurned easy chances from Mick Hill and Keith Dyson – the latter hitting the side netting when he really should have scored. On both occasions the provider was the influential Mickey Burns. At half-time it was goalless, but Blackpool appreciated the scoreline more than Roma.

The second half started with the temperature rising, and it was clear that the 'Pool players were struggling. Within two minutes they had gone a goal down. Capelino took advantage of a loose ball from Dave Hatton and scored comfortably. The home side's fans turned up the volume, and Blackpool now had their backs to the wall and yet again had two decent chances to equalise through a header from Glyn James and a spectacular effort from Burns.

It was to no avail, though, as Roma held firm under the rare pressure and increased their lead through Scaratti and Zigoni. Terry Alcock got a late consolation for Blackpool, but the Seasiders had been well beaten. The feeling was that the players had lacked the passion and commitment to take on the intimidating atmosphere.

They did leave the tournament with their heads held high, though, being congratulated as perfect ambassadors for English football. Also, as well as winning the Cup the previous year, they did also create a scoring record when beating Lanerossi Vicenza 10–0 in a group-stage qualifier. They and others had gone some way to restoring dignity to a competition that had been tainted by violent play in the past, but sadly it was scrapped two years later and Blackpool never got the chance to regain the Cup.

AS Roma: Ginvilli, Capelli, Liquori, Salvori, Bet, Santarini, Capellino, Spadani, Rigani, Cordeva, Franzot.
Blackpool: Burridge, Hatton, Bentley, Suddaby, James, Ainscow, Hutchison, Suddick, Dyson, Hill, Burns.
Attendance: 75,000 (approx.)

Blackpool 3 Sunderland 2

Second Division – 1 February 1975

One of the most exciting and dramatic games seen at Bloomfield Road was this top-of-the-table clash in the Second Division with Sunderland in 1975. It had everything, and it was the type of game that those who witnessed it would never forget.

Sunderland came to Blackpool as Division Two pacesetters, with Blackpool just a few places and points behind them. The Wearsiders were cheered on by 4,000 fans, who provided a superb atmosphere. The game, unsurprisingly, started frantically with late tackles and off-the-ball incidents, but eventually a feast of football was exposed as both teams calmed down.

It was Blackpool who scored the opener through Terry Alcock after 19 minutes. A corner from Bill Bentley had been nodded on by Mickey Walsh, and Alcock was there to head home. Blackpool then took control and came close through Alan Ainscow (twice) and Bentley, but on 42 minutes they doubled their lead. A Walsh cross was not dealt with and Wyn Davies was able to stab the ball home. It could, and should, have been 3–0 minutes later when Bentley missed a glorious opportunity, but Blackpool were good value for their half-time lead.

The second half saw huge pressure from Sunderland after a half-time lambasting from manager Bob Stokoe, and it was no surprise when they scored on 51 minutes. Halom's powerful shot gave Burridge no chance, and then followed wave after wave of striped-shirt attacks, although just when it looked like Blackpool had weathered the storm, Bobby Kerr

Terry Alcock opens the scoring against Sunderland after catching the Wearsiders' defence naping.

Wyn Davies scores the Seasiders' second after a mistake by Jim Montgomery in the Sunderland goal.

equalised on 68 minutes. The game ebbed and flowed, and it would now need something special to settle it. That something came with three minutes remaining.

Mickey Walsh broke free from his markers on the halfway line, shrugged off the attentions of Moncur and Guthrie and, from a full 35 yards, unleashed a fierce left-foot shot that flew into the top corner of the net, past a despairing Montgomery. The goal became famous and won that season's BBC *Match of the Day* Goal of the Season. At the final whistle, the Blackpool fans spilled on to the pitch as their team had snatched a remarkable 3–2 victory and thus continued their promotion challenge.

One other incident took place during this incredible game that has since been forgotten among the football thrills and spills. Just after Sunderland had equalised, they were awarded a penalty, taken by Billy Hughes. This was saved easily by Burridge, but afterwards on television it was noted by pundit Jimmy Hill that a white-coated groundsman behind the goal was waving his arms and had clearly distracted Hughes. This, according to Hill, was unfair and was ungentlemenly conduct, but when the man in question, Bert Taylor, was asked about the incident, he just smiled, 'I was trying to tell the referee that I thought he'd made a poor decision.' His collegue Clifford Collier just nodded and smiled.

Blackpool: Burridge, Curtis, Hatton, Hart, Harrison, Alcock, Ainscow, Davies, Walsh, Bentley, Evanson.
Sunderland: Montgomery, Malone, Bolton, Moncur, Watson, Guthrie, Kerr, Hughes, Halom, Robson, Towers.
Attendance: 16,151

Darlington 0 Blackpool 4

Fourth Division – 1 May 1985

Blackpool came to this top-of-the-table clash knowing that victory would almost certainly secure promotion back to Division Three. Darlington were a place behind the Seasiders, and with only four games remaining it was essential that Blackpool came away without defeat.

Over 3,000 fans travelled with the team that evening, and they witnessed one of the most positive and certainly most efficient performances of the season. It was a perfect lesson in finishing power, as Blackpool completely overwhelmed their opponents.

Darlington did seem dangerous in the first half, actually wasting three easy chances, before allowing Mike Conroy to give Blackpool the lead on 25 minutes. A home attack had broken down, and Ian Britton had sent Paul Stewart away on the right. His cross for Conroy was perfect, and the number eight smashed the ball past the despairing Barber in goal.

The home side responded by attacking, which was unusual as they had been criticised all season for their negative play, especially by Blackpool manager Sam Ellis, and this played into the 'Pool's hands. On 37 minutes Eamon O'Keefe received a through ball from Dave Windridge and calmly slotted home to make it 2–0. It killed off the game as a contest, and just before half-time Windridge was denied a clear penalty, but Blackpool went in at half-time completely in command.

The second half was totally in Blackpool's control. They scored on 60 minutes when a Windridge cross was deflected on to Stewart by 'keeper Barber, and 17 minutes later the fourth

Champagne celebrations in the Feethams' dressing-room after the Seasiders' return to the Third Division.

came. Another cross from Windridge – playing his best football – was met by John Deary. His first-time header was brilliantly saved, but the follow-up was decisive. It was so one-sided that Blackpool 'keeper Billy O'Rourke had only one save to make in the second period.

Blackpool's 4–0 victory had gained them three valuable points, and after the game the 3,000 'Pool fans chanted Sam Ellis's name and would not leave the ground until he acknowledged them. It was an important victory, even more so bearing in mind that three weeks later Darlington joined Blackpool's promotion party with just one point less than the Seasiders.

Darlington: Barber, Aldred, Johnston, Smith, Macdonald, Tupling, McLean, Forster, Haire, Airey, Todd.
Blackpool: O'Rourke, Moore, Price, Deary, Hetzke, Greenall, Britton, Conway, Stewart, O'Keefe, Windridge.
Attendance: 7,021

Blackpool 2 Torquay United 2 (Torquay won 5–4 on penalties)

Fourth Division Play-off Final – 31 May 1991

Thirty-eight years after their last, and indeed most famous, appearance at Wembley, Blackpool returned to the old stadium for a less glamorous but important game. The Fourth Division Play-off Final of 1991 offered Blackpool a second chance to gain promotion after they had thrown away automatic promotion so miserably at Walsall three weeks previously.

Blackpool players line-up for a minute's silence in memory of the great Stan Mortensen before their 1991 Wembley game against Torquay United.

Over 15,000 fans made the journey to London on a bitterly cold May evening, and they witnessed a night of high drama. Both sides were expected to approach with caution, knowing how important the game was, as it effectively decided their immediate future, but it was an entertaining and free-flowing match that was served up that evening.

It was Blackpool who made the perfect start after just eight minutes when captain Paul Groves latched on to a through ball from the already impressive Mark Taylor and coolly slipped the ball under the outstretched arms of 'keeper Gareth Howells. Blackpool were ahead against a team that finished seven points adrift of them in the regular season. Promotion was there for the taking.

Torquay had other ideas, though; they attacked constantly, and the equaliser was inevitable, coming on the half-hour mark. A corner was not cleared and was met by Wes Saunders from five yards out. The scores were level, but after another period of sustained pressure from the Devon side it looked like Blackpool had steadied themselves and were getting back into the contest. Then disaster struck, as on 40 minutes Dave Bamber handled in his own area while trying to clear a cross. Referee George Courtney pointed to the spot, and Dean Edwards easily converted. It was the start of a personal nightmare for Bamber; back in the squad after injury, the team's top scorer was to have a hand in the eventual outcome of the match, but with dire results.

The second period saw Blackpool push hard for the equaliser, but poor finishing and excellent goalkeeping kept them at bay. When it did come, however, it was in a bizarre fashion. Mike Davies floated a free-kick into the box, Bamber nodded it down and David Eyres tried a spectacular overhead kick that crashed against the bar, hit 'keeper Howells, and rolled into the net.

Blackpool pushed for the winner, but full-time saw the teams level. There were 30 minutes of extra-time, which saw a Dave Bamber goal disallowed for offside, and an outstanding save by Steve McIlhargey at the death to keep Torquay out. With the time approaching 10.30pm, a penalty shoot-out would decide the 49-match season.

The penalties were taken at the end with the small band of Torquay fans, and it always looked like the Devon side were the more positive. At 4–4, sudden death ensued, and after 'keeper Gareth Howells had despatched his, up stepped Bamber. The Blackpool hero capped off his personal night of despair by putting his kick well wide of the goal. The Torquay fans celebrated, while the Blackpool majority stood in disbelief. Promotion had been snatched away, and in another cruel fashion.

It was left to manager Billy Ayre to sum up the feelings of everyone when interviewed after the game. He said, 'I've never had a worse moment in my life, never mind in football.' It was the perfect description of a night of despair.

Blackpool: McIlhargey, Davies, Wright, Groves, Horner, Gore, Rodwell, Taylor, Bamber, Garner, Eyres.
Torquay United: Howells, Curran, P. Holmes, Saunders, Elliot, Joyce, Myers, M. Holmes, Evans, Edwards, Loran.
Attendance: 21,615

Blackpool 1 Scunthorpe United 1 (Blackpool won 4–3 on penalties)

Fourth Division Play-off Final – 23 May 1992

Twelve months after their 1991 disappointment, Blackpool returned to Wembley for another Play-off Final. Unlike the last occasion, though, this was not greeted in the celebratory fashion as before, but the anti-climax of again throwing away automatic promotion and having to try again at Wembley was something that did not appeal.

Only around 13,000 fans made the trip on a scorchingly hot day, but they were amply rewarded. Blackpool were completely committed, epitomised by Mike Davies being booked after 80 seconds for an overzealous challenge. The game was open, and it was Blackpool who created the most and better chances. Andy Garner and Dave Bamber (desperate to make amends for the previous year) both came close. Scunthorpe should have taken the lead through Ian Hamilton, who blasted over the bar when it seemed easier to score, and within 60 seconds they were punished when Bamber headed in from a Tony Rodwell cross. It was Bamber's 37th goal of the season, and of course the most important.

In the second period Blackpool had to contain constant Scunthorpe pressure, with McIlhargey called upon time and time again. He was beaten on 52 minutes, though, as Tony Daws unleashed a fierce 25-yard shot following a nice one-two with Ian Helliwell. That made the game more open and Blackpool came close through Eyres and Phil

Blackpool players celebrate their play-off win over Scunthorpe United.

Horner, and had a legitimate penalty claim turned down when it looked like Bamber had been fouled. For their part, Scunthorpe also worried the Blackpool goal, with Dave Hill particularly unfortunate toward the end.

Extra-time followed with 30 minutes of leg-sapping action in increasing temperatures. Blackpool pushed for the winner and should have wrapped up the game, but somehow Bamber shot wide from three yards out. That was followed by a Rodwell miss after a 20-yard run through the defence. The whistle blew again, and it was penalties once more.

The tension was just as great, and a number of Tangerine fans could not bear to watch, with memories of the previous season still fresh. As it was, Blackpool (kicking toward their own fans) looked more assured, and at 3–4 Scunthorpe substitute Jason White stepped up and blasted his kick over the bar. It was a cruel ending once more, but this time Blackpool had benefited. They had been promoted to the new Second Division, and the 13,000 fans who had made the journey could celebrate long and hard.

Blackpool: McIlhargey, Burgess, Cook, Groves, Davies, Gore, Rodwell, Horner, Bamber, Garner, Eyres.
Scunthorpe United: Samways, Joyce, Longden, Hill, Elliot, Humphreys, Martin, Hamilton, Daws, Buckley, Helliwell.
Attendance: 22,741

Blackpool 0 Bradford City 3

Division Two Play-off semi-final second leg – 15 May 1996

Whatever Blackpool Football Club has achieved down the years, and whatever it achieves in the future, there will always be a stain that has left its indelible mark on the club's great history. 15 May 1996 is a date that will stay with Blackpool fans for as long as they live, and for totally the wrong reasons.

After throwing away automatic promotion in the most dramatic of circumstances, Blackpool went into this second leg with a 2–0 lead from Valley Parade and were surely only 90 minutes from Wembley. The Bradford City manager, Chris Kamara, had already promised that his team would attack, as the tie was effectively still at half-time. He had wound up his players by pinning to the dressing room door the directions to Wembley from the night's programme, something which Blackpool officials, who had printed it, were later criticised for. In their defence, it made complete sense to print the directions in the final match programme of the season, no matter what the score from the first leg.

If it could go wrong for the home side that evening, then it was guaranteed to in a major way. A capacity crowd witnessed a performance of such nervousness, timidity and fright that it was hardly surprising that a blatant penalty for Bradford was turned down within the first two minutes. It was clear how the evening was to progress. The goals, when they came, were scrappy affairs. They came from Des Hamilton – to give Bradford a half-time lead, but still trailed Blackpool overall – and Carl Shutt and Mark Stallard. Blackpool never competed, although they did hit the bar through Andy Preece, and Tony Ellis had come close too, but it was the Blackpool side that had thrown away a seemingly unassailable lead at the end of the season, as opposed to the team that had taken control the previous Sunday in the first leg.

Bradford City won the game 3–0 and 3–2 on aggregate. Their fans celebrated and went on to greater glory by beating Notts County 2–0 in the Final at Wembley. Blackpool reacted badly; manager Sam Allardyce was sacked just a few days later by chairman Owen Oyston (who was in prison at the time) and the club took nearly 12 years to recover.

Since the game, numerous 'conspiracy' theories have arisen as to how the team could have played so abysmally. There were reports of players seen after the game drinking and enjoying their evening, but that is hardly a basis for some of the conjecture. Whatever the reason, the Blackpool team that had played so well for most of the season let themselves and the fans down that cold May evening. They also managed to get Sam Allardyce the sack, although that was just one of the many regrettable decisions by the board down the years.

Blackpool: Nixon, Bryan, Bradshaw, Linighan, Gouck, Morrison, Mellor, Bonner, Watson, Ellis, Preece.
Bradford City: Gould, Husford, Mohan, Brightwell, Jacobs, Hamilton, Duxbury, Mitchell, Kiwomya, Shutt, Stallard.
Attendance: 9,593

Blackpool 4 Leyton Orient 2

Division Three Play-off Final – 26 May 2001

Blackpool had arrived at the Millennium Stadium after the proverbial 'rollercoaster' season in the basement division. Steve McMahon's men had fallen to 91st in the Football League, been humiliated at Barnet 7–0, and yet had produced a late-season run that saw them scrape into the Play-offs on the final day. After despatching Hartlepool United easily in the semi-finals, they were faced with Leyton Orient in Cardiff (while Wembley was being rebuilt), a team that had not been out of the top six all season.

Around 14,000 Blackpool fans travelled to Wales and certainly created the atmosphere in the huge stadium and the surrounding streets before the game, but it was Orient who surprisingly opened the scoring. It happened within 30 seconds when 'Pool 'keeper Phil Barnes made a howler of a mistake, and Chris Tate nipped in to score in front of the Orient fans. It was the worst possible start, but Blackpool kept composed and played the type of football that McMahon had introduced since he arrived. It was free flowing and entertaining, but not always clinical.

On 35 minutes captain Ian Hughes levelled for the Seasiders, completely with the run of play, yet agonisingly they went behind two minutes later after allowing Scott Houghton too much space. His effort was pinpoint and Blackpool trailed again.

As half-time approached, the Tangerine fans were ecstatic again as Brian Reid converted a Gary Parkinson cross, and the scores were level once more. It had been an astonishing 45 minutes and evenly fought.

The Blackpool fans celebrating after the final whistle at Cardiff. (Courtesy of Danny Roper)

The second half was mostly Blackpool's, and their third goal came with 13 minutes remaining from veteran and fans' favourite Paul Simpson. Richie Wellens had supplied a beautiful pass, and Simpson, struggling with injury, finished it off perfectly, beating 'keeper Ashley Bayes. It was wonderful and selfless from Wellens, who could have strode through the area alone and scored, but his vision was excellent.

As the minutes ticked away and the Blackpool fans started celebrating, Brett Ormerod sealed promotion with a stunning goal made by John Hills and Simpson with some delightful touch play. Ormerod's finish was clinical, and his somersaulting celebrations summed up the feelings of the fans, who had been starved of success for so long.

It had been a wonderful ending to a dramatic season, and Steve McMahon had provided promotion in his first full season in charge. Blackpool were back in Division Two and surely on the road to a sustained period of success.

Blackpool: Barnes, Hills, Parkinson, Hughes, Reid, Coid, Wellens, Clarkson, Simpson, Ormerod, Murphy.
Leyton Orient: Bayes, Joseph, Lockwood, Smith, Downer, Harris, Walschaerts, McGee, Houghton, Ibehre, Tate.
Attendance: 23,600

Blackpool 4 Cambridge United 1

Football League Trophy Final – 24 March 2002

One year after gaining promotion to Division Two, Blackpool returned to the Millennium Stadium for the Final of the LDV Vans Trophy. It was a tournament in which they had failed to make any impression in the past – save for a Northern Area Final against Bolton Wanderers in the late 1980s – and for most clubs, the attractions are far outweighed by inconvenience in the early rounds. It is only when the club makes the Final that it takes it seriously.

As it was, 13,000 fans travelled again to Cardiff and this time in celebratory mood. The expectation was high as Cambridge were weaker opponents and on a downward slide at that time. The Blackpool fans were not to be disappointed.

Before the game, manager Steve McMahon had rested nine players in a League match with Brentford, something which did not make him popular with other clubs fighting for points, but it meant that his side were fresh and ready for the challenge. In fact, they so dominated proceedings that the scoreline was flattering to their opponents.

After early misses from John Murphy and Scott Taylor, Murphy made amends by opening the scoring on six minutes. He threw himself at a Lee Collins's cross and headed bullet-like past the 'keeper. It seemed only a matter of time before the second came, yet Cambridge reorganised themselves and scored an equaliser through a penalty just after the half-hour mark. Tommy Jaszczun brought down Tom Youngs in the box, and Paul Wanless converted the spot-kick. It was harsh on Blackpool, but the second period saw a completely one-sided display that brought three goals.

Chris Clarke headed in a John Hills free-kick, with a deflection from Taylor, past the despairing Lionel Perez in goal, and Blackpool were on their way. Hills scored the third after a lovely pass from Wellens, and then five minutes later, on 82 minutes, Scott Taylor slid a through ball from Jaszczun perfectly past the oncoming Perez.

It was as simple as that. Blackpool had overwhelmed their opponents and had won their first trophy for 31 years. Steve McMahon had managed two successful Finals in two years, and at that point he could do no wrong with the Blackpool faithful.

Blackpool: Barnes, Jaszczun, Marshall, Clarke, O'Kane, Collins, Hills, Wellens, Bullock, Murphy, Taylor.
Cambridge United: Perez, Angus, Murray, Tann, Duncan, Guttridge, Wanless, Tudor, Ashbee, Kitson, Youngs.
Attendance: 20,287

The players parade the LDV Vans Trophy around the Cardiff pitch. (Courtesy of Danny Roper)

Blackpool 2 Southend United 0

Football League Trophy Final – 21 March 2004

For the third time in four years, Blackpool had reached a Final at the Millennium Stadium – matched only by Arsenal at that point – and again it was for the LDV Trophy. This time, though, the interest from the Blackpool fans was slow, and for the first time in a major Final they were outnumbered by their opponents, although there were still 16,000 present that day. The love affair between manager Steve McMahon and the Tangerine faithful was wavering, and this 'day out' was seen as a final act in the relationship. For Southend, fighting for the League status, it was the biggest game in their 98-year history – hence 18,000 fans travelling from Essex.

The game was almost as comfortable as two years previously. Under the roof – closed to keep out the horrendous elements outside – Blackpool took the lead within two minutes when a Scott Taylor shot was deflected to an offside John Murphy, who swept the ball home.

To be fair to Southend, they did not complain and went about playing their best football, but their finishing was woeful, with Maher, Hunt and Gower all wasting chances. Blackpool weathered the storm and went 2–0 up early in the second half. Mike Sheron was sent clear by Martin Bullock, his cross passed three Blackpool shirts until Danny Coid, unmarked, latched on to the ball and swept it home. Game over.

Southend had only one chance of note after that, when Leon Constantine fluffed a shot after good work in the build-up, and Blackpool had regained the Cup they had won two years previously.

The celebrations were a little muted this time. The fans were now demanding more from the team and manager, and this was scant reward for a season that was again unravelling in the League. McMahon was soon to depart Bloomfield Road after a hugely successful era, and within three years Blackpool would be on the verge of a great period in their history.

Blackpool: Jones, Grayson, Flynn, Elliot, Coid, Bullock, Wellens, Dinning, Jaszczun, Sheron, Murphy.
Southend United: Flahavan, Jupp, Cort, Warren Wilson, Hunt, Gower, Maher, Pettefer, Constantine, Broughton.
Attendance: 34,031

Blackpool 2 Yeovil Town 0

League One Play-off Final – 27 May 2007

Blackpool arrived at Wembley for their biggest game in years on the back of nine consecutive wins and 13 victories from the previous 15 games. Simon Grayson's men had struggled at the beginning of the season, only recording one victory in their opening 12 games, but their form in the final stages of the 2006–07 season was almost irresistible. Their opponents, Yeovil Town, had overcome all the odds with a stunning fightback against Nottingham Forest in the semi-finals, while Blackpool had easily despatched Oldham Athletic over two legs.

Around 31,000 Blackpool fans bedecked a soaking Wembley stadium in tangerine that day, and they were rewarded with a performance that was about as perfect as possible. There will be few games played at Wembley quite as one-sided as this one, and the only surprise was that the scoreline stayed at 2–0.

Blackpool all but overwhelmed their opponents and came close to scoring on many occasions, even as early as the fourth minute, when Keigan Parker had a legitimate penalty appeal turned down. There were then chances for Claus Jorgenson, Andy Morrell and Wes Hoolahan, all of whom should have scored. Keigan Parker came close after 30 minutes, but his shot went straight to the 'keeper, and Hoolahan once more made an easy chance look difficult and pulled his shot wide from just eight yards.

The amount of pressure Blackpool had would surely deliver a goal, and it came on 43 minutes with a superb free-kick from Robbie Williams. Parker, waltzing his way past the Yeovil defence, was unceremoniously brought down, and Williams fired the ball past the despairing Mildenhall from a full 20 yards. It was a perfect free-kick and the perfect ending to a dominant first half, yet Blackpool nearly allowed Yeovil an equaliser right on half-time when Paul Rachubka tipped over a Davies effort. The half-time highlights on the big screen showed wave after wave of Blackpool attacks; the only concern was that the Seasiders had just a one-goal lead.

The second half continued the way the first had ended, and barely seven minutes in Parker scored what is surely one of the greatest goals seen at the new stadium. He shimmied past a couple of defenders and from around 30 yards unleashed an unstoppable shot into the top corner of the net. It was a sublime strike and one that will grace the archives for years to come. In that moment, Keigan Parker showed the talent and promise that had endeared him to Blackpool fans, yet it was a promise that was never realised once the team moved to a higher level of football.

From then on it was almost complete domination from the men in tangerine, and the Blackpool faithful could dream of Championship football for the first time in 29 years. Parker should have scored a third soon after, but a fine save from Mildenhall denied him, and then the same from Morrell kept the score respectable.

Yeovil did contribute to an entertaining afternoon, but with the exception of a late Marcus Stewart effort that bounced over the bar, they never really threatened Rachubka's goal. It mattered not for the 31,000 ecstatic Blackpool fans. The whistle blew from Andy D'Urso, and the Seasiders had finally returned to the top half of English domestic football. It was a remarkable achievement by manager Simon Grayson, who just 19 months previous had taken over a side seemingly destined for League Two football following the disastrous reign of Colin Hendry. His skills turned a team, always struggling, into a free-flowing and attractive side that could now pit its wits against the best in the Championship.

The celebrations were long and passionate, with the prospect of local 'derbies' against Preston North End and Burnley to look forward to, but, as the PA announcer said at the end of the game, 'Blackpool are back!' He was so right.

Blackpool: Rachubka, Barker, Jackson, Evatt, Williams, Forbes, Jorgenson, Southern, Hoolahan, Parker, Morrell.
Yeovil Town: Mildenhall, Lindergaard, Forbes, Guyett, Jones, Gray, Barry, Cohen, Davies, Stewart, Morris.
Attendance: 59,313

Blackpool 3 Cardiff City 2

Championship Play-off Final – 22 May 2010

Three years after the League One Play-off Final, Blackpool were back on a sun-soaked May afternoon to participate in possibly the biggest game in the history of the club. It was a game that dwarfed the 1953 FA Cup Final in terms of its rewards with a suggested £90 million for the winners, and a game that few Blackpool fans could barely have dreamt about some five years previously.

The fact that Blackpool were just 90 minutes away from the 'promised land' of the Premier League was in itself a source of amazement to most 'experts'. The pundits had all suggested that Blackpool would be firm favourites for relegation that season, and no matter how many times Blackpool flirted with or joined in the promotion race, they were never on the national media's radar. Ian Holloway's side was playing a type of football that enthralled, entertained and, most importantly, won matches.

Their run-in had been similar to 2007, with a late-season surge seeing them snatch the final Play-off place. Despatching Nottingham Forest in mesmerising fashion over two legs in the semi-finals was proof enough, but they still went into the Final against Cardiff – winners over Leicester City in the semis – as underdogs. Around 37,000 Blackpool fans – the largest gathering ever in one place to support the team – made a blazing Wembley a colourful and passionate place to be.

The game turned out to be one of the most thrilling that the stadium, old and new, had ever seen. Both sides, mindful of the rewards, abandoned any caution and frankly went for the jugular with a brand of football that delighted as well as frightened. It was Cardiff who settled first, and after one close effort they took the lead after nine minutes through Michael Chopra. He exchanged passes with Peter Whittingham and then finished inch-perfectly past Matt Gilks.

Within four minutes Blackpool were level. Stephen McPhail handled needlessly, and the resulting free-kick from Charlie Adam was stunning. A left-foot placed shot from just outside the box and the Blackpool fans were ecstatic. The white-shirted men then took control of the contest and should have taken the lead, but for DJ Campbell's miskick, yet it was Cardiff who scored the next goal. Chris Burke was guilty of a bad miss but atoned soon afterwards as he played in Joe Ledley, who slipped the ball past the advancing Gilks.

The lead did not last long, as Blackpool pushed forward. A fine save from Marshall resulted in a corner, and after a goalmouth mêlée that saw Ian Evatt's effort blocked on the line, Gary Taylor-Fletcher pushed the ball over for the equaliser. It was not over, however, as on the stroke of half-time Campbell wriggled free of two defenders and played in Brett Ormerod, who slipped it past the advancing 'keeper. It was poetic that Ormerod should score

A fan's view of the trophy celebration at Wembley. (Courtesy of Steve Higginbottom)

as it was nine years since he had scored the fourth goal in Blackpool's 4–2 in over Leyton Orient in the Third Division Play-off Final.

Amazingly, there was time for one more goal, but thankfully for Blackpool fans Darcy Blake's effort was rightly ruled for offside. A breathless 45 minutes had brought five goals and enough entertainment to fill a whole season.

Of course, with the temperatures reaching 110 degrees Fahrenheit on the pitch, the second half could not possibly hope to match the first. Blackpool were content to allow Cardiff to attack, but they never looked likely to concede, despite Chopra hitting the post on 57 minutes. In fact, the Seasiders could have wrapped it up at the end when substitute Ben Burgess was put clean through, but his finish was frustratingly weak.

When the final whistle blew, the celebrations were like nothing seen before. Grown men and women fell to their knees and cried. They cried because it was a day that no Blackpool fan seriously thought that they would see in their lifetime. Ian Holloway had turned a good team into something quite special, and now Blackpool were in the Premier League. Among the celebrating fans was a certain Mr Valeri Belokon, the Latvian President of the club. When he bought a stake four years previously, the team were struggling in League One and he promised Premier League football in five years. Most laughed, yet his dream came true.

Two days after the game, an estimated 80,000 fans crammed on to Blackpool promenade to welcome the team back. A special cheer was reserved for Holloway, who, after a tongue-in-cheek question, asking where they had all been all season, then promised that Blackpool would approach the Premier League in the same way: they would attack it. He was true to his word.

Blackpool: Gilks, Baptiste, Crainey, Evatt, Coleman, Southern, Adam, Vaughan, Taylor-Fletcher, Campbell, Ormerod.
Cardiff City: Marshall, McNaughton, Hudson, Kennedy, Burke, Whittingham, Ledley, Blake, McPhail, Chopra, Bothroyd.
Attendance: 82,244

BLACKPOOL STARS

Charlie Adam

Midfielder: 94 + 4 appearances, 32 goals
Born: 10 December 1985, Dundee, Scotland
Career: Rangers, Blackpool (2009–present day).

The £500,000 that Blackpool paid to Rangers for Charlie Adam at the start of the 2009–10 season must surely be some of the best money spent by the club in its entire history. Charlie Adam has become such an important part in the success of the Tangerines over the past couple of years that it now seems impossible to imagine the side without him.

For six years Adam played for his boyhood club, Rangers, making 61 appearances and scoring 13 goals, including one in an Old Firm Derby. Under managers Paul Le Guen and Walter Smith, it seemed that Adam had a future at Ibrox Park, even being part of the team that made the UEFA Cup Final in 2008. He did find himself on loan at Ross County and St Mirren, but his future always seemed to be with Rangers. Sadly for him, financial problems at the club and the fact that he had fallen down the pecking order as far as Smith concerned meant that he was surplus to requirements.

So it was that in February 2009 he joined Blackpool on loan until the end of the season, and it is not an exaggeration to say that it was a piece of footballing genius by caretaker manager Tony Parkes to recognise the worth of the player. He played for the rest of the campaign, actually being sent off against Doncaster Rovers on his debut, but he became a huge fans' favourite when he scored the only goal in the Derby Day victory at Preston North End. At the end of the season, with survival in the Championship confirmed and Adam receiving many plaudits and constant nominations in the 'Team of the Week', he returned to Ibrox Park unsure of his future. The fans wanted him at Bloomfield Road, and with the arrival of Ian Holloway as manager it was only a matter of time before Adam became a permanent Blackpool player.

Adam was instrumental in Blackpool's promotion to the Premier League. His performances were stunning, begging the question as to how Rangers could have been so willing to release him. His goal in the Play-off Final, a screaming free-kick just minutes after Cardiff had taken the lead, will be remembered as one of the best seen at the stadium. He was clearly Blackpool's best player of the season. Inevitably he has attracted some of the bigger clubs, but despite figures being suggested, so far no club has matched the valuation that Blackpool have placed, and it was fitting that Adam should see Premier League football with the club that showed so much faith in him.

His future is assured, and already he has made the international breakthrough with caps for Scotland. At the time of writing he is still a Blackpool player, and we can only hope that he stays for many years to come.

Adam took to Premier League football with ease and was the star of the team. Off the field, he was involved in a disappointing court case with Karl Oyston over a non-payment of bonus from the previous season, which he won, and in January he was the subject of many big-money offers from other clubs. All approaches were turned down, and Adam saw out the season with Blackpool. He was one of only a few players from the Blackpool team who would walk immediately into another Premier League side, but he gave his all for Blackpool Football Club and it was an honour to have the man wear the tangerine shirt.

Alan Ainscow

Midfielder: 193 + 16 appearances, 28 goals
Born: 15 July 1953, Bolton, England
Career: Blackpool (1971–78), Birmingham City, Everton, Barnsley, Wolves, Blackburn Rovers, Rochdale, Horwich RMI.

Alan Ainscow was a promising youngster who rose through Blackpool's ranks and was tipped to be as successful as Tony Green. Ainscow, born in Bolton in 1953, was a midfielder of outstanding ability who joined the Seasiders as an apprentice in July 1971. Without a League appearance, he was picked for the Anglo-Italian Final against Bologna in that same year and showed his incredible talent and potential,

only being substituted after 90 minutes through sheer exhaustion. His League debut came in the following season when he scored in a victory over Swindon Town, but it took some time for him to establish himself in the first team. After the departure of Tommy Hutchison, however, he became almost constant in the first-team line up.

He could play on either side, although he soon found himself in a much deeper role, and in 1972–73 he was joint top scorer with Alan Suddick. His main talent, however, was in midfield, where he could supply the telling passes for the front men.

In July 1978 he was transferred to Birmingham City, as Blackpool had now become a spent force and were facing life in the Third Division. He played over 100 times for the Blues and then had spells with Everton, Barnsley (on loan), Wolves, Blackburn, a stint in Hong Kong before Rochdale, and finally non-League Horwich. It seemed a sad ending to what should have been a glittering career. When he first burst on to the scene at the beginning of the 1970s, he was constantly compared to both Alan Ball and Tony Green – his stature and demeanour similar – but he never quite realised the potential expected of him, and the dreams of international honours never materialised. He was always very popular with the Blackpool fans, however, who remember him fondly.

'Geordie' Anderson

Centre-half/forward: 78 appearances, 29 goals
Born: Scotland
Career: Leith Athletic, Blackburn Rovers, New Brighton, Blackpool (1900–04).

When 'Geordie' Anderson arrived in Blackpool in 1899, he was, according to the local newspaper, a little 'worse for wear'.

That did not refer to his state of mind, but to the fact that he was regarded as a veteran. Anderson had made nearly 200 appearances for his previous club, Blackburn Rovers, where he had also been captain. He was signed because he had recently moved to the seaside and had expressed a preference for playing for Blackpool in the clean and bracing air. Blackpool were, of course, happy to sign a strong and reliable defender. As it turned out, he played mostly in attack, due to the presence of Harry Stirzaker at centre-half. Anderson revelled in his new role, and during 1901–02 he was top scorer with 12 goals – the only man to achieve double figures. He worked with the youngsters at the club, and after his playing days ended he was given a temporary position as coach. Anderson played some great games for Blackpool, none more so than in February 1904 at home to Burton United, when, along with new signing Whittle, he destroyed the opposition and scored a hat-trick in a 4–1 victory. The local newspaper heaped praise on him, suggesting that with 11 Andersons in the team Blackpool could win the League, the Cup and the Boat Race too!

Jimmy Armfield

Full-back: 627 appearances, 6 goals.
England 43 appearances, 0 goals
Born: 21 September 1935, Denton
Career: Blackpool (1954–71).

After the 1962 World Cup in Chile, Jimmy Armfield was voted by the press corps as 'the best right-back in the world'. It was a supreme accolade and one that was thoroughly deserved. Born in Denton, Manchester, in September 1935, his family moved to Blackpool, where he spent his school years and quickly began to shine at field sports, notably rugby and football. It was during a practice match at Bloomfield Road that manager Joe Smith spotted

Armfield and offered him a trial. On 27 December 1954 he made his debut at Portsmouth and began a 17-year association with the club, during which time he made a record 627 appearances, including 10 years as captain. If any player could be described as a 'one-club man', it is Jimmy Armfield.

His main attributes were speed, superb distribution, outstanding tackling and an enormous capacity for hard work. Time and time again, especially during the team's difficult years in the 1960s, he would somehow find an extra ounce of energy when all seemed lost, and in turn motivate the team around him. This was one of the many attributes that made him such a superb the captain, not only for Blackpool, but for England too. He developed the overlap, so loved by defenders today, to such an art form that fans used to flock to the grounds to see him in action. He struck up a partnership with Stanley Matthews in the late 1950s, and the duo would go on to mesmorise opposing markers. Armfield was voted 'Young Player of the Year' in 1959 and was unlucky not to become Footballer of the Year in 1966, narrowly beaten by Bobby Charlton. He achieved Blackpool Player of the Year instead – a tribute to his marvellous loyalty and leadership.

Unfortunately, he saw little in the way of success for Blackpool, with the exception winning promotion in 1969–70. After the victorious game at rivals Preston, he was chaired off the field by celebrating supporters. There was a smile on his face and pride in his heart, as he, more than anyone, had helped Blackpool back to Division One.

His international career began in 1956 when he appeared for the Under-23 England side, and he made his full debut on 13 May 1959 against Brazil in front of over 120,000 fans. There then followed 43 caps – a record for the club – which included 15 as captain. As well as 'the best right-back in the world' honour, he was also voted 'the best right-back in Europe' for three successive seasons from 1962 to 1964. He bowed out of international football in 1966, to be replaced by George Cohen of Fulham, and sadly missed out on an opportunity to appear in the World Cup Finals in England.

He played his last game for Blackpool in May 1971 against Manchester United, and was awarded a testimonial on his 35th birthday. Thousands turned out to pay tribute to him.

After his playing career ended, he managed Bolton Wanderers, where he gained promotion, and then later Leeds United, taking them to the European Cup Final in 1975. Surprisingly, he was sacked three years later, and then continued his football involvement via the media, notably Radio Five Live, where he is an established and respected pundit. He was also a consultant at the Football Association, and in 2000 was awarded an OBE for his services to football. A CBE was added in 2010.

He is still hugely popular at Blackpool Football Club, where he can be seen on match days as often as his time will allow, and of course he has been inducted in the Blackpool's 'Hall of Fame' at Bloomfield Road. To show the respect he is afforded by Blackpool, the South Stand – completed in 2010 – is named after him, and a new statue has been commissioned for outside the ground.

He has recently overcome a serious illness when he was diagnosed with lymphoma of the throat, but he battled on and was seen at Wembley in May 2010, celebrating the team's promotion to the Premier League. If one looked closely, you could see a tear from his eye. Jimmy Armfield and Blackpool Football Club will always be entwined, and no club has had a greater servant.

Jack Ashurst

Defender: 59 appearances, 4 goals
Born: 12 October 1954, Renton, Scotland
Career: Sunderland, Blackpool (1979–81), Carlisle United, Leeds United, Doncaster Rovers, Rochdale.

Jack Ashurst is mentioned because at the time of his arrival at Bloomfield Road he was Blackpool's most expensive player at £116,666, joining from Sunderland in October 1979. Born in Coatbridge in Scotland, Ashurst started his career at the Roker Park club, joining as an apprentice in 1971. He went on to make 140 appearances for them, and would have made many more but for the presence of Dave Watson at centre-half. Ashurst was in the squad for the 1973 FA Cup Final, although injury ruled him out of the Wembley game.

He joined Blackpool under Stan Ternent in November 1979 and made his debut in a draw with Gillingham, replacing the veteran Peter Suddaby at centre-half. Over the next season or so he was used as a utility player, but then suffered bad

injuries, which curtailed his Blackpool career. Also, the pressure of being the club's most expensive player weighed heavily, and it is fair to say that his time at Bloomfield Road was one of disappointment.

When Allan Brown rejoined as Blackpool manager, he sold Ashurst to Carlisle United for a small £40,000 fee in August 1981. He went on to make nearly 200 appearances for Carlisle, before spells at Leeds United and Doncaster Rovers. His last professional club was Rochdale, for whom he made just one appearance. Ashurst was unlucky to have joined Blackpool in their darkest days and, sadly, his time is not remembered with any fondness.

Alan Ball

Midfielder: 126 appearances, 44 goals. England 72 appearances, 8 goals
Born: 12 May 1945, Farnworth, Lancashire
Died 25 April 2007, Warsash, Hampshire
Career: Blackpool (1962–66), Everton, Arsenal, Southampton, Bristol Rovers.

Alan Ball was quite simply one of the most exciting players ever seen at Bloomfield Road, a tireless midfielder who became one of the most famous English footballers of the 1960s and 1970s. In 1966 he was transferred to Everton for a British record fee of £112,000 and then five years later went to Arsenal for another record fee, this time £220,000. Ball played 76 times for England, including the 1966 World Cup Final when he was only 21 years of age, and continued playing right through to the early 1980s. Born in Farnworth, he had trials at Wolves and Bolton Wanderers before joining Blackpool in 1962. He made his League debut under manager Ron Suart in August in a win at Liverpool. It took some time before his permanent breakthrough to the first team, but with his eventual partnership with Ray Charnley he proved irresistible. In 1963–64 and 1964–54 he was the club's top scorer as they fought desperately against relegation.

His England debut came in 1965 against Yugoslavia, and following a triumphant World Cup his transfer to Everton was confirmed. At Goodison Park he won a Championship medal and an FA Cup runners'-up medal, and with Arsenal

he gained runners'-up medals in the League and FA Cup again. He later helped Southampton into Division One, before spells in America and Canada. His last playing duties were for Bristol Rovers in 1984, and when he finally retired he had played an unbelievable 975 competitive games. During that time he had represented England in two World Cups – 1966 and 1970 – and had also captained his country six times. He seemed to be an integral part of the national line up under Sir Alf Ramsey and then Joe Mercer, but it was ended dramatically by Don Revie, who it seems did not afford him the courtesy of a phone call to tell him that his England career had ended.

As described elsewhere in this book, Ball's management career – especially at Blackpool – was not a resounding success, but as a player he is one of the club's greats. He was inducted into Blackpool's Hall of Fame in 2006, and his death was mourned by an older generation of Blackpool supporters who had the privilege of seeing him wear the Tangerine shirt. Many players have since played for Blackpool and been described as 'the next Alan Ball', but it is a tribute to him that none of them – no matter how talented – have ever lived up to that accolade. As a player, there was only one Alan Ball.

Dave Bamber

Striker: 189 appearances, 89 goals
Born: 1 February 1959, Prescott
Career: Blackpool (1979–83 and 1990–94), Coventry City, Walsall, Portsmouth, Swindon Town, Watford, Stoke City, Hull City.

Graham Carr's last act as manager in 1990 was to secure former 'Pool favourite Dave Bamber on a month's loan. Four weeks later, Billy Ayre agreed to pay Hull City £35,000 and complete a full circle in the player's career. Born in St Helens, Bamber joined Blackpool from Manchester University, signing for Stan Ternant. During the next four seasons of struggle he scored 36 goals in 100 games under four different managers. In 1981–82 and 1982–83 he was the club's top scorer, before joining Coventry City for £50,000 after the emergence of Paul Stewart. For Coventry he made 19 appearances with three goals, before transfers to Walsall (seven goals in 20 games), Portsmouth (four appearances, one goal) and Swindon (31 goals from 106 appearances). Then high-flying Watford paid £105,000 for him, but after just 18 games and three goals he went to Stoke City for £190,000. With only eight goals in 43 games, Bamber moved to Hull City, where a return of five goals in 28 games was a disappointment.

His career was almost at a halt when Blackpool came calling for a second time. He scored on his second debut against Hereford United and ended the season as top scorer again. An injury probably cost Blackpool promotion in 1991–92, but the following season he was instrumental in

gaining advancement to the Second Division. Bamber continued to play for two more seasons, but ended his career in 1994. He stayed in the Blackpool area and went into property development. A much-loved player, inextricably linked to the great Billy Ayre, Bamber was inducted to the Hall of Fame in 2006.

Steve Banks

Goalkeeper: 153 appearances
Born: 9 February 1972, Hillingdon
Career: West Ham United, Gillingham, Blackpool (1995–99), Bolton Wanderers, Rochdale, Bradford City, Stoke City, Wimbledon, Hearts, Dundee United.

Steve Banks joined Blackpool in August 1995, and went on to make over 150 appearances for the Seasiders in a time of trouble for the club. He started his career at West Ham United, where he played just once before being transferred to Gillingham in 1993. Two years later he was snapped up by Sam Allardyce before the start of the 1995–96 season. He played regularly, but was not part of the team that capitulated so dramatically in the play-offs at the end of the season.

He was reliable and seemingly a star of the future, so much so that he was reportedly the subject of a six-figure bid from Celtic in 1998. So it was with some anger from the Blackpool fans that chairman Vicky Oyston accepted a bid of just £50,000 from Bolton Wanderers in March 1999. Mrs Oyston reasoned that the player was a free agent at the end of the season, so it made sense to release him and accept needed funds. It was, with the advantage of hindsight, a poor business decision for the club.

Sadly for Banks, the big move to a Premier League club failed to work, and he only played 20 times for the Trotters in four years. There then followed numerous loan spells with various clubs, before ending up at SPL Hearts. This move was inevitably traumatic, with the eccentric owner, Vladimir Romanov, publicly stating in 2008 that Banks, now a goalkeeping coach, could 'no longer be trusted'. He soon joined Dundee United in a similar role, where he still is today.

Banks was a goalkeeper who looked like he could join the long list of talented stoppers at Bloomfield Road, but there was always the feeling that somewhere along the way he lost out. Being at Blackpool during a time when the side was struggling to adapt following the 1995–96 season debacle did not help, but the rest of his career failed to live up to its high billing.

Shaun Barker

Defender: 134 appearances, 5 goals.
Born: 19 September 1982, Trowell
Career: Rotherham United, Blackpool (2006–09), Derby County.

Shaun Barker was transferred to Derby County from Blackpool in July 2009, just two months after chairman Karl Oyston publicly stated that there had been no offers from any club for the team captain and that he would definitely be staying at Bloomfield Road for the 2009–10 season. A fee of approaching £1 million seemed to have changed his mind.

It was inevitable that Barker would look to a bigger stage to parade his obvious talents, yet it is ironic that he should have left just as Blackpool were on the verge of great things, with the subsequent promotion to the Premier League.

Barker started his career at Rotherham United and made over 120 appearances for the Millers in a six-year period. He played as either a centre-half or right-back, and was soon attracting the attention of higher-League clubs. One was Blackpool, managed by Simon Grayson at the time, and after turning down a new contract with Rotherham, he joined Blackpool on a free transfer in August 2006. It was the best money the club has not spent in many a year.

Barker went on to make over 130 appearances for Blackpool, and in 2007–08 he was a constant in the side. After promotion to the Championship, he was made team captain, and was clearly destined for greater things. As the club embarked on a new era with Ian Holloway as manager, Barker decided to leave and join Derby County. He has been asked regularly since leaving Bloomfield Road whether he regretted the decision, as Derby struggled to avoid relegation while Blackpool reached the promised land of the Premier League. His answers have always been the same: he believed that Derby were the bigger club, and with more money he could surely provide a better future for him and his family. There must be moments when he sits down and wonders...

Phil Barnes

Goalkeeper: 141 appearances
Born: 2 March 1979, Sheffield
Career: Rotherham United, Blackpool (1997–04), Sheffield United, Torquay United, Queen's Park Rangers, Grimsby Town, Gainsborough Trinity.

Phil Barnes joined Blackpool in August 1997 from Rotherham United for a fee of £100,000. He was brought in as cover for number-one 'keeper Tony Caig, but soon made the position his own.

He stayed at Blackpool for seven years, becoming a fans' favourite, and was part of the team that gained promotion to Division Two in 2001, contributing with some fine performances and a number of clean sheets. Unfortunately for him, he lost his place in the first team, and in 2003 requested a transfer, which manager Steve McMahon did not oppose. He then joined Sheffield United on a free transfer the following summer, but his stay there was less than successful. Despite the Blades' promotion to the Premier League, he hardly figured, and after a couple of loan spells he ended up at Grimsby Town. There he made 120 appearances, before joining non-League Gainsborough Trinity.

Another fine goalkeeper while at Bloomfield Road, he could be compared to Steve Banks in that his potential never seemed to be fully realised once he left the club.

Harry Bedford

Striker: 180 appearances, 118 goals. England 2 appearances, 1 goal
Born: 15 October 1899, Calow
Died: 24 June 1976
Career: Nottingham Forest, Blackpool (1921–25), Derby County, Newcastle United, Sunderland, Bradford Park Avenue, Chesterfield.

When Harry Bedford joined Blackpool he did more than just fill the gap left by Joe Lane's departure, he surpassed Lane's amazing records for the club. Born near

Chesterfield, Bedford joined Nottingham Forest in 1919, and it was after he had caused havoc in Blackpool's defence at the City Ground that the promotion-seeking Seasiders signed him in March 1921. Bedford scored seven goals in his first 10 League matches, and although it was not enough to bring First Division football (the team faltered badly in the run-in), Bedford was obviously a star of the future. In 1922–23 and 1923–24 he was the country's top scorer – a feat that only Jimmy Hampson equalled with Blackpool. In 1924–25 Bedford's goals helped Blackpool to reach the FA Cup fourth round for the first time. He could snatch a half chance, had tremendous strength (which made up for a comparative lack of speed) and possessed a fierce shot.

Surprisingly, he gained only two England caps, but once scored four goals for the Football League against the Irish League. In September 1925 he moved to Derby County for a fee of over £3,000, Blackpool again bowing to financial pressures. For five consecutive seasons Bedford was Derby's top scorer, and he later played for other top clubs, including Newcastle and Sunderland.

He died in Derby in 1976, and in 2006 was another Blackpool player to be inducted into the Hall of Fame.

Bill Bentley

Defender: 318 + eight appearances, 14 goals
Born: 21 October 1947, Stoke-on-Trent
Career: Stoke City, Blackpool (1969–77), Port Vale, Stafford Rangers.

Bill Bentley was one of football's hard men; at first he was an aggressive defender who relished the crunching tackle, and later developed into an overlapping full-back. He was born in Stoke in 1947 and began his career with his home-town club,

for whom he made 48 appearances, before being transferred to Blackpool in January 1969 for £30,000. He remained at Bloomfield Road for seven seasons, making almost 300 League appearances following his debut in a home defeat to Charlton Athletic.

Bentley soon established a partnership with Terry Alcock and struck up a formidable midfield understanding with him, although at first he worked with Jimmy Armfield, preferring the famous overlap that Armfield had made his trademark. Over the years, Bentley played in a variety of roles: in the heart of defence; in midfield; and occasionally in attack, where, although he rarely scored, when he did it was usually quite spectacular. The winner in the FA Cup third round against Burnley in 1976 will never be forgotten.

In the 1971 Anglo-Italian Cup Final he stifled the Bologna defence for long periods, and also supplied the through ball for John Craven to score the equaliser. Sadly, his career was plagued by injury, and in July 1977 he moved to Port Vale, back in his hometown. He ended his Football League career there, but then had a brief spell with non-League Stafford Rangers. Bentley now lives in the Stoke area but is always welcomed warmly at Bloomfield Road whenever he returns.

Gary Briggs

Midfielder: 137 appearances, 4 goals
Born: 21 June 1959, Leeds
Career: Middlesbrough, Oxford United, Blackpool (1989–95), Chorley.

Gary Briggs was a no-nonsense, hard-tackling tough midfielder who could intimidate opposing players just by his presence. Born in Leeds, he joined Blackpool after a successful career at Oxford United, where he made over 400 appearances. He was signed by Jimmy Mullen (one of the few things that Mullen managed to get right during his short spell as manager at Bloomfield Road), but it was under the guidance of Billy Ayre that Briggs really flourished. It was the never-say-die attitude of both manager and team that made Briggs the player so loved by Blackpool fans, and during the four years under Ayre he was an integral part of the side that made two successive Wembley Play-off Final appearances. Unfortunately for Briggs, he was forced to miss both games due to injury, but his contribution had been enormous.

Briggs had been named 'Rambo' by Oxford fans, and it was not difficult to see why. He was one of the most fearsome players in the lower Leagues, and you get the impression that he was born a couple of decades too late. His all-or-nothing attitude and mentality seemed to belong to the bygone age of the 1950s, where his hard approach would have been tolerated and lauded a little more. As it was, his cult status had been guaranteed at Oxford United, and a similar appreciation had been garnered at Blackpool. Sadly for Briggs, once Billy Ayre departed, his own career stalled. He was not part of Sam Allardyce's plans, and in May 1995 he left the club. He then joined Chorley to finish his playing days, and in 2005 he had an executive box at Oxford United's new ground named in his honour.

Briggs was a player who was loved by Blackpool fans. Remembered fondly, his reputation has been embellished with time, yet it is fair to say that his tough approach would be lost in today's Blackpool team. He is, though, a genuine choice for great Blackpool players in history.

Tommy Browell

Striker: 71 appearances, 29 goals
Born: 19 October 1892, Newcastle-upon-Tyne
Died: 5 October 1955
Career: Hull City, Everton, Manchester City, Blackpool (1926–30).

By the time Tommy Browell came to Bloomfield Road in 1926, he was already a veteran in football terms, yet he served Blackpool admirably for three seasons. Born in Walbottle, he joined his two brothers at Hull City, making his debut for

the Anlaby Road club in September 1910. A year later, after scoring 72 goals in 52 games for Hull, he was transferred to Everton for £1,650 – a huge fee for the day.

'Boy' Browell, as he was known throughout his career, moved to Manchester City for £1,500 in October 1913 and played for them in the 1926 FA Cup Final, before Major Frank Buckley paid £1,100 for him – part of a huge rebuilding process undertaken by the ambitious manager. Browell made his debut in September in a home draw with Darlington. Teaming up with Downes on the left wing, he scored 14 times to become the team's second-highest scorer that season. His goals included a stunning hat-trick against Notts County in the final game of the season, where the Seasiders recorded a 5–0 win.

In 1927–28 he switched to the right and teamed up with Meredith and the prolific Jimmy Hampson, but eventually age got the better of him, and with the emergence of Jack Oxberry, he was released by the club. He stayed in the area, signing as a player-coach for Lytham and then Morecambe, and then became a tram driver on the seafront. He died in 1955.

He is remembered especially by Manchester City, where he played for 13 years, and even has a road named after him. Tommy Browell Close is located near the old Maine Road ground.

Allan Brown

Midfield: 185 appearances, 74 goals. Scotland 13 appearances, 5 goals
Born: 12 October 1926, Kennoway
Died: 19 April 2011
Career: East Fife, Blackpool (1950–56), Luton Town, Portsmouth, Wigan Athletic.

During Allan Brown's time as a player at Blackpool, the club reached two FA Cup Finals, but despite playing a major part in getting them there, he missed both due to injury. In 1951 he was forced out after damaging his knee against Huddersfield Town, and in 1953 he broke his left leg in scoring the 88th-minute winner against Arsenal in the sixth round.

Born in Fife in 1926, Brown was a Scottish international with East Fife when

Blackpool paid £26,500 for him in December 1950. The fee was the largest received by a Scottish club at the time and proved how highly he was rated.

Brown, a burly inside-forward, could drop the ball exactly on the spot from almost any distance, and he also possessed a fine shot. His debut came in December 1950 in a victory at Charlton Athletic, where he replaced Bill Slater. Soon he made the position his own. When he later teamed up with Stan Mortensen, they accounted for most of Blackpool's goals as the team began to take a hold of English football. Brown, an almost constant in the side, joined a Scottish invasion that included Mudie, Fenton, Kelly and Farm.

He played for Scotland in the 1954 World Cup Finals, and during his time at Blackpool the club enjoyed their most successful years. With Matthews, Mortensen, Perry and Taylor, Brown played in a formidable front line during the heady 1950s.

In December 1957 he was transferred to Luton Town for £10,000, and appeared in the 1959 FA Cup Final against Nottingham Forest – so making up for his disappointment in the earlier Finals. Sadly for him, Luton were beaten. He then moved to Portsmouth, before joining non-League Wigan Athletic as a player-manager. It was then that his managerial career took off, which of course included two spells at Blackpool.

He is also a member of Blackpool's Hall of Fame and lived in the area until his death in April 2011.

Martin Bullock

Midfielder: 153 appearances, 4 goals
Born: 5 March 1975, Derby
Career: Barnsley, Port Vale, Blackpool (2001–05), Macclesfield Town, Wycombe Wanderers.

Martin Bullock was one of the fastest and most elusive midfielders in the lower divisions, and his standing at Blackpool will always be immense.

Signed from Barnsley by Steve McMahon in 2001, he became a regular during the period that saw promotion to Division Two and two more Millennium Stadium appearances in the Football League Trophy Finals. He was tricky and elusive, and a regular playmaker, capable of turning a game single-handedly. He was quite often the Blackpool player that opponents feared and fans loved to bait, but he was also incredibly talented, and it is with amazement that he was never afforded a shot at higher-level football.

Despite his obvious talents, manager Colin Hendry decided to release him in 2005 after over 150 appearances for the club. It was one of the first of the many regrettable decisions taken by the former Scottish international as he attempted to stamp his authority on his first managerial post. The fans, always impressed by tricky midfielders (Alan Ball and Tony Green to name but two), were outraged. Sadly, Bullock's career never recovered, and he joined struggling Macclesfield Town and then Wycombe Wanderers before emigrating to New Zealand to see out his career.

Bullock was immensely talented, and it is sad that his potential was never fully realised, but he can claim to have been part of the revival of Blackpool FC. It is just a shame that he was not allowed to stay to see that revival truly take root.

Ben Burgess

Striker: 126 appearances, 23 goals
Born: 9 November 1981, Buxton
Career: Blackburn Rovers, Brentford, Stockport County, Oldham Athletic, Hull City, Blackpool (2006–10), Notts County.

Like John Murphy a few years before him, Ben Burgess was a burly and imposing centre-forward who liked to get among the opponents and use his physical presence. Also like Murphy, he was popular with most Blackpool fans, but unlike Murphy there was a minority that criticised him constantly, effectively driving him out of the club.

He started his career at Blackburn Rovers, but failed to make an impact, with only two starts in four years. He went on loan to an Australian club for a year, where he found his scoring touch, and then, on his return to England, joined Brentford on loan. There he scored freely, and in 2003 he joined Hull City. He became a regular first-teamer, but after an injury forced him to miss most of the team's League One promotion campaign, he sportingly refused a promotion award. In the Championship he continued to score goals for Hull until a £100,000 move to Blackpool.

Manager Simon Grayson was looking for a centre-forward who could eventually replace John Murphy, and Burgess was an obvious candidate. It took him some time to break through to the first team on a regular basis, especially as the likes of Keigan Parker and Andy Morrell were first choices. Sadly for him, he was an unused substitute in the League One Play-off Final victory over Yeovil Town at Wembley, but once in the Championship, Burgess made the centre-forward role his own.

He was never a prolific scorer, but what he brought to the game was an ability to hold the ball for others, a skill that a section of the Blackpool support could not understand. They barracked him on a regular basis, which forced manager Ian Holloway in 2010 to publicly criticise the fans who vented their anger on Burgess. To be fair to Burgess, he never complained, merely continuing to play his way.

After Blackpool's promotion to the Premier League, Holloway was keen to keep him at Bloomfield Road, but it was clear that his first-team opportunities would be extremely limited. With that in mind, he joined newly promoted League One outfit Notts County.

Burgess is an intelligent footballer both on and off the field, and his contribution to the club has been huge. Sadly, a section of fans failed to appreciate him.

Mickey Burns

Striker: 196 + 7 appearances, 62 goals
Born: 21 December 1946, Preston
Career: Skelmersdale United, Blackpool (1969–74), Newcastle United, Cardiff City, Middlesbrough.

This former England amateur international, picked up by Les Shannon from non-League football, was Blackpool's top scorer in three of the five seasons he was at Bloomfield Road, before moving to Newcastle United for £175,000. Burns, who has a teaching degree, was persuaded to join Blackpool in 1969. He was a fast winger who scored goals regularly, and

older fans were quickly comparing him with the great Bill Perry. He scored on his League debut, a win over Portsmouth in August 1969, and helped the club win promotion back to Division One.

He could play on either flank, and top scored in three of the next four seasons, including the disastrous campaign in the First Division. His finest spell at Blackpool was in 1971–72, where he netted 17 times in the League, plus he was prolific in the Anglo-Italian successes. He scored four in the 10–0 defeat of Lanerossi Vicenza, and had also scored the extra-time winner against Bologna in the 1971 Final.

Amazingly, he was never popular with a particularly vociferous section of the fans, who regarded his style as too individualistic and not helpful for the team. So it was not surprising that in the summer of 1974 he asked for a transfer, and soon after he found himself at Newcastle United. With the Magpies he played in the 1976 League Cup Final, before spells at Cardiff City as player-coach, but he never settled, and he finished his career at Middlesbrough.

In later years he joined Middlesbrough's coaching staff, and was also the PFA's education officer, before resigning in 2003. Burns is another player inducted into Blackpool's Hall of Fame – a fine footballer who contributed greatly to the dashing Blackpool side of the early 1970s, but sadly he was never really appreciated during his time at Bloomfield Road.

John Burridge

Goalkeeper: 148 appearances
Born: 3 December 1951, Workington
Career: Workington, Blackpool (1971–75), Aston Villa, Southend United, Crystal Palace, Queen's Park Rangers, Wolverhampton Wanderers, Derby County, Sheffield United, Southampton, Newcastle United, Hibernian, Scarborough, Lincoln City, Enfield,

Aberdeen, Dunfermline Athletic, Dumbarton, Falkirk, Manchester City, Notts County, Witton Albion, Darlington, Grimsby Town, Gateshead, Northampton Town, Queen of the South, Purfleet, Blyth Spartans.

At the start of 1971 John Burridge was playing for Workington Reserves in the Northern Alliance, yet in April that year he made his First Division debut at Goodison Park against Everton in a goalless draw after being brought to Blackpool on loan. He was called as cover for the injured Neil Sidebottom, who had broken his arm, and Seasiders boss Bob Stokoe had already seen his potential when he had tried to sign the player for Carlisle United during Stokoe's time as manager there.

On his debut Burridge almost single-handedly kept the Everton strikers at bay, and one save in particular from Alan Ball was simply world-class. His performance persuaded the club to make the signing permanent, and they paid the Cumbrians £10,000 for his services. It was certainly money well spent.

A tremendously popular figure with the Blackpool supporters, he stayed at

Bloomfield Road for five years, despite the presence of George Wood. Rather small for a goalkeeper, he would spend many hours on the training pitch reaching for crosses and high balls. Always spectacular, he was the obvious showman of the team and loved to play to the crowd. One of his finest moments at Blackpool came in the 1971 Anglo-Italian Cup Final against Bologna, where he earned the praise of the normally highly critical Italian fans and media.

In 1975 he made a switch to Aston Villa, mindful of George Wood's presence, where he stayed for two years and helped to win the League Cup Final for Ron Saunders's side. There then followed spells at so many clubs over the next 20 years or so that you almost get the feeling that Burridge was hoping to achieve his own 92-League club record. In total he played for 22 English, six Scottish and one Irish club before finally retiring. He actually managed his final club, Blyth Spartans, for a while, and brought them to Blackpool for an FA Cup tie in 1997, which Blackpool won 4–3.

He is another member of Blackpool's Hall of Fame, and never has there been a more charismatic player at Bloomfield Road, or indeed at the myriad of clubs that have used his services. He once said that he loved football so much that he would sleep with a ball in his bed. Odd as that seems, it is probably true.

DJ Campbell

Striker: 67+2 Appearances 30 goals
Born: 12 November 1981, London
Career: Brentford, Birmingham City, Leicester City. Blackpool (2009–2010 and 2010–present day), Derby County.

DJ Campbell is included as a Blackpool star, not just because at the time of writing he is the club's record signing at £1.25 million, but because in his three spells at

Bloomfield Road he has made such a mark that it seems inconceivable to omit him.

Campbell has had a chequered football career. He was bought by Martin Allen at Brentford from non-League Yeading for £5,000 in 2005, after spending the first five years of his career at that level. He scored on his debut and immediately his stock rose, so much so that within five months Birmingham City had bought him for £500,000 – a good piece of business for the West London club and manager. He scored nine times for the Blues, but despite signing a three-year contract, he found himself at Leicester City within a year after they paid £1.6 million for his services. It was a meteoric rise for the player, and this might go some way to understanding why the expectations of him were never really realised. The then Plymouth Argyle manager, Ian Holloway, described the fee as 'madness'.

Campbell's time at Leicester was anything but successful, and after niggling injuries and few first-team appearances he was loaned out to Blackpool. He managed to score on both his debut and his home debut – against former club Birmingham City – and his nine goals in 20 games went some way to helping the Seasiders avoid relegation from the Championship.

For 2009–10 he returned to Leicester, but it was clear that he had no future there. He went out on loan again, this time to Derby County, before a second return to Blackpool – again on loan. This time, under Holloway, he was instrumental in getting Blackpool to the Premier League, scoring eight goals in 15 games, including a remarkable second-half hat-trick at Nottingham Forest in the Play-off semi-final second leg.

After the Play-off Final victory at Wembley – in which he had played a huge part without scoring – he made public his desire to join Blackpool permanently. It was clear that he had fallen in love with the club, and the club reciprocated. The move was prolonged, though, due to the Leicester manager Paulo Souza being keen on him staying. Eventually a deal was agreed and Campbell became a full-time Blackpool player on the 31 August 2010. Inevitably, he scored on his third 'debut' in the 2–0 win at Newcastle United. He has already become a Blackpool legend in his short time at the club.

Campbell proved his worth by being Blackpool's top scorer in the Premier League, although his sending off at Wolves toward the end of the season seriously hampered Blackpool's relegation fight. He was one of the fans' favourites, and it is hoped he will stay long enough to experience top flight football with the club again.

Clarke Carlisle

Midfielder: 93 appearances, 7 goals
Born: 14 October 1979, Preston
Career: Blackpool (1997–2000), Queen's Park Rangers, Leeds United, Watford, Luton Town, Burnley.

In 2002 Clarke Carlisle was voted 'Britain's Brainiest Footballer' in a television show. It is fair to say that his intelligence off the pitch is matched on it. A talented centre-back, his career has seen many highs and lows, and his strong and imposing frame belies the fact that he has footballing ability as well as the strength to shore up the midfield.

He joined Blackpool as a youth player and made his debut in a remarkable 4–3 victory at Wrexham, after the side had come from 3–0 down. He then actually scored his first goal in the following match, fittingly at home to Carlisle United, and within a year he had become a regular first-team player. Sadly, he was never given the chance to shine at a higher level with Blackpool as in the three seasons he was at Bloomfield Road, they struggled. Manager Nigel Worthington was unable to stem the downwards tide of the team, and when he was replaced by Steve McMahon, it was clear that Blackpool would be heading for the lower basement. Carlisle was too good a player to ply his trade there, and after scoring in the 1–1 draw at Oldham Athletic that confirmed Blackpool's relegation, he was the subject of a £250,000 bid from Queen's Park Rangers. It was money the club could not afford to turn down, and gave the player the chance to impress at the top level.

Sadly his career hit a low. Despite being chosen for the England Under-21 team, he suffered a catalogue of injuries, and then was released by manager Ian Holloway following a drunken episode on a team coach. Realising his problems, he turned to his Christian faith to help overcome them, and it is to his credit that he came through counselling for alcohol addiction and reignited his career.

A spell at Leeds United followed by Watford (where he helped them gain promotion to the Premier League, only to suffer an injury and miss virtually the entire next season), and then finally a move to Blackpool's neighbours Burnley. He is there today, and his performances have made him a Claret favourite, actually winning the Man of the Match in the Play-off Final victory over Sheffield United that saw Burnley back in the top division.

A fine player, an intelligent man and much loved at Blackpool.

Ray Charnley

Centre-forward: 407 appearances, 222 goals. England 1 appearance, 0 goals
Born: 29 May 1935, Lancaster
Died: 15 November 2009, Rossall
Career: Morecambe, Blackpool (1957–67), Preston North End, Wrexham, Bradford Park Avenue.

Ray Charnley is Blackpool's most prolific goalscorer, behind Jimmy Hampson and Stan Mortensen. Unlike Hampson and Mortensen, though, Charnley's goals came in a struggling team. The tall, stylish

centre-forward was born in Lancaster and bought from non-League Morecambe for £1,000 in May 1957.

His debut came that September, in a defeat at Luton Town, and four weeks later he scored twice in Blackpool's 7–0 home victory over Sunderland, before leaving the pitch with a serious head injury. Eventually he teamed up with Jackie Mudie, a move inspired by Joe Smith and later used to good effect by Ron Suart.

Charnley was Blackpool's top scorer in seven seasons, and scored his 100th League goal in his 156th game – a record only marginally bettered by Harry Bedford. He played his best football alongside Alan Ball, and in October 1962 he received a belated England call-up against France, but it was perhaps too late in his career and he was not picked again.

After an infamous home defeat by Millwall in 1967, the then new manager, Stan Mortensen, made drastic changes, which included dropping Charnley. Charnkey immediately asked for a transfer and soon moved to rivals Preston after 10 years at Bloomfield Road. It was ironic that it was Preston, who had initially rejected him before his move to the seaside, and it was even more ironic that nine days after his transfer he returned to Bloomfield Road and scored for Preston!

He ended his playing career with Wrexham, Bradford PA and a final return to Morecambe. In football retirement he started his own business and died after a short illness in 2009. He was given a minute's applause by both sets of fans before the local derby with Preston that year and is a member of the Blackpool FC's Hall of Fame.

Peter Clarke

Midfielder: 100 appearances, 14 goals
Born: 3 January 1982, Southport
Career: Everton, Blackpool (2002 and

2004–06), Port Vale, Coventry City, Southend United, Huddersfield Town.

Peter Clarke is a strong and tall centre-back who played for Blackpool on two separate occasions and became a fans' favourite almost immediately. Starting his career at Everton, he struggled to break into the first team on a regular basis and in 2002 was loaned to Blackpool. In 16 starts he scored three times, including two on his debut, and became a player that manager Steve McMahon earmarked for the future. In fact the manager tried desperately to secure Clarke on a permanent basis, but a deal could not be agreed upon. Clarke returned to Everton, where he was then sent out to Port Vale on loan.

On 17 September 2004, then manager Colin Hendry brought Clarke back on loan and then managed to sign him full time for £150,000. Clarke became a mainstay of the midfield and played his part in helping the Seasiders secure safety in League One. He was made club captain and played 84 times for the club in a time of difficulty on the pitch for the team.

At the beginning of the 2006–07 campaign, despite being offered a new contract, he signed for Southend United. They had just been promoted to the Championship, and he publicly stated that he felt they could go all the way to the Premier League. As it was, they were relegated and Blackpool were promoted under Simon Grayson and three years later were in the Premier League themselves! It must have been galling for the player as he surely would have played his part, but these are the decisions that define our lives.

Clarke now plays at Huddersfield Town in League One, where he is captain. He is a talented player, who really should be show-casing those talents at a higher level.

Phil Clarkson

Midfielder: 171 appearances, 35 goals
Born: 13 November 1968, Hambleton
Career: Crewe Alexandra, Scunthorpe United, Blackpool (1997–2002), Bury, Halifax Town, Lancaster City.

Phil Clarkson was one of the most popular players to wear the tangerine shirt during a time when the club found itself falling to the depths of the Football League, only to rise and to start the remarkable recovery. Phil Clarkson's time at Bloomfield Road coincided with both, and it is fitting that he is still employed at Blackpool as youth-team coach.

He started his career in non-League football and then joined Crewe Alexandra under manager Dario Gradi. There he stayed for five years, helping the club to win promotion, but in February 1996, after a short loan spell, he joined Scunthorpe United. In his one year there, he managed to score 18 goals in 48 appearances, quite prolific for a midfielder. It was then that he was noticed by Blackpool, and in February 1997 he was signed by manager Nigel Worthington for £80,000.

He will always be remembered by Blackpool fans for the two goals he scored (his first two for the club) against Preston North End in the 2–1 victory, but the image of a famous back-heel goal against Northampton Town is one that is regularly replayed on television archive. He was a huge favourite with the fans, and his 35 goals in over 170 appearances (he was actually top scorer in 1998–99), showed he had talent and ability as both a midfielder and in the forward line if required.

He helped Blackpool gain promotion under Steve McMahon, but after a brief loan spell, he was sold to Halifax Town. Then a move to Lancaster City, while working as a postman at the same time, before taking his coaching degree and a return full circle to Bloomfield Road. Clarkson is a member of Blackpool's 'Hall of Fame'.

Harry 'Gyp' Cookson

Forward: 33 appearances, 8 goals
Born: 28 January 1869, Blackpool
Died: 27 May 1922
Career: Burslem Port Vale, South Shore, Blackpool (1902–03), Accrington Stanley.

Harry 'Gyp' Cookson played only one full season for Blackpool, but for many years he had been involved with South Shore FC. Cookson was a big, strong forward who liked to score goals. He had been the mainstay for South Shore's forward line for many seasons and helped the club win the Fylde Cup in 1888. When the famous Blackburn Olympic team visited the town, Cookson apparently had the game of his life, scoring the goal in a 1–1 draw, which had followed a remarkable 3–0 victory over the same side seven days earlier.

In 1892–93 Cookson had played for Accrington in the First Division, scoring 15 goals in 30 League and Cup games – including a hat-trick in a 5–2 win at Stoke City – before Accrington dropped out of

the Football League. At the start of the 1902–03 season he signed for his home-town club, Blackpool, and during that time he played alongside Geordie Anderson and Jack Parkinson, becoming top scorer with eight goals. It was not a successful season for the club, though, as once again they fought relegation, before finishing 14th.

Cookson retired from playing, although he remained at the club to help coach the youngsters, and he also kept his connection with the town, living there until his death in 1922, aged just 53. Cookson was one of the many players who contributed greatly to the town's two clubs' successes, although the majority of it was with neighbours South Shore.

Jack Cox

Winger: 86 appearances, 18 goals. England 3 appearances, 0 goals.
Born: 27 December 1877, Liverpool
Died: 11 November 1955
Career: Blackpool (1897–98 and 1909–12), Liverpool.

Jack Cox was the first big transfer deal involving a Blackpool player. In February 1898 he went to Liverpool for the then large fee of £150, so enabling Blackpool to announce a loss of 'only' £441 for the season, as opposed to £1,000 for the previous campaign.

Liverpool-born Cox went to Blackpool via neighbours South Shore in the close season of 1897. He made his debut in October against Burton Swifts, scoring both goals in the 2–1 home victory, and went on to score 12 in 17 appearances. He was a fast and tricky outside-left who combined with Jack Parkinson to form a formidable partnership.

Soon far wealthier clubs looked at him, and Blackpool, mindful of financial restraints, let him go after less than one season. He helped Liverpool to two League Championships and a Second Division title, and he also gained international honours with England during this time.

In 1909, after scoring 80 goals in 360 appearances for Liverpool, he returned to Blackpool on a free transfer and effectively became the club's first player-manager. He had lost none of his speed, but his goalscoring had deserted him and he bowed out three years later. Despite having his success in Merseyside, he is remembered as one of Blackpool's greats in the fledgling years of the club.

John Craven

Midfielder: 174 + 12 appearances, 27 goals
Born: 15 May 1947, Lytham
Died: 14 December 1996
Career: Blackpool (1965–71), Crystal Palace, Coventry City, Plymouth Argyle.

When John Craven made his debut for Blackpool in August 1965, in a defeat at Tottenham Hotspur, he did so as left-back. When he was transferred to Crystal Palace some six years later, it was as a centre-forward and Blackpool's club captain. Craven was a hard-tackling defender when he joined the Seasiders, and at first he teamed up with skipper Jimmy Armfield, but after failing to displace Tommy Thompson at left-back, he switched to half-back, with some success. Then, after a period in the forward line with Gerry Ingram and Alan Skirton, he was put back into the heart of the defence by Ron Suart.

It was Les Shannon who converted

Craven to the forward line on a permanent basis, and it was Craven's success in teaming up with Fred Pickering and Mickey Burns that helped Blackpool to promotion. Over the next two years Craven was high in the scoring charts for the club, and when Bob Stokoe took over, he made him captain following Jimmy Armfield's retirement. Craven led Blackpool to Anglo-Italian success in Bologna in 1971, scoring the equalising goal in the Final, and was later voted Player of the Year at the club.

In September he asked for a transfer and joined Crystal Palace for £37,000. He later had spells at Coventry City and Plymouth Argyle, before settling in Canada and then the United States. It was there, in 1996, that he died of a heart attack at the age of just 49.

John Crossland

Defender: 74 appearances, 0 goals
Born: Lytham
Career: Ansdell Rovers, Blackpool (1946–54), Bournemouth.

John Crossland was signed by Joe Smith from Ansdell Rovers during World War Two. A strapping six-footer who could switch from centre-back to full-back, he was unable at first to break into the first team due to the excellent form of Ron Suart and Harry Johnston. After his debut in September 1946 at Brentford, he managed only three more appearances that season.

The following year again saw him make only a handful of appearances, yet one of them was in the FA Cup Final against Manchester United, replacing the injured Ron Suart. He coped admirably with winger Jimmy Delaney and might even have scored himself when, after running the entire length of the field, he ballooned his shot wide. Despite these encouraging signs, he did not appear the following

season at all, but eventually replaced the veteran Eric Hayward after the centre-half succumbed to injury.

The England selectors capped him at B level in 1950, before he was given regular first-team football at Blackpool. A series of injuries curtailed his career and he was soon sold to Bournemouth for a nominal fee, a decision that was unpopular with the fans.

Crossland was never a great player, but he deserves a mention because of his commitment to the club, where he was rarely given the opportunity to shine.

Tony Cunningham

Striker: 84 appearances, 24 goals
Born: 12 November 1957, Kingston, Jamaica
Career: Lincoln City, Barnsley, Sheffield Wednesday, Manchester City, Newcastle United, Blackpool (1987–89), Bury, Bolton Wanderers, Rotherham United, Doncaster Rovers, Wycombe Wanderers, Gainsborough Trinity.

In his brief stay at Bloomfield Road, Tony Cunningham became something of a hero, for he was a strong, tall, well-built striker who loved to get among the goals. Born in Jamaica, he was playing for non-League Stourbridge when Lincoln City signed him in May 1979. Cunningham scored 32 goals in 123 League games for the Imps, before moving to Barnsley in September 1982. After scoring 11 goals in 42 games, his career took him to Sheffield Wednesday (five goals in 27 games), Manchester City (one goal in 18 games) and Newcastle (four goals in 47 games), before joining Blackpool in July 1987 for a tribunal-fixed fee of £25,000.

He made his debut on the opening day of the 1987–88 season in a draw at Gillingham, and his potential as a prolific striker for the team was apparent. It is perhaps the level of expectation surrounding him that caused problems, and it seemed that he was constantly in trouble with referees. As Blackpool struggled in the League, Cunningham became the scapegoat, and after a remarkable scoring record of a goal in every three games, he rejoined Sam Ellis at Bury, where he continued to have considerable success.

He then found himself playing at numerous clubs, but never for long, and eventually retired to become a solicitor in the mid–1990s. He was regarded highly by the Blackpool fans but was the one player who would be criticised when things on the pitch were going wrong. His final act at Bloomfield Road was one that delighted the supporters, though; after being transferred to Bury he returned to Blackpool and promptly got himself sent off!

Mike Davies

Defender: 310 appearances, 16 goals
Born: 19 January 1966, Stretford
Career: Blackpool (1984–95).

Mike Davies, like Jimmy Armfield before him, was a true 'one-club man'. He played his entire career with Blackpool from his debut in May 1984 in a home win over Halifax Town, to his final appearance in 1995. Initially a winger, he won a regular place in the first team within a year and ably replaced the experienced Ian Britton, teaming up with John Deary. Davies continued playing wide on the right for the next few seasons under Sam Ellis, scoring important goals as they gained promotion back to Division Three.

For 1987–88 he was at full-back, prompted by the arrival of Tony Cunningham. He adapted well, and despite a brief return to the wing he made the position his own and became a regular. A fast, tricky player who had tremendous commitment, the flame haired terrier was often in trouble with over zealous referees, who did not always appreciate his approach. The fans did though, and regular plaudits were heaped on him, including 'Player of the Year'. When this book was originally written, Mike Davies was still playing, and I said 'One feels that if every man to have worn a Blackpool shirt over the years had showed as much

commitment to the cause as Mike Davies, then the Seasiders would never have fallen from grace'. Those words remain true today.

Davies still has links with the club. He is a coach and is a member of the 'Hall of Fame'. He may not have won the accolades of Jimmy Armfield, or indeed played in a successful team at the top level, but his contribution to the history of Blackpool Football Club is as great. A true legend of Bloomfield Road.

John Deary

Midfielder: 322 + 19 appearances, 53 goals
Born: 18 October 1962, Ormskirk
Career: Blackpool (1980–89), Burnley, Rochdale, Southport.

John Deary was one of Alan Ball's youngsters during Ball's brief and traumatic time as Blackpool manager. Unlike the rest though, Deary made the grade, and went on to make over 300 appearances for the Seasiders.

He started as an apprentice, signing for Blackpool in March 1980, and made his debut in September of that year. It was a win against Fulham, and then he played in a handful of games for the rest of the season, mostly in midfield. The management seemed uncertain as to whether he should be played in defence or the heart of midfield, but it proved he had the versatility to cope. Eventually he settled for the centre of the park, and spent many successful years there. A tough tackler, who loved to go forward, in the Fourth Division promotion season of 1984–85, he top scored.

Although Deary was a regular scorer, he was more comfortable in a supporting role for the likes of Paul Stewart, Eamon O'Keefe and later, Tony Cunningham. His leadership qualities were used to good effect, with manager Sam Ellis, while not making him captain, often relying on him to provide inspiration when the team was struggling.

At the end of 1988–89, after 10 years at Blackpool, he decided to move on, his place in the team now coming under increasing pressure. Burnley snapped him up for £30,000, and he then spent five years at Turf Moor and helped the Clarets to promotion from the Fourth Division. He then spent two years in the lower tier with Rochdale, before playing just five games

for Southport. He actually scored in his first four, but then a bad injury in the fifth forced his playing retirement.

Deary now owns a double-glazing firm in Liverpool.

Jock Dodds

Striker: 15 appearances, 13 goals
Born: 7 September 1915, Grangemouth
Died: 23 February 2007
Career: Huddersfield Town, Lincoln City, Sheffield United, Blackpool (1939–46), Shamrock Rovers, Everton, Lincoln City.

During World War Two, Ephraim 'Jock' Dodds became a legendary sporting figure nationwide because of his phenomenal goalscoring feats. In six years at Bloomfield Road, Dodds scored well over 200 goals, including 66 in 1941–42 alone. He scored eight in a cup game against Stockport County in 1941, seven against Oldham Athletic the previous season, and another seven against Tranmere Rovers in their 15–3 thrashing at Bloomfield Road. In that match, he scored his first hat-trick in less than three minutes, and a week later scored another almost as quickly.

Despite being a massive figure with huge thighs and a thick neck, he was one of the fastest centre-forwards in the game. Dodds was born in Scotland in 1915, but his family moved to Durham when he was 12. In 1932, he signed for Huddersfield Town, but two years later joined Sheffield United on a free transfer. It was at Bramall Lane where his career took off – he was the Blades' leading scorer for four seasons, and played in the 1936 FA Cup Final against Arsenal. That was the season he was the Second Division's joint top scorer with Blackpool's Bobby Finan.

Blackpool signed Dodds in March 1939 for the huge fee of £10,500, and he made his debut in a defeat at Charlton Athletic, where he scored the Seasiders' only goal. He then went on to score four more in the home victory over Middlesbrough and quickly became a firm favourite. Alas, war intervened, and he did most of his scoring for Blackpool in the regional competitions. He also made all of his international appearances during the war, once scoring a hat-trick to help Scotland to a 5–4 victory over England.

After the war ended, he briefly joined Irish side Shamrock before Everton signed him for £7,500. They had recently lost Dixie Deans and Tommy Lawton, so Dodds was an ideal replacement, and he went on to score 36 times in 55 League games, before ending his career with Lincoln City. Even there, as he became one of the oldest players, his goalscoring record was impressive, with 39 goals from 60 games.

Following retirement, he fell foul of the FA after attempting to lure players to a new League in Bogota. He was banned in 1950 for bringing the game into disrepute, but later cleared. He lived the rest of his life in Blackpool and was inducted in the 'Hall of Fame' at Bloomfield Road. He died in 2007 – the oldest living FA Cup finalist at the age of 91.

Peter Doherty

Striker: 88 appearances, 29 goals. Ireland 16 appearances, 3 goals
Born: 15 June 1913, Magherafelt
Died: 6 April 1990
Career: Blackpool (1933–36), Manchester City, Derby County, Huddersfield Town, Doncaster Rovers.

When Peter Doherty joined Blackpool in November 1933 from Glentoran for £1,500, he already had a reputation as a brave forward, and in an age of burly defenders he was never known to shirk a tackle. Doherty was also a master of the long pass and was capable of shooting accurately from just about any position. His partnership with the great Jimmy Hampson was legendary, although it is fair to say his greatest successes came after he left Bloomfield Road.

Born in Ireland in June 1913, he was turned down by Coleraine before joining Glentoran in June 1930. Blackpool signed him from under the noses of rivals Preston and he soon made his debut, against Bradford. Although Blackpool won 2–1, Doherty failed to impress and it was some time before he gained a regular first team place. When he did, he struck a rich partnership, not only with Hampson, but also with Scottish inside-forward Bobby Finan, and their goals in 1934–35 nearly brought promotion.

Doherty made his debut for Ireland in 1935, but it was surprising that he made such few appearances for his country while with Blackpool. In February 1936, against his own wishes, he was transferred to Manchester City for £10,000. The board at Blackpool were again looking at the financial windfall, and Doherty had little say in the matter. He loved the town and had recently started seeing a local girl, so he was reluctant to leave. He soon repaid the fee though by helping City to the League Championship the following season. During World War Two he guested for Derby County, before signing for £6,000 and teaming up with Raich Carter. They won the FA Cup in 1946.

He joined Huddersfield, and then later as player-manager he helped Doncaster Rovers win the Third Division North title. He held a number of coaching posts and was Northern Ireland's manager when they reached the World Cup Finals in 1958 – they actually got as far as the last eight in the tournament. He died in Fleetwood in 1990 – a wonderful player who Joe Mercer regarded as the greatest ever.

Dave Durie

Forward: 380 appearances, 93 goals
Born: 13 August 1931, Blackpool
Career: Blackpool (1952–64), Chester City, Fleetwood Town.

Dave Durie came to Bloomfield Road as a deputy to Allan Brown, but eventually succeeded him altogether. Durie joined

Blackpool in May 1952 and made his League debut in March the following year in a 3–3 draw with Charlton Athletic. He made two more appearances that season, but when Brown struggled with injury a year later, Durie stepped up as inside-forward.

A strong, speedy player, he was probably under-rated by supporters – hardly surprising bearing in mind the number of stars in the team at the time. He was a loyal servant to the club and one of the fittest men in the squad, despite remaining a part-time professional with many outside business interests.

With the departure of Brown, Durie became a regular, mostly as a creative inside-forward, and in 1956–57, he and Jackie Mudie scored 52 goals between them, with Durie notching 20. One of his best performances came in the third round of the FA Cup against Mansfield Town in January 1960, when he destroyed the opposition almost single-handedly and scored a hat-trick. That season, manager Ron Suart switched him to left-half and Durie adapted easily.

His nickname of 'legs divine' came about because he had seemingly telescopic legs that gave his body a strange rocking motion when he ran. He was also a Methodist Sunday school teacher, which meant he could not play football on Christian holidays. That meant he missed the 'derby' with Preston on Good Friday 1958. He played over 300 games for Blackpool and was never booked, never mind sent off.

Keith Dyson

Forward: 101 + 3 appearances, 32 goals
Born: 10 February 1950, Consett
Career: Newcastle United, Blackpool (1971–76), Lancaster City.

Keith Dyson joined Blackpool in the deal that took Tony Green to Newcastle United for a record fee. A former England Under-21 international, the tall centre-forward had played over 70 times for the Magpies. He found it difficult to maintain a regular place at St James' Park and made his Blackpool debut in October 1971 soon after arriving. It was defeat against Fulham, but he then displaced Glyn James from his temporary number nine shirt.

Dyson made a great start to his Blackpool career, scoring 12 goals in his first season, including a hat-trick against Burnley on Easter Saturday, and then teamed up with the new signing Billy Rafferty and Alan Suddick. He was a strong player with an excellent temperament, but somehow he became unpopular with a section of the highly critical Blackpool fans. The goals dried up and after a time he became under pressure from the veteran Wyn Davies, and later Mickey Walsh. With a series of niggling injuries, his appearances became irregular and Dyson never really realised his true potential at Bloomfield Road, despite his talent and enthusiasm.

After a spell battling for fitness, he was advised to retire and after a playing in the United States – where he teamed up successfully with Jackie Mudie – he returned to manage Lancaster City.

A player who inevitably was compared to the man he had swapped clubs with, Tony Green – which was unfair – but a player who always gave his all for the tangerine cause.

Tony Ellis

Striker: 147 appearances, 55 goals
Born: 20 October 1964, Salford
Career: Oldham Athletic, Stoke City, Preston North End, Blackpool (1994–97), Bury, Stockport County, Rochdale, Burnley.

Tony Ellis was one of an unique group of players on the Fylde coast. He was one of the few in recent years to switch clubs from one arch-rival to the other and so instantaneously become a legend at his new home. When Ellis signed for Blackpool in 1994 for £165,000, he had already had a successful career at Preston North End. Born in Salford, he was playing for Oldham Athletic reserves when Preston manager John McGrath spotted him and took him to

Deepdale. There then followed two separate spells at Preston where he managed to score 75 goals in a total of 158 appearances, but a much publicised falling out with the then manager John Beck resulted in him asking for a transfer. That resulted in him moving up the M55 to play for Blackpool.

Ellis's arrival was greeted ecstatically by Blackpool fans, but less so by the Preston supporters he had left behind. One of the earliest games he played in a tangerine shirt was an FA Cup tie at Deepdale, where he was inevitably given a rough welcome by the fans who once adored him. Ellis had made his choice and for the next three seasons he was the new star at Bloomfield Road. Teaming up with Andy Preece and James Quinn, he was part of the team that aimed, and ultimately failed in dramatic fashion, for promotion. Off the field, his relations with the club were a little fractious, with him asking for a transfer as early as November 1995, but the club resolved that by offering him an extension to his contract.

Ellis was a fans' favourite, and his goalscoring talents really should have been rewarded with experience at a higher level, but after the disastrous promotion failure under Sam Allardyce the team faded away and he fell out of favour. In 1997, manager Nigel Worthington sold him to Bury for £70,000 before a similar move to Stockport County. He then found himself at Rochdale, seemingly drifting from one lower League club to another, but everywhere he went he scored goals.

In 2001 he was released by the Spotland club and seemed to be on the verge of retirement, until a last-minute call from Stan Ternant at Burnley. He played one season for the Clarets before hanging up his boots for good, although he did play non-League football for a while.

In 2007 he joined Rochdale as a youth coach, but his career seems to have been one of missed opportunities. A talented striker who scored regularly, he was adored by Blackpool supporters and is a member of the 'Hall of Fame'.

David Eyres

Midfield: 147 appearances, 38 goals
Born: 26 February 1964, Liverpool
Career: Blackpool (1989–93), Burnley, Preston North End, Oldham Athletic.

Like Tony Ellis, David Eyres was another example of a player who switched clubs between rivals Blackpool and Preston, but in his case he went from Bloomfield Road to Deepdale, with a detour to Turf Moor for good measure!

He came into the professional game late and was playing non-League football for Rhyl when Blackpool manager Jimmy Mullen signed him for £10,000 in 1989. A fast and tricky midfielder, he was in the mould of Alan Ball and Tony Green and was able to add goalscoring to his talents too. He made his debut against Burnley in the League Cup in August 1989 and stayed at Blackpool for four seasons. During that time he made two Wembley appearances, the second securing promotion back to the Second Division, and in 1992–93 was the club's top scorer with 16 goals. He was a huge favourite with the fans, and so it was with dismay that they learned in the summer of 1993 that Jimmy Mullen – now manager of Burnley – had signed him for the Clarets. The fee was just £90,000, which seemed ludicrously low, but the player himself had initiated the move, believing that things had 'gone stale' at Blackpool.

Eyres stayed for seven years at Burnley and became a huge favourite there too, and then in 1997 he signed for Preston North End as his tour of Lancashire continued. He stayed there for three years, before a six-season spell at Oldham Athletic, which eventually resulted in him being co-manager with John Sheridan after the departure of Iain Dowie.

Eyres was a player who typified the Billy Ayre era – passionate, committed and determined. He was talented and popular, but that waned with his subsequent moves to firstly Burnley and then Preston. Sadly, despite his time at Blackpool, he is now one of the less-welcomed ex-players at Bloomfield Road.

Horace Fairhurst

Defender: 50 appearances, 0 goals
Born: 2 June 1893, Bolton
Died: 7 January 1921
Career: Darwen, Blackpool (1919–21).

Horace Fairhurst was a stocky, hard-tackling right-back who struck fear into approaching forwards, but his greatest attribute was his enormous courage. When he joined Blackpool, he struck up a partnership with Bert Tulloch, and it was their solid defending that helped the team's fortunes to turn around so dramatically.

During World War One he was stationed, like so many other footballers, at Blackpool and appeared in many army games at Bloomfield Road. On his return from Egypt, where he later served, he was signed by Blackpool and made his debut against Oldham Athletic in the 1917 Principal Tournament. From then on he was an almost ever-present, replacing Jimmy Jones, who had joined Bolton Wanderers.

Blackpool were playing particularly well at this stage, making a strong push for promotion to the First Division, with one of the meanest goals against columns in the League. Fairhurst could dispossess a forward almost by looking at him, as he was such an imposing figure. Yet, off the field, he was mild mannered and even tempered and very much a family man.

His career came to a tragic end on Boxing Day 1920, when he was stretchered off in the game against Barnsley. He had gone into a tackle in typically courageous fashion but had been left unconscious after a severe bang on the head from an opponent's boot. It was an accident, but he never recovered and on 7 January 1921 he died at his home. In May that year, Blackpool played a benefit match against Preston for his widow and for the children of Bert Tulloch, whose wife had died the same weekend as Fairhurst.

Horace Fairhurst was only 26, and a promising footballing career had been ended so abruptly.

George Farm

Goalkeeper: 512 appearances, 1 goal. Scotland 10 appearances, 0 goals
Born: 13 July 1924, Edinburgh
Died: 18 July 2004
Career: Hibernian, Blackpool (1948–60), Queen of the South.

George Farm was probably Blackpool's best-ever goalkeeper. Born in Scotland, Farm came to Bloomfield Road in September 1948, from Hibernian for £2,700. He stayed for 12 years, breaking appearance records, and appeared in two FA Cup Finals – not bad for a player who had been third choice for Hibs.

Well built, he had a distinctive way of holding the ball, preferring to catch it with one hand above and one hand below, as opposed to the orthodox style used by most goalkeepers. He was a perfectionist and could be found at the training ground well after the others had left. He was brave, and it did not matter how he kept the ball out – if that meant heading it, then fine.

Farm made his debut in September 1948 at Bolton Wanderers, replacing out-of-form Joe Robinson. He went on to make more than 500 first-team appearances, including 47 consecutive FA Cup matches. Unfortunately his performance in the 1953 FA Cup Final was criticised, yet manager Joe Smith always kept faith in him. The only time he was replaced – by fellow Scot Bob Wyle – was through injury. He played for Scotland on 10 occasions, including three times in 1959 when he was at the age of 35. A year later he was granted a transfer. Manager Ron Suart, who had been one of Farm's teammates, was reluctant to let him go, but as soon as Blackpool's precarious League position improved, Queen of the South took him for £3,000 – more than Joe Smith had paid twelve years previously.

Farm is one of the few 'keepers to have scored a goal. In the 6–2 home defeat by Preston, he injured a shoulder and

replaced Jackie Mudie at centre-forward, where he proceeded to open the scoring. From then on his teammates were never to hear the last of it.

At Queen of the South he became player-manager, guiding them to the First Division, but was sacked two years later. He then had spells at Raith Rovers and Dunfermline Athletic, where he won the Scottish Cup in 1968 and then reached the semi-finals of the Cup-Winners' Cup the following season.

His retirement years were spent as a football pundit and oddly as a lighthouse keeper. He died in Edinburgh, five days after his 80th birthday.

George Farrow

Defender: 154 appearances, 15 goals
Born: 4 October 1913, Whitburn
Died: 1980
Career: Stockport County, Wolverhampton Wanderers, Bournemouth, Blackpool (1936–48), Sheffield United.

In the years before, during and after World War Two, the half-back line of George Farrow, Eric Hayward and Harry Johnston became legendary. At this time Blackpool were one of the most powerful teams in the country, and the famous trio were feared by every team they faced.

George Farrow joined Blackpool from Bournemouth in 1936 and made his debut in September that year in the home victory over West Ham United. Initially an inside-left, he soon switched to wing half where his fierce tackling was of more use. That season he helped the club gain promotion to Division One and for the next 12 seasons contributed to turning the team into one of the best ever seen at Bloomfield Road.

His main attributes were strong tackling, accurate long-range passes and a rapid shot. His reputation grew, culminating in him being dubbed 'the best uncapped half-back

in England'. He was also one of the earliest exponents of the long throw in.

Farrow played for Blackpool for 13 seasons including the war years, but was unfortunate to be transferred to Sheffield United just a few weeks before Blackpool's FA Cup run which lead to a first Wembley appearance. He then only played one game for the Blades.

Farrow probably did not receive the recognition due to him, mainly because of the presence of Captain Harry Johnston, but he was an integral part of the side that was so successful in the wartime years.

Ewan Fenton

Defender: 214 appearances, 20 goals
Born: 17 November 1929, Dundee
Died: 3 April 2006
Career: Blackpool (1946–59), Wrexham, Limerick.

Ewan Fenton was one of Blackpool's unsung heroes during the successful years of the 1950s, and he played for the Seasiders for over 13 years. Born in Scotland, Fenton played for Jeanfield Swifts before signing professional terms in November 1946. He made his debut in September 1948 in a home draw with Derby County, He was a cultured right-half and was brought in as understudy to Harry Johnston, so it was some time before he broke through to the first team.

In 1952–53 his patience was rewarded and he played throughout the campaign to finish with an FA Cup-winners' medal, his steadiness going a long way in inspiring the fightback against Bolton Wanderers at Wembley. Indeed, calmness was his great strength and in 1956–57 he was appointed captain of the side. Fenton was a shrewd

passer of the ball and enjoyed joining the attack, scoring some crucial goals.

He was never capped by his country, and the nearest he came to a representative honour was in the powerful British Army X1. After having a transfer request turned down in 1958, he was finally released in May 1959, joining Wrexham for a small fee. He spent over a year at the Racecourse Ground, although a serious injury had threatened to end his career. In 1960–61 he played for Limerick in the European Cup and so boasting that he was the only member of Blackpool's FA Cup-winning side from 1953 who went on to play European football.

After his playing career ended, he stayed in Ireland and managed both Limerick and Linfield with a degree of success. He eventually started his own driving school and died in 2006 at the age of 76.

Bobby Finan

Forward: 180 appearances, 89 goals. Scotland one appearance, 0 goals
Born: 1 March 1912, Old Kilpatrick
Died: 1983
Career: Blackpool (1933–47), Crewe Alexandra, Wigan Athletic.

Bobby Finan was another of Blackpool's prolific goalscorers in the years leading up to World War Two, eventually taking over the mantle held by the great Jimmy Hampson. Born in Scotland, Finan began his career as a middle forward with Yoker Athletic before manager Alex McFarlane persuaded him to join Blackpool in 1933. His League debut in April 1934 was memorable only for the fact that Blackpool lost 7–0 at Grimsby Town, but the following season he excelled and became a regular first-team player.

In 1933–34, with Jimmy Hampson injured, Finan deputised at centre-forward and responded to the challenge so well that

he ended the season as the Second Division's joint top scorer with 34 goals. When Hampson returned midway through the season he went to inside-right as Finan continued to lead the attack.

Finan was fast and strong and not only had a similar style to Hampson, but also shared a remarkable resemblance to him too. He continued scoring freely the next season and once again topped the scoring charts at Bloomfield Road. As he grew older and his speed began to wane, he was moved to outside-left, where he laid on goals for the strike force of Buchan and Dodds.

During the war, Finan's appearances were spasmodic, although he was in the famous Cup Final against Arsenal in 1943 at Stamford Bridge, scoring one of the goals. After leaving Blackpool he played for both Crewe and then Wigan before returning to Bloomfield Road as a scout.

Bobby Finan as only capped once for Scotland and that was during the war, but to Blackpool supporters he was one of the finest forwards the club had seen.

Andy Garner

Midfield: 179 + 10 appearances, 44 goals
Born: 6 March 1966, Stonebroom
Career: Derby County, Blackpool (1988–92), Gresley Rovers

Andy Garner was a favourite with the fans from the moment he moved to Blackpool from Derby County in August 1988 for £75,000. Garner made his debut in the opening game of that season in a 1–1 draw with Chester City and, although playing in his first season as centre-forward, he enjoyed greater success in midfield. He had good ball skills and was able to score crucial goals, although a lack of pace troubled him at times.

After the disappointment of the Play-off Final at Wembley in 1991, Garner was the subject of much transfer speculation and it seemed his time at Blackpool would be coming to an end, but thankfully for the fans he continued to wear the tangerine shirt. He was then instrumental in the club gaining promotion at Wembley the following season, but the next year he made only seven first team appearances and left the club. He played out his career at non-League Gresley Rovers.

Garner has always had an association with Derby County. He joined them as an apprentice and played in their promotion season of 1985–86 – actually scoring a winner at Blackpool for them – and returned there once his playing career had finished. He is now first-team coach at Pride Park. At Blackpool he is remembered well and is a member of the 'Hall of Fame'.

Tommy Garrett

Defender: 334 appearances, 4 goals, England 3 appearances, 0 goals
Born: 28 February 1926, South Shields
Died: 16 April 2006
Career: Blackpool (1946–61), Millwall, Fleetwood Town, Wigan Athletic.

Tommy Garrett was a polished, skilful defender who never wilted under pressure. He was a miner playing for Horden Colliery when Blackpool signed him in 1942. Initially as a forward, it was at full-back that he became established. He was a 'footballing' defender, always playing his way out of trouble, never slamming the ball aimlessly away. He would spend hours practicing heading and was a tower of strength in the air.

Garrett made his debut in March 1947 but with Ron Suart playing regularly, he had to wait until his departure to Blackburn Rovers before making the

position his own. He could perform equally well on either flank and played in the 1951 and 1953 FA Cup Finals, appearing in the latter with a broken nose sustained the week before. During this time he made a handful of international appearances, partnering Alf Ramsey in the England defence.

In the 1953 FA Cup run, Garrett scored a remarkable goal against Huddersfield Town, lobbing the ball home from his own half to put Blackpool into the fifth round. After 19 years with the Seasiders he was given a free transfer and signed for Millwall in May 1961, making 12 appearances before retiring from League football. After a short time with Fleetwood and Wigan, he emigrated to Australia where he died in 2006. A fine player for Blackpool in a time when the club was at its peak.

Roy Gatrix

Defender: 436 appearances, 0 goals
Born: 9 February 1932, Salford
Died: 2002
Career: Blackpool (1953–64), Manchester City.

Roy Gatrix was always described as the 'centre-half England never chose'. He was a player who appeared over 400 times for Blackpool, yet never fully received the credit he deserved. He was playing for a local Manchester works team – Taylor Bros – when he was signed by Blackpool manager Joe Smith. A tall, strong defender, Gatrix succeeded Eddie Shimwell at right-back, making his debut in March 1954 in a goalless draw with Middlesbrough. He then played in every match until the end of that season.

In 1954–55, he retained his position, teaming up with Tommy Garrett, although occasionally being asked to play at left-back. The following season, with Harry Johnston leaving to manage Reading, Gatrix moved to centre-half, where he remained for the rest of his playing days.

He created an unusual record at Blackpool, for despite his 436 appearances, he never found himself on the score sheet, unless you count an own-goal against Sheffield Wednesday. During the 1950s, the half-back line of Gatrix and the two Kellys was a formidable one. The contrasting styles of Hugh and Jimmy worked perfectly with the rugged but effective style of Gatrix, and it is no coincidence that Blackpool had some of

their most successful seasons while they were together.

In September 1964 Gatrix signed for Manchester City, where he made 15 appearances. He then went to Toronto for a time before playing in non-League Welsh football. He died in 2002.

Ian Gore

Defender: 200 appearances, 0 goals
Born: 10 January 1968, Prescott
Career: Birmingham City, Southport, Blackpool (1988–95), Torquay United, Doncaster Rovers.

Ian Gore joined Blackpool on a free transfer from non-League Southport in January 1988 and went on to make 200 appearances for the Seasiders. He had started his career as an apprentice at Birmingham City but was released without playing a single game for them. A tall, no-nonsense defender, he was part of the Blackpool side that made two Wembley appearances in Play-off Finals, and won promotion in the season of 1991–92. One year previously, he had been voted as Player of the Year by Blackpool supporters.

He continued to appear in the tangerine shirt for the next three seasons, becoming a regular fixture in the teams managed by Billy Ayre, but in August 1995 manager Sam Allardyce saw his first team appearances as limited and so he was taken on by Torquay United on a free transfer. He stayed a season, before a slightly longer period at Doncaster Rovers. He eventually ended up in non-League football.

Never a star at Bloomfield Road, he was certainly a reliable player and one that will always be linked to the Tangerines.

Tony Green

Midfielder: 136 + one appearances, 19 goals. Scotland 6 appearances, 0 goals
Born: 13 October 1946, Glasgow
Career: Albion Rovers, Blackpool (1966–71), Newcastle United.

Tony Green was described as the 'new Alan Ball' when he moved to Blackpool, a title that was hard to live up to, but he managed it with something to spare and is now regarded as one of the club's most exciting and talented players in the last 50 years.

He was still at school in Glasgow when he became a part-time player at Albion Rovers, and his speed and goalscoring soon attracted the top English clubs, notably Fulham and Blackburn Rovers. It was on Scottish Cup Final day in 1967 that Blackpool manager Stan Mortensen signed him for £15,000. It was to be one of the bargain buys of the century for the club, as Green made his debut almost immediately, and despite the 3–1 home loss to West Bromwich Albion, he was cheered off the field. He was obviously a star in the making.

In 1967–68, his partnership with Alan Suddick took the Seasders to a whisker of promotion to Division One, and although he rarely scored himself in a tangerine shirt he did manage to lay on most of Gerry Ingram's goals. Sadly, just when it looked

like he would break into the Scotland squad, he suffered a serious ankle injury in training and was out of action for over a year, completely missing Blackpool's promotion season of 1969–70.

He stayed cheerful, and when he re-appeared in the home match with champions Everton he brought new vitality to the team and hope to the hearts of supporters who were already enduring a miserable season. Later, in the FA Cup he almost single-handedly destroyed West Ham United at Bloomfield Road in a 4–0 win, sadly rather over shadowed by the news of the exploits of various Hammers players in Blackpool town centre the night before.

Green eventually made his international debut in 1971, playing magnificently against England at Wembley, and on the back of that there were bids of over £100,000 from clubs keen on signing him. To Blackpool's credit they held out, but at the beginning of 1971–72, Green turned down a new contract, and after helping the team to a 4–1 League Cup victory over Aston Villa, he moved to Newcastle United for a club-record £150,000 – over 10 times the amount that Blackpool had paid for him.

Not long afterwards he suffered another serious injury which was to eventually force his retirement from playing at the age of just 25. It was tragic as Green was one of the most talented players of his generation and was surely ready for great things in the game.

Since then, he took up teaching full time in the Blackpool area, where he still lives today. He is a member of the 'Hall of Fame' and surely one of the most-loved Blackpool players of all time.

Colin Greenall

Defender: 200 + 4 appearances, 11 goals
Born: 30 December 1963, Billinge
Career: Blackpool (1980–86), Gillingham, Oxford United, Bury, Preston North End, Chester City, Lincoln City, Wigan Athletic.

On 23 August 1980 at the age of 16 years and 237 days, Colin Greenall made his debut for Blackpool and so becoming the club's then youngest-ever League player. Three days later he appeared in a League Cup game at Goodison Park.

Born near Wigan, Greenall eventually signed full time for Blackpool in 1981, one of a host of young players brought to the

club by manager Alan Ball. Unlike most of the others though, he stayed the course, developing into a dependable defender. Eventually he took over the central role, combining with Captain Steve Hetzke and Mike Conroy to form a successful defensive partnership.

Greenall won England Youth honours, and at 20 he was voted the Fourth Division Player of the Year by the PFA. Under new manager Sam Ellis, he became a stylish player with just the right amount of aggression. Unfortunately, after 200 appearances for Blackpool, he had a contractual dispute and in September 1986 he moved to Third Division Gillingham for £40,000 and Blackpool lost one of its most influential players.

Greenall joined Oxford United in 1988 for £235,000, and they soon made him captain following the departure of Tommy Caton. He then moved to Bury two years later for £100,000. There were then short spells at Preston North End, Chester City, Lincoln City before a prolonged period at Wigan Athletic. He was ever present in their promotion season in 1997 (he had also seen promotion at Chester too), and actually came out of retirement to help the Latics win the Auto-Windscreen Shield at Wembley in 1999, beating Millwall 1–0.

There was a brief time as coach at Wigan, but he then went to Rochdale as part of their back room staff. He now coaches for the Lancashire FA.

Jimmy Hampson

Striker: 373 appearances, 252 goals. England three appearances, 5 goals.
Born: 23 March 1906, Little Hulton
Died: 10 January 1938
Career: Nelson, Blackpool (1927–38).

Before the glory days of Matthews and Mortensen, there was one player that Blackpool supporters treated with similar reverence. Jimmy Hampson was an extraordinary goalscorer, feared by defenders, and to this day still Blackpool's record scorer.

Hampson started his League career with Nelson, making his debut in 1925. At inside-right, he soon became their top scorer and attracted the interest of many of the top clubs. It was Second Division Blackpool who secured his services though in October 1927. They agreed a fee of £1,000 with Nelson, and Hampson was tracked down to a local cinema to be told he had become Blackpool's latest, and certainly shrewdest, signing. Despite being only 5'6" tall, Hampson was converted to centre-forward and proved his worth with 31 goals in the remaining 32 games of the season.

Among his many attributes were incredible acceleration and a bullet-like shot from either foot. He was often on the receiving end of some rough treatment, but accepted it as part of the game. The following season he scored 40 goals to become the Second Division topscorer, and that summer Arsenal made a near-record bid of £10,000 for him. It is fair to

say that Hampson, a quiet man, would perhaps not have been at home among the bright lights of London, so he remained a Blackpool player.

In 1929–30 the club won the Second Division title and Hampson's goals – 45 in the League – were the key to the club reaching the First Division for the first time. His partnership with centre-half Billy Tremelling, who would often supply the through ball for Hampson, was almost irresistible.

Jimmy Hampson was now a household name and was even honoured by a wax model of himself in Louis Tussaud's Waxworks on the promenade. Fame was not something that came easilyy to him though, and after the team returned from Oldham on the train – where they had gained promotion – he got off at an earlier station to avoid the crowds that were waiting.

During three seasons of struggle in Division One, Hampson still managed 72 goals, and after the team were finally relegated, he was the club's top scorer for a further two seasons, even though injury plagued him and he missed quite a few games. Indeed, since his arrival he had scored approximately 60 per cent of all Blackpool goals. He also held the record for the fastest century of goals, scoring 101 in 97 games between 1927 and 1930.

His international career was brief, due to the presence of 'Dixie' Deans and the fact that Hampson played most of his career in Division Two, but he scored five goals in his three England games, plus nine in four appearances for the Football League. Jimmy Hampson was physically small, but his standing in English football in the 1930s could not be exaggerated. He was idolised in Blackpool, and when he drowned in a fishing boating accident in January 1938, at the age of just 32, the whole town was stunned. It was said that grown men cried, knowing that the greatest player the club had seen had been lost forever. His body was never found, but his legend lives on and his 248 League goals in 361 appearances is a club record unlikely to be beaten.

He was, of course, inducted into Blackpool's 'Hall of Fame'.

Harold Harman

Midfielder: 71 appearances, 10 goals. England 4 appearances, 1 goal
Born: 4 April 1882, Newton Heath
Died: 9 June 1965
Career: Blackpool (1900–03), Everton, Manchester United, Bradford City, Stoke City.

Harold Harman was another one of the Blackpool players in the early part of the 20th century, who went on to greater success after leaving the club. He was discovered as a schoolboy in Manchester, and after signing for Blackpool, was thrown into the first team during the club's one-year exile in the Lancashire League in 1899–1900, when he also appeared for the Northern Nomads.

He made his Football League debut in September 1900 in the home draw with

Gainsborough Trinity, and for the next three seasons became an almost ever present. Essentially an outside-left, he had the ability to switch flanks and sometimes turned out on the right wing. Fast and tricky, although not a great goalscorer himself, he provided the through ball for many of the goals scored by Birkett and Parkinson.

Blackpool though were a team constantly struggling in the Second Division, and Hardman was far too good for the club to retain. In 1903 Everton bought him for just over £100 and he played for them in the 1906 and 1907 FA Cup Finals before joining Manchester United in 1908. That year he also won an Olympic soccer gold medal with Great Britain. He later played for Bradford City and Stoke City, but after his playing days ended he became a well known administrator and later the much-loved chairman of Manchester United.

Blackpool never saw the best of Hardman, all of his England appearances taking place while he was at Everton, but he was proud of the new talent policy the club had introduced during the early 1900s, which he got involved with heavily. He was also a solicitor in the Manchester area, where he died in 1965.

Paul Hart

Defender: 156 appearances, 16 goals
Born: 4 May 1953, Golbourne
Career: Stockport County, Blackpool (1973–78), Leeds United, Nottingham Forest, Sheffield Wednesday, Birmingham City, Notts County.

Son of Johnny Hart, a former Manchester City forward, Paul Hart was an immensely talented defender, skilful enough to play at times in midfield, who signed for Blackpool from Stockport County in June 1973 for £25,000. He made his debut in a home win over Fulham four months later, but only played twice more that season.

Eventually, though, he established himself as a regular first-team player, and in 1976–77 he scored six times for Blackpool – when they made a serious challenge for promotion to the First Division – and was ever present. Hart's reputation grew, especially as the side started to struggle, and with relegation to the Third Division virtually assured one year later, he moved to Leeds United as a replacement for Gordon McQueen. The fee of £300,000 was hard for the Blackpool board to turn down.

After a shaky start, he made nearly 200 appearances for Leeds before moving to Nottingham Forest in 1983. Hart actually scored for Forest in the controversial 1983–84 UEFA Cup semi-final against Anderlecht, but the goal was disallowed for seemingly no reason. Later Anderlecht admitted they had bribed the official. There then followed spells with Sheffield Wednesday, Birmingham City (where he broke his leg in his only appearance for them) and then Notts County. He retired in 1987 after making over 560 appearances.

Hart then went into management and,

after starting his career at Chesterfield, he then went on to manage numerous clubs, including Nottingham Forest, but in recent years he seems to have become something of a 'firefighter', arriving at clubs in crisis with a remit to 'steady the ship', notably Portsmouth, Queen's Park Rangers and Crystal Palace.

Dave Hatton

Defender: 273 + one appearances, eight goals.
Born: 30 October 1943, Farnworth
Career: Bolton Wanderers, Blackpool (1969–76), Bury.

Wing-half Dave Hatton arrived at Blackpool from Bolton Wanderers in September 1969 for £40,000, and by the end of the season he had helped the Seasiders to a return to Division One. Hatton made nearly 260 appearances for the Trotters before Blackpool manager Les Shannon signed him. He made his debut in a home win over Swindon Town and teamed up with Glyn James and John McPhee, adding an extra dimension to the midfield as a skilful ball winner.

Sadly, the following season was something of a disaster for Blackpool with relegation back to Division Two, and Hatton's worst moment came in the 4–3 home defeat by Chelsea. The visitors had come from 3–0 down, and Hatton somehow managed to score a last-minute own-goal in the most remarkable of circumstances. It haunted him, but in the following summer he was able to help the club reach European success with the Anglo-Italian trophy.

The arrival of Peter Suddaby saw him move back to the full-back position, where he played some of his best football for Blackpool. His partnership with Bill Bentley continued at Bloomfield Road until he left to join Allan Brown at Bury in

August 1976. A year later he became player-manager at Gigg Lane but was sacked after they narrowly avoided relegation to Division Four in 1979.

Bob Hatton

Striker: 84 appearances, 35 goals
Born: 10 April 1947, Hull
Career: Wolverhampton Wanderers, Bolton Wanderers, Northampton Town, Carlisle United, Birmingham City, Blackpool (1976–78), Luton Town, Sheffield United, Cardiff City.

Although Bob Hatton only played for Blackpool for two seasons, he will never be forgotten by those who witnessed his goalscoring feats and partnership with Mickey Walsh. By the time Hatton arrived at Bloomfield Road in 1976, he had already enjoyed a varied career at Wolves, Bolton Wanderers, Carlisle United and Birmingham City (for whom he scored 58 goals in 175 League games, helping them into Division One in 1972 and to two FA Cup semi-finals). Allan Brown brought

him to Blackpool, and in his first game he scored twice in a 4–1 victory over Bristol Rovers. When the injured Mickey Walsh returned, the two created a frightening attacking partnership, scoring 36 goals between them that season. Hatton was the perfect foil for the speedy Walsh with his excellent control, aerial power and boundless energy.

The following season was a personal triumph for Hatton with 22 goals, including two successive home matches where he scored seven in total. Amazingly, despite this and a further 14 goals from Mickey Walsh, Blackpool dropped into the Third Division in the most dramatic fashion, completely collapsing after the departure of Brown.

Hatton then moved to Luton Town, where he was still prolific in front of goal, followed by Sheffield United before ending his career at Cardiff City. Since his retirement, he has been involved with the Professional Footballers Association in the Midlands, where he still lives today.

Eric Hayward

Defender: 297 appearances, 0 goals
Born: 2 August 1917, Newcastle-under-Lyme
Died: 1976
Career: Port Vale, Blackpool (1937–52).

During World War Two, and for a few years beyond, Blackpool had what was regarded as the best half-back line up in the country in George Farrow, Eric Hayward and Harry Johnston. Of that trio, Hayward was the one who received the least publicity and the fewest accolades, yet his contribution was as great in the team of the 1940s and early 1950s.

He first played for Hanley and Port Vale when manager Joe Smith signed him. A strong, skilful centre-half, he was totally dependable, always there with a last ditch tackle or a timely clearance. He joined Blackpool in 1937 and during the war played in one of the finest sides in the country, although service in India restricted the number of games he could appear in. He played in the 1943 War Cup Final and also appeared in both the 1948 and 1951 FA Cup Finals. The latter saw him marking the

legendary Jackie Milburn, with Blackpool unsuccessfully deploying an offside game to compensate for Hayward's comparative lack of speed. Two goals and another defeat were testament to the failure.

Hugh Kelly had now taken over from Farrow, and he and Hayward worked as well together, Hayward breaking up the attack and placing the pass for Kelly to start the counter attack. Hayward remained loyal to Blackpool and after his playing days ended, he returned as assistant manager to another old boy, Ron Suart. It was in that capacity that helped to nurture the talent of Alan Ball, turning a youngster with potential into a player of immense talent. Eric Hayward died in 1976.

Iain Hesford

Goalkeeper: 230 appearances, 0 goals.
Born: 4 March 1960, Ndola, Zambia
Career: Blackpool (1977–83), Sheffield Wednesday, Fulham, Notts County, Sunderland, Hull City, Maidstone United.

Iain Hesford was the son of Bob Hesford, who kept goal for Huddersfield Town in the 1938 FA Cup Final, and when he joined Blackpool he seemed to have his own glittering career ahead of him. Somehow his potential was never realised, despite winning seven England Under-21 caps. A well-built goalkeeper, who was never spectacular, but certainly one of the safest pair of hands in the lower divisions.

He joined Blackpool as an apprentice in August 1977 and was understudy to George Woods until his transfer to Everton. Hesford's debut came in the opening game of the 1977–78 season, a draw with Oldham Athletic, and despite coming under pressure from Ward, McAllister and Rush he went on to play 230 times for Blackpool in a little over five years. He had certainly caught the eye of bigger clubs, especially with his international appearances – which came

about due to his parentage – so it was not surprising that he moved to Sheffield Wednesday in August 1983 for a large fee. Surprisingly, he did not play a single game for the Owls and was loaned out to Fulham and Notts County, before Sunderland manager Lawrie McMenemy signed him in August 1986 for £80,000.

He played for two seasons and then moved to Hull City but was part of the team that was relegated from the old Division Two in 1991. He ended his playing career in this country for Maidstone United and actually scored a goal. It came against Hereford United on a windy day in 1991 when a huge drop kick went straight into the opponent's net, helping his side to a 3–2 victory.

For the next six years he played in Hong Kong for Eastern, Sing Tao and South China with some success. Eventually he returned to England and now runs a hotel near Rochdale. His brother, Bob, won 10 Rugby Union caps at international level for England.

It is difficult to understand how Hesford's career faltered, as he was a superb 'keeper, and the future always looked bright. His time at Sheffield Wednesday seemed to cause the problem and it was at that time when his career stalled. For Blackpool, though, he will be a player fondly recalled.

Steve Hetzke

Defender: 160 appearances, 19 goals
Born: 3 June 1955, Marlborough
Career: Reading, Blackpool (1982–86), Sunderland, Chester City, Colchester United.

Steve Hetzke made over 250 League appearances for Reading, the club he signed for as an apprentice in June 1973, before being transferred to Blackpool nine years later. A tall, strong central-defender, he came to Bloomfield Road for a modest £12,500 tribunal-settled fee, which turned out to be a bargain purchase.

Hetzke, who had a summer in the NASL in 1976 with the Vancouver Whitecaps, made his Blackpool debut on the opening day of the 1982–83 season, in a defeat at Mansfield Town, taking over from the departed Paul Hart. He was a tower of strength in what was a leaky defence as Blackpool finished in 21st position in Division Four. Gradually, though, the team progressed and under his captaincy they made a concerted push for promotion. In 1984–85, the Seasiders were finally promoted, conceding only 39 goals in 46 matches.

Hetzke was never a spectacular centre-half, as he always preferred the measured pass as opposed to the hopeful boot out of defence. Midway through the following season his place came under threat from Nicky Law, and in March 1986 he moved to Sunderland. He only played 31 times at Roker Park before ending his career at Chester City and then Colchester United.

Steve 'Mandy' Hill

Winger: 85 appearances, 1 goal
Born: 15 February 1940, Blackpool
Died: 29 November 2010
Career: Blackpool (1959–64), Tranmere Rovers, Wigan Athletic.

'Mandy' Hill's was a career that showed great promise when he was young, but eventually a catalogue of injuries deprived him of the success he deserved. Born in Blackpool, he joined his home-town club in May 1959 as a winger with a reputation for speedy pace and a magical touch. He had a deceptive body swerve that made some supporters compare him to the great Stanley Matthews. In fact, the management groomed him as a potential successor to the maestro, and indeed four appearances in England's Under-21 side underlined Hill's ability.

He made his first-team debut in October 1959, deputising for the injured Matthews in a home defeat by Manchester City, but then spent the next two years trying to break into the first team as Matthews continued long after most pundits had predicted that he would hang up his boots. Eventually, in 1961–62, with

Matthews transferred to Stoke City, Hill broke into the side on a regular basis. Unfortunately, he was injury prone, and one particular knock forced him to miss the majority of the next two seasons. Once it had cleared, his place had been taken by Leslie Lea, and so Hill was sold to Tranmere Rovers in September 1964.

He made 130 League appearances for the Wirral club, but his career never realised the enormous potential that was seen at the beginning. He ended his playing days at Wigan Athletic, but the mantle of 'the next Stanley Matthews' was not one that was easy to wear. He died in hospital on 29 November 2010.

Emlyn Hughes

Defender: 33 + 1 appearances, 0 goals. England 62 appearances, one goal
Born: 28 August 1947, Barrow-in-Furness
Died: 9 November 2004, Sheffield
Career: Blackpool (1964–67), Liverpool, Wolverhampton Wanderers, Rotherham United, Hull City, Mansfield Town, Swansea City.

Emlyn Hughes only made 28 League appearances for Blackpool before being transferred to Liverpool in February 1967, but he is regarded as one of the best players to have graced Bloomfield Road. Son of a Rugby League international, Hughes joined the Seasiders from Roose FC in September 1964. His debut came in the final game of the 1965–66 season, a victory over Blackburn Rovers, and the following campaign saw manager Ron Suart team up Hughes with the experienced Jimmy Armfield – a tremendous opportunity for the youngster to learn his trade.

Soon he was attracting the attentions of other managers and Liverpool's Bill Shankly paid £65,000 for the 19-year-old in February 1967. It was with the Reds that Hughes had his most successful time. He went on to collect the game's greatest honours, captaining the side to a host of domestic and European victories as well as being capped by England 62 times, where for a brief spell he was Captain too.

His style of play was unusual, a full-back with a strange galloping action when

he ran, and coupled with his infectious enthusiasm, he was always a fans' favourite no matter where he played. He earned the nickname of 'Crazy Horse' after a lunging tackle on Newcastle United's Albert Bennett, a name that stayed with him throughout his career.

After 657 games for Liverpool, where he had won four League titles, one FA Cup, two European Cups, two UEFA Cups, one European Super Cup and three Charity Shields, he joined Wolves in August 1979 for £90,000. He then helped them to a League Cup Final success before taking over as player-manager at Rotherham United before being sacked two years later as the team struggled in the Second Division. He then moved to Hull City (where he later became a Director of the club), Mansfield Town (although he did not play a single game for them) and Swansea City, before ending his playing career.

In later life he forged a very successful television career, especially on the BBC's *A Question of Sport* with the episode featuring Princess Anne regularly repeated. He continued to keep a high profile throughout his later years, appearing in a whole variety of TV programmes, plus regularly appearing as a football pundit on radio.

In 2003 it was revealed that he had a brain tumour, and one year later he died in hospital in Sheffield. He was an inspirational player and certainly much loved at Anfield, and even though his time at Blackpool was brief he is still fondly remembered. He is one of only four England players to have played at international level over three decades, alongside Jesse Pennington, Stanley Matthews and Bobby Charlton. A wonderful player, and certainly worth inclusion in Blackpool's Stars.

Tommy Hutchison

Midfielder: 185 + 2 appearances, 14 goals.
Scotland 17 appearances, 1 goal.
Born: 22 September 1947, Cardenden
Career: Alloa Athletic, Blackpool (1967–72), Coventry City, Manchester City, Bulova, Burnley, Swansea City, Merthyr Tydfil.

Tommy Hutchison was one of the most gifted players to have appeared at Bloomfield Road. Bought from Scottish club Alloa Athletic in February 1968 for £10,000, he almost immediately took the place of Graham Oates at outside-left, making his debut against Plymouth Argyle. Hutchison was bought by manager Stan Mortensen to boost Pool's flagging promotion hopes, and in the final nine games of the season, with 'Hutch' playing, they won eight. Promotion was missed on the final day, but Hutchison had impressed.

He teamed up with Alan Suddick in midfield, often winning the ball deep in his own half and taking it forward before supplying the perfect pass. When Bob

Stokoe took over, he worked on Hutchison's crossing ability, believing it was the players' only weak spot. He did not score many goals, but one of his most spectacular was in a home game against Portsmouth in 1972, crashing the ball home after a brilliant solo run. Later that year, Coventry City offered £140,000 plus Billy Rafferty, and Blackpool let him go.

At Coventry – where he stayed for eight seasons – and at Manchester City, he enjoyed most of his success, also winning international honours. His most famous moment came in the 1981 FA Cup Final for Manchester City against Tottenham Hotspur, when he scored for both sides! He later appeared for Burnley, after a spell in Hong Kong, Swansea City and then ended his playing days in non-League football in Wales. When he retired – at the age of 43 – he had made over 1,000 appearances.

Hutchison was inducted into Blackpool's 'Hall of Fame' as one of the club's most popular players. He currently works as a football development officer with Bristol City.

Glyn James

Centre Half: 440 + 6 appearances, 25 goals.
Wales 9 appearances, 0 goals
Born: 17 December 1941, Llangollen.
Career: Blackpool (1959–74).

Glyn James served Blackpool as a centre-half and captain, played for 15 seasons and made over 400 appearances in a one-club career. A strong, tall player, he made his debut at Preston North End in October 1960, standing in for the injured Roy Gatrix, whose monopoly of the number-five shirt meant that the youngster had to wait nearly four years to succeed him.

James was never spectacular, but his height proved invaluable at the heart of the defence. With the hard John McPhee alongside him, they made a fearsome duo,

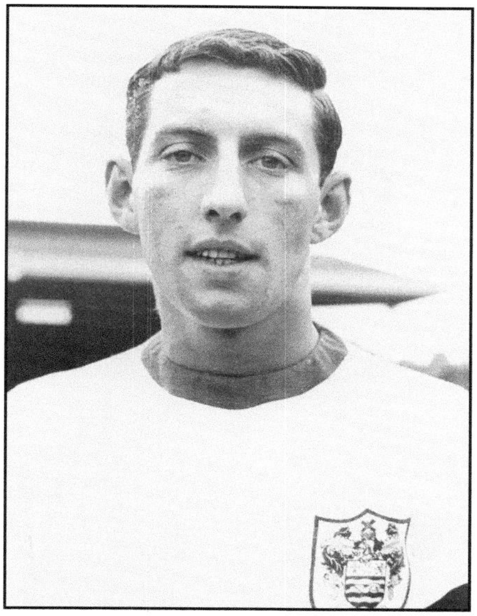

although James preferred the more cultured approach. His leadership qualities earned him Welsh caps, but his greatest moment came in the 1972 Anglo-Italian Cup Final against AS Roma when he held the defence together as the Italians threatened to overwhelm Blackpool. Although they lost, it made up for James's disappointment 12 months previously when he was forced to miss the Bologna Final due to injury.

At the start of 1971–72, Bob Stoke tried him at centre-forward and James managed to score six goals in his first five games, but after the arrival of Keith Dyson he reverted to his former role. Towards the end of his career, the club arranged for a testimonial game to be played in his honour, in which thousands of Blackpool fans turned up at Bloomfield Road. He is a member of the 'Hall of Fame', and following his retirement he set up his own business in the town, where he still lives today.

Harry Johnston

Defender: 438 appearances, 14 goals.
England 10 appearances, 0 goals

Born: 26 September 1919, Manchester
Died: 12 October 1973
Career: Blackpool (1934–55).

Between 1937 and 1955 Harry Johnston was 'Mr Blackpool', for during that time he made over 400 appearances and captained the club in three FA Cup Finals. He started his career at Droylsden Athletic but, despite being in the shadow of Maine Road, he was a fanatical Manchester United supporter. It was Blackpool, though, who signed him when he was 15 as a member of the ground-staff, and three years later he made his debut at Deepdale.

He was one of the youngest players to appear for Blackpool, but by the following season he was a regular in the first team. During his career he appeared in all three half-back positions and even moved up to centre-forward when circumstances demanded. After the war, during which he served in the Middle-East, he became the rock with which the successful Blackpool team was built, and as captain he led them to FA Cup Final appearances in 1948 and 1951, and of course victory in 1953.

Although a hard tackler, he was also a perfect gentleman, and it was often said that if Johnston, Matthews and Mortensen were playing, then the away attendance would normally be doubled. In 1950–51 he was voted Footballer of the Year and so confirming his popularity all over the country. Johnston was inevitably the subject of several big bids from other clubs, but he always remained a one-club player. He played his last game for Blackpool on 25th April 1955 at Newcastle United, and later that year became manager of Reading.

Harry Johnston was always a Blackpool man, so it was no surprise to see him back at Bloomfield Road seven years later as chief scout and assistant manager to Stan Mortensen. His international career was all too short, at least as far as caps were concerned. He gained only 10 in a seven-year period, although had it not been for the consistent Billy Wright he would have appeared many more times.

Harry Johnston played for Blackpool more times than any other player until Jimmy Armfield broke his record. He was an essential part of the great team of the 1950s and commanding leadership was the inspiration to those around him. When one talks of great players of the post war era, the names of Matthews, Mortensen and Johnston are synonymous. When he died, at the age of only 54, the whole town mourned, for Harry Johnston was truly one of the greatest players ever to wear the tangerine shirt. He is, of course, a member of the 'Hall of Fame'.

Herbert Jones

Defender: 105 appearances, 0 goals.
England 6 appearances, 0 goals
Born: 3 September 1896, Blackpool
Died: 11 September 1973
Career: South Shore, Blackpool (1922–25), Blackburn Rovers, Brighton.

Herbert 'Taffy' Jones became an integral part of the Blackpool defence in the 1920s, and later gained full international honours while playing for Blackburn Rovers. He started his playing career at South Shore and Fleetwood before joining Blackpool in 1922, making his debut for the club on 16th December against Hull City.

A hard full-back, he made a formidable partnership with Leaver and their ability at the back helped Blackpool's 'goals against' column look so impressive. He made only 100 appearances for the Seasiders before being lured away by the mighty Blackburn Rovers for a then huge fee of £3,850, one of the largest paid for a full-back at the time. While at Ewood Park, Jones made appearances for England and played over 200 times for Rovers. Later he was transferred to Brighton before ending his career at Fleetwood, whom he led to a Lancashire Junior Cup Final at the age of 40.

He continued to follow the fortunes of Blackpool and lived on the Fylde Coast until his death in 1973. He was never regarded as a star at Bloomfield Road, more of a solid and reliable player, but then all good teams are built on those attributes.

Jimmy Jones

Defender: 116 appearances, 0 goals
Born: 9 July 1889, Newburn-on-Tyne.
Career: Gateshead, Blackpool (1912–20), Bolton Wanderers, New Brighton.

Jimmy Jones was a sharp tackling full-back who joined Blackpool from Gateshead in June 1912. Although relatively small for a defender, he had tremendous pace and a cannon-like shot. He made his debut in September 1912, in a home win over Fulham, and proceeded to take over the left-back position vacated by Charlie Gladwin. From that moment he was almost ever present in a team that was constantly changing, and he kept his place throughout the next few years, which included the first two seasons of wartime football.

Jones was reliable if unspectacular, aggressive but fair. He was popular with the Blackpool supporters, and they were

sad when he left for Bolton Wanderers in March 1920 for £1,000. His position had come under pressure from the talented Horace Fairhurst, and as he was no longer regarded as the first choice he decided to move. After 70 appearances for Bolton, he joined New Brighton of the Lancashire Combination in August 1922 and the following season became their first captain in the Football League. Jones retired in the close season of 1927, after 141 games for the Rakers and returned to Blackpool as a publican.

Sammy Jones

Defender: 170 appearances, 6 goals.
Ireland 4 appearances, 1 goal
Born: 11 June 1911, Lurgan, Ireland
Died: 1993
Career: Distillery, Blackpool (1933–39).

During the early part of the 1933–34 season, manager Alex McFarlane was looking to boost his side's already flagging promotion hopes. He looked for players to strengthen the squad and found two in Ireland – Peter Doherty and Sammy Jones. Jones was playing for Distillery and needed no persuading to cross the water and play in English League football. A few weeks later, Doherty also joined Blackpool and the two of them became firm friends, sharing digs near Bloomfield Road.

Jones was a stylish but tough-tackling half-back who played 170 games for Blackpool. He was, like his friend Doherty, a complete fitness fanatic and would spend hours in extra training. Due to his upbringing he never drank or smoked, believing both to be hazardous to his health at a time when neither activity was particularly frowned upon by sportsmen.

He played alongside a number of centre-halves, but his partnership with Louis Cardwell was especially successful, particularly in 1936–37 when Blackpool

regained First Division status. He made is debut in October 1933 in the goalless draw with Oldham Athletic, and continued playing right through to the war. He also played in the team that lifted the War Cup in 1943.

He could often be seen marshalling his players and urging them to even greater efforts. He only played for his country four times and scored on his debut, but always believed he had not received the recognition he deserved. A good solid, no frills type of player who for 10 years was one of the mainstays of the Blackpool team.

Hugh Kelly

Defender: 468 appearances, 9 goals.
Scotland 1 appearance, 0 goals
Born: 23 July 1923, Valleyfield
Died: 28 March 2009, Lytham St Annes
Career: Blackpool (1943–60).

Hugh Kelly joined Blackpool for a £10 signing on fee from Scottish junior club Jeanfield Swifts in 1943 and went on to make nearly 470 appearances for the club. Kelly, who was born in Scotland, was a sturdy wing-half and a superb passer of the ball. He guested for several clubs during the war, notably East Fife before making his League debut for Blackpool in September 1946 in the home victory over Aston Villa, although he had appeared in the previous season's marathon FA Cup tie against Middlesbrough.

It took some time for him to become established, but by 1948–49 the half-back line of Johnston-Hayward-Kelly was becoming admired and respected. Kelly played in the 1948 and 1951 FA Cup Finals, but an ankle injury saw him miss the 1953 Final, although the club asked the FA to produce a special winners' medal for his nomination as '12th man'. In 1955 he took over from Harry Johnston as captain and helped Blackpool to finish in their highest-ever League position of second to Manchester United.

Kelly won one Scottish cap, in the 6–0 victory over the USA in 1952, but sadly was not called again. In 1960–61, unable to command a first-team place any more, he was given a free transfer and non-League Ashton United snapped him up as player-manager. He later returned to Bloomfield Road as part of the back room staff, and was also a businessman in the town as a grocer and ice cream merchant.

He was often called 'Mr Loyal' by supporters, and no football club could have wished for a better servant. He died in 2009 after contracting pneumonia following a short illness.

Joe Lane

Forward: 99 appearances, 67 goals.
Born: 11 July 1892, Hereford.
Died: February 1959, Abbots Langley.
Career: Watford, Sunderland, Blackpool (1913–20), Birmingham City, Millwall.

Joe Lane was Blackpool's first prolific goalscorer, and in the season immediately after World War One he helped the Seasiders to their highest-ever finish to that point. He joined Watford as an amateur in 1906 and then played in

Hungary before signing for Sunderland in 1912. A year later he moved to Blackpool for £400, and went straight into the first team as centre-forward, where he struck a rich partnership with inside-right Charlton.

Lane scored on his debut against Leeds City and went on to net a further 10 that season, helping Blackpool progress up the table after a shaky start. It soon became obvious that the club had unearthed a talent of some considerable skill, who also had a knack of scoring regularly. The following year his goals helped Blackpool to a respectable mid-table position and the club managed to hold on to him despite strong interest elsewhere.

During the war, Lane served in Egypt with the Herefordshire Yeomanry, and then in the first post war season he helped Blackpool up to second, their highest since joining the Football League. In March 1920 the board finally bowed to increasing financial pressure and sold him for a club record £3,300 to Birmingham City. The move caused uproar among Blackpool supporters and the season subsequently collapsed with promotion missed and a fourth place finish. The directors though had no choice, attendances were poor and the club was financially embarrassed.

At Birmingham, Lane scored 26 goals in 67 games to help the Blues gain First Division status. He later played for Millwall, coached Barcelona and was still scoring goals for Watford Printing FC when he was 43. He died in 1959 at the age of just 66. The first of the club's great goalscorers down the years.

Leslie Lea

Midfielder: 177 + 2 appearances, 16 goals
Born: 5 October 1942, Manchester
Career: Blackpool (1960–67), Cardiff City, Barnsley.

Leslie Lea was another player heralded as Stanley Matthews's replacement. Sadly he never realised his earlier potential and had his best days after he left Bloomfield Road. A nippy outside-right, he joined Blackpool from a Manchester junior club and made his debut in August 1960 in the opening game of the season against Leicester City. Ron Suart's idea was that Lea would compliment Matthews on the right, but he only played a handful of games that season, and the combination of niggling injuries and the form of Mandy Hill kept him out of the first team for some time.

That both Hill and Lea were described in the press as the natural successors to Matthews is interesting, as sadly neither lived up to the billing. Lea's breakthrough came in 1962–63 when he teamed up with Pat Quinn, but then the emergence of Alan Ball restricted his appearances. Lea was a talented player with fluent ball control, an accurate cross and he enjoyed running at an opponent.

In November 1967, Stan Mortensen, mindful of new signing Alan Skirton, transferred Lea to Cardiff City for £20,000. While at Ninian Park he became a huge fans' favourite before ending his career with over 200 games for Barnsley. A player that is again fondly remembered, but like Mandy Hill, a talent that was never fully realised.

Jimmy McIntosh

Forward: 87 appearances, 27 goals
Born: 5 April 1918, Dumfries
Died: 2000
Career: Droylsden, Blackpool (1935–37 and 1946–48), Preston North End, Everton, Distillery.

Jimmy McIntosh could be described as one of Blackpool's unluckiest players. During the 1947–48 FA Cup campaign, he scored five goals to help the club reach Wembley, and so it was a crushing blow hen he was told by manager Joe Smith that due to injury and a recent loss of form he would not be playing against Manchester United. Blackpool lost the Cup, and a week later McIntosh was recalled for the final match of the season. In a re-arranged game at Preston North End, he tore the home defence apart and scored five in a 7–0 rout. The great Jimmy Hampson is the only other Blackpool player to have scored five goals for the club, and the victory still stands out as Blackpool's biggest away victory – and at Preston too!

McIntosh was discovered at non-League Droylsden, playing alongside Harry Johnston. A fast, strong and well-built player, he was ideally suited to step into Hampson's shoes, yet his appearances were few. He made his debut in September 1935 in a defeat at Swansea City, and played only three more times that season. Two years, and one appearance later, he was part of the deal that brought Frank O'Donnell from Preston, with Dickie Watmough joining McIntosh on his way to Deepdale.

Immediately after the war, McIntosh rejoined Blackpool and struck a partnership with Stan Mortensen. In 1947–48 he scored 13 goals in 35 games plus those five FA Cup goals. A year after his Wembley disappointment, with the arrival of namesake Willy McIntosh – also from Preston – he moved to Everton for a nominal fee.

In later years he managed a number of Irish clubs, plus Greenock Morton in Scotland.

John McPhee

Defender: 281 + 10 appearances, 18 goals
Born: 21 November 1937, Motherwell
Career: Motherwell, Blackpool (1962–70), Barnsley, Southport.

John 'Chopper' McPhee was one of football's hard men. He joined Blackpool from his home town club Motherwell – where he was one of Bobby Ansell's 'babes' – in July 1962 for a bargain £10,000.Hard tackling and fully committed, he was also versatile and during his eight years with Blackpool he played in virtually every position except goal.

He made his League debut in September 1962, at inside-right in a draw

with Aston Villa, but soon reverted to half-back, swapping roles with Bobby Crawford. His place came under threat a couple of years later when Graham Rowe joined the club, but McPhee's all-round ability won the day. In 1965 and 1968 he was voted the club's Player of the Year.

He earned his 'chopper' reputation because of his crunching tackles and there were not many forwards who relished going into battle with the Scotsman, yet he rarely found himself in trouble with referees. In July 1969 McPhee was initially blamed for the injury that virtually crippled the brilliant Tony Green, but it was soon established by Green that his tendon had snapped as he ran past McPhee in a pre-season friendly. McPhee's popularity survived and his passion and enthusiasm went a long way to helping the team gain promotion the following season.

In June 1970 he moved to Barnsley and ended his career at Southport. He returned to the town as a businessman and is now owner of the Hotel Sheraton on the promenade.

Craig Madden

Striker: 85 + 22 appearances, 27 goals
Born: 25 September 1958, Manchester
Career: Bury, West Bromwich Albion, Blackpool (1986–90), Wrexham, York City, Fleetwood Town.

Craig Madden was one of the lower divisions' most prolific scorers in the early 1980s. At 5'8" he was small for a striker, but deceptively quick, especially around the penalty area, with superb ball control. He started his professional career with Bury in March 1978, joining from Northern Nomads. For the Gigg Lane club, Madden re-wrote the record books, scoring 129 goals in 296 League appearances, including 35 in 1981–82.

His prowess was eventually recognised by a bigger club, and West Bromwich Albion signed him in March 1986 for £50,000. The move did not work out, though, and after just 12 appearances, where he scored three times, he moved to Blackpool in February 1987 for the same fee of £50,000. He made his debut in a

heavy defeat at Wigan Athletic, scoring the Seasiders' only goal. From then he was almost ever present, working well alongside Keith Walwyn and Tony Cunningham.

In 1987–88 Madden was the club's third highest scorer, but he started to suffer niggling injuries, and each time he dropped out of the team he found it increasingly difficult to re-establish himself. Midway through the disastrous 1989–90 season, manager Jimmy Mullen allowed him to leave the club and join non-League neighbours Fleetwood Town after loan periods with Wrexham and York City. There he regained his scoring touch and continued to enjoy his football. He also kept his connection with Blackpool, becoming community officer at Bloomfield Road. He is now assistant manager at Fleetwood Town, alongside Micky Mellon.

Stanley Matthews

Midfielder: 440 appearances, 18 goals. England 54 appearances, 11 goals

Born: 1 February 1915, Hanley
Died: 23 February 2000
Career: Stoke City, Blackpool (1947–61).

Stanley Matthews is regarded as one of the greatest players the game has seen, and for most of his career Matthews and Blackpool were inextricably linked, the two enjoying more success than any other time. He was the man who played League football longer than any other, 33 years, and the man who had the longest England international career.

The son of boxer Jack Matthews, the 'Fighting Barber of Hanley' as he was billed, Matthews senior was a fitness fanatic, and Matthews junior inherited his father's dedication, although young Stan preferred football and joined Stoke City as an amateur in September 1930. Within two years he had signed professional terms and in 1933 helped Stoke City to the Second Division title. In September 1934 he marked his England debut with a goal against Wales.

Throughout his long career, he was famous for his elusiveness, and there was no faster player over 20 yards. He had superb balance, his slightly hunched figure over the ball almost inviting opponents to tackle him. They could try, but Matthews more often than not left them on their backsides after a body swerve and pushing the ball the other way. If he was tackled unfairly, he would never retaliate, but just got up and continued to humble opponents in the only way he knew.

In 1934, after an England game against Italy, a journalist said that he lacked the 'big game temperament', but Matthews continued to play for his country well past his 42nd birthday. The first time he played for Blackpool was during World War Two. He was in the RAF and was stationed in the town and willingly accepted Colonel William Parkinson's invitation to guest for the club. His first match was in a defeat at Preston North End in August 1941, but he went on to star in a Blackpool team that excelled in wartime football.

In the 1943 War Cup challenge match against Arsenal at Stamford Bridge, he virtually destroyed the Gunners' defence single handedly. Matthews signed officially for Blackpool on 10 May 1947 for a fee of £11,500 when he was at the age of 32. Some suggested that his best years were behind him, but Stoke fans turned up at a public meeting in their thousands in an attempt to persuade him to stay in the Potteries.

The next six years saw Matthews play in three FA Cup Finals and win many more international caps. The greatest moment of his career came on 2 May 1953, when he engineered an incredible Blackpool fightback as the team came from 3–1 down to beat Bolton Wanderers 4–3 in the dying seconds of the FA Cup Final at Wembley. That game will always be remembered as the 'Matthews Final' despite Stan Mortensen's hat-trick and Ernie Taylor's great display.

Blackpool were a tremendous draw wherever they went, and if Matthews was playing then one could almost guarantee the highest gate of the season for their opponents. In the 1957 New Year's honours list he was awarded the CBE and eight years later became football's first knight. He was Footballer of the Year in 1948 and again in 1963, while playing for Stoke City at the age of 48. His international career spanned 22 years, and while playing for Blackpool he made 36 England appearances, the last coming against Denmark in 1957.

He returned to Stoke City in 1961 and continued playing for another four years, helping them regain First Division status and significantly help to improve their attendances. He appeared as fit as ever, and when he finally retired at the age of 50 all the great stars of the day turned up in his testimonial game at Stoke. He later managed Port Vale and coached around the world, notably Malta and Canada before returning to live in his beloved Potteries.

When the first edition of this book was published, Sir Stan appeared as a guest at Bloomfield Road at an official book signing. Despite being asked the same question time and again from older star-struck supporters, he answered every one with grace and friendliness. He was a true gentleman as well as a great footballer, and the like that Blackpool Football Club will not see again. He is of course in the Blackpool Hall of Fame. He died in 2000.

Georgie Mee

Outside-left: 230 appearances, 21 goals
Born: 12 April 1900, Bulwell
Died: July 1978, Poulton-le-Fylde
Career: Notts County, Blackpool (1920–26), Derby County, Burnley, Mansfield Town, Rochdale.

Between December 1920 and September 1925 Georgie Mee created a club record by appearing in 195 consecutive League matches for Blackpool. Mee signed from Notts County in July 1920 and made his debut on 18 September that year in the 2–0 victory at Coventry City when he replaced Donachie at outside-left and made the position his own.

Mee was small, well built and incredibly fast. His bursts down the wing were legendary, and his ability to cross the ball accurately helped Harry Bedford to score many of his goals. Mee was not a great scorer himself, preferring to make them (or assist as modern football parlance dictates), but in March 1922 he scored one of the greatest goals ever seen at Bloomfield Road, hitting the ball home from fully 40 yards in the win over Nottingham Forest.

He was an essential part of the forward line that included Bedford, Barrass, Charles and the man with whom he worked especially well on the left, Heathcote. Despite being Blackpool's top scorer, Bedford was criticised for being 'too lazy' off the ball and too slow to react to

crosses. Of course it was Mee who made up for Bedford's weaknesses with his remarkable speed and accurate centres.

In February 1926 Mee joined Derby County for £3,750 along with Jimmy Gill. He helped Derby into Division One that season and to the First Division runners'-up spot in 1929–30 before moving to Burnley in September 1932. He later played for Mansfield Town, Accrington Stanley (two spells), Great Harwood and Rochdale before retiring and managing a pub in Blackpool. His brother, Bertie, managed Arsenal's double-winning side of 1970–71. George Mee died in Poulton in 1978 and is another member of the 'Hall of Fame'.

Micky Mellon

Midfielder: 125 appearances, 14 goals
Born: 18 March 1972, Paisley
Career: Bristol City, West Bromwich Albion, Blackpool (1994–97), Tranmere Rovers, Burnley, Kidderminster Harriers, Witton Albion, Lancaster City.

Micky Mellon, a tall and combative midfielder started his career at Bristol City, and was part of the side that gained promotion to the First Division in 1989–90. He spent four years at Ashton Gate before a £75,000 transfer to West Bromwich Albion. Again he helped the club to promotion, but in 1994 new Blackpool manager Sam Allardyce brought him to Bloomfield Road for £50,000. It was there that he shone, and his contribution to two promotion-challenging seasons was immense.

In the 1995–96 season he was voted Player of the Year by Blackpool supporters, and so it was hugely disappointing that, following Allardyce's sacking after the disastrous promotion failure that season, Mellon was sold to Tranmere Rovers for £300,000. He then went on to play for the Wirral club on three separate occasions,

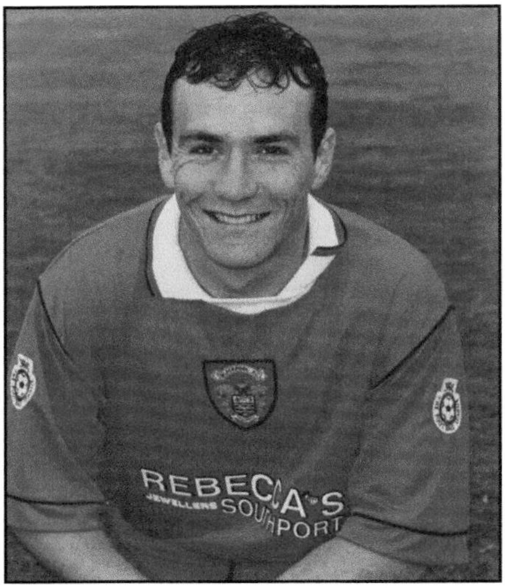

interspersed by a £350,000 move to Burnley, where he helped them gain promotion to the Championship.

In later years, he played in lower League and non-League football, before taking on the coaching role at Lancaster City. He then joined non-League Fleetwood Town, where he has enjoyed tremendous success, getting them promoted to the Conference. In fact, he was tipped as the next Blackpool manager after the departure of temporary boss Tony Parkes in 2009, but eventually the role fell to Ian Holloway.

Mellon was hugely popular with the fans, and is still remembered fondly for his style of play, but sadly the era in which he played in a tangerine shirt is regarded as a huge failure under Sam Allardyce.

Colin Methven

Centre-half: 194 + eight appearances, 13 goals
Born: 10 December 1955, India
Career: East Fife, Wigan Athletic, Blackpool (1986–90), Carlisle United, Walsall, Barrow.

By the time Colin Methven came to Bloomfield Road in July 1986, he had already made over 500 League appearances with his two previous clubs, East Fife and Wigan Athletic. Although born in India, Methven was a true Scot with an unrivalled passion for football. He moved to Wigan in October 1979 and was club captain at Springfield Park when Blackpool signed him for £20,000. He made his debut at centre-half in a home draw with Chesterfield, replacing Nicky Law, and was a virtual ever present for the next four seasons.

Methven was strong, skilful and had tremendous leadership qualities. His contribution in the heart of the defence was outstanding, his age not slowing his drive or enthusiasm. He was also a footballing centre-half who enjoyed going into the box for corners. He played right through to the end of 1989–90, being voted as the club's Player of the Year for two consecutive seasons by the supporters. They in turn were angry when he was sold to Walsall in November 1990 after an earlier loan spell with Carlisle United. Graham Carr, in his brief time as manager, declared that Methven was 'neither fast enough nor good enough for Fourth

Division football'. Methven had the last laugh, though, as in the last game of the season he played in the Walsall side that beat Blackpool 2–0 and so deny the Seasiders automatic promotion. Methven ended his career at non-League Barrow. He was later voted by Wigan fans as the 'Best Football League Player of all time'.

Gordon Milne

Defender: 66 + 7 appearances, 5 goals. England 14 appearances, 0 goals
Born: 29 March 1937, Preston
Career: Morecambe, Preston North End, Liverpool, Blackpool (1967–70), Wigan Athletic.

Gordon Milne's best playing days were behind him when he came to Bloomfield Road in May 1967, but his strong defensive work proved invaluable in the club's first season back in Division Two. Milne played for Preston Amateurs, Morecambe and Preston North End before joining Liverpool for £16,000 in August 1960.

At Anfield he enjoyed his greatest successes. A strong, constructive wing-half, he was capped 14 times by England and was included in the 1966 World Cup squad. Although he missed the 1965 FA Cup Final against Leeds United due to injury, he played in two League Championship sides, a Second Division title side and a European Cup-Winners' Cup Final before joining Blackpool for £30,000.

He made his debut in the opening match of the 1967–68 season at his old club Preston – a 2–0 win – and he immediately worked a partnership with Glyn James and John McPhee. Blackpool missed promotion back to Division One on the final day of the campaign, although by then John Craven had taken over Milne's role at half-back. The next season saw injury and loss of form severely curtail his appearances and towards the end of the

season manager Stan Mortensen tried, unsuccessfully, in the forward line.

In January 1970 new manager Les Shannon let Milne go to Wigan Athletic as player-manager, and he later held managerial posts at Coventry City, Leicester City, the English youth team and with Besiktas of Turkey.

Ian Moir

Winger: 66 appearances, 14 goals
Born: 30 June 1943, Aberdeen
Career: Manchester United, Blackpool (1964–67), Chester City, Wrexham, Shrewsbury Town.

Joining Blackpool in February 1965 from Manchester United, for whom he made 45 League appearances, Ian Moir was immediately thrown into the first team in a desperate effort to stave off relegation. An exciting winger, Moir made his debut on the left in the drawn game with Leicester City on 13 February and thereafter alternated between the left and right flanks.

He found himself competing with

Leslie Lea, a player who had wrongly been heralded as the replacement for Stanley Matthews, but when he did play Moir forged a rewarding partnership with Alan Ball. Many of the brilliant midfielder's goals were the result of Moir's work, and supporters were puzzled that he never enjoyed greater success in his career. He had excellent ball skills and could beat his man with ease, although he was sometimes accused of being 'greedy'.

At the end of the 1966–67 relegation season, Stan Mortensen began his rebuilding process and sold Moir to Chester City for just over £10,000. He moved to Wrexham in January 1968 for a similar fee, and helped them to promotion from Division Four in 1970 before being surprisingly released to Shrewsbury Town in March 1972. Sixteen months later he returned to Wrexham for a short spell and then played in South Africa.

Steve Morgan

Defensive midfielder: 164 + 7 appearances, 12 goals

Born: 19 September 1968, Oldham

Career: Blackpool (1985–90), Plymouth Argyle, Coventry City, Bristol Rovers, Wigan Athletic, Bury, Burnley, Hull City, Halifax Town.

Steve Morgan was an excellent product of Blackpool's youth policy in the 1980s and was capped at an early age by England's Under-21s. He made his first-team debut in April 1986 in an away defeat to Bristol Rovers. A strong, well-built player, he was comfortable as either a defensive or midfield position and spent much of his earliest career deep in defence alongside Dave Burgess and Mike Davies.

Fast and skilful, he possessed an accurate cross, often after an overlapping sprint down the left wing. Morgan was virtually ever present throughout his first three seasons, although his popularity waned after supporters questioned his attitude. Indeed, his style often gave the impression that he was too relaxed, and with Blackpool struggling in the Third Division, he was often made a scapegoat by fans. Toward the end of the 1988–89 season, Wimbledon reportedly offered around £300,000 for him. Cash-starved Blackpool could have used the money, but Morgan could not agree personal terms. A year later, in July 1990, he joined Plymouth

Argyle for less than one third of that amount. He spent some time at Home Park and then became a player who hardly settled at one club. Spells at Coventry City, Bristol Rovers, Wigan Athletic, Bury, Burnley, Hull City and Halifax Town all followed.

He was an excellent player, but one who saw his best days once he had left Bloomfield Road.

Colin Morris

Midfielder: 100 appearances, 32 goals
Born: 22 August 1953, Blyth
Career: Burnley, Southend United, Blackpool (1980–82), Sheffield United, Scarborough.

Colin Morris arrived at Bloomfield Road in January 1980 in the £125,000 part-exchange deal that took old favourite Derek Spence to Southend United. Morris made his debut that month in a home defeat by Oxford United, and immediately proved that he was worth every penny of the fee. Fast and strong, he started in midfield, supplying the front men of Fletcher and Bamber, but soon to be just as adept at scoring goals. The following season he was top scorer with 12 League goals in a relegation year, and manager Alan Ball praised him as the side spiralled towards Division Four.

His commitment to a lost cause was remarkable as no other player scored more than five goals in a disastrous campaign. With the club in the basement division, and Ball departed, it became only a matter of time before Morris was snapped up by a top side. In February 1982, Blackpool accepted a fee of £100,000 from Sheffield United, a figure that represented the amount the taxman had demanded be paid within seven days, but a sum nowhere near representing the worth of the player.

He went on to make 240 League

appearances for the Blades, scoring 68 goals and ended his career with non-League Scarborough.

Andy Morrison

Defender: 53 appearances, 4 goals
Born: 30 July 1970, Inverness
Career: Plymouth Argyle, Blackburn Rovers, Blackpool (1994–96 and 2000), Huddersfield Town, Manchester City, Crystal Palace, Sheffield United.

Although Andy Morrison only played two seasons for Blackpool and made just over 50 appearances, he is a justifiable member of Blackpool's 'Hall of Fame' due to his immense contribution to the Sam Allardyce era.

He started his career at Plymouth Argyle, where he made over 100 starts, and then was transferred to Kenny Dalglish's Blackburn Rovers. Sadly for the player, he failed to break through to the first team when they were at their peak in the Premier League. That led to Sam Allardyce buying him for a then club-record fee of

£245,000 in December 1994, making his debut a few days later in the 3–1 victory over Bournemouth.

A hard-tackling defender, who could play in midfield, he became the lynch pin that the Blackpool side depended on during the failed promotion bids under Allardyce. He quickly became a fans' favourite due to his full-blooded commitment and his never-say-die attitude. Unfortunately, following the departure of Allardyce, he was sold to Huddersfield Town for £500,000. It was good business for the club, but a confirmation that the team that had failed to make it under 'Big Sam' was now being dismantled by new manager Nigel Worthington.

After Huddersfield, Morrison ended up at Manchester City, where he was hugely successful. He led them to promotion as captain in the Division Two Play-off Final against Gillingham at Wembley. In fact, he was so popular at Maine Road that City fans have voted him as their third-best captain in history. He was close to achieving a Scotland call up by coach Craig Brown in 2000, but a serious injury frustrated him. There then followed a period of 18 months trying to get back into the City side, and he even requested a loan move back to Blackpool in 2000 to keep up his fitness.

Sadly, his career declined, and a number of loan moves to Crystal Palace and Sheffield United and a trial with Bury resulted in yet more injuries and eventually his retirement from the game as a player. His career was clouded with many disciplinary problems on the field too, meaning he was regularly out of the first team with suspension, and off the field he also had his problems. He was found guilty of fraud in 2006, and while assistant manager of Worcester City – to former Blackpool teammate Andy Preece – he was sacked after a dressing room incident.

Morrison was recently appointed as the new coach of Seychelles on a two-year contract. Despite his brief stay at Bloomfield Road, he is a player who every fan has good memories of.

Stan Mortensen

Striker: 354 appearances, 222 goals. England 25 appearances, 23 goals
Born: 26 May 1921, South Shields
Died: 2 May 1991
Career: Blackpool (1938–55), Hull City, Southport, Bath City, Leicester City.

Stan Mortensen is one name who can truly live up to the often over-used term of 'great' footballer. One of the fastest, most powerful forwards in the game, Mortensen scored over 200 goals for Blackpool, including his famous hat-trick in the 1953 FA Cup Final, and he managed virtually a goal per game when wearing an England shirt.

He was playing local football in South Shields when Blackpool signed him in May 1938 to begin an association that was to last for virtually the rest of his life. At first he showed little promise, and after 12 months the club were close to terminating his contract. Then, after individual training sessions with Georgie Mee and Bobby Finan, Mortensen found new pace and gradually became the player that was admired so widely. Fast, determined and skilful, he worked his way through the reserve team before war interrupted his progress and he found himself playing in a makeshift Blackpool team and also guesting for other clubs, notably Bath City.

Mortensen made his League debut on 31 August 1946, scoring the opening goal in a victory over Huddersfield Town, and going on to net 29 that season to become Blackpool's top scorer. The following season, as the team began to make a serious impact, his 31 goals again put him top of the list, including a hat-trick in the

FA Cup semi-final at Villa Park and a goal in the Final at Wembley against Manchester United. At this time he had been joined by Stanley Matthews. It was Matthews for centres and Mortensen for goals every weekend as far as the fans were concerned. Blackpool were now a powerful force, and 'Morty's' goals helped them maintain their challenge.

He was top scorer right through to 1955, but his greatest moment came in 1953, when he scored the famous hat-trick that helped Blackpool win the FA Cup Final against Bolton Wanderers. His last-minute equaliser is now legendary – a 25-yard free-kick straight past the defensive wall and into the goal, despite Ernie Taylor's insistence that there was 'no gap'.

His international career started in the war when he made a guest appearance for Wales after Ivor Powell went off injured and the Blackpool man generously stepped in. He made his England debut in May 1947, scoring four goals against Portugal, and went on to score 23 times in 25 games. In late 1955 he was transferred to Hull City, yet chose to continue training at Bloomfield Road. Later, he played for Southport, Bath City again and Leicester City, but he was always lured back to his first love, Blackpool. He of course returned as manager, and after just missing out on promotion in 1967–68 he was sacked a year or so later after a regrettable and unexplainable decision by the board. He then became a successful local businessman and a town councillor.

He was a brilliant player, had a lethal shot, incredible speed, a remarkable body swerve and also a torpedo-like header. He was also truly a Blackpool man, loved and admired by everyone in the town. Interestingly, the month of May was always significant to Mortensen. He was born in May, signed professional terms in May, made his international debut in May, scored his famous Cup Final hat-trick in May and, finally, in May 1991 he died. The whole town mourned his passing, and it was particularly ironic that he passed away on the day that his beloved club had reached Wembley – in the Fourth Division Play-off Final – for the first time since 1953. He will never be forgotten and is inevitably a member of Blackpool's 'Hall of Fame'.

Henry Mowbray

Defender: 100 + 4 appearances, 1 goal
Born: 1 May 1947, Hamilton
Career: Cowdenbeath, Blackpool (1967–71), Bolton Wanderers, St Mirren.

Three weeks before the great Tony Green was signed for Blackpool by Stan Mortensen, Henry Mowbray was acquired from Scottish club Cowdenbeath. Mortensen had gone to watch Mowbray, signed him and then noticed Green. The rest is history.

Mowbray was a young full-back with tremendous determination and a lot of skill. He could run with the ball and had a perfectly timed tackle. He was the ideal replacement for Tommy Thompson, who had given such sterling service. He was signed on his 20th birthday, and in August 1967 he made his debut in a draw with Ipswich Town. He fitted in perfectly with Jimmy Armfield for the next couple of years. He was then hampered by injury and found himself battling to regain his place from Bill Bentley. It was a difficult dilemma for Mortensen, and later Les Shannon – the culture of Mowbray or the aggression of Bentley? Sadly for Mowbray, he often lost out, and in April 1971 he played his last match for Blackpool. New manager Bob Stokoe sold him to Bolton Wanderers, where he made 31 appearances before joining Scottish club St Mirren. He then went to Australia and had spells playing for a couple of clubs before retiring from football.

Jackie Mudie

Centre-forward: 356 appearances, 155 goals. Scotland 17 appearances, 9 goals
Born: 10 April 1930, Dundee
Died: 2 March 1992, Stoke-on-Trent
Career: Blackpool (1947–61), Stoke City, Port Vale.

Jackie Mudie started his football career with the amateur Scottish club Lochee Harp, before becoming a full time professional in June 1947. On his League debut, at Liverpool in March 1950, he scored the only goal. A year later, after being second highest scorer to Mortensen, Mudie played in the FA Cup Final against Newcastle United, but after the game, Blackpool signed Ernie Taylor and Mudie lost his place. Eventually he worked his way back and scored the last minute winner in the 1953 FA Cup semi-final against Tottenham Hotspur. He then went on to win a Cup-winners' medal.

In 1955 Mudie took over from the departed Mortensen, at centre-forward, scoring 22 goals in the first season and 32 the next – still a top tier record for a Blackpool player. He made 17 appearances for Scotland, scoring nine goals including a hat-trick against Spain that secured Scotland's World Cup Finals place.

In March 1961 he was sold to Stoke City for £8,500 and scored on his debut after only five minutes. He was small for a centre-forward – 5ft 6in – yet many of his goals were headers, and he played in every forward position except outside-left for Blackpool.

He later joined Stoke's rivals Port Vale and eventually became joint manager with Stanley Matthews, but it was not successful. He then spent time in America and South Africa in coaching roles. He died in 1992 after a short illness.

John Murphy

Striker: 229 appearances, 83 goals
Born: 18 October 1976, Whiston
Career: Chester City, Blackpool (1999–2006), Macclesfield Town.

John Murphy was a hugely popular centre-forward who played for Blackpool at the beginning of the century and contributed massively to the start of the success that the club has enjoyed.

He started his career at Chester City, where for four years from 1995 he made over 100 appearances and scored effectively once every four games. It was this strike rate that first caught the eye of Blackpool manager Nigel Worthington. A big, burly player, the old-fashioned type of centre-forward, he blossomed once Steve McMahon took over the reins. Combining with the likes of Brett Ormerod and Paul Simpson, Murphy became prolific scoring 83 times in six years. His highest point was at the Millennium Stadium in the Football League Trophy Finals against Cambridge United in 2002 and Southend United in 2004 where he scored in 4–1 and 2–0 wins respectively. He also played in the Third Division Play-off Final against Leyton Orient in 2000, where Blackpool were promoted after a 4–2 victory. Also his hat-trick against Luton Town at Kenilworth

Road on a cold February evening in 2003 will always be remembered.

After McMahon's departure, Colin Hendry and then Simon Grayson continued to use his services, but in 2007, after a loan spell, he was allowed to join Macclesfield Town. Blackpool were aiming for promotion to the Championship, and Murphy was now surplus to requirements. He played at the Moss Rose side for six months before rejoining Chester City.

He was a popular player at Bloomfield Road and one that is remembered well by all Blackpool fans.

Graham Oates

Midfielder: 127 + 3 appearances 28 goals
Born: 4 December 1943, Scunthorpe
Career: Blackpool (1961–68), Grimsby Town, Wigan Athletic.

Graham Oates signed as an apprentice for Blackpool in May 1961. He had been approached by the club earlier, but they were fined for 'poaching' him. Oates, a nippy winger able to dribble with the ball and a regular goalscorer, was seen as one

for the future for a team that was changing rapidly in a vain attempt to halt the slide from the glory days.

After making his debut in September 1961, in a home defeat by Nottingham Forest, he played in a handful of games over the next year or so as veterans Bill Perry and Ray Parry continued their good form. Eventually Oates broke through, and for the next four seasons he was a regular on the left wing, scoring eight goals in his first 12 games before playing a supporting role to Charnley's goalscoring talents.

Injury then kept Oates's appearances down, and with competition from Des Horne he found it difficult to break back into the side. In 1968–69 manager Stan Mortensen was in the process of rebuilding the side, and Oates was one of the players who no longer figured in his plans. In October 1968 he was sold to Grimsby Town for £10,000. He stayed there for three years before joining non-League Wigan Athletic.

A player who is still remembered by Blackpool supporters, he was one of the unsung heroes of the 1960s at Bloomfield Road.

Jack O'Donnell

Defender: 59 appearances, 0 goals
Born: 25 March 1897, Gateshead
Died: 1952
Career: Darlington, Everton, Blackpool (1930–32), Hartlepools United, Wigan Athletic.

Jack O'Donnell joined Blackpool in June 1930 and made his debut on 20 December in the home game against Grimsby Town. For the next two seasons he became a mainstay for the defence as Blackpool tried desperately to preserve their recently won First Division status.

He started his career, like so many others from the North East, by playing for his local colliery team, in his case Felling.

Darlington soon signed him, and he earned a reputation as a hard-tackling full-back, the kind who could ruin a top striker's game by close marking and ruthless tackling. Everton paid around £3,000 for his services soon afterwards, showing how highly he was rated, particularly as that kind of fee was rare for a defender.

Unfortunately for O'Donnell, the move did not work out, and in the autumn of 1930 Blackpool bought him for a similar price. Almost immediately he struck a partnership with the captain Walter Grant. Sadly, it was a torrid time for the defenders as those first few years of higher League football they conceded 231 goals in just two seasons. The team was woefully out of its depth, and the defenders took the majority of the criticism. O'Donnell also had a serious disciplinary problem, and it was reported on three occasions that the club had suspended him for various matters. Eventually it was agreed to end his contract by mutual consent, and O'Donnell played out his career in the lower Leagues.

O'Donnell was a fine player, but the belief was that Blackpool never really saw him at his best.

Eamon O'Keefe

Forward: 38 appearances, 23 goals.
Republic of Ireland 5 appearances, 1 goal
Born: 3 October 1953, Manchester
Career: Plymouth Argyle, Hyde United, Mossley, Everton, Wigan Athletic, Port Vale, Blackpool (1985–86), Chester City.

Eamon O'Keefe was a free-scoring centre-forward who began in non-League football before joining Plymouth Argyle in February 1974. He failed to make the grade at Home Park and returned to non-League with Hyde United a year later. There then followed a spell in Saudi Arabia before his 29 goals helped Mossley win the Northern Premier League title. This earned him England semi-professional honours, something which caused trouble a year later when he attempted to make his Republic of Ireland debut against Wales, although he went on to win five caps for Eire.

Everton had signed him in July 1979, and he played in 40 League games before

joining Wigan Athletic (25 goals in 58 games) and then Port Vale (17 goals in 59 games). Blackpool manager Sam Ellis paid £17,500 for him in March 1985, and he made a scoring debut in a home win over Peterborough United. He helped the club gain promotion to Division Three and the following season saw him at his best with 17 goals in 22 matches.

Sadly, injury now bothered him and after making only two appearances in 1986–87, he retired. That summer, 5,000 fans saw Blackpool meet League champions Everton in his benefit game at Bloomfield Road. O'Keefe scored for Blackpool that night, and two years later he made a comeback, returning with his new club Chester City to score a last-minute equaliser to deny Blackpool two points in their battle against relegation.

He only featured in three more games for Chester before drifting out of the game. He is a member of the 'Hall of Fame' at Bloomfield Road.

Brett Ormerod

Striker: 167+50 appearances, 71 goals
Born: 18 October 1976, Blackburn
Career: Accrington Stanley, Blackpool (1997–2001 and 2009–present day), Southampton, Leeds United, Wigan Athletic, Preston North End, Nottingham Forest, Oldham Athletic.

Brett Ormerod is one of Blackpool's favourite current players, who started his successful career at Bloomfield Road and seems to be ending it in a more successful fashion at his 'spiritual' home. He started his career at his home-town club but failed to make the grade and ended up with non-League Accrington Stanley. There he supplemented his income by working in a cotton mill, but he had already started to attract attention. A fast and pacy front man, he was adept at scoring goals, getting 32 for Stanley in two seasons. Gordon Strachan had noticed his ability and promised he would sign him when he returned to football management. As it was, Nigel Worthington paid £50,000 for him, and he made his Blackpool debut on 21 March 1997 in a draw at Chesterfield. From then on, he became a regular first-team player.

His four years at Bloomfield Road had its highs and lows. The high definitely was scoring the final goal in the 4–2 Play-off Final victory over Leyton Orient at the Millennium Stadium in 2001 and so gaining promotion for Blackpool, but the low was certainly breaking his leg in October 1999 and so missing out the entire season. He was a favourite with the fans, especially after his winning goal at Deepdale in the last few minutes in a famous derby day victory over Preston North End, but inevitably he was now attracting attention from bigger clubs.

In December 2001, despite repeated rejections and the promise from Chairman Karl Oyston that he would be staying at Blackpool, he signed for Southampton for £1.75 million, a then club-record fee for a player signed from Blackpool. He went on to stay at the South Coast club – under Gordon Strachan initially – for five years and appeared in the 2003 FA Cup Final defeat to Arsenal.

Soon his appearances were becoming limited, and he found himself sent out on

loan to Leeds United and Wigan Athletic. In 2006 he joined arch rivals Preston North End on a free transfer and stayed at Deepdale for two seasons, making over 60 appearances, but also found himself sent out on loan to Nottngham Forest and Oldham Athletic, but in January 2009 he returned to Blackpool on a free transfer. He was signed by caretaker manager Tony Parkes, and at first there was a great deal of scepticism from the supporters who questioned his pace. It turned out that he had not lost his knack of scoring goals and got his 100th against Norwich City two months later.

The following season he was instrumental in helping to secure Blackpool's place in the Premier League and scored what turned out to be the winner against Cardiff City at Wembley in the 3–2 Play-off Final victory.

Ormerod is unique in that he played for the club, actually ended up at Preston and returned to Blackpool and still seen as a folk hero by the fans. In 2001 he scored the goal that confirmed Blackpool's promotion from League Two. Nine years later he scored the winner that confirmed Blackpool's promotion to the top tier. He is a true club legend.

It was fitting that in the Premier League, Ormerod scored against Tottenham Hotspur and so became the only Blackpool player to score in all four divisions.

Keigan Parker

Striker: 141 appearances, 34 goals
Born: 8 June 1982, Livingston
Career: St Johnstone, Blackpool (2004–08), Huddersfield Town, Hartlepool United, Oldham Athletic, Bury, Mansfield Town.

Keigan Parker's Blackpool career was as spectacular as it was unpredictable. Signed by Colin Hendry on a free transfer from St Johnstone in 2004, the nimble forward made his debut in the 2–0 opening day defeat at Doncaster Rovers, and gradually worked his way into the team as a regular choice. The first two seasons were always difficult as Hendry struggled to mould a successful unit in League One, but a second half hat-trick against Torquay United at Bloomfield Road showed what the player was capable of.

It was after Simon Grayson took over as manager that Parker really started to shine, and his superb second goal in the League One Play-off Final against Yeovil Town at Wembley in 2007 was the highlight of his career. At that point it seemed his future was secure. Sadly for the player, his time at Blackpool started to unravel. Off-the-field problems led to a loss of form, and he struggled to regain his place in a team that was now playing at Championship level, and after only making 17 appearances that season, and also turning down a move to Barnsley, he left the club and joined Huddersfield Town.

There his career seemed to follow a sad pattern. Early promise and then a loss of form. He only scored twice for them before going on loan to Hartlepool United and then a permanent move to Oldham Athletic. Again, in just under a year, he scored twice and was the victim of financial cuts at the club, and after a loan to Bury, he found himself at non-League Mansfield Town.

There is no doubt that Parker is a talented footballer, but his temperament let him down at Bloomfield Road when he should have gone on to greater things. Sadly, it seems his potential may never be truly realised.

Jack Parkinson

Forward: 375 appearances, 53 goals
Born: 1869, Blackpool
Died: 20 December 1911, Blackpool
Career: Blackpool (1896–99 and 1900–10), Liverpool, Barrow.

Jack Parkinson was top scorer in Blackpool's first-ever League season and went on to make over 360 appearances for them. He devoted nearly his whole career to his home-town club, playing at centre-forward or middle right. Later he was the perfect foil for prolific scorers like Jack Cox and Bob Birkett, and then later moved to midfield and centre-half, as the selection committee felt that the modern game was becoming too fast for the veteran centre-forward.

He became a celebrity around Blackpool, and when the team returned from their victorious Cup tie with Sheffield United it was Parkinson who was lifted shoulder high by his adoring fans. In 1899–1900, after Blackpool failed to gain re-election, he played one game for Liverpool in a Merseyside derby with Everton at Anfield but returned a year later when Blackpool were back in the League. From then on he was virtually ever present until his free transfer to Barrow in 1910.

In April 1905, after 10 years service, he was given a benefit match against Liverpool. Afterwards he was presented with a gold watch by the directors. He then became a superintendent at Cocker Street baths and lost his life in a tragic accident. He was attempting to rescue a colleague from a tank of boiling sea water when a plank on which he was standing snapped and Parkinson also fell in. He died shortly afterwards. He is also a member of Blackpool's 'Hall of Fame'.

Bill Perry

Midfielder: 436 appearances, 129 goals. England 3 appearances, 2 goals
Born: 10 September 1930, Johannesburg
Died: 27 September 2007
Career: Blackpool (1949–62), Southport, Hereford United.

Bill Perry was the most successful of the South African players who joined Blackpool after the war. He was recommended by Billy Butler, manager of Perry's team, Johannesburg Rangers. A year

earlier in 1948, Perry had turned down a move to Charlton Athletic, but now lured by a big club, he moved to England.

He made his League debut in March 1950, in a win at Manchester United, and for the next few years virtually made the outside-left position his own. He was fast, had an accurate centre and after he teamed up with Allan Brown during the team's most successful seasons, those two figured prominently.

Perry was never a prolific scorer, but in 1955–56 he netted 20 goals to help Blackpool to their highest-ever League position. His goal deep into injury time in the 1953 FA Cup Final, when he pounced on a Matthews cross, gave Blackpool their famous FA Cup success.

Due to his father's birthplace, he was able to play for England and won three caps, scoring twice in a 4–1 victory over Spain. In 1960 a cartilage operation virtually brought his career to an end, and after struggling to regain his position he was transfer listed in the summer of 1962. Southport bought him for around £3,500 and he stayed at Haig Avenue for a year before joining Hereford United.

After a spell in Australia, he returned to Blackpool where he became a director of Fleetwood Town and then a local businessman. He died in 2007.

A player of such immense stature has inevitably been inducted into Blackpool's 'Hall of Fame'.

Fred Pickering

Forward: 57 appearances, 25 goals. England 3 appearances, 5 goals
Born: 19 January 1941, Blackburn
Career: Blackburn Rovers, Everton, Birmingham City, Blackpool (1969–71), Brighton and Hove Albion.

Although Fred Pickering was at Blackpool for only two seasons, he played an important role in the club at the turn of the 1970s. He began his career with his home-town club Blackburn Rovers and stayed for five years when he scored 59 goals. He joined Everton for £85,000 in March 1964 and at that time became an England international, scoring a hat-trick on his debut against the USA. Surprisingly he was only selected once more for his country.

In 1967, after 56 goals in 97 starts for Everton, he moved to Birmingham City where he continued to score on a regular basis. It was that goalscoring prowess that persuaded Blackpool manager Les Shannon to pay £45,000 for him in 1969.

A big, powerful centre-forward, and with the decline of Tom White, he was seen as an ideal replacement as Blackpool made a push for promotion back to the First Division. He made his debut with Mickey Burns in August 1969 in a home win over Portsmouth, and went on to become topscorer that season. Three of his goals came at the famous promotion decider at Deepdale when Blackpool won 3–0, gaining First Division status and in turn

consigning their bitter rivals to the Third Division. It made him hugely popular with the fans.

Back in Division One, he only played in a handful of games, and the controversial match with Chelsea will always be remembered. Blackpool were cruising against the high flyers from West London. They had taken a 3–0 lead, with two from Pickering, when with 15 minutes to go and the lead still at 3–1, Les Shannon substituted him. There were howls of derision from the crowd and somehow Blackpool lost 4–3, a last-minute goal causing heartbreak. Shannon resigned two days later.

When Bob Stokoe took over, he sold Pickering back to Blackburn for £10,000. It did not work out, and after a disagreement with the manager Ken Furphy, he ended his playing career with Brighton and Hove Albion.

Andy Preece

Striker: 129 appearances, 35 goals
Born: 27 March 1967, Evesham
Career: Northampton Town, Wrexham, Stockport County, Crystal Palace, Blackpool (1995–98), Bury, Carlisle United.

Andy Preece was a part of the Sam Allardyce side that included the likes of Tony Ellis, James Quinn and Andy Morrison, and will always be thought of fondly by fans, despite the ultimate failings of the team at that time.

A strong and tall forward, he started his career in non-League before being snapped up by Wrexham. A year later he joined Stockport County for £10,000 and impressed enough to be signed by Crystal Palace three years later for £350,000. He had scored in a giant-killing FA Cup victory at Queen's Park Rangers and managed 42 goals in just under 100 appearances for County.

At Palace he was less than successful, and in June 1995 he was signed by Allardyce for £200,000, where he immediately formed a partnership with Tony Ellis. They looked to be irresistible at times, and their scoring exploits guaranteed that Blackpool, would be pushing for promotion, but sadly the capitulation toward the end of the season ended any such hopes and effectively brought about the end of what should have been a 'golden era' for Blackpool. Allardyce was sacked and Preece continued under new boss Gary Megson.

The team struggled and Preece became disillusioned and in July 1998 he joined Bury on a free transfer. It was a sad ending to his time at Bloomfield Road and, after a falling out with manager Nigel Worthington, he refused to play in the final match at Chesterfield, so denying the fans a chance to say goodbye to one of their favourites.

He spent some time at Bury and Carlisle United before entering management, as player-manager at Bury and then non-League football. Preece was hugely popular with the Blackpool supporters.

James Quinn

Striker: 151 appearances, 36 goals. Northern Ireland 50 appearances, 4 goals
Born: 15 December 1974, Coventry
Career: Birmingham City, Blackpool (1993–98), Stockport County, West Bromwich Albion, Notts County, Bristol Rovers, Willem 11, Sheffield Wednesday, Peterborough United, Bristol City, Northampton Town, Scunthorpe United.

James Quinn was a tall and imposing centre-forward who played alongside Tony Ellis and Andy Preece during the mid-1990s, but after his move from Blackpool seemed to lose his direction.

He joined Blackpool from Birmingham City in 1993 for £25,000 and stayed for nearly five years. At first it did not look like he would make the grade, and he was loaned out to Stockport County, but under Billy Ayre, and then especially Sam Allardyce, he blossomed and scored some important goals. Against Bristol City in the opening fixture of the 1995–96 season, he scored within 11 seconds, and his two goals in the two League Cup legs against Chelsea in 1996 gave the high flyers some nervous moments as Blackpool nearly caused an upset.

Quinn was part of the expensively arrayed team that pushed for promotion under Allardyce in 1995–96, but its failure led to the departure of the manager and the gradual breakup of the side. At this time, Quinn had gained international honours with Northern Ireland, and over an 11 year period he played 50 times for his country.

He left Blackpool in 1998 for West Bromwich Albion for £500,000 – a fee that the club found impossible to turn down. It was not a success as he found goals harder to come by at a higher level, and he was loaned out numerous times before trying his hand in Dutch football. He spent three years in Holland, but missed the UK and so returned in 2005. After that he moved from one club to another, but in 2007 he announced that he was retiring from football. He is now a coach in Jersey.

Graham Rowe

Defender: 112 + four appearances, 14 goals
Born: 28 August 1945, Southport
Career: Blackpool (1963–71), Tranmere Rovers, Bolton Wanderers.

At 6ft 2in, Graham Rowe was the perfect size for a centre-half, and indeed at his former club Southport, he mostly played in that position. At Blackpool, though, he became a utility player moving from wing-half to centre-half and also on occasion at centre-forward.

He joined Blackpool in the early part of 1961, signing professional forms in July 1963 and making his debut in February the following year against Wolves, although it took some time for him to break into the first team regularly as John McPhee was in such good form. Rowe was heavily built, and his weight often contributed to the heavy tackles that he so enjoyed, although like McPhee, he was never a dirty player.

He came into his own while partnering Glyn James and McPhee in the half-back

line, yet on the occasions he was asked to perform in attack he always coped admirably. In November 1968, while playing at centre-forward, he scored a hat-trick in the 6–0 demolition of Bury. A solid and reliable player, he never enjoyed popular status, yet was always appreciated by the fans. In November 1970, he moved to Tranmere Rovers on loan, and ended his career with Bolton Wanderers, for whom he signed at the end of Blackpool's disastrous 1970–71 campaign

Eddie Shimwell

Defender: 324 appearances, 7 goals.
England 1 appearance, 0 goals
Born: 27 February 1920, Birchover
Died: October 1988
Career: Sheffield United, Blackpool (1946–57), Oldham Athletic, Burton Albion, Matlock Town.

When Sheffield United refused Eddie Shimwell permission to run a pub, Blackpool jumped in to sign the unsettled defender for £7,000 in December 1946. It was to be a shrewd purchase as Shimwell went on to play in all three FA Cup Finals for the Seasiders.

A tough-tackling full-back, good in the air and possessing a powerful clearance ball, he played for the Blades throughout the war before Blackpool signed him. His debut was delayed when the train from his Chesterfield home was snow bound, and he did not arrive at The Valley until half-time. Instead, he opened his Blackpool account four days later on Christmas Day against Blackburn Rovers, replacing Eric Sibley. From that moment he made the position his own, teaming up in later years with Tommy Garrett, when their contrasting styles were most effective. Garrett was the polished defender, Shimwell preferring the sliding tackle and the shoulder charge.

He scored two important FA Cup goals for Blackpool. The first against Chester City in January 1948 saw him lob the ball home from fully 60 yards, the following wind and a frozen pitch seeing it bounce over the 'keeper's head. Later that year he became the first full-back to score in a Wembley Cup Final when his 14th-minute penalty gave Blackpool the lead against Manchester United.

A dislocated shoulder brought about a premature end to his Blackpool days, although for some time he played for the

reserves, still travelling from his Chesterfield home for games. In May 1957 he was given a free transfer to Oldham Athletic, and he later played non-League football for Burton Albion and Matlock Town.

After his career ended, where he played once for England in 1949 against Sweden, he retired and ran a pub in Derbyshire.

Alan Skirton

Midfielder: 86 + 1 appearances, 28 goals
Born: 23 January 1939, Bath
Career: Bath City, Arsenal, Blackpool (1966–68), Bristol City, Torquay United.

At nearly 6ft, Alan Skirton did not look like a typical outside-right, yet he had great speed, marvellous ball skills, an accurate cross and a fierce shot. His size and weight deterred defenders from tackling him.

He joined Arsenal from Bath City for £5,000 in January 1959 and scored 53 goals in 145 League games for the Gunners before being transferred to Blackpool in September 1966 for £65,000, although had the club listened to Stan Mortensen, then they could have had him for a lot less. Mortensen, a former Bath player himself, had earlier recommended Skirton to the Seasiders.

He scored on his debut – at Highbury of all places – and the next season saw the club back in Division Two with Skirton their second highest scorer. That made him popular with the fans, and he was also a good influence in the dressing room. In November 1968 however, Mortensen, seeing the emergence of Ronnie Brown on the wing, allowed Skirton to return to the West Country and he joined Bristol City for £15,000. It was a shame for the Bloomfield Road faithful as Skirton had brought enjoyment to their football and had become something of a folk hero.

He later played for Torquay United, in South Africa for Durban City, for Weymouth and held commercial posts at the same club plus Bath City and Yeovil Town.

Bill Slater

Defender: 35 appearances, 12 goals. England 12 appearances, 0 goals
Born: 29 April 1927, Clitheroe
Career: Blackpool (1949–51), Brentford, Wolverhampton Wanderers.

Bill Slater, or W.J. Slater as he was known in his Blackpool days, holds two interesting records. He is the last amateur to have appeared in an FA Cup Final at Wembley, for Blackpool in 1951, and he scored Blackpool's quickest ever goal up to that point – 11 seconds in December 1949 against Stoke City.

He joined Blackpool as a schoolboy just after the war and made his debut in September 1949 in a goalless draw at Aston Villa. As a nippy inside-forward, he found himself competing with Allan Brown for the number-10 position for most of his time at the club. In the Cup Final against Newcastle United he partnered South African Bill Perry, but unable to guarantee

a first-team place he joined Brentford in December 1951. He then moved to Wolves in August the following year, finally becoming a part-time professional.

With Wolves he switched to half-back and was capped 12 times at full level by England, being voted Footballer of the Year in 1960, when he led Wolves to victory in the FA Cup Final against Blackburn Rovers. He also won three Championship medals with the Molineux club. In July 1963 he returned to Brentford after 339 appearances for Wolves, and then later played for the Northern Nomads. Slater held several posts in physical education and in 1982 was awarded an OBE for his services to sport. His daughter, Barbara, was chosen as the first female Director of Sport for the BBC in 2009.

Derek Spence

Forward: 95 + 3 appearances, 24 goals.
Northern Ireland 29 appearances, 3 goals
Born: 18 January 1952, Belfast
Career: Crusaders, Oldham Athletic, Bury, Blackpool (1976–78 and 1978–80), Olympiakos, Southend United, Sparta Rotterdam, Hong Kong Rangers.

The tall, lanky striker was most unfortunate in his career at Bloomfield Road. The former Oldham Athletic forward was signed by Allan Brown from Bury at the beginning of the 1976–77 season, and he made his debut against Nottingham Forest that October. He complimented the twin striking powers of Mickey Walsh and another new signing, Bob Hatton, although at the end of the season he found his position under pressure from Stan McEwan.

A serious injury then kept him out for the whole of the next campaign, significantly the season that saw the club relegated to Division Three for the first time in their history. His international career was also on hold after he had made six appearances for Northern Ireland, all of them as substitute.

He then went to Greece and joined Olympiakos, scoring six goals in 21 appearances, before rejoining Blackpool for £27,000. He teamed up with Tony

Kellow, a signing from Exeter City, and they made a formidable pair, scoring 27 goals between them, and nearly half of the team's total with Spence top scorer on 16.

He returned to the international scene and went on to win 29 caps, scoring three goals. Blackpool, though, were struggling, and there were constant team changes, with Spence's place coming under pressure from Gary Jones. During 1979–80, he sustained an injury serious enough to force his premature retirement from the game. He did, however, continue to play for Southend United for two years, helping them to the Fourth Division title in 1981.

Following his playing career, he ran his own business in Bury before returning to Bloomfield Road as the club's Football in the Community officer.

Paul Stewart

Forward: 205 + 13 appearances, 61 goals.
England 3 appearances, 0 goals
Born: 7 October 1964, Manchester
Career: Blackpool (1981–87), Manchester City, Tottenham Hotspur, Liverpool, Crystal Palace, Wolverhampton Wanderers, Burnley, Sunderland, Stoke City, Workington.

In 1986–87, Paul Stewart joined the ranks of the prolific centre-forwards that Blackpool have produced, when he scored 21 goals before being sold to Manchester City for £250,000, then a Blackpool record. He was brought to Bloomfield Road by Allan Brown and made his debut as substitute for Dave Bamber in a home draw with Rochdale in February 1982. For the rest of the season, he alternated between midfield and the forward line, and it was not until the arrival of Sam Ellis as manager that Stewart found his true role – that of centre-forward. Ellis can take credit for making Stewart the player he became, even though it took some time for his

goalscoring prowess to be found. He was at first the provider for Deary and O'Keefe, but in his final season he scored those 21 goals and helped Mark Taylor bag 14.

In March 1987, hard up Blackpool were forced to sell him, and as he had always supported Manchester City as a boy it was natural he would move to Maine Road. Within two years he had been sold for £1.7 million to Tottenham Hotspur (a proportion going to Blackpool), where he found a new role in midfield. It was also at this time that he gained international honours for England under Bobby Robson and then Graham Taylor.

He returned to Bloomfield Road with Spurs in the FA Cup in 1991 and scored the only goal in the third round game. He was welcomed back by the fans who bore him no malice. A year later he was transferred to Liverpool for £2.3 million as a replacement for the departed Dean Saunders. His time at Anfield was not successful, and after numerous loan moves he eventually found himself at Sunderland in 1996. He helped them to promotion to the Premier League before a move to Stoke City and ending his playing career at non-League Workington.

Always a popular player at Bloomfield Road, he is another inducted into the 'Hall of Fame'.

Harry Stirzaker

Defender: 154 appearances, 13 goals
Born: 1869, Fleetwood
Died: Blackpool (1894–1903)
Career: Blackpool (1894–1903).

Signed from Fleetwood Rangers in 1894, Harry Stirzaker played in Blackpool's very first League game against Lincoln City in September 1896, and became a regular first teamer for the next five seasons.

A well-built player, he started his career at centre-half, but also appeared at the heart of the defence, and occasionally as an attacker. One of those times he scored a remarkable goal against Burslem Port Vale. It came midway through the first half, when after receiving a pass from Bob Birkett he cannoned the ball toward goal from fully 30 yards. It was hit with such ferocity that it rebounded off one post against the goalkeeper's head, and then against the opposite post before rolling over the line. While Sturzaker and his team mates celebrated, the poor 'keeper was being stretchered off unconscious, unaware of what had happened.

Stirzaker was rewarded for his commitment with the captaincy for the 1901–02 season, and that commitment was amply displayed in the opening game when he volunteered to stand in goal after regular 'keeper Joe Dorrington was injured and there was no replacement. Blackpool lost that day, but Stirzaker performed brilliantly and conceded only two goals.

Along with two other imports from Fleetwood Rangers, Birkett and Jack Scott, he was the mainstay of Blackpool's fledgling Football League team in the early part of the last century.

Ron Suart

Defender: 112 appearances, 0 goals
Born: 1920, Barrow in Furness
Career: Blackpool (1938–49), Blackburn Rovers.

Ron Suart was the first Blackpool player to return to manage the club. He joined the Seasiders from Netherfield in the summer of 1938 and spent his first season playing in the reserves. Then, just as it seemed he was ready to break into first-team football, war intervened.

He was a strong full-back with a reputation as a hard but fair defender, and Blackpool were grooming him for the future. He started his career in junior sides in his hometown of Barrow before moving to Netherfield, where he had attracted the attentions of many top clubs. Suart established himself in Blackpool's first team during the war, first at centre-half where he played alongside

the likes of George Farrow and Harry Johnston.

He made his League debut on 31 August 1946 in the victory at Huddersfield Town, and eventually moved to full-back. In 1948, Suart suffered the same fate as Jimmy McIntosh when, after playing in all of the knock out stages of the FA Cup, he was forced to miss the Final with Manchester United with a foot injury. Many fans felt that one of the reasons for defeat that day was the defensive frailties that had shown themselves without the sturdy Suart.

In 1949 he was granted a transfer as he was now unable to command a first-team place, and so Blackburn Rovers secured his services for £12,000, where he was to spend six seasons. He later went into management, including Blackpool, as described elsewhere in the book.

Peter Suddaby

Defender: 370 + 1 appearances, 10 goals
Born: 23 December 1947, Stockport
Career: Wycombe Wanderers, Blackpool (1970–80), Brighton and Hove Albion, Wimbledon.

Peter Suddaby was a great servant of Blackpool during the 1970s. He graduated as a teacher and was playing for non-League Skelmersdale United when he was spotted by Blackpool, whom he joined in May 1970. He made his debut under Bob Stokoe the following February in a defeat at Coventry City, playing in a back four before taking over as centre-half to team up superbly with Glyn James. He continued at number five for the rest of his career, replacing the experienced Dave Hatton, who moved to full-back.

Suddaby was strong in the air, possessed a biting tackle and was an excellent leader. He also enjoyed going forward for corners, although goalscoring

was not one of his greatest talents. He played for Blackpool right through to the midway point of the 1979–80 season, including of course the disastrous campaign that led to Third Division football for the first time. To his credit, he did not desert the sinking ship that was Blackpool as others had in those dark days, but was a true club man. Eventually, under Alan Ball, he moved on. His place was under increasing pressure with the arrival of record signing Jack Ashurst from Sunderland, and so he felt it was time to forge a new career elsewhere. He joined Brighton & Hove Albion and then moved to Wimbledon.

After a spell at Wycombe Wanderers, he became manager, but it was unsuccessful and he left after less than a year. He now teaches maths at a school in Chalfont St Giles.

Alan Suddick

Midfielder: 341 + 7 appearances, 76 goals
Born: 2 May 1944, Chester le Street
Died: 16 March 2009

Career: Newcastle United, Blackpool (1966–76), Stoke City, Southport, Bury, Barrow, Lancaster City.

On 22 October 1966, Blackpool beat Newcastle United 6–0 at Bloomfield Road. Playing for the Magpies was inside-forward Alan Suddick, and so impressed were Blackpool of his commitment that two months later they paid a club record fee of £66,000 for him.

Suddick was an outstanding talent. He had a wealth of skills, including superb passing ability and a famous 'banana' shot – well before the likes of David Beckham – and became one of Blackpool's most popular players.

He made his debut on Boxing Day, in a home defeat to West Ham United and was virtually ever present thereafter, teaming up with Tommy Hutchison on the left or deep in midfield. In the 1971 Anglo-Italian Cup Final against Bologna, he quite simply took the opposition apart. Three of the best goals ever seen at Bloomfield Road were from Suddick. Against Verona in the aforementioned tournament, where he kept the ball airborne for an age before crashing it into the net, against Arsenal in an FA Cup replay and against Oxford United with one of his familiar 'bending' free-kicks. It was after that goal that television picked up on his remarkable skill and tried to analyse how a player could bend the ball round a defensive wall. Suddick was the first.

In 1968–69, he was top scorer with 12 goals, most of them spectacular. He missed most of 1970–71 with a leg injury, and then again in 1974–75 with a similar problem. For all of his talent though, his erratic form could infuriate – like all footballing geniuses – and that probably contributed to his lack of international appearances. He played at Under-21 level for England twice, but he scored an own-goal in one of them.

His talent and potential was never truly realised and, like many stars, his temper sometimes got the better of him. Toward the end of his career at Blackpool, he created an unofficial 'keepy-up' record, completing three laps of the ground in 20 minutes without letting the ball touch the ground.

In 1976, he was transferred to Stoke City for £12,000, a pitiful fee for such a talent. His career hit a downward slide with few appearances, and then spells at Southport, Bury and more non-League football with Barrow and Lancaster City.

After his playing career ended, he stayed in the town and went to Bloomfield Road regularly, but sadly in 2008 he was diagnosed with cancer. He died the following March.

Suddick was a true hero at Blackpool, one of the most talented players ever to wear the tangerine shirt, and if he had played today would have been one of the best paid players in the country. He scored his 100th goal for Blackpool against Preston North End in a 3–0 victory, something which in itself would endear him to Blackpool fans for evermore. He is a member of the 'Hall of Fame' at Bloomfield

Road and regularly tops the fans' polls for best player. For the author, he was my all-time favourite, and when the first edition of this book was released in 1992 I was honoured to have him as a guest at a book signing. Sadly, it was a very wet Thursday evening, and hardly anyone turned out due to a lack of publicity, but it was three of the best hours I have ever experienced. A true gentleman, a true football great and sadly missed. The greatest in my eyes.

Alan Taylor

Goalkeeper: 106 appearances, 0 goals
Born: 17 May 1953, Cleveleys
Career: Blackpool (1963–71), Oldham Athletic, Stockport County, Southport.

Goalkeeper Alan Taylor was unfortunate to be at Bloomfield Road under the shadow of two other excellent 'keepers in Tony Waiters and Harry Thompson. Taylor, an acrobatic 'keeper with a superb temperament, signed for the Seasiders in October 1963 and spent most of his early days as an understudy for Waiters.

He made his first-team debut in 1966, when Waiters was injured, but despite keeping a clean sheet in the two games he played he had to wait nearly a year before being selected again. This time he played three times, but was denied again by the brilliance of Waiters. His breakthrough came after Waiters retired, and his first full season was one of near promotion in which Taylor was outstanding.

He continued to be first choice for another 12 months until the arrival of Harry Thompson, and then it was back to the reserves. By 1971, John Burridge was beginning to make a name for himself, and manager Bob Stokoe decided that Taylor and another reserve 'keeper, Adam Blacklaw, could leave. Taylor, who had been on loan at Oldham Athletic and Stockport County, signed for Southport in July 1971, and ended his career after over 100 appearances for the Haig Avenue club.

Ernie Taylor

Forward: 242 appearances, 55 goals. England 1 appearance, 0 goals
Born: 2 September 1925, Sunderland
Died: 9 April 1985, Birkenhead
Career: Newcastle United, Blackpool (1951–58), Manchester United, Sunderland, Altrincham, Derry.

It is believed that after Blackpool's defeat to Newcastle United in the 1951 FA Cup Final, Stanley Matthews told manager Joe Smith that he would like the Magpies' inside-right in the team. It is unsure if that is true, but on 10 October that year, Ernie Taylor signed for Blackpool for £25,000 and went on to become one of the club's greatest-ever players.

He was a naval submariner when he joined Newcastle in 1942, and at only 5ft 4in, he was one of the smallest players in the game. His defence-splitting passes caused havoc among opponents, and it was his cheeky back heel that laid on the goal for Jackie Milburn in the '51 Final.

He made his debut for Blackpool three days after signing, and when Matthews recovered from injury, the pair created one of the most respected of right-wing partnerships. In the 1953 FA Cup Final, Taylor played brilliantly in one of the greatest comebacks of all time. That year England decided to use the Taylor-Matthews partnership, but it was in the 6–3 home defeat to Hungary, and Taylor, like others, was discarded from the international scene afterwards. He continued to dominate First Division defences, though.

In the FA Cup in January in 1956 he scored after only 13 seconds at Maine Road, but the match was later abandoned due to fog. Although not known for his goalscoring, the ones he did score were usually spectacular, notably the equaliser against Arsenal in the 1953 FA Cup sixth round. In 1958 he joined the devastated Manchester United club, still in mourning following the Munich Air Disaster, but soon afterwards he moved to Sunderland for £6,000.

He ended his career at Altrincham and Derry before emigrating to New Zealand where coached as well as played. He returned to England and died at his home of Birkenhead in 1985.

Mark Taylor

Forward: 121 + 16 appearances, 46 goals
Born: 20 November 1964, Hartlepool
Career: Hartlepool United, Crewe Alexandra, Blackpool (1986–92), Cardiff City, Wrexham.

Mark Taylor may have come to Blackpool on a free transfer from Hartlepool United, but he soon had fans thinking about the days when Tony Green showed his brilliance. Taylor joined his home-town club from junior football in January 1984 and stayed for two years before falling out with the management. After a month on loan with Crewe Alexandra, he arrived at Bloomfield Road in August 1986, and made his debut the following month in a draw at Doncaster Rovers.

Taylor was fast and tricky and could also score goals. He started on the wing before moving to a central role, backing up Paul Stewart, but still managing to score 14 times in his first full season. It was surprising that Hartlepool had allowed him to leave without demanding a fee, as in 1987–88, Taylor top scored with 21 goals and his partnership with the emerging Keith Walwyn proved effective.

Sadly, midway through the following season, Taylor suffered an injury that sidelined him for nearly two years. Eventually he fought his way back, but the long lay off had left him short of pace and the familiar light touch on the ball was missing. In March 1992, after a month's loan with Cardiff City, he was transferred to Wrexham for a small fee. It was a disappointing and sad end to a Blackpool career that promised so much, and only delivered a fraction. After his playing days ended, he took a degree in physiotherapy and returned to Bloomfield Road in that capacity. He has also worked at Blackburn Rovers, Bolton Wanderers, Newcastle United and Fulham.

Scott Taylor

Forward: 115 + 23 appearances, 61 goals
Born: 5 May 1976, Chertsey
Career: Staines Town, Millwall, Bolton Wanderers, Rotherham United, Blackpool (1998 and 2002–04), Tranmere Rovers, Stockport County, Plymouth Argyle, MK Dons, Brentford, Rochdale, Grays Athletic, Lewes.

Scott Taylor's time at Blackpool – briefly on loan in 1998 and then a two-year stint from 2002 – was hugely successful and constantly begs the question as to why the player did not go on to greater things once leaving Bloomfield Road.

A tall and rangy striker, he started his professional career at Millwall before being signed by Bolton Wanderers for £150,000 in 1996. He failed to break into the first team and was quickly sent out on loan to Rotherham United and Blackpool. In just 6 appearances in a tangerine shirt, he scored twice and was clearly a player needed at the struggling club. Sadly, Blackpool fans had to wait four years before his return.

He joined Tranmere Rovers in October 1998 for £350,000 and played well over 100 times for them, including the 2000 League Cup Final, before moving to Stockport County on a free transfer in July the following year. His spell was brief, and he rejoined Blackpool permanently in January 2002. It was in the next two year period that he enjoyed his best time in his career. He scored the last goal in the 4–1 victory over Cambridge United in the Football League Trophy at the Millennium Stadium, and eventually netted 61 times in 138 appearances.

In early 2004, under Colin Hendry, Taylor decided to leave the club. There had been suggestions of family problems for the player and the travelling involved, and so it was with surprise that he ended up in Devon, playing for Plymouth Argyle after a £100,000 move. He struggled to establish himself at Home Park and then joined MK Dons two years later, actually scoring for his new club against Blackpool in a League match.

He had a couple of years there, but failed to re-ignite his fire power and eventually drifted around a number of clubs, ending his career at non-League Staines Town – where he had started. His last moment of glory was scoring for them in a Play-off Final against Carshalton Athletic to gain promotion to the Conference South.

Since his retirement from football, he has become an electrician and is no longer involved in the game. A sad ending to a very promising career.

Harry Thomson

Goalkeeper: 68 appearances, 0 goals
Born: 25 August 1940, Edinburgh
Career: Burnley, Blackpool (1969–71), Barrow.

Between 1968 and 1972, Blackpool had some fine goalkeepers, and perhaps the most popular was Harry Thomson. He was bought from Burnley by manager Les Shannon in July 1969 and made his debut on the opening day of the following season against Portsmouth, immediately displacing Alan Taylor.

At 5ft 9in, Thomson was small for a goalkeeper, yet he was one of the most spectacular that Bloomfield Road had seen. He loved to play to the crowd and on more than one occasion was censured by the club for his on-field antics. Like most showmen, however, he was erratic and sometimes fell out with referees too. Once he had overcome his initial nervousness, he could be quite brilliant.

During the disastrous 1970–71 campaign, he sometimes kept Blackpool in the game single handed. When Bob Stokoe took over, Thomson had just been disciplined, but the new manager brought him back to the first team. It did not work, though, and after a poor performance against Ipswich Town when he let in a bad goal near the end, Stokoe terminated his contract and he ended his career with Barrow.

Thomson had started his career at Burnley, joining them in August 1959 from Bo'ness United, and spent nearly six years as understudy to Adam Blacklaw at Turf Moor. He eventually made around 150 appearances for the Clarets before the arrival of Peter Mellor. His most famous game for them was in the 1967 Fairs Cup, after which an Italian newspaper called him 'a god in a green jersey'.

Billy Tremeling

Forward/Defender: 119 appearances, 44 goals
Born: 9 May 1905, Newhall
Died: 1961
Career: Mansfield Town, Retford Town, Blackpool (1925–30), Preston North End.

Billy Tremeling started as a centre-forward, but after an inspired tactical move at the start of the 1927–28 season he became an attacking centre-half who helped Jimmy Hampson to a record number of goals. Tremeling joined Blackpool in the summer of 1924 and made his League debut in March the following year against

Manchester United, but made only one more appearance that season. He needed constant service from midfield men, and in the 1920s Blackpool had no one to supply it.

He continued to score for the reserves and his chance came again the following season after an injury to Sid Binks. Tremeling only managed three appearances before breaking a leg in the home win over Barnsley. It was not until well into the 1926–27 season that he regained his place, but he scored 31 goals in 27 League and Cup games, becoming the club's top scorer. He scored a hat-trick in the 6–0 thrashing of Clapton Orient and he looked to be an obvious successor to Harry Bedford.

Strangely the next season saw him start at centre-half, proving to be an inspired move by new manager Sydney Beaumont. He believed that Tremeling could service Jimmy Hampson and enable the centre-forward to be even more prolific in front of goal. The change worked, and over the next few seasons, Tremeling helped Hampson to be top scorer each time.

His career at Blackpool came to an end in December 1930 when he transferred to Preston North End for a nominal fee. He later captained Preston in an FA Cup Final, but later he joined the growing number of players who returned to Bloomfield Road in a coaching role. His brother, Dan, was a Birmingham City goalkeeper who played for England.

Bert Tulloch

Defender: 186 appearances, 0 goals
Born: 23 February 1889, Blaydon
Died: 15 February 1953, Blackpool
Career: Blackpool (1914–24).

Bert Tulloch was one of Blackpool's finest full-backs and for around 10 seasons either side of World War One he was the mainstay of the defence. Strong and

committed, his strong defensive tactics unnerved opponents to such an extent that subsequent raids on the Blackpool goal would invariably come down the opposite flank to where Tulloch was operating.

He joined Blackpool in the summer of 1914 and made his debut in a 2–1 home defeat to Leicester Fosse, immediately establishing a regular place. He was two footed, enabling him to appear on either wing, and quickly struck a partnership with Bert Jones. He was skilful and would often dribble the ball out of danger.

During his time at the club, Blackpool had some of their most successful seasons with four concerted pushes for promotion, and it was no coincidence that the 'goals against' column showed a marked improvement.

Some days after his playing days ended, he returned to Bloomfield Road as a trainer and masseur, joining a growing number of players lured back by the friendly atmosphere.

Tony Waiters

Goalkeeper: 286 appearances, 0 goals. England 5 appearances, 0 goals
Born: 1 February 1937, Southport
Career: Bishop Auckland, Macclesfield Town, Blackpool (1959–67), Burnley.

In a long line of splendid Blackpool 'keepers, Tony Waiters was probably one of the best. He won England amateur honours with Bishop Auckland and Macclesfield Town before signing for Blackpool in 1959, making his debut on Boxing Day against Blackburn Rovers. Waiters, who eventually displaced the great George Farm, was a fitness fanatic and was always practising taking high crosses and saving fierce shots. Lean and agile, tall and strong, he soon developed into one of the country's top goalkeepers and in 1964–65 won five England caps, taking the place of the great Gordon Banks.

Somehow he never achieved the greatness predicted for him, and many believed he gave up the game too quickly when he retired in May 1967 to become the FA's North West regional coach. Coaching and managerial posts followed with Liverpool, Burnley (for whom he made 38 League appearances), Plymouth Argyle, Vancouver Whitecaps, the Canadian Olympic team, Tranmere Rovers and Chelsea.

Waiters played for seven seasons at Bloomfield Road and was a firm favourite with the fans, yet he enjoyed none of the top club honours. Maybe it was this that persuaded him to retire early. He now works and lives as a football coach in North America.

Jock Wallace

Goalkeeper: 250 appearances, 0 goals
Born: 13 April 1911, Deantown
Died: 1978
Career: Raith Rovers, Blackpool (1934–48), Derby County, Leith Athletic.

Blackpool have had many excellent goalkeepers, and one of the best was Jock Wallace. He joined Blackpool from Raith Rovers in March 1934 and was on the Seasiders books for over 14 years. A giant of a man and amazingly agile, he was capable of making quite incredible last-ditch saves.

Wallace made his debut at Lincoln City in February 1934 and became an almost ever present. Sandy McFarlane, the man who signed him, described him as a 'natural talent in goal, and a man born to be a goalkeeper'. The following season he played in every game, but then a knee injury saw him challenged for his place by Andy Roxburgh, although Wallace was always first choice.

During the war he was stationed abroad for a spell, and his appearances were brief.

Off the field he was a joker and at times a controversial character. More than once he fell out with the board or management, and in one notorious occasion he refused to join the team to play Leeds United in the FA Cup. His argument was over contractual terms, and he eventually joined Derby County for a nominal fee of £500 in February 1948. Derby had a goalkeeping crisis, and the veteran Wallace, who was not Cup-tied, played for the Rams in the sixth round and semi-final. Ironically, Derby were knocked out, and it was Blackpool who went on to Wembley from the other semi-final. Many fans believed he should have been playing for Blackpool in that 1948 Cup Final.

His job done, he left Derby County for Leith Athletic in August 1948. He died in 1978.

His son, Jock junior, successfully managed Rangers, Leicester City and Motherwell, among others.

Mickey Walsh

Forward: 186 + 8 appearances, 76 goals. Republic of Ireland 21 appearances, 3 goals
Born: 13 August 1954, Chorley
Career: Blackpool (1973–78), Everton, Queen's Park Rangers, Porto, Salgueiros, Espinho.

Mickey Walsh scored one of the greatest goals ever seen at Bloomfield Road. It was three minutes from time in a thrilling game with Sunderland in February 1975. A run from the halfway line that ended with a terrific shot and was voted 'Goal of the Season' on BBC's *Match of the Day*.

Walsh joined Blackpool in the summer of 1973 and made his League debut in September, in a draw at Fulham. He was meant to compliment Wyn Davies upfront, but circumstances meant he moved to outside-left where he was unhappy and struggled to keep his place. During 1974–75, he became a virtual ever present, switching

from centre-forward to outside-right, and he was top scorer with 12 League goals in an overall tally of only 38.

A strong player with good skill, he netted 17 in 1975–76 in an unsuccessful promotion bid, but his best spell came in the next campaign when he teamed up with veteran striker Bob Hatton. They scored 36 goals – 26 to Walsh – for the highest individual tally since Ray Charnley's in 1961–62. Blackpool tried to keep their star forward, but after the disastrous 1977–78 season, when they were relegated despite Walsh's 14 goals, he was sold to Everton for a six-figure fee. A Republic of Ireland international, he also played for QPR before spending six seasons in Portugal. The highlight was playing in the 1984 European Cup-Winners' Cup Final for Porto against Juventus.

Walsh is a member of Blackpool FC's 'Hall of Fame'.

Mike Walsh

Defender: 163 + 9 appearances. Republic of Ireland 5 appearances, 0 goals
Born: 20 June 1956, Manchester
Career: Bolton Wanderers, Everton, Norwich City, Burnley, Manchester City, Blackpool (1984–89), Bury.

Like his namesake from the 1970s, Mike Walsh contributed much to Blackpool Football Club. He started his career with Bolton Wanderers in 1974 and made 177 League appearances for the Trotters, helping them to win the Second Division title in 1977–78.

A strong, skilful defender, he captained most of his clubs, including Blackpool. In August 1981 he joined Everton in a £90,000 plus player deal, and while at Everton he gained the first of his five Republic of Ireland caps. There then followed loans spells with Norwich City and Burnley and a summer with Fort Lauderdale in the NASL before he signed for Manchester City in October 1983.

He joined Blackpool for only £6,000 in January 1984, and his debut the following month was in a 3–0 home victory over leaders York City, where he took a deep, defensive role alongside David Moore. During five happy years at Blackpool, he led the Seasiders to promotion during 1984–85, but injuries sometimes hindered him. He was influential in a well-organised defence, and one of his best games came in a 1988 FA Cup replay at Maine Road, where Blackpool nearly scored a shock win over his former club Manchester City.

At the end of 1988–89,with the dismissal of manager Sam Ellis, Walsh decided to move, and so it as no surprise that he ended up at Bury, where Ellis had taken over. Walsh helped the promotion charge for the Shakers that season and in 1991–92 he was made manager following Eliis's departure.

In his five years there, he got the club into the Play-offs three times, including a first-ever trip to Wembley, but constant financial restraints meant he was forced to sell players. He was eventually sacked by an impatient board, and found himself at Barrow, then assistant to Steve McMahon at Swindon Town, plus another managerial appointment at Southport, before retiring from the game. He now runs a restaurant in Javea, Spain.

Dickie Watmough

Midfielder: 105 appearances, 34 goals
Born: 1912, Bradford
Died: 7 September 1962
Career: Bradford City, Blackpool (1934–37), Preston North End.

Outside-right Dickie Watmough was signed by Alex McFarlane from Bradford City late in 1934 for a large fee of £3,300, and immediately struck a partnership with Tommy Jones and Jimmy Hampson. A fast and tricky winger, who as well as being able to score goals, later found a new role by supplying the telling crosses for Hampson's successor, Bobby Finan. His lightening bursts down the right wing became a trademark, and after scoring the winner in his debut in October 1934 at home to Norwich City he became almost an ever present.

He scored a further eight goals that season, and more significantly – in the following campaign – he helped Finan to become the Second Division's top scorer. Watmough played for the majority of the

1936–37 season, helping Blackpool back to Division One, although after being dropped, he was selected for the final game against Doncaster Rovers for purely sentimental reasons.

He did not adapt to First Division football and a recurring injury also meant his appearances were limited. When Alex Munro arrived from Hearts, it soon became obvious that he was to be preferred to Watmough. In December 1937 he moved to Preston North End in a £8,000 exchange deal that brought Frank O'Donnell to Blackpool and also took Jim McIntosh to Deepdale.

At Preston, Watmough resurrected his career and won an FA Cup-winners' medal. The 1938 FA Cup Final was his last senior game, for after missing the whole of the following season through injury, he retired. Once 12th man for Yorkshire County Cricket Club in a Championship match, Watmough later became a publican and scouted for Bradford Park Avenue. He died in 1962.

Albert Watson

Midfielder: 390 appearances, 22 goals
Born: 19 August 1903, Felling
Career: Blackpool (1923–36), Halifax Town, Gateshead.

Albert Watson will always be remembered for scoring the '£10,000 goal'. It came seven minutes from the end of Blackpool's crucial home game with fellow relegation candidates Manchester City in May 1931. The scored was 2–1 to City, and in an act of almost total desperation Blackpool's inside-right Jack Oxberry exchanged places with wing-half Watson. He took a square pass from Jimmy Hampson and shot a 20-yarder into the corner of the net to save First Division football for the Seasiders. The goal ensured free meals in local restaurants for Watson for the rest of his life.

A strong, heavily built wing-half who liked to attack, he made nearly 400 appearances for Blackpool, helping them to two promotions. He made his debut in April 1923, in a home in over Rotherham County, and was virtually ever present from then on. He played alongside the captain, Billy Benton, but never really had the flair or speed of his skipper. This is maybe why his contributions were overlooked by the local media and supporters.

He stayed at Bloomfield Road until 1936, when he was granted a free transfer, and in later years he scouted for Blackpool and was responsible for discovering many young and talented players.

Andy Watson

Striker: 104 + 30 appearances, 49 goals
Born: 1 April 1967, Leeds
Career: Halifax Town, Swansea City, Carlisle United, Blackpool (1993–96), Walsall, Doncaster Rovers.

Andy Watson was the product of a successful 'buy a player' scheme introduced by the board in 1993 where the proceeds from the gate receipts – in the home game with Rotherham United – were given to manager Billy Ayre to purchase a new player. It was a controversial idea with the fans, but more than 6,000 turned up and gave the manager the chance to delve into the transfer market, something he had been unable to do at that time. He chose a player he had managed while at Halifax Town five years earlier in tall and rangy striker Andy Watson.

Watson started his professional career at the Shay, where he immediately became a prolific striker. Two years later, in 1990, he moved to Swansea City for £40,000, but the move was not as successful, and within a year he joined Carlisle United, where he scored a remarkable 22 goals in just over 50 appearances. It was that strike rate that attracted Ayre, and in January 1993 he joined Blackpool for £55,000. He very quickly provided the goalscoring prowess that had been missing and scored his first goals for the club in a thrilling 3–3 draw with rivals Preston North End. In later years he forged a partnership with Tony Ellis and became a fans' favourite, although also the brunt of criticism when things were not always going according to plan.

He scored 49 times for Blackpool in his four years at Bloomfield Road under Ayre, Sam Allardyce and Gary Megson, but in 1996 it was Megson who deemed him surplus to requirements and sold him to Walsall for £60,000. He continued to score for the Bescott stadium side and eventually saw out his career with Doncaster Rovers. A fine, if under-rated, player.

Phil Watson

Defender: 178 appearances, 12 goals. Scotland 1 appearance, 0 goals
Born: 27 February 1907, Dykehead
Died: 1990
Career: Hamilton Academical, Blackpool (1932–37), Barnsley, Queen of the South.

After Billy Tremeling's departure, Blackpool tried Eric Longden at centre-half for a season before settling on Phil Watson, a £3,000 signing from Hamilton Academical. Watson, who was a strong and hard player with lots of skill for a centre-half, joined Blackpool in February 1932 and made his debut that month in a home win over Everton. It was a baptism of fire as he was marking the great Dixie Dean, but he acquitted himself well.

Watson spent most of his career at Bloomfield Road, moving to full-back in 1935–36. One of his greatest moments though, came as a stand-in centre-forward against Aston Villa in March 1933. He took over from the injured Jimmy Hampson and scored a hat-trick in Blackpool's 6–2 victory.

A native of Scotland, he was capped once at international level against Austria in 1934. In December 1937 he moved to Barnsley and ended his career with Queen of the South where he was part of the team that recorded its first-ever League victory over Rangers. He also played for the Scottish League.

Richie Wellens

Midfielder: 203 + 23 appearances, 25 goals
Born: 29 March 1980, Moston
Career: Manchester United, Blackpool (2000–05), Oldham Athletic, Doncaster Rovers, Leicester City.

Richie Wellens was a hard-tackling and fiercely competitive midfielder who played for Blackpool at the beginning of the remarkable revival the club has enjoyed, yet did not share in the spoils due to his desire to find success elsewhere.

He started his career at Manchester United in 1999, but with no likelihood of breaking into the first team he joined Blackpool within a year. He immediately created a rapport with the fans due to his commitment and desire, and under manager Steve McMahon he helped the team to promotion in 2001 and two further appearances in the Millennium Stadium for victories in the Football League Trophy. He was a regular first-team player in midfield and one of the first on the list, yet when Colin Hendry took over, the team's backward slide concerned him and he left to join Oldham Athletic in 2005. The deal saw Scott Vernon coming to Bloomfield Road, and so also prevented a 50% pay on clause to United should he move on.

He was popular and successful at Boundary Park, but his return to Blackpool – especially in the League One Play-off semi-final – was one where he found himself at the centre of constant abuse from the Blackpool fans. From a much loved tangerine, he had become the subject of loathing.

He spent two years with Oldham before joining Doncaster Rovers and helping them to promotion to the Championship. After signing a new three-year contract, he was then bought by Leicester City for £1.2 million as part of their rebuilding process following their promotion back to the Championship.

Wellens was, and is, an excellent player whose enthusiasm can sometimes get the better of him. It was ironic that after giving five years to Blackpool, he should leave at a point when the club were on the verge of incredible success.

Tom White

Forward: 37 appearances, 11 goals
Born: 12 August 1939, Musselburgh
Career: Raith Rovers, St Mirren, Hearts, Aberdeen, Crystal Palace, Blackpool (1968–69), Bury, Crewe Alexandra.

Tom White, brother of the late Tottenham Hotspur and Scotland star John, came to Bloomfield Road in March 1968 from Crystal Palace for £20,000. He made his debut in a home win over Aston Villa,

immediately taking over the centre-forward role vacated by the departing Gerry Ingram.

White was a tall, skilful payer whose aerial command led to many of his goals, and although he had lost a lot of his speed when he came to Blackpool he could still play havoc with opposing defenders. In his first season he teamed up brilliantly with Tony Green and Alan Suddick, although toward the end of the campaign he found his position under pressure from Graham Rowe and eventually moved to outside-left.

Perhaps White did not score as many goals as expected, but he did lay on many for Suddick. Injury curtailed his playing days with Blackpool, and he ended his career with Bury and Crewe Alexandra. After his career, he continued his association with Blackpool, becoming a businessman in the town and serving as a director of the club until 1992. In 1990 he was called upon to act as temporary manager after the dismissal of Jimmy Mullen, with the team hurtling toward Division Four. It was a task that he did not relish, but he showed total commitment in what proved to be a lost cause.

He started his career with Raith Rovers, but it was shortened by two years due to National Servce. After a time at St Mirren, he joined Hearts for £8,000 and as soon dubbed 'goal-a-game White' by the local media. Thirty goals in 37 appearances was impressive.

After a year at Aberdeen, he went south to Crystal Palace, where he scored 13 times in 39 games before his move to Blackpool. After leaving Bloomfield Road, he joined Bury and managed 13 goals in 48 appearances, more than he had achieved with Blackpool.

George Wood

Goalkeeper: 144 appearances, 0 goals. Scotland 4 appearances, 0 goals
Born: 28 September 1952, Douglas
Career: East Stirling, Blackpool (1971–77 and 1989–90), Everton, Arsenal, Crystal Palace, Cardiff City, Hereford United, Merthyr Tydfil, Inter Cardiff.

A giant of a man at over 6ft tall and weighing 14st, goalkeeper George Wood was bought from East Stirling in January 1972 for £10,000 as cover for the tremendously popular John Burridge. After spending some time in the reserves, Wood made his debut that April in a home victory over Oxford United, and then spent the next four years vying for the number-one spot with Burridge before establishing himself in 1975–76.

Wood was never a spectacular goalkeeper, but a safer pair of hands you were not likely to see, reminding many older fans of the legendary George Farm.

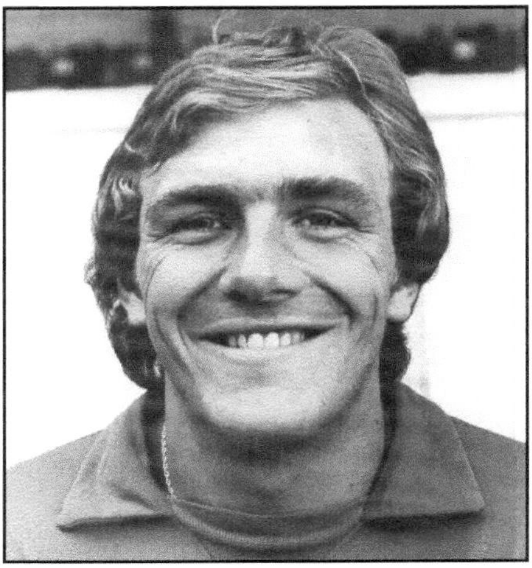

At the end of 1976–77 he was transferred to Everton for £150,000, and it was then that he became a Scottish international. There was then a big-money move to Arsenal and after failing to displace Pat Jennings, he moved to Crystal Palace. He spent five happy years there, before moving to Cardiff City, where he helped them win the Welsh Cup.

In 1989 he returned to Bloomfield Road on loan as the team were heading toward Fourth Division football. He said at the time that it was like he was coming home, but sadly even he could not halt Blackpool's slide.

After finishing his career in non league football, he took up goalkeeping coaching and is now at Swindon Town in that capacity. He was a fine goalkeeper and fondly remembered by Blackpool fans, and sadly his international career never matched his ability due to the presence of Alan Rough and Jim Leighton.

Alan Wright

Defender: 112 + 9 appearances, 0 goals
Born: 28 September 1971, Ashton-under-Lyne
Career: Blackpool (1989–91), Blackburn Rovers, Aston Villa, Middlesbrough, Sheffield United, Derby County, Leeds United, Cardiff City, Doncaster Rovers, Nottingham Forest, Cheltenham Town, Fleetwood Town.

Alan Wright was one of the game's most exciting prospects when he joined Blackpool as a trainee. He made his debut, as a substitute, in May 1988 in a home game with Chesterfield, being just 16 at the time. He had risen from the YTS ranks to the first team in a remarkably short time and was soon challenging Steve Morgan in the heart of the defence.

Small at 5ft 4in, he had outstanding speed, good ball control and a maturity

beyond his years. Wright signed as a full-time professional in 1989, gaining a regular first-team place. He soon brought stability to a shaky defence and in the 1991 Play-off Final at Wembley he was a calm head under intense pressure. He had a cultured left foot and his bursts down the wing were his trademark.

After Blackpool failed to gain promotion in the aforementioned game, big clubs started to enquire after him, and so it was no surprise that Blackburn Rovers – then being guided by owner Jack Walker and manager Kenny Dalglish – bought him for £450,000. His time at Ewood Park was not successful, and he left before they won the Premier League title, joining Aston Villa for £1 million in 1995. It was at Aston Villa where his career highlighted, making 260 appearances, playing in Europe and winning the League Cup.

After eight years he left Villa and joined Middlesbrough, but his career was on a downward slope and in the next six years he played for no fewer than eight different clubs. Wright now plays for Fleetwood Town, a few miles north of Blackpool, so his career has effectively come full circle. He was part of the team that gained promotion to the Conference for the first time. He was tremendously popular with the fans and another member of the 'Hall of Fame'.

BLACKPOOL MANAGERS

Bill Norman

1919–1923

At the beginning of the 1919–20 season, Blackpool joined the growing number of football clubs to appoint a full-time manager, whereas previously team selection had been the responsibility of a committee comprising directors, captain and vice-captain. Blackpool's first full-time boss was Bill Norman, and in his four years in charge he would help the club to challenge seriously for promotion on three occasions.

Norman had been the trainer of the Barnsley side that won the FA Cup in 1912, and he held a similar post at Huddersfield Town before joining Blackpool in the summer of 1919. He was an imposing figure with his waxed moustache, and was always dressed impeccably – expecting his players to do the same. He immediately organised spartan training routines, helped by his son-in-law Allan Ure, who was also the club's trainer, and this disciplined approach soon earned him the nickname 'Sergeant Major'.

Rebuilding the team after World War One was always going to be a difficult job, and although Norman could rely on a number of established players he was also prepared to delve into the transfer market. He did this on frequent occasions, with his best signing being that of Harry Bedford.

In his first season, Blackpool only just missed out on promotion after making the running for most of the campaign. The sale of top scorer Joe Lane had hardly endeared him to supporters, but in that same season, 1919–20, the club won the Central League, proving that the reserve side was rich with talent.

The following season saw a similar story with a concerted promotion push, but a poor end-of-season run-in dented their hopes, and success eluded the manager and team again. He then spent heavily ahead of the 1921–22 season, so it was a huge disappointment to see the club fight relegation, with only a double victory over West Ham United at the end of the campaign guaranteeing them survival, and so avoiding a drop to the Third Division North.

This had given Norman's critics – and there were many – all the ammunition they needed, but he stuck at his task and took the team to the top of the table for the majority of the 1922–23 season. Sadly, though, and perhaps inevitably, Blackpool collapsed toward the end of the campaign, and promotion was missed once more. Whether it was because of this or because of the loud criticism, but the following summer he and his assistant, Allan Ure, left Blackpool and

headed for Leeds United. Norman became assistant manager to Arthur Fairclough, with whom he had worked at Barnsley.

Norman helped Leeds into Division One, but when they were relegated in 1927, both he and Fairclough resigned. Norman joined Hartlepools United as manager, and although his years in the North East were a struggle, he did discover the great W.G. Richardson, who later starred for West Bromwich Albion. He stayed at Hartlepools until his death in September 1931, while Ure had returned to Blackpool as trainer five years earlier.

One story perhaps sums up Norman's approach: one day at Hartlepools, the players complained that it was too cold to train, so to prove them wrong, Norman stripped naked and rolled in the snow!

Major Frank Buckley

1923–27

After Bill Norman's departure, the Blackpool board successfully lured Major Frank Buckley to Bloomfield Road with the promise of an extremely high salary and enough money available to strengthen the squad. In the event, and despite a total change of tactics Buckley did not really have much more success than his predecessor.

Buckley's previous management experience had been limited to a spell with Norwich City, but after leaving them in July 1920, he was out of football and working as a commercial traveller when Blackpool took him on.

As a centre-half, he had achieved England honours in a career that encompassed Aston Villa, Brighton, Manchester United, Manchester City, Birmingham, Derby County and Bradford City. He retired during World War One but played one game for Norwich City in September 1919, when he was the Canaries'

secretary-manager. His one international cap came in 1914, when England suffered a shock 3–0 defeat to Ireland at Ayresome Park.

During the war, Buckley had risen to the rank of major in the 17th Middlesex regiment – the famous footballers' battalion – and he used the rank for the remainder of his life. One of his five brothers, Chris, played for Aston Villa and was later chairman of the club.

Major Buckley's managerial style was controversial and, some say, years ahead of its time. Indeed, on more than one occasion he found himself in trouble with the footballing authorities for his methods. He was an imposing figure, nearly 6ft tall, and was always well dressed, his favourite fashion being 'plus fours'. Despite this, though, he was a 'tracksuit manager' and had a special talent for developing young players, with his youth policy being the first of its kind at Bloomfield Road.

In his first season in charge, he improved on the previous year by taking Blackpool to fourth place in Division Two, but once again this was something of a disappointment as the team had led the table for most of the campaign. Sadly, the following season saw a fight against relegation, and there was dissent among the supporters. One group founded the original Blackpool Supporters Club, and their main complaint was against the style of management introduced by Buckley. The fans suggested that the players had lost their enjoyment of the game and that this was the reason for the team's lack of success; Buckley ignored them

He went about rebuilding the side, which included selling established stars such as Herbert Jones and top scorer Harry Bedford, and in the following season of 1925–26 the team did well and finished in sixth – this time hampered by a poor start to the campaign. They failed to improve the following year when, after spending freely on new players, Blackpool could only finish just above midway in the table. It was a huge let-down for the fans, and indeed the manager, and when Wolverhampton Wanderers courted him, he did not think twice about moving.

He had made a major contribution to Blackpool, though, and even though he failed to bring First Division football to Bloomfield Road, Buckley did bring about a new professional approach and, most importantly, a successful youth policy.

At Molineaux he guided Wolves from the lower reaches of Division Two to runners'-up spot in Division One and to an FA Cup Final. In 1944 he became manager of Notts County – at the staggering wage of £4,000 per year – and later managed Hull City, Leeds United and Walsall. Despite little success at Blackpool, he has now become regarded as one of the finest managers the game has produced, notably for his 17 years in charge at Wolves. He died in Walsall in December 1964.

Sydney Beaumont

1927–28

Sydney Beaumont's reign as Blackpool manager was as short as it was unsuccessful. He took over from Frank Buckley in the summer of 1927 and immediately made changes to the side by bringing in big-money signings. This was despite the club being in financial difficulty once more. His ideas were different from those of his predecessor, and his radical change of tactics caused problems as the team struggled, losing five of the first six League games in his charge.

At times, his team selection seemed unusual to say the least and, coupled with new tactics, it meant that the team that started the 1927–28 season was far different to the one that had ended the previous campaign, in both personnel and shape. One change that did work very effectively, however, was that of moving Billy Tremeling from centre-forward to the half-back line, and so striking up a rich partnership with Jimmy Hampson. Indeed, Beaumont could claim responsibility for bringing the great Hampson to Blackpool in the first place.

Sydney Beaumont was a former Preston North End player, which probably did not cause as much unease among the Blackpool supporters in the early part of the 20th century as it would now, but Beaumont came with the pressure already heaped upon him. A native of Wrestlingworth, he had an unremarkable playing career, making 25 League appearances for Watford, one for Preston and 15 for Merthyr Town, before drifting into non-League football in Wales.

He joined Blackpool after a spell managing Third Division South club Aberdare Athletic, where he had seen unemployment in the town, a miners' strike and the club's wooden grandstand burn down before they were voted out of the Football League. They finished 19th and were replaced by Torquay United.

He never really made a positive impact at Bloomfield Road, and as Blackpool struggled even more in the depths of Division Two criticism of the manager intensified. Despite scoring freely, helped by Jimmy Hampson, they were to end up conceding 101 goals that season, and so it was no surprise that in the spring of 1929, with the team in the bottom three, he resigned. Two months later he took over as secretary of Bangor City.

The directors, mindful of financial pressures, decided against replacing him with a full-time manager, and instead appointed Harry Evans to carry the title of honorary manager for the next five seasons, aided by the club's trainers.

Alex 'Sandy' McFarlane

1933–35

After Blackpool had been relegated to the Second Division at the end of the 1932–33 season, there were strong calls from supporters for the reintroduction of a full-time manager.

Since the departure of Sydney Beaumont in 1928, the club had relied on the services of one of the directors, Harry Evans, who had acted as 'honorary manager'. Although this had been a success – particularly as in 1930 Blackpool had gained promotion to Division One for the first time – it was felt by the fans and club alike that a full-time manager was needed to give the side the sense of direction they had been missing in the previous couple of seasons.

The directors searched and finally settled on Alex McFarlane, a former Scottish international inside-forward who had played for Airdrie, Newcastle United, Dundee (with whom he had won a Scottish Cup winners' medal in 1910) and Chelsea.

A tactician extraordinaire, McFarlane had plenty of managerial experience, with two spells each in charge of Dundee and Charlton Athletic. He first joined Dundee as manager in March 1919 and guided them to the Scottish Cup Final in 1925, before taking over as secretary-manager of Charlton in May that year.

He saw Charlton relegated in his first season, but after rejoining the club following another spell with Dundee, he steered them to the Third Division South Championship in 1929. With little money to spend, his feat at the Valley had been remarkable, but he resigned midway through a quite disastrous 1932–33 season.

McFarlane arrived at Blackpool with a reputation for sternness, a strong sense of discipline and an ability to spot up-and-coming youngsters. He was a fine judge of a player, and when he signed a two-year contract in the summer of 1933 Blackpool had every reason to feel optimistic.

McFarlane was never a popular manager with the players, and indeed the local newspaper was full of stories of dressing-room discontent. He did, however, bring a period of stability to the club.

In his first season in charge – and Blackpool's first back in Division Two – he guided them to a mid-table position, quite respectable but not good enough for the perfectionist manager. That summer he completely dismantled the side, allowing no fewer than nine players to leave Bloomfield Road as he brought in fresh faces. One of his best signings was that of Peter Doherty for £1,000, a player later to be sold for 10 times that amount.

The following season was a success, with the club just missing out on promotion, finishing in fourth place. The seeds had been sown for the future, and McFarlane could certainly look back on a job well done. He had injected new pride into the club, and had given the fans a new hope. He was a perfectionist in everything he did, and some may say that it was his relentless quest for perfection that not only made him unpopular with the players, but also led the board to decide not to renew his contract.

Whatever the reason for his departure, his time at Bloomfield Road could be regarded as a success, and when he left in 1935 the team were on the verge of good things. Blackpool was his last football appointment, and he apparently drifted out of the game at the age of 57.

Joe Smith

1935–58

Joe Smith was arguably Blackpool's greatest-ever manager, his 33-year reign being not only the longest, but also the most successful in the club's history.

Smith was born in 1890 and spent nearly all of his playing days with Bolton Wanderers, either as an inside or centre-forward. He helped them reach two FA Cup Finals in 1923 and 1926, and also played for England before and after World War One. Smith was acknowledged as one of the best players ever to play for the Trotters, and with the help of teammate Ted Vizard he scored a (then) club record 38 goals in one season for them.

When he retired from playing, he became manager of Third Division South Reading, and in four years at Elm Park he proved that he could make the transition with ease. He led Reading to a runners'-up spot twice and to third and fourth in the other two seasons.

In August 1935 Smith was invited to take over as manager at Bloomfield Road, an offer which he accepted immediately – a love of the seaside apparently being one of the main deciding factors. The transformation that he brought to the club was nothing short of remarkable, as the sternness and harshness associated with his predecessor were replaced by smiles and informality. Smith was never a 'tracksuit manager', and it has to be said that tactics were not his strongest point, but he did have an incredible ability to motivate, and nearly everyone who played for him had the utmost respect for Joe Smith.

His record speaks for itself. In his second season in charge he engineered a promotion-winning side, and then, with shrewd purchases and the moulding of exciting players, he created one of the greatest sides in the country. The famous 'M' forward line of the 1950s was responsible for three FA Cup Final appearances and regular challenges for the League Championship. In fact, well before that, in the 1930s Smith built a side that was so superior that many people believe that if it had not been for the intervention of the Second World War, Blackpool would have swept all before them.

He was responsible for bringing many of the country's top stars to Blackpool, notably Stanley Matthews, who many believed at the age of 31 was past his best. That opinion, of course, turned out to be ill-informed.

As a manager, Smith never bullied his men, preferring to motivate or even massage their egos. He was a good loser, and even in defeat he was ready with a joke and a 'never mind, we'll win the next one' attitude. His informality set a precedent at the club, and many managers who followed tried to emulate him, but with nowhere near the same success.

His greatest achievement was, of course, guiding Blackpool to their dramatic FA Cup Final victory over Bolton Wanderers at Wembley in 1953, but in many ways a greater achievement was the transformation of a struggling Second Division club into one of the most powerful in the country. For 21 of the 23 seasons that he was in charge, Blackpool were in the First Division, and it is fair to say that the club's gradual decline coincided with his retirement due to ill health in 1958.

Blackpool Football Club never forgot him, awarding him a hefty golden handshake and also buying him a home in the town. It was the least they could have done, as he was – and still is – the greatest manager Blackpool have had in their long history.

Joe Smith died on 11 August 1971, and it is said that grown men wept at his funeral. His like will probably never be seen again – more is the pity.

Ron Suart

1958–67

Ron Suart was the first player to return to Bloomfield Road as a manager, and for nine years he sat in the hot seat, during what could only be described as a turbulent time for the club.

When Joe Smith announced his retirement due to ill health, the club looked around for a suitable successor – a man who would be capable of continuing the good work of Smith in the previous 23 years. A daunting task for anyone, especially because by this stage the maximum wage had been abolished and Blackpool, like other clubs, were to suffer at the hands of their wealthier neighbours.

Ron Suart came with an impeccable pedigree. As well as being an excellent player, while at Bloomfield Road, he had successfully made the transition to football management. After his playing days ended at Blackburn Rovers, he travelled a few miles down the road to become player-manager of Wigan Athletic, before taking over at Scunthorpe and Lindsey United.

A mild-mannered and quietly spoken man, the appointment was well received by

the fans and press alike. He had a keen eye for young talent, and during his spell he brought such players as Alan Ball, Ray Charnley and Graham Rowe to the club. Unfortunately, though, with the abolition of the maximum wage and the new freedom that players now had, he was unable to prevent many of his players from moving on. Also, the club could never hope to match the success of the previous decade, and indeed, after Suart's first season in charge the team never again finished in the top half of Division One.

Attendances started to fall, and Blackpool were soon to become known as a spent force in English football. The critics rounded on Suart, and after a 6–2 Cup humiliation at Scunthorpe United, he was asked to resign. He refused and tried desperately to restore pride to the team and the club, but as each season passed it became increasingly obvious that relegation was an eventuality.

The fact that relegation did not occur until the end of the 1965–66 campaign was a testament to Suart's ability to motivate his players and the mix of youth and experience that he had created. With apparently a great deal of interference from the board over team selections and transfers, Suart found the job almost impossible. In 1966–67 Blackpool won only six League games – and only one of those at Bloomfield Road – and were relegated to Division Two for the first time in 30 years. In January 1967 Suart offered his resignation, and it was accepted immediately.

He joined Chelsea and spent seven years there as assistant-manager to Tommy Docherty and then Dave Sexton, before becoming full-time manager at Stamford Bridge in October 1974. It was never intended to be a long-term appointment, and in April 1975, as Chelsea struggled at the foot of Division One, he was replaced by Eddie McCreadie. He later became a scout for Wimbledon, but as that club struggled financially, he was released in 2002. Suart was an unsung hero of Blackpool Football Club, both as player and manager, and to this day he holds the record of the second longest-serving manager at Bloomfield Road. Sadly, his talent was never rewarded with sustained success on the field.

Stan Mortensen

1967–69

Stan Mortensen's appointment as manager of Blackpool in February 1967 was universally popular with the fans. Always a huge favourite during his playing days, he remained a Blackpool man, even during his time at Hull City, Bath City and Southport. He was still a local businessman and town councillor, so when he was asked to save the sinking ship that was Blackpool Football Club in 1967, he took to the task with relish and unbounded enthusiasm.

Unfortunately, Mortensen's appointment came too late to preserve First Division status, yet within 12 months he had transformed the same side into regular winners, and was denied promotion only on the final day of the season in the most dramatic and cruel of circumstances. He quickly proved that he had a keen eye for young talent, for while buying Henry Mowbray from Albion Rovers, he noticed a young lad called Tony Green.

Within a week, Green was at Bloomfield Road for a fee of just over £15,000, and he went on to play a fulsome part in Blackpool's revival the following year. Four years later, the same player was transferred to Newcastle United for a fee 10 times the amount that Blackpool had paid.

Mortensen blended youth and experience in his team. He gave them the confidence to believe in themselves, and more than anything, he told them to enjoy the game. He was also not afraid to make unpopular decisions – one of the least popular being the sale of crowd-favourite Ray Charnley after a miserable home defeat to Millwall. Charnley had played over 200 times for Blackpool and was a folk hero with the fans, but after the 4–1 home defeat (in which he scored the only goal), Mortensen could see that something was wrong and released him. He was replaced by Gerry Ingram, and it worked well as Blackpool became a force again in Division Two.

Their first season ended in despair for 'Morty' and his players, however. Despite seven consecutive victories and a points total of 58, the team were pipped to promotion by Queen's Park Rangers by just 0.21 of a goal. It was a bitter blow to the club and the man, but to Mortensen's credit he never complained, but just congratulated his players and promised the fans that they would be successful the following season.

For the 1968–69 campaign there were many comings and goings at the club, with one of the manager's shrewdest signings being Tommy Hutchison from Alloa Athletic. The team looked good and were one of the pre-season favourites for promotion, yet unfortunately they flattered to deceive. The final League position of eighth was a disappointment.

'Morty' was still hugely popular with the fans and most believed that success was just a matter of time. With this in mind, the decision by the board to terminate his contract in April 1969 seems inexplicable. There had been rumours of discontent among the players, and talk of a lack of discipline, yet in the aftermath of his departure, not one of the players seemed to have a bad word to say about the manager. It was probably one of the worst and most inexcusable decisions taken by a board in the long history of the club – only matched

years later by the subsequent sackings of Allan Brown, Billy Ayre and Sam Allardyce. The reasons have to this day still not been disclosed, but 'Morty', being the gentleman that he was, never showed any bitterness. In fact, he stayed close to the club for the rest of his life, often sitting in the stands to cheer on the team.

Many people believe that his dismissal was the start of the downward spiral that the club embarked on. One thing is for certain, though, it was a long time before Blackpool found a manager of Stan Mortensen's calibre.

Les Shannon

1969–70

After Stan Mortensen's departure, the Blackpool board searched long and hard for a suitable replacement. They eventually settled on the former Burnley and England B international inside-forward and wing-half Les Shannon, who had managed Bury to Division Two in 1968.

Shannon was a man light years away from his predecessor at Blackpool. He was quiet and seemingly distant from his players, yet he quickly commanded their respect. Shannon did little to change the team at first, except for adding some very experienced players to the squad, notably Fred Pickering and Dave Hatton. He also managed to pick up from Skelmersdale, for no fee, Mickey Burns, a player who was to blossom while at Bloomfield Road.

The expectations of the manager were high, as only promotion back to the First Division would be enough to satisfy a now highly critical set of supporters, yet by October that seemed unlikely. Only three wins in their opening 10 League games saw the team near the bottom of the table, but gradually form arrived, and with it a concerted push for promotion. Eventually, promotion was achieved, in the penultimate game of the season, and at Deepdale of all places, on a celebratory Monday evening in April 1970. Shannon and the team were heroes to the fans, and the manager had, impressively, given First Division football to Blackpool in his first season in charge. Promotion was all the more remarkable as it had been gained without the help of the great Tony Green, who had missed the entire season with injury.

The euphoria lasted barely few months, as the team failed miserably to adapt to top-level football. They were hopelessly out of their depth, and in despairing moves, Shannon changed the team constantly, using no fewer than 22 players in their first 14 games. The critics turned on him, and the fans, never the most patient in the country, now called for his dismissal, whereas just a few months previously he had been the saviour of the club. The crisis came to a head in October after a quite astonishing home defeat to high-flying Chelsea. After taking a remarkable 3–0 lead in the first half, Shannon then substituted Fred Pickering to howls of protest from the fans. It effectively changed the game and ended Shannon's Blackpool career, as Chelsea went on to win 4–3. A few days later, the board refused to back him and he resigned after just 17 months in charge. The managerial merry-go-round had truly begun, and fans were to endure it for years to come.

Shannon then spent the next six years managing in Greece with huge success, and is still now regarded in that country as one of the most outstanding foreign managers in their domestic football. He was also an advisor on the Channel Four series *The Manageress* in the early 1990s, with a reference – albeit inaccurate – to Blackpool's Anglo-Italian exploits in one of the episodes.

Shannon returned to the UK permanently in 1984 and scouted for Luton Town. He died in December 2007 at the age of 81.

Bob Stokoe

1970–73 and 1978–79

Bob Stokoe was first approached by Blackpool in the summer of 1969, after the departure of Stan Mortensen. At the time he declined, preferring to remain at Carlisle United, but just over 18 months later he became the ninth official manager in the club's history.

Stokoe, who appeared in Newcastle United's 1955 FA Cup-winning side, was almost a one-club man as a player, making nearly 300 League and Cup appearances for the Magpies as a versatile half-back, before being transferred to Bury in 1961. He eventually became manager at Gigg Lane, and was also boss at Charlton Athletic, Rochdale (twice), Carlisle (three times) and Sunderland, as well as his two stints at Blackpool.

Stokoe was a strict disciplinarian, and one of his first tasks on arriving at Bloomfield Road was to clear out the 'dead wood', as he called it. Too late to save First Division status, he began to systematically rebuild the side to his liking. Out went goalkeepers Taylor, Blacklaw and Thompson, plus Graham Rowe and the ever-popular Fred Pickering, and in their place came Dave Lennard, Chris Simpkin and big George Wood in goal. Stokoe also agreed to the sale of Tony Green to his old club Newcastle, with Keith Dyson coming the other way.

In the meantime, he took Blackpool on a successful European jaunt, winning the Anglo-Italian Cup in 1971, beating Bologna in the Final. Stokoe seemed to be the answer to Blackpool fans' prayers.

His first season in charge saw a respectable sixth place, but again this was not welcomed by the supporters. They had become disenchanted with the style of football, plus numerous stories appearing on the back pages of the national press were certainly harming the club. Blackpool needed a good second season, but before that there was another summer of Italian football, with the team reaching the Final once more, this time beaten by Roma. They had made many friends with their attitude, but domestically it was clear that the following campaign was make or break.

There were changes made by Stokoe to the playing staff, notably the arrival of Billy Rafferty, and Tommy Hutchison going to Coventry City. The season started reasonably well, with the team handily placed for a promotion push, but then Stokoe resigned. He had been lured back to his native North East by Sunderland, a club he felt had much more potential than Blackpool. It was annoying to the fans, as Stokoe had publicly stated that he intended to stay at Bloomfield Road for at least five years. Sunderland went on to win a famous FA Cup Final against the mighty Leeds United, while Blackpool faded away.

Five years later he returned to Bloomfield Road with Blackpool in

desperate trouble. They were facing Third Division football for the first time, and he was brought in to steady the sinking ship with all aboard drowning. Unfortunately, he could not save them, not helped by having to offload the better players, such as Wood, Hart, Hatton and Walsh – none of them having the appetite for third-tier football – and replacing them with youngsters. Blackpool finished mid-table and Stokoe resigned again.

He was a manager never loved at Blackpool, but he was certainly effective. Elsewhere he was adored by fans of Carlisle United and Sunderland, plus Newcastle United for his playing exploits. A statue stands outside Sunderland's Stadium of Light in his honour, a place where he is still revered to this day. Bob Stokoe died in February 2004 after a long illness. It is a fitting testament to the man that as a manager, despite being in charge of numerous clubs, he was never sacked.

Harry Potts

1973–76

Blackpool quickly appointed Harry Potts as manager following Bob Stokoe's untimely departure in 1973, and so established a link that had been suggested back in the 1950s. At that time Potts was an effective inside-forward for Burnley, with whom he gained an FA Cup winners medal in 1947. Blackpool, looking to strengthen their team, made a record £25,000 bid for him, only to be turned down by the Burnley board.

Potts eventually went to Everton, before being appointed chief coach at Wolves. He managed Shrewsbury Town before becoming manager of Burnley in January 1958, spending 12 years in charge at Turf Moor and guiding Burnley into Europe as League Champions and to an FA Cup Final; they were heady days indeed for the Clarets. He was eventually moved upstairs to become general manager, but then took up the offer of the Blackpool post of manager.

Potts was a genial man, even-tempered and certainly a football thinker. Yet after a particularly good start, he allowed the team to deploy negative tactics, which eventually proved to be his undoing. His first season in charge nearly saw him emulate Les Shannon by taking Blackpool to promotion, but after leading 1–0 at Sunderland with seven minutes to go in their final match, they lost 2–1 and so missed out to Carlisle United – a team they had beaten the previous week 4–0.

Potts bought wisely but expensively, most notably on players such as John Evanson, Paul Hart and the old campaigner Wyn Davies. These players were worth the fees, but the club and fans demanded instant return in the form of good results, and Potts was constantly under pressure.

After the good start, it was disturbing to see the team deteriorate into a negative unit, unable to sustain any real kind of promotion challenge. In the next two seasons, they could only manage 38 and 40 goals respectively, despite the obvious scoring talents of Mickey Walsh. Also, the sale of Mickey Burns to Newcastle for £175,000 hardly endeared Potts to the fans, even though the transaction was for financial reasons.

At the end of the 1975–76 campaign, a strong 'Potts out' faction made themselves heard and, with the team only managing to finish 10th, the board sacked him in May that year. It was difficult to understand how a successful team could have become so insular and lacking in ambition, and if Potts had continued the good work shown in his first season, he and the side could have been together for longer.

One of the highlights of his tenure was a memorable FA Cup win over his old club Burnley in January 1976, a result that hastened the departure of the Clarets' boss Jimmy Adamson. Potts returned for second spell at Turf Moor from June 1977 to October 1979, and then was a scout for the now defunct non-League side, Colne Dynamos. He is remembered fondly by Burnley fans, and the 'Harry Potts Way' at Turf Moor is testament to that. He died in the town in January 1996 at the age of 75 after a long illness.

Allan Brown

1976–78 and 1981–82

After Harry Potts's dismissal, Blackpool turned to one of its most popular players to manage the team. Allan Brown had already proved himself in football management at non-League Wigan Athletic, Luton Town, Torquay United, Bury and Nottingham Forest, and older

supporters, remembering his exploits on the field in the 1950s, looked to the future with optimism.

Brown strengthened the attack, something that was not difficult bearing in mind the paucity of goals under Potts, and in came Derek Spence and the veteran Bob Hatton. Once again the team looked likely to be in the heart of a promotion push.

Brown's style was relaxed, helped by the knowledge that he was popular with the fans, and this was transmitted to the team. In his first season, Blackpool finished fifth, just one point short of promotion, and a new pride was blossoming around Bloomfield Road. In those first 12 months he had sold the likes of Alcock, Dave Hatton and 'keeper Burridge, to be replaced by youngsters as Brown continued a complete rebuilding of the squad.

The start of the 1977–78 season saw Blackpool favourites for promotion, with Brown making encouraging and positive statements about the future. The team's play was open and entertaining, and although they conceded regularly they scored as many, if not more. It was a refreshing change. This was all part of Brown's philosophy of enjoying the game, and the fans loved it, turning up in greater numbers. He sold George Wood to Everton for a large fee but quickly replaced him with future international Iain Hesford. Also joining as an apprentice was Jeff Chandler, who was later sold to Leeds United for £100,000.

The team and the season were shaping up nicely, and Blackpool were in the position expected – on the verge of the promotion race – when the unthinkable happened and Brown was sacked. It came after an acrimonious meeting with the board, and the reasons are still unclear today. It seems that Brown had become weary of constant board interference in team matters, and public statements that followed made his position untenable. Inevitably, and understandably, it provoked a backlash from the fans, especially as in the previous two home games Blackpool had won both and scored 10 goals! Whatever the reason, it was another example of the board acting rashly – something that was to be repeated on many occasions in the future. Blackpool only managed one more victory and were then relegated to the Third Division for the first time. When Brown left in February, they were seventh.

After managing briefly in Kuwait, Brown returned to Bloomfield Road in 1981 following the hugely unsuccessful Alan Ball era. The club was in financial difficulties and were facing the prospect of Fourth Division football, so it was hoped that Brown could weave his magic once more. It was not to be, and in April 1982 Brown left. He never managed a football club again. Allan Brown died on 19 April 2011.

Stan Ternent

1979–80

Like Jimmy Meadows before him, Stan Ternent was asked to step into the managerial position at short notice after the untimely departure of the previous occupant. Unlike Meadows, though, Ternant was given the job on a full-time basis.

Ternent, a former Burnley and Carlisle United winger, had worked well with Bob Stokoe as coach at Blackpool, so his familiarity with the players was an asset as far as the board was concerned, and his appointment was seen by the fans as an attempt to bring some stability to the now shaky vessel that was Blackpool Football Club in August 1979.

Ternent immediately started to reshape the side, spending large sums on new players. Jack Ashurst was secured from Sunderland for a club record fee, and also brought in were Dave Bamber, Colin Morris and Peter Noble. Despite these signings, the team's fortunes refused to improve, and by the early 1980s Blackpool were in the bottom half of Division Three. Also, for some time the board had been actively pursuing former Blackpool favourite Alan Ball, so it was no surprise that in February Ternent was sacked. He had been the sixth different name on the manager's door in 10 years. Unsurprisingly, Ternent has had little good to say about his time at Bloomfield Road, but he did prove his effectiveness as a football manager in the later years. He had spells at Hull City, Burnley (where he won automatic promotion), Gillingham and an ill-starred spell at Huddersfield Town. He also had coaching spells at Bradford City and Derby County, and can now be found scouting for Sunderland.

Alan Ball

1980–81

Alan Ball was one of Blackpool's greatest players, yet his 12-month managerial reign must go down as one of the most traumatic and disappointing in the club's history.

Ball's appointment was well received by Blackpool supporters. This was a man who had started his footballing career at Bloomfield Road and had gone on to great things in the game, yet had always publicly expressed his desire to manage Blackpool at the end of his playing days. He returned with enthusiasm, a passion to bring the good times back to the club, and the energy to be able to take to the field as and when he felt it was necessary. Sadly, the year that followed saw it all evaporate as the club's fortunes sunk even lower.

Large sums were spent on players, yet the quality of players seemed to be suspect, plus Ball was prepared to take gambles on youngsters. Add to that the unpopular sale of Tony Kellow, a huge favourite with the fans, and the love affair turned sour very quickly. Joining a club towards the end of a season is always difficult, even with an experienced manager, and for Ball it proved almost impossible. The team was sliding towards the trapdoor into Division Four, and only some spirited performances in the last six games ensured survival. The fans at first showed little dissent, but that was to change in the following season.

Ball brought in experienced players such as Ted McDougall and Willie Morgan, neither of whom were to make any kind of impact, yet the signing of John Deary proved that he was capable of spotting talent. Sadly, the season started the same way that the last had ended – with a battle against relegation. By now the fans had turned against him, followed very quickly by the local press. Ball did not help his cause when he bitterly attacked the supporters after an FA Cup victory over neighbours Fleetwood Town, complaining that the majority of the 10,000 crowd had not wanted Blackpool to win as much as he had. There were calls for him to change his tactics, yet he stubbornly refused. In later years, when reflecting on his time as manager, he admitted that he should have kept Stan Ternent on as his assistant, yet had decided not to, believing that he had enough ability to overcome his lack of experience. Such are the decisions that life is made of...

Ball lost the backing of the fans and, after a defeat at Brentford in February 1981, the backing of the board too. He was dismissed with immediate effect. The dream had quickly become a nightmare, and Ball's first foray into football management had been an unmitigated disaster. There is film footage of Ball on the training ground during his days at Blackpool, where he is on the verge of exasperation as he barks out orders to his

less talented players, who all look totally bemused. Maybe that was the reason for his failure – asking players to do the things that came naturally to him, and really never understanding why they failed.

Ball did resume a playing career with Southampton and then picked up the management reigns at Portsmouth (where he was hugely successful), Colchester United, Stoke City (where he was not successful) and Exeter City, followed by a spell as coach under Graham Taylor at England. Then he made another return to Southampton as manager, where, among other notable achievements, he signed Matt Le Tissier on a full-time contract, before a high-profile move to Manchester City. This last move turned out to be nearly as disastrous as his time at Blackpool.

His final management position was back at Portsmouth, but severe financial problems hampered him, and despite managing to save them from relegation two years running, he was dismissed in December 1999. It was his last foray into management. Always a controversial figure, many would say that his reputation was tarnished by his many managerial failures, yet at Bloomfield Road he will always be fondly remembered for his playing exploits and not his management. Ball died of a heart attack in April 2007 aged 61.

Sam Ellis

1982–89

Sam Ellis arrived at Bloomfield Road in the summer of 1982 with no management experience, but a keenness to learn. He stayed, remarkably for the time, for seven years, and within three years had achieved what no previous manager had done for 15 seasons – gained promotion.

Ellis was a fine player for Sheffield Wednesday in the 1960s, starring at centre-half. As a teenager he made an FA Cup debut in the 1966 Final against Everton, when his team lost 3–2, and then moved to Mansfield Town, Lincoln City and eventually Watford. At Vicarage Road he became coach and assistant manager to future England boss Graham Taylor, and played a great part in Watford's meteoric rise through the divisions. Then Ellis turned down a new contract with the club, preferring to gain first-hand management experience with a club in the lower divisions. When the Blackpool job was advertised, he applied and was accepted.

At this time, Blackpool were trying desperately to improve their fortunes, which had by now reached rock bottom following the dismissal of Alan Ball. A new board had promised stability and were now looking to the future, a welcome change from the in-house bickering of previous years. Ellis was hardly given any money to spend and so was forced to use the free transfer market extensively. He also helped a lot of the young players at the club to blossom, but sadly he was also forced to sell established stars, notably Colin Greenall to Sheffield United. This was effectively to pay the tax man, meaning that it was a real baptism of fire for the new manager.

His first season was certainly a learning experience, as the team finished in the bottom four of the Football League and were forced to apply for re-election, but Sam Ellis had a belief in what he was doing and, just as importantly, so did the board and the fans. One year on, and Blackpool finished sixth, just out of the promotion places. This had been achieved with minimal outlay on players, but there had been some excellent acquisitions, such as Mike Walsh from Everton and Ian Britton. In fact, in his first two years in charge Ellis had spent barely £60,000 on new players and was of course obliged to sell others just to alleviate the constant financial shortfall.

One of the noteworthy triumphs was an incredible FA Cup victory over Manchester City at Bloomfield Road, which was sadly overshadowed by Manchester United losing to Bournemouth on the same weekend!

Promotion was gained in 1985 and Ellis's popularity with the supporters was at an all-time high. It had been done, once again, with little financial outlay and with stunning new signings in the shape of Alex Dyer and Eamon O'Keefe. Ellis also brought on a strong new centre-forward in Paul Stewart, who would be sold to Manchester City two years later for a quarter of a million pounds. Sadly, his management style was not always appreciated, and again there were tales of dressing-room unrest, but the fact was that Ellis had brought Third Division football back to the club again.

The first season back in the higher tier was acceptable, but it was clear that the long-ball game employed was not tuned enough for success, and Ellis went into the transfer market to strengthen the side. Also, there had been approaches from Manchester City for his services, which Ellis had turned down, so it was clear that stability was faltering somewhat.

The next few seasons were uninspiring, and as each new campaign began the expectations were high, the team were flattering to deceive, and the result was a let-down. All of this conspired to end the love affair between Sam Ellis and the Blackpool fans, something that had repeated itself over and over down the years. Despite some good additions to the squad, in the shape of Tony Cunningham, Andy Garner and Colin Methven, the team were now struggling and again looking at the prospect of basement football once more. After a heavy home defeat over the Easter period – 4–2 to Reading – Sam Ellis's contract was terminated by mutual consent in April 1989.

He went to Bury, where he had a fair amount of success, before joining Peter Reid as assistant at Manchester City, some five years after the Maine Road club had initially approached him. There then followed a year at Lincoln City, followed by spells as number two at Burnley, Leeds United, Luton Town and finally Sheffield United.

Ellis was hit by personal tragedy in 2001 when his 28-year-old-son, Timothy, was killed in a car accident.

He was a typical Blackpool manager in a way, loved at first, despised towards the end. But he could look back on his time at Bloomfield Road with pride, as he transformed an ailing club into a respectable and desirable unit. Maybe he stayed too long, but that was to his credit.

Jimmy Mullen

1989–90

Jimmy Mullen was appointed manager of Blackpool largely on the strength of the last five games of the 1988–89 season. After the departure of Sam Ellis, Mullen was asked to take charge of the team until the end of the season, with the unenviable task of ensuring Third Division survival. With the help of Len Ashurst, he guided Blackpool to four victories in the last five matches and so just avoided relegation. Soon afterwards, his appointment was confirmed.

Jarrow-born Mullen, a defender with Sheffield Wednesday, Rotherham United and Cardiff City, was assistant manager at Cardiff and Aberdeen and player-manager of Newport County, before joining Blackpool in May 1989, and his appointment was, at first, very popular with the fans. This enthusiasm did not last though.

In his one season in charge, the team seemed to lurch from one crisis to another. The problems had been forewarned with the opening game, at home to Wigan Athletic, where a dreary goalless draw had seen Blackpool unable to either win a corner or even have a shot on goal until the final three minutes. Players had been brought in, but not a single one seemed to impact in the expected way. Strikers Gordon Owen and Gary Brook struggled, Carl Richards found Mullen's management style difficult and the team looked disjointed and unsteady. The only truly successful signing was that of David Eyres from Rhyl, but it was clear that Blackpool were heading downwards, and within 11 months of his appointment Mullen's contract was terminated.

There were few bright spots, but certainly one worth mentioning was an incredible FA Cup run that saw Blackpool reach the fifth round for the first time in over 30 years, only to lose a second replay to Queen's Park Rangers. Unfortunately, it could not make up for the fact that Blackpool were relegated back to the Fourth Division and started the new decade in the lowest tier once more.

Mullen went to Burnley, where ironically, at the expense of Blackpool, he took the Clarets to the Fourth Division title. He then had further success by achieving another promotion to the new First Division in 1994, but after a couple of mediocre seasons he was sacked by the Turf Moor club in 1996. There then followed numerous managerial roles in non-League football, plus a sojourn to Ireland with Sligo Rovers. He returned to English football with Walsall in 2008 as manager, but was dismissed after just eight months in charge. He now assists at Rotherham United.

Mullen was enthusiastic at Blackpool, but sadly one of the least successful managerial appointments made by the club.

Graham Carr

1990

Graham Carr's reign as manager at Bloomfield Road was as short as it was unsuccessful. He arrived in the close season, and left just four months later, in November, so becoming Blackpool's shortest-serving manager.

Carr had arrived with a good reputation following his success at Northampton Town. He had transformed the unfashionable club into Fourth Division title-winners in 1987, with a record number of points gained and goals scored, and was certainly looked upon with affection by the club's fans. Sadly for him, it had all spiralled downwards after the sale of key players, and he was sacked in May 1990. It was then that he joined Blackpool.

The style of football he had deployed at Northampton was never pretty, but it had been effective, and this went some way to his failure at Blackpool. He immediately alienated the fans with the sale of Colin Methven to Carlisle United, saying that he was not good enough for League football – a decision that was stunning bearing in mind the popularity of the player in question. He had also failed to make a decision on relocating to the area, and after a heavy defeat by Tranmere Rovers in the Leyland DAF Cup, he was dismissed after only 16 League matches in charge.

Soon afterwards, Carr joined Maidstone United, but he only survived eight months before being sacked. He then had a three-year spell at Kettering Town, which was relatively successful, before returning to one of his playing clubs, Weymouth. He resigned after only four months at the helm, however. In more recent times he has scouted, with a large degree of success, at Tottenham Hotspur, Manchester City and Newcastle United.

As an aside, his son, Alan Carr, is well known for presenting the TV programmes *The Friday Night Project* and *Alan Carr: Chatty Man*.

Billy Ayre

1990–94

After Graham Carr's speedy departure, his assistant, Billy Ayre, was thrown into the hot seat. Almost unknown outside the lower Leagues, his appointment was greeted reservedly by Blackpool supporters. But in the space of one year Ayre became the club's most popular and certainly most successful manager since Stan Mortensen.

As a player he had spells with Scarborough, Hartlepools United, Halifax Town and Mansfield Town, and as a manager his only previous experience was at Halifax, where he had enjoyed little success. It hardly seemed the most inspired appointment, but the northeasterner's no-nonsense attitude worked with the players, and he proceeded to turn around the team's fortunes almost immediately. He re-signed Dave Bamber permanently and dragged the team from their 18th position in October to second place on the last day of the season, only losing three games in the process.

He had become a folk hero at Bloomfield Road, and his showbiz entrance onto the pitch before each game perfectly summed up his desire, passion and enthusiasm. He had quite literally transformed the club in a remarkably short space of time. Even the loss on the final day of the season at Walsall, where Blackpool dropped from second to fifth place in 90 minutes, failed to dampen the fans' love of him. The Play-off Final at Wembley, where

a penalty shoot-out disaster against Torquay United consigned Blackpool to lower League football for another season, perfectly summed up his attitude. As he stood on the pitch with the time approaching midnight, he reflected that he 'hadn't had a worse moment in life, never mind in football.'

The following season the team created all kinds of records, especially at home, as they again pushed for promotion. Once more, though, they failed in the final match – maybe an inherent weakness stopped them from becoming the successful side that everyone expected – and so Play-offs beckoned again. This time it was a winning penalty shoot-out against Scunthorpe United at Wembley, and Ayre had got Blackpool promoted to the new Second Division. His stock at Bloomfield Road was at an all-time high, and the task of survival in the higher division was greeted with unbridled enthusiasm.

Sadly, and regrettably, he was never given the financial backing needed by the board. In fact, in his time in charge he was forced to sell the likes of Alan Wright, Paul Groves (before the new season had even begun) and Trevor Sinclair, big-name players who were always going to be hard to replace. Despite this, sheer graft and hard work ensured that Blackpool survived, and an 18th-place finish was certainly respectable.

The following season was incredibly difficult, as little money was made available, and only a last-day victory over Leyton Orient ensured safety for another season. Chairman Owen Oyston publicly stated that this would not happen again, and sadly he made the decision to sack Ayre in the summer of 1994. It was a hugely unpopular decision with the fans, summed up in a home League Cup game the following season when Sam Allardyce's Blackpool side had to play to the chants of 'Billy Ayre's

Tangerine Army' from the home faithful.

Ayre did not really achieve much in the way of managerial success thereafter. He went to Scarborough and was sacked within months, before a short stint at non-League Southport. He then had spells as assistant at Swansea City and Cardiff City under Jan Molby and Frank Burrows respectively, before taking over the reins at Ninian Park in January 2000. He left the club for good 10 months later. His last job in football was as assistant to ex-player Andy Preece at Bury, but by this time his health was failing badly. He had been diagnosed with lymph node cancer back in 1995, and by 2002 the disease had overcome his fighting spirit and on 16 April, aged 49, he died.

Ayre is regarded as possibly the most popular manager of Blackpool in recent memory, and his popularity was summed up when he was spotted in the crowd at the Millennium Stadium for the Football League Trophy Final with Cambridge United. He was mobbed by Blackpool fans, and his name was sung around the concourse, much to his embarrassment. As far as the author is concerned, and I believe that I speak for many of the fans, it is sad that his achievements and popularity were never acknowledged by the club. Such a high-calibre manager will never be seen again.

Sam Allardyce

1994–96

Sam Allardyce is regarded today as one of the most forward-thinking football managers in the domestic game, yet when he was appointed at Blackpool in 1994, his pedigree amounted to little, with a brief yet successful spell at Irish club Limerick, and a temporary tenure at rivals Preston North End.

A useful centre-half who appeared for many clubs, most notably and successfully Bolton Wanderers, he arrived at Bloomfield Road with little enthusiasm from the fans. Not only was he an ex-Preston player and manager, but he was replacing the hugely popular Billy Ayre.

Rather surprisingly, the board gave him money to spend as the club had struggled in Division Two during the previous two years, and Allardyce spent wisely. The partnership of Tony Ellis and Andy Preece was paying dividends, and the emerging James Quinn was part of a team that was gelling nicely. That first season saw a respectable mid-table position, despite a horror-type Christmas period that saw Blackpool lose to York City (0–4), Stockport County (1–2) and Birmingham City (1–7). They stayed in contention for the Play-offs up until March, and after a home defeat to Bristol Rovers the fans again showed their displeasure with a demonstration aimed at the manager. Allardyce had not won any friends, and the season was typified by the opening game of the season, a loss to Huddersfield 1–4 at home, and the penultimate home fixture, 0–5 against York City. Yet there had been

highs, and the new campaign was looked towards with a little more enthusiasm than expected.

The next season saw 'Big Sam' reign over one of the most traumatic campaigns in the history of the club. With the team in the top six for most of the season, and at one stage actually leading the division, Blackpool were well placed for automatic promotion. That they failed to achieve their goal in a most spectacular fashion – as already described – is something that even today is not totally understood. There were rumours of the manager asking the chairman for funds for a player, only to be turned down in the crucial run-in at the end of the season, but the truth to that story was never revealed. At that time, the chairman, Owen Oyston, was in prison following his conviction for sexual assault, so any dealings with him must have been difficult. None of that could explain Blackpool's astonishing capitulation in the second leg of the Play-off semi-final at home to Bradford City. Leading 2–0 from the first, they inexplicably lost 3–0, and so ended Sam Allardyce's career at Blackpool Football Club.

Big Sam has always said that he was called into a meeting to discuss the following season, and at the time there seemed to be no indication that a change of manager was likely, despite the anger from the fans over the Bradford debacle. Indeed, if Allardyce had been kept on, surely promotion would have been gained significantly earlier than the eventual 2007! As it was, Allardyce was sacked by the chairman, residing in a prison cell, and later moved to Notts County. There he proved his ability by gaining promotion in his first full year. He then had a successful time at Bolton Wanderers, actually bringing European football to the Trotters as well as regular Premier League football, and is regarded extremely highly by the club and its fans.

A short spell at Newcastle United was deemed a failure, but he was employed at Blackburn Rovers to build a foundation at Ewood Park to provide regular Premier League football.

Allardyce never won over the Blackpool fans for reasons already explained, but as time has passed most supporters look back and realise the talent the club had at its disposal, and the rashness of Allardyce's sacking.

Midway through the 2010–11 season, Allardyce was sacked by the new Indian owners of the club. It was an astonishing decision and very nearly cost Blackburn their Premier League status.

Gary Megson

1996–97

Gary Megson's appointment was totally underwhelming for most Blackpool supporters, but it is fair to say that he had an almost impossible job following the debacle of the previous season. A tough-tackling midfielder who had played for many clubs, notably Sheffield Wednesday, he arrived at Bloomfield Road with limited managerial experience. His only managerial stint had been at Norwich City, where he had initially been a player, but after one full season in charge had been sacked to make way for Mike Walker.

He brought in Mike Phelan as his assistant, as the club tried to recover from the hangover from the promotion-failing disaster, but within a few weeks it was clear that he was not going to be able to stop what had rapidly become a downward spiral. His standing with the fans, not the most patient when it comes to managers, was never high, and was not helped by a public complaint after they had barracked him. There were few highlights in the season, but one, a 3–1 win at Chelsea in the League Cup, stands out. The League campaign stuttered, and a team that was pre-season favourites for the title, found itself in the bottom half by Christmas. Only a good run saw Blackpool edge toward the promotion race, but the play-offs were missed on the last day of the season. That effectively saw the end of Megson's time at Bloomfield Road. He left to join a 'bigger club', as he described it. That club was Stockport County, who happened to be in Division One at the time, and could not in any way be described as 'bigger' as far as Blackpool fans were concerned. Legal issues followed between the two clubs, which were not resolved for some time, and Megson had left Blackpool with few fond memories.

Since then, he has managed at the highest level. From Stockport, where he left after two years, he went for a brief spell at Stoke City. There was then success at West Bromwich Albion, which included two promotions to the Premier League, before a disastrous stint at Nottingham Forest. Then followed a month at Leicester City, before a much longer and more successful time with Bolton Wanderers. He was sacked in December 2009.

Nigel Worthington

1997–99

As Blackpool Football Club started its descent with its refusal to learn from the mistakes of the infamous 1995–96 season, the managerial appointments had become unexpected to say the least. After the short Gary Megson era, the club decided that Nigel Worthington, a full-back who had played mostly for Sheffield Wednesday and who had made nine appearances for the Tangerines, should be appointed as player-manager. It was not what the fans had desired, and sadly heralded an era of total underachievement for the club.

Worthington had never managed, but he was given the opportunity at Blackpool – a club now deep in crisis, with Owen Oyston's wife, Vicky, in charge, and the fans so disillusioned that 'funeral marches' were made to the ground and the Oyston's home. At one stage, a League game was interrupted as fans entered the pitch and staged a sit-down protest on the centre circle. With this taking place, it needed a strong manager at the helm, but unfortunately Nigel Worthington was not that man. Almost immediately, Worthington ended his playing days so he could concentrate fully on his managerial duties, but there was so little that was positive in the Worthy-era, that there is little to describe. Performances by the team deteoriated to such an extent that mid-table mediocrity was considered the norm. The former Leeds United assistant Mick Henigan was brought in to help, but nothing could change the stale and dour football that was on offer. After a couple of seasons, the team found themselves deep in a relegation battle once more, and after a heavy defeat at Preston – just four days after a creditable performance at Arsenal in the FA Cup – Worthington resigned, stating that he had taken the club 'as far as he could.' He left after two and a half years, during which time the team had gradually worsened, and return to the basement division seemed inevitable.

Worthington was not out of work for long as he joined Norwich City, firstly as assistant to Bryan Hamilton, and then as full-time manager. He enjoyed remarkable success by taking the Canaries to the Premier League, leaving the Blackpool fans to wonder why on earth ex-managers seemed to have so much success once they left Bloomfield Road! Worthington stayed at Carrow Road for six years but was sacked after another attempt to regain Premier League status seemed doomed to failure. He then joined the band of managers who entered the revolving door at Leicester City, before taking charge of Northern Ireland. He has had minimal success, but the Irish Football Association have been suitably impressed.

Steve McMahon

2000–04

The success that Blackpool Football Club has experienced in recent years can arguably be traced back to the appointment of Steve McMahon as manager. Following the resignation of Nigel Worthington, the club was in disarray. Plummeting towards relegation, they needed someone to galvanise and enthuse everyone involved, and they found that in former England international McMahon. Successful as a creative and combative midfielder for Everton, Aston Villa and especially Liverpool – where he won many honours for the club – followed by spells at Manchester City and then Swindon Town, McMahon had only had one previous managerial position. That was at Swindon, where he had presided over both promotion and relegation, and effectively polarised opinion among the Town supporters. Four years later, the same could be said of Blackpool fans.

His arrival was greeted with delight by most Blackpool supporters. A big name who was prepared to sweep through the club and stamp his mark. Too late to save Second Division status, he embarked on rebuilding the club's and his own reputation. The following season, with the help of numerous loan deals and astute transfer buys, he won promotion back via a Play-off Final against Leyton Orient at Cardiff's Millennium Stadium. The season had not been without its dramas, though, a 4–1 victory at Kidderminster Harriers being described as a 'make or break' for the manager, as Blackpool were at that time in 91st position in the Football League. That was followed by a 7–0 defeat at Barnet, but the style of attacking football was paying dividends and eventually brought success.

Back in the third tier, the omens looked good, and with another trip to Cardiff for victory in the Football League Trophy against Cambridge United, Blackpool's success seemed assured. Off the field, McMahon's influence had spread well enough to hasten the rebuilding of Bloomfield Road, with the North and West Stands rising and opening during his tenure. He had constantly maintained that it was impossible to attract decent players to the old and dilapidated ground, and he can take huge credit for Bloomfield Road's regeneration.

On the field, though, there were concerns. Mirroring exactly what had taken place at the County Ground, Blackpool followed the same pattern: stunning early-season performances that flattered to deceive, only for the team to suffer inconsistency and lack any kind of strength of character, which was quite astonishing, bearing in mind the personality of the manager. Even another Football League Trophy two years later, at the expense of Southend United, failed to paper over the cracks, as many fans now questioned if McMahon could take the club further. There were the familiar rows with the chairman behind the scenes over finances, and one particularly comedic farce took place on the 15 January 2004, when after resigning he burst into the televised press conference to say that he had changed his mind! It did him, and the club, no favours.

The relationship between chairman and manager stayed tense, and before the last match of the season, where Blackpool had again failed to live up to their League billing, McMahon resigned once more, this time without return. Afterwards he had a very brief and unsuccessful spell at Perth Glory, before returning to the UK to work as a pundit for radio and television. He is now part of an investment group that recently attempted, and failed, to launch a takeover of Newcastle United.

McMahon could and should have been a great manager. He had all the attributes: the experience of football at the highest level and the enthusiasm to get the job done. Sadly, there was something missing, and despite three trophies in four years at Blackpool, there is a general feeling that he underachieved.

Colin Hendry

2004–05

In the 10 years of success that Blackpool Football Club has enjoyed since the turn of the century, there has only been one blip, and that was the tenure of Colin Hendry. The Scottish International defender came with great playing pedigree. Tough-tackling and inspirational on the pitch, he had success at both domestic level and international. Blackburn Rovers is where he will always be associated as a player, but he had spells at Dundee, Manchester City, Rangers and, towards the end of his playing career, Blackpool. His appointment to succeed Steve McMahon should have been inspired; it turned out to be a disaster.

It is difficult to understand why Hendry failed so spectacularly, but his first three competitive games resulted in defeat, with Blackpool bottom of the division. The season did not improve much, although a mid-season revival did drag the team to just below mid-table, but it was clear to see that Hendry did not have the support of the fans or, according to the rumours, the players. He had an eye for talent, notably the acquisition of Keigan Parker, but too many players were brought in and failed to gel, or were played out of position.

With the 2005–06 season heading downwards once more, and after a heavy defeat in the FA Cup to Doncaster, Hendry

was put on gardening leave by Karl Oyston. In one of the longest dismissals on record, an agreement was finally reached and Hendry left the club in November 2005. He then went to Boston United as assistant manager, before winning a full-time position at Clyde. The Clyde tenure was not successful and he resigned in January 2008, but that was more to do with the serious illness that his wife, Denise, was suffering from.

Blackpool fans, although disappointed by his failure as a manager, will always have fond feelings towards Hendry. The same can be said for many around the country, as he has suffered more in his private life than any person should. His wife died in July 2009, and in 2010 he was declared bankrupt – seemingly as a result of hospital bills for Denise.

It is hoped that all football fans remember Colin Hendry as a great football player and forget his lack of success as a manager.

Simon Grayson

2005–08

Simon Grayson was an unlikely appointment to succeed Colin Hendry, despite being his assistant, but went on to become one of the most successful managers in Blackpool's history. It was an unlikely appointment because the chairman, Karl Oyston, had publicly said that he would not favour the cheap option and would look far and wide for a new manager. Grayson may or may not have been cheap, but he was on the doorstep when the chairman began his search.

Simon Grayson was a defender who had spent most of his career at Leicester City, before arriving at Blackpool – the last of his nine clubs – in 2002. He made over 120 appearances for the Seasiders and was established as the club captain. When Steve McMahon resigned before the final game of the 2003–04 season, Grayson took charge, and as Hendry remoulded the side he then moved from defence to midfield and was also installed officially as Hendry's assistant manager. So it was fitting that he should take over temporarily once Hendry had gone.

Grayson's first game in charge was the televised home fixture with Scunthorpe United, which Blackpool duly won 5–2. This victory set the standard for the remainder of the season, and relegation – seemingly a certainty when Colin Hendry left – was avoided on the penultimate weekend. It was a remarkable achievement, and one which effectively matched anything on Grayson's CV in the next few years at Blackpool and Leeds United.

For the next season he was given the role permanently, and he retired from playing duties to concentrate on managing. He was an immediate success. After a slow start to the season, he guided Blackpool to a remarkable 10 successive victories at the end of the campaign, and promotion to the Championship via a Play-off Final win over Yeovil Town at Wembley. It was the club's first appearance back in the top half of the Football League since 1978, and Grayson can take enormous credit for the way he moulded the side into one of the most attractive and creative teams in the Division. He did it without spending money, although the appearance of a new investor in Latvian Valeri Belokon gave him the chance to spend a little more freely than previous managers had been able to do.

The next season saw consolidation in the Championship, although relegation was only avoided on the final day, but the team did enjoy a League Cup run that only saw defeat at Tottenham Hotspur in the fourth round. A win at Preston North End was the highlight of the season, courtesy of a young Wes Hoolahan, who had been spotted by Grayson playing for Livingston, and the large majority of fans supported the manager fully. Inevitably, his name was being linked with bigger clubs, one of them being Leicester City, where he had spent five years as a player. Each overture was turned down, much to the relief of everyone connected to Blackpool, but as Christmas 2008 approached it was clear that the love affair was ending. A poor home performance against rivals Preston had seen a few of the supporters now openly question Grayson, and his abundance of loan players in the team became open to criticism. Added to that, the team were again looking over the shoulder at possible relegation, and it was no surprise that when his boyhood favourite club, Leeds United, came calling, he did not think twice about leaving Blackpool.

It was no surprise that Grayson should have gone to Leeds, despite them being in a lower division. He had always supported them and lived close to the City. Also, even the most rabid of Blackpool fans could see that Leeds United is a huge club with massive potential. Most fans wished him well, even if his timing left something to be desired. Temporary manager Tony Parkes – picking up the baton in his career for the umpteenth time – was faced with nearly a dozen players returning to their parent clubs in the new year of 2009, just days after Grayson's departure.

A legal battle followed, which was eventually resolved, and Simon Grayson continued to show his managerial talents. After a Play-off defeat to Millwall in his first season, he guided Leeds back to the Championship the next year. He and the club are clearly destined for greater things.

What Steve McMahon had started back in 2000, Simon Grayson continued. He was, and is, a great manager, and Blackpool can feel grateful that he started at Bloomfield Road.

Ian Holloway

2009–present day

What can be said about Ian Holloway? Charismatic, quirky, eccentric, witty, but most of all a football genius. The list of managers at Blackpool Football Club includes two who have become part of the fabric of the club and its fans – Joe Smith and Billy Ayre. It is fair to say that Ian Holloway is very close to joining that small, elite group of Blackpool managerial successes.

Bristol-born Holloway was a midfielder who played for 18 years and made over 300 appearances for his beloved Bristol Rovers. His managerial record saw him at Rovers, with minimal success, then Queen's Park Rangers, where he oversaw promotion, before moving back to Devon and Plymouth Argyle. He became hugely popular with the fans and seemed to be on the verge of success at Home Park before making what he describes as a terrible decision – leaving for Leicester City. Leicester were a club deep in crisis, with a managerial record that resembled a Christmas card list, but he chose to leave a club where he was loved for one that was lurching from one crisis to another. Inevitably, he was sacked after they were relegated to League One (ironically, Blackpool avoided the drop on the same day) and Holloway then found himself out of work for a year, watching football,

Ian Holloway and the 2010–11 squad.

thinking about his footballing philosophy, and providing witty words of wisdom as a radio pundit. Then Blackpool came calling.

There are still stories as to how Holloway and Blackpool FC came together, but the fact is that Karl Oyston – who had surprisingly decided against installing Tony Parkes as full-time manager, despite helping the team avoid relegation – saw something in Holloway that appealed, and the relationship thrived.

Holloway came with his own brand of football, which was basically to attack. He made on-loan star Charlie Adam a permanent signing for a club-record fee, and then bought players who all added to the strength of the team. The return of favourite Brett Ormerod was a master stroke, when many felt that he had seen his best; 'Olly' knew better. He utilised the loan market excellently, and despite not appearing at any time on the national media's radar he kept Blackpool right on the verge of the promotion race throughout the season, despite the smallest budget and low crowds due to the ground still being underdeveloped. He forged a successful relationship with the chairman, and it was clear that the two of them had great respect for each other.

Holloway and Blackpool were made for each other, and his greatest achievement in football was to bring top-flight football back to the town for the first time since 1971. This feat was done in an attractive and flowing way. The semi-final second leg of the Play-offs at Nottingham Forest was one of the finest displays of football seen by a Blackpool side for many years, and the famous Wembley Final will live long in the memory of Blackpool and football fans alike.

Ian Holloway is unique. There is frankly no one quite like him. Press conferences and interviews with him can be a lesson in randomness, but beneath his media persona is a manager who has the ability to go on the great things. At a time when England are preparing for a new English manager, it is typical of the national media – who ignored Blackpool in their promotion season until they were forced kicking and screaming to acknowledge what was happening – that 'Olly' is not mentioned. Ian Holloway is quite simply the best English manager in England, and his achievements at Bloomfield Road, in such a short space of time, can easily stand scrutiny alongside the great Joe Smith. Long may he reign.

Holloway was true to his word and attacked the Premier League at every opportunity, both on the pitch and at times in his usual dramatic press conferences. He found himself in trouble after making 10 changes for the visit to Aston Villa (a game they lost 3–2 and frankly could have won if a stronger side was chosen), and for that he was fined £25,000. There was a suggestion that he was ready to resign over the matter, but thankfully he continued. Holloway became the darling of the media and, as Blackpool became everyone's 'second team' due to their flair and vibrancy, so 'Olly' became more and more popular. His tactical and motivational powers were second to none at times, and if he had achieved the incredible and kept Blackpool in the Premier League, then surely he would have been named Manager of the Year. As it was, relegation was only confirmed 20 minutes from the end of the season, an amazing achievement bearing in mind he still had effectively a Championship side at his disposal. His next test was still to come. Could he resurrect the club to push for promotion again?

1896-97

Division Two

Did you know that?

Charlie Mount scored Blackpool's first-ever League goal against Lincoln City – but they lost 3–1.

Burton Wanderers were the first visitors to Raikes Hall for a Football League game. The match on 19 September resulted in a 5–0 win for Blackpool.

On Boxing Day, Blackpool played in front of a crowd of around 10,000, when they lost 2–0 at Newton Heath.

William Douglas, Tommy Bowman and Bob Norris were the only ever-presents for Blackpool this season.

Match No.	Date	Venue	Opponents	Result		Scorers	Attendance
1	Sep 5	A	Lincoln City	L	1-3	Mount	1,500
2	12	A	Darwen	W	3-2	Donnelly 2, Mount	
3	19	H	Burton W	W	5-0	Connor, Donnelly, Stirzaker, Mount, Clarkin	3,000
4	26	H	Manchester City	D	2-2	J Parkinson, Bowman	4,000
5	Oct 3	A	Leicester Fosse	L	1-2	Donnelly	6,000
6	17	H	Newton Heath	W	4-2	Mount, J Parkinson 2, Martin	5,000
7	24	H	Burton Swifts	D	2-2	Martin, J Parkinson	3,000
8	Nov 7	A	Manchester City	L	2-4	J Parkinson, Martin	4,000
9	14	H	Lincoln City	W	3-1	Birkett, Mount, Clarkin	1,500
10	28	H	Notts County	W	3-2	Stirzaker, Martin 2	2,200
11	Dec 19	A	Woolwich Arsenal	L	2-4	R Parkinson, Donnelly	6,000
12	26	A	Newton Heath	L	0-2		10,000
13	Jan 1	H	Grimsby Town	W	1-0	Norris	5,000
14	4	H	Woolwich Arsenal	D	1-1	Martin	1,000
15	16	A	Newcastle United	L	1-4	Bowman	8,000
16	23	H	Small Heath	L	1-3	Bradshaw	2,000
17	30	A	Loughborough T	L	1-4	Stirzaker	
18	Feb 13	H	Walsall	W	3-2	J Parkinson, Clarke, Parr	1,000
19	20	A	Grimsby Town	D	2-2	Martin, Clarke	5,000
20	27	H	Leicester Fosse	W	3-0	Bradshaw, J Parkinson,Clarke	
21	Mar 6	A	Small Heath	W	3-1	Clarke, J Parkinson, Martin	5,000
22	13	H	Newcastle United	W	4-1	J Parkinson, Clarke 2, Bradshaw	3,000
23	20	A	Notts County	L	1-3	Bradshaw	7,000
24	27	H	Loughborough T	W	4-1	Clarke 2 , Bradshaw, Clarkin	2,500
25	29	A	Burton W	L	1-3	Martin	
26	Apr 3	A	Gainsborough T	L	0-2		
27	10	A	Walsall	L	0-2		
28	14	H	Darwen	W	1-0	J Parkinson	5,000
29	19	H	Burton Swifts	W	3-0	J Parkinson 2, Martin	3,000
30	24	H	Gainsborough T	D	1-1	Clarkin	3,000

Final League Position: 8th in Division Two

Apps

Gls

Douglas	Parr	Bowman	Stuart	Stirzaker	Norris	Clarkin	Donnelly	Parkinson J	Parkinson R	Mount	Connor	Thompson	Martin	Birkett	Colville	Gillett	Bradshaw	Winstanley	Clarke	Scarr
1	2	3	4	5	6	7	8	9	10	11										
1	2	3	4	5	6	7	8	10		11	9									
1	2	3	4	5	6	7	8	10		11	9									
1	2	3	4	5	6	7	8	10		11	9									
1	2	3	4	5	6	11	10	9		7	8									
1	2	3	4	5	6	7	8	9		11			10							
1	2	3	4	5	6	7	8	9		11			10							
1	2	3	4	5	6	7	8	9		11			10							
1	2	3	4	5	6	7	8	9		11				10						
1	2	3	4	5	6	7	8	9	10				11							
1	2	3	4	5	6		8	9	11				10							
1	2	3	4	5	6	7	8		9				11				10			
1	2	3	4	5	6	7	8		9				10							
1	2	3		5	6	7		9	10				11		4	8				
1	2	3		5	6	7	8	9	10				11		4					
1		3		5	6	7		9	8			2	11		4		10			
1	2	3	4	5	6								11		9	7	10	8		
1	2	3	4	5	6	7		10					8				11		9	
1	2	3	4	5	6	7		10					8				11			
1	2	3	4	5	6	7		10									11	8	9	
1	2	3	4	5	6	7		10					8				11		9	
1	2	3	4	5	6	7		10					8				11		9	
1	2	3	4	5	6	7		10					8				11		9	
1	2	3	4	5	6	7		10					8				11		9	
1	2	3		5	6	7		10					8		4		11		9	
1	2	3		4	6	7		10				5	8				11		9	
1	2	3		4	6	7		10				5	8		4				9	
1	2	3			6	7		10				5	8				11		9	4
1	2	3			6	7		10				5	8				11		9	4
1	2	3			6	7		10				5	8				11		9	4
30	29	30	21	27	30	28	14	27	8	9	4	6	23	1	5	2	17	2	13	3
	1	2		3	1	6	5	12	1	5	1		10	1			5		6	

League Table

	P	W	D	L	F	A	Pts
Notts County	30	19	4	7	92	43	42
Newton Heath	30	17	5	8	56	34	39
Grimsby Town	30	17	4	9	66	45	38
Small Heath	30	16	5	9	69	47	37
Newcastle United	30	17	1	12	56	52	35
Manchester City	30	12	8	10	58	50	32
Gainsborough Trinity	30	12	7	11	50	47	31
Blackpool	30	13	5	12	59	56	31
Leicester Fosse	30	13	4	13	59	57	30
Woolwich Arsenal	30	13	4	13	68	70	30
Darwen	30	14	0	16	67	61	28
Walsall	30	11	4	15	54	69	26
Loughborough	30	12	1	17	50	64	25
Burton Swifts	30	9	6	15	46	61	24
Burton Wanderers	30	9	2	19	31	67	20
Lincoln City	30	5	2	23	27	85	12

1897-98

Division Two

Did you know that?

The final game of the season, at home to Luton Town, saw only 200 spectators witness a 1–0 victory.

The first win of the season was at the Athletic Grounds where Blackpool beat Burton Swifts 2–1 at home.

The club announced a loss of 'only' £441 this season, compared to £1184 12 months previous.

Goalkeeper William Douglas played in every match, meaning that he had appeared in every Blackpool League game so far.

Match No.	Date		Venue	Opponents	Result		Scorers	Attendance
1	Sep	4	A	Burnley	L	1-5	Own-goal	2,000
2		11	H	Burnley	D	1-1	Martin	4,000
3		18	H	Manchester City	L	0-2		3,000
4		25	A	Newton Heath	L	0-1		3,000
5	Oct	2	A	Gainsborough T	L	1-4	Halsall	
6		9	H	Burton Swifts	W	2-1	Cox 2	3,000
7		16	H	Small Heath	W	4-1	Clarkin, Cox 2, Birkett	1,500
8		23	A	Newcastle United	L	0-2		7,000
9	Nov	6	A	Leicester Fosse	L	1-4	Martin	6,000
10		13	A	Darwen	L	1-2	Martin	2,000
11		27	A	Woolwich Arsenal	L	1-2	Martin	6,500
12		29	A	Luton Town	L	1-3	Clarkin	
13	Dec	18	H	Gainsborough T	W	5-0	Cox, Stirzaker, Parkinson, Own-goal 2	
14		25	H	Newcastle United	L	2-3	Cox 2	3,000
15		27	A	Walsall	L	0-6		
16	Jan	1	H	Woolwich Arsenal	D	3-3	Cox 2, Birkett	1,500
17		8	H	Leicester Fosse	W	2-1	Parkinson, Martin	3,000
18		15	H	Newton Heath	L	0-4		4,000
19		29	A	Small Heath	W	3-2	Parkinson, Martin, Cox	6,000
20	Feb	5	A	Lincoln City	L	2-3	Wilson, Birkett	
21		19	H	Lincoln City	W	5-0	Birkett 2, Cox 2, Parkinson	1,000
22		26	A	Burton Swifts	L	1-2	Birkett	
23	Mar	19	A	Grimsby Town	L	0-3		4,000
24		26	A	Loughborough T	W	2-0	Birkett, Leadbetter	
25		30	A	Manchester City	D	3-3	Clarkin, Parkinson 2	1,000
26	Apr	2	H	Walsall	D	1-1	Martin	
27		9	H	Darwen	W	1-0	Clarkin	4,000
28		16	H	Grimsby Town	D	1-1	Leadbetter	1,000
29		23	H	Loughborough T	W	4-0	Parkinson 2, Birkett, Leadbetter	300
30		30	H	Luton Town	W	1-0	Clarkin	300

Final League Position: 11th in Division Two

Apps

Gls

Douglas	Parr	Bowman	McHardie	Stirzaker	Norris	Clarkin	Martin	Wilson	Keach	Halsall	Parkinson	Leadbetter	Stuart	Cox	Birkett	Cardwell	Scarr	Banks
1	2	3	4	5	6	7	8	9	10	11								
1	2	3	4	5	6		7	9	10		8	11						
1	2	3	4	5		7	8	9	4	10								
1	2	3		5	6	7	8		4	10	9	11						
1	2	3		5		7		8	6	9	10		4	11				
1	2	3		5	6	7	8		4	9	10			11				
1	2	3		5		7	8		4			10		11	9			
1	2	3	6	5		7	8	10	9				4	11				
1	2		6	5		7	8	10	9				4	11		3		
1	2		6	5		7	8	10	2				4	11	9			
1	2		5		6	7	10	8	3		9		4	11				
1	2		5		6	7	10	8	3		9		4	11				
1	2		5	3	6	7	10	8			9		4	11				
1			5	3	6	7	2	8	4		9	10		11				
1			5	3	6	7	2	8	4		9	10		11				
1	2		5		6	7	4	8				11		9	10	3		
1	2		5		6	7	8	4	9		10				11	3		
1	2		5	3	6	7	8	4	9		10			11				
1	2		5	3	6	7	9	4			10			11	8			
1	2		5	3	6	7	9	4			10			11	8			
1	2		5	3	6	7	9	4			10			11	8			
1	2		5	3	6	7	9	4			10	11			8			
1	2		5	3	6	7	9	4			10	11			8			
1	2		5	3	6	7	9	4			10	11			8			
1	2		5	3	6	7	9	4			10	11	8					
1	2		5	3	6	7	9	4			10	11			8			
1	2		5	3	6	7	9	4			10	11			8			
1	2			5	6		9				10	11	8		7	3	4	
1	2				5		9				10	11	8		7	4	3	
1	2			5			9				10	11	8		7	4	3	6
30	28	8	24	25	23	26	29	23	18	5	24	17	10	17	14	6	3	1
				1		5	7	1		1	8	3		12	8			

League Table

	P	W	D	L	F	A	Pts
Burnley	30	20	8	2	80	24	48
Newcastle United	30	21	3	6	64	32	45
Manchester City	30	15	9	6	66	36	39
Newton Heath	30	16	6	8	64	35	38
Woolwich Arsenal	30	16	5	9	69	49	37
Small Heath	30	16	4	10	58	50	36
Leicester Fosse	30	13	7	10	46	35	33
Luton Town	30	13	4	13	68	50	30
Gainsborough Trinity	30	12	6	12	50	54	30
Walsall	30	12	5	13	58	58	29
Blackpool	30	10	5	15	49	61	25
Grimsby Town	30	10	4	16	52	62	24
Burton Swifts	30	8	5	17	38	69	21
Lincoln City	30	6	5	19	43	82	17
Darwen	30	6	2	22	31	76	14
Loughborough	30	6	2	22	24	87	14

1898-99

Division Two

Did you know that?

Blackpool suffered eight consecutive defeats this season, a record that stood for 67 years.

Only 10 players appeared for Blackpool in the 6–1 defeat at Burslem Port Vale on 21 January.

Seven home games were played at Raikes Hall and the remaining 10 at the Athletic Grounds.

The club was relegated out of the Football League with Gainsborough and Darwen.

Match No.	Date		Venue	Opponents	Result		Scorers	Attendance
1	Sep	3	A	Grimsby Town	L	1-4	Own-goal	
2		10	H	Walsall	L	1-2	Leadbetter	1,000
3		17	A	Burton Swifts	L	1-3	Parkinson	3,000
4		24	H	Burslem Port Vale	L	0-4		1,000
5	Oct	8	H	Loughborough T	W	2-1	Birkett 2	500
6		22	A	Grimsby Town	L	1-2	Birkett	4,000
7	Nov	5	A	New Brighton Town	L	0-4		500
8		12	H	Lincoln City	W	3-0	Stirzaker, Birkett 2	1,000
9		26	H	Luton Town	L	2-3	Cartmell, Leadbetter	500
10	Dec	3	A	Leicester Fosse	L	0-4		4,000
11		10	A	Newton Heath	L	1-3	Birkett	4,000
12		17	A	Gainsborough T	L	0-7		
13		24	H	Manchester City	L	2-4	Hateley, Hoyle	1,000
14		26	A	Small Heath	L	0-5		4,000
15		31	H	Glossop	L	1-2	Parkinson	
16	Jan	7	A	Walsall	L	0-6		
17		14	H	Burton Swifts	W	3-0	Parkinson 2, Scott (pen)	2,000
18		21	A	Burslem Port Vale	L	1-6	Parkinson	
19	Feb	4	A	Loughborough T	W	3-1	Scott, Birkett 2	5,000
20		11	A	Barnsley	L	1-2	Stuart	
21		18	H	Grimsby Town	L	3-6	Birkett 2, Parkinson	4,000
22	Mar	4	H	New Brighton Town	L	1-2	Parkinson	
23		8	H	Small Heath	D	1-1	Scott	1,000
24		11	A	Lincoln City	D	0-0		
25		15	H	Barnsley	W	3-1	Parkinson, Gamble 2	600
26		18	A	Woolwich Arsenal	L	0-6		3,000
27		22	H	Woolwich Arsenal	D	1-1	Gamble	1,000
28		25	A	Luton Town	L	2-3	Leadbetter, Birket	
29		31	H	Darwen	W	6-0	Parkinson, Parr, Morris 2, Birkett, Williams	
30	Apr	1	H	Leicester Fosse	D	2-2	Scott, Morris	
31		3	A	Newton Heath	L	0-1		3,000
32		8	A	Darwen	W	2-0	Leadbetter, Morris	
33		15	H	Gainsborough T	W	2-0	Leadbetter 2, Birkett 2	
34		23	A	Manchester City	L	1-4	Birkett	10,000

Final League Position: 16th in Division Two (failed re-election)

Apps

Gls

1899-1900

Lancashire League

League Table

	P	W	D	L	F	A	Pts
1. Stockport County	28	21	3	4	80	23	45
2. Stalybridge Rovers	28	16	8	4	61	23	40
3. Blackpool	28	16	6	6	79	36	38
4. Crewe Alexandra	28	16	4	8	87	48	36
5. Darwen	28	13	10	5	56	31	36
6. Chorley	28	15	6	7	49	28	36
7. Southport Central	28	14	5	9	49	32	33
8. White Star Wanderers	28	11	4	13	51	56	26
9. Rochdale	28	9	7	12	50	53	25
10. Haydock	28	9	5	14	40	57	23
11. Earlestown	28	7	5	16	40	64	19
12. Wigan County	28	5	8	15	26	59	18
13. South Liverpool FC	28	5	7	16	32	66	17
14. Horwich	28	5	6	17	27	70	16
15. Middleton	28	5	2	21	18	99	12
16. South Shore*	0	0	0	0	0	0	0

*Merged with Blackpool.

Fletcher	Stirzaker	Scott	Scarr	Howson	Mayor	Harrison	Jones	Leadbetter	Birkett	Parkinson	Dickson	Cartmell	Gosling	Banks	Exton	Williams	Harrison F	Harrison W	Parr
1	2	3	4	6	5	7	10	11	8	9									
1	2	3	4	6	5	7	10	11	8	9									
1	2	3	4	5			10	11	7	9	6	8							
1	2	3	4	6				11	7	9			5	8	10				
1	2	3		4				11	9	10		7		8		5	6		
1	2	3		4				11	9	10				8		5	6	7	
1	5	3		4				11	7	10				8		9			2
1	5	3		4				11	9	10		7		8					2
1	5	3		6				11		10		7		9		8			2
1	3	9		7				11	8	10						5			2
1	3	9		7				11	8	10						5			2
1	3	9		8				11		10						5			2
1	4	3						11	9	8						5			2
1	4	3						11	9	8						5			2
	4	3						11	9	8						5			2
	4	3		9				11		8						5			2
1	3	8						11	9	10				7		5			2
1	3	8						11	9	10				7		5			2
1	3	8						11	9	10				7		5			2
1	3	8						11	9	10				7		5			2
1	3	10		6					9	8						5			2
1	3	8						11	9	10						5			2
1	3	10						11		9						5			2
1		8						11	9	10						5			2
1		3						11		10						5			2
1	5	3						11		10						5			2
1	5	3						11		10									2
1		3						11	9	10									2
1	5	3						11	8	10						5			2
1	5	3						11		10									2
1	5	3						11		10									2
1	5	3						11		10									2
1	5	3						11	9	10									2
1	5	3						11	8	10									2
32	32	34	4	14	2	2	3	33	24	34	1	4	1	10	1	22	2	1	28
	1	4						6	15	9		1				1			1

League Table

	P	W	D	L	F	A	Pts
Manchester City	34	23	6	5	92	35	52
Glossop	34	20	6	8	76	38	46
Leicester Fosse	34	18	9	7	64	42	45
Newton Heath	34	19	5	10	67	43	43
New Brighton Tower	34	18	7	9	71	52	43
Walsall	34	15	12	7	79	36	42
Woolwich Arsenal	34	18	5	11	72	41	41
Small Heath	34	17	7	10	85	50	41
Burslem Port Vale	34	17	5	12	56	34	39
Grimsby Town	34	15	5	14	71	60	35
Barnsley	34	12	7	15	52	56	31
Lincoln City	34	12	7	15	51	56	31
Burton Swifts	34	10	8	16	51	70	28
Gainsborough Trinity	34	10	5	19	56	72	25
Luton Town	34	10	3	21	51	95	23
Blackpool	34	8	4	22	49	90	20
Loughborough	34	6	6	22	38	92	18
Darwen	34	2	5	27	22	141	9

1900-01

Division Two

Did you know that?

Blackpool and South Shore had amalgamated the previous year, and most of the South Shore players joined the new club.

It was the final season that Raikes Hall was used by the club.

There was a record League defeat – 1–10 at Small Heath – on 2 March. The game had ended 9–1, but the referee realised he had blown four minutes early and made the players return to the pitch. Blackpool conceded another goal straightaway.

Another goalkeeper, Joe Dorrington, was again the only ever-present.

Match No.	Date		Venue	Opponents	Result		Scorers	Attendance
1	Sep	1	A	New Brighton Town	D	0-0		3,000
2		8	H	Gainsborough T	D	1-1	Birkett	good'
3		15	A	Walsall	W	2-1	Birkett, Evans	5,000
4		22	H	Burton Swifts	W	2-0	Stirzaker, Birkett	2,000
5		29	A	Barnsley	W	1-0	Evans	4,000
6	Oct	6	H	Woolwich Arsenal	D	1-1	Hardman	4,000
7		13	H	Chesterfield	D	1-1	Parkinson	1,000
8		20	A	Stockport County	W	1-0	Birkett	1,000
9		27	H	Small Heath	D	0-0		good'
10	Nov	10	H	Lincoln City	W	2-0	Birkett 2	
11		24	H	Glossop	D	0-0		1,500
12	Dec	1	A	Middlesbrough	L	1-3	Leadbetter	10,000
13		8	H	Burnley	L	0-1		3,500
14		15	A	Burslem Port Vale	L	0-4		
15		22	H	Leicester Fosse	W	1-0	Birkett	2,000
16		26	A	Newton Heath	L	0-4		10,000
17		29	H	New Brighton Town	L	1-2	Evans	2,000
18	Jan	5	A	Gainsborough T	W	3-1	Hardman, Birchall, Stirzaker	
19		12	H	Walsall	W	1-0	Evans	920
20		19	A	Burton Swifts	W	2-1	Birkett, Stirzaker	
21		26	A	Grimsby Town	L	0-2		
22	Feb	16	A	Chesterfield	L	0-2		
23		23	H	Stockport County	W	3-0	Parkinson, Stirzaker (pen), Birchall	2,000
24	Mar	2	A	Small Heath	L	1-10	Anderson	5,000
25		9	H	Grimsby Town	L	0-1		2,000
26		16	A	Lincoln City	L	0-3		
27		20	H	Barnsley	D	1-1	Birkett	500
28		23	H	Newton Heath	L	1-2	Birkett	1,000
29		30	A	Glossop	L	0-6		
30	Apr	5	H	Burslem Port Vale	W	2-1	Stirzaker, Parkinson	800
31		6	A	Middlesbrough	W	3-0	Anderson, Parkinson, Own-goal	2,000
32		8	A	Woolwich Arsenal	L	1-3	Stirzaker	6,000
33		9	A	Leicester Fosse	L	1-3	Parkinson	3,000
34		13	A	Burnley	L	0-4		2,000

Final League Position: 12th in Division Two

Apps

Gls

Dorrington	Boulton	Burden	Threlfall	Stirzaker	Birchall	Speight	Baxendale	Birkett	Parkinson	Evans	Hardman	Howson	Scott	Leadbetter	Anderson	Taylor	Jones
1	2	3	4	5	6	7	8	9	10	11							
1	2	3	4	6	5	7		9	10	8	11						
1	2	3	4	5	6	7	8	9	10	11							
1	2	3	4	5	6	7	8	9	10	11							
1	2	3	4	5	6	7	8		9	10	11						
1	2	3	4	5	6		8	9	10	11	7						
1	2	3	4	5	6		7	9	8	10	11						
1	2	3	4	5	6		8	7	9	10	11						
1	2	3	4	5	6		8	7	9	10	11						
1	2	3	4	5	6			9	10	8	11	7					
1	2	3	4	5	6			8	9	10	11	7					
1	2	3	4	5	6			9		8		7	10	11			
1	2	3	4	5	6			9	10	8		7		11			
1	2	3	4	5	6			9	10	8		7		11			
1		3	4	5	6			9	8	10	7		2	11			
1	2	3	4	5			10		8	11			6	7			
1	6	3	4	5				9	8	11	7		2	10			
1	6	3	4	5				9	8	11	7		2	10			
1	4	3		5	6			9	8	11	7		2	10			
1	2	3		5	6			9	8	11	7		4	10			
1	2			5	6			9	8	11	7	4	3	10			
1	2			5	6			9	8	11	7	4	3	10			
1	2		7	5	6			9	8	10	11	4	3				
1	2	3	4	5	6			9	10	11	7				8		
1	2	3	4	5	6			9	10	11	7				8		
1	2	3	4		6			9	10	11	7		5		8		
1	2	3	4	5				8	10	11	7		9		6		
1	2		4	5	6			9	10		7		3	11		8	
1	7	3	4	5	6		8	9			11		2		10		
1	7	3	4	5	6		8		9		11		2		10		
1		3	4	10	6			9	5		7		2		11	8	
1		3	4	5	6			9	10		7		2	11		8	
1		3	4	5	6			9	10		7		2	11		8	
1		3	4	5	6			9	10		7		2	11			8
34	29	30	30	33	30	5	11	32	32	22	27	8	19	15	7	4	1
	1	4		6	2			10	5	4	2			1	2		

League Table

	P	W	D	L	F	A	Pts
Grimsby Town	34	20	9	5	60	33	49
Small Heath	34	19	10	5	57	24	48
Burnley	34	20	4	10	53	29	44
New Brighton Tower	34	17	8	9	57	38	42
Glossop	34	15	8	11	51	33	38
Middlesbrough	34	15	7	12	50	40	37
Woolwich Arsenal	34	15	6	13	39	35	36
Lincoln City	34	13	7	14	43	39	33
Burslem Port Vale	34	11	11	12	45	47	33
Newton Heath	34	14	4	16	42	38	32
Leicester Fosse	34	11	10	13	39	37	32
Blackpool	34	12	7	15	33	58	31
Gainsborough Trinity	34	10	10	14	45	60	30
Chesterfield	34	9	10	15	46	58	28
Barnsley	34	11	5	18	47	60	27
Walsall	34	7	13	14	40	56	27
Stockport County	34	11	3	20	38	68	25
Burton Swifts	34	8	4	22	34	66	20

1901-02

Division Two

Did you know that?

Bloomfield Road became the club's permanent home.

Blackpool and Preston North End played each other in the League for the first time that season. Preston won 4–1 at Bloomfield Road, and the return fixture was drawn.

For the opening game of the season, against Bristol City, Blackpool did not have a fit goalkeeper, so Harry Stirzaker took up the duties, but conceded twice in a 2–0 defeat.

The club's biggest crowd in League football up that point was recorded twice – 6,000 – against Preston and Burnley.

Match No.	Date	Venue	Opponents	Result		Scorers	Attendance
1	Sep 7	H	Bristol City	L	0-2		4,000
2	14	A	Burton W	D	1-1	Foster	3,000
3	21	A	Stockport County	L	1-3	Birkett	
4	28	H	Newton Heath	L	2-4	Anderson 2	3,300
5	Oct 5	A	Glossop	L	1-3	Brooks	
6	12	H	Doncaster Rovers	W	3-1	Evans, Hardman, Anderson	1,000
7	19	A	Lincoln City	D	0-0		4,000
8	26	H	West Brom Albion	D	2-2	Foster, Hardman	5,000
9	Nov 9	H	Barnsley	W	2-1	Stirzaker, Birkett	3,000
10	23	H	Preston NE	L	1-4	Foster	6,000
11	30	A	Burnley	L	0-2		600
12	Dec 21	H	Gainsborough T	W	3-0	Foster, Evans, Stirzaker	1,500
13	25	A	Woolwich Arsenal	D	0-0		5,000
14	28	A	Middlesbrough	L	1-2	Parkinson	8,000
15	Jan 1	H	Burslem Port Vale	W	1-0	Anderson	4,000
16	4	A	Bristol City	L	0-3		2,000
17	11	H	Burton W	W	1-0	Parkinson	2,200
18	18	H	Stockport County	W	1-0	Parkinson	3,300
19	25	A	Newton Heath	W	1-0	Anderson	3,000
20	Feb 1	H	Glossop	D	1-1	Threlfall	2,000
21	8	A	Doncaster Rovers	L	3-4	Anderson, Parkinson, Anderton	1,500
22	15	H	Lincoln City	W	3-0	Anderson 2, Anderton	
23	22	A	West Brom Albion	L	2-7	Anderson 2	7,000
24	Mar 1	H	Woolwich Arsenal	L	1-3	Parkinson	good'
25	8	A	Barnsley	L	0-2		
26	15	A	Leicester Fosse	L	0-1		
27	22	A	Preston NE	D	1-1	Boulton	3,000
28	28	H	Leicester Fosse	W	4-0	Anderson, Foster 2, Parkinson	3,000
29	29	H	Burnley	W	2-1	Anderton, Anderson	6,000
30	31	A	Chesterfield	L	1-3	Anderton	
31	Apr 5	A	Burslem Port Vale	W	1-0	Scott	100
32	12	H	Chesterfield	D	0-0		
33	19	A	Gainsborough T	L	0-3		
34	26	H	Middlesbrough	L	0-2		2,000

Final League Position: 12th in Division Two

Apps
Gls

Stirzaker	Scott	Burden	Brooks	Threlfall	Birchall	Hardman	Anderson	Birkett	Foster	Evans	Higginson	Boulton	Dorrington	Gillett	Parkinson	Anderton	Allen	Barcroft	Billington
1	2	3	4	5	6	7	8	9	10	11									
5	8	3		4	6	7		9	10	11	1	2							
5	3		8	4	6	7		9	10	11	1	2							
5	3			4	6	7	8	9	10	11	1	2							
5	3		7		6	11	4	9	10	10		2	1	8					
5	3			4	6	7	8		10	11		2	1	9					
5	3			4	6	11	8	7	9			2	1		10				
5	3			4	6	11	8	7	9			2	1		10				
5	3			4	6	11		7	8		11	2	1	9	10				
5	3			4	6	7		9	8	11		2	1		10				
5	3			4	6	11	8	7	9	10		2	1						
5	3			4	6		8		10	11		2	1		9	7			
5	3			4	6		8		10	11		2	1		9	7			
5	3			4	6		8	11				2	1		9	7	10		
5	3			4	6	11	8	9				2	1		10	7			
5	3				6		4	7	11			2	1		9	8	10		
5	3			4	6	11	8		7	10		2	1		9				
5	3			4	6	7			10	11		2	1		9		8		
5	3			4	6		8		10	11		2	1		9	7			
5	3			4	6		8	10		11		2	1		9	7			
5	3			4	6		8	2	10	11			1		9	7			
5	3			4	6		8	2	11				1		9	7	10		
5	3			4	6		8	2	11				1		9	7	10		
5	3			4	6		8	10		11		2	1		9	7			
5	3			4	6		8			11		2	1		9	7	10		
5	3			4	6		10	2		11					9	8		1	7
	3			4	6		8	2	10	11		5	1		9	7			
5	3			4	6		8	2	11	10			1		9	7			
5	3			4	6		8	2	11	10			1		9				
5	3			4	6		8	2	11	10			1		9				
	5	3		4	6		8		11	10		2	1		9	7			
	5			4	6		8	3	11	10		2	1		9	7			
	5			4	6		8	3	11			2	1		9	7			
	10	3		4	6		8	5	11			2	1		9	7			
29	34	4	3	32	34	14	29	26	28	23	3	27	29	3	27	21	6	1	1
2	1		1	1		2	12	2	6	2		1			6	4			

League Table

	P	W	D	L	F	A	Pts
West Bromwich Albion	34	25	5	4	82	29	55
Middlesbrough	34	23	5	6	90	24	51
Preston North End	34	18	6	10	71	32	42
Woolwich Arsenal	34	18	6	10	50	26	42
Lincoln City	34	14	13	7	45	35	41
Bristol City	34	17	6	11	52	35	40
Doncaster Rovers	34	13	8	13	49	58	34
Glossop	34	10	12	12	36	40	32
Burnley	34	10	10	14	41	45	30
Burton United	34	11	8	15	46	54	30
Barnsley	34	12	6	16	51	63	30
Burslem Port Vale	34	10	9	15	43	59	29
Blackpool	34	11	7	16	40	56	29
Leicester Fosse	34	12	5	17	38	56	29
Newton Heath	34	11	6	17	38	53	28
Chesterfield	34	11	6	17	47	68	28
Stockport County	34	8	7	19	36	72	23
Gainsborough Trinity	34	4	11	19	30	80	19

1902-03

Division Two

Did you know that?

Blackpool played Manchester United for the first time this season. Previously, the club had been known as Small Heath.

Tom Barcroft arrived at Bloomfield Road as a temporary secretary, but he remained in his role for over 30 years.

Harry Stirzaker retired at the end of the season, after nine years at the club.

Match No.	Date		Venue	Opponents	Result		Scorers	Attendance
1	Sep	6	A	Burslem Port Vale	D	1-1	Heywood	3,500
2		13	H	Barnsley	D	3-3	Anderson 3 (1 pen)	2,000
3		20	A	Gainsborough T	D	0-0		
4		27	H	Burton W	D	3-3	Anderson, Parkinson, Duckworth	2,000
5	Oct	11	H	Glossop	D	2-2	Parkinson, Cookson	2,000
6		25	H	Stockport County	W	2-0	Birchall, Own-goal	1,500
7	Nov	8	A	Woolwich Arsenal	L	1-2	Threlfall	8,000
8		22	A	Lincoln City	W	2-0	Parkinson, Anderson	
9		29	H	Small Heath	L	0-1		3,500
10	Dec	6	A	Leicester Fosse	L	1-2	Cookson	2,000
11		13	H	Manchester City	L	0-3		4,000
12		20	A	Burnley	D	1-1	Cookson	600
13		25	H	Doncaster Rovers	W	4-0	Hardman 2, Parkinson, Anderton	4,000
14		26	A	Manchester Utd	D	2-2	Heywood 2	
15		27	H	Preston NE	D	2-2	Heywood, Cookson	4,000
16	Jan	1	H	Bristol City	L	0-1		3,000
17		3	H	Burslem Port Vale	L	2-5	Anderson, Cookson	1,000
18		10	A	Barnsley	L	0-6		
19		17	H	Gainsborough T	W	4-0	Anderson 2, Hardman, Anderton	800
20		24	A	Burton W	L	0-2		3,000
21		31	A	Bristol City	W	1-0	Clarkson	4,600
22	Feb	7	H	Burnley	W	2-0	Scott (pen), Hardman	600
23		14	H	Manchester Utd	W	2-0	Cookson, Threlfall	3,000
24		17	A	Glossop	L	0-1		2,000
25		21	A	Stockport County	L	0-4		
26		28	A	Chesterfield	D	1-1	Anderton	
27	Mar	7	H	Woolwich Arsenal	D	0-0		2,000
28		14	A	Doncaster Rovers	L	0-3		2,100
29		21	H	Lincoln City	L	2-3	Hardman, Parkinson	1,500
30		28	A	Small Heath	L	1-5	Hardman	7,000
31	Apr	4	H	Leicester Fosse	W	2-0	Duckworth 2	poor'
32		10	A	Preston NE	L	1-3	Scott (pen)	
33		11	A	Manchester City	L	0-2		4,000
34		13	H	Chesterfield	W	2-1	Cookson, Parkinson	3,000

Final League Position: 14th in Division Two

Apps

Gls

Dorrington	Birkett	Scott	Threlfall	Anderson	Birchall	Duckworth	Cookson	Parkinson	Heywood	Hardman	Stirzaker	Anderton	Wolstenholme	Wright	Parr	Evans	Hull
1	2	3	4	5	6	7	8	9	10	11							
1	2	3	4	8	6	7	9		10	11	5						
1	2	3	4	8	6	7	9		10	11	5						
1	2	3		5	6	7	8	9	10	11		4					
1		3	2	5	6		8	9	10	11		7	4				
1	2	3	4	8	6			9	10	11		7	5				
1	2	3	4	5	6		8	9	10	11		7					
	2	3	4	5	6		8	9	10	11		7		1			
	2			5	6		8	9	10	11		7	4	1	3		
1	2			5	6		8	9	10	11		7	4		3		
	2	3		5	6		8	9	10	11		7	4	1			
	2	6		5			8	9	10	11		7	4	1	3		
	2	3		5	6		8	9	10	11		7	4	1			
	3	2		5	6		8	9	10	11		7	4	1			
	3	2	4	5			8	9	10	11		7	6	1			
1	2	3	4	5			8	9	10			7	6			11	
1	2	3	4	5		7	8	9	10				6			11	
		3	4	2		7	8	9	10		5		6			11	1
	2	3	4	8	6		9		10	11		7	5				1
	2	3	4		6	7	8	9	10	11			5				1
	2	3			6		8	9	10	11	5	7	4				1
	2	3	4				8	9	10	11	5	7	6				1
	2	3	4		5		8	9	10	11		7	6				1
	2	3	4		5		8	9	10	11		7	6				1
	2	3	4		5		8	9	10	11		7	6				1
1	2	3	4		5		8	9	10	11		7	6				
		3	4	2			7	9	10	11	5	8	6				1
		3	4	2			7	9	10	11	5	8	6				1
	2	3	4		9		8	5	10	11		7	6				1
1	2	3	4		5		9	10		11		8	6				7
	2	3	4			7	9	5	10	11		8	6				1
	2	3	4			7	9	5	10	11		8	6				1
	2	3	4			7	8	9	10		5	11	6				1
	2	3	4				8	9	10	11	5	7	6				1
12	30	32	26	21	22	10	33	31	33	30	9	28	28	7	3	3	16
		2	2	8	1	3	8	6	4	6		3					

League Table

	P	W	D	L	F	A	Pts
Manchester City	34	25	4	5	95	29	54
Small Heath	34	24	3	7	74	36	51
Woolwich Arsenal	34	20	8	6	66	30	48
Bristol City	34	17	8	9	59	38	42
Manchester United	34	15	8	11	53	38	38
Chesterfield	34	14	9	11	67	40	37
Preston North End	34	13	10	11	56	40	36
Barnsley	34	13	8	13	55	51	34
Burslem Port Vale	34	13	8	13	57	62	34
Lincoln City	34	12	6	16	46	53	30
Glossop	34	11	7	16	43	57	29
Gainsborough Trinity	34	11	7	16	41	59	29
Burton United	34	11	7	16	39	59	29
Blackpool	34	9	10	15	44	59	28
Leicester Fosse	34	10	8	16	41	65	28
Doncaster Rovers	34	9	7	18	35	72	25
Stockport County	34	7	6	21	38	74	20
Burnley	34	6	8	20	30	77	20

1903-04

Division Two

Did you know that?

Over 7,000 turned up for the visit of Bolton Wanderers, but the gate was boosted by 3,000 visiting supporters.

The home game against Grimsby Town on 27 February only attracted 200 spectators, but they did see a 3–0 win.

The great 'keeper Joe Dorrington did not make a single appearance for the Seasiders this season.

Match No.	Date	Venue	Opponents	Result		Scorers	Attendance
1	Sep 5	A	Woolwich Arsenal	L	0-3		12,000
2	12	H	Barnsley	L	0-2		4,000
3	19	A	Lincoln City	D	0-0		
4	26	H	Stockport County	W	4-1	Pentland, Rooke, Scott (pen), Parkinson	2,500
5	Oct 3	A	Chesterfield	L	1-2	Pentland	
6	10	H	Bolton Wanderers	L	1-4	Pentland	7,000
7	17	A	Burnley	W	4-1	Pentland 2, Anderson, Threlfall	3,000
8	24	H	Preston NE	L	0-3		6,000
9	Nov 7	H	Leicester Fosse	L	1-2	Carthy	2,500
	21	A	Gainsborough T	L	1-3	Anderson	
11	Dec 5	A	Bristol City	L	0-5		
12	19	A	Glossop	W	1-0	Bennett	
13	25	H	Glossop	W	3-2	Anderson 2, Bennett	3,500
14	26	H	Bradford City	L	0-1		
15	Jan 1	A	Bolton Wanderers	L	0-3		11,000
16	2	H	Woolwich Arsenal	D	2-2	Own-goal, McEwan	4,000
17	9	A	Barnsley	D	2-2	Bennett 2	
18	16	H	Lincoln City	W	2-1	Scott, Parkinson	
19	23	A	Stockport County	L	1-2	Birkett	
20	30	H	Chesterfield	D	0-0		700
21	Feb 13	H	Burnley	L	0-5		1,500
22	20	H	Burton U	W	4-1	Anderson 3, Bennett	
23	27	H	Grimsby Town	W	3-0	Birkett (pen), Bennett, Scott (pen)	200
24	Mar 5	A	Leicester Fosse	L	1-5	Bennett	
25	9	H	Manchester Utd	W	2-1	Rooke, Bennett	1,000
26	12	A	Burslem Port Vale	L	0-5		
27	19	H	Gainsborough T	W	2-1	Bennett, Threlfall	500
28	26	A	Burton U	D	1-1	Rooke	
29	Apr 1	H	Burslem Port Vale	W	1-0	Anderson	1,500
30	2	H	Bristol City	L	0-1		1,000
31	4	A	Grimsby Town	L	0-4		4,500
32	9	A	Manchester Utd	L	1-3	Spencer	10,000
33	23	A	Bradford City	W	2-0	Rooke 2	7,000
34	30	A	Preston NE	L	0-1		

Final League Position: 15th in Division Two

Apps

Gls

Hull	Birkett	Scott	Threlfall	Wolstenholme	Pickford	Anderton	Rooke	Pentland	Parkinson	Bennett	Davies	Jones	Anderson	Carthy	Hughes	Miller	Swarbrick	McEwan	Kilean
1	2	3	4	5	6	7	8	9	10	11									
1	2	3	4	6		7	8	9	5	10	11								
1	2	3	4	5		7	8	9	10	11		6							
1	2	3	4	5		7	8	9	10	11		6							
1	2	3	4	5		7	8	9	10	11		6							
1	2	3	4	5		7	8	9	10	11		6							
1	2	3	4	5		7	8	9		11		6	10						
1	2	3	4	5		7	8	9		11		6	10						
1	2	3	4	5		7	8			11		6	10	9					
1	2	3				8				10		4	5	9	6	7	11		
1	2	3	4	6		10	8					5		9		7		11	
1	2	3		4		7			5	10		6	8	9				11	
1	2	3		4		7			5	10		6	8	9				11	
1		2		4		7			5	10		6	8	9				11	3
1	2		4			7	8		5			10	8	9				11	3
1	2	3	4			7	8		5	10		6		9				11	
1	2	3	4			7			5	10			8					11	6
1	2	3	4						5	10			8	9		7		11	6
1	2	3	4	6		7			5	10			8	9				11	
1	2	3	4	6		7			5	9		10	8					11	
1	2	3	4	6		7			5	9		10	8					11	
	2	3	4	6		7	8		5	11		1	10						
	2	3	4	6		7	8		5	11			10						
	2	3	4	6		7	8		5	11			10						
1	2	3	4	6		7	8		5	9				10				11	
1		3	4	2		7	8		5	9				10				11	6
1	2	3	4	6		7			5	9			10	8				11	
1	2	3	4	6		7	8		5	9			10					11	
1	2	3	4	6		7	8		5	9			10					11	
1	2	3	4	6		7	8		5	9								11	
1	2	3	4	6		7	8		5					9				11	
1	2	3	4	6		7			5	10				9				11	
1	2	3	4	6		7	8		5	9			10					11	
1	2	3	4	6		7	8		5				10	9				11	
31	22	33	30	29	1	23	23	8	29	30	1	17	21	16	1	3	1	21	5
	2	3	1			1	5	5	2	9			7	1				1	

League Table

	P	W	D	L	F	A	Pts
Preston North End	34	20	10	4	62	24	50
Woolwich Arsenal	34	21	7	6	91	22	49
Manchester United	34	20	8	6	65	33	48
Bristol City	34	18	6	10	73	41	42
Burnley	34	15	9	10	50	55	39
Grimsby Town	34	14	8	12	50	49	36
Bolton Wanderers	34	12	10	12	59	41	34
Barnsley	34	11	10	13	38	57	32
Gainsborough Trinity	34	14	3	17	53	60	31
Bradford City	34	12	7	15	45	59	31
Chesterfield	34	11	8	15	37	45	30
Lincoln City	34	11	8	15	41	58	30
Burslem Port Vale	34	10	9	15	54	52	29
Burton United	34	11	7	16	45	61	29
Blackpool	34	11	5	18	40	67	27
Stockport County	34	8	11	15	40	72	27
Glossop	34	10	6	18	57	64	26
Leicester Fosse	34	6	10	18	42	82	22

1904-05

Division Two

Did you know that?

The game with Bolton Wanderers had an attendance of 9,500 at Bloomfield Road, making the Trotters the main attraction annually for the fans.

Blackpool appeared in the FA Cup proper for the first time since becoming a League club, but they were beaten at Bristol City 2–1 in the first round.

Geordie Anderson retired in this season after arriving in 1899 and being described by the local newspaper as being 'a little worse for wear'.

A boardroom upheaval took place at the end of the season following discontent from the supporters over the team's failings in the League.

Match No.	Date		Venue	Opponents	Result		Scorers	Attendance
1	Sep	3	H	Leicester Fosse	D	0-0		4,300
2		5	A	Burslem Port Vale	D	2-2	Hogg, Chadwick	
3		10	A	Barnsley	L	1-2	Chadwick	3,000
4		17	H	West Brom Albion	D	0-0		5,000
5		24	A	Burnley	W	1-0	Kearns	4,000
6	Oct	1	H	Grimsby Town	D	1-1	Chadwick	3,500
7		8	A	Bolton Wanderers	L	0-3		10,000
8		15	A	Doncaster Rovers	D	0-0		3,000
9		22	H	Gainsborough T	D	2-2	Hogg 2	1,500
10	Nov	5	H	Liverpool	L	0-3		5,500
11		7	A	West Brom Albion	L	2-4	Birkett (pen), Waddington	4,951
12		19	H	Bristol City	L	2-4	Scott, Hogg	4,000
13	Dec	3	H	Glossop	W	4-1	Kearns, Chadwick, Birkett (pen), Waddington	
14		17	H	Bradford City	W	2-0	Own-goal, Waddington	2,000
15		24	A	Lincoln City	L	0-1		
16		26	A	Burton U	D	0-0		
17		31	A	Leicester Fosse	L	1-3	Scott (pen)	
18	Jan	7	H	Barnsley	W	6-0	Chadwick 2, Morgan, Kearns, Parkinson, Threlfall	
19		21	H	Burnley	W	2-0	Morgan, Waddington	3,000
20		28	A	Grimsby Town	L	0-2		3,000
21	Feb	11	H	Doncaster Rovers	W	1-0	Birkett	2,000
22		18	A	Gainsborough T	D	1-1	Chadwick	
23		25	H	Burton U	W	1-0	Hogg	2,000
24	Mar	5	A	Liverpool	L	0-5		6,000
25		11	H	Burslem Port Vale	W	3-0	Waddington 2, Morgan	1,400
26		18	A	Bristol City	L	0-2		7,000
27		25	H	Manchester Utd	L	0-1		6,500
28	Apr	1	A	Glossop	D	0-0		
29		8	H	Chesterfield	D	1-1	Chadwick	
30		15	A	Bradford City	L	1-3	Pratt	12,000
31		21	H	Bolton Wanderers	L	0-2		9,500
32		22	H	Lincoln City	W	1-0	Pratt	3,800
33		24	A	Manchester Utd	L	1-3	Morgan	10,000
34		29	A	Chesterfield	L	0-2		2,000

Final League Position: 15th in Division Two

Apps

Gls

FA Cup

1	Jan	14	A	Bristol City	L	1-2	Morgan	8,000

Apps

Gls

Hull	Birkett	Scott	Threlfall	Parkinson	Wolstenholme	Morgan	Kearns	Hogg	Chadwick	McEwan	Lowe	Gettins	Heywood	Waddington	Dorrington	Jolly	Crewdson	Cook	Pratt
1	2	3	4	5	6	7	8	9	10	11									
1	2	3	4	5	6	7	8	9	10	11									
1		3	4	5	6	7	8	9	10	11	2								
1	2	3	4	5	6	7	8		10	11		9							
1	2	3	4	5	6	7	8	9	10	11									
1	2	3	4	5	6	7	8	9	10	11									
1	2	3	4	5	6	7	8		10	11			9						
1	2	3	4	5	6	7	8	9	10	11									
1	2	3	4	5	6		8	9	10	11				7					
	2	3	4	5	6	8		9	10	11				7	1				
1	2		4	5	6	8		9	10	11					1	3			
	2	3		5	6	8		9	10	11				7	1		4		
1	2	3	4	5	6		9		10	11				8				7	
1		3	4	5	6			9	10	11	2			8				7	
1	2	3	4	5	6			9	10	11				8				7	
1	2	3	4	5	6			9	10	11				8				7	
1	2	3	4	5	6		8		10	11				9				7	
1	2	3	4	5	6	9	8		10	11								7	
1	2	3	4	5	6	9			10	11				8				7	
1	2	3	4	5	6	9	7		10	11				8					
1	2	3	4	5	6	8		9	10	11				7					
1	2	3	4	5	6	8		9	10	11						7			
1	2	3	4	5	6	8		9	10					11		7			
1	2	3	4	5	6	8		9	10	11						7			
1	2	3	4	5	6	8		9	10					11		7			
1	2	3		5	6	8	7	9	10					11			4		
1	2	3	4	5	6		7	9	10					11					8
1	2	3	4	5	6			9	10										8
1	2	3	4	5	6	7		9	10					11					8
1	2	3	4	5	6	7		9	10					11					8
1	2	3	4	5	6	7		9	10					11					8
1	2	3	4	5	6	7		9	10										8
1	2	3	4	5	6	7		9	10					11					8
1	2	3	4	5	6			9	10					11					8
31	32	33	32	34	34	25	15	27	34	23	2	1	1	21	3	5	2	7	8
	3	2	1	1		4	3	4	8					6					2

Hull	Birkett	Scott	Threlfall	Parkinson	Wolstenholme	Morgan	Kearns	Hogg	Chadwick	McEwan	Lowe	Gettins	Heywood	Waddington	Dorrington	Jolly	Crewdson	Cook	Pratt
1	2	3	4	5	6	9			10	11				8				7	
1	1	1	1	1	1	1			1	1				1				1	
						1													

League Table

	P	W	D	L	F	A	Pts
Liverpool	34	27	4	3	93	25	58
Bolton Wanderers	34	27	2	5	87	32	56
Manchester United	34	24	5	5	81	30	53
Bristol City	34	19	4	11	66	45	42
Chesterfield	34	14	11	9	44	35	39
Gainsborough Trinity	34	14	8	12	61	58	36
Barnsley	34	14	5	15	38	56	33
Bradford City	34	12	8	14	45	49	32
Lincoln City	34	12	7	15	42	40	31
West Bromwich Albion	34	13	4	17	56	48	30
Burnley	34	12	6	16	43	52	30
Glossop	34	10	10	14	37	46	30
Grimsby Town	34	11	8	15	33	46	30
Leicester Fosse	34	11	7	16	40	55	29
Blackpool	34	9	10	15	36	48	28
Burslem Port Vale	34	10	7	17	47	72	27
Burton United	34	8	4	22	30	84	20
Doncaster Rovers	34	3	2	29	23	81	8

1905-06

Division Two

Did you know that?

Charles Ramsden became the new Chairman of Blackpool FC while Tom Barcroft remained the 'temporary' secretary.

Blackpool had a remarkable FA Cup run. They beat Crystal Palace after three games and reached the third round where they lost to Newcastle United at St James' Park in front of 35,000. In the second round they had been drawn at home to Sheffield United, but sold the rights and played at Bramall Lane where they won famously 2–1. They had also made around £300 from the tie and so justifying their decision.

This season saw the first reprimand from the authorities over crowd behaviour at Bloomfield Road. Around 200 fans had invaded the pitch after a defeat by West Bromwich Albion and the referee W. Gilgryst was escorted from the field. The Football League gave the club a severe warning.

Match No.	Date		Venue	Opponents	Result		Scorers	Attendance
1	Sep	2	H	Burton U	W	2-0	Connor 2	3,000
2		4	A	Manchester Utd	L	1-2	Bennett	9,000
3		9	H	Chelsea	L	0-1		3,000
4		11	A	Burslem Port Vale	W	2-1	Bennett, Duckworth	
5		16	H	Gainsborough T	D	2-2	Bennett, Johnson	
6		23	A	Bristol City	L	1-2	Bennett	9,000
7		30	H	Manchester Utd	L	0-1		7,500
8	Oct	7	A	Glossop	L	1-4	Birkett	700
9		14	H	Stockport County	W	2-0	Hancock, Birkett	1,500
10		21	A	Grimsby Town	D	1-1	Birkett (pen)	
11		28	A	Bradford City	L	1-2	Bate	10,000
12	Nov	4	H	West Brom Albion	L	0-3		2,500
13		11	A	Leicester Fosse	L	0-2		
14		25	A	Lincoln City	D	1-1	Connor	
15	Dec	2	H	Chesterfield	W	2-1	Duckworth, Gow	2,800
16		16	H	Barnsley	D	0-0		3,000
17		23	H	Clapton Orient	D	0-0		
18		25	A	Burnley	L	1-4	Lavery	6,000
19		30	A	Burton U	D	1-1	Connor	
20	Jan	1	H	Leeds C	L	0-3		3,000
21		6	A	Chelsea	L	0-6		6,000
22		20	A	Gainsborough T	W	1-0	Francis	
23		27	H	Bristol City	L	1-3	Gow	5,000
24	Feb	10	H	Glossop	W	1-0	Hancock	2,100
25		17	A	Stockport County	L	1-2	Francis	
26	Mar	3	H	Bradford City	D	2-2	Hancock 2	3,500
27		7	H	Grimsby Town	W	2-0	Connor, Sanderson	2,000
28		10	A	West Brom Albion	L	0-5		6,500
29		14	H	Hull City	L	1-2	Francis	1,500
30		17	H	Leicester Fosse	L	0-1		
31		24	A	Hull City	D	2-2	Parkinson, Francis	5,000
32		31	H	Lincoln City	W	2-0	Scott (pen), Francis	2,000
33	Apr	7	A	Chesterfield	L	0-2		
34		13	H	Burnley	L	0-1		4,500
35		14	H	Burslem Port Vale	W	2-1	Hancock, Francis	
36		16	A	Leeds C	L	0-3		10,000
37		21	A	Barnsley	D	1-1	Connor	
38		28	H	Clapton Orient	W	3-0	Hancock, Threlfall, Lavery	

Final League Position: 14th in Division Two

Apps
Gls

FA Cup

1	Jan	13	H	Crystal Palace	D	1-1	Hancock	2,500
R		17	A	Crystal Palace	D	1-1#	Threlfall	4,000
2R		22	N	Crystal Palace	W	1-0	Francis	2,500
2	Feb	3	A	Sheffield United	W	2-1	Hancock 2	10,219
3		24	A	Newcastle United	L	0-5		35,000

after extra-time

N Played at Aston Lower Grounds, Birmingham

Sheffield United drawn at home, but sold ground rights

Apps
Gls

Hull	Birkett	Scott	Threlfall	Parkinson	Raisbeck	Duckworth	Connor	Hancock	Bennett	Darlington	Johnson	Gow	Bate	Francis	Reilly	Lowe	Lavery	Crewdson	Jones
1	2	3	4	5	6	7	8	9	10	11									
1	2	3	4	5	6	7	8	9	10	11									
1	2	3	4	5	6	7	8	9	10	11									
1	2	3	4	5	6	7	8	9	10	11									
1	2	3	4		6		8	9	10		5	7	11						
1	2	3	4	5	6		8	9	10			7	11						
1	2	3	4	5	6		8	9	10			7	11						
1	2	3	4	5	6	7	9		10			8	11						
1	2	3	4	5	6	7	8	9	10				11						
1	2	3	4	5	6		8	9	10			7	11						
1	2	3	4	5	6			8	10			7	11	9					
1	2	11	4	5	6			8	10			7		9	3				
1	2	3	4	5	6	7	10	9				8	11						
1	2	3	4	5		7	10	9			6	8	11						
1	2	3	4	5		7	10	9			6	8	11						
1		3	4	5		7	10	9			6	8	11			2			
1		3	4	5		7	10				6	8	11			2	9		
1		3	4	5		7	10				6	8	11			2	9		
1		3	4	5		7	10				6	8	11			2	9		
1		3	4	5		7	10				6	8	11			2	9		
1		3	4	5		7	10				6	8	11			2	9		
1	2			5	4		8					7	11	9			10	3	6
1	2	3	4	5			10				6	8	11				9		
1		3	4	5			10	8			6	7		9				2	
1		3	4	5			10	8			6	7		9				2	
1		3	4	5		7	10	8			6			9				2	
1		3	4	5		7	8				6			9				2	
1		3	4	5		7	10	8			6			9				2	
1		3	4	5		7	10	8			6			9				2	
1		3	4	5		7		8			6			9			11	2	
1		3	4	5	6		7				8			10				2	
1		3	4	5			7				6			10				2	
1		3	4	5		7	10	8			6			9				2	
1		3	4	5		7	10	8			6							2	
1			4	5		7		8			6			10				2	
1	2		4	5		7	10	8			6						11		
1	2	3	4	5			8				6		11				9		
1	2	3	4	5				8			6		11				9		
38	20	35	37	37	15	24	33	27	12	4	25	20	20	14	1	6	11	13	1
	3	1	1	1		2	6	6	4		1	2	1	6			2		

Hull	Birkett	Scott	Threlfall	Parkinson	Raisbeck	Duckworth	Connor	Hancock	Bennett	Darlington	Johnson	Gow	Bate	Francis	Reilly	Lowe	Lavery	Crewdson	Jones
1	2	3	4	10		7	5	8			6	11		9					
1	2	3	4	10		7	5	8			6	11	9	9					
1	2	3	4	10		7	5	8			6	11	9	9					
1		3	4	5		7	10	8			6		11	9				2	
1		3	4	5			10	8			6	7	9	9				2	
5	3	5	5	5		4	5	5			5	4	1	5				2	
			1					3						1					

League Table

	P	W	D	L	F	A	Pts
Bristol City	38	30	6	2	83	28	66
Manchester United	38	28	6	4	90	28	62
Chelsea	38	22	9	7	90	37	53
West Bromwich Albion	38	22	8	8	79	36	52
Hull City	38	19	6	13	67	54	44
Leeds City	38	17	9	12	59	47	43
Leicester Fosse	38	15	12	11	53	48	42
Grimsby Town	38	15	10	13	46	46	40
Burnley	38	15	8	15	42	53	38
Stockport County	38	13	9	16	44	56	35
Bradford City	38	13	8	17	46	60	34
Barnsley	38	12	9	17	60	62	33
Lincoln City	38	12	6	20	69	72	30
Blackpool	38	10	9	19	37	62	29
Gainsborough Trinity	38	12	4	22	44	57	28
Glossop	38	10	8	20	49	71	28
Burslem Port Vale	38	12	4	22	49	82	28
Chesterfield	38	10	8	20	40	72	28
Burton United	38	10	6	22	34	67	26
Clapton Orient	38	7	7	24	35	78	21

1906-07

Division Two

Did you know that?

The club sold its FA Cup rights again. This time to West Ham United in the first round, where 13,000 turned up and gave Blackpool another £300 windfall. They lost the game 2–1.

The first 'exact' attendance was announced at Bloomfield Road when 5,772 was given for the victory over West Bromwich Albion on 10 November.

The team continued to play in maroon shirts and white shorts. They had adopted the colours five years earlier after wearing a combination of blue-and-white stripes from the turn of the century.

Match No.	Date	Venue	Opponents	Result		Scorers	Attendance
1	Sep 1	A	Barnsley	L	2-3	Connor, Francis	
2	8	H	Chelsea	D	0-0		5,000
3	15	A	Wolves	D	1-1	Francis	6,000
4	22	H	Clapton Orient	L	1-3	Copestake	
5	29	A	Gainsborough T	L	0-2		
6	Oct 1	A	Burton U	D	0-0		
7	6	H	Stockport County	L	0-1		2,500
8	13	A	Hull City	L	0-3		8,000
9	20	H	Glossop	W	4-1	Connor 2, Threlfall, Dunkley	
10	27	H	Chesterfield	D	0-0		
11	Nov 3	A	Bradford City	L	0-3		
12	10	H	West Brom Albion	W	2-1	Grundy, Anderton	5,772
13	17	A	Leicester Fosse	L	1-5	Grundy	
14	24	H	Nottingham Forest	L	1-2	Threlfall	6,000
15	Dec 1	A	Lincoln City	W	1-0	Francis	2,000
16	5	H	Leeds C	W	1-0	Scott	1,000
17	15	A	Grimsby Town	D	0-0		3,000
18	22	H	Burslem Port Vale	L	0-1		2,000
19	25	A	Burnley	L	1-2	Dunkley	7,000
20	29	H	Barnsley	L	2-3	Anderton, Grundy	2,000
21	Jan 1	H	Gainsborough T	W	1-0	Scott (pen)	
22	5	A	Chelsea	L	0-3		15,000
23	19	H	Wolves	L	1-2	Connor	3,000
24	26	A	Clapton Orient	D	0-0		5,000
25	Feb 2	A	Leeds C	D	1-1	Dunkley	5,000
26	9	A	Stockport County	D	0-0		
27	16	H	Hull City	D	1-1	Francis	1,500
28	23	A	Glossop	D	0-0		
29	Mar 2	A	Chesterfield	W	1-0	Own-goal	
30	9	H	Bradford City	W	1-0	Morris	2,000
31	16	A	West Brom Albion	L	0-3		5,500
32	23	H	Leicester Fosse	W	1-0	Grundy	
33	29	H	Burnley	W	2-0	Grundy, Morris	7,000
34	30	A	Nottingham Forest	L	0-3		
35	Apr 6	H	Lincoln City	W	2-0	Grundy, Francis	2,000
36	13	H	Burton U	D	1-1	Grundy	2,000
37	20	H	Grimsby Town	W	4-3	Morris 2, Grundy (pen), Threlfall	700
38	27	A	Burslem Port Vale	L	0-3		

Final League Position: 13th in Division Two — 13th — Apps / Gls

FA Cup

1	Jan 12	A	West Ham Utd	L	1-2	Parkinson	13,000

Drawn at home - sold ground rights — Apps / Gls

Wilcox	Birkett	Scott	Threlfall	Parkinson	Johnson	Copestake	Connor	Francis	Morris	Dunkley	Rimmer	Swan	Wake	Crosswaithe	Lowe	Clarke	Gow	Lavery	Bate
1	2	3	4	5	6	7	8	9	10	11									
1	2	3		5	6	7			10	11	4	8	9						
1	2	3	4	5	6	7		9	10	11		8							
1	2	3	4	5	6	7		9	10	11		8							
		3	4	5				9		11		8		1	2	6	7	10	
1		3	4	5				9		11	2	8				6	7	10	
1		3	4	5				9		11	2	7				6	7	10	
1			4	5				9		11	2	8			3	6	7	10	
1		3	4	5			8		11	10		9				6	7		
1		3	4	5			8		11	10		9				6	7		
1		3	4			7	8					10				6			11
1		3	4									10				6			11
1		3	4						8			10				6			
1		3	4			7	8					10				6			
1		3	4	5			8	9				10				6	7		
1		3	4	5			8					10				6	7		
1		3	4	5			8	10								6	7		
1			4	5			8	10			3					6	7		
1			4	5			8	9		10	3					6	7		
1		3	4		5		8			10						6	7		
1		3	4	5		7		8		10	2					6			
1		3	4		5		8	9								6	7	10	
1			4		5		8	11					9			6	7	10	
1		3	4	5				8					9			6	7	10	11
1		3		5	4	7		9		11						6	8	10	
1		3	4	5		7		10		11						6	8	9	
1		3	4	5		7		10								6	8	9	
1		3	4	5	11	7		10								6	8	9	
1		3	4	5		7		10	11							6	8	9	
1		3	4	5		7			10							6	8	9	
1		3	4	5		7			10							6	8	9	
1		3	4	5					10			8				6	7		
1		3	4	5					10			8				6	7		
1		3	4	5		7			10			8				6		9	
1		3	4	5		7		8	10							6			
1		3	4	5		7		8	10							6			
1		3	4	5				8	10							6	7		
1		3	4	5					10	11		8				6	7	9	
37	4	34	36	31	9	17	13	23	17	15	7	19	3	1	2	34	26	16	4
		2	3			1	4	5	4	3									

Wilcox	Birkett	Scott	Threlfall	Parkinson	Johnson	Copestake	Connor	Francis	Morris	Dunkley	Rimmer	Swan	Wake	Crosswaithe	Lowe	Clarke	Gow	Lavery	Bate
1		3	4	5			8	10		11						6	7		
1		1	1	1			1	1		1						1	1		
				1															

League Table

	P	W	D	L	F	A	Pts
Nottingham Forest	38	28	4	6	74	36	60
Chelsea	38	26	5	7	80	34	57
Leicester Fosse	38	20	8	10	62	39	48
West Bromwich Albion	38	21	5	12	83	45	47
Bradford City	38	21	5	12	70	53	47
Wolverhampton W	38	17	7	14	66	53	41
Burnley	38	17	6	15	62	47	40
Barnsley	38	15	8	15	73	55	38
Hull City	38	15	7	16	65	57	37
Leeds City	38	13	10	15	55	63	36
Grimsby Town	38	16	3	19	57	62	35
Stockport County	38	12	11	15	42	52	35
Blackpool	38	11	11	16	33	51	33
Gainsborough Trinity	38	14	5	19	45	72	33
Glossop	38	13	6	19	53	79	32
Burslem Port Vale	38	12	7	19	60	83	31
Clapton Orient	38	11	8	19	45	67	30
Chesterfield	38	11	7	20	50	66	29
Lincoln City	38	12	4	22	46	73	28
Burton United	38	8	7	23	34	68	23

1907-08

Division Two

Did you know that?

Bob Whittingham was signed from Goldenhill Wanderers and immediately became the team's top scorer.

Another board was appointed with Charles Ramsden being replaced by Fred Seed. More money was promised for new players.

Nearly 10,000 fans saw Blackpool beat Burnley 1–0 at Bloomfield Road in April – the highest attendance so far at the ground.

Match No.	Date		Venue	Opponents	Result		Scorers	Attendance
1	Sep	2	A	Stockport County	D	1-1	Whittingham	
2		7	H	Clapton Orient	W	5-0	Whittingham 2, Scott, Owers 2	4,500
3		14	H	Leeds C	L	2-3	Brindley, Parkinson	5,500
4		21	H	Wolves	L	0-2		5,000
5		28	A	Gainsborough T	L	1-2	Owers	
6	Oct	5	H	Stockport County	L	1-3	King	
7		12	A	Glossop	D	2-2	Whittingham, Grundy	
8		19	H	Leicester Fosse	D	2-2	Whittingham, Grundy	
9		26	A	Grimsby Town	D	2-2	Whittingham, Reid	4,500
10	Nov	2	A	Stoke City	L	1-3	Parkinson	
11		9	H	West Brom Albion	L	0-1		9,145
12		16	A	Bradford City	L	0-3		11,000
13		23	H	Hull City	D	1-1	Weston	2,000
14		30	A	Derby County	L	1-2	Grundy	9,000
15	Dec	7	H	Lincoln City	W	4-3	Weston, Grundy 3 (1 pen)	
16		14	A	Fulham	L	0-3		10,000
17		21	H	Barnsley	D	1-1	Grundy	
18		25	A	Burnley	L	1-2	Heywood	12,000
19		26	A	Oldham Athletic	L	2-3	Grundy, Gow	4,000
20		28	A	Chesterfield	L	2-3	Whittingham, Weston	
21	Jan	1	H	Oldham Athletic	W	1-0	Grundy	5,000
22		4	A	Clapton Orient	D	1-1	Brindley	
23		18	A	Wolves	L	0-1		7,000
24		25	H	Gainsborough T	L	0-1		
25	Feb	8	H	Glossop	W	4-0	Whittingham 2, Weston, Grundy	
26		15	A	Leicester Fosse	L	1-2	Gow	
27		29	H	Stoke City	W	1-0	Birch	
28	Mar	7	A	West Brom Albion	L	0-3		7,000
29		14	H	Bradford City	W	2-1	Birch, Weston	3,000
30		21	A	Hull City	L	2-3	Whittingham 2	7,000
31		28	H	Derby County	W	1-0	Grundy	4,000
32	Apr	1	H	Grimsby Town	W	3-0	Threlfall, Birch, Grundy	
33		4	A	Lincoln City	L	0-2		
34		11	H	Fulham	W	2-1	Whittingham, Connor	7,000
35		17	H	Burnley	W	1-0	Whittingham	9,500
36		18	A	Barnsley	D	0-0		
37		20	A	Leeds C	D	1-1	Cookson	7,000
38		28	H	Chesterfield	W	2-0	Whittingham 2	

Final League Position: 15th in Division Two — Apps / Gls

FA Cup

1	Jan	11	A	Manchester Utd	L	1-3	Grundy	12,000

Apps
Gls

Tilotson	Crewdson	Scott	Threlfall	Parkinson	Clarke	Grundy	Whittingham	Owers	King	Brindley	Lowe	Rose	Gow	Cookson	Rimmer	Weston	Reid	Connor	Heywood
1	2	3	4	5	6	7	8	9	10	11									
1	2	3	4	5	6	7	8	9	10	11									
1	2	3	4	5	6	7	8	9	10	11									
1	2	3	4	5	6	7	8	9	10	11									
1		3		5	6		10	9		11	2	4	7	8					
1	2	3		5	6	7	8	9	10	11		4							
1	4	3		5	6	7	8	9	10	11					2				
1	6	3	4	5		7	8		10	11					2	9			
1	6	3	4	5		7	8		10	11					2		9		
1	6	3		5			8		10	11					2	9	7	4	
1	6	3		5			8	9	10	11					2		7	4	
1	6			5	3		8	9		11					2	10	7	4	
1	4	3		5	6	9	8			11					2	10	7		
1	4	3		5	6	9									2	10	7		8
1	4	3		5	6	9									2	10	7		8
1	4	3		5	6	9									2	10	7		8
1	4	3			6	9							7		2	10		5	8
	2	3			6		10					5	7			9		4	8
	2	3			6	9	10					5	7					4	8
	2	3			6		10					5	7			9		4	8
	2	3			6	9				11		5	7			10		4	8
	2			5	6					10			7		3	9		4	8
	2			5	6					10			7		3	9		4	8
	2	3		5	6	9	11						7			10		4	8
	2	3	4	5	6	9	8						7			10			
	2	3	4	5	6		10						7			9			8
	2	3	4	5		9	8			7						10		6	
	2	3	4	5		9	8			7						10		6	
	2	3	4	5		9	8			7						10		6	
	2	3	4	5			8						7			9		6	
	2	3	4	5		9	8									10	7	6	
	2	3	4	5		9	8									10	7	6	
	2	3	4	5			8						7				9	6	10
	2	3	4	5	10	9	8										7	6	
	2	3	4	5	10	9	8										7	6	
	2	3	4	5	10	9	8										7	6	
	2	3	4	5	10		8							9			7	6	
	2	3	4	5	10	9	8										7	6	
17	37	35	20	33	27	26	31	9	10	19	1	6	13	2	13	22	16	23	13
			1	2		12	15	3	1	2			2	1		5	1	1	1

	2	3	4	5		9				11			7			10		6	8
	1	1	1	1		1				1			1			1		1	1
						1													

League Table

	P	W	D	L	F	A	Pts
Bradford City	38	24	6	8	90	42	54
Leicester Fosse	38	21	10	7	72	47	52
Oldham Athletic	38	22	6	10	76	42	50
Fulham	38	22	5	11	82	49	49
West Bromwich Albion	38	19	9	10	61	39	47
Derby County	38	21	4	13	77	45	46
Burnley	38	20	6	12	67	50	46
Hull City	38	21	4	13	73	62	46
Wolverhampton W	38	15	7	16	50	45	37
Stoke	38	16	5	17	57	52	37
Gainsborough Trinity	38	14	7	17	47	71	35
Leeds City	38	12	8	18	53	65	32
Stockport County	38	12	8	18	48	67	32
Clapton Orient	38	11	10	17	40	65	32
Blackpool	38	11	9	18	51	58	31
Barnsley	38	12	6	20	54	68	30
Glossop	38	11	8	19	54	74	30
Grimsby Town	38	11	8	19	43	71	30
Chesterfield	38	6	11	21	46	92	23
Lincoln City	38	9	3	26	46	83	21

1908-09

Division Two

Did you know that?

The club were forced to re-apply for election to the Football League after finishing 20th. They were successful.

Bob Whittingham was sold to Bradford City in January, but he still remained as the top scorer for the season with 13 goals.

The first five-figure crowd was recorded at Bloomfield Road, with 10,000 seeing Blackpool beat Oldham Athletic 1–0 on 12 September.

Match No.	Date	Venue	Opponents	Result		Scorers	Attendance
1	Sep 2	H	Barnsley	D	1-1	R Whittingham	4,000
2	5	A	Wolves	D	2-2	Reid, R Whittingham	8,000
3	12	H	Oldham Athletic	W	1-0	Weston	10,000
4	19	A	Clapton Orient	D	1-1	Weston	
5	26	H	Leeds C	W	1-0	Weston	5,000
6	Oct 3	A	Barnsley	L	0-4		
7	10	H	Tottenham H	D	1-1	R Whittingham	6,000
8	17	A	Hull City	L	0-2		8,000
9	24	H	Derby County	D	2-2	Baddeley, R Whittingham	6,000
10	31	H	Bolton Wanderers	L	1-2	Walker	5,500
11	Nov 7	A	Chesterfield	L	1-3	Walker	
12	14	H	Glossop	W	2-1	R Whittingham 2	
13	21	A	Stockport County	L	0-1		
14	28	H	West Brom Albion	L	0-2		5,500
15	Dec 15	A	Birmingham City	D	2-2	R Whittingham 2 (1 pen)	6,000
16	12	H	Gainsborough T	W	3-0	Grundy 2, R Whittingham	2,000
17	19	A	Grimsby Town	L	1-2	R Whittingham	
18	25	A	Burnley	D	1-1	Whalley	
19	26	H	Fulham	W	2-0	R Whittingham, Beare	5,000
20	Jan 1	A	Bradford City	L	3-4	R Whittingham (pen), Baddeley, Lyon	12,000
21	2	H	Wolves	W	3-1	Grundy 2, R Whittingham	3,000
22	9	A	Oldham Athletic	L	1-3	Beare	6,000
23	23	H	Clapton Orient	L	1-3	Lyon	
24	30	A	Leeds C	L	0-1		8,000
25	Feb 13	A	Tottenham H	L	1-4	Walker	15,000
26	20	H	Hull City	L	2-3	Reid (pen), Baddeley	5,000
27	27	A	Derby County	D	1-1	Swan	3,800
28	Mar 6	A	Bolton Wanderers	L	1-3	Grundy	4,000
29	13	H	Chesterfield	D	2-2	Grundy (pen), Beare	2,000
30	20	A	Glossop	L	0-3		
31	27	H	Stockport County	W	2-1	Grundy, Beare	
32	31	H	Bradford City	W	2-1	Beare 2	
33	Apr 3	A	West Brom Albion	L	1-5	Weston	17,426
34	9	H	Burnley	D	0-0		6,000
35	10	H	Birmingham City	W	2-0	Grundy, Beare	5,000
36	12	A	Fulham	L	0-3		10,000
37	17	A	Gainsborough T	L	0-1		
38	24	H	Grimsby Town	D	2-2	Whalley, Beare	

Final League Position: 20th in Division Two

Apps

Gls

FA Cup

1	Jan 16	H	Hastings and St Leonards	W	2-0	Whalley, Threlfall	2,000
2	Feb 6	A	Newcastle Utd	L	1-2	Weston	32,137

Apps

Gls

Fiske	Crewdson	Scott	Threlfall	Whittingham S	Connor	Reid	Beare	Lyon	Whittingham R	Baddeley	Parkinson	Whiteside	Weston	Miller	Latheron	Swan	Stephenson	Walker	Grundy
1	2	3	4	5	6	7	8	9	10	11									
1	2		4	5	6	7	8		10	11	5	9							
1	2		4	5	6	7			10	11	5	8	9						
1	2		4	5	6	7			10	11	5	8	9						
1	2		4	5	6	7			10	11	5	8	9						
1	2	3	4		6	7			10	11	5	8	9						
1	2		4		6		7		8		5	10	9	3	11				
1	2				6	7	11		9		5			3		4	8	10	
1	2			9	6		7		8	11	5			3		4		10	
1	2		4	3	6	8	7		9	11	5							10	
1	2		4	3	6		7		8	11	5		9					10	
1	2	3	4		6		7		8	11	5		10						9
1	2	3			6	7			8	11	5		10			4			9
1	2	3	4		6	7	11		8		5							10	9
1	2	3	4		6		7		8	11	5		10						9
1		3	4		6		7		8	11	5							10	9
1	2	3	4		6		7		8	11	5		10						9
1	2	3	4		6		7	10	8	11	5								
1	2	3	4		6		7	10	8	11	5								9
1	2	3	4		6		7	10	8	11	5								9
1	2	3	4		6		7	10	8	11	5								9
1	2	3	4	5	6		7	10	8	11									9
1	2	3	4		6		7	10		11	5								9
1	2	3	4		6		10			11	5								9
1	2	3		4	6	7	11			10	5							9	
1	2	3		4	6	7	11	9		10	5					8			
1	2	3		4	5	7	11			10			9			8			
1	2	3		4		7	11			10	5					8			9
1	2	3		4	5		11			10						8			9
1	2		4	3	6		7			10	5		8						9
1	2		4	3	5		8			9			10						7
1	2		4	3	5		8			9			10						7
1			4	3	5	7	8			9			10	2					
1	2		4	3	5		8			9			10						7
1	2		4	3	5		8						10						7
1	2		4	3		7	8			9			10						
	2			3	5		8						10						7
1	2			5			8						10						7
37	36	20	28	23	35	16	33	8	22	32	26	6	20	4	1	7	1	7	21
						2	8	2	13	3			4			1		2	6

1	2	3	4		6		7	10		11	5								
1	2	3		4	6	7	11			10	5		9			8			
2	2	2	1	1	2	1	2	1		2	2		1			1			
			1										1						

League Table

	P	W	D	L	F	A	Pts
Bolton Wanderers	38	24	4	10	59	28	52
Tottenham Hotspur	38	20	11	7	67	32	51
West Bromwich Albion	38	19	13	6	56	27	51
Hull City	38	19	6	13	63	39	44
Derby County	38	16	11	11	55	41	43
Oldham Athletic	38	17	6	15	55	43	40
Wolverhampton W	38	14	11	13	56	48	39
Glossop	38	15	8	15	57	53	38
Gainsborough Trinity	38	15	8	15	49	70	38
Fulham	38	13	11	14	58	48	37
Birmingham	38	14	9	15	58	61	37
Leeds City	38	14	7	17	43	53	35
Grimsby Town	38	14	7	17	41	54	35
Burnley	38	13	7	18	51	58	33
Clapton Orient	38	12	9	17	37	49	33
Bradford Park Avenue	38	13	6	19	51	59	32
Barnsley	38	11	10	17	48	57	32
Stockport County	38	14	3	21	39	71	31
Chesterfield	38	11	8	19	37	67	30
Blackpool	38	9	11	18	46	68	29

1909-10

Division Two

Did you know that?

The great Jack Cox returned to the club as an unofficial player-manager. It coincided with an upturn in the team's fortunes.

A new kit was introduced at the beginning of the season, with Blackpool now wearing red shirts and white shorts.

The team suffered their heaviest FA Cup defeat to date with a 6–0 mauling at the hands of Barnsley in a first-round replay.

Match No.	Date		Venue	Opponents	Result		Scorers	Attendance
1	Sep	2	A	Manchester City	W	2-1	Beare (pen), Dawson	14,000
2		4	H	Wolves	W	2-0	Miller, Connor	7,000
3		11	A	Gainsborough T	L	1-3	Miller	
4		13	A	Fulham	W	1-0	Miller	6,000
5		18	H	Grimsby Town	W	1-0	Beare (pen)	7,000
6		25	H	Manchester City	D	0-0		8,500
7	Oct	2	H	Leicester Fosse	L	0-1		
8		4	H	Fulham	D	1-1	Beare	4,000
9		9	A	Lincoln City	D	2-2	Burt, Dawson	
10		16	H	Clapton Orient	D	2-2	Burt, Cox	
11		23	A	Bradford City	L	1-2	Morley	
12		30	A	Hull City	W	2-1	Morley, Elmore	8,000
13	Nov	6	H	Derby County	D	1-1	Morley	5,000
14		13	A	Stockport County	L	0-2		
15		20	H	Glossop	D	1-1	Cox	
16		27	A	Birmingham City	W	2-1	Morley, Beare	1,000
17	Dec	4	H	West Brom Albion	W	2-1	Beare, Miller	7,700
18		11	A	Oldham Athletic	L	0-2		4,000
19		18	H	Barnsley	D	0-0		
20		25	A	Burnley	L	1-5	Elmore	12,000
21		27	A	Leeds C	L	1-3	Beare	10,000
22	Jan	1	H	Leeds C	W	3-1	Miller 3	4,000
23		8	A	Wolves	L	1-2	Dawson	8,500
24		22	H	Gainsborough T	L	0-2		
25	Feb	12	A	Leicester Fosse	L	2-3	Beare 2	
26		15	A	Grimsby Town	W	1-0	Morley	
27		19	H	Lincoln City	W	3-0	Morley, Connor, Elmore	
28		26	A	Clapton Orient	L	1-2	Miller	
29	Mar	5	H	Bradford City	D	0-0		
30		12	H	Hull City	L	1-2	Connor	3,000
31		19	A	Derby County	L	1-2	Miller	10,000
32		25	H	Burnley	L	2-3	Miller, Morley	10,000
33		26	H	Stockport County	W	2-0	Connor, Elmore	9,500
34	Apr	2	A	Glossop	W	3-2	Elmore 2, Beare	
35		9	H	Birmingham City	W	2-0	Cox, Miller	2,000
36		16	A	West Brom Albion	W	3-0	Miller 2, Wolstenholme	6,103
37		23	H	Oldham Athletic	L	1-3	Dawson (pen)	5,500
38		30	A	Barnsley	L	0-1		

Final League Position: 12th in Division Two

Apps

Gls

FA Cup

1	Jan	15	H	Barnsley	D	1-1	Wolstenholme	5,000
1R		20	A	Barnsley	L	0-6		10,000

Apps

Gls

Fiske	Crewdson	Whittingham	Threlfall	Connor	Clarke	Morley	Beare	Miller	Elmore	Dawson	Gladwin	Cox	Drain	Burt	Evans	Goulding	Didymus	Shaw	Bradshaw
1	2	3	4	5	6	7	8	9	10	11									
1		3	4	5	6	7	8	9	10	11	2								
1	2	3	4	5	6	7	8	9	10	11									
1	2	3	4	5	6	7	8	9	10	11									
1	2	3	4	5	6	7	8	9	10	11									
1	2	3	4	5	6	7	8	9	10	11									
1	2	3	4	5	6	7	8		10	11		9							
1		3	4	5	6	7	8	9	10	11	2								
1	2	3	4		6	8			10	11		7	5	9					
1	2	3	4		6	8	7		10			11	5	9					
1	2	3	4		6	8			10	7		11	5	9					
1		3		4	6	8	7		10		2	11		9	5				
1		3		4	6	8	7		10		2	11		9	5				
1		3		4	6	8	7	9	10		2	11			5				
1		3		4	6	8	7	9	10		2	11			5				
1		3	4	5	6	10	7	9	8		2	11							
1		3	4	5	6	8	7	9	10			11				2			
1		3	4	5	6	8	7	9	10							2	7		
1		3	4	5	6	8	7	9	10							2		7	
1		3	4	5	6	8		9	10			11				2		7	
1		3	4	5	6	7	9	10				11				2	8		
1		3	4	5	6	7	9	10				11				2	8		
1	2			5	6	7		8		11				9		3			4
1		3		5	6	7	9		8		2	11	4						
1			4	5	6		9	8			3	11							
1			4	5	6	7	9	8	10		3	11							
1			4	5	6	7	9	8	10		3	11							
1		3	4	5	6	7	9	8	10			11							
1			4	5	6	7	9	8	10	11	3								
1			4	5	6		7	8	9		3	11							
1			4	5	6	8	7	9	10		3	11							
1		3	4	5	6	8	7	9	10			11							
1				5	6	8	7	9	10			11				3			4
1			4	5	6		7	9	8			11				3			
1			4	5	6		7	9	8			11				3			
1			4	5	6		7	9	8		2	11				3			
1			4	5	6		7	9	8	11	2					3			
1			4	5	6	7	11	9	8							3			
38	10	25	31	35	38	32	34	31	34	13	16	25	4	6	4	13	3	2	2
				4		7	9	13	6	4		3		2					

Fiske	Crewdson	Whittingham	Threlfall	Connor	Clarke	Morley	Beare	Miller	Elmore	Dawson	Gladwin	Cox	Drain	Burt	Evans	Goulding	Didymus	Shaw	Bradshaw
1		3	4	5	6		9	8		11						2			
1		3	4	5	6		9	8		11	2		9						
2		2	2	2	2		2	2		2	1					1			

League Table

	P	W	D	L	F	A	Pts
Manchester City	38	23	8	7	81	40	54
Oldham Athletic	38	23	7	8	79	39	53
Hull City	38	23	7	8	80	46	53
Derby County	38	22	9	7	72	47	53
Leicester Fosse	38	20	4	14	79	58	44
Glossop	38	18	7	13	64	57	43
Fulham	38	14	13	11	51	43	41
Wolverhampton W	38	17	6	15	64	63	40
Barnsley	38	16	7	15	62	59	39
Bradford Park Avenue	38	17	4	17	64	59	38
West Bromwich Albion	38	16	5	17	58	56	37
Blackpool	38	14	8	16	50	52	36
Stockport County	38	13	8	17	50	47	34
Burnley	38	14	6	18	62	61	34
Lincoln City	38	10	11	17	42	69	31
Clapton Orient	38	12	6	20	37	60	30
Leeds City	38	10	7	21	46	80	27
Gainsborough Trinity	38	10	6	22	33	75	26
Grimsby Town	38	9	6	23	50	77	24
Birmingham	38	8	7	23	42	78	23

1910-11

Division Two

Did you know that?

The club sold the ground rights again to another FA Cup tie, this time against Manchester United. The game at Old Trafford realised receipts of £680 for Blackpool, but they lost the tie 2–1.

The team finished in seventh spot, their highest position to date.

After only one defeat in their first nine games, Blackpool were in a top-four position before falling away later in the season.

14,500 fans saw the game at Bloomfield Road with Burnley on 14 April, with the Seasiders winning 1–0.

Match No.	Date		Venue	Opponents	Result		Scorers	Attendance
1	Sep	3	A	Leeds C	W	2-1	Connor, Miller	12,000
2		10	H	Stockport County	W	2-1	Wolstenholme, Cx	
3		17	A	Derby County	D	1-1	Connor	6,000
4		24	H	Barnsley	W	1-0	Connor	7,000
5	Oct	1	A	Leicester Fosse	L	0-2		
6		8	H	Wolves	W	2-0	Clennel, Beare	5,000
7		15	A	Chelsea	D	0-0		30,000
8		23	H	Clapton Orient	D	1-1	Clennel	
9		29	H	Bolton Wanderers	D	1-1	Clennel	6,000
10	Nov	5	A	Glossop	L	1-3	Cox	
11		12	H	Lincoln City	W	5-1	Cox, Morley 3 (1pen), Clennel	3,000
12		26	H	Birmingham City	W	3-1	Morley, Wolstenholme,Clennel	4,500
13	Dec	3	A	West Brom Albion	W	1-0	Hoad	8,840
14		10	H	Hull City	W	2-0	Clennel 2	6,000
15		17	A	Fulham	L	1-2	Clennel	14,000
16		24	H	Bradford City	W	4-1	Clennel 2, Morley 2	
17		26	A	Burnley	D	1-1	Clennel	15,500
18		27	A	Gainsborough T	L	0-2		
19		31	H	Leeds C	L	1-2	Connor	4,500
20	Jan	2	H	Gainsborough T	D	1-1	Clennel	
21		7	A	Stockport County	W	3-1	Bainbridge, Clennel, Connor	
22		21	H	Derby County	L	0-1		5,000
23		28	A	Barnsley	W	2-1	Wolstenhome, Clennel	
24	Feb	4	A	Huddersfield Town	D	2-2	Hoad, Clennel	6,000
25		11	A	Wolves	W	3-0	Clennel, Morley 2	9,000
26		18	H	Chelsea	L	0-2		3,000
27		25	A	Clapton Orient	L	1-2	Wolstenholme	9,000
28	Mar	4	A	Bolton Wanderers	L	0-1		13,500
29		11	H	Glossop	W	1-0	Connor	
30		18	A	Lincoln City	W	1-0	Clennel	
31		25	H	Huddersfield Town	D	1-1	Clennel	4,000
32		29	H	Leicester Fosse	W	2-0	Own-goal, Morley	3,000
33	Apr	1	A	Birmingham City	L	0-2		13,000
34		8	H	West Brom Albion	D	0-0		6,100
35		14	H	Burnley	W	1-0	Morley	14,500
36		15	A	Hull City	D	1-1	Morley	3,500
37		22	H	Fulham	L	1-2	Hoad	5,000
38		29	A	Bradford City	L	0-1		2,000

Final League Position: 7th in Division Two — Apps

Gls

FA Cup

1	Jan	14	A	Manchester Utd	L	1-2	Clennel	20,000

Drawn at home - sold ground rights — Apps

Gls

Fiske	Gladwin	Goulding	Threlfall	Connor	Clarke	Beare	Wolstenholme	Miller	Clennel	Cox	Dale	Dawson	Crewdson	Morley	Bradshaw	Hoad	Walters	Quinn	Burt
1	2	3	4	5	6	7	8	9	10	11									
1	2	3	4	5	6	7	8	9	10	11									
1	3		4	5	6	7	8	9	10	11	2								
1	3		4	5	6	7	8	9	10	11	2								
1	3		4	5	6	7	8	9	10		2	11							
1	3		4	5	6	7		8	10			11	2	9					
1	3		4	5	6	7	8		10	11			2	9					
1	3		4	5	6	7	8		10	11			2	9					
1	3			5	6	7	8		10	11			5	9	4				
1			4	5	6		8		10	11	2		3	9		7			
1	3		4		6		8		10	11			2	9		7	5		
1	3		4	5	6		8		10	11			2	9		7			
1	3		4	5	6		8		10	11			2	9		7			
1	3		4	5	6		8		10				2	9		7		11	
1	3			5	6		8		10	11			2	9	4	7			
1	3			5	6		8		10	11			2	9	4	7			
1	3			5	6		8		10	11			2	9	4	7			
1	3			5	6		8		10				2		4	7		11	9
1	3			5	6		8		10	11			2	9	4	7			
1	3				6		8		10	11			2			7	5		
1				5	6		8		10	11	3		2		4				
1	3			5	6		8		10	11			2		4	7			
1	3		4				8		10	11			2				5		
1	3		4	5			8		10	11			2	9		7			
1	3		4	5			8		10	11			2	9		7			
1	3		4	5			8		10	11			2	9					
1	3		4	5			8		10	11			2	9		7			
1	3			5	4		8		10	11			2	9				9	
1	3			5	4		8		10	11			2	9		7			
1	3			5	4		8		10		2			11		7			
1	3			5	6				10		2			9		7		8	
1	3						8			11	2					7	5	10	
1	3				5		8		10	11			2	9		7			
	3			5			8			11			2	9		7		10	
	3			5			8					11	2	9		7		10	
				5			8				3	11	2	9				10	
	3				10		8						2	9		7	5	11	
	3				10		8						2	9		7	5	11	
33	35	2	18	31	29	9	36	6	32	28	9	4	30	27	8	26	6	11	1
				6		1	4		18	3				11		3			

Fiske	Gladwin	Goulding	Threlfall	Connor	Clarke	Beare	Wolstenholme	Miller	Clennel	Cox	Dale	Dawson	Crewdson	Morley	Bradshaw	Hoad	Walters	Quinn	Burt
1	3			5	6		8		10	11			2	9	4	7			
1	1			1	1		1		1	1			1	1	1	1			
									1										

League Table

	P	W	D	L	F	A	Pts
West Bromwich Albion	38	22	9	7	67	41	53
Bolton Wanderers	38	21	9	8	69	40	51
Chelsea	38	20	9	9	71	35	49
Clapton Orient	38	19	7	12	44	35	45
Hull City	38	14	16	8	55	39	44
Derby County	38	17	8	13	73	52	42
Blackpool	38	16	10	12	49	38	42
Burnley	38	13	15	10	45	45	41
Wolverhampton W	38	15	8	15	51	52	38
Fulham	38	15	7	16	52	48	37
Leeds City	38	15	7	16	58	56	37
Bradford Park Avenue	38	14	9	15	53	55	37
Huddersfield Town	38	13	8	17	57	58	34
Glossop	38	13	8	17	48	62	34
Leicester Fosse	38	14	5	19	52	62	33
Birmingham	38	12	8	18	42	64	32
Stockport County	38	11	8	19	47	79	30
Gainsborough Trinity	38	9	11	18	37	55	29
Barnsley	38	7	14	17	52	62	28
Lincoln City	38	7	10	21	28	72	24

1911-12

Division Two

Did you know that?

15,000 spectators saw Blackpool draw with Burnley 0–0 on 5 April. This was the highest attendance at Bloomfield Road to date.

Blackpool's first FA Cup first-round replay with Crewe Alexandra on 16 January was abandoned after 61 minutes with Blackpool winning 2–0. It took two further games for Blackpool to win through, only to lose at Bolton Wanderers in the second round.

For the first time in five years, no Blackpool player was able to reach double figures in goals scored.

Match No.	Date		Venue	Opponents	Result		Scorers	Attendance
1	Sep	2	H	Hull City	W	3-2	Nesbitt, Milne, Wolstenholme	5,500
2		9	A	Barnsley	L	0-1		
3		15	H	Bradford City	L	0-4		
4		23	A	Fulham	L	0-3		10,000
5		30	H	Derby County	W	1-0	Wolstenholme	5,000
6	Oct	7	A	Stockport County	W	2-1	Nesbitt 2	6,000
7		14	H	Leeds C	W	3-0	Quinn, Nesbitt, Wolstenholme	5,000
8		21	A	Wolves	L	0-3		10,000
9		28	H	Leicester Fosse	D	1-1	Quinn	
10	Nov	4	A	Gainsborough T	D	0-0		
11		11	H	Grimsby Town	L	1-2	Connor (pen)	3,000
12		18	A	Nottm Forest	L	1-2	Wolstenholme	
13		25	H	Chelsea	W	1-0	Wolstenholme	3,000
14	Dec	2	A	Clapton Orient	L	0-2		
15		9	H	Bristol City	W	1-0	Wolstenholme	2,400
16		16	A	Birmingham City	L	1-2	Morley	10,000
17		23	H	Huddersfield Town	W	3-1	Morley 2, Milne	1,500
18		25	A	Burnley	D	1-1	Wolstenholme	22,000
19		26	A	Glossop	D	1-1	Milne	
20		30	A	Hull City	L	0-3		9,000
21	Jan	1	H	Glossop	W	2-0	Milne, Morley	
22		6	H	Barnsley	D	0-0		700
23		27	H	Fulham	W	3-1	W Clarke, Connor (pen), Own-goal	4,000
24	Feb	6	A	Bradford City	D	0-0		
25		10	H	Stockport County	L	0-1		
26		17	A	Leeds C	L	0-2		6,000
27		24	A	Derby County	L	1-5	Quinn	5,000
28	Mar	2	A	Leicester Fosse	L	0-4		
29		9	H	Gainsborough T	D	0-0		
30		16	A	Grimsby Town	L	0-1		4,000
31		23	H	Nottm Forest	W	2-0	Thorpe, Wolstenholme	
32	Apr	5	H	Burnley	D	0-0		15,000
33		6	H	Clapton Orient	W	1-0	Milne	
34		13	A	Bristol City	L	0-2		10,000
35		17	H	Wolves	W	1-0	Wolstenholme	6,000
36		20	H	Birmingham City	W	1-0	Wilson	2,000
37		22	A	Chelsea	L	1-4	Milne	27,000
38		27	A	Huddersfield Town	L	0-4		3,000

Final League Position: 14th in Division Two — Apps

Gls

FA Cup

1	Jan	14	A	Crewe Alexandra	D	1-1	Milne	8,000
R		22	H"	Crewe Alexandra	D	2-2#	Quinn, Wolstenholme	3,500
2R		25	A*	Crewe Alexandra	W	2-1	Bainbridge, Crowe	7,500
2	Feb	3	A	Bolton Wanderers	L	0-1		18,607

" Following an abandoned game on 16 Jan (61 mins) with Blackpool winning 2-0 — Apps

after extra-time — Gls

Fiske	Crewdson	Gladwin	Thorpe	Connor	Evans	Morley	Wolstenholme	Milne	Metcalfe	Nesbitt	Cahill	Clarke W	Owen	Quinn	Dale	Downhall	Cowie	Dollins	Cox
1	2	3	4	5	6	7	8	9	10	11									
1	2	3	4	5	6	7	8	9	10	11									
1	2	3	4	5	6		8	9		11	7	10							
1	2	3	4	5	6		8	9		11		10	7						
1	2	3	4	5	6	7	8	9					11	10					
1	2	3	4	5	6	7	8	9		11				10					
1	2	3	4	5	6	7	8	9		11				10					
1	2		4	5	6	7	8	9		11				10	3				
1	2	3	4	5		7	8				11			10		6	9		
1	2		4	5	6	8	10			7					3			9	11
1	2	3	4	5	6	7	8	9						10					11
1	2	3	4	5			8			7				10				9	11
1	2	3	4	5			8			7				10				9	11
1	2	3	4	5			8			7				10				9	11
1	2	3	4	5			8			7				10				9	11
1	2	3	4	5		10	8	9			7								11
1		3	4	5		10	8	9			7				2				11
1		3	4	5		10	8	9			7				2				11
1	2		4	5		10	8	9			7				3				11
1	2		4	5		10	8	9			7				3				11
1	2	3	4	5		10	8	9			7			11					
1	2	3	4	5		10	8	9			7			11					
1	2	3	4	5		10	8				7			11					
	2	3	4	5							7	10		11			8		
	2	3	4	5		8		9				10		11					
	2	3	4	5								10		11			8		
	2	3	4	5										10					11
	2	3	4	5		8					7			10					11
	2	3	4	5		8					7			10					11
1	2	3	4	5		10	8	9			7								11
1	2		4	5	6		8				7	10		11	3				
1	2		4	5	6		10				7			11	3				
1	2		4	5	6		10				7			11	3				
1	2		4	5	6		10	9			7			11	3				
1	2		4	5	6		10				7			11	3				
1	2		4	5	6		10				7			11	3				
1	2		4	5	6		10	9			7			11	3				
1			4	5	6			9	8					11	2				
32	35	26	38	38	18	21	31	21	3	12	21	6	2	22	16	1	3	5	15
			1	2		4	9	6		4		1		1					

Fiske	Crewdson	Gladwin	Thorpe	Connor	Evans	Morley	Wolstenholme	Milne	Metcalfe	Nesbitt	Cahill	Clarke W	Owen	Quinn	Dale	Downhall	Cowie	Dollins	Cox
1	2	3	4	5		10	8	9			7								11
1	2	3	4	5		9	8				7		9	10					11
	2	3	4	5							7			10			8		11
	2	3	4	5							7	10		11			8		
2	4	4	4	4		2	2	1			4	1		3			2		2
							1	1						1			1		

League Table

	P	W	D	L	F	A	Pts
Derby County	38	23	8	7	74	28	54
Chelsea	38	24	6	8	64	34	54
Burnley	38	22	8	8	77	41	52
Clapton Orient	38	21	3	14	61	44	45
Wolverhampton W	38	16	10	12	57	33	42
Barnsley	38	15	12	11	45	42	42
Hull City	38	17	8	13	54	51	42
Fulham	38	16	7	15	66	58	39
Grimsby Town	38	15	9	14	48	55	39
Leicester Fosse	38	15	7	16	49	66	37
Bradford Park Avenue	38	13	9	16	44	45	35
Birmingham	38	14	6	18	55	59	34
Bristol City	38	14	6	18	41	60	34
Blackpool	38	13	8	17	32	52	34
Nottingham Forest	38	13	7	18	46	48	33
Stockport County	38	11	11	16	47	54	33
Huddersfield Town	38	13	6	19	50	64	32
Glossop	38	8	12	18	42	56	28
Leeds City	38	10	8	20	50	78	28
Gainsborough Trinity	38	5	13	20	30	64	23

1912-13

Division Two

Did you know that?

Yet again Blackpool sold the ground rights for an FA Cup tie. The first round replay at Tottenham Hotspur saw the Seasiders lose 6–1 after a 1–1 draw.

Blackpool were forced to apply for re–election once more after finishing 20th. Again, they were successful.

Blackpool finished bottom of Division Two, while rivals Preston North End won the title. Burnley finished second.

Match No.	Date		Venue	Opponents	Result		Scorers	Attendance
1	Sep	3	A	Grimsby Town	D	1-1	Heslop	5,000
2		7	A	Hull City	L	1-4	Wilson	8,000
3		9	H	Grimsby Town	W	2-1	Connor (pen), Wilson	6,000
4		14	H	Bury	W	2-1	Wilson, Wilkinson	10,000
5		21	A	Glossop	L	0-2		3,000
6		28	H	Fulham	W	2-0	Heslop, Quinn	5,000
7	Oct	5	A	Clapton Orient	L	0-1		14,000
8		12	H	Barnsley	L	0-1		
9		19	A	Lincoln City	L	0-1		
10	Nov	2	A	Nottm Forest	D	1-1	Heslop	12,000
11		9	H	Wolves	L	1-2	Wilson	5,000
12		16	A	Bristol City	D	0-0		10,000
13		23	H	Leicester Fosse	W	2-1	Gillow, Wilson	2,000
14		26	H	Bradford City	L	0-2		
15		30	A	Birmingham City	L	2-3	Wilson, Heslop	10,000
16	Dec	7	H	Stockport County	D	1-1	Clarke	
17		14	A	Huddersfield Town	L	0-3		3,500
18		21	H	Preston NE	L	0-1		6,000
19		25	A	Burnley	L	0-4		13,500
20		26	A	Leeds C	W	2-0	Quinn, Bainbridge	8,000
21		28	H	Hull City	L	1-2	Connor (pen)	3,000
22	Jan	1	H	Leeds C	L	0-3		5,000
23		4	A	Bury	D	1-1	Gillow	4,000
24		18	H	Glossop	D	1-1	Bainbridge	2,000
25		25	A	Fulham	L	2-4	Charles, Bainbridge	7,000
26	Feb	8	H	Clapton Orient	W	2-0	Bainbridge, Wilson	
27		15	A	Barnsley	L	3-5	Bainbridge, Wilson, Gillow	
28		22	H	Lincoln City	D	1-1	Wilson	
29	Mar	1	A	Bradford City	L	2-4	Bainbridge, Booth	
30		8	H	Nottm Forest	W	2-1	Connor (pen),Bainbridge	7,000
31		15	A	Wolves	L	0-4		2,500
32		21	H	Burnley	L	0-2		13,000
33		22	H	Bristol City	D	1-1	Quinn	4,000
34		29	A	Leicester Fosse	L	1-5	Bainbridge	
35	Apr	5	H	Birmingham City	W	2-0	Bainbridge, Charles	10,000
36		12	A	Stockport County	L	0-2		
37		19	H	Huddersfield Town	W	2-1	Dollins, Wilson	2,000
38		21	A	Preston NE	L	1-2	Charles	

Final League Position: 20th in Division Two — Apps / Gls

FA Cup

1	Jan	11	A	Tottenham Hotspur	D	1-1	Charles	18,667
R		14	A*	Tottenham Hotspur	L	1-6	Charles	16,926

* Sold ground rights — Apps / Gls

Fiske	Dale	Gladwin	Thorpe	Connor	Booth	Charles	Heslop	Dollins	Wilkinson	Quinn	Wilson	Chapman	Bainbridge	Jones	Kidd	Gillow	Crewdson	Millership	Davies
1	2	3	4	5	6	7	8	9	10	11									
1	2	3	4	5	6	7	8		10	11	9								
1	2	3	6	5		7	10			11	9	8	4						
1	2	3	4	5		7	8		10	11	9		6						
1	2	3	4	5		7	8		10	11	9		6						
1		2	4	5		7	8		10	11	9		6	3					
1		2	4	5		7	8		10	11	9		6	3					
		2	4	5		7			10	11	9		6	3	1	8			
		2	5		6	7				11	9	8	4	3	1	10			
		2	5		6	7	8		10	11	9		4	3	1				
			5		6	7	8		10	11	9		4	3	1		2		
			5		6	7	8			11	9		4	3	1	10	2		
			5		6	7	8			11	9		4	3	1	10	2		
			5		6	7	8			11	9		4	3	1	10	2		
			4	5	6	7	8			11	9			3	1	10	2		
1			4	5	6	7	8			11	9			3		10	2		
1			4	5	6	7	8			11				3		10	2	9	
1			4	5	6	7		8	10	11				3		9	2		
1			4	5	6	7		8	10	11				3		9	2		
1			4	5	6	7		8		11			9	3		10		2	
1			4	5	6	7		8		11			9	3		10		2	
			5		6	7	9	8		11			4	3	1	10	2		
			4		6	7	5	8			9			3	1	10	2		11
			4			7	6	8					9	3	1	10	2		11
			4			7	6		8				9	3	1	10	2		11
			4	5	6	7				11	8		9	3	1	10	2		
			4	5		7	6			11	8		9	3	1	10	2		
			4	5		7	6			11	8		9	3	1	10	2		
			4	5	6	7	8			11	10		9	3	1		2		
1			4	5		7	6			11	10		9	3				2	
1			4	5		7	6			11	10		9	3				2	
1			4	5		7	6		10	11			9	3				2	
1			4	5		7	6		10	11			9	3				2	
1			4	5		7	6	8	10	11			9	3				2	
1			4	5	6	7		8		11			9	3		10		2	
1			4	5	6	7		8					9	3		10		2	
1			4	5	6	7		8			9			3		10		2	
1			4	5	6	7		8			9			3		10		2	
22	5	10	38	28	23	38	27	13	15	32	24	2	28	32	16	23	17	12	3
				3	1	4	4	1	1	3	10		9			2			

Fiske	Dale	Gladwin	Thorpe	Connor	Booth	Charles	Heslop	Dollins	Wilkinson	Quinn	Wilson	Chapman	Bainbridge	Jones	Kidd	Gillow	Crewdson	Millership	Davies
			4		6	7	5	8			9			3	1	10	2		11
			4		6	7	5	8		11	9		9	3	1	10	2		
			2		2	2	2	2		1	2			2	2	2	2		1
						2													

League Table

	P	W	D	L	F	A	Pts
Preston North End	38	19	15	4	56	33	53
Burnley	38	21	8	9	88	53	50
Birmingham	38	18	10	10	59	44	46
Barnsley	38	19	7	12	57	47	45
Huddersfield Town	38	17	9	12	66	40	43
Leeds City	38	15	10	13	70	64	40
Grimsby Town	38	15	10	13	51	50	40
Lincoln City	38	15	10	13	50	52	40
Fulham	38	17	5	16	65	55	39
Wolverhampton W	38	14	10	14	56	54	38
Bury	38	15	8	15	53	57	38
Hull City	38	15	6	17	60	55	36
Bradford Park Avenue	38	14	8	16	60	60	36
Clapton Orient	38	10	14	14	34	47	34
Leicester Fosse	38	13	7	18	49	65	33
Bristol City	38	9	15	14	46	72	33
Nottingham Forest	38	12	8	18	58	59	32
Glossop	38	12	8	18	49	68	32
Stockport County	38	8	10	20	56	78	26
Blackpool	38	9	8	21	39	69	26

1913-14

Division Two

Did you know that?

The team wore black shorts for this season and retained their red shirts.

Levy Thorpe left the club in October after playing in 98 consecutive games.

Blackpool scored the lowest number of goals in the division – 33.

The team were beaten by a non-League side – Gillingham – in the FA Cup, the first time they had been knocked out of the competition by non-League opposition.

Joe Lane signed from Sunderland for £400 and scored 11 goals in 26 games.

Match No.	Date	Venue	Opponents	Result		Scorers	Attendance
1	Sep 6	H	Hull City	D	2-2	Brown, Charles	3,000
2	13	A	Barnsley	L	1-2	Brown	
3	20	H	Bury	L	0-1		11,000
4	24	A	Notts County	L	0-2		
5	27	A	Huddersfield Town	L	0-1		7,000
6	Oct 4	H	Lincoln City	W	2-1	Quinn, Charles	
7	11	A	Fulham	D	0-0		6,000
8	18	A	Nottm Forest	L	0-3		10,000
9	25	H	Woolwich Arsenal	D	1-1	Quinn	18,000
10	Nov 1	A	Grimsby Town	L	0-2		8,000
11	8	H	Birmingham City	D	2-2	Connor (pen), Charles	5,000
12	15	A	Bristol City	L	0-1		8,000
13	22	H	Leeds C	D	2-2	Lane, Connor (pen)	5,000
14	29	A	Clapton Orient	L	0-2		
15	Dec 6	A	Glossop	W	2-1	Charlton, Lane	
16	13	A	Stockport County	D	0-0		
17	20	H	Bradford City	W	2-1	Pagman, Lane	
18	25	A	Leicester Fosse	W	1-0	Charlton	10,000
19	26	A	Wolves	L	0-1		10,000
20	27	A	Hull City	D	0-0		12,000
21	Jan 1	H	Wolves	W	2-0	Lane 2	7,500
22	3	H	Barnsley	W	3-1	Lane, Charlton, Charles	6,000
23	17	A	Bury	L	0-1		10,000
24	24	H	Huddersfield Town	L	0-1		
25	Feb 7	A	Lincoln City	W	2-1	Charles, Lane	
26	14	H	Fulham	D	1-1	Connor (pen)	5,000
27	21	H	Nottm Forest	W	2-1	Buchan 2	
28	28	A	Woolwich Arsenal	L	1-2	Charles	20,000
29	Mar 7	H	Grimsby Town	D	1-1	Lane	4,000
30	14	A	Birmingham City	D	0-0		7,000
31	21	H	Bristol City	L	0-1		4,000
32	28	A	Leeds C	L	1-2	Lane	12,000
33	Apr 4	H	Clapton Orient	D	0-0		3,500
34	10	H	Leicester Fosse	W	1-0	Connor	4,000
35	11	H	Glossop	D	1-1	Lane	4,000
36	13	H	Notts County	D	0-0		5,000
37	18	H	Stockport County	D	2-2	Charles,Turley	4,000
38	25	A	Bradford City	L	1-4	Lane	25,500

Final League Position: 16th in Division Two

Apps
Gls

FA Cup

1	Jan 10	A	Gillingham	L	0-1		

Apps
Gls

Fiske	Millership	Jones	Thorpe	Heslop	Booth	Charles	Turley	Brown	Gillow	Quinn	Connor	Buchan	Pignam	Sharp	Robson	Bainbridge	Rushton	Burke	Lane
1	2	3	4	5	6	7	8	9	10	11									
1	2	3	4		6	7	8	9	10	11	5								
1	2	3	4		6	7	8	9		11	5	10							
1	2	3	4		6			9		11	5	10	7	8					
1		3	4	10	6			9		11	5		7	8	2				
1		3	4		6	8		9		11	5	10	7		2				
1		3	4		6	8		9		11	5	10	7		2				
1		3	4		6	8		9		11	5	10	7		2				
1		3	4		6	8		9		11	5	10	7		2				
1		3			6	8		9		11	5	10	7		2	4			
1		3			6	8		9		11	5	10	7		2	4			
1		3			6	8				11	5	10	7			9	7	4	
1		3			6	7				11	5	8			2	4			9
1		3			6	7				11	5	8			2	4			9
1		3			6			7		11	5	8			2	4			9
1		3			6					11	5		7	8	2	4			9
1		3			6						5	10	7		2	4			9
1		3			6						5	10	7		2	4			9
1		3			6						5	10	7		2	4			9
1		3			6	7					5				2	4			9
1		3			6	7					5				2	4			9
1	2	3			6	7					5					4			9
1	2	3			6	7					5	10				4			9
		3			6	7					5				2	4			9
		3			6	7					5	10			2	4			9
		3			6	7				11	5	10			2	4			9
		3			6	7		11			5	10			2	4			9
1	2	3			6	7				11	5	10				4			9
1	2	3			6	7				11	5	10				4			9
1	2	3			6	7					5	10	11			4			9
1	2	3			6	7					5	10	11			4			9
1	2	3			6	7	8				5		11			4			9
1	2	3			6	7					5		11			4			9
1	2	3			6	7					5		11			4			9
1	2	3			6	7					5		11			4		10	9
1	2	3			6	7	8					10	11			4			9
1	2	3			6	7	8			11	5					4			9
1	2	3			6	7	8			11	5					4			9
34	16	38	9	2	38	31	7	13	2	21	36	24	20	3	21	29	1	2	26
						7	1	2		2	4	2	1						11
1		3			6	7					5			2	4				9
1		1			1	1					1			1	1				1

League Table

	P	W	D	L	F	A	Pts
Notts County	38	23	7	8	77	36	53
Bradford Park Avenue	38	23	3	12	71	47	49
Woolwich Arsenal	38	20	9	9	54	38	49
Leeds City	38	20	7	11	76	46	47
Barnsley	38	19	7	12	51	45	45
Clapton Orient	38	16	11	11	47	35	43
Hull City	38	16	9	13	53	37	41
Bristol City	38	16	9	13	52	50	41
Wolverhampton W	38	18	5	15	51	52	41
Bury	38	15	10	13	39	40	40
Fulham	38	16	6	16	46	43	38
Stockport County	38	13	10	15	55	57	36
Huddersfield Town	38	13	8	17	47	53	34
Birmingham	38	12	10	16	48	60	34
Grimsby Town	38	13	8	17	42	58	34
Blackpool	38	9	14	15	33	44	32
Glossop	38	11	6	21	51	67	28
Leicester Fosse	38	11	4	23	45	61	26
Lincoln City	38	10	6	22	36	66	26
Nottingham Forest	38	7	9	22	37	76	23

1914-15

Division Two

Did you know that?

For this season, Blackpool wore a kit that involved red, black and yellow hoops in deference to the number of Belgians who were stationed in the town as World War One approached.

Not a single game at Bloomfield Road attracted a five-figure attendance.

Joe Lane scored a remarkable 28 goals in just 38 League games for the Seasiders.

Match No.	Date		Venue	Opponents	Result		Scorers	Attendance
1	Sep	2	A	Bristol City	L	1-2	Lane	3,000
2		5	A	Hull City	W	3-1	Lane 3	6,000
3		12	H	Bury	L	3-4	Yarnall, Charles, Green	
4		19	A	Leeds C	L	0-2		8,000
		26	H	Preston NE	L	0-2		8,000
6	Oct	3	A	Clapton Orient	L	0-2		
7		10	H	Nottm Forest	W	3-0	Lane 2, Green	
8		17	A	Arsenal	L	0-2		17,000
9		24	H	Leicester Fosse	L	1-2	Sibbald	
10		31	A	Derby County	L	0-5		4,000
11	Nov	7	H	Barnsley	D	1-1	Booth	
12		14	A	Lincoln City	W	1-0	Lane	
13		21	H	Glossop	W	3-0	Lane 3	7,000
14		28	A	Birmingham City	L	0-3		5,000
15	Dec	5	H	Wolves	W	1-0	Sibbald	4,500
16		12	A	Grimsby Town	L	0-2		
17		19	H	Fulham	D	2-2	Lane, Green	2,000
18		25	A	Stockport County	W	2-0	Lane 2	
19		26	A	Huddersfield Town	L	0-5		9,500
20	Jan	1	H	Bristol City	W	2-0	Quinn, Lane	4,000
21		2	H	Hull City	L	1-2	Lane (pen)	5,000
22		23	H	Leeds C	W	1-0	Lane (pen)	6,000
23		25	A	Bury	D	2-2	Quinn, Green	3,000
24		30	A	Preston NE	L	0-1		7,000
25	Feb	6	H	Clapton Orient	W	5-1	Lane 2, Booth, Sibbald, Wilson	
26		13	A	Nottm Forest	L	1-2	Wilson	
27		20	H	Arsenal	L	0-2		6,000
28		27	A	Leicester Fosse	D	2-2	Lane 2	
29	Mar	6	H	Derby County	W	2-1	Quinn, Lane	5,000
30		13	A	Barnsley	W	2-1	Lane 2	
31		20	H	Lincoln City	D	0-0		
32		27	A	Glossop	W	3-1	Appleton, Sibbald, Charles	
33	Apr	2	H	Huddersfield Town	W	3-2	Charles, Lane, Quinn	4,500
34		5	H	Stockport County	W	4-2	Appleton, Sibbald, Charles, Lane	5,000
35		10	A	Wolves	L	0-2		7,000
36		14	H	Birmingham City	W	3-1	Charles, Lane 2	5,000
37		17	H	Grimsby Town	W	5-0	Charles, Appleton, Lane, Sibbald 2	4,000
38		24	A	Fulham	W	1-0	Bainbridge	2,000

Final League Position: 10th in Division Two

Apps
Gls

FA Cup

1	Jan	9	H	Sheffield United	L	1-2	Sibbald	7,500

Apps
Gls

Kidd	Robson	Jones	Bainbridge	Connor	Rooks	Charles	Turley	Lane	Yarnall	Quinn	Green	Booth	Millership	Tulloch	Sibbald	Wilson	Appleton	Gregson CWS	Mitchell FJ
1	2	3	4	5	6	7	8	9	10	11									
1	2	3	4	5	6	7		9	10	11	8								
1	2	3	4	5	6	7		9	10	11	8								
1	2	3	4	5		7	8	9	10	11		6							
1	2		4	5		7		9	10	11	8	6	3						
1	2		4	5		7		9	10	11	8	6	3						
1	2	3	4	5		7		9	10	11	8	6							
1	2	3	4	5		7		9	10	11	8	6							
1		3	4	5		7		9	8	11		6		2	10				
1		3	4			7		9		11	8	6		2	10	5			
1	2	3	4			7		9		11	8	6			10	5			
1	3		4			7		9		11	8	6		2	10	5			
1	3		4			7		9		11	8	6		2	10	5			
1	3		4					9		11	8	6		2	10	5	7		
1	3		4					9		11	8	6		2	10	5	7		
1	3		4					9		11	8	6		2	10	5	7		
1	3		4			7		9		11	8	6		2	10	5			
1	3		4			7		9		11	8	6		2	10	5			
1	3		4			7		9		11	8	6		2	10	5			
1	3	2	4			7		9		11	8	6			10	5			
1	3	2	4			7		9		11	8	6			10	5			
1	3		4			7		9		11	8	6		2	10	5			
1			2			7	4	9		11	8	6		3	10	5			
1			2			7	4	9			8	6		3	10	5	11		
1	2		4			7		9		11		6		3	10	5	8		
1	2		4			7		9		11		6		3	10	5	8		
1	2		4			7		9		11		6		3	10	5	8		
1			4		2	7		9		11		6		3	10	5	8		
1	2	3	4		6	7		9		11						5	8	10	
1	2	3	4		6	7		9		11						5	8	10	
		3	4		6	7		9		11				2		5	8	10	1
		3	4			7		9		11		6		2	10		8		
		3	4			7		9		11		6		2	10		8		
		3	4		6	7		9		11				2	10	5	8		
		3	4		6	7		9		11				2	10	5	8		1
		3	4		6	7		9		11				2	10	5	8		1
		3	4		6	7		9		11				2	10	5	8		1
		3	4		6	7		9		11				2	10	5	8		1
30	25	21	38	9	12	35	4	38	9	37	21	27	2	25	27	27	18	3	5
			1			6		28	1	4	4	2			7	2	3		

Kidd	Robson	Jones	Bainbridge	Connor	Rooks	Charles	Turley	Lane	Yarnall	Quinn	Green	Booth	Millership	Tulloch	Sibbald	Wilson	Appleton	Gregson CWS	Mitchell FJ
1	3		4			7		9		11	8	6		2	10	5			
1	1		1			1		1		1	1	1		1	1	1			
															1				

League Table

	P	W	D	L	F	A	Pts
Derby County	38	23	7	8	71	33	53
Preston North End	38	20	10	8	61	42	50
Barnsley	38	22	3	13	51	51	47
Wolverhampton W	38	19	7	12	77	52	45
Arsenal	38	19	5	14	69	41	43
Birmingham	38	17	9	12	62	39	43
Hull City	38	19	5	14	65	54	43
Huddersfield Town	38	17	8	13	61	42	42
Clapton Orient	38	16	9	13	50	48	41
Blackpool	38	17	5	16	58	57	39
Bury	38	15	8	15	61	56	38
Fulham	38	15	7	16	53	47	37
Bristol City	38	15	7	16	62	56	37
Stockport County	38	15	7	16	54	60	37
Leeds City	38	14	4	20	65	64	32
Lincoln City	38	11	9	18	46	65	31
Grimsby Town	38	11	9	18	48	76	31
Nottingham Forest	38	10	9	19	43	77	29
Leicester Fosse	38	10	4	24	47	88	24
Glossop	38	6	6	26	31	87	18

1915-16

Lancashire Section

Did you know that?

With the onset of War, Blackpool were placed in a 14-team group B of the Lancashire League and played in two competitions, finishing second and third.

Blackpool now adopted a white-and-blue kit, which lasted them until 1921.

Most of the players who represented the Seasiders during this season were soldiers who were stationed in the town.

Eddie Latheron, who played officially for Blackburn Rovers, guested and top scored with 16 goals.

Match No.	Date	Venue	Opponents	Result		Scorers	Attendance
1	Sep 4	A	Southport Cen	L	0-2		1,100
2	11	H	Oldham Athletic	W	4-1	Latheron, Chapman 2, Appleton	5,000
3	18	A	Everton	L	2-4	Appleton, Latheron	
4	25	H	Bolton Wanderers	W	2-1	Latheron, Charles	
5	Oct 2	A	Manchester City	L	0-3		
6	9	H	Stoke City	D	1-1	Latheron	
7	16	A	Burnley	L	2-5	Latheron, Chapman	6,000
8	23	H	Preston NE	W	5-1	Hodgkinson 2, Charles, Latheron 2	
9	30	A	Stockport County	L	1-2	Latheron	
10	Nov 6	H	Liverpool	W	5-2	Wilson, Latheron 2, Chapman 2	4,000
11	13	A	Bury	W	2-1	Charles, Chapman	
12	20	H	Manchester Utd	W	5-1	Chapman, Latheron 2, Appleton, Crompton (pen)	4,000
13	27	A	Rochdale	W	3-2	Chapman, Appleton, Crompton	
14	Dec 4	H	Southport Cen	D	0-0		
15	11	A	Oldham Athletic	L	0-2		500
16	18	H	Everton	L	1-4	Chapman	
17	25	A	Bolton Wanderers	W	2-0	Appleton, Hodgkinson	1,000
18	Jan 1	H	Manchester City	W	2-0	Carney, Charles	
19	8	A	Stoke City	L	1-3	Wilson	
20	15	H	Burnley	W	2-1	Hodgkinson, Latheron	4,000
21	22	A	Preston NE	W	2-1	Own-goal, Charles	
22	29	H	Stockport County	W	4-1	Charles, Green 2, Wilson	
23	Feb 5	A	Liverpool	L	0-1		16,000
24	12	H	Bury	W	3-1	Charles, Fairclough, Hodgkinson	
25	19	A	Manchester Utd	D	1-1	Fairclough	10,000
26	26	H	Rochdale	W	4-2	Quinn 2, Green 2	4,000

Final League Position: 3rd in Principal Competition - Lancashire Section

Apps
Gls

Northern Group

Match No.	Date	Venue	Opponents	Result		Scorers	Attendance
27	Mar 4	A	Bury	W	2-1	Carney, Crompton (pen)	3,000
28	11	H	Burnley	L	1-2	Carney	5,000
29	18	A	Preston NE	W	3-1	Hodgkinson, Charles, Latheron	4,500
30	25	H	Bolton Wanderers	W	3-1	Green, Carney, Quinn	3,000
31	Apr 1	A	Southport Cen	W	3-2	Booth, Latheron (pen), Quinn	
32	8	H	Bury	W	4-2	Latheron (pen), Quinn 3	4,000
33	15	A	Burnley	L	1-2	Own-goal	4,000
34	21	H	Southport Cen	W	3-1	Green 2, Charles	4,000
35	22	H	Preston NE	W	2-0	Charles, Quinn	6,000
36	29	A	Bolton Wanderers	W	2-1	Appleton, Green	

Final League Position: 2nd in Subsidary Competition - Northern Group

Apps
Gls

Mitchell	Crompton	Jones	Bainbridge	Wilson	Booth	Charles	Green	Chapman	Latheron	Appleton	Hodgkinson	Carney	Kidd	Quinn	Hampson	Clarke	Lloyd	Smith	Fairclough
1	2	3	4	5	6	7	8	9	10	11									
1	2	3	4	5	6	7	8	9	10	11									
1	2	3	4	5	6	7	8	9	10	11									
1	2	3	4	5	6	7	8	9	10		11								
1	2	3	4		6	7	8	5	10	9	11								
1	2	3	4	5	6	7		9	10	8	11								
1		3	2	5	6	7	8	9	10	11		4							
1	2	3	4	5	6	7		9	10	8	11								
1	2	3	4	5	6	7		9	10	8	11								
		3	2	5	6	7		9	10		11	4	1	8					
	2	3	4	5	6	7		9	10		11	8	1						
	2	3	4	5	6	7		9	10	8	11		1						
	2	3	4	5	6			9	10	8	11		1		7				
	2	3	4	5	6			9	10	8	11		1			7			
		3	2	5	6			9		8	11	4	1			7	10		
	2	3	4	5	6			9	10	11			1			7	8		
	5		4	2	6	8	7		10	9	11	3	1						
	5		4	2	6	8			10	9	11	3	1	7					
	2	3	8	5	6	7			10	9	11	4	1						
	2	3	4	5	6	7		9	10	8	11		1						
	2	3	4	5	6	7	8		10	9			1	11					
	2	3	9	5	6	7	8		10			4	1					11	
	2	3	4	5	6	7	8		10		11		1						9
	2	3		5	6	7	8		10		11	4	1						9
	2	3		5	6	7	8		10		11	4	1						9
	2	3		5	6	7	8		10	11		6		9					
9	24	24	23	25	26	25	13	17	25	16	21	11	17	4	1	3	2	1	3
	2			3		7	4	9	13	5	5	1		2					2

Mitchell	Crompton	Jones	Bainbridge	Wilson	Booth	Charles	Green	Chapman	Latheron	Appleton	Hodgkinson	Carney	Kidd	Quinn
	3	2	6	5	4	11			8		7	10	1	9
	2	3	4	5	6	7			10		11	8	1	9
	2	3	4	5		7	8		10		11	6	1	9
	2	3	4	5		7	8		10		11	6	1	9
		3	2	5	6	7	8		10		11	4	1	9
		3	2	5	6	7	8		10		11	4	1	9
		3	2	5	6	7	8		10		11	4	1	9
		3	2	5	6	7	8					4	1	
		3	2	5	6	7	8					4	1	10
		3	2	5	6		8			7		4	1	9
	4	10	10	10	8	9	8	1	7	1	7	10	10	9
	1				1	3	4		3	1	1	3		6

Note: Exact line-ups for all wartime games are not known.

1916-17

Lancashire Section

Did you know that?

Blackpool struggled to find players to compete this season and were forced to rely on staff and recovering patients from local hospitals to field a team.

Jim Simmons, a Sheffield United player, was on honeymoon in the town and was asked to play in the game with Preston on 2 September. Blackpool won 5–1.

On 25 November, the club could only field nine players, yet somehow drew with Stoke City 1–1. The previous week they had been beaten 11–1 by Burslem Port Vale.

Blackpool used a total of 62 players during a season that had 36 matches.

Match No.	Date	Venue	Opponents	Result		Scorers	Attendance
1	Sep 2	H	Preston NE	W	5-1	Bainbridge 2, Carlisle, Croker, Charles	3,000
2	9	A	Blackburn Rovers	L	0-4		2,000
3	16	H	Burnley	D	1-1	Croker	4,000
4	23	A	Manchester City	L	0-4		10,000
5	30	H	Manchester Utd	D	2-2	Appleton 2	4,000
6	Oct 7	A	Everton	L	1-3	Croker	15,000
7	14	H	Liverpool	L	0-1		1,500
8	21	A	Rochdale	L	1-4	Johnstone	
9	28	H	Stockport County	L	0-2		2,000
10	Nov 4	A	Bolton Wanderers	L	1-4	Appleton	
11	11	H	Bury	D	1-1	Whiting	4,000
12	18	A	Port Vale	L	1-11		
13	25	H	Stoke City	D	1-1	Jones	
14	Dec 2	A	Oldham Athletic	D	1-1	Williamson	1,144
15	9	H	Stockport County	L	0-2		
16	16	A	Preston NE	L	1-2	Spencer	
17	23	H	Blackburn Rovers	W	3-2	Williamson 3	1,000
18	30	A	Burnley	L	0-7		2,000
19	Jan 1	A	Southport Cen	L	0-1		
20	6	H	Manchester City	W	3-1	Bainbridge, Booth, Hartland	3,000
21	13	A	Manchester Utd	L	1-6	Unknown	
22	20	H	Everton	D	1-1	Clifton	3,000
23	27	A	Liverpool	D	2-2	Hartland, Smith	12,000
24	Feb 3	H	Rochdale	L	0-2		1,000
25	10	A	Stockport County	L	0-6		
26	17	H	Bolton Wanderers	W	5-2	Phillips, Jones, Kelly 2, Williamson	
27	24	A	Bury	L	0-2		
28	Mar 3	H	Port Vale	W	4-0	Gilham, Williamson, Hampson 2	3,000
29	10	A	Stoke City	L	0-6		
30	17	H	Oldham Athletic	W	9-0	Williamson, Clifton, Hampson 4, Carlisle, Gilham 2	3,000

Final League Position: 16th in Principal Competition - Lancashire Section

Apps
Gls

Northern Group

Match No.	Date	Venue	Opponents	Result		Scorers	Attendance
31	Dec 25	A	Burnley*	L	0-4		2,000
32	Mar 31	A	Preston NE	L	1-2	Williamson	
33	Apr 6	H	Burnley	L	2-3	Unknown 2	5,000
34	7	H	Blackburn Rovers	W	4-1	Gilham 2, Williamson, Own-goal	4,000
35	14	H	Preston NE	D	0-0		3,000
36	21	A	Blackburn Rovers	W	3-2	Williamson, Davies 2	

* Counted towards Principal and Subsidary Competitions

Final League Position: 11th in Subsidary Competition - Lancashire Section

Final League Position: 2nd in Subsidary Competition - Northern Group

Kidd	Harker	Jones	Connor	Carlisle	Booth	Charles	Simmons	Bainbridge	Appleton	Croker	Collins	Peet	Lyner	Chorley	Sibbald	Johnstone	Mitchell	Kuragh	Wilcox
1	2	3	4	5	6	7	8	9	10	11									
1		3	4	5	6	7			10	11	2	8	9						
1		3	4	5	6	7		2	8	11				9	10				
1		3	4	5	6	7		2	8					9		10	11		
1	2		4	5	6	7			8	3				9		10	11		
1	2		4	5	6	7			9	3				10		8	11		
1	2	3	4	5	6				7	11		4		10		8		9	
		3	4	5				9	10	11				10		8			1
1		3	4	5				9	10	11				10		8			
1		3	4	5	6			2	8	11									
1		3	4		6			2		11									
		3	4		6				8	11									1
		3	4		6					11									1
		3	4		6					11									1
		6	4						8	11									1
		6	4						8	11									1
		6	4						8	11									1
		6	4						8	11									1
		6	4						8	11									1
			4		6			2	8										1
			4		6			2	8										1
			4	5				2	8										
			4	5	6				8										
			4	5	6				8										
1			4		6			2	8										
		3	4		6			2	8										
		3	4	5	6				8										
		3	4	5	6			2											
			4	5	6														
			4	5	6														
10	4	20	30	17	22	6	1	16	22	18	1	2	1	7	1	6	3	1	12
		2		2	1	1		3	3	3						1			

Kidd	Harker	Jones	Connor	Carlisle	Booth	Charles	Simmons	Bainbridge	Appleton	Croker	Collins	Peet	Lyner	Chorley	Sibbald	Johnstone	Mitchell	Kuragh	Wilcox
		3	4						8	11									1

Stansfield, Cuffe, Jones, ConnorCarlisle, Booth, Clifton, Williamson, Fazackerley, Smith, Moscrop

Stansfield, Cuffe, Jones, ConnorCarlisle, Booth, Clifton, Williamson, Fazackerley, Smith, Moscrop

Stansfield, Gilham, Jones, Connor, Carlisle, Booth, Clifton, Williamson, Hampton, Smith, Moscrop

Stevenson, Cuffe, Jones, Connor, Carlsile, Dunn, Gilham, Fazackerley, Williamson, Roach, Moscrop

Stansfield, Cuffe, Jones, Connor, Carlisle, Dunn, Gilham, Fazackerley, Williamson, Roach, Fazackerley

Note: Exact line-ups for all wartime games are not known.

Exact squad numbers for the players in the Northern Group are not known.

1917-18

Lancashire Section

Did you know that?

Due to the lack of footballers in the town, again Blackpool could only field 10 men in the game with Manchester United on 1 December. They lost the game 1–0 after borrowing a player from the home team.

For the game with Burnley on 29 March, Blackpool's team was made up entirely of soldiers.

53 players were used in the 36-match season.

On 2 January Bloomfield Road played host to a military International fixture between England and Scotland, which resulted in a 1–1 draw.

Match No.	Date	Venue	Opponents	Result		Scorers	Attendance
1	Sep 1	H	Oldham Athletic	W	3-2	Kirrage 3	2,000
2	8	A	Oldham Athletic	D	1-1	Kirrage	2,218
3	15	H	Bury	W	1-0	Wilson	
4	22	A	Bury	L	1-2	Campey	
5	29	H	Stockport County	W	3-1	Thomas 2, Kirrage	
6	Oct 6	A	Stockport County	L	1-3	Williamson	
7	13	H	Stoke City	L	0-5		4,000
8	20	A	Stoke City	L	1-3	Thomas	
9	27	A	Liverpool	L	1-4	Thomas	12,000
10	Nov 3	H	Liverpool	L	0-6		3,000
11	10	A	Southport Cen	W	2-0	Bold, Williamson	800
12	17	H	Southport Cen	D	1-1	Clarke	2,000
13	Dec 1	A	Manchester Utd*	L	0-1		
14	15	H	Manchester Utd	L	2-3	Myers, Williamson	3,000
15	22	H	Rochdale	L	1-3	Berry	
16	25	A	Burnley	D	1-1	Unknown	3,000
17	29	A	Rochdale	L	3-6	Beel 2, Moorcroft	
18	Jan 8	H	Everton	W	1-0	Moorcroft	
19	15	A	Everton	L	2-7	Keenan, Moorcroft	
20	22	H	Port Vale*	L	0-1		700
21	29	A	Port Vale	L	0-4		
22	Feb 2	H	Bolton Wanderers	L	0-5		3,000
23	9	A	Bolton Wanderers	D	1-1	Williamson	
24	16	A	Preston NE	L	1-2	Moorcroft	
25	23	H	Preston NE	W	1-0	Connor (pen)	
26	Mar 2	A	Blackburn Rovers	D	2-2	Keenan, Williamson	
27	9	H	Blackburn Rovers	W	4-1	Hunter 4	2,000
28	16	H	Manchester City	W	1-0	Bold	3,000
29	23	A	Manchester City	D	2-2	Booth, Unknown	
30	29	H	Burnley	W	1-0	Hunter	

Final League Position: 12th in Principal Competition - Lancashire Section — Apps

* Team line up imcomplete. — Gls

Subsidary Competition

31	Nov 24	A	Burnley	L	1-3		500
32	Dec 1	H	Burnley	W	5-1	Thomas 2, Keenan, Chadwick 2	1,000
33	Mar 30	H	Blackburn Rovers	W	2-0	Hanson, Banks	500
34	Apr 9	A	Blackburn Rovers	W	4-1	Bold, McBear 2, Hunter	small
35	13	H	Preston NE	L	2-3	Hunter, Berry	3,000
36	20	A	Preston NE	W	4-1	Mitcham 2, Bold, Hunter	

Final League Position: 5th in Subsidary Competition - Lancashire Section

Final League Position: 2nd in Subsidary Competition - Northern Group

Stevenson	Fairhurst	Dunn	McPherson	Connor	Keenan	Robb	Campey	Gilham	Williamson	Kirrage	Wilson	Thomas	Bates	Bold	Stirzaker	Booth	Clarke	Robson	Bell
1	2	3	4	5	6	7	8	9	10	11									
1	2	3	4	5	6	7	8	9	10	11									
1	2	3	4		6	7	8	9	10	11	5								
1	2	3	4	5	6		8	9	10	11	7								
1	2	3	4	5	6	7		9	10	11		8							
1	2	3	4	5	6	7		9	10	11		8							
1	2	3	4	5	6	7		9	10	11		8							
1	2	3	4	5	6	7		9	10	11		8							
1	2	3	4	5	6	7		9	10	11		8							
1	2	3	4	5	6	7		9	10	11		8							
1			4	5	6	7	8	9	11			10	2	3					
1			4		6	7			11			10	2	3	5	8	9		
1				5	6					11		10		3				4	7
1				5	6				10			11	2	3					7
			4	5	6				10			11	2	3					7
1			4	5	6					11		10	2	3		8	9		
				6	5				10				2	3				4	
				6	5				10				2	3				4	
				6	5				10				2	3		8		4	
	2	3			6			8							7				
	2	3		4	6				8										
	2	3		4	6				8							10			
1	2	3		4	6				8							9			
1		3		4	6				8							9			
1	2			4	6				8							9			
1	2			4	6				8							9			
1	2			4	6											9			
				5	9								2	3					
				6	5								2	3		9			
		3		4	5								2			7			
20	17	16	13	28	30	11	5	11	27	11	2	12	11	11	1	12	2	8	3
				1	2		1		5	5	1	4		2		1	1		

Spencer, Bates, Bold, McPherson, Connor, Keenan, Williamson, Booth, Clarke, Thomas, Williamson	1
Stevenson, Bates, Bold, McPherson, Connor, Keenan, Williamson, Booth, Clarke, Thomas, Chadwick	
Mitchell, Bates, Dunn, Connor, Keenan, Booth, Hanson, Banks, McBear, Berry, Grice	
Mitchell, Bates, Bold, Connor, Keenan, Booth, Hanson, Hunter, McBear, Berry, Grice	
Monaghan, Bates, Dunn, Connor, Keenan, Booth, Williamson, Banks, Hunter, Berry, Mitcham	
Monaghan, Bold, Keenan, Connor, Kinsella, Booth, Williamson, Hunter, Banks, Berry, Mitcham	

Note: Exact line-ups for all wartime games are not known.

Exact squad numbers for the players in the Northern Group are not known.

1918-19

Lancashire Section

Did you know that?

Blackpool reached the Final of the Lancashire Senior Cup, losing 1–0 to Liverpool.

Bill Norman became Blackpool's first full-time manager.

Again Blackpool struggled to field a full team and had to borrow a player from opponents Port Vale on 28 September. They went on to lose 6–0.

The largest wartime crowd of 24,000 saw Blackpool lose at Liverpool 3–1 on 15 March.

The defeat to Liverpool in the semi-finals of the Lancashire Senior Cup on 24 May saw another pitch invasion and the referee escorted from the field for some controversial decisions.

Match No.	Date		Venue	Opponents	Result		Scorers	Attendance
1	Sep	7	H	Bolton Wanderers	L	1-4	Berry	
2		14	A	Bolton Wanderers	L	1-2	McBear	
3		21	H	Port Vale	D	1-1	McBear	
4		29	A	Port Vale	L	0-6		
5	Oct	5	H	Preston NE	L	1-2	Hunter	2,000
6		12	A	Preston NE	D	2-2	Unknown 2	
7		19	H	Manchester City	L	0-3		6,000
8		26	A	Manchester City	L	0-4		
9	Nov	2	A	Oldham Athletic	D	1-1	O'Doherty	1,517
10		9	H	Oldham Athletic	W	2-1	Unknown 2	2,500
11		16	A	Blackburn Rovers	W	3-0	McIver, Baker, Jackson	700
12		23	H	Blackburn Rovers	W	2-0	)'Doherty 2	5,000
13		30	A	Everton	L	0-6		10,000
14	Dec	7	H	Everton	L	1-3	Jackson	3,000
15		14	A	Rochdale	L	0-1		
16		21	H	Rochdale	W	5-1	Quinn 2, Hunter 2, Berry	3,000
17		28	H	Manchester Utd	D	2-2	Hunter 2	
18	Jan	6	A	Manchester Utd	D	1-1	Unknown	
19		11	H	Stoke City	L	1-6	O'Doherty	
20		18	A	Stoke City	L	1-2	Lockett	6,000
21		25	H	Bury	W	3-2	Connor, O'Doherty, Appleton	2,000
22	Feb	1	A	Bury	L	0-1		
23		8	H	Burnley	D	1-1	Hunter	
24		15	A	Burnley	L	0-3		6,283
25		22	H	Stockport County	W	2-0	O'Doherty, Hunter	3,000
26	Mar	1	A	Stockport County	W	2-1	Hunter, O'Doherty	
27		8	H	Liverpool	W	3-2	Rooke, Hunter, O'Doherty	5,000
28		15	A	Liverpool	L	1-3	O'Doherty	24,000
29		22	H	Southport Vulcan	W	6-0	O'Doherty, Hunter 4, Unknown	
30		29	A	Southport Vulcan	W	2-0	Hunter, O'Doherty	

Final League Position: 11th in Principal Competition — Apps

Line ups not knon for matches 4, 6 and 18 — Gls

Subsidary Competition

Match No.	Date		Venue	Opponents	Result		Scorers	Attendance
31	Dec	25	A	Burnley	L	1-5	Unknown	7,000
32	Apr	5	A	Blackburn Rovers	D	1-1	O'Doherty	12,000
33		12	H	Blackburn Rovers	W	6-1	Rooke, O'Doherty 2, Hunter2, Wilson	8,000
34		18	H	Burnley	D	0-0		12,000
35		19	H	Preston NE	W	3-0	O'Doherty 2, Hunter	10,000
36		26	A	Preston NE	W	2-0	Heathcote, Hunter	
SF	May	24	H	Liverpool	L	0-1		10,000

Final League Position: 1st in Subsidary Competition - Lancashire Section

Qualified for Final of Lancashire Senior Cup

Final League Position: 2nd in Subsidary Competition - Northern Group

Mahon	Bainbridge	Dunn	Connor	Keenan	Booth	Buckley	Hunter	McBear	Hogan	Berry	Congrove	Bowman	Robinson	Robson	Orrell	O'Doherty	Stevenson	McIver	Baker
1	2	3	4	5	6	7	8	9	10	11									
1	2	3	4	5	6	7	8	9	10	11									
1	2		4	5	6	7	8	9		11	3	10							
1	2			5	6	7	8			11	3	10	4	9					
1	2			5	6	7	8			11	3	10	4	9					
1	2			5	6	7	8				3	10	4	9	11				
1	2			5	6	7	8				3	10	4		11	9			
	2	3		5	6	7	8					10	4		11	9	1		
				5	6	7	8					10			11	9	1	2	3
	2	3		5	6								4		11	9	1	7	8
	2	3		5	6								4		11	9	1	7	8
	2	3		5	6					7			4		11	9	1		8
	2	3		5	6								4		11	9	1		8
	2	3		5	6		8			11			4			9	1		
	3	2		5	6		8			11			4			9			
	3	2		5	6		8			11			4			9	1		
	3	2	4	5	6		8			11							1		
	3	2	4	5	6		8			11						9	1		
	3	2	4	5	6		8			11						9	1		
			4	5	6		8									9			
			8	5	6								4			9	1		
	2			5	6		8						4			9			
	2			5			8			6			4			9			
	2			5			8						4			9			
	2			5			8						4			9			
				4	6		9									10			
				4	6		9									10			
7	18	13	8	27	24	9	22	3	2	14	5	7	17	3	8	20	12	3	5
			1				14	2		2						11		1	1

Team line-up Unknown
Mingay, Fairhurst, Jones, Keenan, Watson, Booth, Appleton, Heathcote, Hunter, O'Doherty, Rooke
Mingay, Fairhurst, Jones, Keenan, Watson, Booth, Appleton, Wilson, Hunter, O'Doherty, Rooke
Mingay, Fairhurst, Jones, Keenan, Watson, Booth, Appleton, Wilson, Hunter, O'Doherty, Rooke
MingayBainbridge, Jones, Keenan, Watson, Booth, Appleton, Wilson, Hunter, O'Doherty, Rooke
MingayBainbridge, Jones, Keenan, Watson, Booth, Heathcote, Wilson, Hunter, O'Doherty, Rooke
MingayFairhurst, Rooke, Keenan, Watson, Quinn, Heathcote, Wilson, Hunter, O'Doherty, Appleton

Note: Exact line-ups for all wartime games are not known.

Exact squad numbers for the players in the Northern Group are not known.

1919-20

Division Two

Manager: Bill Norman

Did you know that?

The prolific Joe Lane was sold to Sunderland in this season, despite scoring another 28 goals in total. It caused uproar among the supporters.

The finishing position of fourth was the Seasiders' best to date.

The West Stand was all but destroyed in a fire, meaning that the profit of £2383 was all but taken up with the rebuild.

Over 17,000 fans turned up for the visit of Bury in April. They were rewarded with a 1–0 win.

Match No.	Date	Venue	Opponents	Result		Scorers	Attendance
1	Aug 30	H	Leeds City	W	4-2	Wilson, Lane 2 (1 pen), Charles	10,000
2	Sep 1	A	Lincoln City	W	3-0	Lane, Heathcote 2	
3	6	A	Leeds City	L	0-1		10,000
4	8	H	Lincoln City	W	6-0	Lane 3 (1 pen), Sibbald 2, Heathcote	9,000
5	13	A	Stoke City	L	0-2		
6	20	H	Stoke City	W	3-2	Heathcote, Lane 2	9,000
7	27	A	Grimsby Town	D	1-1	Heathcote	4,000
8	Oct 3	A	Nottm Forest	L	0-2		4,000
9	4	H	Grimsby Town	W	2-0	Lane 2 (1 pen)	
10	11	A	Birmingham City	L	2-4	Lane 2	16,000
11	18	H	Birmingham City	W	3-0	Heathcote, Lane, Rookes	8,000
12	25	A	Leicester City	W	3-2	Lane 2, Booth	12,000
13	Nov 1	H	Leicester City	W	3-0	Charles, Booth, Lane	
14	8	A	Fulham	W	2-1	Sibbald, Lane	12,000
15	15	H	Fulham	D	1-1	Rooke	7,000
16	22	A	Coventry City	D	0-0		19,000
17	29	H	Coventry City	W	2-0	Heathcote, Lane	5,000
18	Dec 6	A	Huddersfield Town	W	3-1	Quinn, Heathcote, Lane	6,500
19	13	H	Huddersfield Town	L	0-3		5,000
20	20	A	Bristol City	D	0-0		8,000
21	25	A	Bury	W	2-1	Lane 2	15,000
22	27	H	Bristol City	D	0-0		10,000
23	Jan 1	H	Rotherham C	W	5-1	Lane 2, Sibbald, Charles, Quinn	
24	3	H	West Ham Utd	D	0-0		7,000
25	17	A	West Ham Utd	L	0-1		26,000
26	24	H	Clapton Orient	W	3-0	Robson, Quinn, Lane	8,000
27	Feb 7	H	Tottenham Hotspur	L	0-1		12,000
28	14	A	Tottenham Hotspur	D	2-2	Lane 2	38,000
29	21	H	South Shields	L	0-3		8,000
30	28	A	South Shields	L	0-6		28,000
31	Mar 6	A	Wolves	W	3-0	Quinn, Sibbald, McGinn	15,000
32	13	H	Wolves	D	1-1	Hunter	7,000
33	18	A	Clapton Orient	L	0-3		
34	20	A	Hull City	W	1-0	Berry	10,000
35	27	H	Hull City	W	2-1	Sibbald, Hunter	6,000
36	Apr 2	H	Bury	W	1-0	Charles	17,000
37	3	A	Stockport County	D	0-0		
38	5	A	Rotherham C	W	2-1	Heathcote, Hunter	15,000
39	10	H	Stockport County	W	1-0	Heathcote	6,000
40	17	A	Barnsley	D	1-1	Hunter	
41	24	H	Barnsley	L	0-2		8,000
42	May 1	H	Nottm Forest	W	3-2	Heathcote 3	7,000

Final League Position: 4th in Division Two

Apps
Gls

FA Cup

1	Jan 10	H	Derby County	D	0-0		11,000
1R	14	A	Derby County	W	4-1	Sibbald, Lane 2, Charles	20,000
2	30	A	Preston NE	L	1-2	Quinn	25,000

Apps
Gls

Mingay	Tulloch	Jones	Keenan	Wilson	Rookes	Charles	Heathcote	Lane	Sibbald	Quinn	Fairhurst	Booth	Appleton	O'Doherty	Tremeling	Jacklin	McGinn	Burke	Hunter
1	2	3	4	5	6	7	8	9	10	11									
1	2	3	4	5	6	7	8	9	10	11									
1	2	3	4	5	6	7	8	9	10	11									
1	2		5		6	11	8	9	10		3	4	7						
1	2	3	5		6	7	8	9	11			4		10					
1	2	3	4	5	6	11	8	9	10				7						
1	2	3	4	5	6	11	8	9	10				7						
1	2	3	4	5	6	11	8	9	10				7						
1	2	3	4	5	11		8	9	10		6		7						
	2	3	4		6		8	9	10	11			7		5	1			
1	2	3	4		6		8	9	10	11			7		5				
1	2	3	4		6		8	9	10	11			7		5				
1		3			6	11	8	9	10		2	6	7		5				
1		3			6		8	9	10	11	2	6	7		5				
1		3	4		6		8	9	10	11	2		7		5				
1		3	4		6		8	9	10	11	2		7		5				
1		3	4	5	6		8	9	10	11	2		7						
1	2	3	4	5	6		8	9	10	11			7						
1	2	3	4	5	6		8	9	10	11			7						
1	2	3		5	6	7	8	9		11							10	4	
1	2			5	6	7		9	8	11	3						10	4	
1		3		5	6	7		9	8	11	2						10	4	
1		3		5	6	7		9	8	11	2						10	4	
1	2	3		5		7	8	9		11		6					10	4	
1	2			5	6	7	8	9		11	3						10	4	
1	2		4	5	6	7		9	8	11	3						10		
1	2		4	5	6	7		9	8	11	3								8
1	2		4	5			8	9		11	3	6					10		7
1	2		4	5			8	9		11	3	6					10		7
1	2		4	5	11			9	8	10		6							7
1	2		4	5	6	7			8	11	3						10		
1	2		4		6				8		3						10	4	7
1	2		5		6	7			8		3						10	4	
1	2		5		6	7			8		3						10	4	9
1	2		5		6	7			8		3						10	4	9
1	2		5		6	7	8		9		3						10		
1	2		5		6	7	8		9		3						10		
1	2		5		6	7	8				3						10		9
1	2		5		6	7	8				3						10		9
1	2		5		6	7	8				3						10		9
1	2		5		6	7	8				3						10		9
1	2		5		11		8		9		3								
41	35	22	35	22	39	7	31	39	32	24	27	8	15	1	7	1	21	9	11
				1	3	4	13	26	6	4		2					1		4

Mingay	Tulloch	Jones	Keenan	Wilson	Rookes	Charles	Heathcote	Lane	Sibbald	Quinn	Fairhurst	Booth	Appleton	O'Doherty	Tremeling	Jacklin	McGinn	Burke	Hunter
1	2		4	5	6	7	8	9		11	3						10		
1	2		4	5	6	7		9	8	11	3		1				10		
1	2		4	5	6	7		9	8	11	3		1				10		
3	3		3	3	3	3	1	3	2	3	3						3		
						1		2	1	1									

Note: Exact line-ups for all wartime games are not known.

League Table

	P	W	D	L	F	A	Pts
Tottenham Hotspur	42	32	6	4	102	32	70
Huddersfield Town	42	28	8	6	97	38	64
Birmingham	42	24	8	10	85	34	56
Blackpool	42	21	10	11	65	47	52
Bury	42	20	8	14	60	44	48
Fulham	42	19	9	14	61	50	47
West Ham United	42	19	9	14	47	40	47
Bristol City	42	13	17	12	46	43	43
South Shields	42	15	12	15	58	48	42
Stoke	42	18	6	18	60	54	42
Hull City	42	18	6	18	78	72	42
Barnsley	42	15	10	17	61	55	40
Port Vale	42	16	8	18	59	62	40
Leicester City	42	15	10	17	41	61	40
Clapton Orient	42	16	6	20	51	59	38
Stockport County	42	14	9	19	52	61	37
Rotherham County	42	13	8	21	51	83	34
Nottingham Forest	42	11	9	22	43	73	31
Wolverhampton W	42	10	10	22	55	80	30
Coventry City	42	9	11	22	35	73	29
Lincoln City	42	9	9	24	44	101	27
Grimsby Town	42	10	5	27	34	75	25

1920-21

Division Two

Manager: Bill Norman

Did you know that?

Defender Horace Fairhurst suffered a head injury in the game at Barnsley on 27 December and died 11 days later at his home.

Blackpool were atop of the League for a large part of the season, but fell away to finish fourth.

The team were beaten by non-League opposition again in the FA Cup. This time by Southend United 1–0 in the second round.

Match No.	Date		Venue	Opponents	Result		Scorers	Attendance
1	Aug	28	A	Bury	D	2-2	Heathcote, Keenan	20,000
2		30	H	Bristol City	L	1-2	Heathcote	10,000
3	Sep	4	H	Bury	L	0-1		16,000
4		8	A	Bristol City	D	1-1	Barrass	20,000
5		11	H	Coventry City	W	4-0	Benton 3, Donachie	12,500
6		13	H	Clapton Orient	D	2-2	Barass, Heathcote	8,000
7		18	A	Coventry City	W	2-0	Benton, Heathcote	20,000
8		25	H	Leeds United	W	1-0	Heathcote	8,000
9	Oct	2	A	Leeds United	L	0-2		9,500
10		9	H	Birmingham City	W	3-0	Rookes, Heathcote, Benton	9,000
11		16	A	Birmingham City	L	0-3		30,000
12		23	H	West Ham Utd	W	1-0	Reid	10,000
13		30	A	West Ham Utd	D	1-1	Heathcote	25,000
14	Nov	6	H	Fulham	W	1-0	Barrass	8,000
15		13	A	Fulham	W	2-1	Benton, Heathcote	12,000
16		20	H	Cardiff City	L	2-4	Heathcote 2	12,000
17		27	A	Cardiff City	D	0-0		22,000
18	Dec	4	H	Leicester City	W	2-0	Reid, Barrass	8,000
19		11	A	Leicester City	W	1-0	Barrass	16,500
20		18	H	Notts County	L	0-2		7,000
21		25	H	Barnsley	W	1-0	Heathcote	12,000
22		27	A	Barnsley	W	1-0	Barrass	18,000
23	Jan	1	A	Notts County	W	2-1	Heathcote 2	15,000
24		15	A	Nottm Forest	L	1-3	Ratcliffe	10,000
25		22	H	Nottm Forest	W	1-0	Mee	9,000
26	Feb	5	H	Sheffield Wed	D	1-1	Heathcote	9,000
27		7	A	Sheffield Wed	W	1-0	Ratcliffe	8,000
28		12	A	Rotherham C	W	2-0	Keenan, Heathcote	15,000
29		19	H	Rotherham C	L	0-1		
30		26	A	Port Vale	W	1-0	Keenan	
31	Mar	5	H	Port Vale	W	1-0	Heathcote	
32		12	A	South Shields	L	0-1		15,000
33		19	H	South Shields	W	3-2	Bedford, Charles 2	8,000
34		25	H	Stoke City	W	3-1	Heathcote, Barrass, Bedford	15,000
35		26	H	Hull City	L	1-2	Bedford	15,000
36		28	A	Stoke City	D	1-1	Charles	
37	Apr	2	A	Hull City	L	1-2	Barrass	9,000
38		9	H	Wolves	W	3-0	Bedford 2, Mee	10,300
39		16	A	Wolves	L	1-3	Bedford	13,802
40		23	H	Stockport County	D	1-1	Bedford	7,000
41		30	A	Stockport County	D	2-2	Heathcote, Barrass	
42	May	7	A	Clapton Orient	D	0-0		10,000

Final League Position: 4th in Division Two

Apps
Gls

FA Cup

1	Jan	8	A	Darlington	D	2-2	Ratcliffe, Barrass	16,113
1R		12	H	Darlington	W	2-1	McGinn, Ratcliffe	8,000
2		29	A	Southend Utd	L	0-1		9,000

Apps
Gls

Mingay	Fairhurst	Tulloch	Keenan	Halstead	Howard	Charles	Heathcote	Ratcliffe	McGinn	Donachie	Benton	Popplewell	Barras	Burke	Gavin	Brown	Richardson	Bainbridge	Rookes
1	2	3	4	5	6	7	8	9	10	11									
1	3	2		5	6	7	8	9	10	11	4								
1	3	2	4		6	7	8		9	11		5	10						
1	3	2	5		6	7	8			11	9		10	4					
1	3	2	5		6	7	8			11	9		10	4					
1		2	5			7	8			11	9		10	4	3	6			
	3		5			7	8				9		10	4			1	2	6
	3	2	5			7	8			11	9		10	4			1		6
	3	2	5			7	8			11	9			4			1		6
	3	2	5			7	10			11	8			4			1		6
	3	2	5		4		10	9		11	8						1		6
		2	5		4		10			7	8				3		1		6
	3	2	5				10			7	8		9				1		6
	3	2	5				10			7	8		9				1		6
	3	2	5				10			7	8		9				1		6
	3	2	5				10			7	8		9				1		6
	3	2	5			7	10				6		9				1		
	3	2	5			7	8				6		10				1		
	3	2	5			7	10			11	8		9				1		6
	3	2	5			7	10			11	8		9				1		6
	3	2	5				10			7	6		9				1		
	3	2	5				8	9	4	7	6		10				1		
		2	5			7	8	9	4		6		10		3		1		
			5			7		9	4		6		10		3		1	2	
		2	5			7		9	4		8		10		3		1		6
		2	5			7	8	9	4		10				3		1		6
		2	5			7	8	9	4		6				3		1		
		2	5			7	8	9	4		6				3		1		
		2	5			7	8	9	4		6				3		1		
		2	5			7	10	9	6		4		8		3		1		
		2	5			7	10	9	6		4		8		3		1		
		2	5			7	10		4		6		8		3		1		
		2	5			7	10		4		6		8		3		1		
		2	5			7	10		4		6		8		3		1		
		2	5			7	10		4				8		3		1		6
1		2	5			7	10		4		6		8		3				
1		2	5			7	10		4		6		8						
1		2	5			7	10		4		6		8		3				
1		2	5			7	10		4		6		8		3				
1		2	5			7	10		4		6		8						
1		2	5			7	10		4		6		8						3
1		2	5		6		10		4		7		8						3
13	20	40	42	1	8	33	40	13	24	19	39	1	32	7	18	1	29	2	17
			3			3	18	2		1	6		9						1
		2	5			7	8	9	4		6		10		3		1		
			5			7	8	9	4		6		10		3		1		2
		2	5			7	10		4		9		8		3		1		6
		2	3			3	3	2	3		3		3		3		3		2
								2	1				1						

League Table

	P	W	D	L	F	A	Pts
Birmingham	42	24	10	8	79	38	58
Cardiff City	42	24	10	8	59	32	58
Bristol City	42	19	13	10	49	29	51
Blackpool	42	20	10	12	54	42	50
West Ham United	42	19	10	13	51	30	48
Notts County	42	18	11	13	55	40	47
Clapton Orient	42	16	13	13	43	42	45
South Shields	42	17	10	15	61	46	44
Fulham	42	16	10	16	43	47	42
Sheffield Wednesday	42	15	11	16	48	48	41
Bury	42	15	10	17	45	49	40
Leicester City	42	12	16	14	39	46	40
Hull City	42	10	20	12	43	53	40
Leeds United	42	14	10	18	40	45	38
Wolverhampton W	42	16	6	20	49	66	38
Barnsley	42	10	16	16	48	50	36
Port Vale	42	11	14	17	43	49	36
Nottingham Forest	42	12	12	18	48	55	36
Rotherham County	42	12	12	18	37	53	36
Stoke	42	12	11	19	46	56	35
Coventry City	42	12	11	19	39	70	35
Stockport County	42	9	12	21	42	75	30

1921-22

Division Two

Manager: Bill Norman

Did you know that?

Blackpool only avoided relegation by winning their last two games of the season against promotion-chasing West Ham United.

19,000 fans turned up for the home game with Bury on 5 September – they saw a 1–0 defeat.

The club announced a loss of £2944 for the season.

The Spion Kop – now the South Stand – was extended and the capacity rose to around 18,000 (and so making the game against Bury a rather uncomfortable affair).

Match No.	Date	Venue	Opponents	Result		Scorers	Attendance
1	Aug 27	H	Derby County	W	4-2	Benton, Mee 2, Heathcote	12,000
2	31	A	Bury	L	0-3		12,000
3	Sep 3	A	Derby County	L	0-1		10,000
4	5	H	Bury	L	0-1		19,000
5	10	A	Leeds United	D	0-0		18,000
6	17	H	Leeds United	L	1-3	Barrass	13,000
7	24	A	Hull City	L	0-2		8,000
8	Oct 1	H	Hull City	L	0-1		10,000
9	8	A	Notts County	L	1-2	Bedford	
10	15	H	Notts County	L	1-2	Benton	
11	22	A	Crystal Palace	L	0-1		15,000
12	29	H	Crystal Palace	L	1-3	Bedford (pen)	
13	Nov 5	A	Rotherham C	W	1-0	Charles	
14	12	H	Rotherham C	W	3-1	Bedford 2, Sibbald	
15	19	H	Sheffield Wed	L	0-2		
16	26	A	Sheffield Wed	L	1-5	Mee	12,000
17	Dec 3	H	Fulham	L	0-2		6,500
18	10	A	Fulham	L	0-1		15,000
19	17	H	Bradford	D	1-1	Sibbald	7,000
20	24	A	Bradford	D	0-0		6,000
21	26	H	Leicester City	W	2-0	Bedford 2	
22	27	A	Leicester City	L	0-1		
23	31	A	Clapton Orient	L	0-3		20,000
24	Jan 14	H	Clapton Orient	W	2-0	Power, Barrass	6,000
25	21	H	Coventry City	W	2-1	Power, Baverstock	5,000
26	28	A	Coventry City	W	1-0	Mee	15,000
27	Feb 4	H	Barnsley	W	1-0	Power	5,500
28	11	A	Barnsley	L	2-3	Power, Barrass	
29	18	H	Wolves	L	1-3	Power (pen)	7,000
30	25	A	Wolves	L	0-4		11,510
31	Mar 4	H	Nottm Forest	W	2-1	Mee 2	8,000
32	11	A	Nottm Forest	D	0-0		12,000
33	18	A	Bristol City	W	1-0	Barrass	18,000
34	25	H	Bristol City	W	2-0	McGinn, Heathcote	10,000
35	Apr 1	A	South Shields	L	1-2	Barrass	8,000
36	8	H	South Shields	W	4-0	Charles, Power, Mee (pen), Bedford	5,000
37	14	H	Stoke City	W	3-2	Barrass, Benton, Bedford	12,000
38	15	H	Port Vale	L	0-1		15,000
39	17	A	Stoke City	D	1-1	Bedford	20,000
40	24	A	Port Vale	L	0-1		14,000
41	29	A	West Ham Utd	W	2-0	Bedford, Barrass	18,000
42	May 6	H	West Ham Utd	W	3-1	Bedford, Leaver, Barrass	12,000

Final League Position: 19th in Division Two

Apps

Gls

FA Cup

1	Jan 7	H	Watford	L	1-2	Bedford	10,121

Apps

Gls

Richardson	Tulloch	Clough	McGinn	Rooks	Benton	Charles	Heathcote	Bedford	Barrass	Mee	Gavin	Keenan	Mingay	Ford	Curran	Sibbald	Hacking	Dyke	Watkinson
1	2	3	4	5	6	7	8	9	10	11									
1	2		4		6	7	8	9	10	11	3	5							
1	2		4	5	6	7	8	9	10	11	3								
			4		6	7	8	9	10	11	3		1	2	5				
	2		4		6	7		9	10	11	3	5	1			8			
	2		4		6	7		9	8	11	3	5	1			10			
	2		4		6	7	8	9	10	11	3				5		1		
	2		4		6	7	8	9	10	11	3				5		1		
	2		4	6	8			9	10	11	3				5		1	7	
	2		4	6	8	7		9	10	11	3				5		1		
	2		4	6	8	7	10	9		11	3				5		1		
	2		4	6	8	7	10	9		11	3				5		1		
	2		5	6	4	7	10	9		11	3		1			8			
	2		5	6	4	7	10	9		11	3		1			8			
	2		5	6	4		10	9		11	3		1			8			7
	2		4	7			10	9		11	3	5	1			8			
	2			7	4		8			11	3	5	1		6	10			
	2			6		7		8	10	11	3	5	1		4	9			
	2		4	6					9	11	3	5	1			7			
	2		4	6	9	7				11	3	5	1						
	2		4	6		7		9		11	3	5	1						
	2		4	6	9	7				11	3	5	1						
	2		4	7	6			9		11	3	5	1						
	3		4	6		7			8	11			1		5	10			
	3		4	6		7			8	11			1		5	10			
	3		4	6		7			8	11			1		5	10			
	3			6	4	7			8	11			1		5	10			
	3			6	4	7			8	11			1		5	10			
	3		6			7			8	11		6	1		5	10			
	3		4		6	7		9	10	11			1		5				
	2		4		6	7		9	10	11	3		1		5				
	2		4		6	7	8		10	11	3		1		5				
	2		4		6	7	8	9	10	11	3		1		5				
	2		4		6	7	8	9	10	11	3		1		5				
	2		4		6	7	8		10	11	3		1		5				
	2		4		6	7		9	10	11	3		1		5				
	2		4		6	7		9	10	11	3		1		5				
	2			4	6	7	8	9	10	11	3		1		5				
	3				4			9	10	11		5	1						
	3				4			9	8	11		5	1						
	3				5			9	10	11		6	1						
	3		4		6	7		9	10	11		5	1						
3	41	1	34	23	34	33	18	30	31	42	30	15	33	1	25	15	6	1	1
			1		3	2	2	11	8	7						2			

Richardson	Tulloch	Clough	McGinn	Rooks	Benton	Charles	Heathcote	Bedford	Barrass	Mee	Gavin	Keenan	Mingay	Ford	Curran	Sibbald	Hacking	Dyke	Watkinson
	2		4	7	6			9		11	3	5	1						
	1		1	1	1			1		1	1	1	1						
								1											

League Table

	P	W	D	L	F	A	Pts
Nottingham Forest	42	22	12	8	51	30	56
Stoke	42	18	16	8	60	44	52
Barnsley	42	22	8	12	67	52	52
West Ham United	42	20	8	14	52	39	48
Hull City	42	19	10	13	51	41	48
South Shields	42	17	12	13	43	38	46
Fulham	42	18	9	15	57	38	45
Leeds United	42	16	13	13	48	38	45
Leicester City	42	14	17	11	39	34	45
Sheffield Wednesday	42	15	14	13	47	50	44
Bury	42	15	10	17	54	55	40
Derby County	42	15	9	18	60	64	39
Notts County	42	12	15	15	47	51	39
Crystal Palace	42	13	13	16	45	51	39
Clapton Orient	42	15	9	18	43	50	39
Rotherham County	42	14	11	17	32	43	39
Wolverhampton W	42	13	11	18	44	49	37
Port Vale	42	14	8	20	43	57	36
Blackpool	42	15	5	22	44	57	35
Coventry City	42	12	10	20	51	60	34
Bradford Park Avenue	42	12	9	21	46	62	33
Bristol City	42	12	9	21	37	58	33

1922-23

Division Two

Manager: Bill Norman

Did you know that?

A loss of nearly £4000 was announced, but the signing of Harry White from Arsenal for £1225 contributed to the figure.

Manager Bill Norman and his son-in-law Allan Ure – his assistant – both left the club at the end of the season.

Only three wins in the last 10 games saw the Seasiders fall from the promotion race yet again.

Harry Bedford was prolific again, netting 32 goals in 42 League appearances.

Match No.	Date	Venue	Opponents	Result		Scorers	Attendance
1	Aug 26	A	Leeds United	D	1-1	Barrass	20,000
2	28	H	Clapton Orient	D	0-0		14,000
3	Sep 2	H	Leeds United	W	1-0	Bedford	14,000
4	4	A	Clapton Orient	W	1-0	Bedford	
5	9	H	Bradford City	W	3-0	Barrass 3	14,000
6	16	A	Bradford City	W	2-0	Bedford 2	12,000
7	25	H	Southampton	L	1-2	Bedford	13,500
8	30	A	Southampton	D	1-1	Barrass	17,000
9	Oct 7	H	Derby County	W	3-2	Roseboom, Bedford 2	12,000
10	14	A	Derby County	L	0-1		12,000
11	21	A	West Ham Utd	L	0-2		16,000
12	28	H	West Ham Utd	W	4-1	Bedford 2, Barrass 2	10,000
13	Nov 4	A	Notts County	L	0-2		15,000
14	11	H	Notts County	D	1-1	Bedford	12,000
15	18	A	Fulham	D	1-1	McIvenney	15,000
16	25	H	Fulham	W	3-0	Barrass, Bedford, McIvenney	9,500
17	Dec 2	H	Crystal Palace	W	4-0	McIvenney, Barrass, Watkinson, Bedford (pen)	10,000
18	9	A	Crystal Palace	D	1-1	Bedford	5,000
19	16	H	Hull City	D	0-0		8,000
20	23	A	Hull City	D	0-0		8,000
21	25	A	Leicester City	W	2-1	Bedford 2	
22	26	H	Leicester City	L	1-2	McIvenney	15,000
23	30	H	Sheffield Wed	W	3-0	Bedford 2, Barrass	10,000
24	Jan 1	A	Stockport County	D	2-2	Roseboom, Barrass	18,000
25	6	A	Sheffield Wed	W	3-2	Bedford 3	28,000
26	20	A	Barnsley	D	2-2	Barrass, Bedford	7,000
27	27	H	Barnsley	L	0-1		20,000
28	Feb 3	A	Port Vale	L	0-2		9,000
29	10	H	South Shields	W	3-0	Barrass 2, Bedford	9,000
30	17	A	Wolves	W	4-3	Bedford 3, Mee	11,793
31	24	H	Wolves	W	3-1	Charles, Bedford, Barrass	8,500
32	Mar 3	A	Coventry City	W	2-1	Bedford 2	14,000
33	10	H	Coventry City	L	0-1		12,000
34	17	H	Port Vale	L	0-2		11,000
35	21	A	South Shields	L	0-1		
36	30	H	Stockport County	D	0-0		15,000
37	31	H	Manchester Utd	W	1-0	Charles	17,500
38	Apr 7	A	Manchester Utd	L	1-2	Leaver	24,500
39	14	H	Bury	W	5-1	Charles, Barrass, Bedford 3	12,000
40	21	A	Bury	L	0-3		10,000
41	28	H	Rotherham C	W	1-0	Bedford	6,000
42	May 5	A	Rotherham C	L	0-1		

Final League Position: 5th in Division Two

App
Gl.

FA Cup

1	Jan 13	A	Derby County	L	0-2		22,74

App
Gl

Mingay	Baverstock	Tulloch	McGinn	Keenan	Benton	Charles	McIvenney	Bedford	Barrass	Mee	Hird	Watkinson	Roseboum	Edge	Brown	Leaver	Wood	Curran	Baker
1	2	3	4	5	6	7	8	9	10	11									
1	2	3	4	5	6	7		9	10	11	8								
1	2	3	4	5	6			9	10	11	8	7							
1	2	3	4	5	6			9		11	8	7	10						
1	2	3	4	5	6			9	8	11			10	7					
1	2	3	4	5	6			9	8	11			10	7					
1	2	3	4	5	6			9	8	11		7	10						
1	2	3	5		6	7		9	8	11			10		4				
1	2	3	4		6	7		9	8	11			10			5			
1		3	4		6	7		9		11	8		10			5	2		
1		3			6	7		9	8	11			10		4	5	2		
1		3			6			9	8	11				7	4	10	2	5	
1		3			6			9	8	11				7	4	10	2	5	
1		3			6			9	8	11				7	4	10	2	5	
1		3	4		6		8	9	10	11		7					2		5
1		3	4		6		8	9	10	11		7				5	2		
1		3	4		6		8	9	10	11		7				5	2		
1		3	4		6		8	9	10	11		7				5	2		
1			4		6		8	9	10	11		7				5	2		
1			4		6		8	9	10	11		7				5	2		
1			4		6	7	8	9	10	11							2		
1		3	4		6	7	8	9	10	11							2		
1		3	4		6	7		9	10	11			8				2	5	
1			4		6	7		9	10	11			8				2	5	
1		2	4		6	7		9	10	11			8					5	
1		3	4		6	7	8	9	10	11						5	2		
1		3	4		6	7		9	8	11			10			5	2		
1		3	4		6	7	8	9	10	11						5	2		
1			4		6	7	8	9	10	11						5	2		
1			4		6	7	8	9	10	11						5	2		
1			4			7	8	9	10	11					6	5	2		
1			4			7		9	10	11					6	5	2		
1			4			7		9	10	11					6	5	2		
1			4				8	9	10	11						5	2		
1			4			7	8	9	10	11						5	2	6	
1		2	4		6			9		11			8			5			
1		2	4		6	7		9	10	11						5			
1		2	4		6	7		9	10	11						5			
1		2	4		6	7		9	10	11						5	3		
1		3	4		6	7		9	10	11						5	2		
1					6	7		9	8	11						5	2		
1					6	7		9	8	11						5	2		
42	9	29	36	7	37	25	16	42	39	42	4	9	13	5	8	28	29	7	1
						3	4	32	16	1		1	2			1			

1		3	4		6	7	8	9	10	11							2	5	
1		1	1		1	1	1	1	1	1							1	1	

League Table

	P	W	D	L	F	A	Pts
Notts County	42	23	7	12	46	34	53
West Ham United	42	20	11	11	63	38	51
Leicester City	42	21	9	12	65	44	51
Manchester United	42	17	14	11	51	36	48
Blackpool	42	18	11	13	60	43	47
Bury	42	18	11	13	55	46	47
Leeds United	42	18	11	13	43	36	47
Sheffield Wednesday	42	17	12	13	54	47	46
Barnsley	42	17	11	14	62	51	45
Fulham	42	16	12	14	43	32	44
Southampton	42	14	14	14	40	40	42
Hull City	42	14	14	14	43	45	42
South Shields	42	15	10	17	35	44	40
Derby County	42	14	11	17	46	50	39
Bradford City	42	12	13	17	41	45	37
Crystal Palace	42	13	11	18	54	62	37
Port Vale	42	14	9	19	39	51	37
Coventry City	42	15	7	20	46	63	37
Clapton Orient	42	12	12	18	40	50	36
Stockport County	42	14	8	20	43	58	36
Rotherham County	42	13	9	20	44	63	35
Wolverhampton W	42	9	9	24	42	77	27

1923-24

Division Two

Manager: Frank Buckley

Did you know that?

The team adopted a new Orange (not Tangerine) shirt after director Albert Hargreaves – an international referee – had officiated at a Holland v Belgium game. Black shorts and collars and cuffs gave Blackpool a striking look.

A new manager – Major Frank Buckley – took over team affairs.

Harry Bedford scored another 32 League goals and was the only player bar one to reach double figures.

Despite failing to win any of their first seven games, Blackpool still managed to finish fourth.

Bert Tulloch retired at the end of the season, after 10 years at Blackpool – his only professional club.

Match No.	Date	Venue	Opponents	Result		Scorers	Attendance
1	Aug 25	H	Oldham Athletic	D	2-2	Bedford, Leaver	14,000
2	27	A	South Shields	L	0-1		
3	Sep 1	A	Oldham Athletic	D	1-1	Bedford (pen)	17,000
4	3	H	South Shields	D	1-1	White	15,000
5	8	A	Stoke City	D	2-2	Mee, Bedford	16,000
6	15	H	Stoke City	D	1-1	Charles	15,000
7	22	A	Crystal Palace	L	1-3	Bedford	
8	29	H	Crystal Palace	W	2-0	Barrass, Mee	12,000
9	Oct 6	A	Sheffield Wed	D	2-2	Thompson, Bedford	15,000
10	13	H	Sheffield Wed	W	1-0	Barrass	12,000
11	20	H	Coventry City	W	5-0	Mee, Watson 2, White 2	10,000
12	27	A	Coventry City	L	1-3	Barrass	15,000
13	Nov 3	H	Bristol City	W	2-0	Barrass, Bedford	9,500
14	10	A	Bristol City	D	1-1	Barrass	10,000
15	17	A	Southampton	L	2-3	Bedford 2 (1 pen)	10,000
16	24	H	Southampton	W	2-0	Bedford 2	10,000
17	Dec 1	A	Fulham	W	3-2	Barrass 2, Meredith	17,000
18	8	H	Fulham	W	3-0	Mee, Bedford, Watson	10,000
19	15	A	Derby County	L	0-2		18,000
20	22	H	Derby County	W	4-0	Bedford 2, Watson, Benton	12,000
21	25	A	Stockport County	L	1-2	Bedford	15,000
22	26	H	Stockport County	D	0-0		12,000
23	29	H	Nelson	D	1-1	Bedford	9,000
24	Jan 5	A	Nelson	W	3-2	Bedford, Barrass	10,000
25	19	H	Bury	W	3-2	Bedford, White, Barrass	10,000
26	26	A	Bury	L	0-2		15,000
27	Feb 6	H	Manchester Utd	W	1-0	Bedford	7,000
28	9	A	Manchester Utd	D	0-0		20,000
29	16	H	Barnsley	L	0-2		10,000
30	23	A	Barnsley	L	1-3	Bedford	10,000
31	Mar 1	H	Bradford City	W	2-1	Bedford 2	8,000
32	8	A	Bradford City	W	2-0	Bedford, White	13,000
33	15	A	Port Vale	W	6-2	Bedford 3 (1 pen), White, Butler, Meredith	
34	22	H	Port Vale	W	6-1	Bedford 3, White 2, Meredith	9,500
35	29	A	Leeds Utd	D	0-0		25,000
36	Apr 5	H	Leeds Utd	D	1-1	Bedford	14,000
37	12	A	Leicester City	W	2-1	Butler, Bedford	15,000
38	18	H	Hull City	D	0-0		16,000
39	19	H	Leicester City	W	3-1	White 2, Watson	15,000
40	21	A	Hull City	L	1-2	Bedford (pen)	30,000
41	26	A	Clapton Orient	L	0-1		10,000
42	May 3	H	Clapton Orient	W	3-0	Mee, White, Mackenzie	

Final League Position: 4th in Division Two

Apps
Gls

FA Cup

1	Jan 12	H	Sheffield Utd	W	1-0	White	12,567
2	Feb 2	A	Southampton	L	1-3	Bedford	19,519

Apps
Gls

Mingay	Wood	Tulloch	Martin	Leaver	Benton	White	Mackenzie	Bedford	Barrass	Mee	Jones	Charles	Carruthers	Thompson	Curran	Gadsden	Forbes	Meredith	Watson
1	2	3	4	5	6	7	8	9	10	11									
1	2		4	5	6			9	10	11	3	7	8						
1	2		4	5	6	8		9	10	11	3	7							
1	2		4	5	6	8		9	10	11	3	7							
1	2		4	5	6			9	10	11	3		8	7					
1	2		4	5	6			9	10	11	3	7		8					
1	2		4	5	6			9	10	11	3	7		8					
1	2	3	4		6			9	10	11		7		8	5				
1	2		4		6			9	10	11				8		3	5	7	
1	2		4		6			9	10	11	3			8			5	7	
1	2				6	9			10	11	3						5	7	8
1			4	2	6	8		9	10	11	3						5	7	
1				2	6	8		9	10	11	3						5	7	
1				2	6	8		9	10	11	3						5	7	
1			4	2	6			9	10	11	3						5	7	8
1		3		2	6			9	10	11					4		5	7	8
1		3		2	6			9	10	11					4		5	7	8
1				2	6			9	10	11					4	3	5	7	8
1				2	6			9	10	11					4	3	5	7	8
1			5	2	6		10	9		11					4	3		7	8
1		3	5	2	6		10	9	8	11					4			7	
1		3	5	2	6		10	9	8	11					4			7	
1		3		2	6			9	10	11					4		5	7	8
1				2	6	8		9	10	11	3						5	7	
1		2			6	8		9	10	11	3						5	7	
1				2	6	8		9	10	11	3						5	7	
	2				6	8		9	10	11							5	7	
					6	8		9	10	11	3						5	7	
				3	6	8		9	10	11							5	7	
				5	6	8		9	10	11	3							7	
				2	6	8		9	5	11	3							7	4
				2	6	8		9	5	11	3							7	
	2				6	8		9	5	11	3							7	
	2				6	8		9	5	11	3							7	
	2				6	8		9	5	11	3							7	
	2				6	8		9	5	11	3							7	
	2					8		9	5	11	3							7	6
	2					8	10	9	5	11	3							7	6
	2			5		8		9	7	11	3								6
				5		8		9		11	3							7	6
				2		8		9		11						3	5	7	6
					6	9	8		5	11	3					2		7	4
28	20	8	16	28	37	26	6	40	39	42	28	6	2	6	9	6	19	33	15
				1	1	11	1	32	9	5		1		1				3	5

1				2	6	8		9	10	11	3	7			5				
1				2	6	8		9	10	11	3	7	10		5				
2				2	2	2		2	2	2	2	2			2				
						1		1											

League Table

	P	W	D	L	F	A	Pts
Leeds United	42	21	12	9	61	35	54
Bury	42	21	9	12	63	35	51
Derby County	42	21	9	12	75	42	51
Blackpool	42	18	13	11	72	47	49
Southampton	42	17	14	11	52	31	48
Stoke	42	14	18	10	44	42	46
Oldham Athletic	42	14	17	11	45	52	45
Sheffield Wednesday	42	16	12	14	54	51	44
South Shields	42	17	10	15	49	50	44
Clapton Orient	42	14	15	13	40	36	43
Barnsley	42	16	11	15	57	61	43
Leicester City	42	17	8	17	64	54	42
Stockport County	42	13	16	13	44	52	42
Manchester United	42	13	14	15	52	44	40
Crystal Palace	42	13	13	16	53	65	39
Port Vale	42	13	12	17	50	66	38
Hull City	42	10	17	15	46	51	37
Bradford City	42	11	15	16	35	48	37
Coventry City	42	11	13	18	52	68	35
Fulham	42	10	14	18	45	56	34
Nelson	42	10	13	19	40	74	33
Bristol City	42	7	15	20	32	65	29

1924-25

Division Two

Manager: Frank Buckley

Did you know that?

A writ was issued to the club by the builders of the South Stand. Only £1,000 had been paid of a bill totalling £4,618, so the board doubled the share capital to raise £10,000.

A new board was elected and Alderman John Bickerstaff was made President.

Blackpool Supporters Club was formed with an initial 300 members.

The players complained of not being able to see each other in the fog at Blackburn in the FA Cup on the 7 March. The colours of orange and black had made the kit look 'uneven', and this was blamed for the defeat. Blackpool lost 1–0 in front of around 60,000 fans.

Blackpool won the inaugural Victoria Hospital Cup at the end of the season, beating Everton 2–1 at Bloomfield Road.

Match No.	Date	Venue	Opponents	Result		Scorers	Attendance
1	Aug 30	H	Clapton Orient	W	1-0	Bedford	15,000
2	Sep 1	A	South Shields	W	3-1	Barrass, White, Bedford	
3	6	A	Hull City	D	1-1	Bedford (pen)	12,000
4	8	H	South Shields	W	5-0	Bedford 4, Meredith	15,000
5	13	H	Portsmouth	D	1-1	White	
6	15	H	Derby County	W	5-1	Barrass 2, White, Bedford 2	14,000
7	20	A	Fulham	L	0-1		22,000
8	27	H	Wolves	L	2-4	Barrass, Bedford (pen)	13,000
9	Oct 4	A	Barnsley	W	4-2	Butler 3, Meredith	11,000
10	11	H	Middlesbrough	D	1-1	Mee	14,000
11	18	A	Port Vale	W	2-1	White 2	
12	23	H	Crystal Palace	L	0-1		
13	Nov 1	A	Southampton	L	1-2	Meredith	4,000
14	8	H	Chelsea	L	1-2	White	12,000
15	15	A	Stockport County	L	0-1		
16	22	H	Manchester Utd	D	1-1	Bedford	10,000
17	29	A	Leicester City	W	2-0	Bedford, Meredith	20,000
18	Dec 6	H	Stoke City	L	1-2	Barrass	
19	20	H	Oldham Athletic	L	1-2	Bedford (pen)	10,000
20	25	A	Sheffield Wed	W	6-2	Barrass 3, Bedford 2, Meredith	
21	26	H	Sheffield Wed	D	2-2	Curran, Bedford	15,500
22	27	A	Clapton Orient	L	0-1		15,000
23	Jan 3	H	Hull City	D	0-0		7,000
24	17	A	Portsmouth	D	1-1	Barras	
25	24	H	Fulham	W	4-1	Bedford 2 (1 pen), Streets 2	6,000
26	Feb 7	H	Barnsley	L	1-2	White	9,000
27	14	A	Middlesbrough	L	1-4	Barrass	12,000
28	28	A	Crystal Palace	W	2-1	Meredith, Bedford	15,000
29	Mar 9	A	Coventry City	L	1-2	Barrass	
30	14	A	Chelsea	L	0-3		27,000
31	21	H	Stockport County	L	0-1		
32	23	A	Wolves	L	0-2		7,450
33	28	A	Manchester Utd	D	0-0		30,000
34	Apr 1	H	Southampton	W	1-0	Bedford (pen)	8,000
35	4	H	Leicester City	W	2-1	Bedford (pen), Meredith	9,000
36	10	H	Bradford City	L	1-2	Bedford	17,000
37	11	A	Stoke City	L	1-3	Butler	
38	14	A	Bradford City	L	0-1		15,000
39	18	H	Coventry City	W	3-1	Watson, Butler, Curran	9,000
40	22	H	Port Vale	W	4-1	Butler, Bedford, Mee 2	8,000
41	23	A	Oldham Athletic	L	1-4	Bedford	8,988
42	May 2	A	Derby County	D	2-2	Butler, Mee	8,000

Final League Position: 17th in Division Two

Apps
Gls

FA Cup

1	Jan 10	H	Barrow	D	0-0		11,755
1R	13	A	Barrow	W	2-1	Bedford, Streets	7,154
2	31	A	Bradford City	D	1-1	Meredith	21,500
2R	Feb 4	H	Bradford City	W	2-1	Streets, Meredith	13,800
3	21	A	West Ham Utd	D	1-1	Bedford	31,000
3R	25	H	West Ham Utd	W	3-0	Meredith, Bedford 2	15,190
4	Mar 7	A	Blackburn Rovers	L	0-1		60,011

Apps
Gls

Hacking	Leaver	Jones	Watson	Thorpe	Benton	Meredith	White	Bedford	Butler	Mee	Barrass	Wilkinson	Gadsden	Wood	Curran	Bradshaw	Crompton	Streets	Warren
1	2	3	4	5	6	7	8	9	10	11									
1	2	3	4	5	6	7	8	9		11	10								
1	2	3	4	5	6	7	8	9		11	10								
	2	3	4		6	7	8	9	10	11	5	1							
	2	3	4		6	7	8	9	10	11	5	1							
	2	3	4	5	6	7	8	9		11	10	1							
	2		4	5	6	7	8	9		11	10	1	3						
	2		4	5	6	7	8	9		11	10	1	3						
1			4	5	6	7	9		10	11	8			2	3				
1			4	5	6	7	9		10	11	8			2	3				
1			4		6	7	8	9	10	11	5			2	3				
1			4		6	7	8	9	10	11	5			2	3				
1	5	3	4		6	7	8	9		11	10					2			
1	5	3	4		6	7	8	9		11	10					2			
1	5	3	6			7	8	9	10	11	4					2			
	5	3	6			7	8	9	10	11	4					2	1		
	5	3	4		6	7	8	9		11	10					2	1		
	5	3	4		6	7	8	9		11	10					2	1		
	2	3	4		6	7	8	9		11	10				5		1		
	2	3	4		6	7	8	9		11	10				5		1		
	2	3	4		6	7	8	9		11	10				5		1		
	2	3	6			7	8	9	10	11					5		1	4	
	2	3	4		6	7	8	9		11	10				5		1		
	2	3	4		6	7		9		11	10				5		1	8	
	2	3	4		6	7		9		11	10				5		1	8	
	2	3	4	10	6	7	8	9		11							1		5
	2	3	4		6	7	8	9		11	10				5		1		
	2		4		6	7	8	9		11					5	3	1	10	
	2	3		5	6			9		11	10						1	8	
	2	3			6	7	8	9		11	10				5		1	4	
	2	3	4		6	7		9		11					5		1	8	
	2	3	4		6	7		9		11					5		1	8	
	2	3	4		6	7	8	10		11					5		1		
	2	3	4		6	7	8	10		11					5		1		
	2	3	4		6	7	8	9	10	11					5		1		
	2	3	4		6	7	8	9	10	11					5		1		
	2	3	4		6	7	8	9	10	11					5		1		
1		3	4		6	7	8	9	10	11				2	5				
		3	8		6	7		9	10	11				2	5		1		
		3	8	4	6	7		9	10	11				2	5		1		
		3	8		6	7		9	10	11					5	2	1	4	
		3	8	4	6	7		9	10	11				2	5	3	1		
11	33	34	40	12	39	41	33	40	18	42	26	5	2	8	26	9	26	9	1
			1			7	7	24	7	4	11				2			2	

Hacking	Leaver	Jones	Watson	Thorpe	Benton	Meredith	White	Bedford	Butler	Mee	Barrass	Wilkinson	Gadsden	Wood	Curran	Bradshaw	Crompton	Streets	Warren
	2	3	4		6	7	8	9		11	10				5		1		
	2	3	4		6	7		9		11	10		10		5		1	8	
	2	3	4		6	7		9		11	10		8		5		1	8	
	2	3	4		6	7		9		11	10		1		5		1	8	
	2	3	4		6	7	8	9		11	10		1		5		1		
	2	3	4		6	7	8	9		11			1		5		1	10	
	2	3	4		6	7	8	9		11	10		1		5		1		
	7	7	7		7	7	4	7		7	6				7		7	4	
						3		4										2	

League Table

	P	W	D	L	F	A	Pts
Leicester City	42	24	11	7	90	32	59
Manchester United	42	23	11	8	57	23	57
Derby County	42	22	11	9	71	36	55
Portsmouth	42	15	18	9	58	50	48
Chelsea	42	16	15	11	51	37	47
Wolverhampton W	42	20	6	16	55	51	46
Southampton	42	13	18	11	40	36	44
Port Vale	42	17	8	17	48	56	42
South Shields	42	12	17	13	42	38	41
Hull City	42	15	11	16	50	49	41
Clapton Orient	42	14	12	16	42	42	40
Fulham	42	15	10	17	41	56	40
Middlesbrough	42	10	19	13	36	44	39
Sheffield Wednesday	42	15	8	19	50	56	38
Barnsley	42	13	12	17	46	59	38
Bradford City	42	13	12	17	37	50	38
Blackpool	42	14	9	19	65	61	37
Oldham Athletic	42	13	11	18	35	51	37
Stockport County	42	13	11	18	37	57	37
Stoke	42	12	11	19	34	46	35
Crystal Palace	42	12	10	20	38	54	34
Coventry City	42	11	9	22	45	84	31

1925-26

Division Two

Manager: Frank Buckley

Did you know that?

The prolific goal scorer Harry Bedford was sold to Derby County for £3,500.

The final cost of the South Stand was £13,146, but it raised the capacity of Bloomfield Road to 20,000.

The team changed their black shorts and replaced them with white following the complaints from the previous season.

Only 9 home games were played in front of a five-figure crowd.

Match No.	Date		Venue	Opponents	Result		Scorers	Attendance
1	Aug	29	H	Southampton	W	2-1	Meredith, Bedford	18,195
2	Sep	2	A	Middlesbrough	L	2-3	Bedford (pen), Williams	18,108
3		5	A	Nottm Forest	D	1-1	Wright	8,685
4		7	H	Middlesbrough	L	2-3	Bedford 2 (1 pen)	17,036
5		12	H	Derby County	L	1-2	Watson	14,850
6		14	H	Darlington	L	0-1		11,791
7		19	A	Bradford City	L	0-1		11,006
8		23	A	Darlington	W	3-1	Bedford 2, Williams	7,977
9		26	H	Port Vale	D	2-2	Leaver, Benton	9,502
10	Oct	3	A	Barnsley	L	0-2		7,663
11		10	H	Clapton Orient	W	3-0	Banks, Butler, Meredith	9,620
12		17	A	Portsmouth	L	0-2		15,199
13		24	H	Wolves	W	4-0	Gill, Banks 2, Mee	10,724
14		31	A	South Shields	W	4-3	Fishwick 2, Binks, Gill	10,178
15	Nov	7	H	Preston NE	W	3-1	Fishwick 2, Meredith	10,207
16		14	A	Stoke City	W	3-1	Meredith, Fishwick, Mee	8,548
17		21	A	Oldham Athletic	L	2-3	Gill, Fishwick	12,058
18		28	A	Stockport County	L	3-4	Fishwick, Gill, Williams	4,500
19	Dec	5	H	Fulham	W	2-0	Meredith, Binks	6,786
20		12	A	Wolves	D	0-0		12,692
21		19	H	Sheffield Wed	W	1-0	Binks	8,931
22		25	H	Chelsea	D	0-0		13,690
23		26	A	Chelsea	W	3-2	Thorpe (pen), Meredith, Fishwick	29,139
24	Jan	2	A	Southampton	D	2-2	Downes 2	8,637
25		16	H	Nottm Forest	W	3-0	Thorpe (pen), Fishwick 2	6,686
26		23	A	Derby County	L	2-5	Downes 2	14,694
27		30	H	Bradford City	W	3-0	Fishwick 2, Williams	8,061
28	Feb	6	A	Port Vale	L	0-5		9,207
29		13	H	Barnsley	W	4-0	Williams 3, Fishwick	8,620
30		25	A	Swansea T	L	1-6	Williams	16,999
31		27	H	Portsmouth	D	2-2	Fishwick, Downes	6,754
32	Mar	8	A	Clapton Orient	D	2-2	Crook, Watson	4,500
33		13	H	South Shields	W	1-0	Meredith	7,640
34		20	A	Preston NE	L	4-6	Own-goal, Williams 2, Butler	20,000
35		27	H	Stoke City	D	0-0		7,756
36	Apr	2	H	Hull City	D	2-2	Thorpe (pen), Fishwick	13,676
37		3	H	Oldham Athletic	W	2-1	Fishwick, Butler	14,636
38		5	A	Hull City	W	2-1	Wellock, Fishwick	7,365
39		10	H	Stockport County	W	4-1	Wellock, Fishwick 2, Meredith	7,610
40		17	A	Fulham	D	1-1	Butler	14,682
41		24	H	Swansea T	D	0-0		9,994
42	May	1	A	Sheffield Wed	L	0-2		20,575

Final League Position: 6th in Division Two

Apps

Gls

FA Cup

1	Jan	9	H	Swansea T	L	0-2		13,520

Apps

Gls

Crompton	Leaver	Jones	Mercer	Curran	Benton	Meredith	Watson	Bedford	Williams	Mee	Jennings	Wright	Hamilton	Thorpe	Butler	Downes	Streets	Tremelling	Binks
1	2	3	4	5	6	7	8	9	10	11									
	2	3		5	6		8	9	10	11	1	4	7						
	2	3		5	6	7	8	9	10	11	1	4							
	2	3		5	6	7	8	9	10	11	1	4							
1		3		5	6	7	8	9	10	11		4		2					
1	5	3			6	7	8		9			4		2	10	11			
1		3		5	6	7	4	8	9	11				2	10				
1		3		5	6	7	4	9	10	11				2			8		
1	9	3		5	6	7	4			11				2			8	10	
1		3		5	6		4			11		6		2	10		7		9
1		3		5	6	7	4			11		6		2	10		8		9
1		3		5	6	7	4			11		6		2	10		8		9
1		3		5	6	7	4			11				2					9
1		3		5	6	7	4			11				2					9
1		3		5	6	7	4			11				2					9
1		3		5	6	7	4			11				2					9
1		3		5	6	7	4			11				2					9
1				5	6	7	4		11					2					9
1				5	6	7	4			11				2					9
1		3		5	6	7	4			11				2					9
1	2			5	6	7	4		10	11				3					9
1	2			5	6	7	4							3		11			9
1	2			5	6	7	4							3		11			9
1				5	6	7	4							3		11			9
				5	6	7	4		10		1			2		11			9
				5	6	7	4		10					2		11			
				5	6	7	4		10					2		11			
					6	7	4		10					2		11			
1					6	7	4		10					2		11		9	5
1					6	7	4		10					2		11		9	5
1					6	7	4		10					2		11			5
1					6	7	4		10							11			5
1					6	7	4					2			10	11			5
1					6	7	4		9			2			10	11			5
1					6	7	4		9			3		2	10	11			5
1					6	7	4					3		2	10	11			5
1						7	4							2	10	11			5
1						7	4					2			10	11			5
1						7	4					2			10	11			5
1					6	7	4					2			10	11			5
1					6	7	4					2			10	11			5
1					6		4					2			10	11			5
35	10	18	1	27	39	39	42	7	20	19	4	15	1	30	15	22	5	3	30
	1				1	8	2	6	10	2		1		3	4	5			6
1	2			5	6	7	4		8					3		11			9
1	1			1	1	1	1		1					1		1			1

League Table

	P	W	D	L	F	A	Pts
Sheffield Wednesday	42	27	6	9	88	48	60
Derby County	42	25	7	10	77	42	57
Chelsea	42	19	14	9	76	49	52
Wolverhampton W	42	21	7	14	84	60	49
Swansea Town	42	19	11	12	77	57	49
Blackpool	42	17	11	14	76	69	45
Oldham Athletic	42	18	8	16	74	62	44
Port Vale	42	19	6	17	79	69	44
South Shields	42	18	8	16	74	65	44
Middlesbrough	42	21	2	19	77	68	44
Portsmouth	42	17	10	15	79	74	44
Preston North End	42	18	7	17	71	84	43
Hull City	42	16	9	17	63	61	41
Southampton	42	15	8	19	63	63	38
Darlington	42	14	10	18	72	77	38
Bradford City	42	13	10	19	47	66	36
Nottingham Forest	42	14	8	20	51	73	36
Barnsley	42	12	12	18	58	84	36
Fulham	42	11	12	19	46	77	34
Clapton Orient	42	12	9	21	50	65	33
Stoke City	42	12	8	22	54	77	32
Stockport County	42	8	9	25	51	97	25

1926-27

Division Two

Manager: Frank Buckley

Did you know that?

Tommy Browell joined from Manchester City. He had played in the previous season's FA Cup Final.

After only one season, the team reverted to black shorts with orange shirts.

Billy Tremelling was the new goalscoring sensation with 30 League goals from just 26 appearances. The next season he was moved to centre-half to accommodate the new signing, Jimmy Hampson.

Match No.	Date		Venue	Opponents	Result		Scorers	Attendance
1	Aug	28	A	Nottm Forest	L	0-2		11,542
2		30	H	Reading	W	3-1	Downes, Wellock 2	12,958
3	Sep	4	H	Barnsley	W	6-1	Fishwick 3, Thorpe (pen), Ayres, Wellock	12,673
4		8	A	Reading	W	1-0	Wellock	16,005
5		11	A	Manchester City	L	1-2	Fishwick	34,885
6		18	H	Darlington	D	1-1	Fishwick	13,545
7		20	A	Swansea T	L	0-2		14,264
8		25	A	Portsmouth	L	0-5		14,429
9	Oct	2	H	Oldham Athletic	W	2-0	Browell 2	14,599
10		9	A	Fulham	L	0-1		16,237
11		16	H	Wolves	L	2-3	Wellock,Fishwick	9,486
12		23	A	Hull City	L	0-3		11,363
13		30	H	Preston NE	L	2-3	Browell, Ayres	16,542
14	Nov	6	A	Chelsea	D	1-1	Binks	25,366
15		13	H	Bradford City	W	3-0	Curran,Crook (pen),Tremelling	5,498
16		20	A	Southampton	L	3-5	Tremelling 2, Crook (pen)	8,721
17		27	H	Port Vale	D	2-2	Tremelling, Crook	7,656
18	Dec	4	A	Middlesbrough	D	4-4	Downes 2, Fishwick, Tremelling	19,456
19		11	H	Clapton Orient	W	6-0	Fishwick, Tremelling 3, Crook, Downes	7,551
20		18	A	Notts County	W	3-2	Crook,Meredith,Tremelling	8,108
21		25	A	Grimsby Town	L	1-2	Thorpe	15,492
22		27	H	Grimsby Town	W	6-2	Crook 3, Tremelling 2,Downes	13,980
23	Jan	1	H	Swansea T	W	3-1	Tremelling, Fishwick,Browell	13,754
24		15	H	Nottm Forest	D	2-2	Tremelling 2	7,536
25		22	A	Barnsley	L	1-6	Fishwick	7,533
26		29	H	Manchester City	L	2-4	Kelly,Fishwick	9,223
27	Feb	5	A	Darlington	W	3-1	Neal,Tremelling, Meredith	8,695
28		12	H	Portsmouth	W	2-0	Fishwick, Tremelling	8,465
29		19	A	Oldham Athletic	W	3-1	Tremelling 2, Fishwick	14,446
30		26	H	Fulham	D	0-0		7,958
31	Mar	12	H	Hull City	W	4-0	Browell,Binks 2, Neal	9,195
32		19	A	Preston NE	L	1-4	Browell	24,089
33		21	A	Wolves	L	1-4	Browell	8,698
34		26	H	Chelsea	W	3-1	Neal, Tremelling 2	8,251
35	Apr	2	A	Bradford City	L	1-4	Tremelling	9,840
36		9	H	Southampton	W	3-2	Browell, Tremelling, Meredith	7,825
37		15	H	South Shields	W	6-1	Tremelling 2, Meredith 2, Browell, Downes	15,450
38		16	A	Port Vale	W	4-2	Tremelling 3, Meredith	10,749
39		18	A	South Shields	D	2-2	Tremelling, Browell	5,283
40		23	H	Middlesbrough	D	2-2	Tremelling, Browell	12,657
41		30	A	Clapton Orient	L	0-1		16,025
42	May	7	H	Notts County	W	5-0	Browell 3, Ayres, Tremelling	5,653

Final League Position: 9th in Division Two

Apps

Gls

FA Cup

1	Jan	8	H	Bolton Wanderers	L	1-3	Tremelling	16,297

Apps

Gls

Crompton	Thorpe	Bradshaw	Watson	Binks	Benton	Meredith	Fishwick	Wellock	Ayres	Downes	Butler	Browell	Barnett	Tremelling	Neal	Wright	Crook	Best	Curran
1	2	3	4	5	6	7	8	9	10	11									
1	2	3	4	5	6	7	8	9	10	11									
1	2	3	4	5	6	7	8	9	10	11									
1	2	3	4	5	6	7	8	9		11	10								
1	2	3	4	5	6	7	8	9	10	11									
1	2	3	4	5	6	7	8	9		11		10							
1	2	3	4	5	6	7	8	9		11		10							
1		3	4	5	6	7	8			11		10	2	9					
1		3	4	5	6	7	8	9		11		10	2						
1		3	4	5	6	7	8	9				10	2		11				
1		3	4	5	6	7	8	9				10	2		11				
1	2	3		5		7			8			9	6		11	4	10		
	2	3	4	5		7	8	6	9	11		10						1	
	2	3		9	6	7			8			10			11			1	4
	2	3	8	5	6	7								9	11		10	1	4
	2	3	6	5		7						8		9	11		10	1	4
	2	3	4			7	8							9	11		10	1	6
	2		4	5		7	8		6	11				9			10	1	
	2		4	5	6	7	8			11				9			10	1	
	2		4	5	6	7	8			11				9			10	1	
	2		4	5	6	7	8			11				9			10	1	
	2		4	5		7			6	11		8		9			10	1	
	2		4	5		7	8		6	11		10		9				1	
1	2				4	7	8		6	11				9			10		
1	2		4			7	8		6	11				9			10		
1	2	3	4	5	6	7	8			11					10				
	2		4		6	7	8		5	11				9	10			1	
	2		4		6	7	8		5	11				9			10	1	
	2		4		6	7	8		5	11				9			10	1	
	2		4		6	7	8		5	11				9			10	1	
	2		4	9	6	7			5	11		8			10			1	
	2		4	9	6	7			5	11		8					10	1	
	2		4		6	7			5	11		8	3	9			10	1	
	2		4		6	7			5			8		9	11		10	1	
	2		4		6	7			5			8		9	11		10	1	
	2		4		6	7			5			8		9	11		10	1	
	2		4		6	7			5	11		8		9			10	1	
	2				6	7						8	4	9	11		10	1	
	2		4		6	7						8	3	9	11		10	1	
1	2		4		6	7						8		9	11		10		
1	2		4		6	7			5	11		10		9			8		
1	2		4		6	7			5			8	3	9	11		10		
18	38	18	38	25	34	42	25	11	25	28	1	24	9	26	17	1	25	24	4
	2			3		6	13	5	3	6		14		30	3		8		1

Crompton	Thorpe	Bradshaw	Watson	Binks	Benton	Meredith	Fishwick	Wellock	Ayres	Downes	Butler	Browell	Barnett	Tremelling	Neal	Wright	Crook	Best	Curran
	2		4	5		7			6	11		10		9			8	1	
	1		1	1		1			1	1		1		1			1	1	
														1					

League Table

	P	W	D	L	F	A	Pts
Middlesbrough	42	27	8	7	122	60	62
Portsmouth	42	23	8	11	87	49	54
Manchester City	42	22	10	10	108	61	54
Chelsea	42	20	12	10	62	52	52
Nottingham Forest	42	18	14	10	80	55	50
Preston North End	42	20	9	13	74	72	49
Hull City	42	20	7	15	63	52	47
Port Vale	42	16	13	13	88	78	45
Blackpool	42	18	8	16	95	80	44
Oldham Athletic	42	19	6	17	74	84	44
Barnsley	42	17	9	16	88	87	43
Swansea Town	42	16	11	15	68	72	43
Southampton	42	15	12	15	60	62	42
Reading	42	16	8	18	64	72	40
Wolverhampton W	42	14	7	21	73	75	35
Notts County	42	15	5	22	70	96	35
Grimsby Town	42	11	12	19	74	91	34
Fulham	42	13	8	21	58	92	34
South Shields	42	11	11	20	71	96	33
Clapton Orient	42	12	7	23	60	96	31
Darlington	42	12	6	24	79	98	30
Bradford City	42	7	9	26	50	88	23

1927-28

Division Two

Manager: Sydney Beaumont

Did you know that?

Jimmy Hampson was signed from Nelson in October and went on to score 31 goals in 32 League appearances. He cost just £1,000.

Blackpool had a new manager in Sydney Beaumont, replacing Frank Buckley who moved to Wolves. Beaumont only lasted for one season.

The 2–2 draw at Fulham on Christmas Eve was Blackpool's 1,000th Football League game.

Blackpool just avoided relegation by winning two of their last three games, 4–1 and 4–0 respectively.

Match No.	Date	Venue	Opponents	Result		Scorers	Attendance
1	Aug 27	H	Swansea T	D	2-2	Tremelling, Downes	15,771
2	29	H	Oldham Athletic	L	1-2	Own-goal	16,699
3	Sep 3	A	Chelsea	L	0-3		36,529
4	5	A	Oldham Athletic	L	0-6		14,542
5	10	H	Clapton Orient	L	0-1		12,337
6	17	A	West Brom Albion	L	3-6	Tufnell 2, Williams	19,605
7	24	H	Bristol City	W	6-2	Browell 3, Watson, Tufnell, Williams	12,509
8	Oct 1	A	Stoke City	L	0-2		9,293
9	8	H	Southampton	W	1-0	Williams	11,875
10	15	A	Notts County	L	1-3	Hampson	11,885
11	22	H	Manchester City	D	2-2	Hampson 2	17,013
12	29	A	Hull City	D	2-2	Neal, Hampson	9,067
13	Nov 5	H	Preston NE	W	4-1	Benton 2 (2 pens), Meredith, Tufnell	10,789
14	12	A	Nottm Forest	L	1-4	Hampson	8,602
15	19	H	Leeds United	L	0-2		9,008
16	20	A	Wolves	W	4-2	Hampson 3, Downes	13,200
17	Dec 3	H	Port Vale	L	1-6	Hampson	7,662
18	10	A	South Shields	D	2-2	Downes, Hampson	5,130
19	17	H	Barnsley	L	1-3	Hampson	7,629
20	24	A	Fulham	D	2-2	Hampson, Neal	10,853
21	26	H	Reading	W	3-1	Fishwick 3	13,233
22	27	A	Reading	L	0-1		11,841
23	31	A	Swansea T	L	0-1		9,185
24	Jan 2	H	Grimsby Town	L	4-5	Crook 2 (1 pen), Hampson, Ayres	10,347
25	7	H	Chelsea	L	2-4	Browell, Tremelling	8,704
26	21	A	Clapton Orient	W	5-2	Neal 2, Howell, Hampson 2	11,401
27	28	H	West Brom Albion	W	4-1	Hampson 2, Benton (pen), McIntyre	8,102
28	Feb 4	A	Bristol City	D	2-2	McIntyre, Browell	11,395
29	11	H	Stoke City	W	3-1	Meredith, Hampson, Browell	8,744
30	18	A	Southampton	L	0-2		12,229
31	25	H	Notts County	D	3-3	Fishwick, Neal, Meredith	9,423
32	Mar 3	A	Manchester City	L	1-4	Hampson	40,906
33	10	H	Hull City	W	2-1	Oxberry, Downes	9,988
34	17	A	Preston NE	L	1-2	Benton (pen)	22,341
35	24	H	Nottm Forest	W	5-2	Hampson 4, Ramsay	8,977
36	31	A	Leeds United	L	0-4		19,630
37	Apr 6	A	Grimsby Town	D	3-3	Tremelling, Hampson 2	15,097
38	7	H	Wolves	W	3-0	Neal, Browell, Oxberry	18,030
39	14	A	Port Vale	L	0-3		5,321
40	21	H	South Shields	W	4-1	Browell, Hampson 2, Tremelling	8,539
41	28	A	Barnsley	L	1-2	Hampson	4,949
42	May 5	H	Fulham	W	4-0	Hampson 3, Oxberry	14,466

Final League Position: 19th in Division Two — Apps / Gls

FA Cup

1	Jan 14	H	Oldham Athletic	L	1-4	Neal	10,349

Apps
Gls

Crompton	Thorpe	Tilford	Watson	Ayres	Benton	Meredith	Browell	Tremelling	Crook	Downes	Malpas	Hobbs	Grimwood	Cowan	Williams	Tufnell	Hampson	Barrett	Neal
1	2	3	4	5	6	7	8	9	10	11									
1	2	3	4	5	6	7	8	9	10	11									
1	2	3	4	5	6	7	8	9	10	11									
1	2	3	4		6	7	8	9	10	11	5								
	2	3	4		6	7	8		10	11		1	5	9					
	2	3	4		6	7	8			11		1	5		9	10			
	2	3	4		6	7	8			11		1	5		9	10			
	2	3	4		6	7	8			11		1	5		9	10			
	2	3	4		6	7	8			11		1	5		9	10			
	2	3	4		6	7				11		1	5		9	10	8		
	2	3	4		6	7	8			11		1				10	9	8	
	5	3	4		6	7	8					1				10	9	2	11
	5	3	4		6	7	8					1				10	9	2	11
	5	3	4		6	7	8					1				10	9	2	11
	5	3	4		6	7		9				1				10	9	2	11
	5	3	8		6	7	10			11		1				4	9		
	5	3	8		6	7	10			11		1				4	9		
	2	3	4				8			11		1				6	9		7
	2	3	4		8	7				11		1				6	9		
	2				4	7						1				6	9	3	11
	2				4	7						1	5			6	9		11
			4			7						1	5			6	9	3	11
	2		4		6	7						1	5				9		11
	2			6	4	7			10			1					9		11
					4	7	10	8				1					9	3	11
					4	7	8	6				1					9	3	11
					4	7	8	6				1					9	3	11
						7	8	6				1					9	3	11
						7	8	6									9	3	11
					4	7	8	6									9	3	11
			4			7	8	6										3	11
					4	7		6									9	3	11
	2		4	5		7		6		11							9	3	
	2		4	5		7				11							9	3	
1	2		4	5		7		6		11							9	3	
1	2		4	5		7		6		11							9	3	
	2	3	4					6	7								9		11
1	2		4				10	6	7								9	3	11
1	2		4				10	6	7								9	3	11
	2		4				10	6	7								9	3	11
	2		4				10	6	7								9	3	11
	2		4				10	6	7								9	3	11
8	33	20	32	8	28	35	28	22	12	19	1	24	9	1	5	18	32	24	24
			1	1	4	3	9	4	2	4					3	4	31		6

Crompton	Thorpe	Tilford	Watson	Ayres	Benton	Meredith	Browell	Tremelling	Crook	Downes	Malpas	Hobbs	Grimwood	Cowan	Williams	Tufnell	Hampson	Barrett	Neal
1					6	7	8	10								6	9	3	11
1					1	1	1	1								1	1	1	1
																			1

League Table

	P	W	D	L	F	A	Pts
Manchester City	42	25	9	8	100	59	59
Leeds United	42	25	7	10	98	49	57
Chelsea	42	23	8	11	75	45	54
Preston North End	42	22	9	11	100	66	53
Stoke City	42	22	8	12	78	59	52
Swansea Town	42	18	12	12	75	63	48
Oldham Athletic	42	19	8	15	75	51	46
West Bromwich Albion	42	17	12	13	90	70	46
Port Vale	42	18	8	16	68	57	44
Nottingham Forest	42	15	10	17	83	84	40
Grimsby Town	42	14	12	16	69	83	40
Bristol City	42	15	9	18	76	79	39
Barnsley	42	14	11	17	65	85	39
Hull City	42	12	15	15	41	54	39
Notts County	42	13	12	17	68	74	38
Wolverhampton W	42	13	10	19	63	91	36
Southampton	42	14	7	21	68	77	35
Reading	42	11	13	18	53	75	35
Blackpool	42	13	8	21	83	101	34
Clapton Orient	42	11	12	19	55	85	34
Fulham	42	13	7	22	68	89	33
South Shields	42	7	9	26	56	111	23

1928-29

Division Two

Manager: Harry Evans (Honorary title)

Did you know that?

Due to costs, the club decided not to appoint a full-time manager, so director Harry Evans was given the honorary title.

With yet more tinkering with the colours, the team again adopted the unpopular black shorts.

In October and November the inconsistent side recorded results of 1–4, 4–0, 2–8 and 7–0!

They were embarrassed by Plymouth Argyle in the FA Cup, losing 3–0 on the South Coast.

Jimmy Hampson scored another 40 goals, including five in the 7–0 hammering of Reading.

Match No.	Date		Venue	Opponents	Result		Scorers	Attendance
1	Aug	25	A	Preston NE	L	1-3	Hampson	23,225
2		27	A	Swansea T	D	5-5	Hampson 2, Browell, Brookes 2	12,152
3	Sep	1	H	Chelsea	L	0-1		17,653
4		3	H	Swansea T	D	2-2	Hampson 2	12,899
5		8	A	Barnsley	L	1-3	Browell	7,312
6		15	H	Bristol City	W	2-1	Watson 2	14,135
7		22	A	Nottm Forest	L	0-2		12,615
8		29	H	West Brom Albion	L	0-2		16,415
9	Oct	6	A	Clapton Orient	W	4-2	Hampson, Crook, Martin 2	12,222
10		13	H	Stoke City	W	2-0	Hampson, Watson	17,942
11		20	A	Middlesbrough	L	1-4	Hampson	15,727
12		27	H	Oldham Athletic	W	4-0	Oxberry 2, Benton, Hampson	10,624
13	Nov	3	A	Southampton	L	2-8	Ramsay, Hampson	15,146
14		10	H	Reading	W	7-0	Hampson 5, Oxberry 2	6,638
15		17	A	Notts County	L	1-3	Wilson	13,987
16		24	H	Millwall	W	3-0	Hampson 2, Benton (pen)	6,829
17	Dec	1	A	Port Vale	L	0-1		8,244
18		8	H	Hull City	W	2-1	Oxberry, Benton (pen)	9,033
19		15	A	Tottenham Hotspur	W	2-1	Oxberry, Tremelling	15,729
20		22	H	Wolves	W	3-0	Hampson, Tremelling 2	7,262
21		25	A	Grimsby Town	W	4-1	Hampson 3, Downes	15,437
22		26	H	Grimsby Town	D	1-1	Hampson	15,337
23		29	H	Preston NE	W	3-2	Tremelling, Neal, Hampson	16,339
24	Jan	5	A	Chelsea	W	3-2	Neal, Tremelling, Hampson	20,069
25		19	H	Barnsley	L	0-1		8,937
26		26	A	Bristol City	L	2-3	Hampson 2	13,748
27	Feb	2	H	Nottm Forest	D	2-2	Benton (pen), Hampson	6,997
28		9	A	West Brom Albion	D	2-2	Benton, Taylor	10,625
29		16	H	Clapton Orient	L	0-1		6,236
30		23	A	Stoke City	D	1-1	Hampson	12,538
31	Mar	2	H	Middlesbrough	W	3-0	Neal, Downes, Browell	10,440
32		9	A	Oldham Athletic	L	2-4	Hampson, Neal	23,824
33		16	H	Southampton	W	3-0	Upton 2, Hampson	9,279
34		23	A	Reading	L	1-4	Upton	7,517
35		29	H	Bradford	W	3-0	Upton, Hampson 2	17,977
36		30	H	Notts County	W	3-2	Hampson, Brookes, Own-goal	16,049
37	Apr	1	A	Bradford	L	2-5	Hampson 2	14,125
38		6	A	Millwall	L	1-2	Browell	16,933
39		13	H	Port Vale	W	4-0	Hampson, Downes, Upton, Benton (pen)	8,696
40		20	A	Hull City	W	3-1	Brookes, Benton, Hampson	4,945
41		27	H	Tottenham Hotspur	D	2-2	Hampson, Upton	8,744
42	May	4	A	Wolves	W	5-1	Hampson 2 (1 pen), Upton, Downes, Neal	7,936

Final League Position: 8th in Division Two

Apps
Gls

FA Cup

1	Jan	12	A	Plymouth Argyle	L	0-3	Neal	30,300

Apps
Gls

Mercer	Wilson	Barnett	Watson	Grant	Tremelling	Ritchie	Oxberry	Hampson	Ramsay	Crook	Tilford	Benton	Browell	Brookes	Downes	Purdy	Hamilton	Tufnell	Robinson
1	2	3	4	5	6	7	8	9	10	11									
1	2		4	5		7		9			3	6	8	10	11				
1	2		4	5		7		9			3	6	8	10	11				
1	2		4	5		7		9			3	6	8	10	11				
	2		4	5		7		9	10		3	6	8		11	1			
1			4	5		11	9		10	7	3	6	8				2		
1			4	5		11	8	9		7	3	6					2	10	
1			4	5		7	8	9			3	6		10	11		2		
1			4				8	9		7	3	6					2		5
1			4				8	9		7	3	6					2		5
1			4				8	9		7	3	6					2		5
1			4				8	9		7	3	6					2		5
1			4	5			10	9	8	7	3	6					2		
1	5		4	6		7	8	9									3	10	
1	5		4		10	7	8	9				6					3		
1	5	3	4		10		8	9				6			7				
1	5	3	4		10		8	9				6			7				
	5	3	4		10		8	9				6			11	1			
	5	3	4		10		8	9				6			11	1			
	5	3	4		10		8	9				6			11	1			
	5	3	4		10		8	9				6			11	1			
		3	4		10		8	9				6			11	1			5
	5	3	4		10			9				6	8		11	1			
	5	3	4		10		8	9				6			11	1			
	5	3	4		10		8	9				6			11	1			
	5	3	4	2				9				6		10	11	1			
	5		4	2				9				6		10	11	1	3		
	5		4	2				9		7		6		10		1	3		
	5		4	2				9		7		6		10		1	3		
			4	2			8	9	5			6		10	11	1	3		
			4	2			8	9	5			6	10		11	1	3		
			4	2			8	9	5			6	10		11	1	3		
			4	2				9	5			6	10		11	1	3		
			4	2				9	5			6	10		11	1	3		
			4	2				9	5			6	10		11	1	3		
			4	2		7		9	5			6	8	10	11	1	3		
			4	2		7		9	5			6	10		11	1	3		
			4	2				9	5			6	10		11		3		
1		3	4	2				9	5			6		10	11				
1			4	2				9	5			6		10	11		3		
1			4	2				9	5			6		10	11		3		
			4	2			10	9	5			6			11		3		
19	20	13	42	27	12	12	24	41	17	10	12	39	14	14	30	21	25	2	5
	1		3		5		6	40	1	1		7	4	4	4				

	5	3	4		10		8	9				6			11	1			
	1	1	1		1		1	1				1			1	1			

League Table

	P	W	D	L	F	A	Pts
Middlesbrough	42	22	11	9	92	57	55
Grimsby Town	42	24	5	13	82	61	53
Bradford Park Avenue	42	22	4	16	88	70	48
Southampton	42	17	14	11	74	60	48
Notts County	42	19	9	14	78	65	47
Stoke City	42	17	12	13	74	51	46
West Bromwich Albion	42	19	8	15	80	79	46
Blackpool	42	19	7	16	92	76	45
Chelsea	42	17	10	15	64	65	44
Tottenham Hotspur	42	17	9	16	75	81	43
Nottingham Forest	42	15	12	15	71	70	42
Hull City	42	13	14	15	58	63	40
Preston North End	42	15	9	18	78	79	39
Millwall	42	16	7	19	71	86	39
Reading	42	15	9	18	63	86	39
Barnsley	42	16	6	20	69	66	38
Wolverhampton W	42	15	7	20	77	81	37
Oldham Athletic	42	16	5	21	54	75	37
Swansea Town	42	13	10	19	62	75	36
Bristol City	42	13	10	19	58	72	36
Port Vale	42	15	4	23	71	86	34
Clapton Orient	42	12	8	22	45	72	32

1929-30

Division Two

Manager: Harry Evans (Honorary title)

Did you know that?

The Second Division Championship is still Blackpool's only League title to date.

Jimmy Hampson's 45 League goals was the highest in the country.

A record crowd of 24,144 saw Blackpool beat fellow promotion candidates Oldham Athletic at Bloomfield Road.

Blackpool claimed the title on the final day with a goalless draw with Nottingham Forest. Chelsea were beaten by Bury and so went up in second place, pipping Oldham Athletic.

The final points total of 58 was only matched once more before the advent of three-for-a-win in the early 1980s.

Match No.	Date	Venue	Opponents	Result		Scorers	Attendance
1	Aug 31	H	Millwall	W	4-3	Downes, Neal, Hampson, Ritchie	15,760
2	Sep 3	H	Bury	W	2-1	Hampson, Downes	16,918
3	7	A	Southampton	L	2-4	Hampson 2	10,113
4	9	H	Nottm Forest	W	5-1	Upton 2, Downes, Hampson 2	14,182
5	14	H	Tottenham Hotspur	W	3-2	Hampson 2, Upton	14,913
6	21	A	West Brom Albion	L	1-5	Hampson	17,168
7	28	H	Bradford	W	1-0	Downes	18,870
8	Oct 5	A	Barnsley	W	4-2	Hampson 3, Lauderdale	8,353
9	12	H	Cardiff City	W	3-0	Tremelling, Hampson, Quinn	15,900
10	19	A	Preston NE	W	6-4	Lauderdale, Hampson 3, Downes 2	21,183
11	26	H	Bristol City	W	7-1	Downes 3, Hampson 2, Lauderdale, Upton	11,192
12	Nov 2	A	Notts County	W	2-0	Lauderdale, Hampson	13,282
13	9	H	Reading	W	4-2	Hampson 2, Upton, Quinn	10,757
14	16	A	Charlton Athletic	W	4-1	Hall, Hampson, Upton 2	4,493
15	23	H	Hull City	L	1-2	Hampson	10,364
16	30	A	Stoke City	W	1-0	Hampson	11,546
17	Dec 7	H	Wolves	W	3-2	Neal, Hampson, Upton	9,608
18	14	A	Bradford City	D	1-1	Downes	21,644
19	21	H	Swansea T	W	3-0	Hampson 2, Downes	10,139
20	25	H	Chelsea	D	1-1	Ritchie	14,882
21	26	A	Chelsea	L	0-4		53,819
22	28	A	Millwall	L	1-3	Upton	21,745
23	Jan 1	A	Bury	W	1-0	Ritchie	17,963
24	4	H	Southampton	W	5-1	Hampson 3, Tremelling, Ritchie	12,574
25	18	A	Tottenham Hotspur	L	1-6	Quinn	24,946
26	Feb 1	A	Bradford City	L	0-5		17,970
27	8	H	Barnsley	W	2-1	Downes, Hampson	11,785
28	15	A	Cardiff City	L	2-4	Watson, Broadhurst	12,730
29	22	H	Preston NE	W	5-1	Ritchie, Broadhurst, Upton 2, Hampson	15,347
30	Mar 1	A	Bristol City	W	1-0	Broadhurst	11,925
31	5	H	West Brom Albion	W	1-0	Hampson	10,225
32	8	H	Notts County	L	1-2	Broadhurst (pen)	13,733
33	15	A	Reading	D	1-1	Hampson	12,741
34	22	H	Charlton Athletic	W	6-0	Hampson 4, Ratray, Upton	12,614
35	29	A	Hull City	W	3-0	Hampson 2, Broadhurst	10,113
36	Apr 5	H	Stoke City	L	0-2		13,679
37	12	A	Wolves	W	2-1	Hampson, Tremelling	13,444
38	18	H	Oldham Athletic	W	3-0	Oxberry, Hampson, Downes	24,114
39	19	H	Bradford City	W	3-0	Hampson 2, Oxberry	18,163
40	21	A	Oldham Athletic	W	2-1	Hampson, Oxberry	45,304
41	26	A	Swansea T	L	0-3		16,433
42	May 3	A	Nottm Forest	D	0-0		6,044

Final League Position: 1st in Division Two

Apps

Gls

FA Cup

3	Jan 11	H	Stockport County	W	2-1	Browell 2	14,000
4	25	A	Hull City	L	1-3	Hampson	23,000

Apps

Gls

Swift	Grant	Hamilton	Watson	Ramsay	Benton	Neal	Ritchie	Hampson	Oxberry	Downes	Wolfe	Upton	Tremelling	Quinn	Lauderdale	Tufnell	Hall	Jennings	Wilson
1	2	3	4	5	6	7	8	9	10	11									
	2	3	4	5	6	7	8	9	10	11	1								
	2	3	4	5	6	7	8	9		11	1	10							
	2		4	3	6	7	8	9		11	1	10	5						
	2		4	3	6		8	9		11	1	10	5	7					
	2		4	3	6		8	9		11	1	10	5	7					
	2		4	3	6			9		11	1	8	5	7	10				
	2		4	3	6			9		11	1	8	5	7	10				
	2		4	3	6			9		11	1	8	5	7	10				
	2		4	3				9		11	1	8	5	7	10	6			
	2		4	3				9		11	1	8	5	7	10	6			
	2		4	3				9			1	8	5	7	10	6	11		
	2		4	3				9			1	8	5	7	10	6	11		
	2		4					9			1	8	5	7	10	6	11	3	
	2		4	3				9			1	8	5	7	10	6	11		
	2		4	3				9		11	1	8	5		10	6	7		
	2		4	3		7		9		11	1	8	5		10	6			
	2		4	3				9		11	1	8	5		10	6	7		
	2		4	3				9		11	1	8	5		10	6	7		
	2		4	3			10	9		11	1	8	5			6	7		
	2		4	3			7	9	8	11	1		6		10				5
	2		4	3				9		11	1	8	5	7					
	2		4	3			10	9		11	1		5	7		6			
	2		4	3			10	9		11	1		5	7		6			
	2		4	3			10	9		11	1		5	7		6			
	2		4	3			7	9		11	1	8	5		10	6			
	2			5			10	9		11			6	7		4		3	
	2		7	5				9		11	1		6			4		3	
	2		4	3			7	8		11		10	5			6			
	2		4	3			7	9		11		10	5			6			
			4	3			7	9		11		10	5			6			
			4	3			7		9	11		10	5			6			
	2			3				9		11		10	5			6			4
	2			3				9		11		10	5			6			4
	2			3				9		11		10	5			6			4
	2			3				9		11		10	5			6			4
	2		4	3				9	10	11			5						6
	2		4	3				9	10	11			5						6
	2		3					9	10	11		8	5			6			4
	2		3			11		9	10				5			6			4
	2		3					9	10	11			5			6			4
	2		3			7		9	10	11						6			4
1	40	3	37	37	9	7	17	41	10	37	26	29	38	16	15	29	8	3	11
			1			2	5	45	3	13		12	3	3	4		1		

Swift	Grant	Hamilton	Watson	Ramsay	Benton	Neal	Ritchie	Hampson	Oxberry	Downes	Wolfe	Upton	Tremelling	Quinn	Lauderdale	Tufnell	Hall	Jennings	Wilson
	2		4	3			10	9		11	1		5	7		6			
	2		4				11	9			1	8	5	7		6		3	
	2		2	1			2	2		1	2	1	1	2		2		1	
								1											

League Table

	P	W	D	L	F	A	Pts
Blackpool	42	27	4	11	98	67	58
Chelsea	42	22	11	9	74	46	55
Oldham Athletic	42	21	11	10	90	51	53
Bradford Park Avenue	42	19	12	11	91	70	50
Bury	42	22	5	15	78	67	49
West Bromwich Albion	42	21	5	16	105	73	47
Southampton	42	17	11	14	77	76	45
Cardiff City	42	18	8	16	61	59	44
Wolverhampton W	42	16	9	17	77	79	41
Nottingham Forest	42	13	15	14	55	69	41
Stoke City	42	16	8	18	74	72	40
Tottenham Hotspur	42	15	9	18	59	61	39
Charlton Athletic	42	14	11	17	59	63	39
Millwall	42	12	15	15	57	73	39
Swansea Town	42	14	9	19	57	61	37
Preston North End	42	13	11	18	65	80	37
Barnsley	42	14	8	20	56	71	36
Bradford City	42	12	12	18	60	77	36
Reading	42	12	11	19	54	67	35
Bristol City	42	13	9	20	61	83	35
Hull City	42	14	7	21	51	78	35
Notts County	42	9	15	18	54	70	33

1930-31

Division One

Manager: Harry Evans (Honorary title)

Did you know that?

A new Spion Kop, erected on the north side of the ground, added 12,000 to the capacity and so Bloomfield Road now held 30,000 spectators.

Nearly 29,000 saw the opening game of the season against Arsenal.

Blackpool conceded 125 goals in their first season in the top flight, including 10 at Huddersfield Town.

Albert Watson's '£10,000 goal' at home to Manchester City saw Blackpool survive relegation in the final game of the season.

The club had an overdraft of over £17,000

Jimmy Hampson still managed to score 32 goals in the First Division.

Match No.	Date	Venue	Opponents	Result		Scorers	Attendance
1	Aug 30	H	Arsenal	L	1-4	Hampson	28,723
2	Sep 3	A	Manchester City	W	4-2	Carr, Hampson 2, Neal	34,908
3	6	A	Blackburn Rovers	L	0-5		25,388
4	10	H	Portsmouth	D	2-2	Hall 2	20,611
5	13	H	Middlesbrough	W	3-2	Hampson 2, Quinn	20,050
6	17	A	Portsmouth	L	3-4	Hampson 2, Quinn	11,838
7	20	H	Leeds United	L	3-7	Upton, Benton, Hampson	25,743
8	27	A	Sunderland	W	4-2	Hampson 2, Quinn, Upton	20,087
9	Oct 4	H	Leicester City	W	5-4	Hampson 3, Oxberry, Upton	24,105
10	11	A	Birmingham City	D	1-1	Hampson	23,453
11	18	A	Bolton Wanderers	L	0-1		26,651
12	25	H	Liverpool	L	1-3	Benton	14,998
13	Nov 1	A	Chelsea	L	0-3		32,775
14	8	H	Newcastle United	D	0-0		14,516
15	15	A	Manchester United	D	0-0		14,765
16	22	H	Aston Villa	D	2-2	Hutchison, Tremelling	12,054
17	29	A	Sheffield Wednesday	L	1-7	Broadhurst	17,393
18	Dec 6	H	West Ham Utd	L	1-3	Hutchison	12,115
19	13	A	Huddersfield Town	L	1-10	Upton	11,952
20	20	H	Grimsby Town	W	3-1	Hampson 2, Oxberry	11,427
21	25	H	Sheffield United	W	2-1	McMahon, Upton	18,575
22	26	A	Sheffield United	L	1-5	Oxberry	20,963
23	27	A	Arsenal	L	1-7	Carr	35,113
24	Jan 3	H	Blackburn Rovers	D	1-1	Hampson	16,294
25	17	A	Middlesbrough	L	1-5	Hampson	16,060
26	28	A	Leeds United	D	2-2	Hampson 2	7,750
27	31	H	Sunderland	W	3-1	Lauderdale 2, Hampson	7,310
28	Feb 7	A	Leicester City	L	0-6		14,581
29	18	H	Birmingham City	L	0-1		10,136
30	21	H	Bolton Wanderers	D	3-3	Oxberry, McLelland, Hampson	16,695
31	28	A	Liverpool	L	2-5	Oxberry, Hampson	13,732
32	Mar 7	H	Chelsea	W	2-1	Hampson (pen), McLelland	12,271
33	14	A	Newcastle United	W	2-0	Hampson, Ratray	13,303
34	21	H	Manchester United	W	5-1	Hampson 3 (1 pen), McLelland 2	13,612
35	28	A	Aston Villa	L	1-4	Longden	27,245
36	Apr 3	H	Derby County	W	1-0	Longden	22,993
37	4	H	Sheffield Wednesday	L	0-4		23,391
38	6	A	Derby County	L	2-3	Hampson 2	12,149
39	11	A	West Ham Utd	L	2-3	Oxberry, Hampson	15,514
40	18	H	Huddersfield Town	D	1-1	Smalley	15,111
41	25	A	Grimsby Town	L	2-6	Longden, Hampson	8,042
42	May 2	H	Manchester City	D	2-2	Oxberry, Watson	18,688

Final League Position: 20th in Division One

Apps

Gls

FA Cup

3	Jan 10	A	Hull City	W	2-1	Hampson, Upton	20,000
4	24	A	Southport	L	1-2	Downes	10,500

Apps

Gls

Pearson	Grant	Watson	McMahon	Tremelling	Tufnell	Neal	Carr	Hampson	Oxberry	Downes	Ramsay	Benton	Quinn	Upton	Hall	Brookes	Shankley	Hutchison	Broadhurst
1	2	3	4	5	6	7	8	9	10	11									
1	2	3	4	5	6	7	8	9	10	11									
1	2	3	4	5	6	7	8	9	10	11									
1	2		4	5			10	9			3	6	7	8	11				
1	2		4	5			10	9			3	6	7	8	11				
1	2		4	5			10	9			3	6	7	8	11				
1	2		4	5			10	9			3	6	7	8	11				
1	2	4	5					9	10		3	6	7	8	11				
1	2	4	5	6				9	10		3		7	8	11				
1	2	4	5					9	10		3	6	7	8	11				
1	2	4	5					9	10	11	3	6	7	8					
1	2	4	5					9	10		3	6		8			7	11	
1	2	4	5					9	10		3	6		8			7	11	
1	2	4	5				8	9	10		3	6					7	11	
1	2	4	5					9	10		3	6		8			7	11	
1	2	4	6	5			8		10		3						7	11	9
1	2	4	6	5			10	9			3						7	11	8
1	2	4	6	5			10	8			3							11	9
1	2	4	5					9	10	11	3	6		8					
1	2	4	5					9	10	11		6		8					
1	2	4	5					9	10	11		6		8					
1	2	4	5					9	10	11		6		8					
1	2	4	5				10	9		11						6			
1	2	4	5				10	9		11						6			
1	2				6		10	9		11				8					
	2	4	5					9	8	11		6							
	2	4	5					9	8	11		6							
1	2	4						9		11	5	6							
1	2	4						9	8	11	6								
1	2	4						9	8		6				11				
1	2	4			6			9	8		5				11				
1	2	4			6			9	8		5				11				
1	2	4			6			9			5				11				
1	2	4			6			9			5				11				
1	2	4			6			9			5				11				
1	2	4			6			9			5				11				
1	2	4			6			9			5		7		11				
1	2	4				11		9			5		7						
1	2	4			6			9	8		5		7						
1	2	4			6			9			5		7						
1	2	4			6			9			5		7						
1	2	4			6			9	8				7						
40	42	37	26	11	15	4	14	41	23	16	30	18	15	16	15	3	5	6	3
		1	1	1		1	2	32	7			2	3	5	2			2	1

1	2				6			9		11				8	
1	2		5					9		11		6	5	8	
2	2		1		1			2		2		1		2	
								1		1					

League Table

	P	W	D	L	F	A	Pts
Arsenal	42	28	10	4	127	59	66
Aston Villa	42	25	9	8	128	78	59
Sheffield Wednesday	42	22	8	12	102	75	52
Portsmouth	42	18	13	11	84	67	49
Huddersfield Town	42	18	12	12	81	65	48
Derby County	42	18	10	14	94	79	46
Middlesbrough	42	19	8	15	98	90	46
Manchester City	42	18	10	14	75	70	46
Liverpool	42	15	12	15	86	85	42
Blackburn Rovers	42	17	8	17	83	84	42
Sunderland	42	16	9	17	89	85	41
Chelsea	42	15	10	17	64	67	40
Grimsby Town	42	17	5	20	82	87	39
Bolton Wanderers	42	15	9	18	68	81	39
Sheffield United	42	14	10	18	78	84	38
Leicester City	42	16	6	20	80	95	38
Newcastle United	42	15	6	21	78	87	36
West Ham United	42	14	8	20	79	94	36
Birmingham	42	13	10	19	55	70	36
Blackpool	42	11	10	21	71	125	32
Leeds United	42	12	7	23	68	81	31
Manchester United	42	7	8	27	53	115	22

1931-32

Division One

Manager: Harry Evans (Honorary title)

Did you know that?

'Only' 102 goals were conceded this season.

The team avoided relegation by winning their final two games against Huddersfield Town and Sheffield United.

Billy Tremelling moved to neighbours Preston North End.

Match No.	Date	Venue	Opponents	Result		Scorers	Attendance
1	Aug 29	H	Derby County	W	2-1	Hampson, Wilkinson	22,970
2	31	H	Sheffield Utd	W	2-0	Hampson, McLelland	19,052
3	Sep 5	A	West Brom Albion	L	0-4		19,320
4	9	H	Blackburn Rovers	W	2-1	Wilkinson, Hampson	23,444
5	12	H	Birmingham City	D	1-1	Wilkinson	19,063
6	19	A	Sunderland	L	0-4		14,901
7	21	A	Blackburn Rovers	L	1-5	Oxberry	15,149
8	26	H	Manchester City	D	2-2	Hampson 2	25,031
9	Oct 3	A	Everton	L	2-3	McLelland 2	31,651
10	10	H	Arsenal	L	1-5	McLelland	29,576
11	17	H	Middlesbrough	L	1-2	Rattray	17,481
12	24	A	Liverpool	L	2-3	Hampson 2	20,742
13	31	H	Leicester City	L	2-3	Hampson 2	9,542
14	Nov 7	A	Aston Villa	L	1-5	Longden	40,448
15	14	H	Shefiield Wednesday	L	1-2	Douglas	12,160
16	21	A	West Ham Utd	D	1-1	Douglas	14,800
17	28	H	Grimsby Town	W	4-3	Harrison, Hampson, Wilkinson, Longden	12,700
18	Dec 5	A	Bolton Wanderers	W	2-1	Hampson 2	14,294
19	12	H	Newcastle United	W	3-1	Hampson 2, Longden	13,410
20	19	A	Huddersfield Town	L	0-5		11,072
21	25	H	Chelsea	L	2-4	Douglas 2	20,378
22	26	A	Chelsea	L	1-4	Hampson	38,569
23	Jan 2	A	Derby County	L	0-5		8,533
24	16	H	West Brom Albion	L	1-2	Douglas	12,269
25	30	H	Sunderland	W	3-2	Wilkinson, Douglas, Own-goal	14,547
26	Feb 3	A	Birmingham City	L	0-3		5,829
27	6	A	Manchester City	L	1-7	Everest	24,739
28	13	H	Everton	W	2-0	Hampson 2	16,346
29	20	A	Arsenal	L	0-2		39,045
30	27	A	Middlesbrough	W	3-0	Douglas, Watson A 2	11,371
31	Mar 5	H	Liverpool	D	2-2	Hampson, Watson P	14,562
32	12	A	Leicester City	D	2-2	Watson A 2 (1 pen)	14,558
33	19	H	Aston Villa	L	1-3	Watson A (pen)	15,585
34	25	H	Portsmouth	D	1-1	Hampson	23,272
35	26	A	Sheffield Wednesday	L	0-3		13,101
36	28	A	Portsmouth	D	2-2	Hampson, Wilkinson	17,805
37	Apr 2	H	West Ham Utd	W	7-2	Douglas 2, Watson A 2, Wilkinson 2, Hampson	13,092
38	9	A	Grimsby Town	D	0-0		8,651
39	16	H	Bolton Wanderers	L	0-3		16,890
40	27	A	Newcastle United	D	2-2	Hampson 2	31,348
41	30	H	Huddersfield Town	W	2-0	Longden, McLelland	15,675
42	May 7	A	Sheffield Utd	W	3-1	Douglas, McLelland, Wilkinson	12,388

Final League Position: 20th in Division One

Apps

Gls

FA Cup

3	Jan 9	H	Newcastle United	D	1-1	Hampson	14,000
3R	13	A	Newcastle United	L	0-1		46,104

Apps

Gls

Maggs	Grant	O'Donnell	Watson A	Longden	Tufnell	Wilkinson	Upton	Hampson	McLelland	Lax	Quinn	Morfitt	Reece	Oxberry	Smalley	Rattray	Ramsay	Douglas	Wilson
1	2	3	4	5	6	7	8	9	10	11									
1	2	3	4	5	6		8	9	10	11	7								
1	2	3	4	5	6	7	8	9	10	11									
1	2	3	4	5	6	7	8	9	10	11									
1	2	3	4	5	6	7		9	10	11		8							
1	2	3	4	5	6	7	8	9	10	11									
1	2		4	5	6			9	8	11	7		3	10					
1	2	3	4	5			8	9		11	7			10	6				
1	2	3	4	5	6	7	8	9	10	11									
1	2	3	4	5			8	9	10	11					6	7			
1	2	3	4	5			8	9	10	11					6	7			
1	2	3	4	8				9	10		11				6	7	5		
1	2	3	4	8				9	10		11				6	7	5		
1	2			5			4	9			11			8	6	7	3	10	
1	2			8	6	7		9							4		3	10	5
1	2	3		8	6	7		9							4			10	5
1	2	3		8	6	7		9							4			10	5
1	2			8	6	7	4	9									3	10	5
1	2			8	6	7	4	9									3	10	5
1	2			8	6	7	4	9									3	10	5
1	2		4	8		7		9									3	10	5
1	2			4	6	7		9						10			3	8	5
1	2	3		4	6	7		9						10				8	5
1	2	3		4	6	7		8		11								9	5
	2	3		4	6	7		8		11								9	5
	2	3		4	6	7		8										10	5
	2	3	4	5	6	7		8										10	
	2	3	8	4		7		9									6	10	
	2	3	8	4		7		9									6	10	
	2	3	8	4		7		9		11							6	10	
	2	3	8	4		7		9									6	10	
	2	3	8	4		7		9		11							6	10	
	2	3	8	4	6	7		9		11				10					
	2	3	8	4	6	7		9	10	11									
	2		8	4	6	7	10	9		11									5
	2		8	4		7	10	9		11							6		5
	2	3	8	4		7		9		11								10	5
	2	3	8	4		7		9		11								10	5
	2	3	8	4		7		9		11								10	5
	2	3	8	4		7		9		11								10	5
	2	3		4	6	7		9	8							11		10	
	2	3		4	6	7		9	8							11		10	
24	42	32	28	42	25	34	15	42	15	23	6	1	1	6	11	5	15	25	18
			7	4		9		23	6					1		1		10	

Maggs	Grant	O'Donnell	Watson A	Longden	Tufnell	Wilkinson	Upton	Hampson	McLelland	Lax	Quinn	Morfitt	Reece	Oxberry	Smalley	Rattray	Ramsay	Douglas	Wilson
1	2	3	4	8	6	7		9										10	5
1	2	3	4	8	6	7		9					5					10	5
2	2	2	2	2	2	2		2										2	2
								1											

League Table

	P	W	D	L	F	A	Pts
Everton	42	26	4	12	116	64	56
Arsenal	42	22	10	10	90	48	54
Sheffield Wednesday	42	22	6	14	96	82	50
Huddersfield Town	42	19	10	13	80	63	48
Aston Villa	42	19	8	15	104	72	46
West Bromwich Albion	42	20	6	16	77	55	46
Sheffield United	42	20	6	16	80	75	46
Portsmouth	42	19	7	16	62	62	45
Birmingham	42	18	8	16	78	67	44
Liverpool	42	19	6	17	81	93	44
Newcastle United	42	18	6	18	80	87	42
Chelsea	42	16	8	18	69	73	40
Sunderland	42	15	10	17	67	73	40
Manchester City	42	13	12	17	83	73	38
Derby County	42	14	10	18	71	75	38
Blackburn Rovers	42	16	6	20	89	95	38
Bolton Wanderers	42	17	4	21	72	80	38
Middlesbrough	42	15	8	19	64	89	38
Leicester City	42	15	7	20	74	94	37
Blackpool	42	12	9	21	65	102	33
Grimsby Town	42	13	6	23	67	98	32
West Ham United	42	12	7	23	62	107	31

1932-33

Division One

Manager: Harry Evans (Honorary title)

Did you know that?

Chelsea finished with only six players on the pitch at the end of the 4–0 drubbing at Bloomfield Road in October.

When relegation was confirmed, honorary manager Harry Evans was relieved of his duties.

Evans became chairman of the club after a boardroom coup.

Six long-standing directors resigned at the end of the season after a vote of 'no confidence' in them.

Match No.	Date	Venue	Opponents	Result		Scorers	Attendance
1	Aug 27	A	Sheffield Wednesday	L	1-4	Wilkinson	15,152
2	29	H	Leeds United	W	2-1	Hampson, McLelland (pen)	20,315
3	Sep 3	H	West Brom Albion	L	2-4	Hampson, McLelland	20,646
4	5	A	Leeds United	L	1-3	Hampson	9,171
5	10	A	Birmingham City	L	1-2	McLelland (pen)	16,048
6	17	H	Sunderland	W	3-1	McLelland 2, Douglas	18,234
7	24	A	Manchester City	L	1-5	McLelland	25,175
8	Oct 1	H	Arsenal	L	1-2	McLelland (pen)	30,218
9	8	A	Everton	L	0-2		18,359
10	15	H	Leicester City	W	2-1	Hampson, Crawford	16,898
11	22	A	Portsmouth	L	1-2	Wilkinson	14,422
12	29	H	Chelsea	W	4-0	Hampson 3, Wilkinson	7,311
13	Nov 5	A	Aston Villa	L	2-6	Hampson, McLelland	29,371
14	12	H	Middlesbrough	W	3-1	Hampson 2, McLelland	12,104
15	19	A	Bolton Wanderers	L	0-1		14,468
16	26	H	Liverpool	W	4-1	Butterworth 2, Hampson 2	12,162
17	Dec 3	A	Huddersfield Town	W	1-0	Butterworth	8,623
18	10	H	Sheffield Utd	L	0-3		12,909
19	17	A	Wolves	W	3-2	Hampson 2, Wilkinson	21,377
20	24	H	Newcastle United	L	0-4		14,053
21	26	A	Derby County	D	1-1	Wilkinson	21,862
22	27	H	Derby County	W	4-1	McLelland, Hampson, Douglas, Smailes	19,017
23	31	H	Sheffield Wednesday	L	3-4	Hampson 2, Wilkinson	13,689
24	Jan 2	A	Blackburn Rovers	L	5-6	McLelland 2, Wilkinson, Douglas,Smailes	22,471
25	7	A	West Brom Albion	L	1-2	McLelland	17,280
26	21	H	Birmingham City	L	0-1		10,352
27	Feb 1	A	Sunderland	D	1-1	McLelland	19,873
28	4	H	Manchester City	W	1-0	Hampson	13,399
29	11	A	Arsenal	D	1-1	McLelland	35,180
30	22	H	Everton	W	2-1	Watson A, Own-goal	12,050
31	Mar 4	H	Portsmouth	L	0-2		12,623
32	11	A	Chelsea	L	0-1		31,222
33	18	H	Aston Villa	W	6-2	Watson P 3, Smailes 2, Crawford	15,729
34	28	A	Middlesbrough	L	0-2		10,724
35	30	A	Leicester City	L	0-3		7,904
36	Apr 1	H	Bolton Wanderers	L	1-3	Crawford	15,849
37	8	A	Liverpool	L	3-4	Watson P 2, Crawford	16,384
38	14	H	Blackburn Rovers	W	3-0	Smailes, Watson P 2	26,365
39	15	H	Huddersfield Town	D	1-1	Douglas	22,867
40	22	A	Sheffield Utd	L	0-1		8,945
41	29	H	Wolves	D	2-2	Upton, Douglas	16,007
42	May 6	A	Newcastle United	W	2-1	Upton, Reid	11,443

Final League Position: 22nd in Division One

Apps
Gls

FA Cup

3	Jan 14	H	Port Vale	W	2-1	McLelland (pen), Hampson	15,800
4	28	H	Huddersfield Town	W	2-0	McLelland, Douglas	16,187
5	Feb 18	A	Sunderland	L	0-1		46,900

Apps
Gls

McDonough	Grant	Everest	Longden	Watson P	Smalley	Wilkinson	McLelland	Hampson	Douglas	Bridge	Smith	Tufnell	Upton	Wassell	Reece	Watson A	Crawford	Butterworth	Lax
1	2	3	4	5	6	7	8	9	10	11									
1	2	3	4	5	6	7	8	9	10	11									
1	2	3	4	5		7	8	9	10	11	6								
1	2	3	4	5		7	8	9		11		6	10						
1			6	5		7	8	9		11			10	2	3	4			
1			4	5		7	8	9	10	11				2	3		6		
1			4	5		7	8	9	10	11				2	3		6		
1		3		5		7	10	9						2		4	6	8	11
1		3		5		7	10	9						2		4	6	8	11
1		3		5	11	7	10	9						2		4	6	8	
1		3		5	11	7	10	9						2		4	6	8	
1		3		5	11	7	10	9						2		4		8	
1		3		5		7	8	9	10					2		4	6		
1		3		5		7	8	9	10					2		4	6		
1		3		5		7	8	9	10					2		4	6		
1		3		5		7		9	10					2		4	6	8	
1		3		5			8	9	10					2		4	6	7	
1		3		5			8	9	10					2		4	6	7	
1		3		5		7	10	9						2		4	6	8	
1		3		5		7	10	9						2		4	6	8	
1	4	3		5		7	8	9	10					2			6		
1		3		5		7	8	9	10					2		4	6		
1		3		5		7	8	9	10					2		4	6		
1		3		5		7	8	9	10					2		4	6		
1		3		5		7	8	9	10					2		4	6		
1		3		5		7	8	9	10					2		4	6		
1	2	3		5		7	9		10							4	6	8	
1	2	3		5		7		9	10							4	6	8	
1	2	3		5			8	9	10							4	6		
1	2	3		5			8	9	10							4	6		
1	2	3		5				9	10							4	6	8	
1	2	3		5		7	8	9	10							4	6		
	2	3		9			8		10							4	6		
	2	3		9			8		10							4	6		
1	2	3		5			9	8	10							4	6		
1	2	3		5			9	8	10							4	6		
1	2	4		9			8		10					3		5			
1	2			9			8		10					3		4	6		
1	2			9			8		10					3		4	6		
1		3		9			8	7	10					2		4	6		
1		3		5			9		10				8	2		4	6		
1		3		5				9	10				8	2		4	6		
40	18	37	7	42	5	26	38	35	35	7	1	1	4	28	3	35	35	13	2
				7		7	15	18	5				2			1	4	3	

McDonough	Grant	Everest	Longden	Watson P	Smalley	Wilkinson	McLelland	Hampson	Douglas	Bridge	Smith	Tufnell	Upton	Wassell	Reece	Watson A	Crawford	Butterworth	Lax
1		3		5		7	8	9	10					2		4	6		
1		3		5		7	8	9	10				5	2		4	6		
1	2	3		5			8	9	10				8			4	6		
3	1	3		3		2	3	3	3					2		3	3		
							2	1	1										

League Table

	P	W	D	L	F	A	Pts
Arsenal	42	25	8	9	118	61	58
Aston Villa	42	23	8	11	92	67	54
Sheffield Wednesday	42	21	9	12	80	68	51
West Bromwich Albion	42	20	9	13	83	70	49
Newcastle United	42	22	5	15	71	63	49
Huddersfield Town	42	18	11	13	66	53	47
Derby County	42	15	14	13	76	69	44
Leeds United	42	15	14	13	59	62	44
Portsmouth	42	18	7	17	74	76	43
Sheffield United	42	17	9	16	74	80	43
Everton	42	16	9	17	81	74	41
Sunderland	42	15	10	17	63	80	40
Birmingham	42	14	11	17	57	57	39
Liverpool	42	14	11	17	79	84	39
Blackburn Rovers	42	14	10	18	76	102	38
Manchester City	42	16	5	21	68	71	37
Middlesbrough	42	14	9	19	63	73	37
Chelsea	42	14	7	21	63	73	35
Leicester City	42	11	13	18	75	89	35
Wolverhampton W	42	13	9	20	80	96	35
Bolton Wanderers	42	12	9	21	78	92	33
Blackpool	42	14	5	23	69	85	33

1933-34

Division Two

Manager: Sandy McFarlane

Did you know that?

A new manager was appointed. Sandy McFarlane took over and at the end of his first season released eight of Blackpool's long-standing and popular players.

Jimmy Hampson was top scorer for the seventh successive season.

The team adopted another new kit. The orange and white was now replaced by dark-and-light-blue stripes with white shorts. There was no sign of the previous colour in the new strip.

Blackpool won the Victoria Hospital Cup again, beating Everton once more 2–1.

Match No.	Date	Venue	Opponents	Result		Scorers	Attendance
1	Aug 26	H	Preston NE	L	1-2	Hampson	28,771
2	28	A	Fulham	L	0-1		14,948
3	Sep 2	A	Bradford City	L	0-1		13,199
4	4	H	Fulham	W	4-3	Butterworth 2, Hampson, Jones T	20,791
5	9	H	Port Vale	W	1-0	Crawford	16,988
6	16	A	Notts County	D	1-1	Hampson	18,957
7	23	H	Swansea T	W	2-1	Smailes, Hampson	18,366
8	30	A	Millwall	D	0-0		18,243
9	Oct 7	H	Lincoln City	W	2-0	Hampson 2	18,599
10	14	A	Bury	W	5-2	Hampson 3, Thomson, Bussey	10,497
11	21	H	Oldham Athletic	D	0-0		21,233
12	28	A	Burnley	L	2-3	Hampson, Dougal	18,150
13	Nov 4	H	Brentford	W	3-1	Smailes 2, Bussey	14,229
14	11	A	Bolton Wanderers	W	2-1	Smailes, Bussey	19,947
15	18	H	Manchester Utd	W	3-1	Jones T, Hampson, Smailes	14,384
16	25	A	Plymouth Argyle	W	3-0	Rattray 2, Hampson	21,533
17	Dec 2	H	West Ham Utd	D	1-1	Hampson	13,822
18	9	A	Nottm Forest	D	0-0		10,282
19	16	H	Grimsby Town	L	3-4	Rattray 2, Bussey	15,332
20	23	A	Bradford City	W	2-1	Jones T 2	10,465
21	25	H	Hull City	D	0-0		24,631
22	26	A	Hull City	L	0-3		15,002
23	30	A	Preston NE	L	0-3		23,361
24	Jan 6	H	Bradford City	W	3-2	Rattray, Smailes, Doherty	13,070
25	20	A	Port Vale	L	0-1		14,216
26	Feb 3	A	Swansea T	D	2-2	Bussey, Smailes	8,574
27	7	H	Notts County	W	2-1	Bussey, Jones T	10,188
28	10	H	Millwall	D	2-2	Smailes, Jones S	13,149
29	17	A	Lincoln City	D	2-2	Smailes, Jones T	5,968
30	24	H	Bury	W	2-0	Bussey 2	14,811
31	Mar 3	A	Oldham Athletic	L	0-2		9,393
32	10	H	Burnley	D	1-1	Bralisford	13,278
33	17	A	Brentford	L	0-1		16,461
34	24	H	Bolton Wanderers	D	1-1	Hall	17,464
35	30	H	Southampton	W	4-2	Hall, Jones T, Smailes, Doherty	20,966
36	31	A	Manchester Utd	L	0-2		20,038
37	Apr 2	A	Southampton	L	2-3	Hall 2	10,221
38	7	H	Plymouth Argyle	D	1-1	Hall	13,944
39	14	A	West Ham Utd	W	2-1	Oxberry 2	14,170
40	21	H	Nottm Forest	L	2-3	Rattray, Watson P	10,396
41	28	A	Grimsby Town	L	0-7		7,090
42	May 5	H	Bradford City	D	1-1	Bralisford	8,252

Final League Position: 11th in Division Two

Apps

Gls

FA Cup

3	Jan 13	A	Cheltenham Town	W	3-1	Bussey, Watson P, Doherty	12,000
4	27	A	Stoke City	L	0-3		24,000

Apps

Gls

McDonough	Wassell	Everest	Watson A	Watson P	Crawford	Thompson	Robinson	Hampson	Douglas	Smailes	Shipman	Grant	Upton	Butterworth	Jones T	Varty	Rattray	Dougall	Bussey
1	2	3	4	5	6	7	8	9	10	11									
1	2			5	6	7		9	10	11	3	4	8						
1	2			5	6	7	10	9		11	3	4		8					
1	2			5	6	7		9		11	3	4		10	8				
1	2		4	5	6	7		9			3			8	10	11			
1	2		4	5	6			9		11	3			8	10		7		
1	2			5	6	7		9		11	3			8	10			4	
1	2			5	6	7		9		11	3			10				4	8
1	2			5	6	7		9		11	3			10				4	8
1	2			5	6	7		9		11	3				10			4	8
1	2			5		7		9		11	3				10			4	8
1	2			5		7		9		11	3				10			4	8
1	2			5	6	7		9		11	3				10			4	8
1	2			5	6	7		9		11	3				10			4	8
1	2			5	6			9		11	3				10		7	4	8
1	2			5	6			9		11	3				10		7	4	8
1	2			5				9		11	3				10		7	4	8
1	2			5	6			9		11	3				10		7	4	8
1	2			5	6			9		11	3				10		7	4	8
1	2			5				9		11	3				8		7	4	
1	2			5				9		11	3				8		7	4	
1	2			9	6					11	3			7	10			4	8
1	2			5				9		11	3				10		7	4	8
1	2	3		5						11					10		7	4	8
	2	3		5		7									10	11		4	8
	2			5		7				11	3				8			4	9
	2			5		7				11	3				8			4	9
	2			5		7				11	3			8				4	9
	2			5		7				11					8			4	9
	2			5						11					8			4	9
	2			5						11					8			4	9
	2			5		7				11					10			4	8
	2			5		7				11					10			4	8
	2			5		7				11					8			4	
	2			5		7				11					8			4	
	2			5		7				11					8			4	
	2			5	6					11		4							8
	2			5	6			9		11		4			8				
	2			5						11					8		7	4	
	2			5						11					8		7	4	
	2			5						11								4	
				5	6	7				11	3							4	
24	41	3	3	42	20	24	2	23	2	40	26	5	1	9	33	2	12	34	25
				1	1	1		13		10				2	7		6	1	8

McDonough	Wassell	Everest	Watson A	Watson P	Crawford	Thompson	Robinson	Hampson	Douglas	Smailes	Shipman	Grant	Upton	Butterworth	Jones T	Varty	Rattray	Dougall	Bussey
1	2	3		5						11					10		7	4	8
	2	3		5		7				11			5		10			4	8
1	2	2		2		1				2					2		1	2	2
				1															1

League Table

	P	W	D	L	F	A	Pts
Grimsby Town	42	27	5	10	103	59	59
Preston North End	42	23	6	13	71	52	52
Bolton Wanderers	42	21	9	12	79	55	51
Brentford	42	22	7	13	85	60	51
Bradford Park Avenue	42	23	3	16	86	67	49
Bradford City	42	20	6	16	73	67	46
West Ham United	42	17	11	14	78	70	45
Port Vale	42	19	7	16	60	55	45
Oldham Athletic	42	17	10	15	72	60	44
Plymouth Argyle	42	15	13	14	69	70	43
Blackpool	42	15	13	14	62	64	43
Bury	42	17	9	16	70	73	43
Burnley	42	18	6	18	60	72	42
Southampton	42	15	8	19	54	58	38
Hull City	42	13	12	17	52	68	38
Fulham	42	15	7	20	48	67	37
Nottingham Forest	42	13	9	20	73	74	35
Notts County	42	12	11	19	53	62	35
Swansea Town	42	10	15	17	51	60	35
Manchester United	42	14	6	22	59	85	34
Millwall	42	11	11	20	39	68	33
Lincoln City	42	9	8	25	44	75	26

1934-35

Division Two

Manager: Sandy McFarlane

Did you know that?

Hampson top scored again, this time with 20 goals from 25 League appearances.

Blackpool missed promotion by just three points. Losing two and drawing one of their last three games meant that Bolton Wanderers took second spot to Brentford.

Peter Doherty was signed from Glentoran for £1,000 and scored 13 goals in his first season.

The planned forward line of Hampson, Doherty and Bobby Finan never happened due to injuries.

Match No.	Date		Venue	Opponents	Result		Scorers	Attendance
1	Aug	25	A	Bury	W	5-1	Hampson 3, Finan, Smailes	13,006
2		27	H	Newcastle United	W	4-1	Thomas, Hampson 2, Smailes	25,303
3	Sep	1	H	Hull City	W	2-1	Hampson 2	18,447
4		8	A	Nottm Forest	D	0-0		17,179
5		12	A	Newcastle United	L	1-4	Thomas	23,404
6		15	H	Brentford	D	2-2	Hampson, Dougall	24,223
7		22	A	Fulham	L	1-4	Hampson	26,656
8		29	H	Bradford City	W	1-0	Oram	15,354
9	Oct	6	A	Plymouth Argyle	W	2-1	Doherty, Oram	8,286
10		11	H	Norwich City	W	2-1	Hall, Watmough	15,889
11		20	H	Burnley	W	1-0	Oram	22,096
12		27	A	Swansea T	L	1-2	Jones T	5,689
13	Nov	3	H	Manchester Utd	L	1-2	Hampson	15,663
14		10	A	Port Vale	D	2-2	Bralisford, Finan	11,428
15		17	H	Barnsley	W	3-0	Bralisford 2, Watmough	11,428
16		24	A	Sheffield Utd	D	1-1	Doherty	13,856
17	Dec	1	H	Bradford City	W	2-1	Jones T, Watmough	9,576
18		8	A	Notts County	L	2-3	Hall, Watmough	10,067
19		15	H	Southampton	W	4-1	Smailes, Jones S, Doherty 2	10,016
20		22	A	Bolton Wanderers	L	2-4	Hall, Watson P (pen)	22,255
21		25	H	Oldham Athletic	W	4-0	Smailes 2, Jones T, Hall	18,427
22		26	A	Oldham Athletic	W	3-2	Smailes, Doherty, Watmough	14,075
23		29	H	Bury	D	1-1	Watson P (pen)	12,624
24	Jan	5	A	Hull City	D	2-2	Bralisford 2	10,670
25		19	H	Nottm Forest	W	1-0	Doherty (pen)	11,819
26		26	A	Brentford	L	1-2	Doherty	13,087
27	Feb	2	H	Fulham	D	1-1	Doherty	11,022
28		9	A	Bradford City	D	0-0		9,019
29		16	H	Plymouth Argyle	W	4-1	Hampson 3, Doherty	7,484
30		23	A	Norwich City	D	1-1	Watmough	11,290
31	Mar	5	A	Burnley	W	2-1	Hampson, Smailes	8,992
32		9	H	Swansea T	W	2-1	Hampson, Finan	10,979
33		16	A	Manchester Utd	L	2-3	Doherty 2	25,704
34		23	H	Port Vale	W	3-1	Hampson, Watmough, Smailes	7,268
35		30	A	Barnsley	D	2-2	Watmough, Smailes	11,639
36	Apr	6	H	Sheffield Utd	W	1-0	Smailes	11,509
37		13	A	Bradford City	W	2-0	Doherty (pen), Jones T	8,456
38		19	H	West Ham Utd	W	3-2	Hampson 2, Jones T	29,626
39		20	H	Notts County	W	3-1	Hampson, Doherty (pen), Finan	15,434
40		22	A	West Ham Utd	L	1-2	Hampson	35,161
41		27	A	Southampton	L	0-2		6,758
42	May	4	H	Bolton Wanderers	D	1-1	Watmough	25,550

Final League Position: 4th in Division Two

Apps
Gls

FA Cup

3	Jan	12	A	Leicester City	L	1-2	Hall	18,000

Apps
Gls

Wallace	Wassell	Witham	Dougall	Watson	Jones S	Thomas	Finan	Hampson	Jones T	Smailes	Grant	Brailsford	Doherty	Oram	Watmough	Shipman	Cardwell	Hall
1	2	3	4	5	6	7	8	9	10	11								
1	2	3	4	5	6	7	8	9	10	11								
1	2	3	4	5	6	7	8	9	10	11								
1	2		4	5	6	7	8	9	10	11	3							
1	2		4	5	6	7	8	9	10	11	3							
1	2		4	5	6		8	9		11	3	7	10					
1	2		4	5	6		8	9			3	7	10	11				
1	2		4	5	6	7	8	9			3		10	11				
1	2	3	4	5	6		8	9	10				7	11				
1		3	4	5	6				10		2		8	11	7			9
1		3	4	5	6				10			9	8	11	7	2		
1	2	3	4	5	6			9	10				8	11	7			
1	2	3	4	5	6			9	10				8	11	7			
1		3	4	2	6		8		10			9	11		7		5	
1		3	4	2	6		8		10			9	11		7		5	
1		3	4	2	6		8		10			9	11		7		5	
1		3	4	2	6		8		10			9	11		7		5	
1		3	4	2	6		8		10				11		7		5	9
1		3	4	2	6		8			11			10		7		5	9
1		3	4	2	6				8	11			10		7		5	9
1		3		2	6				8	11	4		10		7		5	9
1		3		2	6				8	11	4		10		7		5	9
1		3		2	6				8	11	4		10		7		5	9
1	2	3			6		8			11	4	9	10		7		5	
1	2	3			6				8	11	4	9	10		7		5	
1	2	3	4	9			10		8		5		11		7		6	
1	2	3		9	6				8	11	4		10		7		5	
1	2	3			6		10	9	8	11	4				7		5	
1	2	3			6			9	8	11	4		10		7		5	
1	2	3			6				8	11	4		10		7		5	9
1	2	3			6			9	8	11	4		10		7		5	
1	2	3			6		8	9		11	4		10		7		5	
1	2	3			6			9	8	11	4		10		7		5	
1		3		2	6			9	8	11	4		10		7		5	
1		3		2	6			9	8	11	4		10		7		5	
1		3		2	6			9	8	11	4		10		7		5	
1		3		2	6			9	8	11	4		10		7		5	
1		3		2	6			9	8	11	4		10		7		5	
1		3		2	6		8	9		11	4	7	10				5	
1		3		2	6			9	8	11	4		10		7		5	
1		3		2	6		10	9	8		4		11		7		5	
1		3		2	6		10	9	8	11	4				7		5	
42	21	37	21	34	41	6	22	25	35	28	28	10	35	7	32	1	29	8
			1	2	1	2	4	20	5	10		5	13	3	9			4

Wallace	Wassell	Witham	Dougall	Watson	Jones S	Thomas	Finan	Hampson	Jones T	Smailes	Grant	Brailsford	Doherty	Oram	Watmough	Shipman	Cardwell	Hall
1	2	3			6				8	11	4		10		7		5	9
1	1	1			1				1	1	1		1		1		1	1
																		1

League Table

	P	W	D	L	F	A	Pts
Brentford	42	26	9	7	93	48	61
Bolton Wanderers	42	26	4	12	96	48	56
West Ham United	42	26	4	12	80	63	56
Blackpool	42	21	11	10	79	57	53
Manchester United	42	23	4	15	76	55	50
Newcastle United	42	22	4	16	89	68	48
Fulham	42	17	12	13	76	56	46
Plymouth Argyle	42	19	8	15	75	64	46
Nottingham Forest	42	17	8	17	76	70	42
Bury	42	19	4	19	62	73	42
Sheffield United	42	16	9	17	79	70	41
Burnley	42	16	9	17	63	73	41
Hull City	42	16	8	18	63	74	40
Norwich City	42	14	11	17	71	61	39
Bradford Park Avenue	42	11	16	15	55	63	38
Barnsley	42	13	12	17	60	83	38
Swansea Town	42	14	8	20	56	67	36
Port Vale	42	11	12	19	55	74	34
Southampton	42	11	12	19	46	75	34
Bradford City	42	12	8	22	50	68	32
Oldham Athletic	42	10	6	26	56	95	26
Notts County	42	9	7	26	46	97	25

1935-36

Division Two

Manager: Joe Smith

Did you know that?

Sandy McFarlane retired from the game and Blackpool appointed Joe Smith as their new manager. He had previously managed Reading and went on to make Blackpool one of the forces of English football, staying for 22 years.

The FA Cup game with Margate was the first Blackpool match at Bloomfield Road captured on film. It was later shown at the Grand Theatre and Winter Gardens in the town.

With injury to Jimmy Hampson, Bobby Finan was top scorer with 34 goals from 41 League appearances.

Match No.	Date	Venue	Opponents	Result		Scorers	Attendance
1	Aug 31	H	Doncaster Rovers	W	5-2	Oram, Finan 2, Jones T, Doherty	20,649
2	Sep 4	H	Norwich City	W	2-1	Finan, Oram	19,229
3	7	A	Bury	D	1-1	Oram	12,276
4	11	A	Norwich City	W	1-0	Finan	22,337
5	14	H	West Ham Utd	W	4-1	Finan 2, Oram, Parr	22,082
6	16	H	Nottm Forest	L	1-4	Doherty (pen)	13,738
7	21	A	Swansea T	L	0-1		13,276
8	28	H	Leicester City	L	3-5	Middleton 2, Watmough	24,409
9	Oct 3	A	Nottm Forest	D	2-2	Doherty, Jones T	8,325
10	5	A	Bradford City	L	2-3	Oram, Watmough	11,410
11	12	H	Sheffield Utd	W	3-0	Watmough 2, Finan	19,684
12	19	A	Charlton Athletic	D	1-1	Hampson	23,171
13	28	H	Hull City	W	4-1	Jones T 2, Finan, Doherty	10,624
14	Nov 2	A	Barnsley	W	2-1	Oram, Watmough	9,075
15	9	H	Plymouth Argyle	W	3-1	Finan 2, Doherty	12,415
16	16	A	Bradford City	L	1-2	Finan	13,231
17	23	H	Fulham	D	1-1	Doherty	12,353
18	30	A	Tottenham Hotspur	L	1-3	Finan	35,031
19	Dec 7	H	Manchester Utd	W	4-1	Doherty 2, Jones T, Finan	13,218
20	14	A	Port Vale	D	2-2	Watmough 2	7,106
21	25	A	Burnley	L	2-3	Hampson, Jones T	19,376
22	26	H	Burnley	W	2-0	Hampson, Doherty (pen)	15,579
23	28	A	Doncaster Rovers	W	3-0	Finan 2, Watmough	12,373
24	Jan 4	H	Bury	L	2-3	Finan, Jones T	11,758
25	18	A	West Ham Utd	L	1-2	Finan	19,362
26	29	H	Swansea T	D	1-1	Finan	7,862
27	Feb 1	A	Leicester City	L	1-4	Jones T	18,095
28	8	H	Bradford City	W	4-2	Finan 2, Doherty 2	9,936
29	20	A	Sheffield Utd	L	0-1		16,291
30	22	H	Charlton Athletic	W	6-2	Finan 2, Hampson, Chandler, Bralisford	10,956
31	29	A	Manchester Utd	L	2-3	Finan 2	18,423
32	Mar 7	H	Bradford City	D	3-3	Finan, Cardwell, Jones S	6,918
33	14	A	Plymouth Argyle	L	2-3	Cardwell, Finan	13,761
34	21	H	Barnsley	W	3-0	Hampson, Cardwell, Own-goal	10,123
35	28	A	Fulham	L	2-4	Finan 2	18,250
36	Apr 4	H	Tottenham Hotspur	L	2-4	Finan, Own-goal	11,044
37	10	H	Southampton	W	2-1	Hampson, Finan	18,447
38	11	A	Hull City	W	3-0	Jones T, Middleton, Cardwell (pen)	4,309
39	13	A	Southampton	L	0-1		11,911
40	18	H	Port Vale	W	3-1	Jones T, Jones S, Chandler	9,326
41	22	H	Newcastle Utd	W	6-0	Cardweel (pen), Finan 2, Jones T 2	7,935
42	28	A	Newcastle Utd	L	0-1		7,765

Final League Position: 10th in Division Two

Apps
Gls

FA Cup

3	Jan 11	H	Margate	W	3-1	Finan, Watmough 2	13,800
4	25	A	Fulham	L	2-5	Finan, Jones T	25,000

Apps
Gls

Wallace	Watson P	Witham	Dougall	Cardwell	Jones S	Watmough	Jones T	Finan	Doherty	Oram	Parr	Middleton	McIntosh	Butler	Shipman	Watson A	Hampson	Chandler	Bokas
1	2	3	4	5	6	7	8	9	10	11									
1	2	3	4	5	6			9	10	11	7	8							
1	2	3	4	5	6		8	9	10	11	7								
1	2	3	4	5	6		8	9	10	11	7								
1	2	3	4	5	6		8	9	10	11	7								
1	2	3	4	5	6		8	9	10	11	7								
1	2	3	4	5	6			9	10		7	8	11						
1	2	3	4	5	6	7		9	10			8	11						
1	2	3		5	6	7	8	9	10	11				4					
1	2			5	6	7	8	9	10	11					3	4			
1	2	3		5	6	7	8	9	10	11						4			
1	2	3		5	6	7	8	10		11						4	9		
1	2	3		5	6	7	8	9	10	11						4			
1	2	3		5	6	7	8	9	10	11						4			
1	2	3		5	6	7	8	9	10	11						4			
1	2	3		5	6	7	8	9	10	11						4			
1	2	3		5	6	7	8	9	10							4		11	
1	2	3		5	6	7	8	9	10							4		11	
1	2	3		5	6	7	10	9	11							4	8		
1	2	3		5	6	7	10	9	11							4	8		
1	2	3		5	6	7	10	9	11							4	8		
1	2	3		5		7	8		10	11						4	9		6
1	2	3		5		7	8	9	10	11						4			6
1	2	3		5	6	7	8	9	10	11									4
1	2	3		5	6	7	8	9	10	11									4
		3		5	6	7	8	9	10					2				11	4
		3		5	6	7	10	9	11					2		4	8		
				5	6	7		9	10	11					3	4	8		
1				5	6	7		9	10						3	4	8	11	
1				5	6			9	10						3	4	8	11	
1			4	5	6		10	9							3		8	11	
1			4	5	6		10	9							3		8	11	
1			4	5	6		10	9							3		8	11	
1	2	3	4	5	6		10	9					7				8	11	
1	2	3	4	5	6		10	9					7				8	11	
1		3		5	6		10	9				7				4	8	11	
	5	3	2	4			10	9			7					6	8	11	
	5	3	2	4			10	9				7				6	8	11	
	5	3	2	4			10	9				7				6	8	11	
	2	3	4	5	6		10	9			7						8	11	
	2	3	4	5	6		10	9		11	7						8		
1	2	3	4	5	6		10	9		11	7						8		
34	33	35	19	42	37	23	36	41	29	27	10	6	4	3	7	22	21	15	6
				5	2	8	12	34	11	6	1	3					6	2	

Wallace	Watson P	Witham	Dougall	Cardwell	Jones S	Watmough	Jones T	Finan	Doherty	Oram	Parr	Middleton	McIntosh	Butler	Shipman	Watson A	Hampson	Chandler	Bokas
1	2	3		5	6	7	8	9	10	11									4
1	2	3		5	6	7	8	9	10	11			5						4
2	2	2		2	2	2	2	2	2	2									2
						2	1	2											

League Table

	P	W	D	L	F	A	Pts
Manchester United	42	22	12	8	85	43	56
Charlton Athletic	42	22	11	9	85	58	55
Sheffield United	42	20	12	10	79	50	52
West Ham United	42	22	8	12	90	68	52
Tottenham Hotspur	42	18	13	11	91	55	49
Leicester City	42	19	10	13	79	57	48
Plymouth Argyle	42	20	8	14	71	57	48
Newcastle United	42	20	6	16	88	79	46
Fulham	42	15	14	13	76	52	44
Blackpool	42	18	7	17	93	72	43
Norwich City	42	17	9	16	72	65	43
Bradford City	42	15	13	14	55	65	43
Swansea Town	42	15	9	18	67	76	39
Bury	42	13	12	17	66	84	38
Burnley	42	12	13	17	50	59	37
Bradford Park Avenue	42	14	9	19	62	84	37
Southampton	42	14	9	19	47	65	37
Doncaster Rovers	42	14	9	19	51	71	37
Nottingham Forest	42	12	11	19	69	76	35
Barnsley	42	12	9	21	54	80	33
Port Vale	42	12	8	22	56	106	32
Hull City	42	5	10	27	47	111	20

1936-37

Division Two

Manager: Joe Smith

Did you know that?

Blackpool were promoted back to the First Division finishing second to Leicester City. They had only paid money for one player in the close season – Alex Munro from Hearts for £3,500.

Peter Doherty was sold to Manchester City for an enormous fee of £10,000.

When Blackpool visited Bury on New Year's Day, they were presented with a box of black puddings in recognition of their eight-match winning streak. Blackpool repaid the Shakers by winning 3–2.

Match No.	Date		Venue	Opponents	Result		Scorers	Attendance
1	Aug	29	A	Leicester City	W	2-1	Finan 2	14,417
2		31	H	Tottenham Hotspur	D	0-0		23,875
3	Sep	5	H	West Ham Utd	W	1-0	Finan	20,671
4		12	A	Norwich City	W	2-1	Farrow, Cook	22,631
5		14	H	Bury	L	1-2	Hampson	17,933
6		19	H	Newcastle Utd	W	3-0	Hampson 2, Finan	26,962
7		21	A	Tottenham Hotspur	W	2-1	Watmough, Hampson	16,308
8		26	A	Bradford City	L	1-2	Finan	11,256
9	Oct	3	H	Barnsley	D	1-1	Finan	22,839
10		10	A	Sheffield Utd	D	2-2	Finan,Watmough	22,399
11		17	H	Burnley	W	2-0	Finan, Watmough	22,529
12		24	A	Southampton	L	2-5	Hampson 2	16,779
13		31	H	Swansea T	W	3-2	Watmough 2, Hampson	12,719
14	Nov	7	A	Bradford City	W	4-1	Jones T, Watmough, Finan 2	12,036
15		14	H	Aston Villa	L	2-3	Hampson, Finan	15,694
16		21	A	Chesterfield	W	4-0	Hampson, Finan 2, Farrow	15,116
17		28	H	Nottm Forest	W	7-1	Finan 2, Jones T 4, Watmough	12,294
18	Dec	5	A	Plymouth Argyle	W	3-1	Hill, Watmough 2	24,737
19		12	H	Coventry City	W	3-0	Jones T, Hill, Own-goal	12,271
20		19	A	Doncaster Rovers	W	4-0	Hill, Jones T, Finan 2	13,435
21		25	A	Fulham	W	3-0	Finan, Hampson, Jones T	22,855
22		26	H	Leicester City	W	6-2	Finan 2, Hill, Farrow (pen), Watmough, Jones T	30,759
23		28	H	Fulham	W	3-1	Jones T, Hampson, Hill	13,186
24	Jan	1	A	Bury	W	3-2	Hill, Finan, Hampson	34,386
25		2	A	West Ham Utd	L	0-3		26,229
26		9	H	Norwich City	L	0-2		12,999
27		23	A	Newcastle Utd	W	2-1	Hill 2	34,122
28		30	H	Bradford City	W	6-0	Own-goal, Finan, Jones T 2, Hampson 2	8,923
29	Feb	6	A	Barnsley	L	1-2	Finan	14,013
30		15	H	Sheffield Utd	W	1-0	Finan	14,321
31		24	A	Burnley	L	0-3		9,053
32		27	H	Southampton	W	2-0	Finan, Watmough	11,058
33	Mar	6	A	Swansea T	D	1-1	Munro	13,686
34		13	H	Bradford City	W	4-2	Hampson, Farrow (pen), Finan, Watmough	12,857
35		20	A	Aston Villa	L	0-4		54,860
36		26	H	Blackburn Rovers	W	2-0	Finan, Hampson	29,059
37		27	H	Chesterfield	L	0-1		21,668
38		29	A	Blackburn Rovers	L	0-2		26,977
39	Apr	3	A	Nottm Forest	D	1-1	Watmough	18,674
40		10	H	Plymouth Argyle	D	1-1	Farrow	17,385
41		17	A	Coventry City	W	2-1	Munro, Finan	16,719
42		24	H	Doncaster Rovers	D	1-1	Bowl	16,333

Final League Position: 2nd in Division Two

Apps

Gls

FA Cup

3	Jan	16	A	Luton Town	D	3-3	Finan, Middleton, Watmough	13,000
3R		20	H	Luton Town	L	1-2	Finan	16,700

Apps

Gls

Wallace	Blair	Witham	Hill	Cardwell	Jones S	Watmough	Hampson	Finan	Jones T	Cook	Butler	Parr	Farrow	Shipman	Bowl	Roxburgh	Hull	Munro	Lyon
1	2	3	4	5	6	7	8	9	10	11									
1	2	3	4	5	6		8	9	10	11	7								
1	2	3	4	5	6		8	9		11		7	10						
1	2	3	4	5	6		8	9		11		7	10						
1	2	3	4	5	6		8	9		11		7	10						
1	2	3	4	5	6		8	9		11		7	10						
1	2	3	4	5	6	7	8	9		11		7	10						
1	2	3	4	5	6	7	8	9		11		7	10						
1	2	3	4	5	6	7	8	9	10	11									
1	2	3	4	5	6	7	8	9	10	11									
1	2	3	4	5	6	7	8	9	10	11									
1	2	3	4	5	6	7	8	9	10	11									
1	2	3	4	5	6	7	8	9	10	11									
1	2		4	5	6	7	8	9	10	11				3					
1	2		4	5	6	7	8	9	10	11				3					
1	2	3	11	5	6	7	8	9	10				4						
1	2	3	11	5	6	7	8	9	10				4						
1	2	3	11	5	6	7	8		10				4		9				
	2	3	11	5	6	7	8	9	10				4			1			
	2	3	11	5	6	7	8	9	10				4			1			
	2	3	11	5		7	8	9	10				4			1	6		
	2	3	11	5		7	8	9	10				4			1	6		
	2	3	11	5			8	9	10	7			4			1	6		
	2	3	11	5	6		8	9	10	7			4			1			
	2	3	11	5	6		8	9	10	7			4			1			
	2	3	11	5			8	9	10	7			4			1	6		
1	2	3	11	5		7	8	9	10				4				6		
1	2	3	11	5		7	8	9	10				4				6		
1	2	3	11	5		7	8	9	10				4				6		
1	2	3	11	5	6	7	8	9	10				4						
1	2	3	11	5	6	7	8	9	10				4						
1	2	3	11	5	6	7	8	9	10				4						
1	2	3	11	5	6	7	8	9					4					10	
1	2	3	11	5	6	7	8	9					4					10	
1	2	3	11	5	6	7	8	9					4					10	
1	2	3	11	5	6	7	8	9					4					10	
1	2	3	11	5	6	7	8	9					4					10	
1	2	3	11	5			8	9					4				6	7	10
1	2	3	11	5	6	7	8	9					4						10
1	2	3	11	5	6	7	8	9					4						10
1	2	3	11	5	6		8	9					4					7	10
1	2	3	11	5	6	7	8	9					4		10				
34	42	40	42	42	34	31	42	41	26	19	1	4	33	2	2	8	8	7	4
			8			13	16	28	12	1			5		1			2	

Wallace	Blair	Witham	Hill	Cardwell	Jones S	Watmough	Hampson	Finan	Jones T	Cook	Butler	Parr	Farrow	Shipman	Bowl	Roxburgh	Hull	Munro	Lyon
1	2	3	11	5		7		9	10				4				6		
1	2	3	11	5		7		9	10				4				6		
2	2	2	2	2		2		2	2				2				2		
						1		2											

League Table

	P	W	D	L	F	A	Pts
Leicester City	42	24	8	10	89	57	56
Blackpool	42	24	7	11	88	53	55
Bury	42	22	8	12	74	55	52
Newcastle United	42	22	5	15	80	56	49
Plymouth Argyle	42	18	13	11	71	53	49
West Ham United	42	19	11	12	73	55	49
Sheffield United	42	18	10	14	66	54	46
Coventry City	42	17	11	14	66	54	45
Aston Villa	42	16	12	14	82	70	44
Tottenham Hotspur	42	17	9	16	88	66	43
Fulham	42	15	13	14	71	61	43
Blackburn Rovers	42	16	10	16	70	62	42
Burnley	42	16	10	16	57	61	42
Barnsley	42	16	9	17	50	64	41
Chesterfield	42	16	8	18	84	89	40
Swansea Town	42	15	7	20	50	65	37
Norwich City	42	14	8	20	63	71	36
Nottingham Forest	42	12	10	20	68	90	34
Southampton	42	11	12	19	53	77	34
Bradford Park Avenue	42	12	9	21	52	88	33
Bradford City	42	9	12	21	54	94	30
Doncaster Rovers	42	7	10	25	30	84	24

1937-38

Division One

Manager: Joe Smith

Did you know that?

The great Jimmy Hampson lost his life on 10 January when his fishing boat collided with a trawler and it sank. His body was never recovered and the whole town mourned. He scored over 250 goals for Blackpool, and a player of his stature is unlikely to be seen again.

Blackpool paid high transfer fees for Frank O'Donnell and Willie Buchan. They both came from Celtic and both cost £10,000.

For the first time in their history, every Blackpool game, both in the League and FA Cup, was played in front of a five-figure attendance.

Match No.	Date	Venue	Opponents	Result		Scorers	Attendance
1	Aug 28	A	Huddersfield Town	L	1-3	Hampson	17,768
2	30	H	Bolton Wanderers	D	2-2	Farrow, Finan	24,939
3	Sep 4	H	Everton	W	1-0	Finan	27,423
4	6	A	Bolton Wanderers	L	0-3		23,606
5	11	A	Wolves	L	0-1		30,820
6	16	A	Brentford	W	4-2	Blair JA 2, Munro, Cardwell	14,816
7	18	H	Leicester City	L	2-4	Hampson, Blair JA	31,443
8	20	H	Brentford	D	1-1	Own-goal	20,732
9	25	A	Sunderland	L	1-2	Own-goal	31,356
10	Oct 2	H	Derby County	D	1-1	Hall	29,662
11	9	A	Manchester City	L	1-2	Watmough	38,846
12	16	H	Chelsea	L	0-2		23,974
13	23	A	Portsmouth	W	2-1	Blair JA, Watmough	11,976
14	30	H	Stoke City	L	0-1		15,119
15	Nov 6	A	Leeds United	D	1-1	Hampson	18,438
16	13	H	Birmingham City	L	0-3		13,975
17	20	A	Preston NE	L	0-2		30,815
18	27	H	Liverpool	L	0-1		14,617
19	Dec 4	A	Middlesbrough	D	2-2	Buchan 2	17,970
20	11	H	Grimsby Town	D	2-2	Finan, Hampson	12,880
21	18	A	West Brom Albion	W	2-1	O'Donnell, Buchan	18,129
22	25	H	Arsenal	W	2-1	Farrow (pen), Buchan	23,229
23	27	A	Arsenal	L	1-2	Finan	54,163
24	Jan 1	H	Huddersfield Town	W	4-0	Munro, O'Donnell 2, Farrow	22,362
25	15	A	Everton	L	1-3	Buchan	22,219
26	26	H	Wolves	L	0-2		13,216
27	29	A	Leicester City	W	1-0	Finan	13,873
28	Feb 5	H	Sunderland	D	0-0		16,682
29	12	A	Derby County	L	1-3	Jones T	12,646
30	19	H	Manchester City	W	2-1	Munro, O'Donnell	19,764
31	26	A	Chelsea	W	3-1	Munro, Finan, O'Donnell	27,301
32	Mar 5	H	Portsmouth	W	2-0	Buchan, O'Donnell	19,407
33	12	A	Stoke City	W	3-1	Finan, Farrow, Buchan	24,961
34	19	H	Leeds United	W	5-2	Own-goal, Finan 2, Farrow, O'Donnell	18,029
35	26	A	Birmingham City	D	1-1	Jones T	19,902
36	Apr 2	H	Preston NE	W	1-0	O'Donnell	26,112
37	9	A	Liverpool	L	2-4	Finan, Buchan	31,475
38	15	H	Charlton Athletic	W	1-0	Buchan	29,961
39	16	H	Middlesbrough	W	4-2	Buchan, O'Donnell, Finan 2	29,822
40	18	A	Charlton Athletic	L	1-4	Buchan	25,602
41	23	A	Grimsby Town	L	0-1		10,042
42	30	H	West Brom Albion	W	3-1	Buchan, O'Donnell, Johnstone	13,506

Final League Position: 12th in Division One

Apps
Gls

FA Cup

3	Jan 8	A	Birmingham City	W	1-0	Jones T	40,000
4	22	A	Aston Villa	L	0-4		69,633

Apps
Gls

Wallace	Blair D	Witham	Farrow	Cardwell	Jones S	Munro	Hampson	Finan	Jones T	McIntosh	Lyon	Hill	Blair JA	Watson	Hall	Watmough	Butcher	Butler	Johnston
1	2	3	4	5	6	7	8	9	10	11									
1	2	3	4	5	6	7	8	9			10	11							
1	2	3	4	5	6	7	8	9				11	10						
1	2	3	4		6	7	8	9				11	10	5					
1	2	3	8	5	6	11		9					10		4	7			
1	2			5	6	11	8	9					10		4	7	3		
1	2			5	6	11	8	9					10		4	7	3		
1	2	3		5	6	11	8				9		10		4	7			
1	2	3		5	6	11	8	9					10		4	7			
1	2	3		5	6	11	8	9					10		4	7			
1	2	3		5	6	11	8	9					10		4	7			
1	2	3		5	6	11	8		10						4	7		9	
1	2	3			6	11	8	9					10	5	4	7			
1	2	3			6	11	8	9					10	5	4	7			
1	2	3			6	11	8		10				9	5	4	7			
1	2	3			6	11	8		10				9	5	4	7			
1	2	3	4		5	11		10								7			6
	2	3	4			11		9	10							7			6
	2	3	4			7	10	11											6
	2	3				7	10	11							4				6
	2	3	4			7		11					10						6
	2	3	4			7	9	11					10						6
	2	3	4		6	7		11	10										
	2	3	4		6	7		11	10										
	2		4			7		11					10				3		6
	2	3	4		6	7		11	10									9	
	2		4			7		9	10				11						6
	2		4		6	7		9	10				11						
	2		4		6	7		9	10				11				5		
	2		4			7			10				11						6
	2		4			7		11	10										6
	2		4		6	7		11	10										
	2		4			7		11	10										6
	2		4			7		11	10										6
	2		4			7		11	10										6
	2		4			7		11	10										6
			4			7		9	10				11					2	6
	2		4			7		11	10										6
	2		4			7		11	10										6
	2		4			7		11	10										6
	2		4			7		11	10										6
	2		4		6	7		10											11
17	41	23	30	11	24	42	18	37	23	1	2	3	21	5	13	14	4	3	20
			5	1		4	4	12	2				4		1	2			1

Wallace	Blair D	Witham	Farrow	Cardwell	Jones S	Munro	Hampson	Finan	Jones T	McIntosh	Lyon	Hill	Blair JA	Watson	Hall	Watmough	Butcher	Butler	Johnston
	2	3	4			7	8	11	10										6
	2	3	4			7		11			9		10						6
	2	2	2			2	1	2	1		1		1						2
													1						

League Table

	P	W	D	L	F	A	Pts
Arsenal	42	21	10	11	77	44	52
Wolverhampton W	42	20	11	11	72	49	51
Preston North End	42	16	17	9	64	44	49
Charlton Athletic	42	16	14	12	65	51	46
Middlesbrough	42	19	8	15	72	65	46
Brentford	42	18	9	15	69	59	45
Bolton Wanderers	42	15	15	12	64	60	45
Sunderland	42	14	16	12	55	57	44
Leeds United	42	14	15	13	64	69	43
Chelsea	42	14	13	15	65	65	41
Liverpool	42	15	11	16	65	71	41
Blackpool	42	16	8	18	61	66	40
Derby County	42	15	10	17	66	87	40
Everton	42	16	7	19	79	75	39
Huddersfield Town	42	17	5	20	55	68	39
Leicester City	42	14	11	17	54	75	39
Stoke City	42	13	12	17	58	59	38
Birmingham	42	10	18	14	58	62	38
Portsmouth	42	13	12	17	62	68	38
Grimsby Town	42	13	12	17	51	68	38
Manchester City	42	14	8	20	80	77	36
West Bromwich Albion	42	14	8	20	74	91	36

1938-39

Division One

Manager: Joe Smith

Did you know that?

Blackpool paid £60,000 on new players for the new season – an unprecedented amount for the era.

The team now officially adopted the Tangerine colour. Tangerine shirts, white shorts and blue socks for the start of the season, and that variation has remained essentially unchanged for the next 70 years or so.

They also adopted a new club crest, the first change since 1923.it stayed on the shirts until 1968.

Jock Dodds was bought from Sheffield United and became one of the club's most prolific scorers in the seasons during World War Two.

Match No.	Date	Venue	Opponents	Result		Scorers	Attendance
1	Aug 27	H	Everton	L	0-2		29,647
2	31	A	Portsmouth	L	0-1		24,998
3	Sep 3	A	Wolves	D	1-1	O'Donnell F	24,795
4	10	H	Aston Villa	L	2-4	Buchan 2	29,128
5	17	A	Sunderland	W	2-1	Buchan, Farrow (pen)	26,295
6	19	H	Brentford	W	4-1	O'Donnell F, Buchan 2, Munro	21,970
7	24	H	Grimsby Town	W	3-1	Buchan, Munro, O'Donnell F	27,349
8	31	A	Derby County	L	1-2	Dawson	21,584
9	Oct 8	H	Chelsea	W	5-1	O'Donnell F 3, Buchan 2	24,878
10	15	A	Manchester Utd	D	0-0		39,723
11	22	H	Stoke City	D	1-1	Munro	23,501
12	29	A	Preston NE	D	1-1	O'Donnell F	29,443
13	Nov 5	H	Charlton Athletic	D	0-0		16,135
14	12	A	Bolton Wanderers	W	1-0	Finan	35,782
15	19	H	Leeds United	L	1-2	Finan	16,612
16	26	A	Liverpool	L	0-1		26,752
17	Dec 3	H	Leicester City	D	1-1	Jones	14,255
18	10	A	Middlesbrough	L	2-9	Eastham Munro	17,166
19	17	H	Birmingham City	W	2-1	Finan, Buchan	11,855
20	24	A	Everton	L	0-4		24,040
21	26	H	Huddersfield Town	D	1-1	Eastham	18,955
22	27	A	Huddersfield Town	L	0-3		27,113
23	31	H	Wolves	W	1-0	Finan	16,134
24	Jan 14	A	Aston Villa	L	1-3	Lewis	34,190
25	25	H	Sunderland	D	1-1	Munro	13,273
26	28	A	Grimsby Town	L	0-2		12,126
27	Feb 4	H	Derby County	D	2-2	Jones, Lewis	15,929
28	18	H	Manchester Utd	L	3-5	Astley 2, Buchan	15,253
29	25	A	Stoke City	D	1-1	Astley	22,886
30	Mar 8	H	Preston NE	W	2-1	Astley, Lewis	10,680
31	11	A	Charlton Athletic	L	1-3	Dodds	16,668
32	15	A	Chelsea	D	1-1	Dodds	12,971
33	18	H	Bolton Wanderers	D	0-0		18,896
34	25	A	Leeds United	L	0-1		21,818
35	Apr 1	H	Liverpool	D	1-1	Astley	17,137
36	7	H	Arsenal	W	1-0	Finan	31,497
37	8	A	Leicester City	W	4-3	Dodds 2, Own-goal, Eastham	14,679
38	10	A	Arsenal	L	1-2	O'Donnell H	30,760
39	15	H	Middlesbrough	W	4-0	Dodds 4	13,733
40	22	A	Birmingham City	L	1-2	Dodds	21,812
41	29	A	Brentford	D	1-1	Own-goal	12,761
42	May 6	H	Portsmouth	W	2-1	Dodds, Astley	15,947

Final League Position: 15th in Division One

Apps
Gls

FA Cup

3	Jan 7	H	Sheffield Utd	L	1-2	Lewis	15,000

Apps
Gls

Roxburgh	Blair D	Sibley	Farrow	Hayward	Johnston	Munro	Buchan	O'Donnell F	Finan	Dawson	Blair JA	Wallace	Parr	Hall	Mauchline	Eastham	Ashworth	Jones	Lewis
1	2	3	4	5	6	7	8	9	10	11									
1	2	3	4	5	6	7	8	9	10	11									
1	2	3	4	5	6	7	8	9	10	11									
1	2	3	4	5	6	7	8	9			10								
	2	3	4	5	6	7	8	9	10	11		1							
	2	3	4	5	6	7	8	9	10	11		1							
	2	3	4	5	6	7	8	9	10	11		1							
	2	3	4	5	6	7	8	9	10	11		1							
	2	3	4	5	6	7	8	9	10	11		1							
	2	3	4	5	6	7	8	9	10	11		1							
	2	3	4	5	6	7	8	9	10	11		1							
	2	3	4	5		8	10	9		11		1	7	6					
	2	3	4	5	6	7	8	10	9			1			11				
	2	3	4	5	6	7	8		9			1			11	10			
	2	3	4	5	6	7			9		10	1			11	8			
	2	3	4	5	6	7			9			1			11	8	10		
	2	3	4	5	11	7	8		9			1				10		6	
	2	3	4	5		7	8		9		11	1				10		6	
	2	3	4	5	6	7	8		9			1				10			11
	2	3	4	5	6	7	8		9			1				10			11
	2		4	5	6	7	8					1				10	9		11
	2			5			8					1		4		10	9	6	11
	2		4	5	6	7	8		11			1				10			9
	2		4	5		7	8					1				10		6	9
	2			5	6	7	8		11			1		4		10			
	2			5		7						1		4		10	9	6	11
	2		4	5		7	8					1				10		6	11
	2		4	5		7	8					1				10		6	11
1		2	4	5	6	7					10					8			11
		2	4	5	6	7	8					1				10			11
		2	4	5	6	7	8					1				10			11
	2	3	4	5	6		8					1							
	2	3	4	5	6	7	8					1							
	2		4	5	6	7	8					1							
1	2		4	5	6	7										10			
1	2		4	5	6				7							10			
1	2		4	5	6				7							10			
1		2		5	6		10		7					4					
	2		4	5	6		10		7			1							
	2	3	4	5	6		10		7			1							
	2	3	4		6				7			1				10			
	2	3	4	5	6		10		7			1							
9	38	29	38	41	35	32	34	13	27	12	4	33	1	5	4	22	4	7	12
			1			5	10	7	5	1						3		2	3

Roxburgh	Blair D	Sibley	Farrow	Hayward	Johnston	Munro	Buchan	O'Donnell F	Finan	Dawson	Blair JA	Wallace	Parr	Hall	Mauchline	Eastham	Ashworth	Jones	Lewis
	2		4	5	6	7	8		11			1				10			9
	1		1	1	1	1	1		1			1				1			1
																			1

League Table

	P	W	D	L	F	A	Pts
Everton	42	27	5	10	88	52	59
Wolverhampton W	42	22	11	9	88	39	55
Charlton Athletic	42	22	6	14	75	59	50
Middlesbrough	42	20	9	13	93	74	49
Arsenal	42	19	9	14	55	41	47
Derby County	42	19	8	15	66	55	46
Stoke City	42	17	12	13	71	68	46
Bolton Wanderers	42	15	15	12	67	58	45
Preston North End	42	16	12	14	63	59	44
Grimsby Town	42	16	11	15	61	69	43
Liverpool	42	14	14	14	62	63	42
Aston Villa	42	16	9	17	71	60	41
Leeds United	42	16	9	17	59	67	41
Manchester United	42	11	16	15	57	65	38
Blackpool	42	12	14	16	56	68	38
Sunderland	42	13	12	17	54	67	38
Portsmouth	42	12	13	17	47	70	37
Brentford	42	14	8	20	53	74	36
Huddersfield Town	42	12	11	19	58	64	35
Chelsea	42	12	9	21	64	80	33
Birmingham	42	12	8	22	62	84	32
Leicester City	42	9	11	22	48	82	29

1939-40

Division One

Manager: Joe Smith

Did you know that?

When War broke out and football was suspended, Blackpool sat at the top of the First Division with a 100 per cent winning record from their first three games.

Jock Dodds scored 7 as Blackpool beat Oldham Athletic 11–2 in the North West Regional League.

Blackpool scored an astonishing 73 goals in 22 League games during the season, with Jock Dodds netting 30.

Match No.	Date	Venue	Opponents	Result		Scorers	Attendance
1	Aug 26	A	Huddersfield Town	W	1-0	Finan	15,558
2	28	H	Brentford	W	2-1	Finan, Dodds	21,633
3	Sep 2	H	Wolves	W	2-1	Dodds 2	17,366

Final League Position: 1st in Division One when World War Two broke out — App / Goals

1	Oct 21	A	Blackburn Rovers	D	1-1	Astley	4,000
2	28	H	Bury	W	1-0	Astley	4,500
3	Nov 11	H	Barrow	W	5-4	Dodds 3, Ashworth, Eastham	6,000
4	18	A	Southport	W	3-0	Hayward 2, Dodds	3,000
5	25	A	Accrington Stanley	D	3-3	Dodds 2, Farrow	1,500
6	Dec 2	A	Bolton Wanderers	L	1-3	Lewis	2,777
7	9	H	Preston NE	W	3-0	Dodds (pen), Farrow, Astley	11,000
8	25	A	Burnley	D	1-1	Dodds	2,668
9	Jan 6	H	Carlisle United	D	2-2	Eastham, Ashworth	5,000
10	Feb 10	H	Blackburn Rovers	W	3-2	Astley 2, Lewis	4,800
11	24	A	Bury	W	2-1	Dodds 2	3,000
12	Mar 9	A	Barrow	W	4-1	Own-goal, Munro, Astley	3,202
13	16	H	Southport	W	3-1	Finan, Eastham, Astley	5,000
14	23	A	Accrington Stanley	W	8-1	Dodds 3, Buchan 4, Farrow	7,000
15	30	H	Bolton Wanderers	W	3-1	O'Donnell 2, Dodds	6,000
16	Apr 6	A	Preston NE	D	1-1	Dodds	4,000
17	13	H	Burnley	W	5-0	Dodds 2, Eastham 2, Ashworth	5,000
18	24	H	Rochdale	W	7-2	Dodds 3, Finan 2, Blair, Hayward	
19	May 13	H	Oldham Athletic	W	11-2	Dodds 7, Astley 3, Finan	3,500
20	28	A	Rochdale	D	3-3	Finan,Dodds, Munro	
21	Jun 1	A	Carlisle United	L	1-3	Finan	
22	7	A	Oldham Athletic	L	2-4	Dodds 2	1,835

Final League Position: 3rd in North West Regional League — Apps / Gls

League War Cup

1	Apr 20	H	Southport	W	4-0	Dodds 3, Astley	6,388
	27	A	Southport	W	5-2	Own-goal 2, Dodds, Eastham, Astley	2,300
2	May 4	A	Burnley	W	2-1	Dodds, Finan	7,857
	11	H	Burnley	W	3-1	Dodds 2, Munro	7,631
3	18	A	Barnsley	W	1-0	Dodds	10,796
QF	25	H	Newcastle United	L	0-2		7,809

Apps
Gls

Wallace	Sibley	Butler	Farrow	Hayward	Johnston	Finan	Astley	Dodds	Buchan	O'Donnell F	Roxburgh	Jones S	Eastham	Munro	Ashworth	Blair	Lewis	Ainsley	O'Donnell H
1	2	3	4	5	6	7	8	9	10	11									
1	2	3	4	5	6	7	8	9	10	11									
1	2	3	4	5	6	7	8	9	10	11									
3	3	3	3	3	3	3	3	3	3	3									
						2		4											

Wallace	Sibley	Butler	Farrow	Hayward	Johnston	Finan	Astley	Dodds	Buchan	O'Donnell F	Roxburgh	Jones S	Eastham	Munro	Ashworth	Blair	Lewis	Ainsley	O'Donnell H
	2		4	5	6	7	8	9			1	3	10	11					
	2		4	5	6	7	8	9			1	3	10	11					
	2		4	5	6	7		9			1	3	8	11	10				
	2		4	5	6	7		9			1	3	8	11		10			
	2		4	5	6	7	8	9			1	3		11		10			
	2		4	5	6						1	3	8	7	9	10	11		
	2		4	5	6	7	8	9	10		1	3		11					
	2		4	5	6	7		9		11	1	3	8			10			
	2		4	5	6	7					1	3	8	10	9		11		
	2		4	5	6		7				1	3		10	9		11	8	
	2		4	5	6	7		9			1	3	10	11				8	
	2		4	5	6	7	9				1	3	10	11				8	
	2		4	5	6	7		9			1	3	10	11				8	
	2		4	5	6	7		9	10		1	3		11				8	
	2		4	5	6	7		9			1	3	8	10					11
	2		4	5	6	7	8	9	10		1	3		11					
	2		4	5		7		9			1	3	8	11	10			6	
	2		4	5		7		9			1	3	8	11	10	6			
	2		4	5	6	7	8	9			1	3	10	11					
	2		4			7		9	8		1	3	10	11				6	
	2		4			7		9			1	3	10	11		6	8		
	2		4			7		9			1	3	10	11		6	8		
	22		22	19	17	20	8	18	3	1	22	22	18	21	5	8	1	9	3
			3	3		6	6	30	4	2			5	3	3	1	2	4	

Wallace	Sibley	Butler	Farrow	Hayward	Johnston	Finan	Astley	Dodds	Buchan	O'Donnell F	Roxburgh	Jones S	Eastham	Munro	Ashworth	Blair	Lewis	Ainsley	O'Donnell H
	2		4	5		7	8	9			1	3	10	11		6			
	2		4		5	7	8	9			1	3	10	11		6			
	2		4		5	7	8	9			1	3	10	11		6			
	2		4		5	7	8	9			1	3	10	11		6			
	2		4		5	7	8	9			1	3	10	11		6			
	2		4		5	7	8	9	10		1	3	1	11		6			
	6		6	1	5	6	6	6	1		6	6	5	6		6			
						1	2	8					1	1					

1940-41

North Regional League

Manager: Joe Smith

Did you know that?

Jock Dodds scored another amazing 26 goals from just 22 games.

Wartime travel restrictions meant for lower attendances, yet Blackpool still attracted respectable 'gates' helped by many guest players for the club.

Match No.	Date		Venue	Opponents	Result		Scorers	Attendance
1	Jan	4	H	Bury	W	3-2	Buchan 2, Dodds	6,000
2		11	A	Bury	W	2-1	Buchan, O'Donnell	3,960
3		18	A	Manchester City	W	4-2	Buchan, Dodds, Johnston, Burbanks	1,000
4		25	H	Manchester City	W	2-1	Dodds 2	12,000
5	Feb	1	A	Stockport County	W	2-1	Dodds, Deverall	
6		8	H	Stockport County	W	9-2	Dodds 8, Deverall	
7	Mar	1	H	Chester City	W	5-2	Dodds 2, Boulton 2, Deverall	5,000
8		8	A	Chester City	L	3-4	Dodds, Burbanks, Buchan	2,000
9		15	H	Liverpool	W	6-4	Russell, Burbanks, Buchan, Dodds 3	7,000
10		22	A	Liverpool	W	6-2	Jones C 3, Buchan 2, Dodds	3,000
11		29	H	Manchester Utd	W	2-0	Dodds 2	4,000
12	Apr	5	A	Manchester Utd	W	3-2	Trigg, Johnston, Burbanks	2,000
13		12	H	Liverpool	D	0-0		4,000
14		14	A	Everton	D	2-2	Trigg 2	
15		19	H	Oldham Athletic	W	6-2	Trigg 3, Buchan, Jones C 2	4,000
16		26	A	Manchester City	L	0-2		4,000
17	May	3	H	Manchester City	D	1-1	Jones C	6,000
18		10	A	Burnley	L	0-1		7,000
19		17	A	Preston NE	L	0-2		4,000
20		24	H	Burnley	W	3-0	Jones C, Pope (pen), Murphy	2,000
21		31	H	Chester City	W	4-2	Dodds 3, Jones C	4,000
22	Jun	22	H	Preston NE	W	4-2	Dodds, Murphy, Stevenson, Jones C	9,800

Final League Position: 6th in North Regional League

Apps

Gls

League War Cup

1	Feb	15	H	Manchester City	L	1-4	Dodds	15,000
		22	A	Manchester City	W	1-0	Dodds	8,967

Apps

Gls

Strong	Pope	Jones S	Russell	Whittaker	Johnston	Finan	Astley	Dodds	Buchan	Burbanks	Deverall	O'Donnell	Lowe	Russell	Hughes	Pugh	Jones P	Boulton	McFadyen	Jones C	Trigg	Powell	Fidden	Ottewell	Murphy	Stevenson	Johnson
1	2	3	4	5	6	7	8	9	10	11																	
1	2	3	4	5	6			9	8	7	10	11															
1	2	3		5	6			9	8	7	10	11	4														
1	2	3		5	6			9	8	7	10	11		4													
1	2	3		5	6			9	8	7	10	11		4													
1	2	3		5	6			9	8	7	10	11		4													
1		3		5	6			9	8		11				2	4	7	10									
1	2	3	4	5	6			9	8	11							7	10									
1		3	4	5	7			9	8	11					2	6			10								
1		3	4	5	7			9	8	11					2	6				10							
1		3	4	5	6			9	8	11					2		7		10								
1		3	4	5	6				8	11					2		7		10		9						
1			4		6				8	11	10		5		3		7			9	2						
1	2	3	4	5	6				8	11	10						7				9						
1	2		4	5	6				8	11					3		7			10	9						
1	2		4	5	6				8	11					3		7			10	9						
1		3	4	5	6					11					2		7	8		10	9						
1	2		4	5	6				8	11					3		7			10	9						
1	2		4	5	10					11					3						9	6	7	8			
1	2	3	4	5	10					11										9		6	7		8		
1	2	3	4	5	6			9	8	11			7							10							
1	2	3	4	5	6			9					7							11					8	10	
22	15	17	17	21	22	1	1	13	18	20	8	5	4	3	11	3	10	3	3	9	8	2	2	1	2	1	
	1		1		2			26	7	6	3	1						2		9	6				2	1	

Strong	Pope	Jones S	Russell	Whittaker	Johnston	Finan	Astley	Dodds	Buchan	Burbanks	Deverall	O'Donnell	Lowe	Russell	Hughes	Pugh	Jones P	Boulton	McFadyen	Jones C	Trigg	Powell	Fidden	Ottewell	Murphy	Stevenson	Johnson
1	2	3	4	5	6			9	8	11	10																
1	2	3	4	5	6			9	8	11			10					10		7							
2	2	2	2	2	2			2	2	2	1							1		1							
								2																			

1941-42

Northern Section

Manager: Joe Smith

Did you know that?

Blackpool won the Lancashire Cup, beating Blackburn Rovers 7–1 in the Final.

They also won the Northern Section First Competition.

Jock Dodds scored another 65 goals in all competitions, including seven in a 15–3 win over Tranmere Rovers.

Blackpool scored 28 goals in two matches, with a 15–3 win over Tranmere followed by a 13–0 win over Burnley a week later. Jock Dodds scored 12.

Blackpool were drawn away to Manchester City on 6 April in the League War Cup, but due to travel restrictions, could not fulfil the fixture.

Match No.	Date	Venue	Opponents	Result		Scorers	Attendance
1	Aug 30	A	Preston NE	L	1-3	Dodds	12,000
2	Sep 6	H	Preston NE	W	2-0	Dodds, Burbanks	20,000
3	13	H	Southport	W	10-1	Dodds 3, Farrow, Jones c 2, Whittaker 2, Own-goals 2	7,000
4	20	A	Southport	W	5-1	Dodds 2, Matthews, Dix, Jones C	3,000
5	27	A	Bury	W	5-0	Johnston, Dodds, Dix 2, Jones C	4,137
6	Oct 4	H	Bury	W	4-2	Pope, Jones C, Dodds, Burbanks	6,000
7	11	A	Bolton Wanderers	W	6-2	Buchan 2, Dodds 3, Finan	5,203
8	18	H	Bolton Wanderers	W	2-1	Dix, Johnston	3,000
9	25	A	Blackburn Rovers	L	1-2	Dodds	7,000
10	Nov 1	H	Blackburn Rovers	W	4-1	Dodds 3, Jones C	6,000
11	8	H	Halifax Town	W	9-1	Jones C 2, Dodds 4, Dix 2, Farrow	4,000
12	15	A	Halifax Town	W	2-1	Dodds 2	10,000
13	22	H	Oldham Athletic	W	5-1	Finan, Burbanks, Jones C 3	6,000
14	29	A	Oldham Athletic	W	3-0	Dodds 2, Dix	6,805
15	Dec 6	A	Burnley	D	2-2	Dodds 2	2,873
16	13	H	Burnley	W	9-0	Dix 2, Finan 3, Jones C 3, Burbanks	4,000
17	20	A	Rochdale	W	5-0	Dodds 2, Buchan 2, Own-goal	1,000
18	25	H	Rochdale	L	0-1		10,000

Final League Position: 1st in Northern Section - First Competition

App
Goals

19	Dec 27	H	Stockport County	W	5-2	Dodds 2, Jones C 2, Dix	6,000
20	Jan 3	A	Stockport County	L	1-2	Dix	2,000
21	10	H	Wolves	W	6-1	Matthews, Mortensen, Dodds 2, Dix, Burbanks	6,026
22	17	A	Wolves	L	0-1		4,972
23	24	A	Huddersfield Town	D	3-3	Jones C, Burbanks, Mortensen	4,375
24	31	H	Huddersfield Town	W	4-2	Mortensen, Dodds 2, Dix	6,000
25	Feb 7	H	Liverpool	W	6-2	Dix 2, Dodds 3, Jones C	10,000
26	14	A	Liverpool	W	3-1	Jones C, Dix, Dodds	14,295
27	21	A	Tranmere Rovers	D	2-2	Dodds, Cuthbertson	2,000
28	28	H	Tranmere Rovers	W	15-3	Dodds 7, Jones C 3, Dix 4, Burbanks	3,000
29	Mar 7	H	Burnley	W	13-0	Dodds 5, Mortensen 4, Jones C 2, Burbanks 2	4,000
30	14	A	Everton	D	2-2	Dodds, Dix	12,000
31	21	A	Burnley	W	6-0	Jones C, Dodds 2, Dix 3	5,091
32	28	H	Stoke City	W	4-0	Dodds 3, O'Donnell	4,000
33	Apr 11	H	Bolton Wanderers	W	7-1	Dix 3, Dodds 3, O'Donnell	4,000
34	18	A	Bolton Wanderers	L	1-2	Dix	3,760
35	25	A	Rochdale	L	0-2		3,000
36	May 2	H	Rochdale	W	5-1	Farrow 2, Lewis, Finan, Mortensen	4,000
37	9	A	Oldham Athletic	W	8-2	Jones C 5, Mortensen, 2, Farrow (pen)	1,850
38	16	H	Oldham Athletic	D	2-2	Dix, Jones C	4,000
39	25	H	Liverpool	W	8-2	Finan 2, Mortensen 2, Dix 2, McEwan 2	4,000
40	30	H	Blackburn Rovers	W	7-1	Dodds 5, Dix, Mortensen	10,000

Final League Position: 2nd in Northern Section - Second Competition

Apps
Gls

Matches 19-28 in the Football League War Cup qualifying section

Blackpool drawn away to Manchester City on 6 April in Football League War Cup first round proper, but could not fulfill fixture due to traveling ban

Matches 34-36 in Lancashire Cup

Match 40 - Lancashire Cup Final - Blackpool given bye in semi-final by Everton

Roxburgh	Pope	Jones S	Powell	Whittaker	Johnston	Matthews	Dix	Dodds	Stevenson	Burbanks	Farrow	Buchan	Jones C	Suart	Finan	O'Donnell	Strong	Mortensen	Savage	Barker
1	2	3	4	5	6	7	8	9	10	11										
1	2	3		5	6	7	8	9	10	11	4									
1	2	3	4	5	6	7		9		11		8	10							
1	2	3		5	6	7	8	9		11	4		10							
1	2	3	4		6	7	8	9		11			10	5						
1	2	3			6		8	9		11	4		10	5	7					
1	2	3			6		8	9		11	4	10		5	7					
1	2	3			6		8				4		9	5	7	11				
1	2	3			6		8	9		11	4		10	5	7					
1	2	3			6	7	8	9		11	4		10	5						
1	2	3			6	7	8	9		11	4		10	5						
	2	3			6	7	8	9		11	4		10	5			1			
	2	3			6		7			11	4		9	5	10			8	1	
	2	3			6	7	8	9		11	4		10	5					1	
	2	3	4	5		7		9		11			10		8				1	6
	2	3	4	5		7	8			11			10		9				1	6
	2	3	4	5		7	8	9		11			10						1	6
	2	3	4	5	6	7		9		11			10						1	6
11	18	18	7	8	16	13	15	13	2	17	11	2	15	10	7	1	1	1	6	4
	1			2	2	1	9	28		6	2	2	14		5					

Savage	Pope	Jones S	Powell	Suart	Johnston	Matthews	Dix	Dodds	Jones C	Burbanks	Barker	Ansell	Farrow	Mortensen	Finan	Whittaker	Roxburgh	McEwan	Cuthbertson	Farrow	O'Donnell	Williams	Hayward	Lewis	Dykes	McEwan
1	2	3	4	5	6	7	8	9	10	11																
1	2	3	4	5	6	7	8	9	10	11																
1				5	6	7	10	9		11	2	3	4	8												
1	2	3			6		8	9	10	11	4		5		7											
1	2	3	4		6	7		9	10	11				8		5										
1	2	3	4		6	7	10	9		11				8		5										
1	2		4		6	7	8	9	10	11	3					5										
	2		4	5	6	7	8	9	10	11	3						1									
	2	3	6	5				9		11				10		4	1	7	8							
	2			5	6	7	8	9	10	11	3						1			4						
	2			5	6	7		9	10	11	3			8		4	1									
1	2		4		6	7	8	9	10	11	3					5										
	2				6	7	8	9	10		3		4			5	1				11					
	2		4		6	7		9						8	10	5	1				11	3				
1	2	3			6	7	8	9	10				4								11		5			
1	2	3	4		6		10		7						9					8	11		5			
1	2	3			6	7	8	9					4		10						11		5			
	2				6				9		3		4	8	7		1				10		5	11		
	2				6		10		9		3		4	8	7		1						5	11		
	2				6		10		9		3		4	8	7		1						5	11		
	2				6	7	10				3		4	8	9		1								5	11
	2				6	7	10	9		11	3		4	8			1								5	
11	21	9	10	7	21	16	17	17	15	13	13	1	10	11	8	8	11	1	1	2	6	1	6	3	2	1
						1	23	37	17	5			3	13	3			2	1		2			1		

1942-43

Northern Section

Manager: Joe Smith

Did you know that?

Arsenal were reported to have had a photo taken with the League War Cup before the Final with Blackpool. They were beaten by the Seasiders 4–2 at Stamford Bridge, and the Cup was never handed over.

The likes of Stanley Matthews and Stan Mortensen were becoming regular guest players for Blackpool this season.

Jock Dodds continued to score at will. He netted another 47 this season.

Blackpool were again the Northern Section First Competition champions.

Match No.	Date	Venue	Opponents	Result		Scorers	Attendance
1	Aug 29	A	Manchester City	W	3-1	Matthews, Mortensen, Dix	6,000
2	Sep 5	H	Manchester City	W	5-2	Dodds 3, Dix, Mortensen	5,000
3	12	H	Bury	W	9-1	O'Donnell 2, Finan 2, Dodds 4, Burbanks	
4	19	A	Bury	W	11-1	Dix 5, Dodds 4, Finan 2	4,500
5	26	A	Stockport County	W	6-0	Finan, Farrow, Burbanks, Johnston, Dix, Withington	3,000
6	Oct 3	H	Stockport County	W	6-2	Dodds 3, Finan 2, Johnston	7,000
7	10	H	Bolton Wanderers	W	2-0	Burbanks, Finan	6,000
8	17	A	Bolton Wanderers	W	2-0	Dodds 2	4,982
9	24	A	Rochdale	W	4-3	Dodds, Burbanks 2, Finan	1,500
10	31	H	Rochdale	W	5-0	Finan 2, Dodds, Dix 2	6,000
11	Nov 7	H	Southport	W	6-2	Dix 3, Dodds, Burbanks, Farrow	10,000
12	14	A	Southport	L	2-3	Dodds, Burbanks	6,000
13	21	A	Burnley	D	4-4	Finan 3, Burbanks	5,054
14	28	H	Burnley	W	5-1	Dodds 3, Farrow 2	5,000
15	Dec 5	H	Oldham Athletic	W	8-3	Mortensen 2, Johnston 3, Burbanks, Colquhoun, Finan	3,500
16	12	A	Oldham Athletic	W	4-1	Buchan 2, Burbanks, Finan	5,000
17	19	A	Blackburn Rovers	W	4-2	Dodds 4	3,000
18	25	H	Blackburn Rovers	W	7-2	Dodds 2, Finan 2, Dix 2, Shields	4,000

Final League Position: 1st in Northern Section - First Competition

App

Goals

19	Dec 26	H	Southport	D	1-1	Finan	15,000
20	Jan 2	A	Southport	W	3-2	Farrow, Finan 2	4,000
21	9	H	Manchester Utd	D	1-1	Finan	5,000
22	16	A	Manchester Utd	L	3-5	Dix, Dodds 2	17,381
23	23	A	Blackburn Rovers	D	3-3	Dodds 2, Dix	6,724
24	30	H	Blackburn Rovers	W	4-2	Dodds 2, Dix 2	5,000
25	Feb 6	H	Oldham Athletic	W	4-0	Burbanks, Dix 2, Dodds	6,000
26	13	A	Oldham Athletic	D	1-1	Dix (pen)	4,304
27	20	A	Bolton Wanderers	D	1-1	Matthews S	9,000
28	27	H	Bolton Wanderers	W	5-0	Dodds 2, Jones C 2, Dix (pen)	5,000
29	Mar 6	H	Everton	W	4-1	Dodds 2, Dix (pen), Gardner	15,173
30	13	A	Everton	L	3-4	Dodds 2, Burbanks	35,000
31	20	A	Liverpool	L	1-3	Dix (pen)	40,000
32	27	H	Liverpool	W	5-0	Dodds 2, Finan 2, Dix (pen)	25,000
33	Apr 3	H	Manchester City	W	3-1	Dix 2, Own-goal	25,000
34	10	A	Manchester City	D	1-1	Dodds	53,205
35	17	H	Aston Villa	W	3-1	Farrow, Finan, Dix	28,000
36	24	A	Aston Villa	L	1-2	Gardner	50,000
37	May 1	H	Sheffield Wednesday	D	2-2	Finan, Burbanks	28,000
38	8	A	Sheffield Wednesday	W	2-1	Dodds, Gardner	47,657
39	15	N	Arsenal	W	4-2	Dix, Burbanks, Dodds, Finan	55,195

Final League Position: 13th in Northern Section - Second Competition

Apps

Gls

Matches 19-26 were Football League War Cup qualifying competition

Matches 27-38 were Football League War Cup knock out competition from first round to final

Match 39 was Challenge Cup Final played at Stamford Bridge, Chelsea

Roxburgh	Pope	Williams	Farrow	Jones S	Hayward	Matthews	Mortensen	Withington	Dix	Burbanks	Johnston	Dodds	Powell	O'Donnell	Finan	McEwan	Jones C	Horton	Shields	Barker	Shaw	Colquhoun	Buchan
1	2	3	4	5	6	7	8	9	10	11													
1	2	3	4		5	7	8		10	11	6	9											
1	2	3			5	7				11	6	9	4	8	10								
1	2	3	4		5	7			8	11	6	9			10								
1	2	3	4		5			7	10	11	6			8	9								
1	2	3	4		5	7			8		6	9		11	10								
1	2	3	4		5				8	11	6			10	9	7							
1	2	3	4		5	7			8	11	6	9			10								
1	2	3	4		5				8	11	6	9			10		7						
1	2	3	4		5	7			8	11	6	9			10								
1	2	3	4		5	7			8	11	6	9			10								
1		3	4		5	7			8	11	6	9			10			2					
1	2	3	4		5				8	11	10		6		9				7				
1		3	8		5	7				11	6	9	4		10					2			
1					5		8		10	11	6		4		9					2	3	7	
1		2			5					11			6		9	10				4	3	7	8
1	2	3	5		6	7			8	11		9			10						4		
1	2	3	4	5		7			8			9	6		10				11				
18	14	17	15	2	17	12	3	2	15	16	14	12	6	4	16	2	1	1	2	3	3	2	1
			4			1	4	1	15	10	5	29		2	18				1			1	2

Roxburgh	Pope	Williams	Farrow	Jones S	Powell	Matthews R	Dix	Dodds	Finan	Shields	Burbanks	Savage	Hayward	Johnston	Matthews S	Barker	Buchan	Jones C	Atkinson	Gardner	Hubbick
1	2	3	4	5	6	7	8	9	10	11											
1	2	3	4	5	6		8	9	7	11	10										
1	2	3	4	5	6		8	9	7	11	10										
	2	3	4				10	9	7	8	11	1	5	6							
1	2	3	4				8	9	10		11		5	6	7						
1		3	4				10	9	8		11		5	6	7	2					
1		3			4		8	9	10		11		5	6	7	2					
1				3	4		8	9	10		11		5	6	7	2					
1	2			3	4			9	10		11		5	6	7		8				
1	2		4	3			8	9	7		11		5	6				10			
	2		4	3			8	9	10		11	1		6					5	7	
1	2		4	3			8	9			11			6	7			10	5		
1		3	4		2		8	9	10		11			6					5	7	
1	2		4	3			8	9	10		11		5	6	7						
1	2		4	3			8	9	10		11		5	6	7						
	2		4	3	6		8	9	10		11	1		5	7						
	2		4	3	6		8		9		11	1		10					5	7	
	2		4	3			8	9	10		11	1	5	6						7	
	2		4	3	6		8	9	10		11	1		5	7						
	2		4				8	9	10		11	1	5	6						7	3
	2		4				8	9	10		11	1	5	6	7						3
13	17	8	18	14	10	1	20	20	20	4	20	8	12	18	11	3	11	2	4	5	2
			2				15	18	9		4				1			2		3	

1943-44

Northern Section

Manager: Joe Smith

Did you know that?

A third successive title in the Northern Section First Competition.

They were beaten by Aston Villa in the final of the League War Cup Northern section over two legs.

Stan Mortensen topped the goal scoring charts for the first time since joining Blackpool.

Match No.	Date	Venue	Opponents	Result		Scorers	Attendance
1	Aug 28	H	Rochdale	W	6-1	Finan 2, Beattie 2, McEwan, Farrow	5,000
2	Sep 4	A	Rochdale	W	6-2	Beattie 3, Farrow 2 (1 pen), McEwan	3,500
3	11	H	Manchester City	W	6-2	O'Donnell F 2, Finan 2, McEwan 2	10,000
4	18	A	Manchester City	W	2-1	Hayward, Mortensen	17,500
5	25	H	Stockport County	W	3-2	Dix 2, Beattie	5,000
6	Oct 2	A	Stockport County	D	0-0		7,000
7	9	A	Bury	L	0-1		6,428
8	16	H	Bury	W	3-1	Beattie 3	6,000
9	23	A	Bolton Wanderers	W	2-1	O'Donnell H, Dix	10,243
10	30	H	Bolton Wanderers	L	1-2	Dix	7,000
11	Nov 6	A	Blackburn Rovers	D	1-1	Dodds	9,259
12	13	H	Blackburn Rovers	W	8-0	Mortensen 4, Farrow 2 (1 pen), Dix, Dodds	8,000
13	20	H	Burnley	W	3-0	Dix 2, O'Donnell H	10,000
14	27	A	Burnley	W	5-3	Mortensen 2, Dodds, Johnston, Matthews	8,744
15	Dec 4	A	Oldham Athletic	D	1-1	Mortensen	7,927
16	11	H	Oldham Athletic	W	3-1	Dodds 2, Mortensen	12,291
17	18	A	Southport	D	1-1	Mortensen	4,000
18	25	H	Southport	W	5-0	Dodds 3 (1 pen), Mortensen 2	25,000

Final League Position: 1st in Northern Section - First Competition

App

Goals

19	Dec 26	H	Blackburn Rovers	D	2-2	Dix, Dodds	19,500
20	Jan 1	A	Blackburn Rovers	L	1-3	Bradley	10,000
21	8	A	Southport	W	4-2	O'Donnell H, Dodds, Mortensen, Dix	5,000
22	15	H	Southport	W	2-1	Dix (pen), Dodds	10,000
23	22	A	Bolton Wanderers	W	6-0	Finan 2, Dodds, Dix, O'Donnell H, Kirkham	8,000
24	29	H	Bolton Wanderers	W	2-0	Dodds, Mortensen	10,254
25	Feb 5	A	Burnley	L	1-2	Finan	10,282
26	12	H	Burnley	L	1-3	O'Donnell H	8,000
27	19	H	Rochdale	W	2-0	Dix, O'Donnell H	8,000
28	26	A	Rochdale	W	2-0	Pearson, Dodds	10,000
29	Mar 4	A	Everton	W	7-1	Dix 3, Mortensen 2, Dodds 2	25,000
30	11	H	Everton	W	3-1	Dix, Mortensen 2	28,013
31	18	H	Rochdale	W	8-0	Mortensen 3, Dix 3, Dodds 2	25,000
32	25	A	Rochdale	L	1-2	O'Donnell H	8,706
33	Apr 1	H	Bradford City	D	2-2	Dodds 2	17,000
34	8	A	Bradford City	W	2-1	Finan, Own-goal	32,810
35	15	H	Manchester City	D	1-1	Dodds	24,800
36	22	A	Manchester City	W	2-1	Finan, Tapping	55,000
37	29	H	Aston Villa	W	2-1	Dodds 2	26,800
38	May 6	A	Aston Villa	L	2-4	Dix, Pearson	54,824

Final League Position: 7th in Northern Section - Second Competition

Apps

Matches 19-28 were Football League War Cup qualifying competition

Gls

Matches 29-38 were Football League War Cup knock out competition from first round to semi final

Savage	Pope	Kinsell	Farrow	Powell	Johnston	Matthews	McEwan	Finan	Beattie	Burbanks	Johnson	O'Donnell F	Hayward	Dix	Mortensen	John	Butler	Cutting	Williams	McGahey	O'Donnell H	Suart	Dodds	Jones S
1	2	3	4	5	6	7	8	9	10	11														
1	2	3	4	5	6	7	8	9	10	11														
1	2	3	4	5	6		8	10		11	7	9												
1	2	3	4		6	7		9		11			5	8	10									
1	2	3	4		6			9	10	11	7		5	8										
	2	3						9	10	11	7		5	8		1	4	6						
1	2		4		6	7			10	11	8		5						3	9				
1	2	3	4		6			9	10	11	7		5	8										
1	2	3	4		6	7			10			9	5	8							11			
1	2		4		6	7			10	11			5	8	9				3					
1	2	3	4		6			7	10					8							11	5	9	
1	2	3	4		6	7							5	8	10						11		9	
1	2	3		4	6	7								8	10						11		9	5
1	2	3		4	6	7		10					5		8						11		9	
1	2	3		4	6	7		10					5		8						11		9	
1	2			4	6	7							5	8	10						11		9	3
1	2		4		6	7							5	8	10						11		9	3
1	2	3	4		6	7							5	8	10						11		9	3
17	18	14	13	7	17	13	3	10	9	9	5	2	13	12	9	1	1	1	2	1	9	1	8	4
			5		1	1	4	4	9			2	1	7	12						2		8	

Savage	Pope	Kinsell	Farrow	Hayward	Johnston	Matthews	Dix	Dodds	Mortensen	O'Donnell H	Sibley	Maxwell	Bradshaw	Whittingham	Williams	Finan	Bradley	Jones S	Tapping	Kirkham	Roxburgh	John	Garrett	Gibbons	Davies	Majdesley	Watkin	Pearson
1	2	3	4	5	6	7	8	9	10	11																		
1	2				6					11	3	4	5	7	8	9	10											
1	2	3		5	4		8	9	10	11						7		6										
1	2	3			6		8	9	10	11						7		5	4									
1	2	3			6		8	9		11						7		5	4	10								
	2	3	4		6		8	9	10	11						7		5			1							
1	2	3			6	7		9		11						10		5	4	8								
							8	9		11	3					7						1	2	4	5	6	10	
1	2	3		4	6		8		9	11						10									4	7		
1	2	3		4	6	7	8	9								10		5										11
1	2	3		4	6	7	8	9	10									5										11
1	2	3		5	6		8	9	10							7			4									11
1	2	3			6	7	8	9	10									5							4			11
1	2	3		5	4	7	8	9	10	11								6										
1	2	3			6		8	9								10		5	7						4			11
1	2	3	4	5		7	8	9								10		6										11
1	2	3		5	6	7	8	9								10		4										11
1	2	3		5	6		8		10							9		4	7									11
1	2	3		5	4	7	8	9								10		6										11
1	2	3		5	4	7	8	9								10		6										11
18	19	18	3	12	18	10	18	17	10	10	2	1	1	1	1	17	1	16	6	2	1	1	1	1	4	2	1	10
							13	15	9	5						5	1		1	1								2

1944-45

Northern Section

Manager: Joe Smith

Did you know that?

Blackpool's overdraft, which stood at £33,704 before the war, was now wiped out with the rents paid by the armed forces.

Match No.	Date	Venue	Opponents	Result		Scorers	Attendance
1	Aug 26	A	Rochdale	W	7-3	Finan 2, Farrow, Mortensen 3, Theurer	7,500
2	Sep 2	H	Rochdale	W	3-0	Eakin, Finan, O'Donnell F	3,000
3	9	H	Bolton Wanderers	L	1-2	Pearson	8,000
4	16	A	Bolton Wanderers	L	0-1		10,148
5	23	A	Accrington Stanley	W	4-3	Finan, Mortensen 3	5,500
6	30	H	Accrington Stanley	W	6-0	O'Donnell F 3, Finan 2, Pearson	8,000
7	Oct 7	H	Preston NE	D	1-1	Matthews	14,000
8	14	A	Preston NE	L	0-1		10,000
9	21	A	Southport	W	5-4	Pearson, Matthews, Finan, Farrow 2	5,000
10	28	H	Southport	W	10-2	Dodds 2, Mortensen 4, O'Donnell F 2, Dix, Matthews	12,000
11	Nov 4	H	Oldham Athletic	L	1-3	Larner	6,000
12	11	A	Oldham Athletic	W	3-2	Own-goal, Farrow, Finan	7,135
13	18	A	Halifax Town	L	3-4	Farrow, Paterson, Tweedy	7,000
14	25	H	Halifax Town	W	4-2	Laing, Walsh 2, Tweedy	6,000
15	Dec 2	H	Burnley	L	0-2		5,000
16	9	A	Burnley	L	1-5	Tapping	6,335
17	16	H	Blackburn Rovers	W	2-1	Davies, Tweedy	3,000
18	23	A	Blackburn Rovers	D	2-2	Laing, O'Donnell F	10,000

Final League Position: 20th in Northern Section - First Competition — App / Goals

19	Dec 25	A	Preston NE	W	3-1	Own-goal, Johnson, O'Donnell F	9,000
20	26	A	Manchester City	D	1-1	O'Donnell F	13,000
21	30	H	Preston NE	D	1-1	Laing	10,000
22	Jan 6	A	Burnley	L	0-2		9,643
23	13	H	Burnley	W	4-0	Mortensen, Dodds, Johnson, Fenton	12,000
24	20	A	Blackburn Rovers	L	4-7	Jones, Walsh 3	800
25	27	H	Blackburn Rovers	W	3-1	Johnson, Jones (pen), Fenton	6,000
26	Feb 3	H	Accrington Stanley	L	0-3		8,000
27	10	A	Accrington Stanley	L	2-4	Laing, Fenton	6,091
28	17	A	Rochdale	W	6-3	Finan 2, Fenton 3, Laing	5,000
29	24	H	Rochdale	W	4-0	Eastham 2, Farrow, Laing	6,000
30	Mar 3	A	Accrington Stanley	L	1-4	Laing	5,500
31	10	H	Accrington Stanley	L	1-2	Finan	8,000
32	17	H	Burnley	L	0-2		8,000
33	24	H	Wrexham	W	2-0	Dodds, Worrall	12,000
34	31	A	Wrexham	D	2-2	Farrow, Worrall	17,081
35	Apr 2	H	Manchester Utd	W	4-1	Fenton 3, O'Donnell H	14,000
36	7	H	Bolton Wanderers	L	1-4	Farrow (pen)	18,000
37	14	A	Bolton Wanderers	W	2-1	Worrall 2	13,613
38	21	A	Manchester City	W	1-0	Worrall	9,500
39	28	H	Manchester City	W	4-0	Mortensen 3, Farrow	5,000
40	May 5	A	Preston NE	W	8-1	Farrow 4, O'Donnell H 3, Slater	3,000
41	12	A	Preston NE	W	4-0	Todd 2, Laing 2	3,000
42	19	A	Liverpool	L	0-2		16,807

Final League Position: 16th in Northern Section - Second Competition — Apps

Matches 19-28 were Football League War Cup qualifying competition — Gls

Matches 32-36 in Football League War Cup knock out competition

There were also 6 Lancashire Cup games played between 25th December 1944 and 5th May 1945. Insufficient records available

Savage	Pope	Jones S	Farrow	Davies	Paterson	Matthews	Mortensen	Finan	Theurer	O'Donnell F	Cross	Eakin	Pearson	Rogerson	Edward	Bradley	Suart	Johnson	Tapping	Sibley	Lamer	O'Donnell H	Franklin	Dix	Slater	Thorpe	Dodds	Tweedy	Kirby	Garrett	Walsh	Revell	Kilgallon	Laing	Eastham	Falla	Roxburgh
1	2	3	4	5	6	7	8	9	10	11																											
1	2	3	4	5	6			9		11	7	8	10																								
1	2		4	5				9		11	7		10	3	6	8																					
1	2	3	4	6				9		10			11				5	7	8																		
1	2	6	4				8	7		9			11	3		10	5																				
1	2	5	4		6			8		9			11					7		3	10																
1	2	3	4	6		7	10	9					11				5					8															
1	2		4	6				10					11				5	7	9			8	3														
1	2		4	5	6	7		9					11										3	8	10												
	2	3	4	5	6	7	10			11														8		1	9										
	2		4	5			7	9		11									6	3	10					1		8									
	2	3	4	5	6			9		10								7	8							1			11								
	2	3	4	5	6			10					11					7	9							1		8									
	2	3		5	6					11																1		7	11		4			9			
		5			6	7													4		10					1			3	2	8	9	11				
		5		2	6					11								7	4							1		10	3			9		8			
			5		6					11								7	4				2			1		8	3			9					
	2		5		6					9								7	4			11							3					8			
9	15	12	15	14	12	5	5	12	1	13	2	1	9	2	1	2	4	8	9	2	3	3	3	2	1	8	1	5	6	1	2	3	1	3			
			5	1	1	3	10	8	1	7		1	3						1		1			1			2	3			2			2			

Roxburgh	Pope	Kirby	Tapping	Davies	Paterson	Johnson	Laing	O'Donnell F	Eastham	O'Donnell H	Sibley	Manley	Thorpe	Jones S	Tweedy	Mortensen	Dodds	Fenton	Walsh	Johnston	Farrow	Finan	Oakes	Galley	Franklin	Cross	Thomas	Suart	Worrall	Bailey	Crook	Miller	Todd	Slater
1	2	3	4	5	6	7	8	9	10	11																								
1	2	3	4	5	6	7	8	9	10	11																								
1	2		4	5		7	8	9	10	11	3	6																						
	2		4	5		7	8		10	11		6	1	3	9																			
	2	3		5	4	7				11			1	6		8	9	10																
1	2	3		5	4	7	8			11				6				10	9															
	2	3		5	4	7	8		10	11			1	6				9																
	2	3		5	4	7	8		10	11			1						9	6														
	2	3					6		7	11			1	5		10		8			4	9												
	2	3		5	6		10		7				1					8			4	9	11											
	2	11			6		10		7				1	5				8			4	9		3										
	2	11			6		10		7				1	5				8			4	9		3										
	2	11			6		10		7				1	5				8			4	9		3										
1				5	4				8	11	2			6			9								3	7	10							
1			10	5	6					11	2						9	8			4							3	7					
1				6						11	2			4		8		9			5				3				7	10				
1				6						11	2			4		8		9			5				3				7	10				
1				5	6					11	2					10	9	8			4								7		3			
1				5	6					11	2					8		9			4								7	10	3			
1			8	5						11	3										4								7	10		2	6	9
1				5	10					11	3					8					4								7			2	6	9
1				5	10					11	3					8					4								7			2	6	9
1				5			10			11	3					8					4								7			2	6	9
1				5	10					11	3					8					4								7			2	6	9
15	13	11	6	20	17	8	13	3	12	20	12	2	9	11	1	10	4	13	2	1	14	5	1	3	3	1	1	1	10	4	2	5	5	5
						3	7	2	2	4				2		4	2	9	3		8	3							5				2	1

1945-46

Football League (North)

Manager: Joe Smith

Did you know that?

At the end of the season, the prolific Jock Dodds was sold to Irish club Shamrock Rovers.

The Football League (north) was a stop gap League before the resumption of full-time football.

The FA Cup returned, and Blackpool played five matches over just two rounds.

Match No.	Date		Venue	Opponents	Result		Scorers	Attendance
1	Aug	25	A	Bury	W	4-1	Mortensen 4	12,000
2		27	H	Preston NE	W	6-3	Fenton 2, O'Donnell H 2, Mortensen, Buchan	15,782
3	Sep	1	H	Bury	W	3-1	Fenton 3	13,496
4		3	A	Preston NE	L	0-5		18,000
5		8	H	Blackburn Rovers	W	5-2	Mortensen 2, Farrow 2, Fenton	16,170
6		12	H	Bolton Wanderers	D	1-1	Eastham	15,207
7		15	A	Blackburn Rovers	D	1-1	Own-goal	6,951
8		22	A	Bradford City	L	0-3		15,897
9		29	H	Bradford City	L	0-1		15,597
10	Oct	6	H	Manchester City	W	5-4	Dodds 4, Fenton	14,228
11		13	A	Manchester City	W	4-1	Fenton 2, Dodds, Farrow	32,830
12		20	A	Newcastle United	D	2-2	Farrow, Mortensen	35,299
13		27	H	Newcastle United	D	1-1	O'Donnell H	14,910
14	Nov	3	H	Sheffield Wednesday	W	5-1	Tapping, Mortensen 3, O'Donnell H	14,087
15		10	A	Sheffield Wednesday	L	2-3	Withington, Mortensen	25,619
16		17	A	Huddersfield Town	W	4-2	Dodds, Mortensen 2, O'Donnell H	16,378
17		24	H	Huddersfield Town	W	1-0	Dodds	14,450
18	Dec	1	H	Chesterfield	L	0-1		15,149
19		8	A	Chesterfield	W	3-0	Mortensen 2, Own-goal	17,953
20		15	A	Barnsley	D	1-1	Blair	22,688
21		22	H	Barnsley	D	1-1	Farrow (pen)	10,248
22		25	H	Everton	W	5-2	O'Donnell H 2, Blair 2, Mortensen	20,772
23		26	A	Everton	L	1-7	O'Donnell H	53,985
24		29	A	Bolton Wanderers	D	1-1	Dodds	31,424
25	Jan	12	A	Leeds United	W	2-1	O'Donnell H, Buchan	14,372
26		19	H	Leeds United	W	4-2	Mortensen 3, Blair	8,734
27	Feb	2	A	Manchester Utd	L	2-4	Mortensen 2	18,033
28		16	H	Sunderland	W	4-0	Mortensen, Farro, Dodds 2	12,882
29		23	H	Sheffield Utd	L	1-2	Dodds	16,855
30	Mar	2	A	Sheffield Utd	L	2-4	Dodds 2	38,742
31		9	A	Middlesbrough	L	2-4	O'Donnell H, Dodds	23,000
32		13	A	Sunderland	L	1-3	Finan	6,000
33		16	H	Middlesbrough	W	3-1	Blair 2, O'Donnell H	10,000
34		23	A	Stoke City	L	3-6	Mortensen 2, Blair	18,000
35		27	H	Manchester Utd	L	1-5	Mortensen	10,000
36		30	H	Stoke City	W	3-2	Mortensen, O'Donnell H, Dodds	15,000
37	Apr	6	A	Grimsby Town	L	2-4	Mortensen 2	12,000
38		13	H	Grimsby Town	W	5-3	Mortensen 3, Blair 2	10,000
39		19	A	Burnley	D	1-1	Mortensen	18,104
40		20	H	Liverpool	D	1-1	Buchan (pen)	7,000
41		22	A	Burnley	D	1-1	Mortensen	14,000
42		27	A	Liverpool	L	0-4		20,000

Final League Position: 9th in Football League (North)

Apps

Gls

FA Cup

3	Jan	5	A	Wrexham	W	4-1	Buchan, Mortensen, Blair, Dodds	14,109
		9	H	Wrexham	W	4-1	Dodds 3, O'Donnell H	11,200
4		26	H	Middlesbrough	W	3-2	Mortensen 2, Dodds	17,160
		30	A	Middlesbrough	L	2-4*	O'Donnell H, Mortensen	46,566
R	Feb	4	N	Middlesbrough	L	0-1		30,000

* after extra-time, N - played at Elland Road, Leeds - after extra-time

Apps

Gls

Roxburgh	Sibley	Lewis	Farrow	Jones S	Paterson	Matthews	Buchan	Mortensen	Eastham	O'Donnell H	Wallace	Butler	Suart	Hobson	Fenton	O'Donnell F	Todd	Thorpe	Withington	Larner	Dodds	Tapping	Laing	McLaren	Munro	Blair	Kelly	Franklin	Burke	Astley	Harper	Kennedy	Finan	Hesford	Johnston	Hayward
1	2	3	4	5	6	7	8	9	10	11																										
		3	4		6		8	9		11	1	2	5	7	10																					
1		3	4	5	6				8	11			2	7	9	10																				
1	2	3	4		6	7			8	11			5		10	9																				
1		3	6			7		8	10	11		2	5		9		4																			
	2	3	4		6		8		10	11	1		5	7	9																					
		3	4		6		8		10	11	1	2	5	7	9																					
		3	4			7			9	11		2	5				6	1	8	10																
		3	4	5	6			8		11		2			10			1	7		9															
		3		5	6					11			2		10			1	7		9	4	8													
		3	4	5				8		11			2		7			1				6	9													
1		3	4	5				8		11			2						7		9	6		10												
1		3	4	5				9		11			2						8			6			7	10										
1		3	4	5				8		11		2							7		9	6				10										
1		3	4	6				8		11		2	5						7			9				10										
1		3	4					8		11		2	5						7		9	6				10										
1		3	4					8		11		2	5								9	6			7	10										
1		3		6				8		11		2	5								9	4			7	10										
1		3						8		11		2	5	7			4				9					10	6									
1		3						8		11		2	5	7			4				9					10	6									
1		3	4					8		11		2	5	7			6							9		10										
1	2	3	4	5			7	8		11											9					10	6									
1	2	3		5			7	8		11											9	4				10	6									
1	4	3		5				8		11							6		7		9					10		2								
1		3	4	5			8			11				7			6									10			2	9						
		3	4					8		11	1			7			6				9					10			2		5					
		3						9	10		1			7			6		11			4			8			5	2							
1		3	4					8	7	11			5				6				9					10			2							
1		3	4				7	8		11			5								9					10	6		2							
1		2	4					8	10	11			5	7							9						6		3							
1		3	4				8			11			5								9					10	6					2	7			
		3	4				8			11			5								9					10	6		2					1		
		3	4				8			11			5	7				1			9					10	6		2							
1		3				7		9	8	11			5													10	4		2						6	
1		3	4				8		10	11				7							9								2						6	5
		3					10		8	11			5	7				1			9						4		2						6	
		3	4				7		8	11		2	5	10				1								9									6	
		3		5			8		10				2					1			9				7	11	4								6	
		3		5			8		9	11			2					1							7	10	4								6	
		3		5			8		9	11			2					1							7	10	4								6	
		3		5			8		9	11			2	7				1								10	4								6	
				5			8		9	11			2	7				1								10	4					3			6	
24	6	41	28	19	8	5	18	33	9	40	5	14	32	17	9	2	10	12	10	1	23	11	2	2	7	26	16	2	11	1	1	2	1	1	9	1
			6				3	34	1	13					9				1		15	1				9							1			

		3	4				7	8		11	1		5				6				9					10			2							
		3	4	5			7	8		11	1						6				9					10			2							
		3	4				7	8		11	1		5				6				9					10			2							
		3	4				7	8		11	1		5				6				9					10			2							
		3	4				7	8		11	1		5								9					10	6		2							
		5	5	1			5	5		5	5		4				4				5					5	1		5							
							1	4		2											5					1										

1946-47

Division One

Manager: Joe Smith

Did you know that?

The game with Blackburn Rovers on Boxing Day was the first all-ticket affair at Bloomfield Road.

Their fifth-placed finish was Blackpool highest ever in history up to that date.

Stan Mortensen was the new prolific scorer for Blackpool, scoring 28 in 40 League games.

Nearly 29,000 saw Blackpool beat rivals Preston 4–0 on 15 February.

Match No.	Date	Venue	Opponents	Result		Scorers	Attendance
1	Aug 31	A	Huddersfield Town	W	3-1	Mortensen, Blair, Munro	14,378
2	Sep 2	H	Brentford	W	4-2	Mortensen, Buchan W 2, McIntosh	24,230
3	7	H	Wolves	W	2-0	Eastham, Mortensen	27,623
4	11	A	Portsmouth	W	1-0	Eastham	27,504
5	14	A	Sunderland	L	2-3	Eastham 2	40,653
6	18	A	Brentford	L	1-2	Mortensen	25,621
7	21	H	Aston Villa	W	1-0	Mortensen	27,452
8	23	H	Portsmouth	W	4-3	Buchan W 3 (1 pen), Blair	18,517
9	28	A	Derby County	W	2-1	Mortensen, McIntosh	25,138
10	Oct 5	H	Arsenal	W	2-1	Mortensen, Dick	24,426
11	12	A	Preston NE	L	0-2		34,488
12	19	H	Manchester Utd	W	3-1	Farrow, Mortensen, Dick	26,307
13	26	A	Bolton Wanderers	D	1-1	McIntosh	35,896
14	Nov 2	H	Chelsea	W	1-0	Blair	23,365
15	9	A	Sheffield Utd	L	2-4	Mortensen (pen), Eastham	31,637
16	16	H	Grimsby Town	L	2-3	McIntosh, Mortensen	17,511
17	23	A	Leeds United	L	2-4	O'Donnell, Mortensen	25,829
18	30	H	Liverpool	W	3-2	McIntosh, Blair, Mortensen	23,565
19	Dec 7	A	Stoke City	L	1-4	Dick	28,624
20	14	H	Middlesbrough	L	0-5		14,571
21	21	A	Charlton Athletic	W	1-0	Buchan W (pen)	13,417
22	25	A	Blackburn Rovers	D	1-1	Mortensen	27,013
23	26	H	Blackburn Rovers	W	1-0	Mortensen	25,576
24	28	H	Huddersfield Town	W	2-1	Dick, Buchan W (pen)	24,558
25	Jan 4	A	Wolves	L	1-3	Mortensen	49,482
26	18	H	Sunderland	L	0-5		20,409
27	25	A	Aston Villa	D	1-1	Mortensen	32,541
28	Feb 1	H	Derby County	W	2-1	Munro, Dick	16,042
29	8	A	Arsenal	D	1-1	Mortensen	31,111
30	15	H	Preston NE	W	4-0	Dick 2, Mortensen 2	28,907
31	22	A	Manchester Utd	L	0-3		30,823
32	Mar 1	H	Bolton Wanderers	L	0-1		20,356
33	8	A	Chelsea	W	4-1	Dick 2, Buchan W, Mortensen	30,365
34	15	H	Sheffield Utd	W	4-2	Mortensen, Munro, Dick 2	17,307
35	22	A	Grimsby Town	W	3-2	Mortensen 2, McKnight	13,452
36	29	H	Leeds United	W	3-0	Mortensen 2, McKnight	14,501
37	Apr 4	A	Everton	D	1-1	Own-goal	63,617
38	5	A	Liverpool	W	3-2	Mortensen 2, Buchan W	47,320
39	7	H	Everton	L	0-3		23,699
40	12	H	Stoke City	L	0-2		17,260
41	19	A	Middlesbrough	W	2-1	Eastham, Mortensen	28,849
42	28	H	Charlton Athletic	D	0-0		16,771

Final League Position: 5th in Division One

Apps

Gls

FA Cup

3	Jan 11	A	Sheffield Wednesday	L	1-4	Mortensen	37,000

Apps

Gls

Wallace	Sibley	Lewis	Buchan T	Suart	Johnston	Munro	Buchan W	Mortensen	Blair	McIntosh	Eastham	Crossland	Kelly	Kennedy	Dick	Farrow	O'Donnell	Hayward	Shimwell	Nelson	McKnight
1	2	3	4	5	6	7	8	9	10	11											
1	2	3	4	5	6		8	9	10	11	7										
1	2	3	4	5	6		8	9	10	11	7										
1	2	3	4	5	6		8	9	10	11	7										
1	2	3	4	5	6		8	9	10	11	7										
1	2	3	4		6		8	9	10	11	7	5									
1	2	3			6		8	9	10	11	7	5	4								
1	2				6		8	9	10	11	7	5	4	3							
1	2				6		8	9	10	11	7	5	4	3							
1	2	3		5	6			9	10	11	7		4		8						
1	2	3		5	6			9	10	11	7		4		8						
1	2	3		5	6	7		9		11	10				8	4					
1	2	3		5	6	7		9	10	11					8	4					
1	2	3		5	6	7		9	10	11					8	4					
1	2	3	4	5	6			9	10	11	7				8						
1	2	3	4	5		7		9		11	10		6		8						
1	2	3		5	6		7	8		9	10					4	11				
1	2				6	7		9	10	11				3	8	4		5			
1	2				6	7		9	10	11				3	8	4		5			
1	2				6	7			10	11	8			3	9	4		5			
1	2	3			6	7	10	9		11					8	4		5			
1		3		5	6	7	10	9		11					8	4			2		
1		3		5	6	7	10	9		11					8	4			2		
1		3		5	6		10	9		11					8	4			2	7	
1		3		5	6		10	9		11					8	4			2	7	
1		3	4	5	6			8	10	11									2	7	8
1		3			6			9	11		10				8	4		5	2	7	
1		3			6	7		9	11		10				8	4		5	2		
1		3			6			9	11		10				8	4		5	2	7	
1		3			6	8		9	11						10	4		5	2	7	
1		3			6	8		9	11						10	4		5	2	7	
1		3			6	8		9	11						10	4		5	2	7	
1		3			6	7	8	9			10				11	4		5	2		
1		3			6	7	8	9			10				11	4		5	2		
1	2	3			6		10	9							11	4		5	2	7	8
1	3				6	7	10	9							11	4		5	2		8
1	3				6	7	10	9							11	4		5	2		8
1	3				6	7	10	9							11	4		5	2		8
1	3				6	7	10	9							11	4		5	2		8
1		6		3		7	8		10						11	4		5	2		9
1				3	6	7		9		11	10				8	4		5			
1				3	6	7		9		11	10				8	4		5			
42	26	31	9	21	40	24	23	40	25	28	22	4	6	5	31	28	1	20	21	9	7
						3	9	28	4	5	6				11	1	1				2

Wallace	Sibley	Lewis	Buchan T	Suart	Johnston	Munro	Buchan W	Mortensen	Blair	McIntosh	Eastham	Crossland	Kelly	Kennedy	Dick	Farrow	O'Donnell	Hayward	Shimwell	Nelson	McKnight
1	3			5	6	7	10	9		11					8	4			2		
1	1			1	1	1	1	1		1					1	1			1	1	
								1													

League Table

	P	W	D	L	F	A	Pts
Liverpool	42	25	7	10	84	52	57
Manchester United	42	22	12	8	95	54	56
Wolverhampton W	42	25	6	11	98	56	56
Stoke City	42	24	7	11	90	53	55
Blackpool	42	22	6	14	71	70	50
Sheffield United	42	21	7	14	89	75	49
Preston North End	42	18	11	13	76	74	47
Aston Villa	42	18	9	15	67	53	45
Sunderland	42	18	8	16	65	66	44
Everton	42	17	9	16	62	67	43
Middlesbrough	42	17	8	17	73	68	42
Portsmouth	42	16	9	17	66	60	41
Arsenal	42	16	9	17	72	70	41
Derby County	42	18	5	19	73	79	41
Chelsea	42	16	7	19	69	84	39
Grimsby Town	42	13	12	17	61	82	38
Blackburn Rovers	42	14	8	20	45	53	36
Bolton Wanderers	42	13	8	21	57	69	34
Charlton Athletic	42	11	12	19	57	71	34
Huddersfield Town	42	13	7	22	53	79	33
Brentford	42	9	7	26	45	88	25
Leeds United	42	6	6	30	45	90	18

1947-48

Division One

Manager: Joe Smith

Did you know that?

Stanley Matthews was signed from Stoke City for £11,500 in the summer of 1947.

Stan Mortensen scored in every round of the FA Cup, including the Final against Manchester United.

A celebration was held for the team at London's MayFair hotel on the night of the Final.

Blackpool finished their season with a 7–0 win at arch rivals Preston North End. Jimmy McIntosh, who had not made the Cup Final team a week previous, scored five. It is still Blackpool's biggest win over Preston.

Blackpool were forced to wear white shirts and black shorts for the Final, with United switching to blue shirts and white shorts.

Only 12,000 tickets were made available to both clubs despite Wembley stadium holding 100,000.

Match No.	Date		Venue	Opponents	Result		Scorers	Attendance
1	Aug	23	H	Chelsea	W	3-0	Mortensen 2, Own-goal	27,389
2		25	A	Huddersfield Town	L	0-2		32,099
3		30	A	Everton	W	2-1	Mortensen, McKnight	59,665
4	Sep	1	H	Huddersfield Town	W	4-0	McCormack 2, Mortensen, Farrow (pen)	29,555
5		6	H	Wolves	D	2-2	Buchan 2	31,663
6		8	H	Blackburn Rovers	W	1-0	Matthews	28,137
7		13	A	Aston Villa	W	1-0	McKnight	56,004
8		15	A	Blackburn Rovers	D	1-1	McCormack	27,790
9		20	H	Sunderland	L	0-1		25,343
10		27	A	Grimsby Town	W	1-0	Mortensen	25,576
11	Oct	4	H	Manchester City	D	1-1	Mortensen	30,930
12		11	A	Burnley	L	0-1		52,869
13		18	H	Portsmouth	W	1-0	Johnston	17,719
14		25	A	Bolton Wanderers	L	0-1		45,037
15	Nov	1	H	Liverpool	W	2-0	McIntosh 2	23,999
16		6	A	Arsenal	L	1-2	McIntosh	67,057
17		15	H	Sheffield Utd	W	2-1	Mortensen, Farrow	19,794
18		22	A	Middlesbrough	L	0-4		38,936
19		29	H	Charlton Athletic	W	3-1	Buchan 2 (1 pen), Mortensen	18,954
20	Dec	6	A	Manchester Utd	D	1-1	Mortensen	64,852
21		13	H	Preston NE	L	0-1		29,587
22		20	A	Chelsea	D	2-2	Farrow (pen), Mortensen	48,421
23		25	H	Stoke City	L	1-2	Mortensen	27,047
24		27	A	Stoke City	D	1-1	McIntosh	47,725
25	Jan	3	H	Everton	W	5-0	Dick 2, Mortensen 2, McIntosh	21,685
26		17	A	Wolves	D	1-1	Own-goal	46,383
27		31	H	Aston Villa	W	1-0	McIntosh	22,203
28	Feb	14	H	Grimsby Town	W	3-1	McIntosh 2, Mortensen	21,612
29		21	A	Manchester City	L	0-1		31,445
30	Mar	6	A	Portsmouth	D	1-1	Mortensen	37,067
31		20	A	Liverpool	L	0-2		48,725
32		26	H	Derby County	D	2-2	Mortensen 2	30,445
33		27	H	Arsenal	W	3-0	Mortensen 2, McCall	32,678
34		29	A	Derby County	D	2-2	Mortensen 2	34,896
35	Apr	3	A	Sheffield Utd	L	1-2	Rickett	48,150
36		5	H	Bolton Wanderers	D	1-1	Mortensen	25,050
37		7	H	Burnley	L	0-1		16,732
38		10	H	Middlesbrough	W	1-0	McKnight	16,330
39		12	A	Sunderland	L	0-1		61,084
40		17	A	Charlton Athletic	L	0-2		49,312
41		28	H	Manchester Utd	W	1-0	Mortensen	32,236
42	May	1	A	Preston NE	W	7-0	McIntosh 5, Munro, Rickett	26,610

Final League Position: 9th in Division One

Apps

Gls

FA Cup

3	Jan	10	H	Leeds United	W	4-0	Dick, McIntosh 2, Mortensen	23,000
4		24	H	Chester City	W	4-0	Shimwell, Mortensen 2,Johnston	26,419
5	Feb	7	H	Colchester United	W	5-0	Munro, McIntosh 2, Mortensen 2	26,000
6		28	A	Fulham	W	2-0	Mortensen, McIntosh	32,000
SF	Mar	13	N*	Tottenham Hotspur	W	3-1#	Mortensen 3	67,500
F	Apr	24		Manchester Utd	L	2-4	Shimwell (pen), Mortensen	99,842

N* - played at Villa Park, # - after extra-time

Final played at Wembley

Apps

Gls

Wallace	Shimwell	Suart	Farrow	Hayward	Johnston	Matthews	Munro	Mortensen	Dick	McIntosh	Kelly	Buchan	McCormack	Lewis	McKnight	McCall	Nelson	Robinson	Rickett	Garrett	Hobson	Crossland	Kennedy
1	2	3	4	5	6	7	8	9	10	11													
1	2	3	4	5		7	8	9	10	11	6												
1	2	3	4	5		7		9			6	8	11		10								
1	2	3	4	5	6	7		9		10		8	11										
1	2	3	4	5	6	7		9		10		8	11										
1	2	3	4	5	6	7		9		10		8	11										
1	2	3	4	5	6	7		9				8	11		10								
1	2	3		5	6	7						8	11	4	9	10							
1	2	3		5	6					7		8	11	4	9	10							
1	2	3		5	6	7	8	9					11	4		10							
1	2	3		5	6	7	8	9					11	4		10							
1	2	3	4	5	6	7	8	9	10	11													
1	2	3	4	5	6		8	9	10				11				7						
1	2	3	4	5	6	7		8		10		9	11										
1	2	3		5	6	7	11	8		9				4		10							
1	2	3		5	6	7	11	8		9				4		10							
1	2	3	4	5	6	7	11	8		9						10							
1	2	3	4	5	6	7	11	8		9						10							
1	2	3		5	6	7		9		11	4	10			8								
1	2	3		5	6	7		9		11	4	10			8								
1	2	3		5	6	7		9		11	4	10			8								
1	2	3	4	5	6	7	11	8		9						10							
1	2	3	4	5	6	7	11	8		9						10							
1	2	3	4	5	6	7	11	8		9						10							
1	2	3	4	5		7	11	8	10	9	6												
	2	3		5	4	7	11	8	10	9	6							1					
	2	3		5	4	7	11	8	10	9	6							1					
	2	3		5	4	7		8	10	9	6							1	11				
	2	3		5	4		7	8	10	9	6		11					1					
	2	3		5	4	7		8	10	9	6							1	11				
	2	3		5	4	7		8	10	9	6							1	11				
	2	3		5	4	7		8	10	9	6							1	11				
	2	3		5	4	7	8	9			6					10		1	11				
	2			5	4		8		9		6					10		1	11	3	7		
		3		5	4	7		8		9	6					10		1	11	2			
		3		5	4	7		8		9	6					10		1	11	2			
		3					7		10	9	6	4			8			1	11	2		5	
		3		5			7		10	9	6	4			8			1	11	2			
	2	3		5	4	7	8	9			6					10		1	11				
				5	4	7		8	10	9	6							1	11			2	3
	2			5	4	7		8		9	6					10		1	11			3	
	2			5			8			9	6	4				10		1	11		7	3	
25	37	38	16	41	36	35	23	36	16	33	23	14	12	6	9	18	1	17	14	5	2	4	1
			3		1	1	1	21	2	13		4	3		3	1			2				

Wallace	Shimwell	Suart	Farrow	Hayward	Johnston	Matthews	Munro	Mortensen	Dick	McIntosh	Kelly	Buchan	McCormack	Lewis	McKnight	McCall	Nelson	Robinson	Rickett	Garrett	Hobson	Crossland	Kennedy
	2	3		5	4	7	11	8	10	9	6							1					
	2	3		5	4	7	11	8	10	9	6		10					1					
	2	3		5	4	7		8	10	9	6							1	11				
	2	3		5	4	7	11	8	10	9	6		10					1					
	2	3		5	4	7	11	8	10	9	6		10					1					
	2			5	4	7	8	9	10		6		1					1	11			3	
	6	5		6	6	6	5	6	6	5	6							6	2			1	
	2				1		1	10	1	5													

League Table

	P	W	D	L	F	A	Pts
Arsenal	42	23	13	6	81	32	59
Manchester United	42	19	14	9	81	48	52
Burnley	42	20	12	10	56	43	52
Derby County	42	19	12	11	77	57	50
Wolverhampton W	42	19	9	14	83	70	47
Aston Villa	42	19	9	14	65	57	47
Preston North End	42	20	7	15	67	68	47
Portsmouth	42	19	7	16	68	50	45
Blackpool	42	17	10	15	57	41	44
Manchester City	42	15	12	15	52	47	42
Liverpool	42	16	10	16	65	61	42
Sheffield United	42	16	10	16	65	70	42
Charlton Athletic	42	17	6	19	57	66	40
Everton	42	17	6	19	52	66	40
Stoke City	42	14	10	18	41	55	38
Middlesbrough	42	14	9	19	71	73	37
Bolton Wanderers	42	16	5	21	46	58	37
Chelsea	42	14	9	19	53	71	37
Huddersfield Town	42	12	12	18	51	60	36
Sunderland	42	13	10	19	56	67	36
Blackburn Rovers	42	11	10	21	54	72	32
Grimsby Town	42	8	6	28	45	111	22

1948-49

Division One

Manager: Joe Smith

Did you know that?

George Farm signed from Hibernian, where he was playing for the third team. He went on to make 465 appearances for Blackpool.

An injury to Stanley Matthews severely curtailed Blackpool's firepower, and contributed to a lacklustre season.

No wins in the last six games saw Blackpool flirt with relegation, but they eventually finished five points clear of Preston, who went down.

Match No.	Date		Venue	Opponents	Result		Scorers	Attendance
1	Aug	21	A	Sheffield Utd	L	2-3	Munro, McCall	45,943
2		23	H	Manchester Utd	L	0-3		31,996
3		28	H	Aston Villa	W	1-0	Mortensen	29,815
4	Sep	1	A	Manchester Utd	W	4-3	Rickett, McIntosh W 2, Kelly	54,046
5		4	A	Sunderland	D	2-2	McIntosh W 2	48,750
6		6	H	Derby County	D	1-1	McCall	30,656
7		11	H	Wolves	L	1-3	Matthews	31,329
8		14	A	Derby County	L	1-3	McIntosh W	32,082
9		18	A	Bolton Wanderers	D	2-2	Mortensen 2 (1 pen)	46,779
10		25	H	Liverpool	W	1-0	McCall	28,870
11	Oct	2	A	Preston NE	W	3-1	Mortensen 2, Matthews	38,280
12		9	H	Everton	W	3-0	Wardle (pen), McIntosh W, Rickett	22,070
13		16	A	Chelsea	D	3-3	Mortensen, McCall 2	77,696
14		23	H	Birmingham City	W	1-0	Rickett	25,126
15		30	A	Middlesbrough	L	0-1		44,780
16	Nov	6	H	Newcastle United	L	1-3	Mortensen (pen)	30,676
17		13	A	Portsmouth	D	1-1	Mortensen (pen)	44,869
18		20	H	Manchester City	D	1-1	McIntosh W	22,412
19		27	A	Charlton Athletic	D	0-0		45,727
20	Dec	4	H	Stoke City	W	2-1	McCall 2	22,984
21		11	A	Burnley	L	0-2		37,969
22		18	H	Sheffield Utd	L	0-3		17,086
23		25	H	Huddersfield Town	D	0-0		29,244
24		26	A	Huddersfield Town	L	0-1		41,232
25	Jan	1	A	Aston Villa	W	5-2	Munro, Mortensen, Kelly, Rickett, Matthews	48,392
26		15	H	Sunderland	D	3-3	Mortensen 2, McCall	18,917
27		22	A	Wolves	L	1-2	Shimwell	54,088
28	Feb	12	H	Bolton Wanderers	W	1-0	McIntosh J	23,210
29		19	A	Liverpool	D	1-1	McIntosh J	52,294
30		26	H	Preston NE	D	2-2	McIntosh J 2	27,487
31	Mar	5	A	Everton	L	0-5		75,548
32		12	H	Chelsea	W	2-1	Mortensen 2	20,292
33		19	A	Manchester City	D	1-1	Mortensen	38,973
34		26	H	Charlton Athletic	L	0-1		18,065
35	Apr	2	A	Newcastle United	L	1-3	Fenton	62,672
36		9	H	Portsmouth	W	1-0	Adams	18,723
37		15	H	Arsenal	D	1-1	Mortensen	28,818
38		16	A	Birmingham City	D	1-1	Mortensen	34,726
39		18	A	Arsenal	L	0-2		45,047
40		23	H	Middlesbrough	D	1-1	Mortensen	23,128
41		30	A	Stoke City	L	2-3	McCall, Shimwell (pen)	18,640
42	May	7	H	Burnley	D	1-1	Mortensen	21,626

Final League Position: 16th in Division One

Apps

Gls

FA Cup

3	Jan	8	A	Barnsley	W	1-0	Mortensen	31,700
4		29	A	Stoke City	D	1-1	Mortensen	47,000
4R	Feb	4	H	Stoke City	L	0-1		29,100

Apps

Gls

Robinson	Shimwell	Suart	Johnston	Hayward	Kelly	Matthews	McCall	Mortensen	Munro	Rickett	Wardle	McIntosh W	Wright	Fenton	Farm	Adams	Davidson	Garrett	McIntosh J	McKnight	Kennedy	Hobson
1	2	3	4	5	6	7	8	9	10	11												
1	2	3	4	5	6	7	10	9	8	11												
1	2	3	4	5	6	7	10	9	8		11											
1	2	3	4	5	6		10	8		7	11	9										
1	2	3	4	5	6		10	8		7	11	9										
1		3		5	6		10	8		7	11	9	2	4								
1		3		5	6	7	10	8			11	9	2	4								
1		3		5	6	7	10	8			11	9	2	4								
	2	3	4	5	6	7	10	8			11	9			1							
	2	3		5	6		10			8	11	9		4	1	7						
	2		4	5	6	7	10	8		9	11		3		1							
	2		4	5	6		10		8	7	11	9	3		1							
	2		4	5	6	7	10	8		9	11		3		1							
	2	3	4	5	6		10		7	9	11				1		8					
	2	3	4	5	6	7	10	8		9	11				1							
	2	3	4	5	6	7	10	8		9	11				1							
	2	3	4	5	6	7	10	8		9	11				1							
	2	3	4	5	6	7		10		8	11	9			1							
	2	3	4	5		7	10	8			11	9		6	1							
	2	3	4	5		7	10	8			11	9		6	1							
	2	3	4	5	6	7	10			8	11	9			1							
	2	3	4	5		7	10			8	11	9		6	1							
	2	3	4	5	6	7	10		8	11		9			1							
	2	3	4	5	6	7	10		8	11					1			9				
	2	3	4	5	6	7		8	10	11					1			9				
	2	3	4	5	6	7	10	8		11					1				9			
	2	3	4	5	6	7	10	8		11					1				9			
	2	3	4	5	6	7		8			11				1				9	10		
	2	3	4	5	6	7		8			11				1				9	10		
		3	4	5	6	7		8			11				1				9	10	2	
	2	3	4	5	6		8	9			11				1					10		7
	2	3	4	5	6		8	9							1	11	10					7
	2	3	4	5	6		8	9							1	11	10					7
	2	3	4	5	6			8							1	11	10		9			7
		3		5	6	7	9	8						4	1	11	10	2				
	2	3		5	6		8				11			4	1	7	10		9			
	2	3	4	5	6			8			11				1	7	10		9			
	2	3	4	5	6			8			11				1	7	10		9			
	2	3	4	5	6		11	8						10	1				9	7		
	2	3	4	5	6		11	8							1	7	10		9			
	2	3	4	5	6	7	11	8							1		10		9			
	2	3	4	5			11	8		7				6	1		10		9			
8	37	39	36	42	38	26	34	34	8	22	27	14	6	11	34	9	11	4	13	4	1	4
	2				2	3	9	18	2	4	1	7		1		1			4			

	2	3	4	5	6	7		8	10	11					1			9				
	2	3	4	5	6	7	10	8		11			10		1				9			
	2	3	4	5	6	7	10	8		11					1				9			
	6	5		6	6	6	5	6	6	5	6							6	2			1
	2				1		1	10	1	5												

League Table

	P	W	D	L	F	A	Pts
Portsmouth	42	25	8	9	84	42	58
Manchester United	42	21	11	10	77	44	53
Derby County	42	22	9	11	74	55	53
Newcastle United	42	20	12	10	70	56	52
Arsenal	42	18	13	11	74	44	49
Wolverhampton W	42	17	12	13	79	66	46
Manchester City	42	15	15	12	47	51	45
Sunderland	42	13	17	12	49	58	43
Charlton Athletic	42	15	12	15	63	67	42
Aston Villa	42	16	10	16	60	76	42
Stoke City	42	16	9	17	66	68	41
Liverpool	42	13	14	15	53	43	40
Chelsea	42	12	14	16	69	68	38
Bolton Wanderers	42	14	10	18	59	68	38
Burnley	42	12	14	16	43	50	38
Blackpool	42	11	16	15	54	67	38
Birmingham City	42	11	15	16	36	38	37
Everton	42	13	11	18	41	63	37
Middlesbrough	42	11	12	19	46	57	34
Huddersfield Town	42	12	10	20	40	69	34
Preston North End	42	11	11	20	62	75	33
Sheffield United	42	11	11	20	57	78	33

1949-50

Division One

Manager: Joe Smith

Did you know that?

Blackpool's reserve side won the Central League Championship, scoring 82 goals in the process.

During the reserve season, over 12,000 saw Blackpool reserves beat Burnley reserves at Bloomfield Road.

Blackpool's attraction was shown in the crowds that came to see them, and specifically Stanley Matthews. Over 71,000 turned up at Goodison Park for Everton's home defeat to Blackpool, but Matthews was injured and so he did not play.

The maximum wage of £12 was in place plus a win bonus. Players had to pick up their wages from the club office on Friday in a brown envelope and sign a chitty to prove he had collected his payment.

Match No.	Date		Venue	Opponents	Result		Scorers	Attendance
1	Aug	20	H	Huddersfield Town	W	4-1	McIntosh, Shimwell (pen), Rickett, McCall	29,712
2		22	H	Middlesbrough	D	1-1	McCall	28,243
3		27	A	Portsmouth	W	3-2	McIntosh, Mortensen 2	46,927
4		31	A	Middlesbrough	L	0-2		47,870
5	Sep	3	H	Wolves	L	1-2	Mortensen	31,854
6		5	H	Newcastle United	D	0-0		27,182
7		10	A	Aston Villa	D	0-0		60,337
8		17	H	Charlton Athletic	W	2-0	Shimwell (pen), Mortensen	31,707
9		24	A	Manchester City	W	3-0	Mortensen, Johnston, McIntosh	57,931
10	Oct	1	H	Fulham	D	0-0		33,340
11		8	A	Sunderland	D	1-1	Mortensen	64,889
12		15	H	Liverpool	D	0-0		33,675
13		22	A	Arsenal	L	0-1		66,391
14		29	H	Bolton Wanderers	W	2-0	Mortensen 2	23,233
15	Nov	5	A	Birmingham City	W	2-0	Mortensen 2	34,045
16		12	H	Derby County	W	1-0	Mortensen	17,257
17		26	H	Manchester Utd	D	3-3	Shimwell (pen), McIntosh, Johnston	27,742
18	Dec	3	A	Chelsea	D	1-1	McCall	47,636
19		10	H	Stoke City	W	4-2	Slater 2, McIntosh, Own-goal	18,430
20		17	A	Huddersfield Town	W	1-0	Mortensen	28,107
21		24	H	Portsmouth	W	2-1	McCall 2	29,953
22		26	A	Burnley	D	0-0		49,115
23		27	H	Burnley	W	2-0	Mortensen, McIntosh	31,074
24		31	A	Wolves	L	0-1		51,400
25	Jan	14	H	Aston Villa	W	1-0	Mortensen	23,743
26		21	A	Charlton Athletic	W	2-1	Mortensen, McIntosh	44,701
27	Feb	4	H	Manchester City	D	0-0		23,780
28		11	A	Fulham	L	0-1		32,131
29		25	H	Sunderland	L	0-1		21,317
30	Mar	8	A	Liverpool	W	1-0	Mudie	33,464
31		11	H	West Brom Albion	W	3-0	Mortensen 2, Slater	23,104
32		18	A	Manchester Utd	W	2-1	Mortensen 2 (1 pen)	55,517
33		23	H	Birmingham City	D	1-1	Mortensen	20,733
34	Apr	1	A	Derby County	D	0-0		28,862
35		7	A	Everton	L	0-3		71,008
36		8	H	Arsenal	W	2-1	Mortensen 2	32,025
37		10	H	Everton	L	0-1		22,942
38		15	A	Bolton Wanderers	D	0-0		25,800
39		22	H	Chelsea	D	0-0		26,006
40		26	A	West Brom Albion	L	0-1		23,671
41		29	A	Stoke City	D	1-1	McKnight	17,444
42	May	6	A	Newcastle United	L	0-3		35,274

Final League Position: 7th in Division One

Apps

Gls

FA Cup

3	Jan	7	H	Southend United	W	4-0	Slater 3 (1 pen), Mortensen	24,532
4		28	H	Doncaster Rovers	W	2-1	McIntosh, McKnight	31,362
5	Feb	11	A	Wolves	D	0-0		53,597
5R		14	H	Wolves	W	1-0	Mortensen	29,050
6	Mar	4	A	Liverpool	L	1-2	Mortensen (pen)	48,000

Apps

Gls

Farm	Shimwell	Suart	Johnston	Hayward	Kelly	Matthews	Mortensen	McIntosh	McCall	Rickett	Garrett	Wright	Lewis	Crosland	Slater	Wardle	Davidson	McKnight	Hobson	Kennedy	Adams	Mudie	Perry	Falconer
1	2	3	4	5	6	7	8	9	10	11														
1	2	3	4	5	6	7	8	9	10	11														
1		3	4	5	6	7	8	9	10	11	2													
1		2	4	5	6	7	8	9	10	11		3												
1		3	4	5	6	7	8	9	10	11			3											
1			4	5	6	7	8	9	10	11			3	2										
1			4	5	6	7	8	9	10				3	2	11									
1	2		4	5	6	7	8	9	10				3			11								
1	2		4	5	6	7	8	9	10				3			11								
1	2		4	5	6	7	8	9	10		3					11								
1	2		4	5	6	7	8	9	10		3					11								
1	2		4	5	6	7		9	8	11	3						10							
1	2		4	5	6	7	8	9	10	11	3													
1	2		4	5	6	7	9		10		3					11		8						
1	2		4	5	6	7	9		8		3				10	11								
1	2		4	5	6	7	9		8		3				10	11								
1	2		4	5	6	7		9	8		3					11	10							
1	2		4	5	6	7	9		8		3					11	10							
1	2		4	5	6	7		9	8		3				10	11								
1	2		4	5	6	7	9	10	8		3					11								
1	2		4	5	6	7	9	10	8		3					11								
1	2		4	5	6	7	9	10	8		3					11								
1	2		4	5	6	7	9	10	8		3					11								
1	2		4	5	6	7	9	10	8		3					11								
1	2		4	5	6	7	9		8						10					3	11			
1	2		4	5	6	7	9	10	8		3										11			
1	2		4		6	7	9		8		3			5			10				11			
1	2		4	5	6		9	10			3					11		8	7					
1			4		6		9	10			3			5				8	7	2	11			
1	2		4		6		8	10				3		5		11			7			9		
1	2		4		6		8	11				3		5	10				7			9		
1	2		5		6		8					3			10			4	7			9	11	
1	2		4		6		8	10				3		5					7			9	11	
1	2		4		6		8					3		5	10				7			9	11	
1	2		4		6		8	10				3							7			9	11	
1			4		6		9		10		2	3		5		11							7	8
1			4		6		9		10		2	3		5		11							7	8
1			4		6			9			2	3		5	10	11							7	8
1	2		4		6	7	9	10				3		5									11	8
1	2		4			7	9		8			3		6			10	5					11	
1	2				6	7	8					3		5		11		4				9	10	
1					6	7	8		10		2	3		5				4				9	11	
42	32	5	40	27	41	31	38	29	31	8	24	14	5	16	9	21	5	7	8	2	4	8	11	4
	3		2				22	7	5	1					3			1				1		

Farm	Shimwell	Suart	Johnston	Hayward	Kelly	Matthews	Mortensen	McIntosh	McCall	Rickett	Garrett	Wright	Lewis	Crosland	Slater	Wardle	Davidson	McKnight	Hobson	Kennedy	Adams	Mudie	Perry	Falconer
1			4	5	6	7	9	8			3				10					2	11			
1	2			5	6	7	9	8			3		10		10	11		4						
1	2		4	5	6	7	9	10				3				11		8						
1	2		4	5	6		9	10				3	10			11		8	7					
1			4		6		9	10				3	10	5				8	7	2	11			
5	3		4	4	5	3	5	5			2	3		1	2	3		4	2	2	2			
							3	1							3			1						

League Table

	P	W	D	L	F	A	Pts
Portsmouth	42	22	9	11	74	38	53
Wolverhampton W.	42	20	13	9	76	49	53
Sunderland	42	21	10	11	83	62	52
Manchester United	42	18	14	10	69	44	50
Newcastle United	42	19	12	11	77	55	50
Arsenal	42	19	11	12	79	55	49
Blackpool	42	17	15	10	46	35	49
Liverpool	42	17	14	11	64	54	48
Middlesbrough	42	20	7	15	59	48	47
Burnley	42	16	13	13	40	40	45
Derby County	42	17	10	15	69	61	44
Aston Villa	42	15	12	15	61	61	42
Chelsea	42	12	16	14	58	65	40
West Bromwich Albion	42	14	12	16	47	53	40
Huddersfield Town	42	14	9	19	52	73	37
Bolton Wanderers	42	10	14	18	45	59	34
Fulham	42	10	14	18	41	54	34
Everton	42	10	14	18	42	66	34
Stoke City	42	11	12	19	45	75	34
Charlton Athletic	42	13	6	23	53	65	32
Manchester City	42	8	13	21	36	68	29
Birmingham City	42	7	14	21	31	67	28

1950-51

Division One

Manager: Joe Smith

Did you know that?

Allan Brown – signed for £26,500 from East Fife, which was a record fee to a Scottish club – missed the FA Cup Final through injury.

Third place was the highest Blackpool had finished in their history.

In May, the club competed in a series of friendly matches as part of the Festival of Britain. They hosted Rennes and comfortably beat them 3–0, just two days after beating Anderlecht 2–0.

Match No.	Date	Venue	Opponents	Result		Scorers	Attendance
1	Aug 19	A	Tottenham Hotspur	W	4-1	Johnston 2, Mortensen, Kelly	64,978
2	21	H	Burnley	L	1-2	Slater	33,161
3	26	H	Charlton Athletic	D	0-0		25,484
4	29	A	Burnley	D	0-0		38,688
5	Sep 2	A	Manchester Utd	L	0-1		55,090
6	4	H	Fulham	W	4-0	Mudie, McKnight 3	28,051
7	9	H	Wolves	D	1-1	Johnston	32,204
8	13	A	Fulham	D	2-2	Slater, Perry	39,761
9	16	A	Sunderland	W	2-0	Mudie, Own-goal	56,204
10	23	H	Aston Villa	D	1-1	Mortensen	33,298
11	30	A	Derby County	L	1-4	Mortensen	32,471
12	Oct 7	H	Chelsea	W	3-2	Slater 2, Mortensen	29,240
13	14	A	Portsmouth	L	0-2		47,829
14	21	H	West Brom Albion	W	2-1	Mudie 2	30,536
15	28	A	Newcastle United	L	2-4	Mortensen, Own-goal	61,008
16	Nov 4	H	Everton	W	4-0	Mudie 2, Mortensen, Perry	20,902
17	11	A	Stoke City	L	0-1		39,894
18	18	H	Huddersfield Town	W	3-1	Withers 3	19,724
19	25	A	Middlesbrough	L	3-4	Mudie 2, Mortensen	40,487
20	Dec 2	H	Sheffield Wed	W	3-2	Mortensen, Johnston, Withers	19,732
21	9	A	Arsenal	D	4-4	Withers, Mortensen, Own-goal	54,445
22	16	H	Tottenham Hotspur	L	0-1		22,203
23	23	A	Charlton Athletic	W	3-2	Mortensen, Mudie 2	27,220
24	25	H	Liverpool	W	3-0	Mortensen 2, Mudie	31,867
25	26	A	Liverpool	L	0-1		54,121
26	30	H	Manchester Utd	D	1-1	Perry	22,864
27	Jan 13	A	Wolves	D	1-1	Mortensen	49,628
28	20	H	Sunderland	D	2-2	Perry, Stephenson	22,797
29	Feb 3	A	Aston Villa	W	3-0	Mudie, Mortensen, Johnston	55,093
30	17	H	Derby County	W	3-1	Mortensen 2, Johnston	21,002
31	28	A	Chelsea	W	2-0	Mortensen, Mudie	36,074
32	Mar 4	H	Portsmouth	W	3-0	Brown 2 (1 pen), Mortensen	23,521
33	17	H	Newcastle United	D	2-2	Mortensen, Mudie	24,825
34	23	H	Bolton Wanderers	W	2-0	Mortensen, Johnston	33,627
35	24	A	Everton	W	2-0	Mortensen 2	61,387
36	26	A	Bolton Wanderers	W	2-1	Mortensen 2	42,265
37	31	H	Stoke City	W	3-0	Mortensen 2, Brown	23,106
38	Apr 4	A	West Brom Albion	W	3-1	Mudie 2, Mortensen	39,459
39	7	A	Huddersfield Town	L	1-2	Mortensen	52,479
40	14	H	Middlesbrough	W	2-1	Mudie, McIntosh	16,300
41	21	A	Sheffield Wed	L	1-3	Mortensen	55,420
42	May 2	H	Arsenal	L	0-1		23,044

Final League Position: 3rd in Division One

Apps

Gls

FA Cup

3	Jan 6	A	Charlton Athletic	D	2-2	Perry, Mortensen	37,000
3R	10	H	Charlton Athletic	W	3-0	Mortensen 2, Mudie	28,000
4	27	H	Stockport County	W	2-1	Mortensen, Mudie	31,190
5	Feb 10	H	Mansfield Town	W	2-0	Mudie, Brown	33,016
6	24	H	Fulham	W	1-0	Brown (pen)	33,000
SF	Mar 11	*	Birmingham City	D	0-0		73,000
SFR	15	^	Birmingham City	W	2-1	Mortensen, Perry	70,114
F	Apr 28	@	Newcastle United	L	0-2		100,000

* Played at Maine Road, Manchester

^ Played at Goodison Park, Liverpool

@ Played at Wembley Stadium

Apps

Gls

Farm	Shimwell	Wright	Johnston	Hayward	Kelly	Matthews	McCall	Mortensen	Slater	Wardle	Mudie	McIntosh	McKnight	Garrett	Hobson	Perry	Withers	Brown	Crosland	Fenton	Ainscough	Stephenson	Adams
1	2	3	4	5	6	7	8	9	10	11													
1	2	3	4	5	6	7	8	9	10	11													
1	2	3	4	5	6	7	8	9	10	11													
1	2	2	4	5	6	7		9	10	11	8												
1	2	3	4	5	6	7			10	11	8	9											
1	2	3	4	5	6	7			10	11	8		9										
1	2	3	4	5	6	7		9	10	11	8												
1	2	3	4	5	6	7		9	10		8					11							
1		3	4	5	6	7		9	10	11	8			2									
1	2	3	4	5	6	7		9	10		8					11							
1	2		4	5	6	7		9	10		8			3		11							
1	2		4	5	6			9	10		8				7	11							
1	2		4	5	6	7		9	10		8			3		11							
1	2		4	5	6	7			10		8	9		3		11							
1	2		4	5	6	7		9	10		8			3		11							
1	2		4	5	6	7		9	10		8			3		11							
1	2		4	5	6	7			10		8	9		3		11							
1	2		4	5	6	7		9			8			3		11	10						
1	2		4	5	6	7		9			8			3		11	10						
1	2		4	5	6	7		9			8			3		11	10						
1	2		4	5	6	7		9			8			3		11	10						
1	2		4	5	6	7		9			8			3		11	10						
1	2	3	4	5	6	7		9			8					11		10					
1	2	3	4	5	6	7		9			8					11		10					
1	2		4		6						8	9		3	7	11		10	5				
1	2				6	7		9			8			3		11		10	5	4			
1	2		4		6	7		9			8			3		11		10			5		
1	2		4		6	7		9			8			3		11			5			10	
1	2		4	5	6	7		9			8					11		10	3				
1	2		4	5	6	7		9			8			3		11		10					
1	2		4	5		7		9			8			3		11		10		6			
1	2			5		7		9			8	4		3		11		10		6			
1	2		4	5				9		11	8			3	7			10		6			
1	2		4	5		7		9		11	8			3				10		6			
1	2		4	5		7		9		11	8			3				10		6			
1	2		4	5	6	7		9		11	8			3				10					
1	2		4	5	6	7		9			8			3		11		10					
1	2		4	5	6	7		9			8			3		11		10					
1	2		4		6	7		9			8			3		11		10			5		
1	2			5	6						8	9	4	3		11	10						7
1	2			5	6	7		9			8		4	3		11	10						
1	2		4	5	6	7		9	10		8			3		11							
42	41	12	38	37	37	38	3	36	18	12	39	6	3	30	3	30	7	16	4	6	2	1	1
			7		1			30	4		17	1	3			4	5	3				1	

Farm	Shimwell	Wright	Johnston	Hayward	Kelly	Matthews	McCall	Mortensen	Slater	Wardle	Mudie	McIntosh	McKnight	Garrett	Hobson	Perry	Withers	Brown	Crosland	Fenton	Ainscough	Stephenson	Adams
1	2		4		6	7		9			8			3		11		10	5				
1	2		4		6	7		9			8		10	3		11		10	5				
1	2		4		6	7		9			8			3		11		10	5				
1	2		4	5	6	7		9			8		10	3		11		10					
1	2		4	5		7		9			8		10	3		11		10		6			
1	2		4	5	6	7		9			8		1	3		11		10					
1	2		4	5	6	7		9			8		1	3		11		10					
1	2		4	5	6	7		9	10		8		1	3		11							
8	8		8	5	7	8		8	1		8			8		8		7	3	1			
								5			3					2		2					

League Table

	P	W	D	L	F	A	Pts
Tottenham Hotspur	42	25	10	7	82	44	60
Manchester United	42	24	8	10	74	40	56
Blackpool	42	20	10	12	79	53	50
Newcastle United	42	18	13	11	62	53	49
Arsenal	42	19	9	14	73	56	47
Middlesbrough	42	18	11	13	76	65	47
Portsmouth	42	16	15	11	71	68	47
Bolton Wanderers	42	19	7	16	64	61	45
Liverpool	42	16	11	15	53	59	43
Burnley	42	14	14	14	48	43	42
Derby County	42	16	8	18	81	75	40
Sunderland	42	12	16	14	63	73	40
Stoke City	42	13	14	15	50	59	40
Wolverhampton W.	42	15	8	19	74	61	38
Aston Villa	42	12	13	17	66	68	37
West Bromwich Albion	42	13	11	18	53	61	37
Charlton Athletic	42	14	9	19	63	80	37
Fulham	42	13	11	18	52	68	37
Huddersfield Town	42	15	6	21	64	92	36
Chelsea	42	12	8	22	53	65	32
Sheffield Wednesday	42	12	8	22	64	83	32
Everton	42	12	8	22	48	86	32

1951-52

Division One

Manager: Joe Smith

Did you know that?

Despite an uninspiring League campaign, the fans were flocking to Bloomfield Road as over 32,000 saw them draw with Arsenal on Easter Monday.

Ernie Taylor, who had impressed in the previous year's FA Cup Final, signed for £25,000.

After the previous season's FA Cup exploits, Blackpool were embarrassed by Second Division West Ham United in the third round.

Match No.	Date	Venue	Opponents	Result		Scorers	Attendance
1	Aug 18	H	Chelsea	L	1-2	Mortensen	31,172
2	22	A	Portsmouth	W	3-1	Perry, Own-goal, Mortensen	41,825
3	25	A	Huddersfield Town	W	3-1	Mudie, Own-goal, Brown	33,584
4	27	H	Portsmouth	D	0-0		30,628
5	Sep 1	H	Wolves	W	3-2	Mortensen 2, Mudie	32,074
6	5	A	Preston NE	L	1-3	Mortensen	40,809
7	8	A	Sunderland	W	3-1	Mortensen, Matthews, Withers	55,163
8	10	H	Preston NE	L	0-3		36,120
9	12	H	Aston Villa	L	0-3		31,783
10	22	A	Derby County	D	1-1	Slater	26,655
11	29	H	Manchester City	D	2-2	Mortensen, Slater	33,858
12	Oct 6	A	Burnley	L	0-2		34,855
13	13	H	Charlton Athletic	L	1-2	Mortensen	35,724
14	20	A	Fulham	W	2-1	Mortensen 2	43,569
15	27	H	Middlesbrough	D	2-2	Mortensen, Brown	23,195
16	Nov 3	A	West Brom Albion	D	1-1	Brown	43,045
17	10	H	Newcastle United	W	6-3	Perry, Mortensen 2, Taylor, Robinson, Brown	28,611
18	17	A	Bolton Wanderers	L	0-1		38,990
19	24	H	Stoke City	W	4-2	Brown 2, Robinson, Hobson	18,538
20	Dec 1	A	Manchester Utd	L	1-3	Perry	35,977
21	8	H	Tottenham Hotspur	W	1-0	Taylor	14,821
22	15	A	Chelsea	L	1-2	Wright W	38,912
23	22	H	Huddersfield Town	W	3-1	Mortensen 2, Brown	14,923
24	25	A	Liverpool	D	1-1	Mortensen	41,198
25	26	H	Liverpool	W	2-0	Mortensen 2	27,414
26	29	A	Wolves	L	0-3		32,496
27	Jan 5	H	Sunderland	W	3-0	Perry, Mortensen 2	22,252
28	19	A	Aston Villa	L	0-4		33,613
29	26	H	Derby County	W	2-1	Taylor 2	18,327
30	Feb 9	A	Manchester City	D	0-0		47,528
31	16	H	Burnley	W	1-0	Mortensen	26,079
32	Mar 1	A	Charlton Athletic	L	0-2		42,572
33	8	H	Fulham	W	4-2	Taylor, Mortensen 3	18,600
34	15	A	Middlesbrough	L	0-1		35,094
35	22	H	West Brom Albion	W	2-0	Mortensen, Own-goal	20,128
36	Apr 5	H	Bolton Wanderers	W	1-0	Mortensen	17,374
37	7	A	Newcastle United	W	3-1	Brown 3	47,316
38	11	H	Arsenal	D	0-0		32,186
39	12	A	Stoke City	W	3-2	Brown 3	24,895
40	14	A	Arsenal	L	1-4	Brown (pen)	48,445
41	19	H	Manchester Utd	D	2-2	Mudie 2	29,118
42	26	A	Tottenham Hotspur	L	0-2		45,991

Final League Position: 9th in Division One

Apps
Gls

FA Cup

3	Jan 12	A	West Ham Utd	L	1-2	Johnston	38,600

Apps
Gls

Farm	Shimwell	Garrett	Johnston	Hayward	Kelly	Matthews	Mudie	Mortensen	Brown	Perry	Hobson	Wright J	Withers	Fenton	McIntosh	Slater	Stephenson	Taylor	Robinson	Wright W	Crosland
1	2	3	4	5	6	7	8	9	10	11											
1	2	3	4	5	6	7	8	9	10	11											
1	2	3	4	5	6		8	9	10	11	7										
1		2	4	5	6	7	8	9	10	11		3									
1		2	4	5	6	7	8	9	10	11		3									
1		2	4	5	6	7		9	10	11		3	8								
1	2			5	6	7		8		11		3	10	4	9						
1	2			5	6	7		8		11		3	10	4	9						
1	2			5	6	7		9		11		3		4		8	10				
1	2			5	6	7	8	9		11		3		4		10					
1	2			5	6	7	8	9		11		3		4		10					
1		2	4	5	6	7		9	10	11		3				8					
1		2		5	6	7		9	10	11		3		4				8			
1	2	3		5	6	7		9	10	11				4				8			
1	2	3		5	6	7		9	10	11				4				8			
1	2	3		5		7		9	10	11				4				8	6		
1	2	3		5		7		9	10	11				4				8	6		
1	2	3		5		7		9	10	11				4				8	6		
1	2	3	4	5				9	10	11	7							8	6		
1	2	3	4	5					10	11	7			6		9		8			
1	2	3	4	5					10	11	7			6				8		9	
1	2	3	4	5					10	11	7							8	6	9	
1	2	3	4	5				9	10	11	7							8	6		
1	2	3	4	5				9	10	11	7							8	6		
1	2	3	4	5	6			9	10	11	7							8			
1	2	3	4	5	6			9	10	11	7							8			
1	2	3	4	5				9	10	11	7							8	6		
1	2	3	4	5	6			9	10	11	7							8			
1	2	3	4	5	6			9	10	11	7							8			
1	2	3	4	5	6			9	10	11	7							8			
1	2	3	4	5	6	7		9	10	11								8			
1	2	3	4	5	6	7		9	10	11								8			
1	2	3	4	5	6			9	8	11								10		7	
1	2	3	4	5	6			9	8	11	7							10			
1	2	3	4	5	6			9	8	11	7							10			
1	2		4	5	6			9	8		7	3	11					10			
1		2	4	5	6			9	8		7	3						10	11		
1		2	4	5	6			9	10		7	3						8	11		
1		2	4		6				10		7	3					9	8		11	5
1		2	4		6				10		7	3					9	8		11	5
1	2	3	4	5	6		9		10		7		11					8			
1	2	3	4	5	6		9		10		7		11					8			
42	33	36	31	40	32	19	9	35	37	35	22	15	6	13	2	5	3	30	10	5	2
						1	4	26	14	4	1		1			2		5	2	1	

Farm	Shimwell	Garrett	Johnston	Hayward	Kelly	Matthews	Mudie	Mortensen	Brown	Perry	Hobson	Wright J	Withers	Fenton	McIntosh	Slater	Stephenson	Taylor	Robinson	Wright W	Crosland
1	2	3	4	5		7		9	10	11								8	6		
8	8		8	5	7	8		8	1		8			8		8		7	3	1	
								5			3					2		2			

League Table

	P	W	D	L	F	A	Pts
Manchester United	42	23	11	8	95	52	57
Tottenham Hotspur	42	22	9	11	76	51	53
Arsenal	42	21	11	10	80	61	53
Portsmouth	42	20	8	14	68	58	48
Bolton Wanderers	42	19	10	13	65	61	48
Aston Villa	42	19	9	14	79	70	47
Preston North End	42	17	12	13	74	54	46
Newcastle United	42	18	9	15	98	73	45
Blackpool	42	18	9	15	64	64	45
Charlton Athletic	42	17	10	15	68	63	44
Liverpool	42	12	19	11	57	61	43
Sunderland	42	15	12	15	70	61	42
West Bromwich Albion	42	14	13	15	74	77	41
Burnley	42	15	10	17	56	63	40
Manchester City	42	13	13	16	58	61	39
Wolverhampton W.	42	12	14	16	73	73	38
Derby County	42	15	7	20	63	80	37
Middlesbrough	42	15	6	21	64	88	36
Chelsea	42	14	8	20	52	72	36
Stoke City	42	12	7	23	49	88	31
Huddersfield Town	42	10	8	24	49	82	28
Fulham	42	8	11	23	58	77	27

1952-53

Division One

Manager: Joe Smith

Did you know that?

Over 36,000 saw the opening home game of the season, a draw with Preston North End.

Allan Brown again missed the FA Cup Final through injury.

Stan Mortensen's hat-trick was the only one scored in an FA Cup Final at the old Wembley stadium.

Despite 'Morty's' hat-trick, the game will always be remembered as the Matthews Final due to the respect the player commanded throughout the country.

It was the first football match that the reigning monarch – Queen Elizabeth the second – had attended.

It was the first time that a team had overcome a two-goal deficit without the aid of extra-time in an FA Cup Final.

Only 13,000 tickets each were made available to both clubs.

Match No.	Date	Venue	Opponents	Result		Scorers	Attendance
1	Aug 22	A	Portsmouth	W	2-0	Brown, Mortensen	43,478
2	25	H	Preston NE	D	1-1	Mortensen	36,159
3	30	H	Bolton Wanderers	W	3-0	Own-goal, Matthews, Taylor	31,317
4	Sep 6	A	Aston Villa	W	5-1	Brown 3, Taylor, Mortensen	52,688
5	10	A	Chelsea	L	0-4		47,632
6	13	H	Sunderland	W	2-0	Mortensen, Perry	35,350
7	15	H	Chelsea	W	3-1	Mortensen, Perry Matthews	28,892
8	20	A	Wolves	W	5-2	Mortensen, Matthews, Perry, Taylor, Brown	48,598
9	27	H	Charlton Athletic	W	8-4	Own-goal, Brown 3, Mortensen, Garrett, Matthews, Taylor	33,498
10	Oct 4	A	Arsenal	L	1-3	Taylor	66,642
11	11	H	Burnley	W	4-2	Mortensen, Perry 2, Brown (pen)	35,671
12	18	A	Tottenham Hotspur	L	0-4		53,928
13	25	H	Sheffield Wed	L	0-1		28,162
14	Nov 1	A	Cardiff City	D	2-2	Hobson, Taylor	43,662
15	8	H	Newcastle United	L	0-2		33,712
16	15	A	West Brom Albion	W	1-0	Mortensen	33,712
17	22	H	Middlesbrough	D	1-1	Brown	19,934
18	29	A	Liverpool	D	2-2	Taylor, Perry	32,336
19	Dec 6	H	Manchester City	W	4-1	Matthews, Taylor, Brown 2	19,496
20	13	A	Stoke City	L	0-4		19,118
21	20	H	Portsmouth	W	3-2	Taylor, Fenton, Perry	13,562
22	25	H	Manchester Utd	D	0-0		27,778
23	27	A	Manchester Utd	L	1-2	Mortensen	49,934
24	Jan 1	A	Preston NE	L	2-4	Hobson, Perry	30,696
25	3	A	Bolton Wanderers	L	0-4		36,572
26	17	H	Aston Villa	D	1-1	Mudie	21,258
27	24	A	Sunderland	D	1-1	Hepton	53,653
28	Feb 7	H	Wolves	W	2-0	Brown 2	21,702
29	21	H	Arsenal	W	3-2	Mudie 2, Brown	30,034
30	23	A	Charlton Athletic	L	0-2		15,913
31	Mar 3	A	Burnley	W	1-0	Perry	20,874
32	8	H	Tottenham Hotspur	W	2-0	Mudie, Perry	26,796
33	15	A	Sheffield Wed	L	0-2		59,794
34	25	H	Cardiff City	L	0-1		15,227
35	28	A	Newcastle United	W	1-0	Taylor	41,205
36	Apr 3	H	Derby County	W	2-1	Mortensen, Taylor	27,382
37	4	H	West Brom Albion	W	2-0	Mortensen 2	30,392
38	6	A	Derby County	D	1-1	Mortensen	24,795
39	11	A	Middlesbrough	L	1-5	Durie	38,847
40	15	H	Stoke City	D	1-1	Perry	13,284
41	18	H	Liverpool	W	3-1	Perry, Garrett, Mudie	20,073
42	25	A	Manchester City	L	0-5		35,507

Final League Position: 7th in Division One

Apps
Gls

FA Cup

3	Jan 10	A	Sheffield Wed	W	2-1	Matthews, Taylor	60,199
4	31	H	Huddersfield Town	W	1-0	Garrett	29,239
5	Feb 14	H	Southampton	D	1-1	Perry	27,543
5R	18	A	Southampton	W	2-1	Own-goal, Brown	30,000
6	28	A	Arsenal	W	2-1	Taylor, Brown	68,000
SF	Mar 21	*	Tottenham Hot	W	2-1	Perry, Mudie	68,221
F	May 2	^	Bolton Wanderers	W	4-3	Mortensen 3, Perry	100,000

* Played at Villa Park, Birmingham. ^ Played at Wembley Stadium

Apps
Gls

Farm	Shimwell	Garrett	Johnston	Crosland	Kelly	Matthews	Taylor	Mortensen	Brown	Perry	Robinson	Mudie	Firth	Sharratt	Fenton	Hobson	Ainscough	Wright W	McKnight	Durie	HeptonHall	
1	2	3	4	5	6	7	8	9	10	11												
1		2	4	5	6	7	8	9	10	11	3											
1		2	4	5	6	7	8	9	10	11			3									
1	2	3	4	5	6	7	8	9	10	11												
1	2	3	4	5	6	7	8	9	10	11												
1	2	3	4	5	6	7	8	9	10	11												
1	2	3	4	5	6	7		9	10	11		8										
1	2	3	4	5	6	7	8	9	10	11												
1	2	3	4	5	6	7	8	9	10	11												
1	2		4	5	6	7	8	9	10	11			3									
1	2		4	5	6	7	8	9	10	11			3									
	2		4	5	6	7	8	9		11		10	3	1								
1	2	3	4	5			8	9	10	11					6	7						
1	2	3	4	5			8	9	10	11					6	7						
1	2	3	4		6		8	9	10	11						7	5					
1	2	3	5		6		8	9	10	11					4	7						
1	2	3	5		6		8	9	10	11					4	7						
1	2	3	5		6		8	9	10	11					4	7						
1	2	3	5		6		8	9	10	11					4	7						
1	2	3	5		6		8	9	10	11					4	7						
1	2	3	4	5			8	9	10	11					6	7						
1	2	3	4	5			8	9	10	11					6			7				
1	2	3	4	5			8	9	10	11					6			7				
1	2	3	4	5	6		8	9	10	11						7						
1	2	3	4	5	6		8	9	10	11						7						
1	2	3	5			7	10		9	11		8			6				4			
1	2	3	5			7	10		9	11		8			6						4	
1	2	3	4	5		7	10		9	11		8			6							
1		3	4	5	6	7	8		10	11		9	2									
1		3	4	5	6	7	8		10	11		9	2									
1	2	3	4	5	6	7	8			11		9								10		
1	2	3	4	5	6	7	8			11		9								10		
1		3			6		8	10		11		9	2		4	7	5					
1	2	3	5		6	7	8	9							4			11		10		
1	2	3	5		6		8	9				10			4	7				11		
1	2	3	5		6	7	8	9				10			4			11				
1	2	3	5		6	7	8	9				10			4			11				
1	2	3	5		6			9				8			4	7		11		10		
1	2	3	5		6	7	8	9				10			4					11		
		3	5		6		8	9		11		10	2		4	7						1
	2	3	5		6	7	8	9		11		10			4							1
1		3	5	6				9		11		10	2		4	7				8		
39	35	39	41	25	33	24	39	35	29	36	1	18	9	1	23	16	3	6	1	7	1	2
		2				4	11	15	15	12		5			1	2				1	1	

Farm	Shimwell	Garrett	Johnston	Crosland	Kelly	Matthews	Taylor	Mortensen	Brown	Perry	Robinson	Mudie	Firth	Sharratt	Fenton	Hobson	Ainscough	Wright W	McKnight	Durie	HeptonHall	
1	2	3	5			7	10		9	11		8			6				4			
1	2	3	4	5		7	10		9	11		8	10		6							
1	2	3	4	5		7	10		9	11		8			6							
1	2	3	4	5		7	10		9	11		8	10		6							
1	2	3	5		6	7	8		10	11		9	10		4							
1	2	3	5		6	7	8	10		11		9	1		4							
1	2	3	5			7	8	9		1	6	10	1		4							
7	7	7	7	3	2	7	7	2	5	7	1	7			7				1	1		
		1				1	2	3	2	3		1										

League Table

	P	W	D	L	F	A	Pts
Arsenal	42	21	12	9	97	64	54
Preston North End	42	21	12	9	85	60	54
Wolverhampton W.	42	19	13	10	86	63	51
West Bromwich Albion	42	21	8	13	66	60	50
Charlton Athletic	42	19	11	12	77	63	49
Burnley	42	18	12	12	67	52	48
Blackpool	42	19	9	14	71	70	47
Manchester United	42	18	10	14	69	72	46
Sunderland	42	15	13	14	68	82	43
Tottenham Hotspur	42	15	11	16	78	69	41
Aston Villa	42	14	13	15	63	61	41
Cardiff City	42	14	12	16	54	46	40
Middlesbrough	42	14	11	17	70	77	39
Bolton Wanderers	42	15	9	18	61	69	39
Portsmouth	42	14	10	18	74	83	38
Newcastle United	42	14	9	19	59	70	37
Liverpool	42	14	8	20	61	82	36
Sheffield Wednesday	42	12	11	19	62	72	35
Chelsea	42	12	11	19	56	66	35
Manchester City	42	14	7	21	72	87	35
Stoke City	42	12	10	20	53	66	34
Derby County	42	11	10	21	59	74	32

1953-54

Division One

Manager: Joe Smith

Did you know that?

Blackpool were beaten 3–1 by Arsenal in the Charity Shield.

Blackpool relinquished their FA Cup with a defeat at Third Division Port Vale.

A Christmas period where only five points were gained from a possible 20 derailed Blackpool's Championship challenge.

Allan Brown missed the entire season following his broken leg.

Match No.	Date		Venue	Opponents	Result		Scorers	Attendance
1	Aug	20	H	Chelsea	W	2-1	Mortensen 2	28,440
2		23	A	Burnley	L	1-2	Mortensen	41,574
3		27	A	Sheffield Utd	W	4-3	Mortensen 3, Mudie	35,171
4		29	H	Burnley	W	2-0	Mortensen 2	18,113
5	Sep	5	H	Huddersfield Town	W	3-1	Mortensen, Mudie, Fenton	34,507
6		7	H	Portsmouth	D	1-1	Mudie	30,914
7		12	A	Aston Villa	L	1-2	Mortensen	37,284
8		16	A	Portsmouth	D	4-4	Mudie 2, Mortensen, Perry	28,793
9		19	H	Wolves	D	0-0		35,074
10		26	A	Sunderland	L	2-3	Perry, Mudie	60,998
11	Oct	3	H	Manchester City	W	2-0	Mudie 2	35,666
12		10	A	Charlton Athletic	L	2-4	Mortensen, Fenton (pen)	56,664
13		17	H	Sheffield Wed	L	1-2	Mortensen	35,910
14		24	A	Middlesbrough	W	1-0	Taylor	39,416
15		31	H	West Brom Albion	W	4-1	Mortensen, Taylor 2, Perry	27,106
16	Nov	7	A	Preston NE	W	3-2	Fenton (pen), Brown, Mortensen	31,886
17		14	H	Tottenham Hotspur	W	1-0	Taylor	19,607
18		21	A	Manchester Utd	L	1-4	Perry	29,464
19		28	H	Bolton Wanderers	D	0-0		29,464
20	Dec	5	A	Liverpool	L	2-5	Taylor 2	47,320
21		12	H	Newcastle United	L	1-3	Perry	19,896
22		19	A	Chelsea	L	1-5	Mudie	34,865
23		26	H	Arsenal	D	2-2	Brown 2	29,347
24		28	A	Arsenal	D	1-1	Perry	63,661
25	Jan	1	A	Newcastle United	L	1-2	Brown	44,343
26		2	H	Sheffield Utd	D	2-2	Taylor 2	20,470
27		16	A	Huddersfield Town	D	0-0		25,735
28		23	H	Aston Villa	W	3-2	Stephenson, Perry 2	16,629
29	Feb	6	A	Wolves	L	1-4	Stephenson	27,795
30		13	H	Sunderland	W	3-0	Perry, Brown 2	23,058
31		24	A	Manchester City	W	4-1	Matthews 2, Brown, Perry	22,515
32		27	H	Charlton Athletic	W	3-1	Stephenson 2, Taylor	21,619
33	Mar	6	A	Sheffield Wed	W	2-1	Mudie, Brown	41,619
34		13	H	Middlesbrough	D	0-0		20,334
35		20	A	West Brom Albion	L	1-2	Mudie	53,019
36		31	H	Preston NE	W	4-2	Taylor 2, Durie, Mortensen	16,674
37	Apr	4	A	Tottenham Hotspur	D	2-2	Perry, Mortensen	43,870
38		11	H	Manchester Utd	W	2-0	Mortensen, Perry	25,996
39		17	H	Cardiff City	W	4-1	Brown, Mortensen, Taylor, Perry	26,194
40		18	A	Bolton Wanderers	L	2-3	Brown, Perry	40,291
41		20	A	Cardiff City	W	1-0	Perry	44,508
42		25	H	Liverpool	W	3-0	Mortensen 2, Brown	18,651

Final League Position: 6th in Division One

Apps

Gls

FA Cup

3	Jan	9	H	Luton Town	D	1-1	Mortensen	25,242
3R		13	A	Luton Town	D	0-0*		20,000
3R2		18	N*	Luton Town	D	1-1*	Johnston	33,000
3R3		25	N^	Luton Town	W	2-0	Perry, Stephenson	39,000
4		30	A	West Ham Utd	D	1-1	Brown	37,000
4R	Feb	3	H	West Ham Utd	W	3-1	Perry 2, Brown	27,120
5		20	A	Port Vale	L	0-2		40,500

* after extra-time. N* Played at Villa Park, Birmingham. N^Played at Molineux, Wolverhampton.

Apps

Gls

Farm	Shimwell	Garrett	Fenton	Johnston	Kelly	Matthews	Taylor	Mortensen	Mudie	Perry	Durie	Hobson	Wylie	Wright	Crosland	Brown	Robinson	McKnight	Harris	Frith	Stephenson	Gratrix	Ainscough
1	2	3	4	5	6	7	8	9	10	11													
1	2	3	4	5	6	7	8	9	10	11													
1	2	3	4	5	6	7	8	9	10	11													
1	2	3	4	5	6	7	8	9	10	11													
1	2	3	4	5	6	7		9	8	11	10												
1	2	3	4	5	6	7	8	9	10	11													
1	2	3	4	5	6		8	9	10	11		7											
1	2	3	4	5	6		8	9	10	11		7											
1	2	3	4	5	6	7	8	9	10	11													
1	2	3	4	5	6	7	8	9	10	11													
	2	3	4	5	6	7	8	9	10	11			1										
1	2		4		6	7	8	9	10	11				3	5								
1	2	3	4	5	6	7	8	9		11						10							
1	2	3	4	5		7	8	9		11						10	6						
1	2	3	4	5		7	8	9		11						10	6						
1	2		4	5	6	7	8	9		11				3		10							
1	2	3	4	5	6	7	8	9		11						10							
1	2	3	4	5	6	7	8	9		11						10							
1	2	3	4	5		7	8	9		11						10	6						
1	2	3	4	5		7	8	9		11						10	6						
1	2	3	4	5			8	9	10	11		7				6							
		3	4				8	9	10	11		7	1	3	5	6							
	2	3		4	6	7		9	8	11			1		5	10							
	2	3		4	6	7		9	8	11			1		5	10							
	2	3		4	6			9	8	11		7	1		5	10							
	2	3		4	6	7	8	9		11			1		5	10							
1	2	3			6		8		9	11					5	10		4	7				
1	2	3			6		8		10	11					5				7	4	9		
1	2		4	6					8	11					5	10			7	3	9		
1	2		4	5	6		8		7	11						10				3	9		
1	2		4	5	6		8		7	11						10				3	9		
1	2		4	5	6		8		7	11						10				3	9		
1	2		4	5	6	7			8	11						10				3	9		
1			4	5	6	7	8			11						10				3	9	2	
1			4	5	6	7	8		9	11						10				3		2	
			4	5	6	7	8	9		11	10		1	3								2	
			4	5	6	7	8	9		11	10		1	3								2	
1			4	5	6	7	8	9		11				3		10						2	
1			4	5	6	7	8	9		11				3		10						2	
1			4	5	6	7	8	9		11				3		10						2	
1		3	4		6				8	11						10			7		9	2	5
1		3	4	5	6	7	8	9		11						10						2	
34	32	28	36	37	35	32	35	32	24	42	3	5	8	8	9	27	4	1	4	8	8	9	1
			3			2	12	21	11	15	1					11					4		

Farm	Shimwell	Garrett	Fenton	Johnston	Kelly	Matthews	Taylor	Mortensen	Mudie	Perry	Durie	Hobson	Wylie	Wright	Crosland	Brown	Robinson	McKnight	Harris	Frith	Stephenson	Gratrix	Ainscough
1	2	3	4	5	6	7	8	9		11						10							
1	2	3	4	5	6	7	8	9		11			10			10							
1	2	3		4	6	7	8		9	11					5	10							
1	2		4			7	8			11			10		5	10	6			3	9		
1	2		4	5		7	8			11			10			10	6			3	9		
1	2		4	5		7	8			11			1			10	6			3	9		
1	2		4	5		7	8			11			1			10	6			3	9		
7	7	3	6	6	3	7	7	2	1	7					2	7	4			4	4		
				1				1		3						2					1		

League Table

	P	W	D	L	F	A	Pts
Wolverhampton W.	42	25	7	10	96	56	57
West Bromwich Albion	42	22	9	11	86	63	53
Huddersfield Town	42	20	11	11	78	61	51
Manchester United	42	18	12	12	73	58	48
Bolton Wanderers	42	18	12	12	75	60	48
Blackpool	42	19	10	13	80	69	48
Burnley	42	21	4	17	78	67	46
Chelsea	42	16	12	14	74	68	44
Charlton Athletic	42	19	6	17	75	77	44
Cardiff City	42	18	8	16	51	71	44
Preston North End	42	19	5	18	87	58	43
Arsenal	42	15	13	14	75	73	43
Aston Villa	42	16	9	17	70	68	41
Portsmouth	42	14	11	17	81	89	39
Newcastle United	42	14	10	18	72	77	38
Tottenham Hotspur	42	16	5	21	65	76	37
Manchester City	42	14	9	19	62	77	37
Sunderland	42	14	8	20	81	89	36
Sheffield Wednesday	42	15	6	21	70	91	36
Sheffield United	42	11	11	20	69	90	33
Middlesbrough	42	10	10	22	60	91	30
Liverpool	42	9	10	23	68	97	28

1954-55

Division One

Manager: Joe Smith

Did you know that?

Stan Mortensen was Blackpool's top scorer for the 11th consecutive season.

Harry Johnston retired from playing after 21 years at the club. He remains Blackpool's longest-serving player.

Blackpool were giant killed by Third Division York City in the FA Cup third round at home.

A 6–1 win at Manchester City effectively saved First Division football for the Seasiders.

Match No.	Date		Venue	Opponents	Result		Scorers	Attendance
1	Aug	21	A	Huddersfield Town	W	3-1	Mortensen, Perry, Taylor	35,793
2		23	H	Bolton Wanderers	L	2-3	Fenton, Taylor	33,915
3		28	H	Manchester Utd	L	2-4	Mortensen, Fenton	31,855
4	Sep	1	A	Bolton Wanderers	L	0-3		47,013
5		4	A	Wolves	L	0-1		50,203
6		11	H	Aston Villa	L	0-1		31,417
7		16	A	Charlton Athletic	D	3-3	Mudie, Durie, Mortensen	16,354
8		18	A	Sunderland	L	0-2		51,556
9		20	H	Charlton Athletic	D	1-1	Perry	20,164
10		25	H	Tottenham Hotspur	W	5-1	Brown 2, Fenton (pen), Stephenson, Perry	34,626
11	Oct	2	A	Sheffield Wed	L	1-2	Stephenson	31,415
12		9	H	Preston NE	L	1-2	Brown	36,264
13		16	A	Sheffield Utd	L	1-2	Stephenson	26,007
14		23	H	Chelsea	W	1-0	Fenton (pen)	19,694
15		30	A	Leicester City	D	2-2	Mortensen 2	40,655
16	Nov	6	H	Newcastle United	W	2-0	Own-goal, Perry	20,701
17		13	A	Everton	W	1-0	Mudie	57,137
18		20	H	Manchester City	L	1-3	Mudie	21,734
19		27	A	Cardiff City	W	2-1	McKenna, Taylor	19,823
20	Dec	4	H	Arsenal	D	2-2	Taylor, Stephenson	16,348
21		11	A	West Brom Albion	W	1-0	Stephenson	33,614
22		18	H	Huddersfield Town	D	1-1	Taylor	17,579
23		25	H	Portsmouth	D	2-2	Mudie 2	25,004
24		27	A	Portsmouth	L	0-3		43,896
25	Jan	1	A	Manchester Utd	L	1-4	Perry	54,774
26		15	H	Wolves	L	0-2		14,704
27		22	A	Aston Villa	L	1-3	Brown	30,161
28	Feb	5	H	Sunderland	D	0-0		21,899
29		12	A	Tottenham Hotspur	L	2-3	Hepton, Wright	47,386
30		19	H	Sheffield Wed	W	2-1	Fenton (pen), Hepton	18,959
31		26	A	Preston NE	L	1-3	Kelly J	30,853
32	Mar	5	H	West Brom Albion	W	3-1	Fenton (pen), Matthews, Brown	20,430
33		12	A	Chelsea	D	0-0		55,227
34		19	H	Leicester City	W	2-0	Mudie 2	24,185
35	Apr	2	H	Everton	W	4-0	Taylor, Mortensen, Perry, McKenna	19,269
36		8	A	Burnley	W	1-0	Mortensen	35,212
37		9	A	Arsenal	L	0-3		59,381
38		11	H	Burnley	W	1-0	Mortensen	32,881
39		16	H	Cardiff City	D	0-0		21,852
40		23	A	Manchester City	W	6-1	Perry 3, Mortensen 2, Brown	44,839
41		25	A	Newcastle United	D	1-1	Mortensen	41,380
42		30	H	Sheffield Utd	L	1-2	Perry	19,681

Final League Position: 19th in Division One

Apps
Gls

FA Cup

3	Jan	8	H	York City	L	0-2		26,039

Apps
Gls

Farm	Shimwell	Garrett	Fenton	Johnston	Kelly H	Matthews	Taylor	Mortensen	Bron	Perry	Withers	Gratrix	Stephenson	Mudie	Robinson	McKenna	Durie	Frith	Armfield	Kelly J	Smith	Hepton	Wylie	Wright	Harris
1	2	3	4	5	6	7	8	9	10	11															
1	2	3	4	5	6	7	8	9	10	11															
1	2	3	4	5	6	7	8	9	10		11														
1	2	3	4	5	6	7	8	9	10		11														
1		3	4	5	6	7	8			11		2	9	10											
1		3	4	5	6	7	8	9		11		2		10											
1		3	4	5			8	9	10			2		10	6	7	11								
1		3	4	5			8	9	10			2		10	6	7	11								
1		3	4	5		7	8	9		11		2		10	6										
1		3	4	5		7	8		10	11		2	9		6										
1		3	4	5			8		10	11		2	9		6	7									
1		3	4	5		7	8	9	10			2			6		11								
1		3	4	5	6	7	8		10			2	9			11									
1	2	3	4	5	6	7	8	9	10	11															
1	2	3	4	5	6	7	8	9		11				10											
1	2	3	4	5	6	7		9		11			10	8											
1	2	3	4	5	6	7	8	9						10		11									
1	2	3	4	5	6	7	8	9		11				10											
1	3		4	5	6		8	9		11		2		10		7									
1		3	4	5	6	7	8	9				2	11	10											
1		3	4	5	6	7	8	9				2	11	10											
1			4	5	6	7	8	9				2	11	10				3							
1			4	5	6	7	8			11		2	9	10				3							
1				5	6		8			11		3	9	10		7			2	6					
1			4	5	6	7	8	9		11		3		10					2						
1		3	4	5	6	7						2	10			11				8	9				
1		3	4	5	6	7			10	11		2								8		9			
1		3	4	5	6	7			10	11		2								8		9			
		3	4	6	6	7			10			2								8		9	1	11	
		3	4	5	6	7			10			2								8		9	1	11	
		3	4	5	6	7			10			2								8		9	1	11	
1		3	4	5	6	7			9	11		2		10						8					
1		3	4	5	6	7	8		9	11		2		10											
1		3	4	5	6	7	8	9		11		2		10											
1		3	4	5	6		8	9		11		2		10		7									
1		3	4	5	6		8	9		11		2		10		7									
1		3	4	5	6		8	9		11		2		10		7									
1		3	4	5		7	8	9				2		10						6					11
1		3	4	5	6	7	8	9		11		2		10											
1		3	4	5	6	7	8	9	10	11		2													
1		3	4	5	6		8	9	10	11		2				7									
1	3	5	4		6	7	8	9	10	11		2													
39	11	37	41	41	35	33	34	28	19	27	2	33	11	24	6	12	3	2	2	9	1	5	3	3	1
			6			1	6	11	6	10			5	7		2	1			1		2		1	

Farm	Shimwell	Garrett	Fenton	Johnston	Kelly H	Matthews	Taylor	Mortensen	Bron	Perry	Withers	Gratrix	Stephenson	Mudie	Robinson	McKenna	Durie	Frith	Armfield	Kelly J	Smith	Hepton	Wylie	Wright	Harris
1		3		5	6	7	10	9		11		2		8						4					
1		1		1	1	1	1	1		1		1		1						1					

League Table

	P	W	D	L	F	A	Pts
Chelsea	42	20	12	10	81	57	52
Wolverhampton W.	42	19	10	13	89	70	48
Portsmouth	42	18	12	12	74	62	48
Sunderland	42	15	18	9	64	54	48
Manchester United	42	20	7	15	84	74	47
Aston Villa	42	20	7	15	72	73	47
Manchester City	42	18	10	14	76	69	46
Newcastle United	42	17	9	16	89	77	43
Arsenal	42	17	9	16	69	63	43
Burnley	42	17	9	16	51	48	43
Everton	42	16	10	16	62	68	42
Huddersfield Town	42	14	13	15	63	68	41
Sheffield United	42	17	7	18	70	86	41
Preston North End	42	16	8	18	83	64	40
Charlton Athletic	42	15	10	17	76	75	40
Tottenham Hotspur	42	16	8	18	72	73	40
West Bromwich Albion	42	16	8	18	76	96	40
Bolton Wanderers	42	13	13	16	62	69	39
Blackpool	42	14	10	18	60	64	38
Cardiff City	42	13	11	18	62	76	37
Leicester City	42	12	11	19	74	86	35
Sheffield Wednesday	42	8	10	24	63	100	26

1955-56

Division One

Manager: Joe Smith

Did you know that?

Blackpool's highest-ever attendance at Bloomfield Road was recorded on 17 September, when 38,098 witnessed a 2–1 home victory over Wolves.

George Farm became one of the few goalkeepers to score a goal when he replaced the injured Jackie Mudie in the home game with Preston North End. It did not help as Blackpool were trounced 6–2.

The second-place finish in the First Division remains the club's highest-ever final League position in its history.

Match No.	Date		Venue	Opponents	Result		Scorers	Attendance
1	Aug	20	H	Arsenal	W	3-1	Taylor, Perry, Mortensen	30,928
2		22	A	Burnley	W	2-0	Perry 2	35,226
3		27	A	Portsmouth	D	3-3	Perry 3	37,072
4		29	H	Burnley	D	1-1	Taylor	25,774
5	Sep	3	H	Sunderland	W	7-3	Perry 3, Mudie 2, Mortensen 2	34,546
6		5	H	Chelsea	W	2-1	Fenton (pen), Mortensen	30,563
7		10	A	Aston Villa	D	1-1	Perry	52,000
8		17	H	Wolves	W	2-1	Mortensen, Matthews	38,098
9		24	A	Manchester City	L	0-2		63,925
10	Oct	1	H	Cardiff City	W	2-1	Fenton (pen), Perry	33,451
11		8	A	Luton Town	L	1-3	Mudie	24,473
12		15	H	Charlton Athletic	W	5-0	Durie 2, Mudie 3	34,247
13		22	A	Sheffield Utd	L	1-2	Mudie	23,753
14		29	H	Preston NE	L	2-6	Fenton (pen), Farm	25,692
15	Nov	5	A	Newcastle United	W	2-1	Brown, Mudie	54,692
16		12	H	Birmingham City	W	2-0	Taylor, Mudie	21,967
17		19	A	West Brom Albion	W	2-1	Brown, Taylor	37,910
18		26	H	Manchester Utd	D	0-0		26,240
19	Dec	3	A	Tottenham Hotspur	D	1-1	Mudie	51,162
20		10	H	Everton	W	4-0	Mudie 3, Perry	16,796
21		17	A	Arsenal	L	1-4	Own-goal	45,086
22		25	H	Portsmouth	L	2-3	Perry, Fenton	24,182
23		26	H	Huddersfield Town	W	4-2	Perry, Brown, Mudie, Lythgoe	27,628
24		27	A	Huddersfield Town	L	1-3	Mudie	41,626
25		31	A	Sunderland	D	0-0		41,626
26	Jan	14	H	Aston Villa	W	6-0	Mudie 2, Matthews, Brown 2 (2 pens), Perry	15,844
27		21	A	Wolves	W	3-2	Mudie, Brown (pen), Taylor	46,322
28	Feb	4	H	Manchester City	L	0-1		17,012
29		11	A	Cardiff City	L	0-1		36,000
30		18	H	Luton Town	W	3-2	Durie 2, Perry	18,562
31		25	A	Charlton Athletic	W	2-1	Taylor 2 (1 pen)	30,234
32	Mar	3	H	West Brom Albion	W	5-1	Matthews, Kelly J, Durie, Mudie 2	19,768
33		10	A	Preston NE	D	3-3	Durie 2, Perry	38,058
34		17	H	Newcastle United	W	5-1	Taylor, Mudie 2, Perry, Durie	23,740
35		24	A	Birmingham City	W	2-1	Durie, Perry	47,933
36		30	H	Bolton Wanderers	D	0-0		34,764
37		31	H	Sheffield Utd	D	1-1	Durie	27,272
38	Apr	2	A	Bolton Wanderers	W	3-1	Durie 2,Perry	35,471
39		7	A	Manchester Utd	L	1-2	Durie	62,277
40		14	H	Tottenham Hotspur	L	0-2		19,257
41		21	A	Everton	L	0-1		57,823
42		28	A	Chelsea	L	1-2	Durie	35,247

Final League Position: 2nd in Division One

Apps
Gls

FA Cup

3	Jan	11	A	Manchester City	L	1-2	Perry	42,517

Original game abandoned after 50 minutes due to fog

Apps
Gls

Farm	Shimwell	Garrett	Fenton	Gratrix	Kelly H	Matthews	Taylor	Mortensen	Mudie	Perry	Wright	McKenna	Armfield	Durie	Brown	Kelly J	Lythgoe	Frith	Fawcett	Snowdon	Harris
1	2	3	4	5	6	7	8	9	10	11											
1	2		4	5	6	7	8	9	10	11	3										
1	2		4	5	6	7	8	9	10	11	3										
1	2		4	5	6		8	9	10	11	3	7									
1	2		4	5	6	7	8	9	10	11	3										
1	2		4	5	6	7	8	9	10	11	3										
1	2		4	5	6	7	8	9	10	11	3										
1	2		4	5	6	7	8	9	10	11	3										
1			4	5	6	7	8	9	10	11	3		2								
1	2		4	5	6		8	9	10	11	3	7	2								
1	2		4	5	6		8	9	10	11	3	7	2								
1			4	5	6	7	8		9	11	3		2	10							
1			4	5	6		8		9	11	3	7	2	10							
1			4	5	6	7	8		9	11	3		2	10							
1			4	5	6	7	8		9	11	3		2		10						
1			4	5	6	7	8		9	11	3		2		10						
1			4	5	6	7	8		9	11	3		2		10						
1			4	5	6	7	8		9	11	3		2		10						
1			4	5	6	7	8		9	11	3		2		10						
1			4	5	6	7	8		9	11	3		2		10						
1			4	5	6	7	8		9	11	3		2		10						
1			4	5	6	7	8		9	11	3		2		10						
1			4	5	6	7			9	11	3		2		10		8				
1		3		5	6	7			9	11			2		10	4	8				
1		3	4	5	6				9	11		7	2		10		8				
1		3		5	6	7	8		9	11			2		10	4					
1				5	6	7	8		9	11	3		2		10	4					
1				5	6	7	8		9	11	3		2		10	4					
1				5	6	7			9	10	3				8	4		2	11		
1				5	6	7			9	11	3		2	10	8	4					
1				5	6	7	8		9	11	3		2	10		4					
1				5	6	7	8		9	11	3		2	10		4					
1				5	6	7	8		9	11	3		2	10		4					
1				5	6	7	8		9	11	3		2	10		4					
1				5	6	7	8		9	11	3			10		4		2			
1				5	6	7	8		9	11	3		2		10	4					
1				5	6	7	8		9	11	3		2	10		4					
1			6	5		7	8		9	11	3		2	10		4					
1				5	6	7	8		9	11	3		2	10		4					
1				5	6	7	8		9		3		2	10	11	4					
1					6	7	8		9	11	3		2	10		4				5	
1					6		8		9	11	3		2	10		4				5	7
42	8	4	25	40	41	36	37	11	42	41	38	5	32	15	18	18	3	2	1	2	1
1			4			3	8	5	22	20				14	6	1	1				

Farm	Shimwell	Garrett	Fenton	Gratrix	Kelly H	Matthews	Taylor	Mortensen	Mudie	Perry	Wright	McKenna	Armfield	Durie	Brown	Kelly J	Lythgoe	Frith	Fawcett	Snowdon	Harris
1		3	4	5	6	7	8		9	11			2	10							
1		1	1	1	1	1	1		1	1			1	1							
										1											

League Table

	P	W	D	L	F	A	Pts
Manchester United	42	25	10	7	83	51	60
Blackpool	42	20	9	13	86	62	49
Wolverhampton W.	42	20	9	13	89	65	49
Manchester City	42	18	10	14	82	69	46
Arsenal	42	18	10	14	60	61	46
Birmingham City	42	18	9	15	75	57	45
Burnley	42	18	8	16	64	54	44
Bolton Wanderers	42	18	7	17	71	58	43
Sunderland	42	17	9	16	80	95	43
Luton Town	42	17	8	17	66	64	42
Newcastle United	42	17	7	18	85	70	41
Portsmouth	42	16	9	17	78	85	41
West Bromwich Albion	42	18	5	19	58	70	41
Charlton Athletic	42	17	6	19	75	81	40
Everton	42	15	10	17	55	69	40
Chelsea	42	14	11	17	64	77	39
Cardiff City	42	15	9	18	55	69	39
Tottenham Hotspur	42	15	7	20	61	71	37
Preston North End	42	14	8	20	73	72	36
Aston Villa	42	11	13	18	52	69	35
Huddersfield Town	42	14	7	21	54	83	35
Sheffield United	42	12	9	21	63	77	33

1956-57

Division One

Manager: Joe Smith

Did you know that?

Only four home games attracted over 30,000, prompting the local press to declare that the town did not deserve First Division football.

Allan Brown joined Luton Town, and he eventually made an FA Cup Final appearance with them.

Jim Kelly retired from League football at the end of the season.

Blackpool played at Barcelona in a friendly on 24 May and drew 3–3.

On 19 April, Blackpool became the first club to fly to a game. It was at Highbury against Arsenal, where they drew 1–1.

Match No.	Date		Venue	Opponents	Result		Scorers	Attendance
1	Aug	18	A	Bolton Wanderers	L	1-4	Durie	33,310
2		22	A	Everton	W	3-2	Durie 3	55,442
3		25	H	Wolves	W	3-2	Durie, Mudie 2	28,482
4		27	H	Everton	W	5-2	Mudie 2, Brown, Matthews, Kelly J	14,709
5	Sep	1	A	Aston Villa	L	2-3	Mudie, Brown	46,000
6		3	H	Tottenham Hotspur	W	4-1	Brown 2, Durie, Matthews	28,460
7		8	H	Luton Town	W	4-0	Mudie, Brown, Durie, Wright	32,112
8		15	A	Sunderland	L	2-5	Mudie 2	45,914
9		22	H	Charlton Athletic	W	3-2	Mudie 2, Kelly J	34,199
10		29	A	Manchester City	W	3-0	Mudie, Fenton, Taylor	39,358
11	Oct	6	A	Burnley	D	2-2	Booth, Mudie	27,678
12		13	H	Preston NE	W	4-0	Fenton, Own-goal, Mudie 2	36,006
13		20	A	Sheffield Wed	W	2-1	Brown, Perry	46,395
14		27	H	Manchester Utd	D	2-2	Durie, Mudie	32,632
15	Nov	3	A	Birmingham City	D	2-2	Taylor, Mudie	35,597
16		10	H	West Brom Albion	L	0-1		18,839
17		17	A	Portsmouth	D	0-0		26,466
18		24	H	Newcastle United	L	2-3	Mudie, Durie	18,258
19	Dec	1	A	Chelsea	D	2-2	Brown, Mudie	45,327
20		8	H	Cardiff City	W	3-1	Brown 2, Durie	16,623
21		15	H	Bolton Wanderers	W	4-2	Durie,Mudie, Fenton (pen), Brown	17,556
22		22	A	Wolves	L	1-4	Brown	21,302
23		25	H	Leeds Utd	D	1-1	Brown	20,517
24		26	A	Leeds Utd	L	0-5		22,689
25		29	H	Aston Villa	D	0-0		16,777
26	Jan	12	A	Luton Town	W	2-0	Mudie, Durie	16,564
27		19	H	Sunderland	L	1-2	Mudie	18,702
28	Feb	2	A	Charlton Athletic	W	4-0	Own-goal, Mudie 2, Brown	31,746
29		9	H	Manchester City	W	4-1	Perry 2, Harris, Mudie	21,101
30		23	A	Manchester Utd	W	2-0	Perry, Durie	42,602
31	Mar	2	H	Sheffield Wed	W	3-1	Perry, Mudie, Durie	18,444
32		9	A	Cardiff City	W	4-3	Durie 4	16,000
33		16	H	Birmingham City	W	3-1	Perry, Taylor, Mudie	17,610
34		30	H	Portsmouth	W	5-0	Mudie 2, Durie, Harris, Own-goal	14,972
35	Apr	3	A	West Brom Albion	W	3-1	Smith 3	6,397
36		6	A	Newcastle United	L	1-2	Smith	31,810
37		13	H	Chelsea	W	1-0	Mudie	17,176
38		19	A	Arsenal	D	1-1	Perry	50,270
39		20	A	Preston NE	D	0-0		35,887
40		22	H	Arsenal	L	2-4	Mudie, Durie	24,118
41		27	A	Tottenham Hotspur	L	1-2	Mudie	49,878
42	May	1	H	Burnley	W	1-0	Mudie	13,919

Final League Position: 4th in Division One

Apps

Gls

FA Cup

3	Jan	5	A	Bolton Wanderers	W	3-2	Mudie 2, Durie	42,515
4		26	H	Fulham	W	6-2	Mudie 4, Own-goal, Durie	26,248
5	Feb	16	H	West Brom Albion	D	0-0		32,707
5R		20	A	West Brom Albion	L	1-2	Perry	48,054

Apps

Gls

Farm	Armfield	Garrett	Kelly J	Gratrix	Kelly H	Matthews	Taylor	Mudie	Durie	Perry	Starkey	Wright	Brown	Barnes	Fenton	Booth	Harris	Frith	McKenna	Shimwell	Smith	Snowdon	Peterson
1	2	3	4	5	6	7	8	9	10	11													
1	2	3	4	5	6	7	8	9	10	11													
1	2	3	4	5	6	7	8	9	10		11												
1	2		4	5	6	7		9	10			3	8	11									
1	2		4	5	6	7		9	10	11		3	8										
1	2		4	5	6	7		9	10	11		3	8										
1	2		4	5	6	7		9	10	11		3	8										
1	2		4	5	6	7		9	10	11		3	8										
1	2		4	5	6	7		9	10	11		3	8										
1	2		4	5		7	8	9	10	11		3			6								
1	2		4	5			8	9	10	11		3			6	7							
1	2		4	5		7	8	9	10	11		3			6								
1	2		4	5		7	8		10	11		3	9		6								
1	2		4	5		7	8	9	10	11		3			6								
1	2		4	5			8	9	10	11		3			6		7						
1	2		4	5		7	8	9	10	11		3			6								
1	2		4	5			8	9	10	11		3			6		7						
1	2		4	5			8	9	10	11		3			6		7						
1	2		4	5		7	8	9		11			10		6			3					
1	2		4	5		7	8	9	11				10		6			3					
1	2		4	5			8	9	11				10		6			3	7				
1	2		4	5			8	9		11			10		6			3	7				
1	2		4	5			8	9		11			10		6			3	7				
1	2		4	5				9	10	11			8		6			3	7				
1	2	3	4	5				9	10	11			8		6				7				
1	2	3	4	5				9	8	11			10		6				7				
1	2		4	5		7		9	8	11			10		6					5			
1	2	3	4	5		7	8	9		11			10		6								
1	2	3	4	5			8	9	10	11					6		7						
1	2	3	4	5		7	8	9	10	11					6								
1	2	3	4	5		7	8	9	10	11					6								
1	2	3	4	5		7	8	9	10	11					6								
1	2	3	4	5		7	8	9	10	11					6								
1	2	3	4	5			8	9	10	11					6		7						
1	2	3	4	5	6		8		10					11	4						9		
1	2	3		5	6		8		10	11					4				7		9		
1	2	3		5	6	7		9	10	11												4	8
1	2	3	4	5	6	7	8	9		11													10
1		3	4	5	6		8	9	10	11								2	7				
1		3	4	5	6		8	9	10	11								2					7
1			4	2	6		8	9	10	11								3				5	7
1				2	6		8	9	10	11		3									4	5	7
42	38	18	39	42	17	24	31	39	37	37	1	16	17	2	27	1	5	9	8	1	3	3	5
			2			2	3	32	20	7		1	13		3	1	2				4		

Farm	Armfield	Garrett	Kelly J	Gratrix	Kelly H	Matthews	Taylor	Mudie	Durie	Perry	Starkey	Wright	Brown	Barnes	Fenton	Booth	Harris	Frith	McKenna	Shimwell	Smith	Snowdon	Peterson
1	2	3	4	5		7		9	8	11			10		6								
1	2		4	5		7	8	9	10	11			10		6			3					
1	2	3	4	5		7	8	9	10	11					6								
1	2	3	4	5		7	8	9	10	11			10		6								
4	4	3	4	4		4	3	4	4	4			1		4			1					
								6	2	1													

League Table

	P	W	D	L	F	A	Pts
Manchester United	42	28	8	6	103	54	64
Tottenham Hotspur	42	22	12	8	104	56	56
Preston North End	42	23	10	9	84	56	56
Blackpool	42	22	9	11	93	65	53
Arsenal	42	21	8	13	85	69	50
Wolverhampton W.	42	20	8	14	94	70	48
Burnley	42	18	10	14	56	50	46
Leeds United	42	15	14	13	72	63	44
Bolton Wanderers	42	16	12	14	65	65	44
Aston Villa	42	14	15	13	65	55	43
West Bromwich Albion	42	14	14	14	59	61	42
Chelsea	42	13	13	16	73	73	39
Birmingham City	42	15	9	18	69	69	39
Sheffield Wednesday	42	16	6	20	82	88	38
Everton	42	14	10	18	61	79	38
Luton Town	42	14	9	19	58	76	37
Newcastle United	42	14	8	20	67	87	36
Manchester City	42	13	9	20	78	88	35
Portsmouth	42	10	13	19	62	92	33
Sunderland	42	12	8	22	67	88	32
Cardiff City	42	10	9	23	53	88	29
Charlton Athletic	42	9	4	29	62	120	22

1957-58

Division One

Manager: Joe Smith

Did you know that?

This was Joe Smith's 23rd and final season as Blackpool manager. His last match in charge was a 2–1 defeat at Tottenham Hotspur.

On 19 October, Blackpool played their 2,000th League game. It was at home to Manchester City, and they lost it 5–2.

Stoke City made an unsuccessful bid to re-sign Stanley Matthews at the end of the season.

Three days after the season ended, Blackpool travelled to Los Angeles and beat an All-Star team 13–2.

Match No.	Date		Venue	Opponents	Result		Scorers	Attendance
1	Aug	24	H	Leeds Utd	W	3-0	Durie, Perry, Taylor	26,700
2		26	H	Luton Town	L	1-2	Perry	21,099
3		31	A	Bolton Wanderers	L	0-3		28,584
4	Sep	4	A	Luton Town	L	0-2		19,511
5		7	H	Arsenal	W	1-0	Taylor	31,486
6		9	H	Manchester Utd	L	1-4	Mudie	34,181
7		14	A	Wolves	L	1-3	Perry	38,496
8		18	A	Manchester Utd	W	2-1	Mudie 2	40,763
9		21	H	Aston Villa	D	1-1	Taylor	31,079
10	Oct	5	H	Sunderland	W	7-0	Durie 2, Charnley 2, Taylor 2, Perry	33,172
11		12	A	Sheffield Wed	W	3-0	Mudie, Peterson, Durie	30,332
12		19	H	Manchester City	L	2-5	Mudie 2	28,322
13		26	A	Nottm Forest	W	2-1	Perry, Durie	41,736
14	Nov	2	H	Chelsea	W	2-1	Durie, Peterson	17,817
15		9	A	Newcastle United	W	2-1	Mudie 2	36,410
16		16	H	Burnley	L	2-4	Mudie, Kelly H (pen)	21,641
17		20	A	Everton	D	0-0		47,665
18		23	A	Birmingham City	D	0-0		32,168
19		30	H	Portsmouth	W	2-1	Mudie, Harris	14,722
20	Dec	7	A	West Brom Albion	D	1-1	Durie	27,900
21		14	H	Tottenham Hotspur	L	0-2		14,938
22		21	A	Leeds Utd	L	1-2	Taylor	32,500
23		25	H	Leicester City	W	5-1	Mudie, Perry 2, Peterson 2	16,699
24		26	A	Leicester City	L	1-2	Durie	33,052
25		28	H	Bolton Wanderers	L	2-3	Mudie, Harris	19,858
26	Jan	11	A	Arsenal	W	3-2	Charnley 2, Own-goal	38,667
27		18	H	Wolves	W	3-2	Taylor, Durie, Perry	17,953
28	Feb	1	A	Aston Villa	D	1-1	Taylor	45,000
29		15	A	Sunderland	W	4-1	Durie 2, Perry, Mudie	28,127
30		22	H	Sheffield Wed	D	2-2	Kelly H (pen), Charnley	13,771
31	Mar	1	A	Manchester City	L	3-4	Perry 2, Durie	30,621
32		8	H	Nottm Forest	W	3-0	Perry 2, Durie	16,492
33		15	A	Chelsea	W	4-1	Mudie 2, Charnley, Perry	49,471
34		22	H	Birmingham City	W	4-2	Mudie, Charnley, Perry 2	11,549
35		29	A	Burnley	L	1-2	Perry	20,771
36	Apr	4	H	Preston NE	L	1-2	Mudie	29,029
37		5	H	Newcastle United	W	3-2	Kelly H (pen), Charnley, Mudie	18,719
38		7	A	Preston NE	L	1-2	Charnley	32,626
39		12	A	Portsmouth	W	2-1	Perry, Durie	25,391
40		19	H	West Brom Albion	W	2-0	Charnley 2	17,327
41		23	H	Everton	L	0-1		12,981
42		26	A	Tottenham Hotspur	L	1-2	Charnley	37,632

Final League Position: 7th in Division One

Apps
Gls

FA Cup

3	Jan	5	A	West Ham Utd	L	1-5	Kelly H (pen)	34,000

Apps
Gls

Farm	Armfield	Wright	Kelly J	Gratrix	Fenton	Matthews	Taylor	Mudie	Durie	Perry	Smith	Kelly H	Charnley	Peterson	Garrett	Harris	Gregson	Martin	Snowdon	Hauser
1	2	3	4	5	6	7	8	9	10	11										
1	2	3	4	5	6	7	8	9	10	11										
1	2	3	4	5	6	7	8		10	11	9									
1	2	3	4	5	6	7				11		6	9	10						
1	2		4	5	6	7	8	9		11				10	3					
1	2		4	5	6	7	8	9		11				10	3					
1	2		4	5	6	7		8		11			9	10	3					
1		3	4	5			8	9		11		6		10	2	7				
1		3	4	5		7	8	9		11		6		10	2					
1	2		4	5		7	8		10	11		6	9		3					
1	2		4	5		7	8	9	10			6		11	3					
1	2		4	5		7	8	9	10	11		6			3					
1	2		4	5		7	8	9	10	11		6			3					
1	2		4	5		7		9	10	11		6		8	3					
1	2	3	4	5		7		9	10	11		6		8						
1	2		4	5		7		9	10	11		6		8	3					
1	2	3	4	5		7		9	10	11		6		8						
1	2	3	4	5		7		9	10	11		6		8						
1	2	3	4	5				9	10	11		6		8		7				
1	2	3	4	5				9	10	11		6		8		7				
1	2	3	4	5		7		9	10	11		6		8						
1	2	3	4	5		7	8	9	10	11		6								
1	2	3		5	4	7	8	9		11		6		10						
1	2	3		5	4	7	8	9		11		6		10						
1	2	3		5	4			9	10	11		6		8		7				
1		3	4	5		7		8	11			6	9	10	2					
1		3	4	5		7	8		10	11		6	9		2					
1		3	4	5		7	8		10	11		6	9		2					
1		3	4	5		7		8	10	11		6	9		2					
1		3	4	5		7		8	10	11		6	9		2					
1		3	4	5		7		8	10	11		6	9		2					
1	2	3	4	5		7		8	10	11		6	9							
1		3	4	5		7		8	10	11		6	9		2					
1		3	4	5				8	10	11		6	9	7	2					
1		3	4	5				8	10	11		6	9	7	2					
1	2	3	4	5				8	10	11		6	9				7			
1	2	3	4	5				8	10	11		6	9				7			
1	2	3	4	5				8	10	11		6	9				7			
1		3	4	5				8	10	11		6	9	7	2					
1		3	4	5		7			10	11		6	9	8	2					
1			4	5					10	11		6	9	7				3	5	8
1			4	5				10		11		6	9	7	2			3		8
42	27	31	39	42	10	30	16	35	33	40	1	36	20	25	23	4	3	2	1	2
							8	18	14	18		3	12	4		2				

Farm	Armfield	Wright	Kelly J	Gratrix	Fenton	Matthews	Taylor	Mudie	Durie	Perry	Smith	Kelly H	Charnley	Peterson	Garrett	Harris	Gregson	Martin	Snowdon	Hauser
1	2	3	4	5		7			10	11		6	9	8						
1	1	1	1	1		1			1	1		1	1	1						
												1								

League Table

	P	W	D	L	F	A	Pts
Wolverhampton W.	42	28	8	6	103	47	64
Preston North End	42	26	7	9	100	51	59
Tottenham Hotspur	42	21	9	12	93	77	51
West Bromwich Albion	42	18	14	10	92	70	50
Manchester City	42	22	5	15	104	100	49
Burnley	42	21	5	16	80	74	47
Blackpool	42	19	6	17	80	67	44
Luton Town	42	19	6	17	69	63	44
Manchester United	42	16	11	15	85	75	43
Nottingham Forest	42	16	10	16	69	63	42
Chelsea	42	15	12	15	83	79	42
Arsenal	42	16	7	19	73	85	39
Birmingham City	42	14	11	17	76	89	39
Aston Villa	42	16	7	19	73	86	39
Bolton Wanderers	42	14	10	18	65	87	38
Everton	42	13	11	18	65	75	37
Leeds United	42	14	9	19	51	63	37
Leicester City	42	14	5	23	91	112	33
Newcastle United	42	12	8	22	73	81	32
Portsmouth	42	12	8	22	73	88	32
Sunderland	42	10	12	20	54	97	32
Sheffield Wednesday	42	12	7	23	69	92	31

1958-59

Division One

Manager: Ron Suart

Did you know that?

Ex-player Ron Suart took over as Blackpool's new manager.

Blackpool embarked on a tour of Australia and China in May and June, and in their 13 victories out of 13 games they scored 74 goals.

Allan Brown scored the only goal as Luton Town dumped Blackpool out of the FA Cup.

Ernie Taylor left Blackpool and joined Manchester United in the wake of the Munich disaster.

Match No.	Date		Venue	Opponents	Result		Scorers	Attendance
1	Aug	23	A	Tottenham Hotspur	W	3-2	Charnley 2, Mudie	57,043
2		25	H	Newcastle United	W	3-0	Gregson, Charnley, Durie	25,231
3		30	H	Manchester Utd	W	2-1	Perry, Kelly H (pen)	36,719
4	Sep	3	A	Newcastle United	L	0-1		45,000
5		6	A	Wolves	L	0-2		46,219
6		8	H	Blackburn Rovers	D	1-1	Mudie	31,752
7		13	H	Portsmouth	D	1-1	Kelly H (pen)	26,035
8		15	A	Blackburn Rovers	D	0-0		30,947
9		20	A	Aston Villa	D	1-1	Charnley	27,000
10		27	H	West Ham Utd	W	2-0	Snowdon, Mudie	32,626
11	Oct	4	A	Nottm Forest	L	0-2		31,784
12		11	H	Burnley	D	1-1	Mudie	31,744
13		18	A	Bolton Wanderers	L	0-4		37,045
14		25	H	Everton	D	1-1	Perry	19,426
15	Nov	1	A	Leicester City	W	3-0	Durie, Kelly J, Garrett	31,642
16		8	H	West Brom Albion	D	1-1	Mudie	18,666
17		15	A	Leeds Utd	D	1-1	Mudie	29,252
18		22	H	Manchester City	D	0-0		19,200
19		29	A	Arsenal	W	4-1	Charnley 2, Mudie, Durie	54,792
20	Dec	6	H	Luton Town	W	3-0	Charnley, Mudie, Perry	14,140
21		13	A	Birmingham City	L	2-4	Charnley, Mudie	16,747
22		20	H	Tottenham Hotspur	D	0-0		12,939
23		25	H	Preston NE	W	4-2	Perry 3, Kelly J	24,411
24		26	A	Preston NE	W	3-0	Charnley 2, Kelly J	36,450
25	Jan	3	A	Manchester Utd	L	1-3	Fenton (pen)	61,720
26		31	A	Portsmouth	W	2-1	Charnley, Perry	23,556
27	Feb	7	H	Aston Villa	W	2-1	Durie, Charnley	13,704
28		16	A	West Ham Utd	L	0-1		28,332
29		21	H	Nottm Forest	W	1-0	Durie	13,228
30	Mar	7	H	Bolton Wanderers	W	4-0	Charnley 2, Durie, Mudie	21,072
31		14	A	Everton	L	1-2	Charnley	34,562
32		17	A	Burnley	L	1-3	Peterson	15,887
33		21	H	Leicester City	W	2-1	Perry 2	11,479
34		27	H	Chelsea	W	5-0	Perry 2, Mudie 2, Charnley	19,887
35		28	A	West Brom Albion	L	1-3	Mudie	30,100
36		30	A	Chelsea	L	1-3	Durie	40,534
37	Apr	4	H	Leeds Utd	W	3-0	Charnley 3	14,089
38		11	A	Manchester City	W	2-0	Durie, Perry	28,118
39		13	H	Wolves	L	0-1		22,328
40		18	H	Arsenal	L	1-2	Mudie	17,118
41		20	H	Birmingham City	W	2-0	Charnley, Durie	12,260
42		28	A	Luton Town	D	1-1	Fenton	17,720

Final League Position: 8th in Division One

Apps

Gls

FA Cup

3	Jan	10	A	Southampton	W	2-1	Charnley 2	29,265
4		24	A	Bristol City	D	1-1	Charnley	42,594
4R		28	H	Bristol City	W	1-0	Durie	25,933
5	Feb	14	H	West Brom Albion	W	3-1	Charnley 2, Durie	30,415
6		28	H	Luton Town	D	1-1	Charnley	30,654
6R	Mar	4	A	Luton Town	L	0-1		30,069

Apps

Gls

Farm	Garrett	Wright	Kelly J	Gratrix	Kelly H	Matthews	Mudie	Charnley	Durie	Perry	Gregson	Armstrong	Snowdon	Barnes	Armfield	Hauser	Starkey	Fenton	Martin	Peterson	Fawcett
1	2	3	4	5	6	7	8	9	10	11											
1	2	3	4	5	6		8	9	10	11	7										
1	2	3	4	5	6	7	8	9	10	11											
1	2	3	4	5	6		8	10				7	9	11							
1	2	3	4	5	6		8	10		11			9	7							
1	2	3	4	5	6	7	8	9	10	11											
1	2	3	4	5	6	7	8	9	10	11											
1	3		4	5	6		8	9	10	11				7	2						
1	3		4	5	6	7	8	9	10	11					2						
1	3		4	5	6	7	8		10	11			9		2						
1	3		4	5	6		8		10	11			9	7	2						
1	3		4	5	6	7	8		10	11			9		2						
1	3		4	5	6		8		11	7			9		2		10				
1	3		4	5	6	7	8		10	11			9		2						
1	3		8	5	6	7	9		10	11					2	4					
1		3	8	5	7	7	9		10	11					2	4					
1		3	4	5	6	7	8	9	10	11					2						
1		3	4	5	6	7	8	9	10	11					2						
1		3	4	5	6	7	8	9	10	11					2						
1		3	4	5	6		8	9	10	11				7	2						
1		3	4	5	6		8	9	10	11				7	2						
1		3	4	5	6	7	8	9	10	11					2						
1		3	10	5	6	7	8	9		11					2	4					
1		3	8	5			7	9	10	11					2	4		6			
1		3		5		7	8	9	10	11					2	4		6			
1	3		8		6		7	9	10	11			5		2	4					
1	3			5	6	7	8	9	10	11					2	4					
1	3		8	5	6		7	9	10	11					2	4					
1	3		8	5	6			9	10	11					2	4				7	
1			10	5	6	7	8	9	11						2	4			3		
1	3		10	5	6		8	9	11						2	4				7	
1	3				6		8	9	10				5	11		4			2	7	
1	3			5	6		8	9	10	11						4			2	7	
1	3			5	6	7	8	9		11					2	4				10	
1	3			5	6		8	9	10	11					2	4				7	
1	3			5	6		8	9	10	11					2	4				7	
1			6	2			8	9	10	11			5			4			3	7	
1	3			5	6		8	9	10	11					2	4				7	
1	3			5	6		8	9	10	11					2	4				7	
1			6	5			8	9	10	11					2	4			3	7	
1			6	5			8	9	10	11					2	4			3	7	
1	3			5				9	10	11					2	4		6		8	7
42	28	17	32	40	36	19	40	35	38	38	1	1	10	7	32	22	1	3	6	13	1
	1		3		2		14	20	9	12	1		1					2		1	

Farm	Garrett	Wright	Kelly J	Gratrix	Kelly H	Matthews	Mudie	Charnley	Durie	Perry	Gregson	Armstrong	Snowdon	Barnes	Armfield	Hauser	Starkey	Fenton	Martin	Peterson	Fawcett
1		3		5	6	7	8	9	10	11					2	4					
1		3		5	6	7	8	9	10	11			10		2	4					
1		3		5	6	7	8	9	10	11					2	4					
1		3		5	6	7	8	9	10	11			10		2	4					
1		3		5	6	7	8	9	10	11			10		2	4					
1		3	10	5	6	7	8	9	11				1		2	4					
6		6	1	6	6	6	6	6	6	5					6	6					
								6	2												

League Table

	P	W	D	L	F	A	Pts
Wolverhampton W.	42	28	5	9	110	49	61
Manchester United	42	24	7	11	103	66	55
Arsenal	42	21	8	13	88	68	50
Bolton Wanderers	42	20	10	12	79	66	50
West Bromwich Albion	42	18	13	11	88	68	49
West Ham United	42	21	6	15	85	70	48
Burnley	42	19	10	13	81	70	48
Blackpool	42	18	11	13	66	49	47
Birmingham City	42	20	6	16	84	68	46
Blackburn Rovers	42	17	10	15	76	70	44
Newcastle United	42	17	7	18	80	80	41
Preston North End	42	17	7	18	70	77	41
Nottingham Forest	42	17	6	19	71	74	40
Chelsea	42	18	4	20	77	98	40
Leeds United	42	15	9	18	57	74	39
Everton	42	17	4	21	71	87	38
Luton Town	42	12	13	17	68	71	37
Tottenham Hotspur	42	13	10	19	85	95	36
Leicester City	42	11	10	21	67	98	32
Manchester City	42	11	9	22	64	95	31
Aston Villa	42	11	8	23	58	87	30
Portsmouth	42	6	9	27	64	112	21

1959-60

Division One

Manager: Ron Suart

Did you know that?

This was the last season that Blackpool were to finish in the top half of the top tier of English football.

Hugh Kelly retired after 17 years at the club, and George Farm joined Queen of the South after becoming the first player to make 500 appearances for Blackpool.

The team toured Nigeria and Rhodesia at the end of the season, winning eight games and losing one, scoring 41 goals in the process.

Match No.	Date		Venue	Opponents	Result		Scorers	Attendance
1	Aug	22	H	Bolton Wanderers	W	3-2	Charnley 2, Mudie	29,216
2		26	A	Luton Town	W	1-0	Charnley	19,695
3		29	A	Fulham	L	0-1		42,611
4		31	H	Luton Town	D	0-0		22,008
5	Sep	5	H	Nottm Forest	L	0-1		25,987
6		9	A	Leicester City	D	1-1	Mudie	28,089
7		12	A	Sheffield Wed	L	0-5		29,328
8		14	H	Leicester City	D	3-3	Kelly J, Mudie, Armfield	20,494
9		19	H	Wolves	W	3-1	Mudie 3	35,303
10		26	A	Arsenal	L	1-2	Mudie	47,473
11	Oct	3	H	Manchester City	L	1-3	Mudie	33,236
12		10	A	Burnley	W	4-1	Kaye, Durie 3	26,620
13		17	H	Leeds Utd	D	3-3	Kaye, Durie, Peterson	22,301
14		24	A	West Ham Utd	L	0-1		32,455
15		31	H	Preston NE	L	0-2		27,796
16	Nov	7	A	West Brom Albion	L	1-2	Mudie	30,700
17		14	H	Newcastle Utd	W	2-0	Charnley, Kaye	15,667
18		21	A	Birmingham City	L	1-2	Charnley	24,783
19		28	H	Tottenham Hotspur	D	2-2	Charnley, Durie	17,085
20	Dec	5	A	Manchester Utd	L	1-3	Kaye	45,558
21		12	H	Chelsea	W	3-1	Durie, Charnley, Martin	12,410
22		19	A	Bolton Wanderers	W	3-0	Perry 2, Peterson	17,308
23		25	A	Blackburn Rovers	L	0-1		27,600
24		26	H	Blackburn Rovers	W	1-0	Charnley	30,071
25	Jan	2	H	Fulham	W	3-1	Perry, Kaye, Durie	17,046
26		16	A	Nottm Forest	D	0-0		20,722
27		23	H	Sheffield Wed	L	0-2		16,343
28	Feb	6	A	Wolves	D	1-1	Charnley	36,347
29		13	H	Arsenal	W	2-1	Mudie, Perry	14,868
30		27	H	Manchester Utd	L	0-6		23,966
31	Mar	5	A	Leeds Utd	W	4-2	Durie, Charnley 3	23,127
32		9	A	Manchester City	W	3-2	Kaye, Charnley 2	19,653
33		12	H	West Ham Utd	W	3-2	Perry 2, Charnley	14,513
34		19	A	Chelsea	W	3-2	Charnley, Perry 2	40,262
35		26	H	West Ham Utd	W	2-0	Durie, Kaye	16,190
36	Apr	2	A	Newcastle Utd	D	1-1	Kaye (pen)	31,182
37		9	H	Birmingham City	L	0-1		13,595
38		15	A	Everton	L	0-4		65,719
39		16	A	Preston NE	L	1-4	Charnley	26,126
40		18	H	Everton	D	0-0		25,697
41		23	H	Burnley	D	1-1	Charnley	23,733
42		30	A	Tottenham Hotspur	L	1-4	Perry	49,823

Final League Position: 11th in Division One

Apps
Gls

FA Cup

3	Jan	9	H	Mansfield Town	W	3-0	Durie 3	18,812
4		30	A	Blackburn Rovers	D	1-1	Kaye	51,223
4R	Feb	3	H	Blackburn Rovers	L	0-3		31,975

Apps
Gls

Farm	Armfield	Martin	Kelly J	Gratrix	Kelly H	Kaye	Mudie	Charnley	Peterson	Perry	Hauser	Durie	Garrett	Snowdon	Hill	Matthews	Waiters	Crawford	Fawcett	Green	Burrows	Smethurst
1	2	3	4	5	6	7	8	9	10	11												
1	2	3	4	5	6	7	8	9	10	11												
1	2	3	4	5	6	7	8	9	10	11												
1	2	3	4	5		7	8	9		11	6	10										
1	2		4	5		7	8	9		11	6	10	3									
1	2		4		6	7	8	9		11		10	3	5								
1	2		4		6	7	8	9		11		10	3	5								
1	2		4	5	6	7	9		8	11		10	3									
1	2	3	4	5	6	7	9		8	11		10										
1	2	3	4	5	6	7	9		8	11		10										
1	2	3	4	5	6		9		8	11		10			7							
1	2	3	4	5	6	11	9		8			10			7							
1	2	3	4	5	6	11	9		8			10			7							
1	2	3	4	5	6	11	9		8			10			7							
1	2	3		5	6	11	9		8		4	10				7						
1	2	3		5	6	11	8	9			4	10				7						
1	2	3	6	5		10	8	9		11	4					7						
1	2	3	6	5		10	8	9		11	4					7						
1	2	3	6	5		7		9	8	11	4	10										
1	2	3	6	5		7		9	8	11	4	10										
1	2	3	6	5		7		9	8	11	4	10										
1	2	3	6	5		7		9	8	11	4	10										
1	2	3	6	5		7	10	9	8	11	4											
	2	3	6	5		7		9	8	11	4	10					1					
	2	3	6	5		7		9	8	11	4	10					1					
1	2	3	6	5		7	8	9		11	4	10										
1	2	3	6	5		7	8	9		11	4	10										
	2	3		5	6		8	9			4					7	1	10	11			
	2	3		5	6		8	9		11	4					7	1	10				
	2	3		5	6		8	9		11	4					7	1	10				
	2	3	4	5		8		9		11		6				7	1			10		
	2	3	4	5		8		9		11		6				7	1			10		
	2	3	4	5		8		9		11		6				7	1			10		
	2	3	4	5		8		9		11		6				7	1			10		
	2	3	4	5		8	10	9		11		6				7	1					
	2	3	4	5		7	8	9		11		6					1			10		
		3	4	5		8	10	9		11		6				7	1				2	
	2	3	4	5	6	8		9		11						7	1			10		
	2	3	4	5			8	9				6			7		1		11			10
	2	3	4	5		11	8	9				6			7		1			10		
	2	3	4	5		8	10	9		11		6			7		1					
	2	3	4	5		8	10	9		11		6				7	1					
25	41	38	37	40	18	37	31	34	18	34	18	32	4	2	7	15	17	3	2	7	1	1
	1	1	1			8	9	18	2	9		10										

Farm	Armfield	Martin	Kelly J	Gratrix	Kelly H	Kaye	Mudie	Charnley	Peterson	Perry	Hauser	Durie	Garrett
1	2	3	6	5		7		9	8	11	4	10	
1	2	3		5	6	7	8	9		11	4	10	10
1	2	3		5	6	7	8	9		11	4	10	
3	3	3	1	3	2	3	2	3	1	3	3	3	
						1						3	

League Table

	P	W	D	L	F	A	Pts
Burnley	42	24	7	11	85	61	55
Wolverhampton W.	42	24	6	12	106	67	54
Tottenham Hotspur	42	21	11	10	86	50	53
West Bromwich Albion	42	19	11	12	83	57	49
Sheffield Wednesday	42	19	11	12	80	59	49
Bolton Wanderers	42	20	8	14	59	51	48
Manchester United	42	19	7	16	102	80	45
Newcastle United	42	18	8	16	82	78	44
Preston North End	42	16	12	14	79	76	44
Fulham	42	17	10	15	73	80	44
Blackpool	42	15	10	17	59	71	40
Leicester City	42	13	13	16	66	75	39
Arsenal	42	15	9	18	68	80	39
West Ham United	42	16	6	20	75	91	38
Everton	42	13	11	18	73	78	37
Manchester City	42	17	3	22	78	84	37
Blackburn Rovers	42	16	5	21	60	70	37
Chelsea	42	14	9	19	76	91	37
Birmingham City	42	13	10	19	63	80	36
Nottingham Forest	42	13	9	20	50	74	35
Leeds United	42	12	10	20	65	92	34
Luton Town	42	9	12	21	50	73	30

1960-61

Division One

Manager: Ron Suart

Did you know that?

The first live televised football League game in the country was at Bloomfield Road on 10 September 1960, with Blackpool losing to Bolton Wanderers 1–0.

Fewer than 9,000 saw Blackpool's 5–1 home victory over Leicester City – the first attendance under 10,000 at Bloomfield Road for 15 years.

Blackpool became one of the first clubs in Europe to sign a player from Asia. Cheung Chi Doy joined from Hong Kong's South China AA and so became the first Chinese player in the Football League.

Blackpool competed in the new League Cup, but exited at the first hurdle.

Match No.	Date	Venue	Opponents	Result		Scorers	Attendance
1	Aug 20	A	Leicester City	D	1-1	Charnley	27,062
2	22	H	Tottenham Hotspur	L	1-3	Mudie	27,656
3	27	H	Aston Villa	W	5-3	Charnley 2, Kaye, Mudie , Durie	16,821
4	31	A	Tottenham Hotspur	L	1-3	Lea	46,684
5	Sep 3	A	Wolves	L	0-1		34,036
6	5	H	Everton	L	1-4	Charnley	24,945
7	10	H	Bolton Wanderers	L	0-1		17,166
8	14	A	Everton	L	0-1		46,923
9	17	A	West Ham Utd	D	3-3	Charnley 2, Mudie	23,521
10	24	H	Chelsea	L	1-4	Charnley	26,546
11	Oct 1	A	Preston NE	L	0-1		17,445
12	8	H	Fulham	L	2-5	Charnley 2	20,623
13	15	A	Sheffield Wed	L	0-4		31,424
14	22	H	Nottm Forest	W	4-0	Charnley 2, Durie, Own-goal	15,733
15	29	A	Burnley	W	2-1	Durie, Perry	28,889
16	Nov 5	H	Cardiff City	W	6-1	Charnley 3, Perry, Durie, Parry	13,457
17	12	A	Newcastle Utd	L	3-4	Charnley, Parry, Durie	26,657
18	19	H	Arsenal	D	1-1	Charnley	15,417
19	Dec 3	H	Birmingham City	L	1-2	Charnley	11,720
20	10	A	West Brom Albion	L	1-3	Charnley	14,300
21	17	H	Leicester City	W	5-1	Charnley 2, Mudie, Kelly J, Perry	8,752
22	24	H	Blackburn Rovers	W	2-0	Perry, Charnley (pen)	19,379
23	27	A	Blackburn Rovers	L	0-2		18,200
24	31	A	Aston Villa	D	2-2	Parry 2	30,000
25	Jan 21	A	Bolton Wanderers	L	1-3	Charnley (pen)	15,909
26	Feb 4	H	West Ham Utd	W	3-0	Crawford, Parry, Charnley	9,947
27	11	A	Chelsea	D	2-2	Crawford, Parry	21,993
28	18	H	Preston NE	L	0-1		20,541
29	25	A	Fulham	L	3-4	Charnley, Hauser 2	19,342
30	Mar 4	H	Wolves	W	5-2	Perry 2, Parry, Durie, Charnley	15,312
31	11	A	Nottm Forest	D	0-0		29,646
32	15	H	Sheffield Wed	L	0-1		17,738
33	21	H	Burnley	D	0-0		19,391
34	24	A	Cardiff City	W	2-0	Charnley, Horne	20,000
35	31	H	Manchester Utd	W	2-0	Peterson, Own-goal	30,885
36	Apr 1	H	West Brom Albion	L	0-1		20,809
37	3	A	Manchester Utd	L	0-2		39,169
38	8	A	Arsenal	L	0-1		36,301
39	15	H	Newcastle Utd	W	2-1	Parry, Charnley	19,381
40	19	A	Manchester City	D	1-1	Crawford	28,269
41	22	A	Birmingham City	W	2-0	Peterson, Crawford	17,834
42	29	H	Manchester City	D	3-3	Hauser 2, Own-goal	20,838

Final League Position: 20th in Division One

Apps
Gls

FA Cup

3	Jan 7	A	Scunthorpe United	L	2-6	Mudie, Charnley	19,303

Apps
Gls

League Cup

2	Sep 28	A	Leeds United	D	0-0		13,064
2R	Oct 5	H	Leeds United	L	1-3*	Durie	9,614

* after extra-time

Apps
Gls

Waiters	Armfield	Martin	Kelly J	Gratrix	Durie	Matthews	Lea	Charnley	Kaye	Campbell	Mudie	Hill	Salt	Crawford	James	Garrett	Hauser	Green	Parry	Perry	West	Chi Doy	Peterson	Horne	Singleton
1	2	3	4	5	6	7	8	9	10	11															
1	2	3	4	5	6	7		9	10	11	8														
1	2	3	4	5	6	7	8	9	11		10														
1	2	3	4	5	6		8	9	11		10	7													
1	2	3	4	5	6		8	9	11		10	7													
1	2	3	4	5	6	7	8	9		11	10														
1	2	3	4	5	10		8	9	11			7	6												
1	2	3	4	5				9	7	11	8		6	10											
1	2	3	4	5		7		9	8	11	10		6												
1	2	3	4	5	11	7		9	8		10		6												
1	2	3	4		10		8		7	11	9		6		5										
1		3	6		10			9		11		7			5	2	4	8							
1	2		4	5	11	7		9	8		10		6			3									
1	2		4	5	8	7		9					6			3			10	11					
1	2		4	5	8	7		9					6			3			10	11					
1	2		4	5	8	7		9					6			3			10	11					
1	2		4	5	8	7		9		11			6			3			10						
1	2		4	5	8	7		9					6			3			10	11					
1	2		4	5	8	7		9					6			3			10	11					
1	2		4		8	7		9					6		5	3			10	11					
1	2		4	5		7		9			8		6			3			10	11					
1	2		4	5		7		9			8		6			3			10	11					
1	2		4	5		7		9			8		6			3			10	11					
1	2		4	5	11	7		9			8		6			3			10						
	2		4	5	6			9			8	7				3			10		1	11			
	2		8	5	6			9		7				10		3	4		11		1				
	2			5	6			9		7				10		3	4		11		1		8		
	2			5	6			9		7				10		3	4		11		1		8		
	2			5	6	7		9								3	4		10	11	1		8		
	2			5	6	7		9								3	4		10	11	1		8		
	2			5	6	7		9								3	4		10	11	1		8		
	2			5	6	7		9								3	4		10		1		8	11	
	2			5	6	7		9								3	4		10		1		8	11	
	2			5	6			9				7				3	4		10		1		8	11	
	2	3		5				9				7	6				4		10		1		8	11	
	2	3		5	6			9				7					4		10		1		8	11	
	2			5	6			9				7				3	4		10	11	1		8		
	2	3		5	6	7		9									4		10		1		8	11	
		3		5	6	7		9						8		2	4		10		1		11		
	2			5	6	7		9						8		3	4		10		1		11		
	2	3		5	6	7		9						8			4		10		1		11		
	2	3		5	6			9				7		8			4		10		1		11		
24	40	18	26	39	36	27	7	41	11	11	15	10	18	8	3	26	18	1	29	13	18	1	16	6	
			1		6		1	27	1		4			4			4		8	6			2	1	

Waiters	Armfield	Martin	Kelly J	Gratrix	Durie	Matthews	Lea	Charnley	Kaye	Campbell	Mudie	Hill	Salt	Crawford	James	Garrett	Hauser	Green	Parry	Perry	West	Chi Doy	Peterson	Horne	Singleton
	2		4	5		7		9			8		6			3			10	11	1				
	1		1	1		1		1			1		1			1			1	1	1				
								1			1														

Waiters	Armfield	Martin	Kelly J	Gratrix	Durie	Matthews	Lea	Charnley	Kaye	Campbell	Mudie	Hill	Salt	Crawford	James	Garrett	Hauser	Green	Parry	Perry	West	Chi Doy	Peterson	Horne	Singleton
1	2	3	4		10		8		7	11	9		6		5										
1		3	4	9	10					11		7	6		5								8		2
2	1	2	2	1	2		1		1	2	1	1	2		2								1		1
					1																				

League Table

	P	W	D	L	F	A	Pts
Tottenham Hotspur	42	31	4	7	115	55	66
Sheffield Wednesday	42	23	12	7	78	47	58
Wolverhampton W.	42	25	7	10	103	75	57
Burnley	42	22	7	13	102	77	51
Everton	42	22	6	14	87	69	50
Leicester City	42	18	9	15	87	70	45
Manchester United	42	18	9	15	88	76	45
Blackburn Rovers	42	15	13	14	77	76	43
Aston Villa	42	17	9	16	78	77	43
West Bromwich Albion	42	18	5	19	67	71	41
Arsenal	42	15	11	16	77	85	41
Chelsea	42	15	7	20	98	100	37
Manchester City	42	13	11	18	79	90	37
Nottingham Forest	42	14	9	19	62	78	37
Cardiff City	42	13	11	18	60	85	37
West Ham United	42	13	10	19	77	88	36
Fulham	42	14	8	20	72	95	36
Bolton Wanderers	42	12	11	19	58	73	35
Birmingham City	42	14	6	22	62	84	34
Blackpool	42	12	9	21	68	73	33
Newcastle United	42	11	10	21	86	109	32
Preston North End	42	10	10	22	43	71	30

1961-62

Division One

Manager: Ron Suart

Did you know that?

Stanley Matthews made his final appearance for Blackpool on 7 October in a 3–0 home defeat to Arsenal. He left Bloomfield Road to rejoin Stoke City.

Blackpool reached the semi-finals of the League Cup, losing to Norwich City over two legs.

Any traces of blue in the home kit all but disappeared as tangerine and white was now the accepted style. Blue was to re-appear in a subtle way in the mid-1980s.

Match No.	Date		Venue	Opponents	Result		Scorers	Attendance
1	Aug	19	H	Tottenham Hotspur	L	1-2	Charnley	29,023
2		21	H	Blackburn Rovers	W	2-1	Charnley (pen), Peterson	21,680
3		26	A	Cardiff City	L	2-3	Horne, Charnley	22,700
4		28	A	Blackburn Rovers	D	1-1	Horne	22,400
5	Sep	2	H	Manchester Utd	L	2-3	Charnley 2 (1 pen)	28,156
6		4	H	West Ham Utd	W	2-0	Horne, Hill	19,838
7		9	A	Wolves	D	2-2	Charnley 2 (1 pen)	22,669
8		16	H	Nottm Forest	L	1-3	Charnley	23,737
9		18	A	West Ham Utd	D	2-2	Hauser, Parry	25,528
10		23	A	Aston Villa	L	0-5		31,700
11		30	H	Chelsea	W	4-0	Charnley 3, Peterson	24,191
12	Oct	7	A	Arsenal	L	0-3		41,166
13		14	H	Bolton Wanderers	W	2-1	Horne, Peterson	22,062
14		21	A	Leicester City	W	2-0	Charnley 2 (1 pen)	17,424
15		28	H	Ipswich Town	D	1-1	Parry	19,773
16	Nov	4	A	Birmingham City	D	1-1	Charnley	19,007
17		11	H	Everton	D	1-1	Durie	23,026
18		18	A	Fulham	W	1-0	Parry	18,592
19		25	H	Sheffield Wed	L	1-3	Chi Doy	16,569
20	Dec	2	A	Manchester City	W	4-2	Charnley 2, Horne, Peterson	15,971
21		9	H	West Brom Albion	D	2-2	Crawford, Peterson	13,076
22		16	A	Tottenham Hotspur	L	2-5	Charnley, Own-goal	42,734
23		23	H	Cardiff City	W	3-0	Parry 2, Charnley	13,961
24		26	A	Sheffield Utd	L	1-2	Peterson	22,757
25	Jan	13	A	Manchester Utd	W	1-0	Hauser	27,082
26		20	H	Wolves	W	7-2	Charnley 4, Hauser, Perry, Crawford	12,852
27	Feb	3	A	Nottm Forest	W	4-3	Charnley, Parry 2, Perry	17,828
28		10	H	Aston Villa	L	1-2	Parry	13,039
29		16	A	Chelsea	L	0-1		24,276
30		24	H	Arsenal	L	0-1		13,728
31	Mar	3	A	Bolton Wanderers	D	0-0		14,831
32		10	H	Leicester City	W	2-1	Charnley, Hauser	10,952
33		17	A	Ipswich Town	D	1-1	Charnley	22,521
34		24	H	Birmingham City	W	1-0	Hauser	11,854
35		30	A	Everton	D	2-2	Peterson, Charnley	38,302
36	Apr	3	H	Sheffield Utd	L	2-4	Parry, Hauser	11,199
37		7	H	Fulham	W	2-1	Charnley, Parry	10,641
38		14	A	Sheffield Wed	L	2-3	Green, Parry	18,099
39		20	A	Burnley	L	0-2		34,132
40		21	H	Manchester City	W	3-1	Charnley, Green, Parry	19,954
41		23	H	Burnley	D	1-1	Charnley	31,660
42		28	A	West Brom Albion	L	1-7	Charnley	17,482

Final League Position: 13th in Division One

Apps
Gls

FA Cup

3	Jan	6	H	West Brom Albion	D	0-0		19,250
3R		10	A	West Brom Albion	L	1-2	Hauser	27,061

Apps
Gls

League Cup

1	Sep	13	H	Port Vale	W	2-1	Charnley, Parry	10,494
2	Oct	4	A	Leyton Orient	D	1-1	Oates	9,910
2R		30	H	Leyton Orient	W	5-1	Parry 2, Charnley 3	6,098
3	Nov	5	A	Workington	W	1-0	Green	10,035
4	Feb	6	H	Sheffield Utd	D	0-0		11,127
4R	Mar	27	A	Sheffield Utd	W	2-0	Parry, Charnley	12,895
SF	Apr	11	A	Norwich City	L	1-4	Peterson	19,231
		16	H	Norwich City	W	2-0	Horne, Charnley	9,124

Apps
Gls

West	Armfield	Martin	Hauser	Gratrix	Durie	Horne	Peterson	Charnley	Parry	Perry	Hill	Green	Oates	Crawford	Matthews	Waiters	Thompson	Chi Doy	Cranston	Harvey	Halsall	James	Napier
1	2	3	4	5	6	7	8	9	10	11													
1	2	3	4	5	6	11	8	9	10		7												
1	2	3	4	5	6	11	8	9	10		7												
1	2	3	4	5	6	11	7	9	10			8											
1	2	3	4	5	6	11	7	9	10			8											
1	2	3	4	5	6	11	8	9	10		7												
1	2	3	4	5	6	11	8	9	10		7												
1	2	3	4	5	6		7	9	10			8	11										
1	2	3	4	5	6			9	10	11	7			8									
1	2	3	4	5	6			9	10	11	7			8									
1	2	3	4	5	6		8	9	10				11		7								
1	2	3	4	5	6		8	9	10				11		7								
		3		5	6	11	8	9	10		7			4		1	2						
		3		5	6	11	8	9	10		7			4		1	2						
	2	3	4	5	6	11	8	9	10		7			4		1							
		3		5	6	11	8	9	10		7			4		1	2						
	9	3		5	6	11	8		10		7			4		1	2						
	2	3		5	6	11		9	10		7	8		4		1							
	2	3		5	6	11		9	10		7			4		1		8					
	2	3		5	6	11	8	9	10		7			4		1							
	2	3		5	6	11	8	9	10		7			4		1							
	2	3		5	6	11	8	9	10		7			4		1							
	2	3		5	6	11	8	9	10		7			4		1							
	2	3		5	6	11	8	9	10		7			4		1							
	2	3	8	5	6			9	10	11	7			4		1							
	2	3	8	5				9	10	11	7			4		1			6				
	2	3	8	5	6			9	10	11	7			4		1							
	2	3	8	5	6			9	10	11	7			4		1							
	2		8	5	6			9	10	11	7			4		1	3						
	2	3		5	10		8	9		11	7			4		1			6				
	2	3	8	5	6			9	10	11	7			4		1							
	2	3	8	5	6	11		9	10		7			4		1							
	2	3	8	5	6	11		9	10		7			4						1			
	2	3	8	5	6	11		9	10		7			4						1			
	2	3	8	5	6		10	9	11		7			4						1			
		3	8	5	6		10	9	11		7			4			2			1			
	2	3		5	6	11	8	9	10		7			4						1			
		3		5	6	11		9	10		7	8		4						1		5	
	2	3		5		11		9	10		7	8		4					6	1			
	2	3		5	6	11		9	10		7	8		4							1		
	2	3		5	6			9	10		7	8	11	4							1		
	2	3		5	6	11		9	10		7	8		4						1			
12	37	41	23	42	40	27	24	42	41	10	36	9	4	32	2	20	6	1	3	8	2	1	
			6		1	5	7	30	12	2	1	2		2				1					

	2	3		5	6	11	8	9	10		7			4		1							
	2	3	8	5	6			9	10	11	7		10	4		1							
	2	2	1	2	2	1	1	2	2	1	2			2		2							
			1																				

1	2	3	4	5	6		7	9	10	11				8									
1	2	3	4	5	6	7	8	9	10				11										
		3		5	6	11	8	9	10		7			4		1	2						
	2	3		5	6	11			10		7	8		4		1							
	2	3	8	5	6			9	10	11	7			4		1							
	2	3	8	5	6	11		9	10		7			4						1			
		3		5	6	11	8	9	10		7			4			2			1			
	2	3		5	6	11		9	10		7	8		4						1			
2	6	8	4	8	8	6	4	7	8	2	6	2	1	7		3	2			3			
						1	1	6	4			1	1										

League Table

	P	W	D	L	F	A	Pts
Ipswich Town	42	24	8	10	93	67	56
Burnley	42	21	11	10	101	67	53
Tottenham Hotspur	42	21	10	11	88	69	52
Everton	42	20	11	11	88	54	51
Sheffield United	42	19	9	14	61	69	47
Sheffield Wednesday	42	20	6	16	72	58	46
Aston Villa	42	18	8	16	65	56	44
West Ham United	42	17	10	15	76	82	44
West Bromwich Albion	42	15	13	14	83	67	43
Arsenal	42	16	11	15	71	72	43
Bolton Wanderers	42	16	10	16	62	66	42
Manchester City	42	17	7	18	78	81	41
Blackpool	42	15	11	16	70	75	41
Leicester City	42	17	6	19	72	71	40
Manchester United	42	15	9	18	72	75	39
Blackburn Rovers	42	14	11	17	50	58	39
Birmingham City	42	14	10	18	65	81	38
Wolverhampton W.	42	13	10	19	73	86	36
Nottingham Forest	42	13	10	19	63	79	36
Fulham	42	13	7	22	66	74	33
Cardiff City	42	9	14	19	50	81	32
Chelsea	42	9	10	23	63	94	28

1962-63

Division One

Manager: Ron Suart

Did you know that?

Ray Charnley was Blackpool's top scorer for the fifth successive season.

The FA Cup third-round tie at Norwich City was postponed 11 times before a 1–1 draw on 3 March. Norwich won the replay.

Bill Perry left the club, but new talent Alan Ball joined.

Blackpool played in the Orange Bowl trophy in June in Valencia, losing to both the hosts and FC Lisbon heavily.

Match No.	Date		Venue	Opponents	Result		Scorers	Attendance
1	Aug	18	A	Liverpool	W	2-1	Charnley, Horne	51,207
2		20	H	Ipswich Town	W	1-0	Horne	23,305
3		25	H	Wolves	L	0-2		23,823
4		28	A	Ipswich Town	L	2-5	Durie, Charnley (pen)	21,079
5	Sep	1	A	Aston Villa	D	1-1	Horne	35,006
6		3	H	Nottm Forest	W	2-1	Horne, Green	19,737
7		8	H	Tottenham Hotspur	L	1-2	Charnley	31,773
8		11	A	Nottm Forest	L	0-2		19,032
9		14	A	West Ham Utd	D	2-2	McPhee 2	24,745
10		22	H	Manchester City	D	2-2	Charnley 2 (1 pen)	29,461
11		29	A	Burnley	L	0-2		28,345
12	Oct	6	H	Manchester Utd	D	2-2	McPhee, Charnley	33,242
13		13	A	Leyton Orient	W	2-0	Parry 2	17,156
14		20	H	Fulham	D	0-0		17,115
15		27	A	Sheffield Wed	D	0-0		20,277
16	Nov	3	H	West Brom Albion	L	0-2		12,528
17		10	A	Everton	L	0-5		39,317
18		17	H	Bolton Wanderers	W	3-1	Durie, Charnley, Quinn	12,272
19		24	A	Leicester City	D	0-0		21,832
20	Dec	1	H	Birmingham City	D	1-1	Durie	12,955
21		8	A	Arsenal	L	0-2		23,767
22		15	H	Liverpool	L	1-2	Quinn	16,271
23	Jan	19	A	Tottenham Hotspur	L	0-2		25,710
24	Feb	23	A	Manchester Utd	D	1-1	Charnley (pen)	43,121
25	Mar	2	H	Leyton Orient	W	3-2	Quinn (pen), McPhee, Own-goal	11,732
26		9	A	Fulham	L	0-2		8,954
27		16	H	Sheffield Wed	L	2-3	Charnley 2	10,141
28		20	H	Burnley	D	0-0		16,445
29		23	A	West Brom Albion	W	2-1	McPhee, Parry	14,829
30		25	A	Blackburn Rovers	D	3-3	Parry, Crawford, Charnley	9,900
31		29	H	Aston Villa	W	4-0	Charnley 3, Parry	10,690
32	Apr	6	A	Bolton Wanderers	L	0-3		14,486
33		8	H	Leicester City	D	1-1	Charnley (pen)	16,765
34		13	H	Everton	L	1-2	Quinn	27,842
35		15	H	Sheffield Utd	W	3-1	Charnley, Quinn 2	16,746
36		16	A	Sheffield Utd	D	0-0		21,637
37		20	A	Birmingham City	W	6-3	Crawford, Durie, Charnley 3, Own-goal	15,396
38		23	H	Blackburn Rovers	W	4-1	Charnley, McPhee, Quinn 2	16,446
39		27	H	Arsenal	W	3-2	Charnley 2, Lea	13,864
40	May	4	A	Manchester City	W	3-0	Crawford 2, Lea	19,062
41		9	A	Wolves	L	0-2		14,889
42		13	H	West Ham Utd	D	0-0		12,424

Final League Position: 13th in Division One

Apps

Gls

FA Cup

3	Mar	4	A	Norwich City	D	1-1	McPhee	26,002
3R		6	H	Norwich City	L	1-2	Quinn	15,599

Apps

Gls

League Cup

2	Sep	24	A	Manchester City	D	0-0		12,064
2R	Oct	8	H	Manchester City	D	3-3	Horne, Watt, Parry	10,508
2R2		15	A	Manchester City	L	2-4	McPhee 2	12,237

Apps

Gls

League

West	Armfield	Martin	Crawford	Gratrix	Durie	Ball	Green	Charnley	Parry	Horne	James	Hill	McPhee	Watt	Thompson	Oates	Cranston	Lea	Quinn	Napier	Turner	Prentis
1	2	3	4	5	6	7	8	9	10	11												
1	2	3	4	5	6	7	8	9	10	11												
1	2	3	4	5	6	7	8	9	10	11												
1	2	3	4		6	7	8	9	10	11	5											
1	2	3	4		6		8	9	10	11	5	7	10									
1	2	3	4		6		8	9	10	11	5	7	10									
1	2	3	4		6		8	9	10	11	5	7	10									
1	2	3	4		6	7	8	9	10	11	5		10									
1	2	3	4		6		8	9	10	11	5		10	7								
1	2	3	4		6		8	9	10	11	5	7	10									
1	2	3	4	5	6			9	10	11		7	8									
1	2	3	4	5	6			9	10	11			8	7								
1		3	4	5	6			9	10	11			8	7	2							
1	2	3	4	5	6			9	10			7	8			11						
1	2	3	4	5				9	10	11			8	7			6					
1	2	3	4	5	10		8	9	11								6	7				
1	2	3	4	5	10			9	11				6					7	8			
1	2	3	4	5	10			9	11				6					7	8			
1	2	3	4	5	10			9	11				6					7	8			
1	2	3	4	5	10			9		11			6					7	8			
1	2	3	4	5	10			9	11			7	6						8			
1	2	3	10	5	6			9	11			7	6						8			
1	2	3		5	6			10		11		7	4						8	9		
1	2	3	4	5	6				11				10					7	8	9		
1	2	3		5	6		10	9	11				4					7	8			
1	2	3	10	5	6			9	11				4					7	8			
1	2	3	10	5	6			9	11				4					7	8			
1	2	3	10	5	6			9	11				4					7	8			
1	2	3	10	5	6			9	11				4					7	8			
1	2	3	10	5	6			9	11				4					7	8			
1		3	10	5	6			9	11				4		2			7	8			
1	2	3	10	5	6			9	11				4					7	8			
1	2	3	10	5	6			9	11				4					7	8			
1	2	3	10	5	6			9	11				4					7	8			
1	2	3	10	5	6			9	11				4					7	8			
1	2	3	10	5	6			9	11				4					7	8			
1	2	3	10	5	6			9	11				4					7	8			
1	2	3	10	5	6			9	11				4					7	8			
1	2	3	10	5	6			9	11				4					7	8			
1	2	3	10	5	6			9	11				4					7	8			
1	2	3	10	5	6			9	11				4					7	8			
1		3	10	5				9	11				4		2		6	7	8			
42	39	42	40	35	40	5	12	41	34	17	7	9	37	5	3	1	3	23	25	2		
			4		4		1	22	5	4			6					2	8			

FA Cup

West	Armfield	Martin	Crawford	Gratrix	Durie	Ball	Green	Charnley	Parry	Horne	James	Hill	McPhee	Watt	Thompson	Oates	Cranston	Lea	Quinn	Napier	Turner	Prentis
1	2	3	4	5	6			9	11				10					7	8			
1	2	3		5	6			9	11				10					7	8		4	
2	2	2	1	2	2			2	2				2					2	2		1	
													1						1			

League Cup

West	Armfield	Martin	Crawford	Gratrix	Durie	Ball	Green	Charnley	Parry	Horne	James	Hill	McPhee	Watt	Thompson	Oates	Cranston	Lea	Quinn	Napier	Turner	Prentis
1	2	3	4	5	6			9		11		7	10					8				
1	2	3	4	5	6			9	10	11			8	7								
1		3	4	5	6			9	10	11			8	7								
3	2	3	3	3	3			3	2	3		1	3	2				1				
									1	1			2	1								

League Table

	P	W	D	L	F	A	Pts
Everton	42	25	11	6	84	42	61
Tottenham Hotspur	42	23	9	10	111	62	55
Burnley	42	22	10	10	78	57	54
Leicester City	42	20	12	10	79	53	52
Wolverhampton W.	42	20	10	12	93	65	50
Sheffield Wednesday	42	19	10	13	77	63	48
Arsenal	42	18	10	14	86	77	46
Liverpool	42	17	10	15	71	59	44
Nottingham Forest	42	17	10	15	67	69	44
Sheffield United	42	16	12	14	58	60	44
Blackburn Rovers	42	15	12	15	79	71	42
West Ham United	42	14	12	16	73	69	40
Blackpool	42	13	14	15	58	64	40
West Bromwich Albion	42	16	7	19	71	79	39
Aston Villa	42	15	8	19	62	68	38
Fulham	42	14	10	18	50	71	38
Ipswich Town	42	12	11	19	59	78	35
Bolton Wanderers	42	15	5	22	55	75	35
Manchester United	42	12	10	20	67	81	34
Birmingham City	42	10	13	19	63	90	33
Manchester City	42	10	11	21	58	102	31
Leyton Orient	42	6	9	27	37	81	21

1963-64

Division One

Manager: Ron Suart

Did you know that?

Blackpool played in a Costa Del Sol tournament in August. They lost heavily to Real Madrid 4–1 but beat Monaco 2–1.

The team suffered seven consecutive defeats in December and January, contributing to another relegation battle.

Alan Ball was the team's top scorer in the League, replacing the prolific Ray Charnley.

Match No.	Date		Venue	Opponents	Result		Scorers	Attendance
1	Aug	24	H	Sheffield Utd	D	2-2	Quinn, Parry	18,057
2		26	A	West Ham Utd	L	1-3	Charnley	25,533
3		31	A	Liverpool	W	2-1	McPhee, Charnley	45,767
4	Sep	2	H	West Ham Utd	L	0-1		18,407
5		7	H	Aston Villa	L	0-4		16,885
6		11	A	Manchester Utd	L	0-3		47,363
7		14	A	Tottenham Hotspur	L	1-6	Charnley	38,138
8		16	H	Manchester Utd	W	1-0	Charnley	29,806
9		21	H	Wolves	L	1-2	Ball	25,231
10		28	A	Stoke City	W	2-1	Ball, Oates	27,377
11		30	H	Fulham	W	1-0	Oates	13,757
12	Oct	5	H	Nottm Forest	W	1-0	Durie	22,397
13		12	A	Burnley	L	0-1		20,023
14		19	H	Ipswich Town	D	2-2	Parry, Charnley	14,666
15		26	A	Bolton Wanderers	D	1-1	Charnley	14,359
16	Nov	2	H	Everton	D	1-1	Charnley	24,834
17		9	A	Birmingham City	L	2-3	Crawford, Ball	17,536
18		16	H	West Brom Albion	W	1-0	Oates	11,047
19		23	A	Arsenal	L	3-5	McPhee, Ball, Charnley	33,871
20		30	H	Leicester City	D	3-3	Ball, Charnley 2	10,534
21	Dec	7	A	Sheffield Wed	L	0-1		20,156
22		14	A	Sheffield Utd	L	0-1		13,868
23		21	H	Liverpool	L	0-1		13,254
24		26	H	Chelsea	L	1-5	Durie	17,653
25		28	A	Chelsea	L	0-1		34,380
26	Jan	11	A	Aston Villa	L	1-3	Ball	14,191
27		18	H	Tottenham Hotspur	L	0-2		13,953
28	Feb	1	A	Wolves	D	1-1	Horne	16,345
29		8	H	Stoke City	W	1-0	Oates	14,452
30		15	A	Nottm Forest	W	1-0	Oates	17,008
31		22	H	Burnley	D	1-1	Green	12,938
32		29	A	Fulham	D	1-1	Oates	12,199
33	Mar	7	H	Bolton Wanderers	W	2-0	McPhee, Ball	12,242
34		13	A	West Brom Albion	L	1-2	Green	22,459
35		20	H	Birmingham City	W	3-0	McPhee, Oates 2	10,203
36		27	A	Blackburn Rovers	W	2-1	Horne 2	23,039
37		28	A	Everton	L	1-3	Horne	49,504
38		30	H	Blackburn Rovers	W	3-2	Ball 2, Rowe	20,165
39	Apr	4	H	Arsenal	L	0-1		14,067
40		11	A	Leicester City	W	3-2	Ball 2, Oates	15,189
41		18	H	Sheffield Wed	D	2-2	McPhee, Horne	12,908
42		25	A	Ipswich Town	L	3-4	Ball 2, Lea	11,187

Final League Position: 18th in Division One

Apps
Gls

FA Cup

3	Jan	4	A	West Brom Albion	D	2-2	Charnley, Own-goal	22,459
3R		8	H	West Brom Albion	L	0-1		21,241

Apps
Gls

League Cup

2	Sep	25	H	Charlton Athletic	W	7-1	Charnley 4, Durie, Oates, Ball	6,771
3	Oct	30	A	Norwich City	L	0-1		15,326

Apps
Gls

Waiters	Armfield	Martin	McPhee	Gratrix	Cranston	Lea	Quinn	Charnley	Crawford	Parry	Horne	Durie	Green	Harvey	Hill	Ball	Oates	Cooper	Thompson	Fisher	James	Turner	Rowe
1	2	3	4	5	6	7	8	9	10	11													
1	2	3	4	5	6	7	8	9		10	11												
1	2	3	4	5		7	8	9		10	11	6											
1	2	3	4	5		7	8	9		10	11	6											
1	2	3	4	5		7	8	9		10	11	6											
1	2	3	10	5		7	8	9		11		6	4										
	2	3	10	5			8	9		11		6	4	1	7								
	2	3		5	6		10	9	4		7			1		8	11						
	2	3		5	6		10	9	4		7			1		8	11						
1	2	3		5	6	7		9	4			10				8	11						
1	2	3		5	6	7		9	4			10				8	11						
1	2	3		5	6	7			4			10				8	11	9					
1		3		5	6	7		9	4			10				8	11		2				
1	2	3		5	6	7		9	4	11		10				8							
1	2	3		5	6			9	4	11					7	8				10			
1	2	3	10		6	7		9	4	11						8					5		
1	2	3	10		6	7		9	4							8	11				5		
1	2		10		6			9					4		7	8	11		3		5		
1			10	2	6			9		11			4		7	8			3		5		
1	2	3	10		6	7		9		11			4			8					5		
1	2	3	10		6	7		9		11			4			8					5		
1	2	3			6			9		10			4			7	11				5	8	
1		3			6			9	4	10					7	8	11		2		5		
1		3			6				8	10		9	4		7		11		2		5		
1		3	4	5	6			9		10	11	8			7				2				
1	2	3	4	5	6			9		10	11				7	8							
1	2	3	4	5	6			9		10	11				7	8							
1	2	3		5		7		9			11		6			8	10						6
1	2	3	4	5		7		9			11		6			8	10						
1	2	3	4	5		7					11		6			8	10	9					
1	2	3	4	5		7					11		6			8	10	9					
1	2	3	8	5		7					11		6				10	9					4
1	2	3	9	5		7					11		6			8	10						4
1	2	3	9	5		7					11		6			8	10						4
1	2	3	9	5		7					11		6			8	10						4
1	2	3	9	5		7					11		6			8	10						4
1	2	3	8	5		7		9		10	11		6										4
1		3	9	5		7					11		6			8	10		2				4
1	2	3	9	5		7			4		11		6			8	10						
1		3	9	5		7					11		6			8	10		2				4
1	2	3	9	5		7					11		6			8	10						4
1	2	3	9	5		7					11		6			8	10						
39	35	40	30	34	22	30	9	28	14	20	24	12	23	3	9	31	25	4	8	1	9	1	11
			5			1	1	10	1	2	5	3	2			13	8						1

Waiters	Armfield	Martin	McPhee	Gratrix	Cranston	Lea	Quinn	Charnley	Crawford	Parry	Horne	Durie	Green	Harvey	Hill	Ball	Oates	Cooper	Thompson	Fisher	James	Turner	Rowe
1	2	3	4	5	6			9		10	11				7	8							
1	2	3	4	5	6			9		10	11		10		7	8							
2	2	2	2	2	2			2		2	2				2	2							
								1															

Waiters	Armfield	Martin	McPhee	Gratrix	Cranston	Lea	Quinn	Charnley	Crawford	Parry	Horne	Durie	Green	Harvey	Hill	Ball	Oates	Cooper	Thompson	Fisher	James	Turner	Rowe
	2	3		5	6	7		9	4			10		1		8	11						
1	2	3			6			9	4	11		10	8		7						5		
1	2	2		1	2	1		2	2	1		2	1	1	1	1	1				1		
								4				1				1	1						

League Table

	P	W	D	L	F	A	Pts
Liverpool	42	26	5	11	92	45	57
Manchester United	42	23	7	12	90	62	53
Everton	42	21	10	11	84	64	52
Tottenham Hotspur	42	22	7	13	97	81	51
Chelsea	42	20	10	12	72	56	50
Sheffield Wednesday	42	19	11	12	84	67	49
Blackburn Rovers	42	18	10	14	89	65	46
Arsenal	42	17	11	14	90	82	45
Burnley	42	17	10	15	71	64	44
West Bromwich Albion	42	16	11	15	70	61	43
Leicester City	42	16	11	15	61	58	43
Sheffield United	42	16	11	15	61	64	43
Nottingham Forest	42	16	9	17	64	68	41
West Ham United	42	14	12	16	69	74	40
Fulham	42	13	13	16	58	65	39
Wolverhampton W.	42	12	15	15	70	80	39
Stoke City	42	14	10	18	77	78	38
Blackpool	42	13	9	20	52	73	35
Aston Villa	42	11	12	19	62	71	34
Birmingham City	42	11	7	24	54	92	29
Bolton Wanderers	42	10	8	24	48	80	28
Ipswich Town	42	9	7	26	56	121	25

1964-65

Division One

Manager: Ron Suart

Did you know that?

Blackpool went 15 games without a win between November and February, including eight successive defeats.

Blackpool made their debut on BBC's *Match of the Day* on 21 November. The viewers were entertained as Fulham and the Seasiders drew 3–3, Alan Ball scoring a hat-trick.

The team beat a Hong Kong XI in the national stadium 7–2 in June 1965.

Blackpool played a 10 game series against Sheffield United in New Zealand during the close season, with the Blades winning six games to four.

Match No.	Date		Venue	Opponents	Result		Scorers	Attendance
1	Aug	22	A	Burnley	D	2-2	Oates 2	15,773
2		24	H	Blackburn Rovers	W	4-2	Charnley, Lea, Rowe, Own-goal	22,381
3		29	H	Sheffield Wed	W	1-0	Ball	18,461
4	Sep	2	A	Blackburn Rovers	L	1-4	Charnley	20,315
5		5	A	Liverpool	D	2-2	Charnley 2	45,646
6		7	H	Leeds Utd	W	4-0	Oates, Charnley 2, Ball	26,310
7		12	H	Aston Villa	W	3-1	Oates, Charnley, Ball	22,793
8		16	A	Leeds Utd	L	0-3		35,973
9		19	A	Wolves	W	2-1	Charnley, Oates	22,260
10		26	H	Sunderland	W	3-1	Lea, Ball (pen), Oates	31,291
11		28	H	Tottenham Hotspur	D	1-1	Oates	26,436
12	Oct	5	A	Leicester City	L	2-3	Oates, Charnley	18,727
13		10	A	Sheffield Utd	W	3-1	Horne, Ball, Charnley	20,839
14		17	H	Everton	D	1-1	Charnley	31,855
15		24	A	Birmingham City	L	0-3		15,800
16		31	H	West Ham Utd	L	1-2	Green	14,383
17	Nov	7	A	West Brom Albion	W	3-1	Rowe, Ball 2	17,500
18		14	H	Manchester Utd	L	1-2	Oates	31,129
19		21	A	Fulham	D	3-3	Ball 3	16,587
20		28	H	Nottm Forest	L	0-2		14,047
21	Dec	5	A	Stoke City	L	2-4	Rowe, Oates	17,369
22		12	H	Burnley	L	2-4	Oates 2	11,000
23		19	A	Sheffield Wed	L	1-4	McPhee	16,172
24		26	A	Chelsea	L	0-2		30,581
25	Jan	2	H	Liverpool	L	2-3	Charnley 2	21,363
26		16	A	Aston Villa	L	2-3	Green, Charnley	17,403
27		23	H	Wolves	D	1-1	Horne	11,992
28	Feb	6	A	Sunderland	L	0-2		36,759
29		13	H	Leicester City	D	1-1	Charnley	10,387
30		20	H	Sheffield Utd	D	2-2	Charnley, Moir	10,166
31		27	A	Everton	D	0-0		35,267
32	Mar	6	H	Birmingham City	W	3-1	Armfield, Moir, Rowe	11,464
33		13	A	Tottenham Hotspur	L	1-4	Moir	26,295
34		20	H	West Brom Albion	W	3-0	Robson, Waddell 2	11,168
35		22	A	Manchester Utd	L	0-2		42,318
36	Apr	3	H	Fulham	W	3-0	Waddell, Armfield, Robson	11,972
37		10	A	Nottm Forest	L	0-2		16,595
38		16	H	Arsenal	D	1-1	Ball (pen)	18,620
39		17	H	Stoke City	D	1-1	Charnley	18,263
40		19	A	Arsenal	L	1-3	Charnley	17,063
41		23	A	West Ham Utd	L	1-2	Moir	22,702
42		26	H	Chelsea	W	3-2	Charnley 3	16,008

Final League Position: 17th in Division One

Apps
Gls

FA Cup

3	Jan	11	A	Stoke City	L	1-4	Ball	38,651

Apps
Gls

League Cup

2	Sep	23	H	Newcastle Utd	W	3-0	Ball (pen), Horne (pen), Lea	13,670
3	Oct	26	A	Sunderland	L	1-4	Charnley	20,540

Apps
Gls

Waiters	Armfield	Thompson	Rowe	Gratrix	Green	Lea	Ball	Charnley	Oates	Horne	Prentis	Turner	James	Cranston	Parry	Fisher	McPhee	Crawford	Loyden	Moir	Robson	Waddell
1	2	3	4	5	6	7	8	9	10	11												
1	2	3	4	5	6	7	8	9	10	11												
1		3	4	5	6	7	8	9	10	11	2											
1	2	3		5	6	7	8	9	10	11		4										
1	2	3			6	7	8	9	10				5	4	11							
1	2	3			6	7	8	9	10				5	4	11							
1	2	3			6	7	8	9	10				5	4	11							
1	2	3			6	7	8	9	10				5	4	11							
1	2	3	4		6	7	8	9	10	11			5									
1	2	3	4		6	7	8	9	10	11			5									
1	2	3	4		6	7	8	9	10	11			5									
1	2	3	4		6	7	8	9	10	11			5									
1	2	3	4		6	7	8	9	10	11			5									
1	2	3	4		6	7	8	9	10	11			5									
1	2	3			6	7	8	9	10	11			5	4								
1	2	3	4		6		8	9	7	11			5			10						
1	2	3	4		6		8	9	10	11			5				7					
1	2	3	5		6	7	8	9	10	11							4					
1	2	3	5		6	7	8	9	10	11							4					
1	2	3	5		6	7	8	9	10	11							4					
1	2	3	4		6	7	8	9	11				5				10					
1	2	3	4		6	7	8	9	11				5				10					
1		3			6	7	8	9	10	11			5				9	4				
1	2	3	4		6	7		9	10	11			5				8					
1	2	3	4		6			8	10	11			5				7		9			
1	2	3			6	7	8	9		11			5			10	4					
1	2	3			6	7	8	9		11			5			10	4					
1	2	3			6	7	8	9	10	11			5				4					
1	2	3			6	7	8	10					5				4		9	11		
1	2	3	10		6		8	9		11			5				4			7		
1	2	3	10		6		8	9		11			5				4			7		
1	2	3	10		6		8	9		11			5				4			7		
1	2	3			6		8	9		11			5				4			7	10	
1	2	3			6		8		11				5				4			7	10	9
1	2	3			6		8		11				5				4			7	10	9
1	2	3			6		8		11				5				4			7	10	9
1	2	3			6			8	11				5				4			7	10	9
1	2	3			6		8			11			5				4			7	10	9
1	2		3		6	7	8	9					5				4			11	10	
1	2	3			6	7	8	9					5				4			11	10	
1	2		3		6	7	8	9					5				4			11	10	
1	2	3			6	10	8	9		11			5				4			7		
42	40	40	23	4	42	30	39	38	30	28	1	1	35	5	4	1	26	1	2	14	9	5
	2		4		2	2	11	21	12	2							1			4	2	3

Waiters	Armfield	Thompson	Rowe	Gratrix	Green	Lea	Ball	Charnley	Oates	Horne	Prentis	Turner	James	Cranston	Parry	Fisher	McPhee	Crawford	Loyden	Moir	Robson	Waddell
1	2	3	4		6	7	10	8		11			5				9					
1	1	1	1		1	1	1	1		1			1				1					
							1															

Waiters	Armfield	Thompson	Rowe	Gratrix	Green	Lea	Ball	Charnley	Oates	Horne	Prentis	Turner	James	Cranston	Parry	Fisher	McPhee	Crawford	Loyden	Moir	Robson	Waddell
1	2	3	4		6	7	8	9		11			5			10						
1		3			6	7	8	9		11	2		5	4		10						
2	1	2	1		2	2	2	2		2	1		2	1		2						
						1	1	1		1												

League Table

	P	W	D	L	F	A	Pts
Manchester United	42	26	9	7	89	39	61
Leeds United	42	26	9	7	83	52	61
Chelsea	42	24	8	10	89	54	56
Everton	42	17	15	10	69	60	49
Nottingham Forest	42	17	13	12	71	67	47
Tottenham Hotspur	42	19	7	16	87	71	45
Liverpool	42	17	10	15	67	73	44
Sheffield Wednesday	42	16	11	15	57	55	43
West Ham United	42	19	4	19	82	71	42
Blackburn Rovers	42	16	10	16	83	79	42
Stoke City	42	16	10	16	67	66	42
Burnley	42	16	10	16	70	70	42
Arsenal	42	17	7	18	69	75	41
West Bromwich Albion	42	13	13	16	70	65	39
Sunderland	42	14	9	19	64	74	37
Aston Villa	42	16	5	21	57	82	37
Blackpool	42	12	11	19	67	78	35
Leicester City	42	11	13	18	69	85	35
Sheffield United	42	12	11	19	50	64	35
Fulham	42	11	12	19	60	78	34
Wolverhampton W.	42	13	4	25	59	89	30
Birmingham City	42	8	11	23	64	96	27

1965-66

Division One

Manager: Ron Suart

Did you know that?

Alan Ball was sold to Everton for a record £112,000, but he had waited until after the 1966 World Cup Final, so he was still a Blackpool player on that famous day.

Ball and Jimmy Armfield were honoured at a civic reception at the Town Hall for their part in England's World Cup victory.

Emlyn Hughes made his debut for the club.

Match No.	Date		Venue	Opponents	Result		Scorers	Attendance
1	Aug	21	H	Fulham	D	2-2	Charnley, Green	15,280
2		24	A	Burnley	L	1-3	Charnley	15,509
3		27	A	Tottenham Hotspur	L	0-4		36,118
4		30	H	Burnley	L	1-3	Robson	17,723
5	Sep	4	H	Liverpool	L	2-3	Charnley, Robson	25,616
6		6	H	Leicester City	W	4-0	Robson, Moir, Ball, Armfield	15,640
7		11	A	Aston Villa	L	0-3		21,615
8		14	A	Leicester City	W	3-0	Ball, Charnley, Robson	24,153
9		18	H	Sunderland	L	1-2	Green	28,277
10		25	A	West Ham Utd	D	1-1	Charnley	20,740
11	Oct	9	A	Chelsea	W	1-0	Charnley	28,022
12		16	H	Arsenal	W	5-3	Charnley 3 (1 pen), Ball (pen), Thompson	19,533
13		23	A	Everton	D	0-0		33,766
14		30	H	Manchester Utd	L	1-2	Ball	24,703
15	Nov	6	A	Newcastle Utd	L	0-2		33,853
16		13	H	West Brom Albion	D	1-1	Robson	12,642
17		20	A	Nottm Forest	L	1-2	Ball	19,549
18		27	H	Sheffield Wed	W	2-1	Lea, Robson	9,807
19	Dec	4	A	Northampton Town	L	1-2	Ball (pen)	14,404
20		11	H	Stoke City	D	1-1	Ball (pen)	11,837
21		25	H	Blackburn Rovers	W	4-2	Turner, Waddell, Charnley, Ball	20,851
22	Jan	1	H	Chelsea	L	1-2	Ball	14,065
23		8	A	Stoke City	L	1-4	Ball (pen)	20,276
24		15	H	Everton	W	2-0	Charnley, Own-goal	14,588
25		29	A	Fulham	D	0-0		12,093
26	Feb	5	H	Tottenham Hotspur	D	0-0		13,103
27		19	A	Liverpool	L	1-4	James	45,047
28		26	H	Aston Villa	L	0-1		11,075
29	Mar	5	A	Arsenal	D	0-0		21,881
30		12	A	Sunderland	L	1-2	Oates	26,246
31		19	H	West Ham Utd	W	2-1	Charnley, Ball	10,559
32		26	A	Leeds Utd	W	2-1	Lea 2	30,727
33		28	H	Leeds Utd	W	1-0	Ball	19,017
34	Apr	4	A	Sheffield Wed	L	0-3		20,945
35		8	H	Sheffield Utd	W	2-1	Ball 2 (1 pen)	17,483
36		9	A	West Brom Albion	L	1-2	Charnley	15,000
37		11	A	Sheffield Utd	W	1-0	Ball	15,196
38		16	H	Nottm Forest	L	0-3		10,354
39		20	H	Newcastle Utd	D	1-1	Charnley	12,446
40		27	A	Manchester Utd	L	1-2	Robson	26,953
41		30	H	Northampton Town	W	3-0	Lea, Moir, Ball (pen)	15,295
42	May	2	A	Blackburn Rovers	W	3-1	Charnley 2, Moir	7,487

Final League Position: 13th in Division One

Apps
Sub Apps
Gls

FA Cup

3	Jan	22	H	Manchester City	D	1-1	James	23,957
3R		24	A	Manchester City	L	1-3	Charnley	52,661

Apps
Gls

League Cup

2	Sep	22	H	Gillingham	W	5-2	Charnley 2, Lea, Ball (pen), Rowe	6,717
3	Oct	13	H	Darlington	L	1-2	Green	8,204

Apps
Gls

Waiters	Armfield	Thompson	McPhee	James	Rowe	Moir	Ball	Charnley	Green	Lea	Oates	Craven	Fisher	Robson	Horne	Turner	Prentis	Waddell	Taylor	Brown	Hughes	Conway
1	2	3	4	5	6	7	8	9	10	11												
1	2	3	4	5	6	7	8	9	10	11												
1	2		4	5			8	9	10	11	7	3	6									
1	2		4	5		7	8	9	6	11		3		10								
1	2				5	7	8	9	6			3	4	10	11							
1	2		6		5	7	8	9				3	4	10	11							
1	2		6		5	7	8	9				3	4	10	11							
1	2		12		5	7	8	9	6			3*	4	10	11							
1	2		12		5*	7	8	9	6			3	4	10	11							
1		2		5		7	8	9	6	10		3	4		11							
1	2		7	5			8	9	6	10*	12	3	4		11							
1	2	3		5		7	8	9	6		11			10		4						
1	2	3		5		7	8	9	6		11			10		4						
1*		3	12	5		7	8	9	6		11			10		4	2					
1	2	3	4	5		7	8	9	6					10	11							
1	2	3	4	5		7	8	9	6	11				10								
1		3	4	5		7	8	9	6	11				10			2					
1		3	4	5			8	9	6	7				10	11		2					
1	2	3	4	5		7	8	9	6					10	11							
1	2	3	4	5		7	8	9	6		11							10				
1		3		5		7	8	9	6		11					4	2	10				
1	2	3		5		7	8	9	6		11*				12	4		10				
1	2	3		5		7	8	9	6				12	10	11	4*						
1	2	3		5			8	9	6	7			4		11			10				
	2	3		5	6	7	8	9		11	10		4						1			
	2	3		5	6		8	9		7	10		4		11				1			
1	2	3		5	4		8	9	6	7	10				11							
1	2	3		5	4	11	8*		6	7			10			12		9				
1	2	3	7	5	4		8	10			11		6	12				9*				
1	2	3	7	5	6		8	9	10		11		4									
1		3	12	5			8	9	6*	7	11		4				2	10				
1	2	3	6	5			8	9		7	11		4					10				
1	2	3	6	5			8	9		7	11		4					10				
1	2	3	6	5			8	9		7	11		4					10				
1	2	3	6	5			8	9		7	11		4	10								
1	2	3	6	5			8	9		7	11		4	10								
1	2	3	6	5		10	8	9		7	11		4									
1	2	3	6	5			8	9		7	11		4	10								
1	2	3	6	5			8	9		11			4					10		7		
1	2	3	6	5			8	9		7			4	12	11*			10				
1	2	3	6	5		7	8	9		11			4					10				
1		2	6	5		11		9		8			4					10		7	2	
40	35	34	26	37	13	25	41	41	26	26	20	9	26	18	15	6	5	14	2	2	1	
			4								1		1	2	1	1						
	1	1		1		3	16	16	2	4	1			7		1		1				

1	2	3		5			8	9	6	7			4		11			10				
1	2	3	10	5			8	9	6	7			4		11							
2	2	2	1	2			2	2	2	2			2		2			1				
				1				1														

1	2					7	8	9	6	10		3			11	4						5
1	2		7	5			8	9	6	10		3	4		11							
2	2		1	1		1	2	2	2	2		2	1		2	1						1
							1	2	1	1					1							

League Table

	P	W	D	L	F	A	Pts
Liverpool	42	26	9	7	79	34	61
Leeds United	42	23	9	10	79	38	55
Burnley	42	24	7	11	79	47	55
Manchester United	42	18	15	9	84	59	51
Chelsea	42	22	7	13	65	53	51
West Bromwich Albion	42	19	12	11	91	69	50
Leicester City	42	21	7	14	80	65	49
Tottenham Hotspur	42	16	12	14	75	66	44
Sheffield United	42	16	11	15	56	59	43
Stoke City	42	15	12	15	65	64	42
Everton	42	15	11	16	56	62	41
West Ham United	42	15	9	18	70	83	39
Blackpool	42	14	9	19	55	65	37
Arsenal	42	12	13	17	62	75	37
Newcastle United	42	14	9	19	50	63	37
Aston Villa	42	15	6	21	69	80	36
Sheffield Wednesday	42	14	8	20	56	66	36
Nottingham Forest	42	14	8	20	56	72	36
Sunderland	42	14	8	20	51	72	36
Fulham	42	14	7	21	67	85	35
Northampton Town	42	10	13	19	55	92	33
Blackburn Rovers	42	8	4	30	57	88	20

1966-67

Division One

Manager: Stan Mortensen

Did you know that?

Blackpool were finally relegated to Division Two and manager Ron Suart resigned in January. He was replaced by the legendary Stan Mortensen.

The team only won once at Bloomfield Road, but oddly twice in Liverpool with wins at Goodison Park and Anfield.

The one home win was against Newcastle United 6–0. Soon after, Blackpool bought Alan Suddick from the Magpies for a club record fee of £63,000.

Despite the dismal season, they still managed to record an amazing 5–1 home win over Manchester United in the League Cup.

Match No.	Date		Venue	Opponents	Result		Scorers	Attendance
1	Aug	20	A	Sheffield Wed	L	0-3		21,008
2		22	H	Leicester City	D	1-1	Charnley	17,031
3		27	H	Southampton	L	2-3	Lea, Charnley	15,258
4		31	A	Leicester City	L	0-3		22,005
5	Sep	3	A	Sunderland	L	0-4		24,941
6		5	H	Liverpool	L	1-2	Waddell	24,377
7		10	H	Aston Villa	L	0-2		15,238
8		17	A	Arsenal	D	1-1	Skirton	28,928
9		24	H	Manchester City	L	0-1		25,701
10	Oct	1	A	Burnley	L	0-1		16,445
11		8	A	Manchester Utd	L	1-2	Charnley	33,555
12		15	A	Tottenham Hotspur	W	3-1	Charnley 2, Skirton	36,459
13		22	H	Newcastle Utd	W	6-0	Moir 2, Skirton 2, Charnley, Robson	21,202
14		29	A	Nottm Forest	L	0-2		22,083
15	Nov	5	H	Tottenham Hotspur	D	2-2	Lea, Moir	16,524
16		12	A	Sheffield Utd	D	1-1	Moir	16,224
17		19	H	Stoke City	L	0-1		16,172
18		26	A	Everton	W	1-0	Skirton	38,127
19	Dec	3	H	Fulham	L	0-1		13,518
20		10	A	Leeds Utd	D	1-1	Skirton	28,466
21		17	H	Sheffield Wed	D	1-1	Robson	10,862
22		26	H	West Ham Utd	L	1-4	Charnley (pen)	26,901
23		27	A	West Ham Utd	L	0-4		29,360
24		31	A	Southampton	W	5-1	Fisher, Charnley 3, Suddick	21,356
25	Jan	7	H	Sunderland	D	1-1	Suddick	14,669
26		14	A	Aston Villa	L	2-3	Suddick 2	16,889
27		21	H	Arsenal	L	0-3		12,028
28	Feb	4	A	Manchester City	L	0-1		27,840
29		11	H	Burnley	L	0-2		16,681
30		25	A	Manchester Utd	L	0-4		47,155
31	Mar	4	H	Nottm Forest	D	1-1	Skirton	14,003
32		18	A	Newcastle Utd	L	1-2	Moir	30,550
33		24	A	Chelsea	W	2-0	Charnley, Skirton (pen)	37,852
34		25	H	Leeds Utd	L	0-2		22,548
35		27	H	Chelsea	L	0-2		16,186
36	Apr	1	A	West Brom Albion	L	1-3	Lea	18,304
37		8	H	Sheffield Utd	L	0-1		6,619
38		15	A	Stoke City	L	0-2		12,259
39		22	H	Everton	L	0-1		13,823
40		29	A	Fulham	D	2-2	Oates, Charnley	14,867
41	May	6	H	West Brom Albion	L	1-3	Charnley	9,986
42		13	A	Liverpool	W	3-1	Charnley, Oates, Robson	28,773

Final League Position: 22nd in Division One

Apps
Sub Apps
Gls

FA Cup

3	Jan	28	A	Birmingham City	L	1-2	Charnley	27,603

Apps
Gls

League Cup

2	Sep	14	H	Manchester Utd	W	5-1	Charnley 3 (1 pen), Lea, Waddell	15,570
3	Oct	5	H	Chelsea	D	1-1	Robson	13,520
3R		17	A	Chelsea	W	3-1	Skirton 2, Moir	20,249
4		26	H	Fulham	W	4-2	Charnley 2, Moir, Robson	15,349
5	Dec	7	H	West Ham Utd	L	1-3	Charnley	15,831

Apps
Sub Apps
Gls

Waiters	Armfield	Thompson	Fisher	James	Green J	Lea	Turner	Charnley	Waddell	Moir	Rowe	Hughes	Brown	Robson	Taylor	Craven	McPhee	Skirton	Oates	Suddick	Ingram	Thomas	Green A
1	2	3	4	5	6	7	8	9	10	11													
1	2	3	4	5	10	7		9	8	11	6												
1	2	3	4	5	10*	7		9	8	11	6	12											
1	2	3	4	5		11		9	8		6	10	7										
1		2	4	5		11		9	8		6	3	7	10									
	2	3		5		11	10	9	8	7	4	6			1								
	2	3	4	5		11		9	8	7		6			1		10						
1		2	12	5	6	11		9	8			4				3		7*	10				
1		2		5	6	11		9	8			4	7			3			10				
1		2	8	5	6	11		9		10		3	7				4						
1		2	4	5*		11		9		10		3	7	8		12	6						
1	6	2	4			11		9		10		3		8			5	7					
1		2	4			11		9		10	6	3		8			5	7					
1		2	4			11		9		10	6	3		8			5	7					
1	6	2	4	12		11*		9		10		3		8			5	7					
1	4	2		5		11		9		10		3		8			6	7					
1	4	2	10	5		7		9				3		8			6		11				
1	2		4	5		11		9		10		3		8			6	7					
1	2		4	5		11		9		10		3		8			6	7					
1	2		4	5		11		9		10		3		8			6	7					
1	2		4	5		11		9		10		3		8			6	7					
1	2*		12	5	6			9		11		3		8			4	7		10			
1		2	4			11		9				3		8			6	7		10			
1		2	4	5	10	7		9				3		8			6			11			
1		2		5	10	7		9			4	3		8			6			11			
1	2	3		5	10	7		9				3		8			6			11			
1	2	3	4	5		7		9		10				8			6			11			
1		2		5				9			4	3	7*	8		6	12		11	10			
1		2	4*	5		11		9		8		3		12		6		7		10			
1	4	2		5				9				3		10		6		7	11	8			
1	2	3		5*	4			9		8				12		6		7	11	10			
1	2	3			4			9		8				5		6		7	11	10			
1	2	3				8		9			5			4		6		7	11	10			
1	2	3				8		9			5			4		6		7	11	10			
1	2	3								8	5			4		6		7	11	10	9		
1	2	3				8		9			5			4		6		7	11	10			
		2		5		8								4		3	6	7	10	11	9	1	
	2			5		8		10						4	1	3	6	7		11	9		
	2	3		5	8	7		9						4			6		11	10		1	
	2	3		5	10	8		9						4			6	7	11			1	
	2	3		5	6	8		9									4	7	11			1	10
	2	3		5		8		9						4			6	7	11	10		1	
34	29	36	21	33	15	36	2	40	9	22	13	26	6	30	3	13	25	25	16	19	3	5	1
			2	1								1		2		1	1						
			1			3		14	1	5				3				8	2	4			

Waiters	Armfield	Thompson	Fisher	James	Green J	Lea	Turner	Charnley	Waddell	Moir	Rowe	Hughes	Brown	Robson	Taylor	Craven	McPhee	Skirton	Oates	Suddick	Ingram	Thomas	Green A
1		2	4	5	10	7		9				3		8			6			11			
1		1	1	1	1	1		1				1		1			1			1			
								1															

Waiters	Armfield	Thompson	Fisher	James	Green J	Lea	Turner	Charnley	Waddell	Moir	Rowe	Hughes	Brown	Robson	Taylor	Craven	McPhee	Skirton	Oates	Suddick	Ingram	Thomas	Green A
1	2*	3	12	5	6	11		9	8			4	7						10				
1		2	4	5		11		9		10		3	7	8			6						
1		2	4			11	6*	9		10		3	12	8			5	7					
1		2	4			11		9		10	6	3		8			5	7					
1	2		4	5		11		9		10		3		8			6	7					
5	2	4	4	3	1	5	1	5	1	4	1	5	2	4			4	3	1				
			1										1									1	
						1		6	1	2				1				2					

League Table

	P	W	D	L	F	A	Pts
Manchester United	42	24	12	6	84	45	60
Nottingham Forest	42	23	10	9	64	41	56
Tottenham Hotspur	42	24	8	10	71	48	56
Leeds United	42	22	11	9	62	42	55
Liverpool	42	19	13	10	64	47	51
Everton	42	19	10	13	65	46	48
Arsenal	42	16	14	12	58	47	46
Leicester City	42	18	8	16	78	71	44
Chelsea	42	15	14	13	67	62	44
Sheffield United	42	16	10	16	52	59	42
Sheffield Wednesday	42	14	13	15	56	47	41
Stoke City	42	17	7	18	63	58	41
West Bromwich Albion	42	16	7	19	77	73	39
Burnley	42	15	9	18	66	76	39
Manchester City	42	12	15	15	43	52	39
West Ham United	42	14	8	20	80	84	36
Sunderland	42	14	8	20	58	72	36
Fulham	42	11	12	19	71	83	34
Southampton	42	14	6	22	74	92	34
Newcastle United	42	12	9	21	39	81	33
Aston Villa	42	11	7	24	54	85	29
Blackpool	42	6	9	27	41	76	21

1967-68

Division Two

Manager: Stan Mortensen

Did you know that?

Manager Mortensen sold Ray Charnley to neighbours Preston North End, despite him being the team's top scorer in all competitions for nine successive seasons.

After winning their last seven games, Blackpool missed out on promotion by 0.21 of a goal to Queen's Park Rangers.

The points total of 58 was the highest for a team not to be promoted before the 'three for a win' change.

For the first time in eight years, Blackpool progressed past the third round of the FA Cup.

Tony Green was emerging as a new star in the tangerine shirt.

Match No.	Date	Venue	Opponents	Result		Scorers	Attendance
1	Aug 19	A	Preston NE	W	2-0	Ingram, Charnley (pen)	21,499
2	27	H	Ipswich Town	D	0-0		19,634
3	26	H	Millwall	L	1-4	Charnley	14,886
4	29	A	Ipswich Town	D	1-1	Ingram	18,286
5	Sep 2	A	Hull City	W	1-0	Skirton	16,558
6	4	H	Huddersfield Town	W	2-0	Ingram, Own-goal	17,674
7	9	H	Middlesbrough	W	3-0	Ingram, Skirton, Oates	24,346
8	16	A	Bristol City	W	4-2	Ingram 2, Skirton 2	13,193
9	23	H	Birmingham City	W	1-0	Ingram	23,572
10	30	A	Bolton Wanderers	W	2-1	Oates, Green	16,452
11	Oct 7	A	Rotherham Utd	W	2-1	Ingram 2	6,725
12	14	H	Crystal Palace	W	2-0	Charnley, Armfield	20,905
13	21	A	Aston Villa	L	2-3	Ingram, Suddick	21,620
14	24	A	Millwall	D	1-1	Ingram	17,189
15	28	H	Queens Park Rangers	L	0-1		21,635
16	Nov 11	H	Cardiff City	W	3-1	Ingram, Robson, Skirton	11,324
17	18	A	Charlton Athletic	W	2-0	Ingram, Robson	12,690
18	25	H	Norwich City	L	0-2		12,554
19	Dec 2	A	Portsmouth	L	1-3	Skirton	35,038
20	9	H	Derby County	D	1-1	McPhee	11,113
21	16	H	Preston NE	W	4-1	Milne, Craven 2, Green	16,291
22	26	H	Carlisle Utd	D	1-1	Suddick	20,732
23	30	A	Carlisle Utd	W	3-1	Oates, Skirton, Ingram	12,679
24	Jan 6	H	Hull City	W	3-1	Ingram 2, Green	13,227
25	13	A	Middlesbrough	D	0-0		19,748
26	20	H	Bristol City	D	1-1	Skirton (pen)	13,032
27	Feb 3	A	Birmingham City	W	2-1	Skirton 2	28,008
28	10	H	Bolton Wanderers	D	1-1	Suddick	19,183
29	24	H	Rotherham Utd	D	1-1	James	13,689
30	Mar 2	A	Crystal Palace	L	1-3	Skirton	11,869
31	9	A	Plymouth Argyle	D	2-2	Ingram, James	8,688
32	16	H	Aston Villa	W	1-0	Milne	14,361
33	21	A	Queens Park Rangers	L	0-2		18,498
34	30	H	Plymouth Argyle	W	2-0	White, Brown	14,586
35	Apr 3	A	Blackburn Rovers	L	1-2	Skirton	13,655
36	6	A	Cardiff City	W	3-1	Skirton, Suddick 2	14,439
37	13	H	Charlton Athletic	W	2-0	Skirton 2	17,095
38	15	H	Blackburn Rovers	W	2-1	Suddick, Own-goal	21,865
39	20	A	Norwich City	W	2-1	Rowe, Suddick	16,501
40	27	H	Portsmouth	W	2-0	White 2	17,042
41	May 4	A	Derby County	W	3-1	White, Skirton, Suddick	20,635
42	11	A	Huddersfield Town	W	3-1	Suddick, Skirton, Own-goal	11,603

Final League Position: 3rd in Division Two

Apps
Sub Apps
Gls

FA Cup

3	Jan 27	H	Chesterfield	W	2-1	Green, Own-goal	21,457
4	Feb 17	A	Sheffield Utd	L	1-2	Skirton	25,517

Apps
Sub Apps
Gls

League Cup

2	Sep 12	A	Newport County	W	1-0	Milne	12,000
3	Oct 11	A	Manchester City	D	1-1	Craven	27,633
3R	18	H	Manchester City	L	0-2		21,405

Apps
Sub Apps
Gls

Thomas	Armfield	Thompson	Milne	James	McPhee	Green	Rowe	Charnley	Ingram	Lea	Craven	Suddick	Skirton	Taylor	Mowbray	Oates	Alcock	Brown	Robson	White	Marsden	Dean	Hutchison
1	2	3	4	5	6	7*	8	9	10	11	12												
1	2	3	4	5	6		8	9	10	11		7											
1	2	3	4	5	6	8		9	10	11			7										
	2	12	4	5	6	10			9*		8		7	1	3	11							
	2		4	5	6	10			9		8		7	1	3	11							
	2		4		6	10*			9	12	8		7	1	3	11	5						
	2		4	5	6	10			9		8		7	1	3	11							
	2		4	5	6	10			9		8		7	1	3	11							
	2		4	5	6	10			9		8		7	1	3	11							
	2		4	5	6	10			9		8		7	1	3	11							
	2		4	5	6	10			9*		8		7	1	3	11		12					
	2		4	5	6	10		9			8		7	1	3	11							
	2		4	5	6	11			9		8	10	7	1	3								
	2		4	5	6	10			9		8	11	7	1	3								
	2		4	5	6	10			9	12	8	11	7	1	3*								
	2		4	5	6	10			9	11	3		7	1					8				
	2		4	5	6	10			9	11	3		7	1					8				
	2		4		6	10			9	11	3		7	1			5		8				
	2		4	5	6	10*	12		9		8		7	1	3	11							
	2		4	5	6				9		8	12	7*	1	3	11		10					
	2		4	5	6	7			9		8	11		1	3	10							
	2		4	5*	6	7			9		8	11	12	1	3	10							
	2	3	4		6	8	5		9			11	7	1		10							
	2	3	4		6	8	5		9			11	7	1		10							
	2*	3	4		6	8	5		9		12	11	7	1		10							
	2	3	4		6	8	5		9		12	11	7*	1		10							
	2	3	4		6	8	5		9			11	7	1		10							
		3	4		6	8	5		9		2	11	7	1		10							
	2	3		5	6	8	10*		9		4	11	7	1								12	
	2	3	4	5	6	7					8		11	1		10					9		
	2	3	4	5*	6	7			9		8		11	1		10	12						
	2		4		6	7			12		8		11	1	3	10*	5			9			
	2		4		6	7			10		8		11*	1	3	12	5			9			
	2		8	5	6						4	10		1	3			7		9			11
	2		8	5	6							10	7	1	3					9			11
	2			5	6	8	4					10	7	1	3					9			11
	2			5	6	8	4					10	7	1	3					9			11
	2			5	6	8	4					10	7	1	3					9			11
	2			5	6	8	4					10	7	1	3					9			11
	2			5	6	8	4*				12	10	7	1	3					9			11
	2			5	6	8					4	10	7	1	3					9			11
	2			5	6	8					4	10	7	1	3					9			11
3	41	12	34	32	42	38	14	4	30	6	29	22	37	39	27	22	4	2	3	11	1		9
		1					1		1	2	4	1	1			1	1	1				1	
	1		2	2	1	3	1	3	17		2	9	17			3		1	2	4			

Thomas	Armfield	Thompson	Milne	James	McPhee	Green	Rowe	Charnley	Ingram	Lea	Craven	Suddick	Skirton	Taylor	Mowbray	Oates	Alcock	Brown	Robson	White	Marsden	Dean	Hutchison
	2*	3	4		6	8	5		9		12	11	7	1		10							
	2	3	4	5	6	8	10				9	11	7	1									
	2	2	2	1	2	2	2		1		1	2	2	2		1							
											1												
						1							1										

Thomas	Armfield	Thompson	Milne	James	McPhee	Green	Rowe	Charnley	Ingram	Lea	Craven	Suddick	Skirton	Taylor	Mowbray	Oates	Alcock	Brown	Robson	White	Marsden	Dean	Hutchison
	2		4	5	6	10			9	7	8			1	3	11							
	2		4	5	6	10		9			8		7	1	3	11							
		2	4	5	6	10		9			8		7	1	3	11*		12					
	2	1	3	3	3	3		2	1	1	3		2	3	3	3							
																		1					
			1								1												

League Table

	P	W	D	L	F	A	Pts
Ipswich Town	42	22	15	5	79	44	59
Queen's Park Rangers	42	25	8	9	67	36	58
Blackpool	42	24	10	8	71	43	58
Birmingham City	42	19	14	9	83	51	52
Portsmouth	42	18	13	11	68	55	49
Middlesbrough	42	17	12	13	60	54	46
Millwall	42	14	17	11	62	50	45
Blackburn Rovers	42	16	11	15	56	49	43
Norwich City	42	16	11	15	60	65	43
Carlisle United	42	14	13	15	58	52	41
Crystal Palace	42	14	11	17	56	56	39
Bolton Wanderers	42	13	13	16	60	63	39
Cardiff City	42	13	12	17	60	66	38
Huddersfield Town	42	13	12	17	46	61	38
Charlton Athletic	42	12	13	17	63	68	37
Aston Villa	42	15	7	20	54	64	37
Hull City	42	12	13	17	58	73	37
Derby County	42	13	10	19	71	78	36
Bristol City	42	13	10	19	48	62	36
Preston North End	42	12	11	19	43	65	35
Rotherham United	42	10	11	21	42	76	31
Plymouth Argyle	42	9	9	24	38	72	27

1968-69

Division Two

Manager: Stan Mortensen

Did you know that?

The board inexplicably sacked Stan Mortensen following rumours of player indiscipline and dressing room unrest. The decision was met with anger from the fans.

Les Shannon was appointed on 1 May as new manager, and one of his first acquisitions was Mickey Burns from Skelmersdale.

Match No.	Date	Venue	Opponents	Result		Scorers	Attendance
1	Aug 10	H	Hull City	W	2-0	White 2	16,755
2	17	A	Derby County	D	1-1	Green	24,760
3	21	A	Oxford Utd	D	0-0		14,120
4	24	H	Bristol City	D	2-2	Milne, Green	15,767
5	28	A	Blackburn Rovers	D	1-1	White	21,062
6	31	A	Aston Villa	W	1-0	Brown	18,919
7	Sep 7	H	Bolton Wanderers	W	1-0	Suddick	22,668
8	14	A	Millwall	W	2-1	Suddick, White	13,198
9	16	H	Preston NE	D	1-1	James	27,975
10	21	H	Fulham	D	2-2	Brown, Hutchison	15,765
11	28	A	Sheffield Utd	L	1-2	Green	15,997
12	Oct 5	A	Huddersfield Town	L	1-2	Suddick	13,023
13	7	H	Blackburn Rovers	L	0-1		21,154
14	12	H	Portsmouth	D	1-1	White	16,407
15	19	A	Carlisle Utd	L	0-1		10,519
16	26	H	Crystal Palace	W	3-0	Suddick, McPhee, James	15,224
17	Nov 2	A	Charlton Athletic	D	0-0		14,906
18	9	H	Cardiff City	L	1-2	Hutchison	12,085
19	16	A	Birmingham City	L	0-1		22,206
20	23	H	Bury	W	6-0	Rowe 3, Brown, Suddick 2	10,499
21	30	A	Norwich City	W	1-0	Rowe	15,128
22	Dec 7	H	Middlesbrough	D	1-1	James	13,356
23	14	A	Portsmouth	L	0-1		16,961
24	21	H	Carlisle Utd	W	1-0	Rowe	11,619
25	28	H	Huddersfield Town	D	0-0		20,319
26	Jan 11	H	Charlton Athletic	L	2-3	Brown, Milne (pen)	11,475
27	25	A	Crystal Palace	W	2-1	Craven, Johnston (pen)	17,003
28	Feb 1	H	Birmingham City	W	2-1	Brown, Suddick	11,294
29	12	A	Cardiff City	L	0-1		24,229
30	22	A	Middlesbrough	L	1-2	Craven	18,672
31	Mar 1	A	Hull City	D	2-2	Alcock, Craven	10,896
32	8	H	Derby County	L	2-3	Brown, Craven	18,853
33	15	A	Bristol City	D	1-1	Suddick	16,079
34	19	H	Norwich City	W	2-1	Green, Brown	9,536
35	22	H	Aston Villa	D	1-1	James	12,148
36	26	A	Bury	L	0-2		6,675
37	29	A	Bolton Wanderers	W	4-1	Suddick 2, Brown (pen),Rowe	9,029
38	Apr 5	H	Sheffield Utd	D	1-1	Suddick	13,857
39	7	H	Oxford Utd	W	1-0	Suddick	11,155
40	8	A	Preston NE	L	0-1		17,233
41	12	A	Fulham	D	0-0		7,154
42	19	H	Millwall	W	1-0	Green	9,524

Final League Position: 8th in Division Two

Apps
Sub Apps
Gls

FA Cup

3	Jan 4	A	Coventry City	L	1-3	Brown	28,357

Apps
Sub Apps
Gls

League Cup

2	Sep 4	A	Wrexham	D	1-1	White	15,102
2R	9	H	Wrexham	W	3-0	Hutchison, Suddick, Craven	17,063
3	25	H	Manchester City	W	1-0	White	23,795
4	Oct 16	H	Wolves	W	2-1	Suddick, Marsden	16,466
5	29	A	Arsenal	L	1-5	Green	32,321

Apps
Sub Apps
Gls

Taylor	Armfield	Mowbray	Milne	James	McPhee	Skirton	Green	White	Suddick	Hutchison	Rowe	Oates	Brown	Craven	Alcock	Thompson	Marsden	Johnston	Bentley	Thomas	Fisher
1	2	3	4	5	6	7	8	9	10	11											
1	2	3	4	5	6	7	8	9	10	11											
1	2	3	4	5	6	7	8	9	10	11											
1	2	3	4	5	6	7	8	9	10	11											
1	2	3	4*	5	6	7	8	9	10	11				12							
1	2	3		5	6			9	10	11		7	8	4							
1	2*	3	4	5	6		8	9	10	11		12	7								
1		3		5	6	11	8	9	10	7	4			2							
1		3		5	6	7	8	9	10	11	4			2							
1		3	4	5	6		8	9	10	11			7	2							
1			4	5	6	7	8	9	10	11				2		3					
1	2		8	5	6	9	7		10	11				4*		3	12				
1			4	5	6	7	8		10	11			12		2	3	9*				
1	2		4*	5	6	7	8	9	10	11	12										
1	2		7*	5	6		8		10	11	4		12			3	9				
1	2			9	6		8		10	11	4		7		5	3					
1	2			5	6	7	8		9	11	4*		10	12		3					
1	2			5	6	7	8	9		11	4		10			3					
1	2		4	5	6	7	8	9	10	11						3					
1	2			5	6		8		10	11	9		7	4		3					
1	2			5	6		8		10	11	9		7	4		3					
1	2		12	5	6		8		10	11*	9		7	4		3					
1		2	10	5	6		8		11		9		7	4		3					
1	2		12	5	6		8	10*	11		9		7	4		3					
1	2			5	6		8	10	11				7	4		3					
1	2		8	9	6				10	11			7	4		5			3		
1	2			5	6		8		10	11	9*			4	12			7	3		
1	2			5			8		9	11			7	4	6			10	3		
1	2			5			8		9	11			7	4	6			10	3		
1	2			5	11		8		9				7	4	6			10	3		
1	2			5			8		9	11			7	4	6			10	3		
1	2			5	12		8		9	11			7	4	6			10*	3		
1	2		10	5	6		8	9	11				7	4					3		
1	2		10	5	6		8	9	11				7	4					3		
		2	10*	5	6		8	9	11		12		7	4					3	1	
				5	6		8	9	10	11			7	4					3	1	2
	2			5	6		8		11		9		7	10	4				3	1	
	2			5	6		8		11		9		7		4			10	3	1	
1	2			5	6		10	9	11	7			8		4				3		
1	2			5	6		10	9	11	7			8		4				3		
1	2			5	6		10		11	7	8				4		9		3		
1	2*		12	5	6		8		11		9		7	10	4				3		
38	34	12	18	42	38	14	40	22	41	32	17	1	27	25	13	16	3	8	17	4	1
			3		1						2	1	2	2	1		1				
			2	4	1		5	5	12	2	6		8	4	1			1			

	2		12	5	6		8	10*	11		9		7	4		3					
	1			1	1		1	1	1		1		1	1		1					
			1																		
						1							1								

1	2	3		5	6			9	10	11		7	8	4							
1		3		5	6	7	8		10	11	4			2				9			
1	2	3*	12	5	6	7	8	9	10	11				4							
1	2			5	6	7	8		10	11	4						3	9			
1	2			9	6		8		10	11	4		7			5	3				
5	4	3		5	5	3	4	2	5	5	3	1	2	3		1	2	2			
			1																		
							1	2	2	1				1				1			

League Table

	P	W	D	L	F	A	Pts
Derby County	42	26	11	5	65	32	63
Crystal Palace	42	22	12	8	70	47	56
Charlton Athletic	42	18	14	10	61	52	50
Middlesbrough	42	19	11	12	58	49	49
Cardiff City	42	20	7	15	67	54	47
Huddersfield Town	42	17	12	13	53	46	46
Birmingham City	42	18	8	16	73	59	44
Blackpool	42	14	15	13	51	41	43
Sheffield United	42	16	11	15	61	50	43
Millwall	42	17	9	16	57	49	43
Hull City	42	13	16	13	59	52	42
Carlisle United	42	16	10	16	46	49	42
Norwich City	42	15	10	17	53	56	40
Preston North End	42	12	15	15	38	44	39
Portsmouth	42	12	14	16	58	58	38
Bristol City	42	11	16	15	46	53	38
Bolton Wanderers	42	12	14	16	55	67	38
Aston Villa	42	12	14	16	37	48	38
Blackburn Rovers	42	13	11	18	52	63	37
Oxford United	42	12	9	21	34	55	33
Bury	42	11	8	23	51	80	30
Fulham	42	7	11	24	40	81	25

1969-70

Division Two

Manager: Les Shannon

Did you know that?

A new club crest was introduced to the team's shirts, showing the white letters of BFC encircled against a tangerine background, and so breaking with the tradition of using the town's official crest.

Promotion to the First Division was gained at Deepdale, and it is estimated that there were around 20,000 Blackpool fans in the ground on that evening.

Preston were not relegated that night as myth now suggests, but in fact went down the following weekend.

Nearly 25,000 saw a remarkable comeback against Arsenal in the FA Cup when Blackpool came from two goals down to beat the Gunners 3–2 in the second half.

Match No.	Date	Venue	Opponents	Result		Scorers	Attendance
1	Aug 9	H	Portsmouth	W	2-1	Burns, Craven	15,844
2	16	A	Norwich City	L	1-3	Pickering	17,149
3	18	H	Blackburn Rovers	D	0-0		21,038
4	23	H	Birmingham City	W	2-0	Brown (pen), Own-goal	17,495
5	26	A	Queens Park Rangers	L	1-6	Pickering (pen)	19,227
6	29	A	Hull City	L	0-1		9,700
7	Sep 6	H	Swindon Town	W	3-2	Brown, Craven, Suddick	17,201
8	13	A	Huddersfield Town	L	0-2		10,575
9	15	H	Preston NE	D	0-0		19,741
10	20	H	Watford	L	0-3		14,859
11	27	A	Middlesbrough	W	2-0	Brown, Suddick	20,268
12	Oct 4	H	Cardiff City	W	3-2	Suddick, Pickering, Craven	18,115
13	6	H	Norwich City	D	0-0		12,485
14	11	A	Millwall	W	3-1	Pickering, James, Suddick	11,516
15	18	A	Sheffield Utd	W	3-2	Burns, Pickering 2	15,876
16	25	H	Bolton Wanderers	D	1-1	Craven	17,179
17	Nov 1	A	Charlton Athletic	W	2-0	McPhee, Craven	13,610
18	8	H	Leicester City	D	1-1	Brown	13,074
19	12	A	Blackburn Rovers	L	1-2	Suddick	17,393
20	15	A	Aston Villa	D	0-0		24,942
21	22	H	Oxford Utd	W	1-0	Johnston	10,968
22	29	A	Bristol City	L	1-2	Hutchison	14,818
23	Dec 6	H	Carlisle Utd	D	1-1	Armfield	9,766
24	13	H	Huddersfield Town	W	2-0	Suddick, Craven	12,587
25	26	A	Birmingham City	W	3-2	Hutchison, James, Suddick	29,548
26	Jan 10	A	Watford	W	1-0	Pickering	12,052
27	17	H	Middlesbrough	D	1-1	Burns	15,154
28	31	A	Cardiff City	D	2-2	Burns, Suddick	24,717
29	Feb 7	H	Millwall	D	1-1	Pickering (pen)	10,297
30	14	A	Portsmouth	W	3-2	Pickering, Craven, Suddick	13,949
31	21	A	Bolton Wanderers	W	2-0	Craven, Pickering	14,131
32	28	H	Charlton Athletic	W	2-0	Pickering 2	13,083
33	Mar 14	H	Bristol City	W	1-0	Bentley	13,657
34	18	H	Hull City	L	0-1		15,724
35	21	A	Carlisle Utd	W	2-1	Suddick, Murray	8,212
36	28	H	Aston Villa	W	2-1	Pickering 2 (1 pen)	17,352
37	30	H	Sheffield Utd	W	1-0	Craven	24,432
38	31	A	Leicester City	D	0-0		32,784
39	Apr 4	H	Queens Park Rangers	D	1-1	Craven	19,516
40	7	A	Swindon Town	D	1-1	Burns	28,520
41	13	A	Preston NE	W	3-0	Pickering 3	34,000
42	18	A	Oxford Utd	L	0-2		9,190

Final League Position: 2nd in Division Two

Apps
Sub Apps
Gls

FA Cup

3	Jan 3	A	Arsenal	D	1-1	Hutchison	32,210
3R	15	H	Arsenal	W	3-2	Suddick, Pickering, Burns	24,801
4	24	H	Mansfield Town	L	0-2		23,715

Apps
Sub Apps
Gls

League Cup

2	Sep 3	H	Gillingham	W	3-1	Suddick, Rowe, Bentley	10,797
3	24	A	Crystal Palace	D	2-2	Suddick, James	17,999
3R	Oct 1	H	Crystal Palace	L	0-1		13,973

Apps
Sub Apps
Gls

Thomson	Armfield	Bentley	Alcock	James	Craven	Burns	Milne	Pickering	Suddick	Hutchison	Brown	McPhee	Hughes	Wann	Rowe	Hatton	White	Mowbray	Johnston	Taylor	Thomas	Murray
1	2	3	4	5	6	7	8	9	10	11												
1	2	3	4	5	6	7	8	9	10	11												
1	2	3	4	5	6	7		9	10	11	8											
1	2	3	4	5	6	7		9	10	11	8											
1	2	3	5		6	7*	12	9	10	11	8	6										
1	2	3	5		12		4		10	11	7*	8	8		9							
1	2	3	5		9		4		10	11	7				8	6						
1	2	3		5	9		4		10	11	7				8	6						
1	2	3		5	6		4		10	11	7			12	8*	6						
1	2	3	4	5	8				10	11	7			12		6	9*					
1	2			5	6	7		9	10	11		12				6		3	8*			
	2			5	6	7	8	9	10	11*		12				6		3		1		
	2			5	9	11	8*		10			4	7			6		3		1	12	
	2			5	8	7		9	10	11		4				6		3		1		
1	2	12		5	8	7		9	10	11*		4				6		3				
1	2			5	8	7*		9	10	11		4	12			6		3				
1	2			5	8			9	10	11	7	4				6		3				
1	2			5	8			9	10	11	7	4				6		3				
1	2			5	8			9	10	11	7	4				6		3				
1	2	12		5	8	7*		9	10	11		4				6		3				
1	2			5	8			9	10	11		4				6		3	7			
1	2	12		5				9	10	11	7*	4			8	6		3				
1	2	12		5		8		9	10	11	7*	4				6		3				
1		3		5	8	7		9	10	11		4				6		2				
1		3		5	8	7		9	10	11		4				6		2				
1	2	12		5	8	7*		9	10	11		4				6		3				
1	2	9		5	8	7			10	11*		4			12	6		3				
1	2	3		5	8	7		9	10	11		4*				6		12				
1	2	3		5	8	7*		9	10	11	12	4				6						
1	2	4		5	8	7		9	10*	11		12				6		3				
1	2	4		5	8	7		9	10	11		12				6*		3				
1	2	4		5	8	7		9	10	11						6		3				
1	2	4		5	8	7*		9	10	11	12					6		3				
1	2	4	5		8*			9	10	11	12					6		3				7
1	2	4		5	8	12		9	10	11*						6		3				7
1	2	4		5	8	12		9	10	11						6		3				7*
1	2	3		5	8	7		9	10	11		4				6						
1	2	3		5	8			9	10	11		4				6						7
1	2	3		5	8			9	10	11		4				6						7
1	2	3		5	8*	7		9	10	11		4				6		12				
1	2	3		5	8	7		9	10	11		4				6						
1	2	3		5	8	7*		9	10	11		4				6						12
39	40	28	9	38	39	27	8	35	42	41	13	25	2		5	36	1	24	2	3		5
		5			1	2	1				3	4	1	2	1			2			1	1
	1	1		2	10	6		17	10	2	3	1							1			1

Thomson	Armfield	Bentley	Alcock	James	Craven	Burns	Milne	Pickering	Suddick	Hutchison	Brown	McPhee	Hughes	Wann	Rowe	Hatton	White	Mowbray	Johnston	Taylor	Thomas	Murray
1	2	6		5	8	7		9	10	11		4						3				
1	2	12		5	8	7		9	10	11		4*	7			6		3				
1	2	3		5	8	7		9	10*	11		4				6		12				
3	3	2		3	3	3		3	3	3		3				2		2				
		1																1				
						1		1	1	1												

Thomson	Armfield	Bentley	Alcock	James	Craven	Burns	Milne	Pickering	Suddick	Hutchison	Brown	McPhee	Hughes	Wann	Rowe	Hatton	White	Mowbray	Johnston	Taylor	Thomas	Murray
1		3	5		2		4		10	11	7	6	9		8							
1	2	3	5		4	7		9	10	11		6							8			
1	2			5	4	7	12	9	10	11		6						3	8*			
3	2	2	2	1	3	2	1	2	3	3	1	3	1		1			1	2			
							1															
		1		1					2						1							

League Table

	P	W	D	L	F	A	Pts
Huddersfield Town	42	24	12	6	68	37	60
Blackpool	42	20	13	9	56	45	53
Leicester City	42	19	13	10	64	50	51
Middlesbrough	42	20	10	12	55	45	50
Swindon Town	42	17	16	9	57	47	50
Sheffield United	42	22	5	15	73	38	49
Cardiff City	42	18	13	11	61	41	49
Blackburn Rovers	42	20	7	15	54	50	47
Queen's Park Rangers	42	17	11	14	66	57	45
Millwall	42	15	14	13	56	56	44
Norwich City	42	16	11	15	49	46	43
Carlisle United	42	14	13	15	58	56	41
Hull City	42	15	11	16	72	70	41
Bristol City	42	13	13	16	54	50	39
Oxford United	42	12	15	15	35	42	39
Bolton Wanderers	42	12	12	18	54	61	36
Portsmouth	42	13	9	20	66	80	35
Birmingham City	42	11	11	20	51	78	33
Watford	42	9	13	20	44	57	31
Charlton Athletic	42	7	17	18	35	76	31
Aston Villa	42	8	13	21	36	62	29
Preston North End	42	8	12	22	43	63	28

1970-71

Division One

Manager: Les Shannon/ Bob Stokoe

Did you know that?

Jimmy Armfield retired at the end of the season after 627 appearances for the club.

Les Shannon resigned as manager after the extraordinary 4–3 defeat to Chelsea. He was eventually replaced by Bob Stokoe.

28 players were used throughout the dismal campaign.

The Anglo-Italian Cup Final victory over Bologna was shown live on TV for 90 minutes, yet the extra-time was not, and so most Blackpool fans were forced to wait for the result to be given on television during a commercial break.

The 4–0 FA Cup victory over West Ham United was clouded in controversy as many of the opposing players had been seen in a Blackpool nightclub the evening before.

Nearly 31,000 saw the champions Everton come to Bloomfield Road. Many fans were forced to sit on the touchlines, and some climbed the floodlight pylons.

Match No.	Date		Venue	Opponents	Result		Scorers	Attendance
1	Aug	15	A	Huddersfield Town	L	0-3		22,787
2		17	H	Liverpool	D	0-0		23,818
3		22	H	West Brom Albion	W	3-1	Pickering 2, Brown	22,163
4		26	A	Manchester City	L	0-2		37,197
5		29	A	Newcastle Utd	W	2-1	Craven 2	33,270
6	Sep	2	A	Crystal Palace	L	0-1		26,298
7		5	H	Southampton	L	0-2		18,035
8		12	A	Tottenham Hotspur	L	0-3		19,894
9		19	H	Everton	L	0-2		30,705
10		26	A	Manchester Utd	D	1-1	Burns	46,647
11	Oct	3	H	Stoke City	D	1-1	Burns	25,324
12		10	A	Nottm Forest	L	1-3	Burns	16,615
13		17	H	Huddersfield Town	D	2-2	Green, Burns	21,006
14		24	H	Chelsea	L	3-4	Pickering 2, Suddick	24,940
15		31	A	West Ham Utd	L	1-2	Green	26,239
16	Nov	7	H	Arsenal	L	0-1		17,115
17		14	A	Leeds Utd	L	1-3	Craven	32,921
18		21	A	Derby County	L	0-2		28,237
19		28	H	Ipswich Town	L	0-2		13,048
20	Dec	5	A	Wolves	L	0-1		22,623
21		12	H	Coventry City	W	1-0	Craven	11,381
22		19	A	West Brom Albion	D	1-1	James	17,862
23		26	H	Burnley	D	1-1	Burns	28,371
24	Jan	9	A	Liverpool	D	2-2	Burns, Pickering	42,939
25		16	H	Manchester City	D	3-3	Craven 2, Pickering	29,356
26		30	A	Ipswich Town	L	1-2	Burns	17,509
27	Feb	6	H	Wolves	L	0-2		19,054
28		13	A	Coventry City	L	0-2		18,633
29		20	H	Derby County	L	0-1		17,892
30		27	H	West Ham Utd	D	1-1	Kemp	15,689
31	Mar	6	A	Chelsea	L	0-2		26,539
32		13	H	Leeds Utd	D	1-1	Craven	27,401
33		20	A	Arsenal	L	0-1		37,372
34		27	A	Southampton	D	1-1	Burns	17,833
35	Apr	3	H	Newcastle Utd	L	0-1		14,637
36		10	A	Burnley	L	0-1		14,495
37		12	H	Tottenham Hotspur	D	0-0		16,541
38		13	A	Stoke City	D	1-1	Hutchison	13,916
39		17	H	Nottm Forest	L	2-3	McGinty, Craven	10,028
40		24	A	Everton	D	0-0		26,286
41		26	H	Crystal Palace	W	3-1	Craven, Burns 2	8,905
42	May	1	H	Manchester Utd	D	1-1	Green	29,857

Final League Position: 22nd in Division One

Apps
Sub Apps
Gls

FA Cup

3	Jan	2	H	West Ham Utd	W	4-0	Green 2, Craven, Mowbray	21,814
4		23	A	Hull City	L	0-2		34,752

Apps
Sub Apps
Gls

League Cup

2	Sep	9	H	Newport County	W	4-1	Suddick, Bentley, Coleman, Rowe	9,878
3	Oct	7	H	Bristol City	L	0-1		10,877

Apps
Sub Apps
Gls

Thomson	Armfield	Bentley	Craven	James	Hatton	Murray	Brown	Pickering	Suddick	Hutchison	Mowbray	Hughes	Nicholson	Rowe	Johnston	Coleman	Alcock	McNicholas	Burns	Green	Blacklaw	Wann	Kemp	Taylor	Ramsbottom	Suddaby	McGrotty	Burridge
1	2	3	4	5	6	7*	8	9	10	11	12																	
1	2	4	8	5	6		7	9	10	11	3																	
1	2	4	8	5	6		7	9	10	11	3																	
1	2	4	8	5	6		7*	9	10	11	3	12																
1	2	4	8	5	6				10	11	3	7*		9	12													
1	2	4	8	5	6				10	11	3			9		11												
1	2	4	8		6			9	10	7	3*	12				11	5											
1	2	4	3		6			9	10*	11				8		7	5	12										
1	2	4	3		6					11		9		8		10*	5		7	12								
1	2*	10	9	5	4				12	11	3						6		7	8								
1	2	10	9	5	4				8	11	3						6		7									
1		10	9	5	4	12				8	3		2			11*	6		7									
		10		5	4			9		11	3		2				6		7	8	1							
1	2	6	12	5	4			9*	10	11	3								7	8								
1	3	6		5	4*				10	11	3	9							7	8		12						
1	2	10	4	5					7	11	3						6		9	8								
1	2	3	9	5						11					4		6		7	8		10						
1	2	3	9	5				7		11					4		6		12	8		10*						
1	2	3	9	5		12				11					8*	10	6			7			4					
	2	3	9		6				12	11*						10	5		7	8			4	1				
	2		9		6		12			11	3					10*	5		7	8			4	1				
		3	9	12	6					11	2					10*	5		7	8			4	1				
		3	9		6					11	2					10	5		7	8			4	1				
	2		9	5	6			12		11*	3					10			7	8			4	1				
	2		8	5	6*			9	12		3					10			11	7			4	1				
1	2		8	5	6			9			3					10			11	7			4					
1	2	12	8	5	6			9			3					10			11*	7			4					
1		3	9	5	6			10*			2					11			12	7			8			4		
	2	3*	10	5	6			9		11					12					7			8		1	4		
	2		9	5	6				12	11						10			7*	7			4		1	3		
	2		9	5	6					11	8				12	10*			7				4		1	3		
		3	9	5					10	11	2								7			8	4		1	6		
			9	5	6				10	11							2		7	8			4		1	3		
			9	5	3				10	11	4						2		7	8					1	6		
		3	9	5	2				10	11	4								7	8					1	6		
		3	9	5	2					11					4				7*	8		10			1	6	12	
		3	9	5	2					11			12		4					8		10*	7	1		6		
		3	9	5						11			4	8	10		2		12				7*	1		6		
		3	9	5	2					11					4				12	8		10		1		6*	7	
		3	9	5	2					11			12		4		6			8		10					7*	1
		3	9	5	2					11			12		4		6		7	8		10*						1
	2	12	9	5	3					11					4*		6		7	8		10						1
21	27	32	39	35	36	1	4	14	16	38	25	3	3	5	10	17	21		26	28	1	9	17	9	8	12	2	3
		2	1	1		2	1	1	4		1	2	3		3			1	4	1		1					1	
			8	1			1	7	1	1									10	3			1				1	

Thomson	Armfield	Bentley	Craven	James	Hatton	Murray	Brown	Pickering	Suddick	Hutchison	Mowbray	Hughes	Nicholson	Rowe	Johnston	Coleman	Alcock	McNicholas	Burns	Green	Blacklaw	Wann	Kemp	Taylor	Ramsbottom	Suddaby	McGrotty	Burridge
	2		9	5	6					11	3					10			7	8			4	1				
	2		8	5	6*			9	12		3		7			11				7			4	1		10		
	2		2	2	2			1		1	2					2			1	2			2	2		1		
									1																			1
			1								1									2								

Thomson	Armfield	Bentley	Craven	James	Hatton	Murray	Brown	Pickering	Suddick	Hutchison	Mowbray	Hughes	Nicholson	Rowe	Johnston	Coleman	Alcock	McNicholas	Burns	Green	Blacklaw	Wann	Kemp	Taylor	Ramsbottom	Suddaby	McGrotty	Burridge
1		4	3	5	6*			9	10	11			2	8		7		12										
1	2		9*	5	6				8	10	3		12			11	6		7									
2	1	1	2	2	2			1	2	1	1		1	1		2	1		1									
							1						1					1										
		1							1					1		1												

League Table

	P	W	D	L	F	A	Pts
Arsenal	42	29	7	6	71	29	65
Leeds United	42	27	10	5	72	30	64
Tottenham Hotspur	42	19	14	9	54	33	52
Wolverhampton W.	42	22	8	12	64	54	52
Liverpool	42	17	17	8	42	24	51
Chelsea	42	18	15	9	52	42	51
Southampton	42	17	12	13	56	44	46
Manchester United	42	16	11	15	65	66	43
Derby County	42	16	10	16	56	54	42
Coventry City	42	16	10	16	37	38	42
Manchester City	42	12	17	13	47	42	41
Newcastle United	42	14	13	15	44	46	41
Stoke City	42	12	13	17	44	48	37
Everton	42	12	13	17	54	60	37
Huddersfield Town	42	11	14	17	40	49	36
Nottingham Forest	42	14	8	20	42	61	36
West Bromwich Albion	42	10	15	17	58	75	35
Crystal Palace	42	12	11	19	39	57	35
Ipswich Town	42	12	10	20	42	48	34
West Ham United	42	10	14	18	47	60	34
Burnley	42	7	13	22	29	63	27
Blackpool	42	4	15	23	34	66	23

1971-72

Division Two

Manager: Bob Stokoe

Did you know that?

Tony Green was sold to Newcastle United for £150,000, with Keith Dyson coming the other way.

Blackpool were beaten in the quarter-finals of the League Cup by eventual winners Tottenham Hotspur.

On the way to another Anglo-Italian Cup Final, Blackpool beat Lanerossi Vicenza 10–0 at Bloomfield Road.

Match No.	Date		Venue	Opponents	Result		Scorers	Attendance
1	Aug	14	H	Swindon Town	W	4-1	James 2, Ainscow, Green	13,004
2		16	H	Cardiff City	W	3-0	Green, James 2	19,253
3		21	A	Milwall	L	0-1		12,053
4		28	H	Sheffield Wed	W	1-0	Hatton	16,557
5	Sep	1	A	Portsmouth	W	3-1	Burns, James 2	16,658
6		4	A	Hull City	L	0-1		18,288
7		11	H	Norwich City	L	1-2	Hatton	15,960
8		18	A	Watford	L	0-1		10,575
9		25	H	Birmingham City	D	1-1	Suddick	22,610
10		28	A	Bristol City	L	0-4		20,352
11	Oct	2	A	Middlesbrough	L	0-1		18,671
12		9	H	Orient	W	4-1	Burns 2, Suddaby, Ainscow	14,657
13		16	A	Swindon Town	L	0-1		10,346
14		23	H	Queens Park Rangers	D	1-1	Lennard	16,417
15		30	A	Fulham	L	1-2	Lennard	11,020
16	Nov	6	H	Carlisle Utd	W	2-0	James, Suddick (pen)	12,769
17		13	A	Sunderland	D	0-0		17,240
18		20	H	Luton Town	L	0-1		8,452
19		27	A	Oxford Utd	L	1-3	Suddick (pen)	7,894
20	Dec	4	H	Preston NE	D	1-1	Dyson	18,912
21		11	A	Charlton Athletic	W	3-2	Lennard, Dyson, Burns	9,598
22		18	H	Hull City	D	1-1	Burns	9,349
23		27	A	Burnley	L	1-2	Lennard	21,977
24	Jan	1	H	Watford	W	5-0	Lennard, Suddaby, Burns 3	10,745
25		8	A	Sheffield Wed	W	2-1	Burns, Hatton	17,113
26		22	H	Bristol City	W	1-0	Suddick	9,923
27		29	A	Cardiff City	W	4-3	Burns, Suddick (pen), Dyson	11,719
28	Feb	12	A	Queens Park Rangers	W	1-0	Dyson	13,690
29		19	H	Fulham	W	2-1	Suddick, Lennard	17,892
30		26	A	Carlisle Utd	L	0-2		9,985
31	Mar	4	H	Sunderland	D	1-1	Suddick	10,989
32		11	A	Orient	W	1-0	Burns	11,582
33		18	H	Millwall	D	0-0		12,916
34		25	A	Norwich City	L	1-5	Burns	23,665
35	Apr	1	H	Burnley	W	4-2	Suddick, Dyson 3	15,931
36		3	H	Middlesbrough	W	3-1	Burns, Bentley, Dyson	13,726
37		4	A	Birmingham City	L	1-2	Dyson	45,181
38		8	A	Luton Town	W	4-1	Dyson, Simpson, Burns, Own-goal	7,279
39		15	H	Oxford Utd	W	2-0	Burns, Suddick	10,133
40		22	A	Preston NE	W	4-1	Suddick (pen), Burns, Ainscow, Dyson	19,819
41		24	H	Portsmouth	L	1-2	Hutchison	10,507
42		29	H	Charlton Athletic	W	5-0	Burns, James, Hutchison, Hatton, Own-goal	8,864

Final League Position: 6th in Division Two

Apps
Sub Apps
Gls

FA Cup

3	Jan	15	H	Chelsea	L	0-1		22,135

Apps
Sub Apps
Gls

League Cup

2	Sep	8	A	Bournemouth	W	2-0	Hutchison, Burns	15,609
3	Oct	5	H	Colchester Utd	W	4-0	Suddick, Green, Burns 2	11,042
4		26	H	Aston Villa	W	4-1	Suddick, Green, James, Hutchison	20,193
5	Nov	17	A	Tottenham Hotspur	L	0-2		30,099

Apps
Sub Apps
Gls

Burridge	Hatton	Bentley	Booth	Alcock	Suddaby	Ainscow	Green	James	Suddick	Burns	Hardcastle	Johnston	Craven	Hutchison	Wann	Ramsbottom	Fuschillo	Harrison	Lennard	Kemp	Simpkin	Dyson	Mann	Wood
1	2	3	4	5	6	7	8	9	10	11														
1	2	3	4	5	6	7	8	9	10	11														
1	2	3	4	5	6	7*	8	9	10	11		12												
1	2	3	4	5	6	7*	8	9	10	11			12											
1	2	3	4	5	6		8	9	10	7				11										
1	2	3	4	5	6		8	9	10	7*			12	11										
	2	3	4	5	6		8	9	10	7*				11	12	1								
	2	3	4*	5	6		8	9	10	7				11	12	1								
	2	3*	4	5	6	12	8	9	10	7				11		1								
	2		4	5	6	7	8	9	10						11	1	3							
1	2		4*	5	6	12	8	9	10	7					11			3						
1	2			5	4	7	8	9	10	11								3	6					
1	2			5	4		8	9	7*	11				12				3	10		6			
1	2			5	4		8	9*	7	11				12				3	10		6			
1	2			5	4			9	10	11				7				3*	11		6	8		
1	2			5	4			3	8	11*				7					10	12	6	9		
1	2		10*	5	4					11				7	12		6			8	6	9	3	
1	2			5	4				8	11				7					10*	12	6	9	3	
1	2			5	4			12	8	11									10*	7	6	9	3	
1	2			5	4			6	8	7	3			11					10			9		
1	3			5*	4			6	8	7	2			11					10		12	9		
1	2				4	12		5	8	7				11			3*		10		6	9		
1	2				4	12		5	8	7	3			11					10		6*	9		
1	2				4	12		5	8	7	3*			11					10		6	9		
1	2	3			4			5	8	7				11					10		6	9		
1	2*	3			4	12		5	8	7				11					10		6	9		
1		3		2	4	12		5	8*	7				11					10		6	9		
1	2	3			4			5	8	7				11					10		6	9		
1		3			4			5	8	7	2			11					10		6	9		
1	2	3			4			5	8	7		12		11*					10		6	9		
1	2	3			4			5	8	7	12			11					10		6	9*		
1	2				4			5	8	11	3			7					10		6	9		
1	2				4			5	8	11	3			7				12	10*		6	9		
1	2			12	4			5	8	11	10			7				3*			6	9		
1	2				4			5	8	11	3	12		7					10*		6	9		
1	2	10			4	12		5	8	11	3			7							6*	9		
1	2	3			4	10		5	8	7				11							6	9		
1	2	3			4			5	8	11	10			7							6	9		
	2	3			4			5	8	11	10			7							6	9		1
	4	3			5	12			8	11	2			7					10*		6	9		1
	2	3			4	12		5	8	11	10			7							6*	9		1
	2	3		4		10		5	8	11	6			7								9		1
34	40	23	12	23	41	8	14	38	41	40	15			32	2	4	2	6	23	2	27	28	3	4
				1		10		1		1	1	3	2	2	3			1		2	1			
	4	1			2	3	2	8	10	17				2					6		1	12		

Burridge	Hatton	Bentley	Booth	Alcock	Suddaby	Ainscow	Green	James	Suddick	Burns	Hardcastle	Johnston	Craven	Hutchison	Wann	Ramsbottom	Fuschillo	Harrison	Lennard	Kemp	Simpkin	Dyson	Mann	Wood
1	2	3			4	12		5	8	7				11					10		6*	9		
1	1	1			1			1	1	1				1					1		1	1		
						1																		

Burridge	Hatton	Bentley	Booth	Alcock	Suddaby	Ainscow	Green	James	Suddick	Burns	Hardcastle	Johnston	Craven	Hutchison	Wann	Ramsbottom	Fuschillo	Harrison	Lennard	Kemp	Simpkin	Dyson	Mann	Wood
	2	3	4	5	6		8	9	10	7				11		1								
1	2		4	5	6	7	8	9	10	11								3						
1	2			5	4		8	9	10	11				7				3			6			
1	2		10	5	4			9*		11				7	12					8	6		3	
3	4	1	3	4	4	1	3	4	3	4				3		1		2		1	2		1	
															1									
							2	1	2	3				2										

League Table

	P	W	D	L	F	A	Pts
Norwich City	42	21	15	6	60	36	57
Birmingham City	42	19	18	5	60	31	56
Millwall	42	19	17	6	64	46	55
Queen's Park Rangers	42	20	14	8	57	28	54
Sunderland	42	17	16	9	67	57	50
Blackpool	42	20	7	15	70	50	47
Burnley	42	20	6	16	70	55	46
Bristol City	42	18	10	14	61	49	46
Middlesbrough	42	19	8	15	50	48	46
Carlisle United	42	17	9	16	61	57	43
Swindon Town	42	15	12	15	47	47	42
Hull City	42	14	10	18	49	53	38
Luton Town	42	10	18	14	43	48	38
Sheffield Wednesday	42	13	12	17	51	58	38
Oxford United	42	12	14	16	43	55	38
Portsmouth	42	12	13	17	59	68	37
Orient	42	14	9	19	50	61	37
Preston North End	42	12	12	18	52	58	36
Cardiff City	42	10	14	18	56	69	34
Fulham	42	12	10	20	45	68	34
Charlton Athletic	42	12	9	21	55	77	33
Watford	42	5	9	28	24	75	19

1972-73

Division Two

Manager: Bob Stokoe

Did you know that?

Despite another League Cup quarter-final and a push for promotion, Bob Stokoe resigned and took over at Sunderland. He was replaced by Harry Potts.

Interest in the Anglo-Italian Cup ended for Blackpool at the fourth-round stage.

Match No.	Date	Venue	Opponents	Result		Scorers	Attendance
1	Aug 12	A	Huddersfield Town	L	0-3		12,840
2	19	H	Brighton @ HA	W	6-2	Hutchison 2, Burns, Lennard, Bentley, Dyson	10,894
3	26	A	Cardiff City	W	2-1	Dyson, Lennard	12,401
4	28	H	Sunderland	D	0-0		14,797
5	Sep 2	H	Millwall	W	2-1	Burns, Dyson	9,494
6	9	A	Swindon Town	D	0-0		10,069
7	16	H	Orient	D	1-1	Burns	10,471
8	23	A	Burnley	L	3-4	Suddick 2, Ainscow	14,591
9	26	A	Carlisle Utd	W	3-2	Ainscow, Suddick, Barton	10,969
10	30	H	Middlesbrough	L	0-1		14,714
11	Oct 7	A	Luton Town	D	2-2	Hutchison, Ainscow	12,073
12	14	H	Oxford Utd	W	2-1	Ainscow, Burns	11,589
13	17	H	Aston Villa	D	1-1	Rafferty	15,043
14	21	A	Fulham	L	0-2		8,644
15	28	H	Queens Park Rangers	W	2-0	Rafferty, Suddick	14,160
16	Nov 4	H	Carlisle Utd	D	0-0		9,564
17	11	A	Aston Villa	D	0-0		31,651
18	18	H	Bristol City	W	3-0	Alcock, Dyson, Suddick	8,341
19	25	A	Hull City	W	2-1	Ainscow, Rafferty	8,988
20	Dec 2	H	Portsmouth	W	3-1	Dyson, Ainscow, Suddick	8,409
21	9	A	Preston NE	W	3-0	Ainscow 3	15,822
22	16	H	Sheffield Wed	L	1-2	Hatton	10,270
23	23	A	Nottm Forest	L	0-4		10,078
24	26	H	Burnley	L	1-2	Rafferty	25,277
25	31	A	Brighton @ HA	W	2-1	Ainscow, Alcock	18,001
26	Jan 20	A	Millwall	D	1-1	Suddick	8,700
27	27	H	Swindon Town	W	2-0	Suddick (pen), Rafferty	8,277
28	Feb 2	A	Middlesbrough	L	0-2		10,464
29	10	A	Orient	L	0-2		4,923
30	17	H	Huddersfield Town	D	1-1	Rafferty	8,593
31	28	A	Sheffield Wed	L	0-2		13,950
32	Mar 3	H	Luton Town	D	1-1	Suddick	6,947
33	7	H	Cardiff City	W	1-0	Rafferty	5,303
34	10	A	Oxford Utd	W	1-0	Dyson	7,911
35	17	H	Fulham	W	2-0	Alcock, Dyson	8,019
36	24	A	Queens Park Rangers	L	0-4		15,714
37	31	H	Hull City	W	4-3	James, Dyson, Burns, Suddick	5,645
38	Apr 7	A	Portsmouth	L	0-1		6,768
39	14	H	Preston NE	W	2-0	Rafferty, Burns	12,195
40	21	A	Bristol City	L	0-3		11,537
41	23	H	Nottm Forest	W	2-0	Dyson, Lennard	8,322
42	28	A	Sunderland	L	0-1		26,921

Final League Position: 7th in Division Two

Apps
Sub Apps
Gls

FA Cup

3	Jan 13	A	Bradford City	L	1-2	Suddick (pen)	14,205

Apps
Sub Apps
Gls

League Cup

2	Sep 6	A	Bournemouth	D	0-0		10,577
2R	11	H	Bournemouth	D	1-1*	Suddick	8,685
2R2	18	N	Bournemouth	W	2-1*	Hatton, Barton	2,337
3	Oct 4	A	Newcastle Utd	W	3-0	Parker, Barton, Suddick (pen)	19,810
4	31	H	Birmingham City	W	2-0	Burns 2	13,332
5	Nov 21	A	Wolves	D	1-1	Dyson	17,312
5R	28	H	Wolves	L	0-1		19,812

* after extra-time. N played at Villa Park, Birmingham

Apps
Sub Apps
Gls

Burridge	Hardcastle	Bentley	James	Suddaby	Barton	Hutchison	Suddick	Dyson	Lennard	Burns	Ainscow	Wood	Hatton	Simpkin	Alcock	Fuschillo	Parker	Rafferty	McGrotty	Tully	O'Neil
1	2	3*	4	5	6	7	8	9	10	11	12										
		3	4	5	6	7	8	9	10*	11	12	1	2								
		3	4	5	6	7	8	9	10		11*	1	2	12							
	12	3	4	5	6	7	8	9	10	11		1	2*								
	2	3	4*	5	6	7	8	9	10	11		1			12						
	2	3		5	6		8	9	7	11		1			4	6					
	2*	3		5	6	7	8		10	11	9	1			4		12				
1		3	9	5	6	7	8		10	11*	12		2		4						
1		3	4	5	10	7	8		6	11	9		2								
1		3	4		10	7	8	9*	6		11		2		5	12					
1		3	4	5	6	7*	8			11	10		2			12	9				
1		3	4	5	6		8		10*	11	7		2					9			
1	12	3	4	5	6		8		10*	11	7		2					9			
1		3	4	5	6		8	9		11	7		2			12	10*				
1	12	3	4	5	6		8	10		7*	11		2					9			
1	7	3		5	6*		8	10			11		2	12	4			9			
1		3		5			8	10	6	7	11		2		4			9			
1		3		5			8	10	6	7	11		2		4			9			
1	12	3	6*	5			8		10	7	11		2		4			9			
1	10	3	12	5			8	10*		7	11		2		4			9			
1	6	3		5			8		10	7	11		2		4			9			
1	6*	3	12	5			8		10	7	11		2		4			9			
1		3	12	5			8	10	6*	7	11		2		4			9			
1	3			5			8	10		7	11		2		4			9		6	
1	3			5	10		8			7	11		2		4			9		6	
1	2	3	5				8			7	11			10	4			9			6
1	2	3	4				8			7	11			6	5			9			10
1	2	3	4				8			7	11			6	5			9			10
	2	3	4	5			8			7	11	1		6*				9	12		10
		3	4	5	2		8			7	10	1						9		11	6
		3	11	6			10	12		7	8	1	2		11			9*			4
		3	5	6			8*			7	11	1	2		4			9		12	10
		3	5	6			8	10		7	11	1	2		4			9			
		3	5	6			8	10		7	11	1	2		4			9			
		3	5	6			8	10		7	11	1	2		4			9			
		3	5	6			8	10		7	11	1	2		4			9			
		3	5	6			8	10		7	11	1	2		4			9			
		3	5	6			8	10	12	7*	11	1	2		4			9			
		3	5	6			8	10		7	11	1	2		4			9			
		3	5	6			8	10	12	7	11*	1	2		4			9			
		3	5	6			8	10	12	7		1	2		4			9*		11	
	12	3	5	6*			8	10	9	7		1	2		4					11	
22	14	40	31	38	18	10	42	25	19	39	34	20	33	4	28	1	2	29		5	7
	5		3					1	3		3			2	2	3	1		1	1	
		1	1		1	3	10	9	3	6	10		1		3			8			

Burridge	Hardcastle	Bentley	James	Suddaby	Barton	Hutchison	Suddick	Dyson	Lennard	Burns	Ainscow	Wood	Hatton	Simpkin	Alcock	Fuschillo	Parker	Rafferty	McGrotty	Tully	O'Neil
1		3	5	4		11	8	9	10	7	12		2	6*							
1		1	1	1		1	1	1	1	1			1	1							
											1										
						1															

Burridge	Hardcastle	Bentley	James	Suddaby	Barton	Hutchison	Suddick	Dyson	Lennard	Burns	Ainscow	Wood	Hatton	Simpkin	Alcock	Fuschillo	Parker	Rafferty	McGrotty	Tully	O'Neil
	2	3		5	10	7	8	9	6	11		1			4						
	2	3		5	6	7	8	9*	12	11	10	1			4						
1		3		5	6	7	8*		10		11		2		4	12	9				
1		3	4	5	6	7	8			11	10		2				9				
1	10	3	4	5	6		8	9		11*	7		2		12						
1	12	3	6	5			8	9*	10	7	11		2		4						
1	12	3	6	5			8	9	10*	7	11		2		4						
5	3	7	4	7	5	4	7	5	4	6	6	2	5		5		2				
	2								1						1	1					
					2		2	1		2			1				1				

League Table

	P	W	D	L	F	A	Pts
Burnley	42	24	14	4	72	35	62
Queen's Park Rangers	42	24	13	5	81	37	61
Aston Villa	42	18	14	10	51	47	50
Middlesbrough	42	17	13	12	46	43	47
Bristol City	42	17	12	13	63	51	46
Sunderland	42	17	12	13	59	49	46
Blackpool	42	18	10	14	56	51	46
Oxford United	42	19	7	16	52	43	45
Fulham	42	16	12	14	58	49	44
Sheffield Wednesday	42	17	10	15	59	55	44
Millwall	42	16	10	16	55	47	42
Luton Town	42	15	11	16	44	53	41
Hull City	42	14	12	16	64	59	40
Nottingham Forest	42	14	12	16	47	52	40
Orient	42	12	12	18	49	53	36
Swindon Town	42	10	16	16	46	60	36
Portsmouth	42	12	11	19	42	59	35
Carlisle United	42	11	12	19	50	52	34
Preston North End	42	11	12	19	37	64	34
Cardiff City	42	11	11	20	43	58	33
Huddersfield Town	42	8	17	17	36	56	33
Brighton & Hove Albion	42	8	13	21	46	83	29

1973-74

Division Two

Manager: Harry Potts

Did you know that?

Blackpool were pipped to promotion by Carlisle United on the last day of the season. They were just seven minutes from the First Division, before losing to two late goals at Sunderland, and so the team they had beaten 4–0 the previous week took their place.

Alan Suddick scored his 100th League goal – a penalty in the 3–0 win at home to Preston North End.

The Under-21 team became the first English side to win the Caligaris tournament in Northern Italy. They beat Napoli in the Final 3–1 with two goals from Stuart Parker and one from David Tong.

Match No.	Date	Venue	Opponents	Result		Scorers	Attendance
1	Aug 25	H	West Brom Albion	L	2-3	Alcock, Suddaby	14,236
2	Sep 1	A	Sheffield Wed	D	0-0		15,834
3	8	H	Millwall	W	1-0	Burns	9,442
4	12	A	Fulham	D	0-0		9,301
5	15	A	Orient	L	2-3	Davies, Burns	7,352
6	17	H	Crystal Palace	W	1-0	Rafferty	9,323
7	22	H	Middlesbrough	D	0-0		14,784
8	29	A	Luton Town	L	0-3		10,365
9	Oct 2	A	Crystal Palace	W	2-1	James, Burns	18,080
10	6	H	Notts County	L	0-1		11,072
11	13	A	Cardiff City	L	0-1		7,693
12	20	H	Nottm Forest	D	2-2	James, Davies	8,107
13	22	H	Fulham	W	2-0	Alcock 2	5,526
14	27	A	Bristol City	W	1-0	Dyson	13,896
15	Nov 3	H	Portsmouth	W	5-0	Suddick, Walsh, Burns 2, Alcock	6,535
16	10	A	Preston NE	W	3-1	Alcock 2, Walsh	21,580
17	17	H	Swindon Town	W	2-0	Alcock, Bentley	7,404
18	24	A	Hull City	L	0-1		9,004
19	Dec 1	H	Sunderland	L	0-2		11,000
20	8	A	Carlisle Utd	W	3-2	Bentley, Suddick, Alcock	6,641
21	15	A	Oxford Utd	D	2-2	Alcock, Hatton	5,001
22	22	H	Luton Town	W	3-0	Burns 3	7,796
23	26	A	Bolton Wanderers	D	1-1	Own-goal	18,150
24	29	A	Millwall	D	2-2	Burns, Dyson	8,848
25	Jan 1	H	Sheffield Wed	D	0-0		11,362
26	12	H	Orient	D	1-1	Burns	8,760
27	19	A	West Brom Albion	D	1-1	Ainscow	17,727
28	Feb 2	H	Oxford Utd	W	2-0	Burns, Suddick	5,508
29	9	A	Middlesbrough	D	0-0		21,913
30	16	H	Cardiff City	W	2-1	Ainscow 2	7,410
31	23	A	Notts County	W	3-0	Dyson 2, Burns	11,092
32	Mar 2	H	Bolton Wanderers	L	0-2		18,575
33	16	A	Nottm Forest	L	0-2		15,724
34	19	H	Bristol City	D	2-2	James, Davies	7,710
35	23	H	Preston NE	W	3-0	Alcock, Walsh, Suddick (pen)	13,243
36	30	A	Portsmouth	D	0-0		9,693
37	Apr 6	H	Hull City	L	1-2	Burns	8,159
38	13	A	Swindon Town	L	0-1		4,655
39	15	A	Aston Villa	W	1-0	Dyson	18,351
40	16	H	Aston Villa	W	2-1	Suddick, Dyson	10,787
41	20	H	Carlisle Utd	W	4-0	Dyson, Alcock 2, Suddick (pen)	15,777
42	27	A	Sunderland	L	1-2	Burns	22,331

Final League Position: 5th in Division Two

Apps
Sub Apps
Gls

FA Cup

3	Jan 5	A	Southampton	L	1-2	Dyson	16,212

Apps
Sub Apps
Gls

League Cup

2	Oct 9	H	Birmingham City	D	1-1	Burns	7,943
2R	16	A	Birmingham City	L	2-4	Burns 2	16,880

Apps
Sub Apps
Gls

Wood	Hatton	Bentley	Alcock	James	Suddaby	Burns	Suddick	Davies	McEwan	Tully	Rafferty	Fuschillo	Walsh	Hardcastle	Curtis	Dyson	Burridge	Hart	Harrison	Ainscow	Evanson
1	2	3	4	5	6	7	8	9	10	11*	12										
1	2	3	4	5	6	7	8	9	10	11											
1	2	3	4	5	6	7	8	9		11		10									
1	2	3	4	5	6	7		9		11		10	8								
1		3	4	5	6	7		9		11		10	8*	12	2						
1	2	3	4	5	6	11		9			8		7		10						
1	2	3	4	5	6	7	8	9			10		11								
1	2	3	4	5	6	7	8	9			10		11*		12						
1	3		4	5	6	7	8	9			10*	11			2	12					
1	2	3	4	5	6	7	8	9			10	11									
1	2	3	4	5	6	7	8	9	11							10					
1		3	4	5	6	7	8	9	11*		10				2	12					
		3	4	5	6	7	8	9					11		2		1	10			
	10	3	4	5	6	7	8						11		2	9	1				
	3	10	4	5	6	7	8						11		2	9	1				
	3	10	4	5	6	7	8						11		2	9	1				
		10	4	5	6	7	8						11		2	9	1		3		
	3	10	4	5	6	7	8						11		2	9	1				
	3	10	4	5	6	7	8						11		2	9	1				
	3	10	4	5	6	7	8						11		2	9	1				
	3	10	4	5	6	7	8						11*		2	9	1		12		
	3	10	4	5	6	7	8						12		2	9	1			11*	
	3	10	4	5	6	7	8								2	9	1			11	
	3	10	4	5	6	7	8								2	9	1			11	
	3*	10	4	5	6	7	8						12		2	9	1			11	
		10	4	5	6	7	8						12		2	9	1		3	11*	
		10	4	5	6	7	8								2	9	1		3	11	
		10	4	5	6	7	8								2	9	1		3	11	
		10	4	5	6	7	8								2	9	1		3	11	
		10	4	5		7	8								2	9	1	6	3	11	
		3	4	5		7	8								2	9	1	6		11	10
		3	4	5	6	7	8								2	9	1			11	10
	12	3	4	5	6	7	8								2	9*	1			11	10
	2	3	4	5	6	7	8	9					12				1			11	10*
	2		4	5	6	7	8	9					11				1		3		10
	2		4	5	6	7	8	9									1		3	11	10
	2		4	5	6	7	8	9					12				1		3	11*	10
	2	4		5	6	7	8						10			9	1		3*	11	12
	2	10	4	5	6	7	8									9	1		3	11	
	2	10	4	5	6	7	8									9	1		3	11*	12
	2	11	4	5	6	7	8									9	1		3	12	10*
	2	11	4	5	6	7	8									9	1		3		10
12	39	38	41	42	40	42	39	17	4	5	6	5	16		25	26	30	3	14	18	9
	1										1		5	1	1	2			1	1	2
	1	2	12	3	1	14	6	3			1		3			7				3	

Wood	Hatton	Bentley	Alcock	James	Suddaby	Burns	Suddick	Davies	McEwan	Tully	Rafferty	Fuschillo	Walsh	Hardcastle	Curtis	Dyson	Burridge	Hart	Harrison	Ainscow	Evanson
		10	4	5	6	7	8								2	9	1		3	11	
		1	1	1	1	1	1								1	1	1		1	1	
																1					

Wood	Hatton	Bentley	Alcock	James	Suddaby	Burns	Suddick	Davies	McEwan	Tully	Rafferty	Fuschillo	Walsh	Hardcastle	Curtis	Dyson	Burridge	Hart	Harrison	Ainscow	Evanson
1	2	3	4	5	6	7	8	9	11							10					
1	2	3	4	5	6	7	8	9	11	10											
2	2	2	2	2	2	2	2	2	2	1						1					
						3															

League Table

	P	W	D	L	F	A	Pts
Middlesbrough	42	27	11	4	77	30	65
Luton Town	42	19	12	11	64	51	50
Carlisle United	42	20	9	13	61	48	49
Orient	42	15	18	9	55	42	48
Blackpool	42	17	13	12	57	40	47
Sunderland	42	19	9	14	58	44	47
Nottingham Forest	42	15	15	12	57	43	45
West Bromwich Albion	42	14	16	12	48	45	44
Hull City	42	13	17	12	46	47	43
Notts County	42	15	13	14	55	60	43
Bolton Wanderers	42	15	12	15	44	40	42
Millwall	42	14	14	14	51	51	42
Fulham	42	16	10	16	39	43	42
Aston Villa	42	13	15	14	48	45	41
Portsmouth	42	14	12	16	45	62	40
Bristol City	42	14	10	18	47	54	38
Cardiff City	42	10	16	16	49	62	36
Oxford United	42	10	16	16	35	46	36
Sheffield Wednesday	42	12	11	19	51	63	35
Crystal Palace	42	11	12	19	43	56	34
Preston North End	42	9	14	19	40	62	31
Swindon Town	42	7	11	24	36	72	25

1974-75

Division Two

Manager: Harry Potts

Did you know that?

The home game with Bolton Wanderers on 24 August was overshadowed by the murder of Blackpool fan Kevin Olsson. It brought about stringent measures from the authorities to combat the rise of football hooliganism.

Glyn James retired at the end of the season after 15 years with the club.

The team only scored in 20 of their 42 League games, scoring just 38 goals.

Just under 5,000 turned up at Bloomfield Road to see Blackpool beat Notts County 3–1.

Match No.	Date	Venue	Opponents	Result		Scorers	Attendance
1	Aug 17	A	Norwich City	L	1-2	Bentley	18,551
2	20	H	Orient	D	0-0		9,314
3	24	H	Bolton Wanderers	W	2-1	Dyson, Ainscow	15,513
4	27	A	Orient	D	0-0		7,314
5	31	A	Southampton	D	1-1	Walsh	14,694
6	Sep 7	H	Millwall	W	1-0	Walsh	5,579
7	14	A	Oldham Athletic	L	0-1		11,926
8	21	H	York City	D	1-1	Walsh	7,927
9	24	H	Cardiff City	W	4-0	Parker, Hart, Davies, Own-goal	5,597
10	28	A	Bristol Rovers	W	3-1	Hart, Walsh (pen), Parker	10,968
11	Oct 5	H	Hull City	L	1-2	Hart	8,406
12	12	A	Aston Villa	L	0-1		25,763
13	19	H	Manchester Utd	L	0-3		22,211
14	22	A	Bolton Wanderers	D	0-0		12,574
15	26	A	Portsmouth	D	0-0		10,143
16	Nov 2	H	Sheffield Wed	W	3-1	Tong 2, Ainscow	6,243
17	9	A	Sunderland	L	0-1		24,939
18	16	H	Oxford Utd	D	0-0		5,342
19	23	A	Bristol City	W	1-0	Hatton (pen)	11,584
20	30	A	Fulham	L	0-1		6,416
21	Dec 7	H	Notts County	W	3-1	Ainscow, Walsh, Dyson	4,922
22	14	H	Norwich City	W	2-1	Hart, Walsh	6,683
23	21	A	Nottm Forest	D	0-0		8,480
24	26	H	Oldham Athletic	W	1-0	Walsh	12,491
25	28	A	West Brom Albion	L	0-2		14,924
26	Jan 11	A	Notts County	D	0-0		10,601
27	18	H	Fulham	W	1-0	Alcock	6,710
28	Feb 1	H	Sunderland	W	3-2	Alcock, Davies, Walsh	16,151
29	8	A	Sheffield Wed	D	0-0		14,342
30	15	H	Bristol City	W	2-0	Ainscow, Bentley	8,687
31	22	A	Oxford Utd	D	0-0		7,476
32	Mar 1	H	Southampton	W	3-0	Walsh 2, Alcock	8,831
33	8	A	Cardiff City	D	1-1	Bentley	8,134
34	15	H	Bristol Rovers	D	0-0		8,019
35	22	A	Millwall	D	0-0		7,506
36	29	H	Nottm Forest	D	0-0		11,640
37	31	H	West Brom Albion	W	2-0	Alcock, Own-goal	11,611
38	Apr 1	A	York City	D	0-0		8,234
39	5	H	Portsmouth	D	2-2	Walsh 2 (1 pen)	6,543
40	22	A	Hull City	L	0-1		6,027
41	19	H	Aston Villa	L	0-3		20,762
42	20	A	Manchester Utd	L	0-4		58,769

Fnal League Position: 7th in Division Two

Apps
Sub Apps
Gls

FA Cup

3	Jan 4	A	Plymouth Argyle	L	0-2		23,143

Apps
Sub Apps
Gls

League Cup

2	Sep 11	A	Chester City	L	1-3	Walsh	5,854

Apps
Sub Apps
Gls

Burridge	Hatton	Bentley	Alcock	James	Suddaby	Tong	Suddick	Dyson	Evanson	Walsh	Curtis	Moore	Parker	Harrison	Evans	Hart	Ainscow	Davies	Wood	McEwan	Ronson
1	2	3	4	5	6	7*	8	9	10	11	12										
1		3	4	5	6		8	9			12	7	10*	11	2						
1	2*	10		5	6		8	9			12	7		3		4	11				
1	7	3		5	6			9	8		2			11		4	10				
1	7	3		5	6			9*	8	12	2			11		4	10				
1	5	3			6		7		8	9	2			11		4	10				
1	5	3		2	6		7		8	9	12		10*	11		4					
1	2	3		5	6	8			10*	7	12			11		4		9			
1	2	3		5*	6	8					10	7	12	11		4		9			
	2	3*			6	8				7	5	10	12	11		4		9	1		
	2	3			6	8			10*	7	5		12	11		4		9	1		
	2	3		4	6	8			10	7*	5			11			9	12	1		
	4*	10		5	6	12			11	7	2			3			8	9	1		
1	4	10			6	9			11	7	2			3		5	8				
1	4	10			6	9			11	7	2			3		5	8				
1	2	10			6	7			11	9	4			3		5	8				
1	2	10			6	7*			11	9	4			3	12	5	8				
1	2	10			6				11	9	4		12	3	7*	5	8				
1	2	10			6				11		4		9	3	7	5	8				
1	2	10			6				11	12	4		9*	3	7	5	8				
1	4	3	6			7		10	11	9	2					5	8				
1	4	3	6			7		10*	11	9	2					5	8	12			
1	4	3	6			7		10	11	9	2					5	8				
1	4	3	6			7		10	11	9	2					5	8				
1	4	3	6			7*		10	11	9		2				5	8			12	
1	3		6	4		7			11*	10	2	12				5	8	9			
1	4		6	3		7			11	9	2					5	8	10			
1	3	10	6						11	9	2			5		4	7	8			
1	3	10	6			12			11	9	2*			5		4	7	8			
1	6	10	5						11	7	2			3		4	8	9			
1	6	10	5			9			11	7	2			3		4	8				
1	6	10	5			11				7	2			3		4	8	9			
1	6	10	5						11	7	2			3		4	8	9			
1	6	10	5			12			11	7	2			3		4	8*	9			
1	4	10	5			8			11	7	2		9	3		6					
1	6	10	5						11	7	2			3		4		9			8
1	6	10	5			8			11	7	2			3		4		9			
1	4	10*	5		12				11	7	2		8	3		6		9			
1	6		8		5				10	7	2			3		4	11	9			
1	6		5*			8			11	7	2	12	9	3		4	10				
1	6*				5	8			11	9	2		12	3		4	10				
1	2		3		5	8			11	7	12		9*	3	6		10				
38	41	36	23	12	23	24	5	10	37	35	36	5	8	34	4	37	31	17	4		2
					1	3				2	5	2	5		2			2		1	
	1	3	4			2		2		12			2			4	4	2			

Burridge	Hatton	Bentley	Alcock	James	Suddaby	Tong	Suddick	Dyson	Evanson	Walsh	Curtis	Moore	Parker	Harrison	Evans	Hart	Ainscow	Davies	Wood	McEwan	Ronson
1	4	3	6			12		11	9	2	7*				5	8	10				
1	1	1	1					1	1	1	1				1	1	1				
						1															

Burridge	Hatton	Bentley	Alcock	James	Suddaby	Tong	Suddick	Dyson	Evanson	Walsh	Curtis	Moore	Parker	Harrison	Evans	Hart	Ainscow	Davies	Wood	McEwan	Ronson
1		3	5	7	6	12			8	9	2			11		4	10*				
1		1	1	1	1				1	1	1			1		1	1				
						1															
										1											

League Table

	P	W	D	L	F	A	Pts
Manchester United	42	26	9	7	66	30	61
Aston Villa	42	25	8	9	79	32	58
Norwich City	42	20	13	9	58	37	53
Sunderland	42	19	13	10	65	35	51
Bristol City	42	21	8	13	47	33	50
West Bromwich Albion	42	18	9	15	54	42	45
Blackpool	42	14	17	11	38	33	45
Hull City	42	15	14	13	40	53	44
Fulham	42	13	16	13	44	39	42
Bolton Wanderers	42	15	12	15	45	41	42
Oxford United	42	15	12	15	41	51	42
Orient	42	11	20	11	28	39	42
Southampton	42	15	11	16	53	54	41
Notts County	42	12	16	14	49	59	40
York City	42	14	10	18	51	55	38
Nottingham Forest	42	12	14	16	43	55	38
Portsmouth	42	12	13	17	44	54	37
Oldham Athletic	42	10	15	17	40	48	35
Bristol Rovers	42	12	11	19	42	64	35
Millwall	42	10	12	20	44	56	32
Cardiff City	42	9	14	19	36	62	32
Sheffield Wednesday	42	5	11	26	29	64	21

1975-76

Division Two

Manager: Harry Potts

Did you know that?

Only 40 goals were scored this campaign, and Harry Potts was sacked in May 1976.

Only two games in the League attracted a five-figure crowd to Bloomfield Road.

Match No.	Date	Venue	Opponents	Result		Scorers	Attendance
1	Aug 16	A	Fulham	D	0-0		8,863
2	19	A	Hull City	L	0-1		5,304
3	23	H	Orient	W	1-0	Tong	6,626
4	30	A	Sunderland	L	0-2		23,576
5	Sep 6	H	Oldham Athletic	D	1-1	Walsh	8,862
6	13	A	Charlton Athletic	D	1-1	Walsh	9,190
7	20	H	Southampton	W	4-3	Walsh 3 (1 pen), Moore	9,564
8	24	A	Blackburn Rovers	W	2-0	Walsh, Moore	11,048
9	27	A	Bristol City	L	0-2		10,240
10	Oct 4	H	Luton Town	W	3-2	Suddaby 2, Walsh	7,854
11	11	H	Portsmouth	D	0-0		8,351
12	18	A	Chelsea	L	0-2		16,924
13	25	H	Bristol Rovers	L	1-4	Suddick	9,019
14	Nov 1	A	Bolton Wanderers	L	0-1		17,274
15	4	H	Nottm Forest	D	1-1	Ainscow	5,851
16	8	H	West Brom Albion	L	0-1		8,271
17	15	A	Oxford Utd	W	3-1	Walsh, Suddaby, Ainscow	4,316
18	22	H	Chelsea	L	0-2		8,595
19	29	H	Notts County	W	1-0	Walsh	6,103
20	Dec 6	A	Plymouth Argyle	W	2-1	Walsh 2	12,422
21	12	A	Orient	W	1-0	Tong	4,337
22	20	H	Fulham	D	1-1	Weston	6,379
23	26	A	Carlisle Utd	L	0-1		11,532
24	27	H	York City	D	0-0		7,939
25	Jan 10	H	Charlton Athletic	W	2-1	Walsh 2 (1 pen)	5,748
26	17	A	Oldham Athletic	L	0-1		11,734
27	31	H	Hull City	D	2-2	Alcock, Ronson	4,966
28	Feb 7	A	Nottm Forest	L	0-3		8,582
29	21	H	Oxford Utd	W	2-0	Walsh, Smith	4,423
30	24	H	Blackburn Rovers	D	1-1	Hart	8,772
31	28	A	Bristol Rovers	D	1-1	Smith	6,686
32	Mar 6	H	Bolton Wanderers	D	1-1	Smith	18,548
33	13	A	Portsmouth	L	0-2		8,394
34	20	A	Notts County	W	2-1	Smith 2	10,427
35	27	H	Plymouth Argyle	D	0-0		5,497
36	31	A	West Brom Albion	D	0-0		20,729
37	Apr 3	H	Bristol City	W	2-1	Moore, Walsh	8,273
38	10	A	Southampton	L	1-3	Suddaby	21,758
39	17	H	Carlisle Utd	W	2-1	Walsh, Hart	8,382
40	19	A	York City	D	1-1	Ronson	3,800
41	20	H	Sunderland	W	1-0	Walsh	16,768
42	24	A	Luton Town	L	0-3		8,757

Final League Position: 10th in Division Two

Apps
Sub Apps
Gls

FA Cup

3	Jan 3	H	Burnley	W	1-0	Bentley	20,753
4	24	A	Southampton	L	1-3	Alcock	21,553

Apps
Sub Apps
Gls

League Cup

2	Sep 10	A	Peterborough Utd	L	0-2		6,987

Apps
Sub Apps
Gls

	Burridge	Curtis	Harrison	Suddaby	Tong	Alcock	Walsh	Suddick	Ronson	Moore	Ainscow	McEwan	Hart	Bentley	Dyson	Hatton	Betts	Wood	Evanson	Weston	Smith
	1	2	3	4	5	6	7	8	9	10	11										
	1	2	3	4	5	6	7	8			11		9	10							
	1	2	3	4	5	6	7	8			11		9	10							
	1	2	3	5	10*	4	7	8		12	11		9	6							
	1	2	3	5	10*	4	7	8	12		11			6	9						
	1	2		5	10		12	8		7	11		4	6	9*	2					
	1	2		5			9	8	7	11	10		4	3		6					
		2		5			9	8	7	11	10		4	3		6		1			
		2		5			9	8	7	11	10		4	3		6		1			
		2	11	5			9	8	7		10		4	3		6		1			
		2	12	5	7*		9	8		11	10		4	3		6		1			
		2	3		5		7	8		10	9		4	11		6		1			
		2	3	5		12	9	8			10		4	11		6		1	7*		
		2	3	5			9	8		7	10		4	11		6		1			
		2	3	5			9	7	10	11	8		4			6		1			
			3	5		2	9	7	10	11	8		6			4		1			
			3	5	2		9	7	10*	11	8		6			4	12	1			
			3	5	11	12	9	8	7*	6	10		4			2		1			
			3*	5	7	6	9	8			11		4			2	10	1		12	
				5	7	6	9				11*		4	3		2	10	1	12	8	
				5	7	6	9					4		3		2	11	1	8	10	
					7	6	9				8*	4	5	3		2	12	1	11	10	
			12	5	7	6	9						4	3		2	11	1	8	10*	
			3	5	7*	6	9		8			12	4	10		2		1	11		
			8	5		6	9			12		4	7	3		2		1	11	10	
			8			6	9			2	5*	4	7	3			12	1	11	10	
			3			6	9		12	8		4	5	2				1	7*	11	10
			3	11		6	9		7	8		4	5	2				1			10
			3	5			9		7	11	8		4	6		2		1			10
			3	5			9		7	11	8		4	6		2		1			10
			3	5			9				8	7	4	6		2		1		11	10
			3	5			9				8	7	4	6		2		1		11	10
			3	5		6	9				11	4		3		2		1	12	10*	7
			3	5		6	9				10	4		11		2		1	7		8
			3	5		6	9	8			10	4		11		2		1	7		
				5		6	9	8	11	10		4		3		2		1	7		
				5		6	9	8		11	10	4		3		2		1	7		
				5		6	9	8		11	10	4		3		2		1	7		
			3	5			9	8			7	4	6	10		2		1	11		
			6	5			9	8	11		10		4	3		2		1	7		
			3	5			9	8	4		7		6	10		2		1	11		
			6	5			9	8	11		10	12	4	3		2		1	7*		
	7	15	30	38	16	22	41	27	17	20	35	15	33	36	2	34	4	35	17	10	8
			2			2	1		2	1		2					3		2	1	
				4	2	1	17	1	2	3	2		2							1	5

	Burridge	Curtis	Harrison	Suddaby	Tong	Alcock	Walsh	Suddick	Ronson	Moore	Ainscow	McEwan	Hart	Bentley	Dyson	Hatton	Betts	Wood	Evanson	Weston	Smith
			8	5		6*	9			12		4	7	3		2		1	11	10	
			3			6	9			8		4	5	10		2		1	7	11	
			2	1		2	2			1		2	2	2		2		2	2	2	
										1											
						1								1							

	Burridge	Curtis	Harrison	Suddaby	Tong	Alcock	Walsh	Suddick	Ronson	Moore	Ainscow	McEwan	Hart	Bentley	Dyson	Hatton	Betts	Wood	Evanson	Weston	Smith
	1	2	3*	5	12		7	8	10		11			6	9	4					
	1	1	1	1			1	1	1		1			1	1	1					
					1																

League Table

	P	W	D	L	F	A	Pts
Sunderland	42	24	8	10	67	36	56
Bristol City	42	19	15	8	59	35	53
West Bromwich Albion	42	20	13	9	50	33	53
Bolton Wanderers	42	20	12	10	64	38	52
Notts County	42	19	11	12	60	41	49
Southampton	42	21	7	14	66	50	49
Luton Town	42	19	10	13	61	51	48
Nottingham Forest	42	17	12	13	55	40	46
Charlton Athletic	42	15	12	15	61	72	42
Blackpool	42	14	14	14	40	49	42
Chelsea	42	12	16	14	53	54	40
Fulham	42	13	14	15	45	47	40
Orient	42	13	14	15	37	39	40
Hull City	42	14	11	17	45	49	39
Blackburn Rovers	42	12	14	16	45	50	38
Plymouth Argyle	42	13	12	17	48	54	38
Oldham Athletic	42	13	12	17	57	68	38
Bristol Rovers	42	11	16	15	38	50	38
Carlisle United	42	12	13	17	45	59	37
Oxford United	42	11	11	20	39	59	33
York City	42	10	8	24	39	71	28
Portsmouth	42	9	7	26	32	61	25

1976-77

Division Two

Manager: Allan Brown

Did you know that?

Allan Brown took over as manager at the start of the season. He was responsible for buying Bob Hatton and partnering him with the prolific Mickey Walsh.

Walsh was top scorer for the third successive season.

Blackpool just missed promotion by two points to Brian Clough's Nottingham Forest. One year later, Forest won the First Division title.

Match No.	Date	Venue	Opponents	Result		Scorers	Attendance
1	Aug 21	A	Bristol Rovers	W	4-1	Hatton 2, Suddick, Own-goal	5,845
2	24	H	Oldham Athletic	L	0-2		12,974
3	28	H	Orient	W	3-0	Hart, Walsh 2 (1 pen)	7,928
4	Sep 4	A	Blackburn Rovers	W	1-0	Walsh (pen)	10,173
5	11	H	Millwall	W	4-2	Ronson, Walsh 2, Suddick	8,881
6	18	A	Notts County	L	0-2		9,598
7	25	H	Chelsea	L	0-1		19,041
8	Oct 2	A	Bolton Wanderers	W	3-0	Hatton, Walsh 2 (1 pen)	18,680
9	9	H	Plymouth Argyle	L	0-2		12,647
10	12	A	Carlisle Utd	D	1-1	Bentley	8,427
11	16	H	Nottm Forest	W	1-0	Walsh	17,089
12	23	A	Cardiff City	D	2-2	Hatton, Spence	12,178
13	30	H	Wolves	D	2-2	Spence, Hart	21,005
14	Nov 6	A	Hull City	D	2-2	Walsh, Hatton	9,541
15	13	H	Sheffield Utd	W	1-0	Walsh	13,506
16	20	A	Charlton Athletic	W	2-1	Hart, Walsh	12,045
17	27	H	Fulham	W	3-2	Hart, Hatton,Walsh	16,779
18	Dec 4	A	Luton Town	D	0-0		9,163
19	18	A	Southampton	D	3-3	Bentley, Walsh 2	14,918
20	27	H	Carlisle Utd	D	0-0		17,075
21	28	A	Burnley	D	0-0		19,640
22	Jan 1	H	Hull City	D	0-0		12,503
23	15	A	Oldham Athletic	L	0-1		12,411
24	22	H	Bristol Rovers	W	4-0	Walsh (pen), Hart, Ainscow, Bentley	9,288
25	Feb 12	H	Blackburn Rovers	D	1-1	Ainscow	14,922
26	14	H	Hereford Utd	W	2-1	Walsh 2	8,535
27	19	A	Millwall	D	1-1	Walsh	10,561
28	26	H	Notts County	D	1-1	Walsh	10,275
29	Mar 1	A	Wolves	L	1-2	Hatton	23,879
30	5	A	Chelsea	D	2-2	Ronson, Spence	27,412
31	12	H	Bolton Wanderers	W	1-0	Ronson	23,659
32	19	A	Plymouth Argyle	L	0-2		8,893
33	26	A	Nottm Forest	L	0-3		16,658
34	Apr 2	H	Cardiff City	W	1-0	Hart	7,351
35	9	H	Burnley	D	1-1	Walsh	14,526
36	12	A	Sheffield Utd	W	5-1	Walsh 3, Hatton, Ronson	18,357
37	16	H	Charlton Athletic	D	2-2	Walsh 2 (1 pen)	8,686
38	23	A	Fulham	D	0-0		10,956
39	30	H	Luton Town	W	1-0	Hatton	9,277
40	May 7	A	Hereford Utd	D	1-1	Finnigan	5,312
41	10	A	Orient	W	1-0	Walsh	4,730
42	14	H	Southampton	W	1-0	Hatton	10,768

Final League Position: 5th in Division Two

Apps
Sub Apps
Gls

FA Cup

3	Jan 8	H	Derby County	D	0-0		19,442
3R	19	A	Derby County	L	2-3	Walsh, Spence	21,433

Apps
Sub Apps
Gls

League Cup

2	Aug 31	H	Birmingham City	W	2-1	Ronson, Hatton	12,203
3	Sep 21	H	Arsenal	D	1-1	Walsh	18,983
3R	28	A	Arsenal	D	0-0		27,195
3R2	Oct 5	A	Arsenal	L	0-2		26,791

Apps
Sub Apps
Gls

Wood	Curtis	Bentley	Hart	Suddaby	Tong	Ronson	Suddick	Ainscow	Hatton	Harrison	Moore	Walsh	Gardner	Farley	Hockaday	Spence	Weston	McEwan	Summerbee	Finigan	Milligan	Wilson
1	2	3	4	5	6	7	8	9	10	11												
1	2	3	5	6	4	7*	8	11	10		12	9										
1	2	3	5	6	4	7	8		10		11	9										
1	2	3	5	6	4	7	8		10		11	9										
1	2	3	5	6	4	7	8		10		11	9										
1	2	3	5	6	4	7	8		10		11*	9			12							
1		3	5	6		4	8		10	12	11*	9	2		7							
1		11	5	6		4	8	7	10*	3		9	2		12							
1		3	5	6		4	8	7	10			9	2	11								
1		11	5	6		4	8	7	10	3		9	2									
1		11	5	6		4		7	10	3		9	2			8						
1		11	5	6		4		7	10	3		9	2			8						
1		11	5	6		4	7		10	3		9	2			8						
1		11	5	6		4			10	3		9	2			8	7					
1		11	5	6		4			10	3	12	9	2			8	7*					
1		11	5	6		4			10	3		9	2			8	7					
1		11	5	6		4			10	3		9	2			8	7					
1		11	5	6		4			10	3		9	2			8	7					
1	2	11*	5	6		4			10	3		9				8	7	12				
1	2	11	5	6		4			10	3		9				8	7					
1	2	11	5	6		4			10	3		9				8	7					
1	2	11	5	6	10	4				3		9				8			7			
1	2	11	5	6	12	4*		7	10	3		9				8						
1	2	11	5	6		4		7	10	3		9				8						
1	2	11	5	6		4		7	10	3		9				8						
1	2	11	5	6		4		7	10*	3	8	9				12						
1	2	11	5	6		4		7	10	3	8	9										
1	2	11	5	6		4		7	10	3	8*	9				12						
1	2	11	5	6		4		7	10	3		9				8						
1	2	11	5	6		4		7	10	3		9				8						
1	2	11	5	6		4		7	10	3		9				8						
1		11	5	6					10	3		9	2			8	7	12	4*			
1	2	11*	5	6	12	4		7	10	3		9				8						
1			5	6	11*	4			10	3		9	2		7			12	8			
1		11	8	6		4				3		9	2		7*	12		5		10		
1		11	5	6		4			10	3		9	2			7		8				
1		11	5	6		4			10	3		9	2			7*		8		12		
1		11	5	6		4			10	3		9	2			7		8				
1		11	5	6		4			10	3		9	2			7*		8		12		
1		11	5	6	12	4			10	3*		9	2					8		7		
1			5	6	11	4						9	2					8		7	3	10
1			5	6	11	4			10			9	2					8		7	3	
42	20	39	42	42	10	41	11	17	39	33	8	41	22	1	3	24	9	8	3	4	2	1
					3					1	2				2	3		3		2		
		3	6			4	2	2	10			26				3				1		

Wood	Curtis	Bentley	Hart	Suddaby	Tong	Ronson	Suddick	Ainscow	Hatton	Harrison	Moore	Walsh	Gardner	Farley	Hockaday	Spence	Weston	McEwan	Summerbee	Finigan	Milligan	Wilson
1	2	11	5	6		4		7	10	3		9				8						
1	2	11	5	6		4		7	10	3		9	10			8						
2	2	2	2	2		2		2	2	2		2				2						
												1				1						

Wood	Curtis	Bentley	Hart	Suddaby	Tong	Ronson	Suddick	Ainscow	Hatton	Harrison	Moore	Walsh	Gardner	Farley	Hockaday	Spence	Weston	McEwan	Summerbee	Finigan	Milligan	Wilson
1	2	3	5	6	4	7	8		10		11	9										
1		3	5	6		4	8		10		11	9	2		7							
1		3	5	6		4	8		10	12		9	2		7		11*					
1		11	5	6		4	12	7	10	3		9	2									8*
4	1	4	4	4	1	4	3	1	4	1	2	4	3		2		1					1
							1			1												
						1			1			1										

League Table

	P	W	D	L	F	A	Pts
Wolverhampton W.	42	22	13	7	84	45	57
Chelsea	42	21	13	8	73	53	55
Nottingham Forest	42	21	10	11	77	43	52
Bolton Wanderers	42	20	11	11	75	54	51
Blackpool	42	17	17	8	58	42	51
Luton Town	42	21	6	15	67	48	48
Charlton Athletic	42	16	16	10	71	58	48
Notts County	42	19	10	13	65	60	48
Southampton	42	17	10	15	72	67	44
Millwall	42	15	13	14	57	53	43
Sheffield United	42	14	12	16	54	63	40
Blackburn Rovers	42	15	9	18	42	54	39
Oldham Athletic	42	14	10	18	52	64	38
Hull City	42	10	17	15	45	53	37
Bristol Rovers	42	12	13	17	53	68	37
Burnley	42	11	14	17	46	64	36
Fulham	42	11	13	18	54	61	35
Cardiff City	42	12	10	20	56	67	34
Orient	42	9	16	17	37	55	34
Carlisle United	42	11	12	19	49	75	34
Plymouth Argyle	42	8	16	18	46	65	32
Hereford United	42	8	15	19	57	78	31

1977-78

Division Two

Manager: Allan Brown

Did you know that?

Blackpool had just beaten Charlton Athletic 5–1 and Blackburn Rovers 5–2 at home when Allan Brown was sacked. The team were in ninth place at the time.

Blackpool only won one of their last 15 games to finish 20th and relegated to the Third Division, their lowest position since 1928.

The Blackpool team were on a tour of America when they heard of their relegation as they had fulfilled their fixtures.

Jimmy Meadows was replaced as caretaker manager for the second time.

Match No.	Date	Venue	Opponents	Result		Scorers	Attendance
1	Aug 20	H	Oldham Athletic	D	1-1	Suddaby	11,021
2	23	A	Orient	W	4-1	Finnigan, Hatton 3	5,328
3	27	A	Charlton Athletic	L	1-3	Walsh	6,449
4	Sep 3	H	Bristol Rovers	W	3-1	Walsh 2, Hatton	8,219
5	10	A	Blackburn Rovers	W	2-1	Walsh, Chandler	8,211
6	17	H	Tottenham Hotspur	L	0-2		17,077
7	24	A	Notts County	D	1-1	Finnigan	7,200
8	Oct 1	H	Cardiff City	W	3-0	Hatton 3	8,704
9	4	H	Crystal Palace	W	3-1	Hart, Hatton 2	9,369
10	8	A	Fulham	D	1-1	Ronson	9,190
11	15	A	Hull City	L	0-2		6,800
12	22	H	Luton Town	W	2-1	Ronson, Ainscow	12,167
13	29	A	Burnley	W	1-0	Ainscow	11,225
14	Nov 5	H	Sheffield Utd	D	1-1	Hatton	10,625
15	12	A	Southampton	L	0-2		18,356
16	19	H	Millwall	D	2-2	Hatton, Hart	7,224
17	26	A	Stoke City	W	2-1	Walsh 2	15,132
18	Dec 3	H	Brighton @ HA	L	0-1		9,704
19	10	A	Mansfield Town	W	3-2	Hatton, Ainscow, Walsh	6,975
20	7	H	Southampton	L	0-1		8,640
21	26	A	Sunderland	L	1-2	Hatton	30,628
22	27	H	Bolton Wanderers	L	0-2		25,789
23	31	H	Orient	D	0-0		6,911
24	Jan 2	A	Oldham Athletic	L	1-2	Walsh	15,308
25	14	H	Charlton Athletic	W	5-1	Hatton 3, Hart, Walsh	6,206
26	21	A	Bristol Rovers	L	0-2		7,304
27	Feb 4	H	Blackburn Rovers	W	5-2	Hatton 4, Waldron	12,416
28	11	A	Tottenham Hotspur	D	2-2	Ronson, Walsh	28,707
29	25	A	Cardiff City	L	1-2	Tong	7,322
30	Mar 7	H	Notts County	D	2-2	Walsh (pen), Groves	6,783
31	11	H	Hull City	W	3-0	Tong, Chandler, Ainscow	6,220
32	18	A	Luton Town	L	0-4		6,041
33	25	A	Bolton Wanderers	L	1-2	Walsh (pen)	20,506
34	27	H	Sunderland	D	1-1	Tong	9,872
35	28	H	Burnley	D	1-1	Walsh	13,393
36	Apr 1	A	Sheffield Utd	D	0-0		12,804
37	8	H	Stoke City	D	1-1	Wilson	12,201
38	15	A	Millwall	L	0-2		5,553
39	18	H	Fulham	L	1-2	Walsh (pen)	4,695
40	22	H	Mansfield Town	L	1-2	Hatton	5,376
41	25	A	Crystal Palace	D	2-2	McEwan, Own-goal	11,115
42	29	A	Brighton @ HA	L	1-2	Hatton	33,431

Final League Position: 20th in Division Two

Apps
Sub Apps
Gls

FA Cup

3	Jan 3	A	West Brom Albion	L	1-4	Hatton	21,306

Apps
Sub Apps
Gls

League Cup

2	Aug 30	H	Sheffield Wed	D	2-2	Walsh (pen), Hatton	10,101
2R	Sep 5	A	Sheffield Wed	L	1-3	Hart	13,260

Apps
Sub Apps
Gls

Hesford	Gardner	Harrison	Hart	McEwan	Suddaby	Ainscow	Tong	Walsh	Hatton	Finnigan	Sinclair	Ronson	Milligan	Chandler	Ward	Weston	Groves	Waldron	Wilson	Thompson	Hockaday
1	2	3	4	5	6	7	8	9	10	11*	12										
1	2	3	4	5	6		8	9	10	11		7									
1	2	3	4	6	5		8	9	10	11		7									
1	2	3	5	7	6		8	9	10	11		4									
	2	3		5	6	7		9	10	11		4		8	1						
	2	3	5	12	6	7*		9	10	11		4		8	1						
	2*	3	4	5	6	7		9	10	11		12			1	8					
		3	4	5	6	7		9	10	11			2		1	8					
		3	4	5	6	8		9	10			7	2		1	11					
		3	4	5	6	8		9	10			7	2		1	11					
		3	4	5	6	8		9	10			7	2		1	11					
	2		4	5	6	8		9	10	12		7	3*		1	11					
	2	3	4	5	6	8		9	10			7			1	11					
	2	3	4	5	6	8		9	10			7			1	11					
	2	3	4	5	6	8		9	10	12		7			1	11*					
	2	3	4	5	6	8		9	10	11		7*			1	12					
	2	3	4	5	6	8		9	10						1	7	11				
	2	3	4	5	6	8		9	10			12			1	7*	11				
		3	5	2	6	7	8	9	10			4			1		11				
		3	5	2	6	7	8	9	10			4*			1		11	12			
			5	2	6	7	8	9	10						1	3	11	4			
	2	3	5		6	7		9	10						1	8	11	4*	12		
	2	3	4	5	6	8		9	10			7			1		11				
	2		4	5	6	8		9	10			7	3		1		11				
		3	4	5	6	8		9	10			7			1			11		2	
		3	4	5	6	8		9	10			7			1	12		11*		2	
	2	3	4	5				9	10			7		8	1			11		6	
	2		4	5		10		9				7		8	1	3		11		6	
			4	5			6	9			12	7	3		1		11	10	8	2*	
				5	6		7	9				4	3	8	1		11	10	2		
	2			5	6*	10	7	9				4	3	8	1			11	12		
	2			5	6	10	7*	9				4	3	8	1			11	12		
1	2			5	6	10	12	9				4		8				11	7*	3	
1	2			5	6	10	7		9			4		8			12	11*		3	
1	2			5	6	8	7	9	10			4	3					11			
1	2				6	8	4	9*	10				3	7			12	11	5		
1	2			5	6	8	4		10				3	7*			12	11	9		
1	2				6	8*	4		10				3	7			9	11	5	12	
1	2			5	6		12	9	10			8		7*		3		11		4	
1	2			5	6	11*	7	9	10			8	3				12			4	
1	2			5	6	11	7	9	10			8				3				4	
1	2			5	6	11	7	9	10			8				3				4	
14	31	23	28	38	39	35	19	39	36	9		32	15	13	28	17	11	17	6	11	
				1			2			1	2	2				2	4	1	3	1	
			3	1	1	4	3	14	22	2		3		2			1	1	1		

Hesford	Gardner	Harrison	Hart	McEwan	Suddaby	Ainscow	Tong	Walsh	Hatton	Finnigan	Sinclair	Ronson	Milligan	Chandler	Ward	Weston	Groves	Waldron	Wilson	Thompson	Hockaday
	2		4	5	6	8		9	10			7	3	12	1		11*				
	1		1	1	1	1		1	1			1	1		1		1				
														1							
									1												

Hesford	Gardner	Harrison	Hart	McEwan	Suddaby	Ainscow	Tong	Walsh	Hatton	Finnigan	Sinclair	Ronson	Milligan	Chandler	Ward	Weston	Groves	Waldron	Wilson	Thompson	Hockaday
1	2	3	5		6		8	9*	10	11	12	4									7
1	2	3	5*	7	6		8	9	10	11		4	12								
2	2	2	2	1	2		2	2	2	2		2									1
											1		1								
			1					1	1												

League Table

	P	W	D	L	F	A	Pts
Bolton Wanderers	42	24	10	8	63	33	58
Southampton	42	22	13	7	70	39	57
Tottenham Hotspur	42	20	16	6	83	49	56
Brighton & Hove Albion	42	22	12	8	63	38	56
Blackburn Rovers	42	16	13	13	56	60	45
Sunderland	42	14	16	12	67	59	44
Stoke City	42	16	10	16	53	49	42
Oldham Athletic	42	13	16	13	54	58	42
Crystal Palace	42	13	15	14	50	47	41
Fulham	42	14	13	15	49	49	41
Burnley	42	15	10	17	56	64	40
Sheffield United	42	16	8	18	62	73	40
Luton Town	42	14	10	18	54	52	38
Orient	42	10	18	14	43	49	38
Notts County	42	11	16	15	54	62	38
Millwall	42	12	14	16	49	57	38
Charlton Athletic	42	13	12	17	55	68	38
Bristol Rovers	42	13	12	17	61	77	38
Cardiff City	42	13	12	17	51	71	38
Blackpool	42	12	13	17	59	60	37
Mansfield Town	42	10	11	21	49	69	31
Hull City	42	8	12	22	34	52	28

1978-79

Division Three

Manager: Bob Stokoe

Did you know that?

Bob Stokoe returned as manager, but lasted for just one season.

The average attendance at Bloomfield Road was the lowest the club had suffered since Wartime football.

At the end of the season, it was agreed to have sponsorship on the team's shirts. Blackpool' s first sponsors were Easywear.

Match No.	Date	Venue	Opponents	Result		Scorers	Attendance
1	Aug 19	H	Oxford Utd	W	1-0	Davidson	6,215
2	22	A	Watford	L	1-5	Wilson	11,812
3	26	A	Rotherham Utd	L	1-2	Davidson	4,572
4	Sep 2	H	Carlisle Utd	W	3-1	Spence 3	7,789
5	9	A	Shrewsbury Town	L	0-2		4,179
6	12	H	Chesterfield	D	0-0		6,244
7	16	H	Walsall	W	2-1	Spence, McEwan (pen)	8,153
8	23	A	Swindon Town	W	1-0	Sermanni	6,607
9	26	H	Gillingham	W	2-0	Wagstaffe, Davidson	5,772
10	30	A	Colchester Utd	L	1-3	Hockaday	3,007
11	Oct 7	H	Lincoln City	W	2-0	Spence, Chandler	7,080
12	14	A	Southend Utd	L	0-4		6,374
13	18	A	Exeter City	L	0-3		3,993
14	21	H	Mansfield Town	W	2-0	Chandler, Weston	6,663
15	28	A	Plymouth Argyle	D	0-0		8,886
16	Nov 4	H	Sheffield Wed	L	0-1		9,403
17	11	A	Carlisle Utd	D	1-1	Chandler	6,505
18	18	H	Rotherham Utd	L	1-2	Suddaby	6,085
19	Dec 9	H	Peterborough Utd	D	0-0		4,280
20	23	H	Chester City	W	3-0	Spence 2, Kellow	4,106
21	26	A	Tranmere Rovers	W	2-0	Ronson, Thompson	3,481
22	30	A	Swansea City	L	0-1		12,549
23	Feb 3	A	Gillingham	L	0-2		6,146
24	6	A	Walsall	L	1-2	Kellow	3,711
25	10	H	Colchester Utd	W	2-1	Spence 2	3,446
26	20	H	Hull City	W	3-1	Kellow, Weston, Spence	3,636
27	24	H	Southend Utd	L	1-2	Spence	4,566
28	Mar 3	A	Mansfield Town	D	1-1	Spence	4,829
29	6	A	Bury	W	3-1	Spence 2, Jones	4,575
30	10	H	Plymouth Argyle	D	0-0		4,879
31	14	A	Chesterfield	W	3-1	Ronson 2, Kellow	4,638
32	20	H	Shrewsbury Town	W	5-0	McEwan 2 (1 pen), Kellow 2, Suddaby	5,330
33	24	H	Watford	D	1-1	McEwan	9,253
34	28	A	Oxford Utd	L	0-1		2,924
35	31	A	Brentford	L	2-3	Weston 2	6,360
36	Apr 7	H	Bury	L	1-2	Kellow	5,451
37	13	A	Chester City	L	2-4	Thompson, Jones	4,439
38	14	H	Tranmere Rovers	W	2-0	Spence, Jones	4,798
39	16	A	Hull City	D	0-0		6,000
40	21	H	Swansea City	L	1-3	Kellow	5,977
41	24	H	Exeter City	D	1-1	Kellow	3,136
42	28	A	Peterborough Utd	W	2-1	Kellow 2	4,004
43	May 5	H	Brentford	L	0-1		3,464
44	7	A	Lincoln City	W	2-1	Hockaday 2	1,949
45	15	H	Swindon Town	W	5-2	Chandler, Malone, McEwan (pen), Hockaday, Spence	4,191
46	17	A	Sheffield Wed	L	0-2		7,310

Final League Position: 12th in Division Three

Apps
Sub Apps
Gls

FA Cup

1	Nov 25	H	Lincoln City	W	2-1	McEwan (pen), Chandler	4,375
2	Dec 16	A	Bury	L	1-3	Kellow	6,519

Apps
Sub Apps
Gls

League Cup

1	Aug 12	A	Carlisle Utd	D	2-2	McEwan 2 (1 pen)	5,100
	16	H	Carlisle Utd	W	2-1	Davidson, Own-goal	6,617
2	30	H	Ipswich Town	W	2-0	Davidson 2	10,029
3	Oct 4	H	Manchester City	D	1-1	Spence	18,868
3R	10	A	Manchester City	L	0-3		26,213

Apps
Sub Apps
Gls

Ward	Gardner	Thompson	Wilson	Suddaby	McEwan	Spence	Tong	Holden	Davidson	Wagstaffe	Hockaday	Waldron	Chandler	Pashley	Ronson	Hesford	Sermanni	Bissell	Weston	Hall	Malone	Milligan	May	Kellow	Jones	Kerr	Dowes
1	2	3	4	5	6	7*	8	9	10	11	12																
1	2	3	4	5	6	9	8		10			7*	12														
1	2	3	4	5	6	9		12	10	11	7*			3													
1	2	4		5	6	9			10		7		11	3	8												
1	2	4		5	6	9		7	10	11*			12	3	8												
1	2	4		5	6	9			10	11	7*		12	3	8												
1	2	4		5	6	9			10	11	7		12	3	8*												
	2	4		5	6	9*			10	11	12		7	3		1	8										
	2	4		5	6	9			10	11*	12		7	3	8	1											
	2	4		5	6	9					11		7	3	8	1	12	10*									
	2	4		5	6	9			10	12	7		11	3	8*	1											
	2	4		5	6	9			10		11*		7	3	8	1			12								
1	2	4	12	5	6	9			10	11*				3	8				7								
1	2	4	10*	5	6	9				11			12	3	8				7								
1	2	4		5	6	9*				11			7	3	8		12		10								
1	2*	4		5	6	9				11			7	3	8		12		10								
1		4		5	6	9				11			7	3	8				10		2						
1				8	6	9					12	10	7	3					11		2		4*	8			
	2	4			6				12				7	3		1	8		10*		12			9	11		
		4		5	6	9			10	12				3	8	1					2			7	11*		
		4		5	6	9			10	11				3	8	1					2			7			
		4		5	6	9			10	11*				3	8	1					2			7	12		
		4	9	5	6				10	11*				3	8	1			12		2				7		
		4*		5	6				10					3	8	1	12		11		2			7	9		
			4	5	6	9			10	11*				3	8	1					2			7	12		
				5	6	9			10				11	3		1	8		4		2			7*	12		
		12		5	6	9			10				11	3		1	8		4		2			7*			
		4		5	6	9			10			8*	12	3		1			11		2				7		
		4		5	6	9			10					3	8	1			11		2				7		
		4		5	6	9			10					3		1			11		2				7	8	
		4		5	6	9								3	10	1			11		2			7		8	
				5	6	9						4		3	10	1			11		2			7		8	
				5	6	9						4		3	10	1			11		2			7		8	
		4		5	6	9			12					3	10*	1			11		2			7		8	
			4*	5	6	9								3	10	1			11		2			7	12	8	
			12	5	6	9							10	3		1			11	4	2			8		7*	
		4		5	6	9					7		10	3*		1			11		2			8	12		
	3	4		5	6	9					7					1			11		2			8	10		
		4			6	9										1	7		11		2	3	5	8			10
		4			6	9									10	1	7*		11		2	3	5	8	12		
	3	4		5	6	9									10	1			11		2			8	7		
	3	4		5	6	9					12				10	1			11		2			8	7*		
	3	4		5	6	9					7				10	1			11*		2			8	12		
		4		5	6	9					7		3		10	1			11		2*			8	12		
	12	4		5*	6	9					7		3		10	1			11		2			8			
	2	4	12		6						7		11		10	1			3*		2		5	8	9		
13	22	38	7	42	46	42	2	2	23	16	13	5	18	35	32	33	6	1	29	1	29	2	4	25	11	7	1
	1	1	3					1	2	2	5		6				4		2		1				7		
		2	1	2	5	16			3	1	4		4		3		1		4		1			11	3		

Ward	Gardner	Thompson	Wilson	Suddaby	McEwan	Spence	Tong	Holden	Davidson	Wagstaffe	Hockaday	Waldron	Chandler	Pashley	Ronson	Hesford	Sermanni	Bissell	Weston	Hall	Malone	Milligan	May	Kellow	Jones	Kerr	Dowes
	4			5	6	9				11*	12		7	3		1	8		10		2						
	2	8		5	6	9			12				10	3	11*	1					4			10	7		
	2	1		2	2	2				1			1	2	1	2	1		1		2			1	1		
									1		1									-		-	-	-		-	
					1								1														

Ward	Gardner	Thompson	Wilson	Suddaby	McEwan	Spence	Tong	Holden	Davidson	Wagstaffe	Hockaday	Waldron	Chandler	Pashley	Ronson	Hesford	Sermanni	Bissell	Weston	Hall	Malone	Milligan	May	Kellow	Jones	Kerr	Dowes
1	2		6	5	4	9*	8	12	10	11	7											3					
1	2		4	5	6	7	8	9*	10	11	12											3					
1	2	4		5	6	9			10		7		11	3	8												
	2	4		5	6	9*			10	12	11		7	3	8	1											
	2	4		5	6	9			10		11		7	3	8	1											
3	5	3	2	5	5	5	2	1	5	2	4		3	3	3	2						2					
								1		1	1										-		-	-	-		
					2	1			3																		

League Table

	P	W	D	L	F	A	Pts
Shrewsbury Town	46	21	19	6	61	41	61
Watford	46	24	12	10	83	52	60
Swansea City	46	24	12	10	83	61	60
Gillingham	46	21	17	8	65	42	59
Swindon Town	46	25	7	14	74	52	57
Carlisle United	46	15	22	9	53	42	52
Colchester United	46	17	17	12	60	55	51
Hull City	46	19	11	16	66	61	49
Exeter City	46	17	15	14	61	56	49
Brentford	46	19	9	18	53	49	47
Oxford United	46	14	18	14	44	50	46
Blackpool	46	18	9	19	61	59	45
Southend United	46	15	15	16	51	49	45
Sheffield Wednesday	46	13	19	14	53	53	45
Plymouth Argyle	46	15	14	17	67	68	44
Chester	46	14	16	16	57	61	44
Rotherham United	46	17	10	19	49	55	44
Mansfield Town	46	12	19	15	51	52	43
Bury	46	11	20	15	59	65	42
Chesterfield	46	13	14	19	51	65	40
Peterborough United	46	11	14	21	44	63	36
Walsall	46	10	12	24	56	71	32
Tranmere Rovers	46	6	16	24	45	78	28
Lincoln City	46	7	11	28	41	88	25

1979-80

Division Three

Manager: Stan Ternant/Alan Ball

Did you know that?

Stan Ternant took over as manager, but was soon replaced by the returning Alan Ball.

A new club crest appeared on the shirts in the shape of a white tower on a tangerine background.

30 players were used during the campaign.

Jack Ashurst joined the club for a record £132,400. He only made 59 appearances before being sold to Carlisle United.

The 2–0 win at Rotherham United on the final day of the season helped Blackpool avoid another relegation.

Match No.	Date		Venue	Opponents	Result		Scorers	Attendance
1	Aug	18	H	Gillingham	W	2-1	Pashley, McEwan	5,253
2		21	A	Bury	L	0-3		4,028
3		25	A	Grimsby Town	L	3-4	Smith B, Kellow, Wilson	7,306
4	Sep	1	H	Wimbledon	W	3-0	Wilson, Kerr, Weston	4,556
5		7	A	Southend Utd	W	2-1	Wilson, Kellow	5,000
6		15	H	Rotherham Utd	W	3-2	Wilson, Kellow, McEwan	7,807
7		18	A	Sheffield Utd	L	1-3	Kellow	15,198
8		22	H	Blackburn Rovers	W	2-1	McEwan 2 (1 pen)	10,193
9		29	A	Plymouth Argyle	D	2-2	Kellow, Jones	5,693
10	Oct	3	H	Sheffield Utd	L	2-3	Doyle, McEwan	10,392
11		6	A	Exeter City	L	0-1		3,769
12		10	H	Bury	L	1-2	Kerr	5,955
13		13	H	Brentford	W	5-4	Pashley, McEwan, Kellow 2, Spence	5,386
14		19	A	Colchester Utd	L	1-3	Weston	4,383
15		23	A	Chesterfield	D	0-0		4,967
16		27	H	Swindon Town	L	0-1		5,741
17	Nov	3	A	Gillingham	D	1-1	McEwan (pen)	6,518
18		7	H	Chesterfield	D	2-2	Doyle, McEwan	3,484
19		10	H	Sheffield Wed	D	1-1	Bowey	8,355
20		17	A	Millwall	L	0-2		5,979
21	Dec	1	A	Mansfield Town	D	1-1	Hockaday	4,324
22		8	H	Reading	W	5-2	Kellow 2, Harrison 2, Spence	3,834
23		21	A	Barnsley	L	1-2	Kellow	8,567
24		26	H	Hull City	D	2-2	Weston, Kellow	4,535
25		29	A	Chester City	L	0-1		4,212
26	Jan	5	H	Oxford Utd	L	1-2	McEwan (pen)	4,003
27		12	A	Wimbledon	W	2-1	Jones, Morris	2,688
28		18	H	Southend Utd	W	1-0	Noble	4,286
29		26	H	Grimsby Town	L	0-3		4,932
30	Feb	9	A	Blackburn Rovers	L	0-2		14,446
31		16	H	Plymouth Argyle	L	1-3	Fletcher	3,302
32		23	A	Brentford	L	1-2	Paisley	6,400
33		29	H	Colchester Utd	W	1-0	Kellow	5,594
34	Mar	8	A	Swindon Town	L	1-2	Morris	9,517
35		15	H	Exeter City	W	1-0	Fletcher	4,155
36		18	A	Carlisle Utd	L	0-2		3,793
37		22	A	Sheffield Wed	L	1-4	Fletcher	19,552
38		29	H	Millwall	D	2-2	Noble, Fletcher	4,357
39	Apr	4	H	Barnsley	D	1-1	Morris	10,049
40		5	A	Hull City	L	1-3	McEwan (pen)	5,428
41		7	H	Carlisle Utd	W	2-1	Bamber, McEwan	6,054
42		12	A	Oxford Utd	W	2-0	Fletcher, Harrison	3,582
43		19	H	Mansfield Town	D	1-1	Fletcher	5,677
44		26	A	Reading	W	1-0	McEwan (pen)	5,865
45	May	3	H	Chester City	D	0-0		5,928
46		6	A	Rotherham Utd	W	2-0	Morris, Fletcher	4,497

Final League Position: 18th in Division Three

Apps
Sub Apps
Gls

FA Cup

1	Nov	24	H	Wigan Athletic	D	1-1	McEwan	11,277
1R		28	A	Wigan Athletic	L	0-2		14,589

Apps
Sub Apps
Gls

League Cup

1	Aug	11	H	Rochdale	D	1-1	McEwan	5,842
		14	A	Rochdale	W	1-0	Spence	3,910
2		29	A	Peterborough Utd	D	0-0		4,326
	Sep	5	H	Peterborough Utd	L	0-1		5,254

Apps
Sub Apps
Gls

McAlister	Thompson	Pashley	Doyle	Suddaby	McEwan	Kerr	Kellow	Spence	Smith B	Weston	Wilson	Malone	Gardner	Jones	Hockaday	Hesford	Ashurst	Harrison	Bowey	Bamber	Noble	Morris	Fletcher	MacDougall	Drummy	Brockbank	Seward	Smith P	Chandler
1	2	3	4	5	6	7	8	9*	10	11	12																		
1	2	3	4	5	6	7	8	9	10	11																			
1	2	3	4	5	6	7	8	9*	10	11	12																		
1	2	3	4	5	6	7	8		10	11	9																		
1		3	4	5	6		8		10	11	9	7	2																
1		3	4	5	6		8		10	11	9	7	2																
1		3	4	5	6		8		10	11	9	7	2																
1		3	4	5	6	12	8		10	11	9*	7	2																
1		3	4	5	6	12	8		10	11*		7	2	9															
1	5	3	4		6		8		10	11*	9	7	2		12														
1	7	3	4*	5	6	12	8		10		9		2		11														
1	6	3		5		4	8	9	10	11*	12	7	2																
1	7	3		5	6	4	8*	9	10	12		11	2																
1	7	3*		5	6	4		9	10	12		11	2	8															
	7			5	6	4		9	10	3		11	2	8		1													
	7		4	5	6		8	9	10	3		11	2			1													
		3	4		6	7	8	9	10	11		2				1	5												
		3	4		6	7	8	9	10	11		2*		12		1	5												
	6	3	8		4		10	9		11			2			1	5		7										
	6	3	8		4		10	9		11	12		2			1	5		7*										
		3	8		4		10	9		11		5*	2		7	1		6		12									
		3	8		4		10	9		11			2		7	1	5	6											
1	12	3	8		4		10	9*		11			2		7		5	6											
1	12	3	8		4		10	9*		11			2		7		5	6											
	6	3	8		4		10			11*			2		12	1	5	7		9									
	6	3	8		4		10						2			1	5	11		9		7							
	6	3	8				10					4	2	9		1	5	11				7							
	6	3	8				10						2	9		1	5	11			4	7							
	6	3	8				10*			12		5	2	9		1		11			4	7							
	6	3	8				10		12			5	2	9*		1		11			4	7							
		3	6				8*			11		5	2			1		10			4	7	9			12			
	5	3	6				8			11		2	12			1		10		9*	4	7							
	5	3	6		12		8						2			1	4	10			11	7	9*						
	5*	3	6		12		8						2			1	4	10			11	7	9						
		3	6		5	12							2			1	4	11				7	8	9*	10				
		3	6		5								2			1	4	11				7	9	8	11				
		3	5		6	8							2			1	4					7	9		10			11	
		3			6								2			1	5	11			4	7	9	8	10				
		3	10		6					11			2			1	5				4*	7	9	8	12				
		3	10		6					11			2			1	5		4			7	9	8					
		3*	4		5					10			2			1	6	11		8		7	9				12		
		3	12		6					10			2			1	5	11		8*	4	7	9						
		3	12		5					10			2			1	6	11		8*	4	7	9						
		3			5					10			2			1	6	11			4	7	9	8					
		3			5					10			2			1	6	11			4	7	9	8					
		3			5					10			2			1	6	11			4	7	9	8					
16	22	44	36	15	37	11	32	16	18	32	7	19	39	7	5	30	25	23	3	6	14	21	15	8	4			1	
	2		2		2	4			1	3	4		1	1	2					1					1	1	1		
		3	2		12	2	12	2	1	3	4			2	1			3	1	1	2	4	7						

McAlister	Thompson	Pashley	Doyle	Suddaby	McEwan	Kerr	Kellow	Spence	Smith B	Weston	Wilson	Malone	Gardner	Jones	Hockaday	Hesford	Ashurst	Harrison	Bowey	Bamber	Noble	Morris	Fletcher	MacDougall	Drummy	Brockbank	Seward	Smith P	Chandler
	6	3	8		4		10	9*		11	12		2		7	1	5												
		3	8		4		10	9		11*			2		7	1	5	6		12									
	1	2	2		2		2	2		2			1		2	2	2	1											
											1									1									
					1																								

McAlister	Thompson	Pashley	Doyle	Suddaby	McEwan	Kerr	Kellow	Spence	Smith B	Weston	Wilson	Malone	Gardner	Jones	Hockaday	Hesford	Ashurst	Harrison	Bowey	Bamber	Noble	Morris	Fletcher	MacDougall	Drummy	Brockbank	Seward	Smith P	Chandler
1	2	3	4	5	6	7	8	9		10					11*														12
1	2	3	4	5	6	7	8	9		10	11																		
1	2	3	8	5	4	7	9		10	11		6																	
1	2	3	4	5	6	7	8		11	10	9*	12																	
4	4	4	4	4	4	4	4	2	2	4	2	1			1														
												1																	1
					1			1																					

League Table

	P	W	D	L	F	A	Pts
Grimsby Town	46	26	10	10	73	42	62
Blackburn Rovers	46	25	9	12	58	36	59
Sheffield Wednesday	46	21	16	9	81	47	58
Chesterfield	46	23	11	12	71	46	57
Colchester United	46	20	12	14	64	56	52
Carlisle United	46	18	12	16	66	56	48
Reading	46	16	16	14	66	65	48
Exeter City	46	19	10	17	60	68	48
Chester	46	17	13	16	49	57	47
Swindon Town	46	19	8	19	71	63	46
Barnsley	46	16	14	16	53	56	46
Sheffield United	46	18	10	18	60	66	46
Rotherham United	46	18	10	18	58	66	46
Millwall	46	16	13	17	65	59	45
Plymouth Argyle	46	16	12	18	59	55	44
Gillingham	46	14	14	18	49	51	42
Oxford United	46	14	13	19	57	62	41
Blackpool	46	15	11	20	62	74	41
Brentford	46	15	11	20	59	73	41
Hull City	46	12	16	18	51	69	40
Bury	46	16	7	23	45	59	39
Southend United	46	14	10	22	47	58	38
Mansfield Town	46	10	16	20	47	58	36
Wimbledon	46	10	14	22	52	81	34

1980-81

Division Three

Manager: Alan Ball/ Allan Brown

Did you know that?

Alan Ball was sacked and replaced by the returning Allan Brown as manager.

On 21 March 1981, Blackpool played their 3,000the League match – they lost at Chesterfield 3–2.

The FA Cup game with Fleetwood Town was originally scheduled to be played at the non-League side's ground, but was switched to Bloomfield Road. Blackpool, as the away side, wore their light blue second kit.

A Manchester supermarket chain were in talks to buy Bloomfield Road and re-locate the club.

Blackpool were relegated to the bottom tier for the first time in their history.

Match No.	Date	Venue	Opponents	Result		Scorers	Attendance
1	Aug 16	A	Swindon Town	W	2-1	Hockaday, Fletcher	7,108
2	20	H	Rotherham Utd	D	0-0		10,427
3	23	A	Huddersfield Town	D	1-1	Morris	9,490
4	30	H	Portsmouth	L	0-2		8,352
5	Sep 5	A	Fulham	W	2-1	Sbragia, Morris	4,940
6	13	H	Hull City	D	2-2	Morris, Harrison	6,138
7	16	A	Sheffield Utd	L	2-4	Hocjaday, Gardner	13,331
8	20	H	Brentford	L	0-3		6,738
9	27	A	Walsall	D	2-2	Morris 2	4,227
10	Oct 1	H	Sheffield Utd	W	2-1	Thompson 2	8,995
11	4	H	Gillingham	W	4-0	Morris 2, Hockaday, Thompson	6,588
12	7	A	Millwall	D	0-0		3,363
13	11	A	Plymouth Argyle	W	2-0	Morris 2	10,698
14	18	H	Colchester Utd	D	1-1	Williams	6,997
15	22	H	Chesterfield	L	0-3		8,062
16	25	A	Charlton Athletic	L	1-2	Morgan	6,838
17	28	A	Carlisle Utd	L	0-2		3,583
18	Nov 1	H	Newport County	L	2-4	McEwan (pen), Ashurst	4,556
19	8	A	Oxford Utd	W	2-0	Ball 2 (1 pen)	3,038
20	11	A	Rotherham Utd	L	0-4		6,367
21	15	H	Swindon Town	D	1-1	Entwistle	3,758
22	29	A	Reading	L	0-3		3,968
23	Dec 6	H	Exeter City	D	0-0		3,597
24	20	A	Barnsley	L	0-2		10,862
25	26	H	Chester City	L	2-3	Morgan, Bamber	4,878
26	27	A	Burnley	L	1-4	Bamber	10,667
27	Jan 10	A	Colchester Utd	L	2-3	Morris, Ball	2,378
28	17	H	Reading	D	0-0		3,273
29	24	A	Portsmouth	D	3-3	Morris, Thompson, Hockaday	13,265
30	31	H	Huddersfield Town	L	1-2	Ball (pen)	9,431
31	Feb 7	A	Hull City	L	1-2	Ball	5,315
32	14	H	Fulham	L	0-2		3,792
33	21	H	Walsall	W	1-0	Ashurst	3,894
34	28	A	Brentford	L	0-2		5,850
35	Mar 4	H	Millwall	D	0-0		5,534
36	7	A	Gillingham	L	1-3	Ashurst	3,424
37	14	H	Plymouth Argyle	W	1-0	Morris	3,933
38	21	A	Chesterfield	L	2-3	Thompson, Noble	5,959
39	25	H	Charlton Athletic	L	0-2		4,230
40	28	H	Carlisle Utd	L	0-1		4,531
41	Apr 4	A	Newport County	L	1-3	Williams	4,514
42	12	H	Oxford Utd	D	1-1	Bamber	3,188
43	17	A	Chester City	L	1-2	Entwistle	2,804
44	18	H	Burnley	D	0-0		7,198
45	25	H	Barnsley	W	1-0	Entwistle	7,648
46	May 2	A	Exeter City	D	0-0		3,864

Final League Position: 23rd in Division Three

Apps
Sub Apps
Gls

FA Cup

1	Nov 22	H	Fleetwood Town*	W	4-0	Entwistle, Morris, Hockaday 2	10,897
2	Dec 13	A	Doncaster Rovers	L	1-2	Williams	6,398

Apps
Sub Apps
Gls

League Cup

1	Aug 9	A	Walsall	W	3-2	McEwan 2 (1 pen), Morris	5,496
	13	H	Walsall	W	3-1	Morris, Fletcher, Ashurst	9,781
2	26	A	Everton	L	0-3		20,156
	Sep 3	H	Everton	D	2-2	McEwan (pen), Morris	10,579

Apps
Sub Apps
Gls

Hesford	Gardner	Williams	Doyle	McEwan	Ashurst	Morris	Hockaday	Fletcher	Ball	Harrison	Noble	Brockhurst	Greenall	MacDougall	Welsh	Sbragia	Deary	Pashley	Bamber	Simmonite	Morgan	Thompson	Rush	Entwistle	Conn	
1	2	3	4	5	6	7	8	9	10	11																
1	2	3	4	5	6	7	8		10*	11	9	12														
1	2	3	4	5		7	8	9*		11	10		6	12												
1	2	3	4	5		7	8	9*			10		6	12	11											
1	2	3	4	5		7	8			11				9		6	10									
1	2	3	4	5		7	8			11				9		6	10									
1	2	3	4	5		7	8		10					9*		6		11	12							
1		3	4	5			8		10	7						6		11	9	2						
1		3		5		10	8	9*	4							6	11			2	7	12				
1		3		5		10	8		4							6	11			2	7	9				
1		3		5		10	8		4							6	11			2	7	9				
1		3		5		10	8		4							6	11			2	7	9				
1		3		6	9	10	8		4							5	11			2	7					
1		3		6	9	10	8		4							5*	11			2	7	12				
1		3		6	5	10	8		4								11			2	7	9				
		3		6	4	9	10		8				5				11*			2	7	12	1			
		3		8	5	10	9		4				6							2	7	11	1			
		11		6	5	10	9		4			3	12						8	2*	7		1			
1		3	9		2	10	8		4				6			5		11			7					
1		3	9		2	10	11*		7	12			5			4		6						8		
1		3	8	5	2	10			4				6					11			7			9		
1		3		6	2	10	8		4				5					11			7			9		
1		3		6	2	10	8		4	7								11				5		9		
1		3		6	2	10			4			12						11	8		7*	5		9		
1	2	3		6		10			4									11	8		7	5		9		
1	2	3		6		10			4									11	8		7	5		9		
1	2				5	10	8		4	9*		12				6		3		11	7					
1	2				6	10	8		4	9						5		3		11	7					
1	2				6	10	8		4	9								3		11*	7	5		12		
					6	10	8		4	9								3	12	2*	7	5	1	11		
1	2						12		4	9		11				6		3	8		7	5		10		12
1					6	10	11		4	9								3		2	7	5		8		
1	12				6	10	11		4	9								3		2*	7	5		8		
1	2				6	10	8		4	9		11						3			7*	5		12		
1	2			7	6	10	11			9		8*				4		3				5		12		
1		3		7	6	10	11*			9	4	8				5		2						12		
1	2			4	5	10					11					6		3	12		7	9*			8	
1	2	12		4	5	10				8	11					6		3				9		7*		
1	2	11		4	5	10	12			7	8					6*		3				9				
1				6	2	10	8			9	4					12		3			7	5			11*	
1		8		6	2	10	7			9	4							3	11			5				
1	2			6		10	12			9	4		5					3	11		7				8*	
1	2			6		10				8	4					5		3	11		7			9		
1	2	4		6		10	12			8						5*		3	11		7			9		
1	2			6		10				8	4		5					3	11		7			9		
1	2			6		10				8	4		5					3	11	7				9		
42	23	30	11	36	28	44	33	4	30	26	13	5	11	3	1	22	10	30	12	18	30	21	4	16	3	
	1	1					3			1		3	1	2		1			3			3		4		
	1	2		1	3	12	4	1	5	1	1					1			3		2	5		3		

1		3	8	6	2	10	12		4				5					11*			7			9	
1		3		6	2	10	8		4	7			2					11				5		9	
2		2	1	2	2	2	1		2	1			1					2			1	1		2	
							1																		
		1				1	2																		

1	3		4	6	2	7	8		10					9	11			5	
1	2	3	4*	5	6	7	8	9	10	11					12				
1	2	3	4	5		7	8	9		11	10		6						
1	2	3	4	5		7	8		10	11				9		6			
4	4	3	4	4	2	4	4	2	3	3	1		1	2	1	1		1	
												1			1				
				3	1	3		1											

League Table

	P	W	D	L	F	A	Pts
Rotherham United	46	24	13	9	62	32	61
Barnsley	46	21	17	8	72	45	59
Charlton Athletic	46	25	9	12	63	44	59
Huddersfield Town	46	21	14	11	71	40	56
Chesterfield	46	23	10	13	72	48	56
Portsmouth	46	22	9	15	55	47	53
Plymouth Argyle	46	19	14	13	56	44	52
Burnley	46	18	14	14	60	48	50
Brentford	46	14	19	13	52	49	47
Reading	46	18	10	18	62	62	46
Exeter City	46	16	13	17	62	66	45
Newport County	46	15	13	18	64	61	43
Fulham	46	15	13	18	57	64	43
Oxford United	46	13	17	16	39	47	43
Gillingham	46	12	18	16	48	58	42
Millwall	46	14	14	18	43	60	42
Swindon Town	46	13	15	18	51	56	41
Chester	46	15	11	20	38	48	41
Carlisle United	46	14	13	19	56	70	41
Walsall	46	13	15	18	59	74	41
Sheffield United	46	14	12	20	65	63	40
Colchester United	46	14	11	21	45	65	39
Blackpool	46	9	14	23	45	75	32
Hull City	46	8	16	22	40	71	32

1981-82

Division Four

Manager: Allan Brown

Did you know that?

Just 1,824 fans turned up for the final game of the season, a draw with Hartlepool United.

Allan Brown was forced to resign at the end of the season.

Another boardroom 'coup' took place in the close season.

Match No.	Date	Venue	Opponents	Result		Scorers	Attendance
1	Aug 29	H	Stockport County	W	2-0	Blair, Morris	4,556
2	Sep 5	A	Scunthorpe Utd	D	1-1	Noble	2,200
3	12	H	Crewe Alexandra	W	5-0	Bamber, Goddard 2, Morris, Hockaday	4,506
4	10	A	Darlington	D	2-2	Bamber, Morris	2,085
5	22	A	Rochdale	D	0-0		2,763
6	26	H	Hull City	W	3-1	Bamber 2, Morris	4,838
7	30	H	Halifax Town	W	7-1	Bamber 3, Hockaday, Simmonite, Noble, Harrison	5,084
8	Oct 3	A	Mansfield Town	D	2-2	Hockaday, McEwan (pen)	3,466
9	10	H	Torquay Utd	W	2-1	Noble, Morris	6,716
10	13	A	Northampton Town	W	1-0	Morris	2,376
11	17	A	Aldershot	L	2-3	Pashley, Bamber	2,000
12	20	A	York City	W	4-0	Hockaday, Morris, Blair, Noble	2,657
13	31	A	Sheffield Utd	L	1-3	McEwan	15,566
14	Nov 4	H	Bury	D	1-1	Blair	7,805
15	7	A	Peterborough Utd	L	1-3	McEwan (pen)	5,442
16	11	H	Port Vale	L	2-3	Noble, Morris	4,785
17	14	H	Bournemouth	L	0-3		4,665
18	Dec 4	A	Colchester Utd	L	1-2	Bamber	3,875
19	Jan 9	H	Scunthorpe Utd	W	2-0	Morris 2	4,136
20	13	H	Tranmere Rovers	L	1-2	Bamber	3,329
21	30	H	Darlington	W	1-0	Entwistle	3,336
22	Feb 1	A	Stockport County	W	3-2	Entwistle, Bamber, Hockaday	3,008
23	5	A	Crewe Alexandra	D	1-1	Own-goal	2,513
24	10	H	Rochdale	D	1-1	Entwistle	3,294
25	13	H	Mansfield Town	L	2-3	McEwan (pen), Hockaday	3,017
26	17	H	Northampton Town	W	1-0	Noble	2,231
27	20	A	Halifax Town	D	0-0		2,245
28	27	A	Torquay Utd	D	1-1	Harrison	2,177
29	Mar 3	H	Bradford City	W	1-0	Stewart	4,009
30	6	H	Aldershot	L	0-2		2,655
31	10	H	York City	W	3-1	Brockbank, McEwan (pen), Bamber	2,164
32	13	A	Port Vale	L	0-2		3,439
33	20	H	Sheffield Utd	L	0-1		7,542
34	27	H	Peterborough Utd	D	2-2	Bamber 2	2,855
35	30	A	Wigan Athletic	L	1-2	Morgan (pen)	7,329
36	Apr 3	A	Bournemouth	L	0-1		5,146
37	9	H	Wigan Athletic	L	1-2	Hockaday	9,439
38	10	A	Tranmere Rovers	L	1-2	Morgan	1,828
39	17	H	Colchester Utd	D	0-0		2,298
40	21	A	Hereford Utd	L	1-2	Own-goal	2,617
41	24	A	Bradford City	L	0-1		4,898
42	28	A	Hartlepool Utd	D	2-2	Noble, Bamber	1,387
43	May 1	H	Hereford Utd	W	1-0	Noble	1,881
44	4	A	Hull City	L	0-1		3,206
45	8	H	Hartlepool Utd	D	2-2	Stewart 2	1,824
46	11	A	Bury	W	1-0	Noble	2,041

Final League Position: 12th in Division Four

Apps
Sub Apps
Gls

FA Cup

1	Nov 21	A	Horden CW*	W	1-0	Harrison	4,465
2	Jan 2	A	Kettering Town	W	3-0	Harrison, Wann, Morris	4,439
3	5	A	Barnsley	W	2-0	Bamber, Morris	13,429
4	23	H	Queens Park Rangers	D	0-0		10,227
4R	26	A	Queens Park Rangers	L	1-5	Entwistle	11,712

*

Apps
Sub Apps
Gls

League Cup

1	Sep 2	A	Bradford City	L	1-3	Bamber	3,374
	16	H	Bradford City	D	0-0		5,722

Apps
Sub Apps
Gls

Hesford	Simmonite	Pashley	Blair	Greenall	McEwan	Morris	Noble	Bamber	Hockaday	Harrison	Morgan	Wann	Hart	Pollard	Goddard	Entwistle	Sbragia	Gardner	Rush	Fletcher	Deary	McEvoy	Stewart	Brockbank	Butler	Bardsley
1	2	3	4	5	6	7	8	9	10*	11	12															
1	2	3		5		7	8	9	10*	11		4	6	12												
1	2	3	4	5		7	8*	9	12	11			6		10											
1	2	3	4		6	7	8*	9	12	11			6		10											
1	2	3	4	5		7	8	9		11			6		10											
1	2	3	4		6	7	8*	9	12	11			5		10											
1	2	3	4*		6	7	8	9	10	11		12	5													
1	2	3	4		6	7	8		10*	11		12	5			9										
1	2	3	4		6	7	8	9	10	11			5													
1	2	3	4		6	7	8	9	10	11							5									
1		3	4		6	7	8	9	10	11		12	5					2*								
1		3	4		6	7	8	9	10*	11		12	5					2								
		3	4		6	7	8		10	11		12	5			9*		2	1							
		3	4		6	7	8		10	11*			5			9		2	1	12						
		3	4*		6	7	8	9	10			11	5				12	2	1							
	2	3	4		6	7	8	9	10*			11	5						1		12					
	2	3	4			7	8	9		11*			5				6		1		12	10				
1	2	3	4			7	8	9	10	11		6	5													
1	2	3	4		6*	7	8	9	10	11		5									12					
1	2	3	4			7	8	9	10	11		5*	12								6					
1		3	4	5		7	8	9	10			6				11					2					
1		3	4	5		7	8	9	10	12		6				11*					2					
1		3	4	5	12		8	9	10*	11		6				7					2					
1		3	4	5			8	9*		11	7	6				10					2		12			
1		3	4		5		8	9	12	11*	7	6				10					2					
1		10	4		6		8		9			5				11		2			7			3		
1		10	4		6		8		9			5*				11		2			7		12	3		
1		10	4	12	6		8		9	5								2			7		11*	3		
1		7	4		6		8	9	10	5								2					11	3		
		7	4		6		8	9	10	5								2	1		12		11*	3		
1		10			6		8	9	4	5	7							2					11	3		
1		10			6		8	9	7	5						12		2			4		11*	3		
1	2	10			6		8	9	7	5*		12				11					4			3		
1	2	11			6			9	10		7		5								4		8	3		
1	2	10	6					9	11	12	7		5								4	8*		3		
1	2	11*	6				4	9	10	12	7		5									8		3		
1	2	11					6	9	10	12	7		5								4	8*		3		
1	2	11		12			6*	9	10	8	7		5								4			3		
1	2	11		5			6			8	7										4	10	9	3		
1	2	11		5			6	9	8	4*	7										12		10	3		
1	2	11	8*	5			6	9	10				7								4		12	3		
	2	11	12	5			10	9	8		7*		6						1		4			3		
1	2	11	4	5			10	9	7				6								8			3		
1	2	11*	4	5			10	9	7				6								8		12	3		
1	2	3	4*	5			10	9	7	11			6								8		12			
1	2	11	4	5			7														8	10	9		3	6
39	29	46	36	16	24	22	44	38	37	29	11	13	26		4	11	2	12	7		22	6	9	19	1	1
			1	2	1				4	4		6	1	1		1	1			1	5		5			
	1	1	3		5	10	9	15	7	2	2				2	3							3	1		

Hesford	Simmonite	Pashley	Blair	Greenall	McEwan	Morris	Noble	Bamber	Hockaday	Harrison	Morgan	Wann	Hart	Pollard	Goddard	Entwistle	Sbragia	Gardner	Rush	Fletcher	Deary	McEvoy	Stewart	Brockbank	Butler	Bardsley
1	2	3	4		6	7	8	9	10	11			5													
1	2	3	4		6	7	8	9	10	11		5	2													
1	2	3	4		6	7	8	9	10	11		5														
1	2*	3	4		6	7	8	9	10	11		5									12					
1		3	4			7	8	9	10	11*		5	6			12					2					
5	4	5	5		4	5	5	5	5	5		4	2								1					
																1					1					
						2		1		2		1				1										

Hesford	Simmonite	Pashley	Blair	Greenall	McEwan	Morris	Noble	Bamber	Hockaday	Harrison	Morgan	Wann	Hart	Pollard	Goddard	Entwistle	Sbragia	Gardner	Rush	Fletcher	Deary	McEvoy	Stewart	Brockbank	Butler	Bardsley			
1	2	3	4*	5	6	7		9	10	11		8	12																
1	2	3	4		6	7	8	9	10	11			5																
2	2	2	2	1	2	2	1	2	2	2		1	1																
													1																1
								1																					

League Table

	P	W	D	L	F	A	Pts
Sheffield United	46	27	15	4	94	41	96
Bradford City	46	26	13	7	88	45	91
Wigan Athletic	46	26	13	7	80	46	91
Bournemouth	46	23	19	4	62	30	88
Peterborough United	46	24	10	12	71	57	82
Colchester United	46	20	12	14	82	57	72
Port Vale	46	18	16	12	56	49	70
Hull City	46	19	12	15	70	61	69
Bury	46	17	17	12	80	59	68
Hereford United	46	16	19	11	64	58	67
Tranmere Rovers	46	14	18	14	51	56	60
Blackpool	46	15	13	18	66	60	58
Darlington	46	15	13	18	61	62	58
Hartlepool United	46	13	16	17	73	84	55
Torquay United	46	14	13	19	47	59	55
Aldershot	46	13	15	18	57	68	54
York City	46	14	8	24	69	91	50
Stockport County	46	12	13	21	48	67	49
Halifax Town	46	9	22	15	51	72	49
Mansfield Town	46	13	10	23	63	81	47
Rochdale	46	10	16	20	50	62	46
Northampton Town	46	11	9	26	57	84	42
Scunthorpe United	46	9	15	22	43	79	42
Crewe Alexandra	46	6	9	31	29	84	27

1982-83

Division Four

Manager: Sam Ellis

Did you know that?

New manager Sam Ellis was introduced to the club by Tom White.

Blackpool were forced to seek re-election to the Football League after finishing in their lowest-ever position of 21st.

The hooliganism that was rife throughout the country was especially prevalent at Blackpool, which were becoming notorious at games involving the Seasiders.

The club were deducted two points for fielding an ineligible player. John Butler had played two League games and a League Cup game without being registered.

Blackpool's lowest-ever home crowd for a League match was on 5 February when 1,747 turned up for the defeat to Colchester United.

Match No.	Date	Venue	Opponents	Result		Scorers	Attendance
1	Aug 28	A	Mansfield Town	L	1-2	Hockaday	2,627
2	Sep 4	H	Swindon Town	W	2-1	Pashley (pen), Bamber	3,593
3	7	H	Bury	D	1-1	Bamber	4,292
4	11	A	Bristol City	D	0-0		4,681
5	18	H	Wimbledon	D	1-1	Hockaday	3,929
6	25	A	Colchester Utd	L	1-4	Pashley (pen)	2,918
7	29	A	Chester City	W	2-1	Bamber, Deary	2,256
8	Oct 2	H	Darlington	W	2-0	Hockaday, Bamber	4,059
9	9	H	Halifax Town	D	0-0		4,150
10	16	A	Rochdale	L	1-3	Bamber	2,001
11	19	H	York City	D	1-1	Deary	2,765
12	23	H	Hereford Utd	W	5-1	Downes (pen), Stewart 2, Bamber 2	3,405
13	30	A	Port Vale	L	0-1		5,449
14	Nov 2	H	Torquay Utd	W	1-0	Bamber	2,734
15	6	H	Crewe Alexandra	W	2-0	Mayo, Bamber	3,443
16	13	A	Northampton Town	L	1-2	Hockaday	1,893
17	27	A	Aldershot	L	1-2	Downes (pen)	2,003
18	Dec 4	H	Hull City	D	1-1	Pashley	3,395
19	18	H	Scunthorpe Utd	W	3-1	Hockaday, Downes (pen), Bamber	2,860
20	27	A	Stockport County	L	0-3		3,673
21	28	H	Tranmere Rovers	L	0-2		3,563
22	Jan 1	A	Hartlepool Utd	L	1-2	Jeffrey	1,569
23	3	H	Peterborough Utd	L	0-3		2,383
24	15	H	Mansfield Town	W	2-1	Richardson I, Own-goal	2,217
25	22	A	Bury	L	1-4	Richardson I	3,263
26	29	H	Chester City	D	1-1	Stewart	2,054
27	Feb 5	H	Colchester Utd	L	1-2	Hetzke	1,747
28	15	A	York City	L	0-2		2,937
29	18	A	Halifax Town	L	0-2		2,366
30	26	H	Rochdale	W	1-0	McNiven	2,373
31	Mar 2	A	Torquay Utd	W	3-1	Hockaday, Noble, Deary	1,802
32	5	A	Hereford Utd	D	0-0		1,755
33	12	H	Port Vale	W	2-0	Noble, Hetzke	4,519
34	19	A	Crewe Alexandra	L	1-2	Stewart	2,538
35	26	H	Northampton Town	D	0-0		2,054
36	Apr 1	H	Stockport County	D	0-0		3,126
37	2	A	Tranmere Rovers	D	1-1	Pritchett	1,831
38	9	A	Hull City	L	1-3	Deary	8,555
39	12	A	Darlington	W	1-0	Stewart	1,333
40	16	H	Bristol City	L	1-4	McNiven	2,209
41	19	A	Swindon Town	D	3-3	McNiven, Hockaday, Deary	2,408
42	23	A	Scunthorpe Utd	L	3-4	McNiven 2, Greenall	2,791
43	30	H	Aldershot	W	4-1	Hockaday, Deary, Stewart, Own-goal	1,994
44	May 4	A	Peterborough Utd	L	1-3	Stewart	1,636
45	7	A	Wimbledon	L	0-5		2,717
46	14	A	Hartlepool Utd	L	1-2	Serella	2,184

Final League Position: 21st in Division Four

Apps
Sub Apps
Gls

FA Cup

1	Nov 20	H	Horwich RMI	W	3-0	Pashley, Bamber, Deary (pen)	5,280
2	Dec 11	A	Preston NE	L	1-2	Broadbank	14,148

Apps
Sub Apps
Gls

League Cup

1	Sep 1	A	Chester City	W	2-1	Bamber, Serella	2,557
	14	H	Chester City	W	5-1	Serella, Hetzke, Deary, Stewart, Pashley (pen)	3,429
2	Oct 5	A	Northampton Town	D	1-1	Bamber	2,490
	26	H	Northampton Town	W	2-1	Downes (pen), Bamber	3,249
3	Nov 9	A	Luton Town	L	2-4	Bamber, Pashley	6,409

Apps
Sub Apps
Gls

Hesford	Simmonite	Brockbank	Deary	Hetzke	Greenall	Noble	Hockaday	Bamber	Pashley	Downes	Stewart	Serella	Butler J	Hart	Jeffrey	Mayo	Bardsley	Pritchett	Scott	Richardson I	Richardson P	McNiven	Bramhall
1	2	3	4	5	6	7*	8	9	10	11	12												
1	2	3	4	5		7*	8	9	10	11	12	6											
1	2	3	4	5			8	9	10	11	7	6											
1	2	3	4	5		7	8		10		9	6	11										
1	2	3	4	5		7	11	9	10		8	6											
1	2	3	4	5		7	11	9	10		8	6											
1	2		4	5			7	9	10	11	8	6		3									
1	2			5			7	9	10	11	8	6		3	4								
1	2		5		6	12	7	9	10	11	8*			3	4								
1	2		10		5		7	9	3	11		6	12		4	8*							
1	2		4	5			7	9	10	11	8	6		3									
1	2		4	5			7	9	10	11	8	6		3									
1	2		4	5			7	9	10	11		6		3		8							
1	2		4	5			7	9	10	11		6		3		8							
1	2		4	5			7	9	10	11	12	6*		3		8							
1	2		4	5			7	9	10	11	12	6		3		8*							
1			4	5			7	9	10	11		6			8		2	3					
1			4*	5		12	7	9	10	11		6			8		2	3					
1		3	4	5		12	7*	9	10	11		6			8		2						
		3	4	5		12		9	10	11*		6			8		2		1	7			
			4	5				9	10		11	6			8		2	3	1	7			
1			4	5			7*	9	10		11	6			8		2	3		12			
1			4	5			7	9	10	11	7	6			8		2	3					
1			4	5			7		10	11	9	6					2	3		8	7		
1			4	5			7		2	11	9	6						3		8	10		
1			4	5	12		7		10	11*	9	6					2	3			8		
1			4*	5	6	12	7		10	11	9						2	3			8		
1			4	5	6	9	7		11		10				8		2	3					
1			4	5	6	10*	7		11		9	12			8		2	3					
1			4	5	6	10	7		11		9						2	3				8	
1			4	5	6	10	7		11		9						2	3				8	
1			4	5	6	10	7*		11		9				12		2	3				8	
1			4	5	6	10	7		11		9				12		2	3*				8	
1			4	5	6	10	7		11	3	9						2					8	
1			4	5	6	10	7		11		9		3				2					8	
1			4	5	6	10	7		11		9						2	3				8	
1			4	5	6*	10	7		11	9							2	3				8	12
1			4		6	10	7		5	11	9						2	3				8	
1			4	5	6	10	7		11		9						2	3				8	
1			4	5	6	10*	7	12	11		9						2	3				8	
1			4	5	6		7	10	11		9						2	3				8	
1			4	5	6	10	7		11		9						2	3				8	
1			4	5	6	10	7		11		9						2	3				8	
1			4	5	6		7		11	12	9		10*				2	3				8	
1			4		6			7*	11	10	9	5					2	3				8	12
1			4	7	6	10		11*	2		9	5						3				8	12
44	16	8	45	42	23	21	40	25	46	23	34	26	3	9	12	5	28	26	2	4	4	17	
					1	5		1		1	4	1	1		2					1			3
			6	2	1	2	8	10	3	3	7	1			1	1		1		2		5	

Hesford	Simmonite	Brockbank	Deary	Hetzke	Greenall	Noble	Hockaday	Bamber	Pashley	Downes	Stewart	Serella	Butler J	Hart	Jeffrey	Mayo	Bardsley
1			4	5		8	7	9	10	11*		6		3	12		2
1		12		5		4	7*	9	10	11		6	3		8		2
2			1	2		2	2	2	2	2		2		1	1		2
		1													1		
		1	1					1	1								

Hesford	Simmonite	Brockbank	Deary	Hetzke	Greenall	Noble	Hockaday	Bamber	Pashley	Downes	Stewart	Serella	Butler J	Hart	Jeffrey
1		3	4	5		7	8	9	10	11		6	2		
1	2	3	4	5		7	8	9	10			6	11		
1	2	3			5		7	9	10	11	8			6	4
1	2		4	5			7	9	10	11	8	6		3	
1	2		4	5			7	9	10	11	8	6		3	
5	4	3	4	4	1	2	5	5	5	4	3	4	2	3	1
			1	1				4	2	1	1	2			

League Table

	P	W	D	L	F	A	Pts
Wimbledon	46	29	11	6	96	45	98
Hull City	46	25	15	6	75	34	90
Port Vale	46	26	10	10	67	34	88
Scunthorpe United	46	23	14	9	71	42	83
Bury	46	23	12	11	74	46	81
Colchester United	46	24	9	13	75	55	81
York City	46	22	13	11	88	58	79
Swindon Town	46	19	11	16	61	54	68
Peterborough United	46	17	13	16	58	52	64
Mansfield Town	46	16	13	17	61	70	61
Halifax Town	46	16	12	18	59	66	60
Torquay United	46	17	7	22	56	65	58
Chester	46	15	11	20	55	60	56
Bristol City	46	13	17	16	59	70	56
Northampton Town	46	14	12	20	65	75	54
Stockport County	46	14	12	20	60	79	54
Darlington	46	13	13	20	61	71	52
Aldershot	46	12	15	19	61	82	51
Tranmere Rovers	46	13	11	22	49	71	50
Rochdale	46	11	16	19	55	73	49
Blackpool	46	13	12	21	55	74	49
Hartlepool United	46	13	9	24	46	76	48
Crewe Alexandra	46	11	8	27	53	71	41
Hereford United	46	11	8	27	42	79	41

1983-84

Division Four

Manager: Sam Ellis

Did you know that?

The 2–1 FA Cup victory over Manchester City was largely ignored by the national media, due to the fact that Bournemouth enjoyed a famous win over Manchester United the same weekend.

The promotion push was thwarted by three defeats in the last four games.

Match No.	Date	Venue	Opponents	Result		Scorers	Attendance
1	Aug 27	H	Reading	W	1-0	Mercer	3,429
2	Sep 3	A	Colchester Utd	L	1-2	Serella	2,169
3	6	A	Bury	D	0-0		2,953
4	10	H	Northampton Town	L	2-3	McNiven, Serella	3,216
5	17	A	Swindon Town	D	0-0		2,867
6	28	H	Crewe Alexandra	W	3-0	Deary (pen), Greenall, Windridge	4,198
7	27	H	Mansfield Town	W	2-0	Hetzke, Mercer	3,467
8	Oct 1	A	York City	L	0-4		4,058
9	8	H	Rochdale	L	0-2		3,126
10	18	A	Wrexham	W	1-0	Deary (pen)	2,005
11	22	H	Chesterfield	W	1-0	McNiven	4,206
12	29	A	Stockport County	W	2-1	Mercer, McNiven	2,662
13	Nov 1	H	Bristol City	W	1-0	Windridge	4,344
14	5	H	Darlington	W	3-1	Greenall, Hetzke, Mercer	3,843
15	9	A	Chester City	W	2-0	Stewart, Mercer	2,286
16	12	A	Doncaster Rovers	L	1-2	Greenall	4,604
17	26	A	Hereford Utd	W	2-1	Windridge, Mercer	2,801
18	Dec 3	H	Peterborough Utd	L	1-2	Deary	4,439
19	17	H	Torquay Utd	W	1-0	Hetzke (pen)	3,955
20	26	A	Tranmere Rovers	L	2-3	Mercer, Windridge	3,492
21	27	H	Hartlepool Utd	W	1-0	Hetzke (pen)	4,562
22	31	A	Halifax Town	L	0-1		1,958
23	Jan 2	H	Aldershot	W	5-0	McNiven, Hetzke (pen), Windridge, Britton 2	3,193
24	14	A	Reading	L	0-2		4,923
25	21	H	Swindon Town	D	1-1	Stewart	3,474
26	Feb 4	H	York City	W	3-0	Mercer, Britton, Moore	6,010
27	11	A	Crewe Alexandra	L	1-2	Stewart	4,042
28	14	A	Bristol City	D	1-1	Hetzke	7,413
29	25	A	Chesterfield	D	1-1	Windridge	3,281
30	Mar 3	H	Wrexham	W	4-0	Own-goal, Britton 2, Walsh	3,798
31	10	H	Doncaster Rovers	W	3-1	Mercer, Stewart 2	6,062
32	17	A	Rochdale	L	0-1		3,115
33	20	A	Northampton Town	W	5-1	Walker 3, Greenall, Stewart	1,318
34	24	H	Chester City	D	3-3	Stewart 3	4,746
35	31	A	Mansfield Town	D	1-1	Hetzke (pen)	2,007
36	Apr 7	H	Bury	D	1-1	Stewart	4,513
37	10	H	Stockport County	D	1-1	Stonehouse	3,971
38	14	A	Peterborough Utd	L	0-4		2,921
39	20	A	Hartlepool Utd	W	1-0	Stonehouse	1,817
40	21	H	Tranmere Rovers	L	0-1		4,055
41	28	H	Hereford Utd	W	3-1	Deary 3	2,413
42	May 1	H	Colchester Utd	W	3-2	McNiven, Stonehouse 2	3,131
43	5	A	Aldershot	L	2-3	McNiven,Britton	2,936
44	7	H	Halifax Town	W	4-0	Britton 3, Stonehouse	2,324
45	12	A	Torquay Utd	L	0-1		1,592
46	18	A	Darlington	L	0-2		1,177

Final League Position: 6th in Division Four

Apps
Sub Apps
Gls

FA Cup

1	Nov 19	A	Gainsborough Trinity	W	2-0	Mercer, McNiven	2,557
2	Dec 10	A	Bangor City	D	1-1	Mercer	3,785
2R	13	H	Bangor City	W	2-1	Deary, Stewart	5,013
3	Jan 7	H	Manchester City	W	2-1	McNiven, Own-goal	15,377
4	28	A	Oxford Utd	L	1-2	Mercer	10,759

Apps
Sub Apps
Gls

League Cup

1	Aug 30	H	Walsall	W	2-1	Bardsley, McNiven	3,353
	Sep 13	A	Walsall	L	1-3	Stewart	2,879

Apps
Sub Apps
Gls

O'Rourke	Bardsley	Pritchett	Rodaway	Hetzke	Greenall	Windridge	Mercer	Stewart	Ferns	McNiven	Deary	Serella	Steele	Dyer	Downes	Siddall	Britton	Pierce	Moore	Walsh	Stonehouse	Walker	Brand	Davies
1	2	3	4	5	6	7	8	9	10	11														
1	2	3	4	5		7	8	12	10	11*	9	6												
1	2	3	4	5		7	8	9	10		11	6												
1	2	3	4	5		7*	8	12	10	11	9	6												
1	2	3	4	5	6	7	8	9	10		11													
1	2	3	4	5	6	7	8	9*	10	12	11													
	2	3	4	5	6	7*	8	12	10	9	11		1											
	2	3	4	5	6	7		8	10	9	11		1											
	2	3	4	5	6	7	8	9	10				1	11										
	2		4	5	6	7	8	9	3	11	10					1								
	2		4	5	6	7	8	9	3	11	10					1								
	2		4	5	6	7	8	9	3	11	10					1								
	2		4	5	6	7	8	9	3	11	10					1								
	2		4	5	6	7	8*	9	3	11	10			12		1								
	2		4	5	6	7	8	9	3	11	10					1								
	2		4*	5	6	7	8	9	3	11	10					1	12							
			4	5	6	7	8		3	11	10	2					9	1						
			4	5	6	7	8	12	3*	11	10	2					9	1						
			4	5	6		8	9	3	11	10*			12			7	1	2					
		10*	4	5	6	12	8	9	3	11							7	1	2					
			4	5	6	10	8	9	3*	11				12			7	1	2					
			4	5	6	10	8	9	3	11*				12			7	1	2					
			4	5	6	10	8	9	3	11							7	1	2					
				5	6	10	8	9	3	11				4			7	1	2					
				5	6		8	9		11		3		4	10		7	1	2					
			4	5	6	10	8	9*		11	12						7	1	2	3				
			4	5		10	8	9	3	11							7	1	2	6				
			4	5		10	8	9	3	11*				12			7	1	2	6				
			4	5	6	11	8	9	10*		12						7	1	2	3				
			4	5	6	11	8	9*		12	10						7	1	2	3				
				5	6	11	8	9	10		4						7	1	2	3				
				5	6	11	8*	9	10	12	4						7	1	2	3				
			4	5	6			9		11	10						7	1	2	3		8		
			4	5	6			9		12	10						7*	1	2	3	11	8		
			4	5	6	12		9			10						7	1	2	3	11	8*		
			4	5	6	7		9	12	8	10							1	2	3*	11			
			4	8	5	10*		9	3								7	1	2	6	11	12		
			4	10	5			9	3								7	1	2	6	11	8		
			4	10	6			9	3								7	1	2	5	11	8		
			4	10	6			9	3		12						7*	1	2	5	11	8		
			4					9	3		8	6		10			7	1	2	5	11			
			4	5				9	3	10	8						7	1	2	6	11			
		12	4	5	6	9				10		3*					7	1	2		11	8		
			4	5	6			9									7		2	3	11	10	1	8
			4	5	6			9	10		12						7*		2	3	11		1	8
				5	6			9	10		4						7		2	3	11		1	8
6	16	10	41	45	39	32	31	40	37	28	27	8	3	4	1	7	29	27	28	20	13	8	3	3
		1				2		4	1	4	4			5			1					1		
				7	4	6	9	10		6	6	2					9		1	1	5	3		

			4	5	6	7*	8		3	11	10			12	2		9	1						
		3	4	5	6		8	9		11	10	2	3				7	1						
			4	5	6		8	9	3	11	10	2					7	1						
			4	5	6	10	8	9	3	11							7	1	2					
				5	6	10*	8	9		11	12	3	6	4			7	1	2					
		1	4	5	5	3	5	4	3	5	3	3		1	1		5	5	2					
											1			1								-	-	-
							3	1		2	1													

1	2	3	4	5	6	7*	8		10	11	9			12										
1	2	3	4	5		7*	8	9	10	12	11	8												
2	2	2	2	2	1	2	2	1	2	1	2	1												
										1				1							-		-	-
	1							1		1														

League Table

	P	W	D	L	F	A	Pts
York City	46	31	8	7	96	39	101
Doncaster Rovers	46	24	13	9	82	54	85
Reading	46	22	16	8	84	56	82
Bristol City	46	24	10	12	70	44	82
Aldershot	46	22	9	15	76	69	75
Blackpool	46	21	9	16	70	52	72
Peterborough United	46	18	14	14	72	48	68
Colchester United	46	17	16	13	69	53	67
Torquay United	46	18	13	15	59	64	67
Tranmere Rovers	46	17	15	14	53	53	66
Hereford United	46	16	15	15	54	53	63
Stockport County	46	17	11	18	60	64	62
Chesterfield	46	15	15	16	59	61	60
Darlington	46	17	8	21	49	50	59
Bury	46	15	14	17	61	64	59
Crewe Alexandra	46	16	11	19	56	67	59
Swindon Town	46	15	13	18	58	56	58
Northampton Town	46	13	14	19	53	78	53
Mansfield Town	46	13	13	20	66	70	52
Wrexham	46	11	15	20	59	74	48
Halifax Town	46	12	12	22	55	89	48
Rochdale	46	11	13	22	52	80	46
Hartlepool United	46	10	10	26	47	85	40
Chester City	46	7	13	26	45	82	34

1984-85

Division Four

Manager: Sam Ellis

Did you know that?

This was Blackpool's first promotion since 1970.

They gained promotion at Darlington with four games to go. The home side joined Blackpool in the Third Division the following weekend.

Manager Sam Ellis was approached by numerous clubs but turned down each offer to stay at Bloomfield Road.

Match No.	Date	Venue	Opponents	Result		Scorers	Attendance
1	Aug 28	A	Halifax Town	W	2-0	Stonehouse 2 (1 pen)	1,870
2	Sep 1	H	Exeter City	W	3-0	Deary 2 (1 pen), Dyer	3,663
3	8	A	Colchester Utd	D	1-1	Deary (pen)	1,772
4	15	H	Darlington	D	0-0		4,722
5	18	H	Port Vale	D	1-1	Deary	4,902
6	22	A	Chesterfield	L	1-2	Dyer	3,947
7	29	H	Chester City	W	3-1	Hetzke, Windridge, Dyer	4,566
8	Oct 2	A	Swindon Town	L	1-4	Dyer	2,501
9	6	H	Aldershot	W	1-0	Stonehouse (pen)	3,824
10	13	A	Scunthorpe Utd	D	1-1	Stonehouse	2,366
11	20	H	Bury	D	0-0		5,100
12	23	A	Tranmere Rovers	L	0-3		2,084
13	27	H	Northampton Town	W	2-1	Britton,Stonehouse (pen)	3,577
14	Nov 3	A	Southend Utd	W	4-1	Dyer,Greenall 2, Windridge	1,904
15	7	A	Peterborough Utd	L	0-2		4,296
16	10	H	Stockport County	W	4-1	Stonehouse 2 (1 pen), Windridge 2	3,428
17	24	A	Hereford Utd	L	1-2	Stonehouse	3,588
18	Dec 1	H	Mansfield Town	W	1-0	Stonehouse	2,798
19	7	A	Stockport County	W	3-1	Dyer, Britton, Own-goal	2,428
20	15	A	Torquay Utd	W	2-0	Hetzke 2	1,252
21	22	A	Wrexham	W	2-1	Britton, Dyer	2,109
22	26	H	Rochdale	W	3-0	Stewart 2, Windridge	5,641
23	29	H	Hartlepool Utd	W	2-1	Walsh, Stewart	4,778
24	Jan 1	A	Crewe Alexandra	W	2-0	Stewart, Own-goal	4,008
25	5	H	Halifax Town	D	1-1	Stonehouse	5,184
26	Feb 2	A	Chester City	D	0-0		3,307
27	19	H	Swindon Town	W	1-0	Stewart	3,382
28	23	H	Southend Utd	W	1-0	Britton	4,272
29	Mar 2	A	Northampton Town	W	1-0	Stewart	1,860
30	5	H	Tranmere Rovers	L	1-2	Teasdale	4,885
31	9	A	Bury	L	0-1		7,978
32	16	H	Scunthorpe Utd	W	1-0	Deary (pen)	3,957
33	23	A	Aldershot	L	0-1		2,260
34	26	H	Colchester Utd	D	1-1	Deary	4,057
35	30	H	Peterborough Utd	W	4-2	Deary 2 (1 pen), Conroy, O'Keefe	3,809
36	Apr 2	H	Chesterfield	W	1-0	O'Keefe	7,144
37	6	A	Rochdale	D	1-1	Windridge	3,555
38	9	H	Crewe Alexandra	W	6-1	Cegieski, Windridge 2, Deary 2, Hetzke	6,653
39	17	A	Exeter City	D	1-1	Stonehouse	1,847
40	20	H	Hereford Utd	W	2-0	Deary (pen),Britton	5,585
41	22	A	Port Vale	D	1-1	Hetzke	3,725
42	27	A	Mansfield Town	D	1-1	Greenall	3,030
43	May 1	A	Darlington	W	4-0	Conroy, O'Keefe, Stewart, Deary	7,021
44	4	H	Torquay Utd	D	3-3	O'Keefe 2, Deary (pen)	7,855
45	6	A	Hartlepool Utd	W	2-0	O'Keefe, Dyer	2,196
46	11	H	Wrexham	D	0-0		6,093

Final League Position: 2nd in Division Four

Apps
Sub Apps
Gls

FA Cup

1	Nov 17	H	Altrincham	L	0-1		4,486

Apps
Sub Apps
Gls

League Cup

1	Aug 28	H	Chester City	W	1-0	Deary	3,318
	Sep 5	A	Chester City	W	3-0	Dyre, Deary (pen), Stewart	3,001
2	25	A	Manchester City	L	2-4	Windridge, Greenall	13,344
	Oct 9	H	Manchester City	L	1-3	Britton	10,960

Apps
Sub Apps
Gls

O'Rourke	Moore	Ferns	Conroy	Hetzke	Greenall	Britton	Stonehouse	Stewart	Deary	Dyer	Davies	Walsh	Windridge	Murphy	Bailey	Donovan	Teasdale	Price	Crainie	Cegielski	O'Keefe
1	2	3	4	5	6	7	8	9	10	11											
1	2		4	5	6	7		9	10	11	8	3									
1	2		4	5	6	7		9	10	11	8	3									
1	2	12	4	5	6	7		9*	10	11	8	3									
1	2		4	5	6	7			10	11	8	3	9*	12							
1	2		4	5*	6	7		9	10	11	8	3	12								
1	2		4	5	6	7		9	10*	11	12	3	8								
1	2	10	4*	5	6	7				11	9	3	8	12							
1	2		4	5	6	7	10			11	9	3	8								
1	2		4	5	6	7	10			11*	9	3	8	12							
1	2		4	5	6	7	10				9		8		3	11					
1	2		4	5	6	7	10				12	9*	8		3	11					
1	2		4	5	6	7	10*			11	9		8	12	3						
1	2		4	5	6	7	10			11	9	3	8*	12							
1	2		4	5	6	7	10			11		3	8	9							
1	2		4	5	6	7	10			11		3	8								
1	2		4	5	6	7	10	9		11		3	8								
1	2		4	5	6	7	10	9		11		3	8								
1	2		4	5	6	7	10	9		11		3	8								
1	2*		4	5	6	7	10	9	12	11		3	8								
1	2		4	5	6	7	10	9		11		3	8								
1	2	3	4		6	7*	10	9	12	11		3	8								
1	2	3	4		6	7	10	9	12	11		3	8*								
1	2		4	5	6	7	10*	9	12	11		3	8								
1	2	12	4	5	6	7	10	9	8*	11		3									
1	2	12		5	6	7	10	9	4*	11		3	8								
1	2	3			6	7	10	9	4	11*		3	8				12				
1	2	5*			6	7	10	9	4	11		3	8				12				
1	2		4		6	7		9	5	11		3	8				10				
1	2		8		6	7	10	9	4	11*		5	8				12				
1	2		8		6	7	10*	9	4	11		5	3				12				
1	2		8		6	7		9	4	11*		5		12				3	10		
1	2		8		6	7		9	4	11*		5		12				3	10		
1	2		8		6	7		9	4			5	11					3	10		
1	2		8		6	7		9	4				12					3	11*	5	10
1	2		8		6	7		9*	4			5	12					3	11		10
1	2		8		6	7	12		4	11*		5	9					3			10
1	2		8	5		7			4				9				12	3	11	6	10*
1	2		4	5		7	11				8*		9				12	3		6	10
1	2		8	5	6	7	11		4			3	9								10
1	2		8	5	6	7	11*		4				9					3		12	10
1	2		8	5	6	7		9	4	12		3*	11								10
1	2		8	5	6	7		9	4				11					3			10
1	2*		8	5	6	7		9	4	12			11					3			10
1					6	7		9	4	11	8		2					3		5	10
1					6	7		9	4	11	8		2					3		5	10
46	44	6	41	30	44	46	26	31	28	34	15	35	36	1	3	2	1	13	6	5	12
		2					1		3	2	2		3	7			6			1	
			2	5	3	5	11	7	13	8		1	8				1			1	6
1	2		4	5	6	7	10		11		9*	3	8	12							
1	1		1	1	1	1	1		1		1	1	1								
														1							
1	2	3	4	5	6	7		9	10	11	8										
1	2		4	5	6	7		9	10	11	8	3									
1	2		4	5	6	7	12	9	10	11*		3	8								
1	2	12	4	5	6	7	10			11	9*	3	8								
4	4	1	4	4	4	4	1	3	3	4	3	3	2								
		1					1														1
					1	1		1	2	1			1								

League Table

	P	W	D	L	F	A	Pts
Chesterfield	46	26	13	7	64	35	91
Blackpool	46	24	14	8	73	39	86
Darlington	46	24	13	9	66	49	85
Bury	46	24	12	10	76	50	84
Hereford United	46	22	11	13	65	47	77
Tranmere Rovers	46	24	3	19	83	66	75
Colchester United	46	20	14	12	87	65	74
Swindon Town	46	21	9	16	62	58	72
Scunthorpe United	46	19	14	13	83	62	71
Crewe Alexandra	46	18	12	16	65	69	66
Peterborough United	46	16	14	16	54	53	62
Port Vale	46	14	18	14	61	59	60
Aldershot	46	17	8	21	56	63	59
Mansfield Town	46	13	18	15	41	38	57
Wrexham	46	15	9	22	67	70	54
Chester City	46	15	9	22	60	72	54
Rochdale	46	13	14	19	55	69	53
Exeter City	46	13	14	19	57	79	53
Hartlepool United	46	14	10	22	54	67	52
Southend United	46	13	11	22	58	83	50
Halifax Town	46	15	5	26	42	69	50
Stockport County	46	13	8	25	58	79	47
Northampton Town	46	14	5	27	53	74	47
Torquay United	46	9	14	23	38	63	41

1985-86

Division Three

Manager: Sam Ellis

Did you know that?

The injury to the popular Eamon O'Keefe all but ended his career and severely hampered another promotion push.

The final home game of the season, against Newport County, was being billed as Blackpool's last at Bloomfield Road as the club were in serious financial difficulty.

For the second successive season, Blackpool were dumped out of the FA Cup by non-League Altrincham at home.

Match No.	Date	Venue	Opponents	Result		Scorers	Attendance
1	Aug 17	A	Reading	L	0-1		3,190
2	24	H	Notts County	L	1-3	O'Keefe	4,011
3	26	A	Darlington	L	1-2	O'Keefe	3,548
4	31	H	Swansea City	W	2-0	Deary (pen),Dyer	3,085
5	Sep 7	A	Derby County	W	2-1	O'Keefe 2 (1 pen)	10,102
6	14	H	York City	L	0-2		4,053
7	17	A	Bournemouth	W	4-1	Dyer 2, O'Keefe, Own-goal	3,039
8	21	H	Cardiff City	W	3-0	Davies, O'Keefe, Deary	3,783
9	28	A	Bristol City	L	1-2	O'Keefe	6,570
10	Dec 1	H	Doncaster Rovers	W	4-0	Dyer, O'Keefe 3 (1 pen)	4,121
11	5	H	Gillingham	D	2-2	Deary, O'Keefe (pen)	4,571
12	12	A	Wigan Athletic	D	1-1	O'Keefe	5,993
13	19	H	Bury	W	5-0	O'Keefe 2 (1 pen), Davies, Deary, Hetzke	5,496
14	22	A	Chesterfield	W	2-1	Windridge, Davies	3,720
15	26	H	Brentford	W	4-0	Hetzke, Stewart 2, Windridge	5,448
16	Nov 2	A	Lincoln City	W	3-0	Hetzke, Stonehouse, Deary	2,373
17	5	A	Wolves	L	1-2	Dyer	3,690
18	9	H	Bristol Rovers	W	4-2	Hetzke, Dyer 2, Windridge	4,707
19	23	A	Walsall	D	1-1	Greenall	5,161
20	30	H	Plymouth Argyle	D	1-1	Stonehouse (pen)	6,184
21	Dec 14	A	Newport County	D	1-1	Stewart	1,991
22	22	A	Notts County	W	2-1	Stonehouse, Dyer	5,926
23	26	H	Bolton Wanderers	D	1-1	Stewart	9,473
24	28	H	Darlington	D	0-0		5,595
25	Jan 1	A	Rotherham Utd	L	1-4	Walsh	4,200
26	11	A	Swansea City	L	0-2		5,705
27	18	H	Reading	D	0-0		5,295
28	Feb 1	H	Derby County	L	0-1		6,732
29	4	H	Chesterfield	L	0-1		2,998
30	22	A	Cardiff City	L	0-1		2,430
31	25	H	Lincoln City	W	2-0	Deary, Own-goal	1,995
32	Mar 1	H	Bristol City	W	2-1	Butler, Deary (pen)	3,366
33	4	A	Doncaster Rovers	D	0-0		2,316
34	8	A	Gillingham	D	2-2	O'Keefe (pen), Own-goal	4,537
35	15	H	Wigan Athletic	L	1-2	O'Keefe (pen)	6,218
36	22	A	Brentford	D	1-1	Britton	3,528
37	29	H	Rotherham Utd	W	2-1	Thomson, Davies	4,007
38	31	A	Bolton Wanderers	W	3-1	Thomson, Stewart, O'Keefe	7,878
39	Apr 5	H	Wolves	L	0-1		4,563
40	12	A	Bristol Rovers	L	0-1		3,472
41	19	H	Walsall	W	2-1	Stewart (pen), Own-goal	2,964
42	22	A	Bury	L	1-4	Stewart (pen)	2,738
43	26	A	Plymouth Argyle	L	1-3	Stewart	14,978
44	29	H	Bournemouth	W	2-0	Law, Davies	2,259
45	May 3	H	Newport County	D	0-0		3,407
46	6	A	York City	L	0-3		3,370

Final League Position: 12th in Division Three

Apps
Sub Apps
Gls

FA Cup

1	Nov 16	A	Lincoln City	W	1-0	Own-goal	2,596
2	Dec 7	H	Altrincham	L	1-2	Stewart	5,037

Apps
Sub Apps
Gls

League Cup

1	Aug 20	A	Preston NE	L	1-2	Davies	4,704
	Sep 3	H	Preston NE	L	1-3	Greenall	5,043

Apps
Sub Apps
Gls

Match	O'Rourke	Moore	Walsh	Deary	Hetzke	Greenall	Britton	O'Keefe	Stewart	Windridge	Dyer	Butler	Conroy	Matthews	Davies	Law	Stonehouse	Thomson	Sendall	Ronson	Morgan
1	1	2	3	4	5	6	7	8	9	10	11										
2	1	2	3	4	5*	6	7	8	9	12	11		8								
3	1	2	3*	8		6	7	10			9	11	4	5	12						
4	1	2		8		6	7	10	9		11	3	4			5					
5	1	2		8		6		10	9		11	3	4		7	5					
6	1	2	3	8		6		10	9		11		4		7	5					
7	1	2	3	8		6		10	9		11		4		7	5					
8	1	2	3	8		6		10	9		11		4		7	5					
9	1	2	3*	8		6		10	9		11		4		7	5	12				
10	1	2		8	3	6		10*	9		11		4		7	5		12			
11	1	2		8	5	6		10	9		11		4		7	3					
12	1	2		8	5	6		10	9		11		4		7	3					
13	1	2		8	5	6		10	9		11		4*		7	3	12				
14	1	2		8	5	6		10*	9	12	11				7	3	4				
15	1	2		8	5	6	12		9	10	11				7*	3	4				
16	1	2		8	5	6	12		9	10	11				7*	3	4				
17	1	2			5	6	8		9	10	11				7	3	4				
18	1	2			5	6	8		9	10	11				7	3	4				
19	1	2			5	6	8		9	10	11				7	3	4				
20	1	2			5	6	8		9	10	11				7	3	4				
21	1	2	3	4	5	6	7		9	10	11						8				
22	1		3	8	5	6	7		9*	8	11	2					10		12		
23	1		3	8	5	6	7*		9	10	11	2				12	4				
24	1		3	8	5	6			9*	10	11	2			7	12	4				
25	1		3	8	5	6				10	11	2			7	9	4				
26	1	2		8	5	6				9	11	10			7	3	4				
27	1	2			5	6	7		9	10*	11				12	3	4			8	
28	1	2		4	5	6	7*		9		11				8	3		12		10	
29	1	2		4	5	6	12		9		11				8*	3		7		10	
30	1	2		4	5	6	7		9		11		8*		12	3		10			
31	1	2		8			10		9		11	3	4		7	5		6			
32	1	2	3	8		6	7	12	9		11	10	4			5					
33	1	2	3	8		6		12	9		11	10	4		7*	5					
34	1	2	5	8		6		12	9		11	3	4		7*			10			
35	1	2	5	8		6	12	10	9		11	3	4*					7			
36	1	2	3*			6	8	10	9		11		4		12	5		7			
37	1	2		8		6	7	10			11	3	4*		12	5		9			
38	1	2*		4		6	7	10	9		11	12			3	5		8			
39	1	2	6	4			7	10	9		11*	3			12	5		8			
40	1	2	6	4			7		9			3*			10	5		8	12		11
41	1	2	3	8		6	7		9				4			5		10*	12		11
42	1	2	3	4		6	7*		9				8			5		10	12		11
43	1	2	3	8		6			9				4		7	5		10	11		
44	1	2	3	4		6	12		9				8		7	5		10*	11		
45	1	2*	3	8		6	10		9				4		7	5			11		12
46	1	2	3	8		6*	10		9			4			7	5			11		12
	46	42	25	40	23	43	25	19	42	14	39	17	25	1	30	37	14	14	4	3	3
							5	3		2		1			6	2	2	2	4		2
			1	7	4	1	1	17	8	3	8	1			5	1	3	2			
	1	2			5	6	8		9	10	11				7	3	4				
	1	2	3	8	5	6			9	10	11			3	7		4				
	2	2	1	1	2	2	1		2	2	2				2	1	2				
									1												
	1	2	3	4		6	7	10		5	11		8		9						
	1	2		8		6	7*	10	9		11	3	4	5			12				
	2	2	1	2		2	2	2	1	1	2	1	2	1	1						
																	1				
						1									1						

League Table

	P	W	D	L	F	A	Pts
Reading	46	29	7	10	67	51	94
Plymouth Argyle	46	26	9	11	88	53	87
Derby County	46	23	15	8	80	41	84
Wigan Athletic	46	23	14	9	82	48	83
Gillingham	46	22	13	11	81	54	79
Walsall	46	22	9	15	90	64	75
York City	46	20	11	15	77	58	71
Notts County	46	19	14	13	71	60	71
Bristol City	46	18	14	14	69	60	68
Brentford	46	18	12	16	58	61	66
Doncaster Rovers	46	16	16	14	45	52	64
Blackpool	46	17	12	17	66	55	63
Darlington	46	15	13	18	61	78	58
Rotherham United	46	15	12	19	61	59	57
Bournemouth	46	15	9	22	65	72	54
Bristol Rovers	46	14	12	20	51	75	54
Chesterfield	46	13	14	19	61	64	53
Bolton Wanderers	46	15	8	23	54	68	53
Newport County	46	11	18	17	52	65	51
Bury	46	12	13	21	63	67	49
Lincoln City	46	10	16	20	55	77	46
Cardiff City	46	12	9	25	53	83	45
Wolverhampton W.	46	11	10	25	57	98	43
Swansea City	46	11	10	25	43	87	43

1986-87

Division Three

Manager: Sam Ellis

Did you know that?

Paul Stewart was sold to Manchester City for £200,000, and so relieving some of the financial pressure on the club.

A new board was in place, with local entrepreneur Owen Oyston taking an increasing stake in the club.

On 26 July, the club celebrated its centenary.

Match No.	Date	Venue	Opponents	Result		Scorers	Attendance
1	Aug 23	H	Chesterfield	D	0-0		4,032
2	30	A	Fulham	W	1-0	Stewart	3,903
3	Sep 6	H	Carlisle Utd	L	1-2	Thomson	4,188
4	14	A	Doncaster Rovers	D	2-2	Stewart 2 (1 pen)	3,338
5	16	A	Swindon Town	W	6-2	Taylor 2, Dyer 2, Mayes, Stewart	6,662
6	20	H	Wigan Athletic	W	5-1	Mayes 3, Taylor, Butler	4,905
7	27	A	Bristol Rovers	D	2-2	Mayes, Methven	3,417
8	30	H	Port Vale	W	2-0	Methven 2	4,585
9	Oct 4	H	Walsall	D	1-1	Dyer	5,554
10	11	A	Middlesbrough	W	3-1	Taylor 2, Stewart	11,470
11	18	H	Notts County	W	3-1	Mayes, Taylor, Stewart	5,325
12	23	A	Bolton Wanderers	L	0-1		6,534
13	Nov 1	H	Bristol City	W	1-0	Butler	4,370
14	4	A	Gillingham	L	1-2	Walsh	5,951
15	8	H	Rotherham Utd	W	1-0	Methven	3,578
16	22	A	Brentford	D	1-1	Taylor	4,471
17	29	H	Newport County	D	1-1	Deary	3,281
18	Dec 6	A	Mansfield Town	D	1-1	Stewart	2,931
19	13	H	Bury	D	1-1	Walsh	3,412
20	26	H	York City	W	2-1	Stewart 2 (1 pen)	4,515
21	27	A	Chester City	W	4-1	Davies, Butler, Deary, Taylor	4,002
22	Jan 3	H	Brentford	W	2-0	Taylor, Stewart (pen)	4,384
23	24	A	Carlisle Utd	L	1-3	Davies	3,048
24	Feb 3	A	Bournemouth	D	1-1	Stewart	6,242
25	7	H	Swindon Town	D	1-1	Stewart (pen)	4,839
26	13	A	Wigan Athletic	L	1-4	Madden	6,857
27	17	A	Chesterfield	D	1-1	Stewart	2,468
28	21	H	Bristol Rovers	W	6-1	Taylor 2, Davies, Madden, Stewart 2 (1 pen)	3,434
29	28	A	Port Vale	W	6-1	Stewart 3 (1 pen), Davies, McGinley, Madden	3,765
30	Mar 3	A	Bristol City	L	1-3	Stewart	10,769
31	7	H	Mansfield Town	L	1-2	Stewart (pen)	3,032
32	10	A	Darlington	D	1-1	Windridge	1,600
33	14	A	Notts County	L	2-3	Thomson, Stewart (pen)	5,920
34	17	H	Bolton Wanderers	D	1-1	Taylor	4,717
35	21	H	Middlesbrough	L	0-1		7,132
36	28	A	Walsall	L	1-2	Madden	5,061
37	Apr 4	A	Rotherham Utd	L	0-1		2,653
38	7	H	Fulham	W	1-0	Thomson	1,902
39	11	H	Gillingham	L	0-1		2,558
40	18	H	Darlington	W	2-1	Thomson, Davies	2,612
41	20	A	York City	D	1-1	Taylor	2,694
42	25	H	Bournemouth	L	1-3	Methven	2,866
43	28	H	Doncaster Rovers	D	1-1	Davies	1,638
44	May 2	A	Newport County	D	1-1	Taylor	1,247
45	4	H	Chester City	W	1-0	Deary	2,069
46	9	A	Bury	L	1-4	Madden	2,198

Final League Position: 9th in Division Three

Apps
Sub Apps
Gls

FA Cup

1	Nov 15	A	Middlesbrough	L	0-3		11,205

Apps
Sub Apps
Gls

League Cup

1	Aug 26	H	Preston NE	D	0-0		3,929
	Sep 2	A	Preston NE	L	1-2	Deary	5,914

Apps
Sub Apps
Gls

Siddall	Matthews	Walsh	Law	Methven	Greenall	Deary	Thomson	Stewart	O'Keefe E	Dyer	Davies	Sendall	Butler	Taylor	Mayes	Moore	McAteer	McGinley	Priest	Powell	O'Keefe V	Windridge	Bradshaw	Morgan	Jones	Madden
1	2	3	4	5	6	7	8	9	10	11																
1		3	4	5	6	7	8	9		11	2	10*	12													
1		3	4	5	6	7	8	9	10*	11	2		12													
1	2*	3	4	5		7	8	9		11	6	12		10												
1		3	4	5		6	8*	9		10	2		12	11	7											
1		3	4	5		6		9		10	2		8	11*	7	12										
1		3	4	5		6		9		10	2		8	11	7											
1		3	4	5		6	8	9		10	2		12	11*	7											
1		3	4	5		6	8	9		10	2*		12	11	7											
1		3	4	5		6	8	9		10			2	11	7											
1		3	4	5		6	8	9		10			2*	11	7			12								
1	12	3	4	5		6	8			10	2	9*		11	7											
1		3	4	5		6	8*	9		10	2		12	11	7											
1	7*	3	4	5		6		9		10	2		8	11	12											
1		3	4	5		6	10	9			2		8	11	7											
1		3		5		6		9		10	2		8	11	7*	4		12								
1		3	4	5		6		9		10	2		8	11	7*			12								
1		3	4	5		6	7	9		10	2		8	11												
1		3	4	5			8	9		10	7		2	11					6							
			4*	5		6	8	9		10	7		2	11			3	12		1						
	4			5		6	8*	9		10	7		2	11			3	12			1					
1	4			5		6	8	9		10	7		2	11			3									
1	6*	3		8		4	7	9		10	8		2				11					12				
1		3	4	5		6	8	9		10	7		2	11												
1		3	4	5		6	8	9		10	7*		2	11			12									
1		3	4	5		6	8*	9			7		2	11				12								10
1	2		4	5		6	8	9			7			11			3									10
1	2		4*	5		6		9			7		10	11			3	12								8
1	2		4	5		6		9			7		8*	11			3	12								10
1	2		4	5		6	8	9			7			11			3									10
1	2		4	5		6	8*	9			7		11				3	12								10
1	2	4		5		6		9			7		10				3					11				8
1		4		5		6	8	9			7			2			3					11				10
1		4		5		6	9				7			11			3	2*				8		12		10
1	2			5		6	9				7		8	11			3					12		4*		10
1	6			5			9				7		2	11								10		3	4	8
1	6			5		7	9*						2	11			3	10						12	4	8
1		6		5		8	9				7		2	11			3							12	4	10*
1		6*		5		7	9				8		2	11			3					12		10	4	
		6		5		7	9				8		2*	11			3			1		12		10	4	
	2	6		5		7	9*				8			11			3			1		12			4	10
	2	6		5		7					8			9			3			1				11	4	10
	4	6		5		8					7		3	9						1		2*	12	11		10
	2	6		5		7	9				8		3	11						1			12		4*	10
	4	6*		5		8	9				7		3	11						1			2	12		10
	2			5		8	9				7		3	11						1		12	4	6*		10
37	21	34	27	46	3	44	36	32	2	24	42	2	22	40	12	1	19	2	1	8	1	5	2	7	8	19
	1											1	6		1	1	1	9				5	3	4		
		2		5		3	4	21		3	6		3	14	6			1				1				5

Siddall	Matthews	Walsh	Law	Methven	Greenall	Deary	Thomson	Stewart	O'Keefe E	Dyer	Davies	Sendall	Butler	Taylor	Mayes	Moore	McAteer	McGinley
1		3*	4	5		6	8	9			2		10#	11	7	12		14
1		1	1	1		1	1	1			1		1	1	1			
																1		1

Siddall	Matthews	Walsh	Law	Methven	Greenall	Deary	Thomson	Stewart	O'Keefe E	Dyer	Davies	Sendall	Butler	Taylor
1	2*	3	4	5	6	7	8	9		11	12	10		
1		5	4		6	7	8	9		11	2	10*	3	12
2	1	2	2	1	2	2	2	2		2	1	2	1	
											1			1
						1								

League Table

	P	W	D	L	F	A	Pts
Bournemouth	46	29	10	7	76	40	97
Middlesbrough	46	28	10	8	67	30	94
Swindon Town	46	25	12	9	77	47	87
Wigan Athletic	46	25	10	11	83	60	85
Gillingham	46	23	9	14	65	48	78
Bristol City	46	21	14	11	63	36	77
Notts County	46	21	13	12	77	56	76
Walsall	46	22	9	15	80	67	75
Blackpool	46	16	16	14	74	59	64
Mansfield Town	46	15	16	15	52	55	61
Brentford	46	15	15	16	64	66	60
Port Vale	46	15	12	19	76	70	57
Doncaster Rovers	46	14	15	17	56	62	57
Rotherham United	46	15	12	19	48	57	57
Chester City	46	13	17	16	61	59	56
Bury	46	14	13	19	54	60	55
Chesterfield	46	13	15	18	56	69	54
Fulham	46	12	17	17	59	77	53
Bristol Rovers	46	13	12	21	49	75	51
York City	46	12	13	21	55	79	49
Bolton Wanderers	46	10	15	21	46	58	45
Carlisle United	46	10	8	28	39	78	38
Darlington	46	7	16	23	45	77	37
Newport County	46	8	13	25	49	86	37

1987-88

Division Three

Manager: Sam Ellis

Did you know that?

On 8 March the club celebrated its centenary again with a banquet at the Imperial Hotel. Russell Harty was the guest speaker, exactly three months prior to his death.

Owen Oyston was made chairman on 31 May 1988, replacing Ken Chadwick.

Another new club crest was introduced, with a seagull on a tangerine background, encircled in red.

Match No.	Date	Venue	Opponents	Result		Scorers	Attendance
1	Aug 15	A	Gillingham	D	0-0		4,430
2	22	H	Walsall	L	1-2	Cunningham	4,614
3	29	A	Bury	L	1-3	Walwyn	3,053
4	31	H	Bristol Rovers	W	2-1	Cunningham 2 (1 pen)	3,319
5	Sep 5	A	Brighton @ HA	W	3-1	Cunningham 2, Taylor	7,166
6	12	H	Chester City	L	0-1		4,035
7	15	A	Doncaster Rovers	L	1-2	Cunningham	1,558
8	19	A	Brentford	L	1-2	Walwyn	3,886
9	26	H	Preston NE	W	3-0	Walwyn 2, Madden (pen)	8,406
10	29	A	York City	W	3-1	Cunningham, Morgan, Madden	2,559
11	Oct 3	H	Fulham	W	2-1	Madden 2 (1 pen)	4,973
12	17	H	Sunderland	L	0-2		8,476
13	20	A	Grimsby Town	D	1-1	Taylor	2,260
14	24	H	Wigan Athletic	D	0-0		4,821
15	31	A	Mansfield Town	D	0-0		3,321
16	Nov 3	H	Bristol City	W	4-2	Morgan, Taylor, Madden 2 (1 pen)	3,140
17	7	H	Rotherham Utd	W	3-0	Deary, Taylor, Madden	3,447
18	22	A	Port Vale	D	0-0		3,594
19	28	H	Northampton Town	W	3-1	Cunningham, Walwyn, Morgan	3,593
20	Dec 12	A	Chesterfield	D	1-1	Taylor	2,279
21	19	H	Southend Utd	D	1-1	Walwyn	3,277
22	26	A	Preston NE	L	1-2	Madden	11,155
23	28	H	Notts County	D	1-1	Coughlin	4,627
24	Jan 1	H	Bury	W	5-1	Butler,Cunningham, Morgan, Madden, Deary	4,240
25	2	A	Chester City	D	1-1	Madden	3,093
26	16	H	Brentford	L	0-1		3,911
27	Feb 6	H	Brighton @ HA	L	1-3	Lester	4,081
28	13	A	Notts County	W	3-2	Morgan, Taylor 2	5,794
29	20	H	Gillingham	D	3-3	Coughlin, Taylor, Walwyn	3,045
30	23	A	Walsall	L	2-3	Taylor 2 (1 pen)	4,252
31	27	A	Fulham	L	1-3	Walwyn	4,072
32	Mar 1	H	York City	W	2-1	Taylor, Methven	2,249
33	5	A	Sunderland	D	2-2	Taylor, Walwyn	15,313
34	12	H	Aldershot	W	3-2	Taylor, Walwyn, Cunningham	2,661
35	19	H	Mansfield Town	W	2-0	Taylor 2 (1 pen)	2,847
36	25	A	Wigan Athletic	D	0-0		4,505
37	29	A	Aldershot	D	0-0		2,091
38	Apr 2	A	Rotherham Utd	W	1-0	Deary	3,001
39	4	H	Port Vale	L	1-2	Taylor	5,516
40	9	A	Bristol City	L	1-2	Taylor	6,460
41	15	H	Doncaster Rovers	W	4-2	Madden, Taylor 2, Walwyn	2,291
42	23	H	Grimsby Town	W	3-0	Walwyn, Taylor 2	2,558
43	27	A	Bristol Rovers	L	0-2		3,546
44	30	A	Northampton Town	D	3-3	Walwyn, Methven, Morgan	5,730
45	May 2	H	Chesterfield	W	1-0	Walwyn	2,950
46	7	A	Southend Utd	L	0-4		5,541

Final League Position: 10th in Division Three

Apps
Sub Apps
Gls

FA Cup

1	Nov 14	A	Bishop Auckland	W	4-1	Deary, Madden, Taylor 2	2,462
2	Dec 6	A	Northwich Victoria	W	2-0	Madden, Walwyn	2,528
3	Jan 9	A	Scunthorpe Utd	D	0-0		6,217
3R	12	H	Scunthorpe Utd	W	1-0	Madden	6,227
4	30	H	Manchester City	D	1-1	Sendall	10,835
4R	Feb 3	A	Manchester City	L	1-2	Deary	26,503

Apps
Sub Apps
Gls

League Cup

1	Aug 18	H	Chester City	W	2-0	Cunningham, Methven	3,114
	26	A	Chester City	L	0-1		2,147
2	Sep 23	H	Newcastle Utd	W	1-0	Cunningham	7,691
	Oct 7	A	Newcastle Utd	L	1-4	Morgan	20,805

Apps
Sub Apps
Gls

Siddall	Davies	Morgan	Matthews	Methven	Jones	Cunningham	Madden	Walwyn	Deary	Taylor	Butler	Bradshaw	Walsh	Rooney	Lancashire	McAteer	Hutchison	Coughlin	Lester	Shaw	Muggleton	Powell	Wright	Sendall
1	2	3	4	5	6	7	8	9	10	11														
1	2	3	4	5	6*	7	8	9	10	11#	12		14											
1	2	3	4	5	14		8*	9	10	11#	7		6	12										
1	2	3	4	5		7		9	10	11	8		6											
1	2	3	4	5		7	8	9	10	11			6											
1	2*	3	4	5	14	7	8	9	10	11	12#		6											
1		3	4	5		7	8	9	10	11*		2	6			12								
1	2	3	4	5*	10	7	8	9		11			6			12								
1		3	4	12	10	7	8#	9		11			6*		14	12	2							
1	2	3	4	12	10*	7#	8			11			6		14	12	9							
1	2	3	4	5		7	8	12		11			6			10	9*							
1	2	3	4	5			8	9	7	11			6			10*	12							
1	2*	3	4	5		7		9	8	11			6			10	12							
1		3	4	5		7		9	8#	11	12		6		2*	10	14							
1		3		5	6	7	2	9	8	11		4				10								
1	2*	3		5		7	8	9	6	11		4			12	10								
1	2	3		5			8	9	6	11	12	4			7*	10								
1	2	3		5	14	6	8*	9	7	11#	12	4				10								
1		3		5#	12	8	2	9	7	11		4	6*		14	10								
1	2	3		5		8		9		11		4	6			10		7						
1	2*	3		5	6	7	14	9		11	12	4#				10		8						
1		3		5	6	7	2	9*		11	12	4				10		8						
1		3		5	6	7	9		12	11	2	4*				10		8						
1	12	3		5	6	7#	9		14	11	2					10		8	6*					
1	12	3		5	6	7	9#		14	11	2*					10		8	4					
1	2	3		5	6	7	9		10						12	11		8	4*					
1	2*	3#			6	9	14		10	11	12		5					8	4	7				
	2	3		12	5*	9	14		10	11			6					8	4#	7	1			
	2*	3		5#	12		10	9		11			6			14		8	4	7	1			
1	2	3			5	10	14	9#		11	12		6					8	4	7*				
1	2	3			5	10	12	9	7	11			6					8	4*					
1	2	3		5		10		9	7	11	4*		6					8		12				
1	2	3		5		10		9	7	11	4*		6					8		12				
1	2	3	6	5	8	10		9	4	11									7					
1	2	3	6	5	8*	10		9	4	11				12					7					
1	2	3	6	5	8	10		9	4	11								7						
1	2	3	4	5	8			9	10	11	6							7						
1	2	3	4	5	6			9	10	11*	7#		12	14				8						
1	2	3	6	5	8*	10		9	7	11			12					4						
1		3*	2	5		10		9	7	11		12	6	8				4						
	2	3	8	5		10	6	9	7*	11		12							4			1		
	2	3	8	5		10	6*	9	7	11				12				4				1		
	2	3	8	5		10	6*	9	7			11	12					4				1		
	2#	3	8	12		10	14	9	7			6*	5	11				4				1		
	2	3	8	12		10		9	7			6#	5*	11				4				1	14	
	2	3	8			10		9	7			6	5	11				4				1		
38	36	46	27	37	22	40	25	38	34	41	9	14	25	4	2	16	3	24	11	4	2	6		
	2			5	5		8	1	3		9	2	4	4	5	5	3			2			1	
		6		2		10	11	14	3	21	1							2	1					

Siddall	Davies	Morgan	Matthews	Methven	Jones	Cunningham	Madden	Walwyn	Deary	Taylor	Butler	Bradshaw	Walsh	Rooney	Lancashire	McAteer	Hutchison	Coughlin	Lester	Shaw	Muggleton	Powell	Wright	Sendall
1	2	3		5	6		8*	9	7	11	14	4		12		10#								
1	2*	3			5		8	9	7	11	12	4	6			10								
1	2	3			6	7	9		10	11			5					8	4					
1	2	3		12	6	7	9		10				5			11*		8	4					
1	2	3			6			9	10	11			5	7*				8	4					12
1	2	3			6		12	9	10	11	7		5					8	4*					
6	6	6		1	6	2	4	4	6	5	1	2	5	1		3		4	4					
				1			1				2			1		1								1
							3	1	2	2														1

Siddall	Davies	Morgan	Matthews	Methven	Jones	Cunningham	Madden	Walwyn	Deary	Taylor	Butler	Bradshaw	Walsh	Rooney	Lancashire	McAteer	Hutchison	Coughlin	Lester	Shaw	Muggleton	Powell	Wright	Sendall
1	2	3	4	5	6	7	8	9	10	11*	12													
1	2	3	4	5			8	9	10	11	7		6											
1	2*	3	4		10	7	8	9		11			6		12	5								
1	2	3	4*	5		7	8	9		11			6			10	12							
4	4	4	4	3	2	3	4	4	2	4	1		3			2								
											1				1		1							
		1		1		2																		

League Table

	P	W	D	L	F	A	Pts
Sunderland	46	27	12	7	92	48	93
Brighton & Hove Albion	46	23	15	8	69	47	84
Walsall	46	23	13	10	68	50	82
Notts County	46	23	12	11	82	49	81
Bristol City	46	21	12	13	77	62	75
Northampton Town	46	18	19	9	70	51	73
Wigan Athletic	46	20	12	14	70	61	72
Bristol Rovers	46	18	12	16	68	56	66
Fulham	46	19	9	18	69	60	66
Blackpool	46	17	14	15	71	62	65
Port Vale	46	18	11	17	58	56	65
Brentford	46	16	14	16	53	59	62
Gillingham	46	14	17	15	77	61	59
Bury	46	15	14	17	58	57	59
Chester City	46	14	16	16	51	62	58
Preston North End	46	15	13	18	48	59	58
Southend United	46	14	13	19	65	83	55
Chesterfield	46	15	10	21	41	70	55
Mansfield Town	46	14	12	20	48	59	54
Aldershot	46	15	8	23	64	74	53
Rotherham United	46	12	16	18	50	66	52
Grimsby Town	46	12	14	20	48	58	50
York City	46	8	9	29	48	91	33
Doncaster Rovers	46	8	9	29	40	84	33

1988-89

Division Three

Manager: Sam Ellis

Did you know that?

Manager Sam Ellis was under increasing pressure and, following fan demonstrations, he left the club after a 4–2 home defeat to Reading on 8 April.

Winning four of the last five games ensured Third Division survival, and also gave caretaker manager Jimmy Mullen the position on a full-time basis.

Match No.	Date	Venue	Opponents	Result		Scorers	Attendance
1	Aug 27	A	Chester City	D	1-1	Cunningham	3,496
2	Sep 3	H	Notts County	L	0-1		4,669
3	10	A	Preston NE	L	0-1		8,779
4	17	H	Mansfield Town	D	1-1	Garner	4,021
5	20	H	Bristol City	D	2-2	Davies, Taylor	3,413
6	24	A	Chesterfield	W	2-0	Garner, Taylor	2,128
7	30	A	Wigan Athletic	L	1-2	Taylor	4,141
8	Oct 4	H	Northampton Town	W	3-1	Cunningham, Thompson, Deary	3,034
9	8	A	Bolton Wanderers	D	2-2	Cunningham, Morgan	7,106
10	15	H	Sheffield Utd	L	1-2	Coughlin (pen)	8,471
11	22	H	Port Vale	W	3-2	Cunningham, Madden, Coughlin (pen)	7,045
12	25	A	Wolves	L	1-2	Morgan	12,104
13	29	H	Cardiff City	W	1-0	Garner	3,849
14	Nov 5	A	Fulham	D	1-1	Garner	4,760
15	8	A	Gillingham	L	0-1		3,541
16	12	H	Aldershot	W	4-0	Garner 2, Coughlin (pen), Deary	2,690
17	26	H	Swansea City	D	0-0		3,443
18	Dec 3	A	Huddersfield Town	D	1-1	Cunningham	5,738
19	17	H	Bristol Rovers	D	1-1	Garner	3,240
20	26	A	Brentford	L	0-1		6,021
21	30	A	Reading	L	1-2	Cunningham	5,554
22	Jan 2	H	Bury	D	2-2	Cunningham, Coughlin (pen)	4,199
23	14	A	Notts County	D	1-1	Morgan	4,748
24	21	H	Preston NE	W	1-0	Thompson	8,951
25	28	A	Mansfield Town	W	1-0	Madden	2,738
26	Feb 4	H	Wigan Athletic	W	2-0	Deary 2	4,221
27	11	A	Northampton Town	L	2-4	Thompson 2	3,033
28	18	H	Bolton Wanderers	W	2-0	Cunningham, Thompson	5,552
29	25	A	Sheffield Utd	L	1-4	Garner	11,317
30	28	H	Wolves	L	0-2		6,482
31	Mar 4	A	Port Vale	L	0-1		6,306
32	11	H	Fulham	L	0-1		3,014
33	18	H	Chester City	D	1-1	Deary	2,795
34	25	A	Bury	D	0-0		3,717
35	27	H	Brentford	L	0-3		3,053
36	Apr 1	A	Bristol Rovers	L	0-1		5,355
37	4	A	Southend Utd	L	1-2	Methven	2,795
38	8	H	Reading	L	2-4	Garner, Davies	2,792
39	15	A	Bristol City	W	2-1	Walwyn 2	5,096
40	22	H	Chesterfield	L	1-2	Garner	3,321
41	29	A	Aldershot	L	0-1		1,763
42	May 1	H	Gillingham	W	4-1	Walwyn, Matthews, Own-goal, Garner	2,152
43	6	H	Huddersfield Town	W	2-1	Thompson, Madden	4,070
44	9	H	Southend Utd	W	3-2	Thompson 2, Madden	3,999
45	13	A	Swansea City	W	2-1	Coughlin, Own-goal	3,494
46	16	A	Cardiff City	D	0-0		3,426

Final League Position: 19th in Division Three

Apps
Sub Apps
Gls

FA Cup

1	Nov 19	H	Scunthorpe Utd	W	2-1	Cunningham, Garner	3,974
2	Dec 10	H	Bury	W	3-0	Cunningham, Garner, Deary	5,324
3	Jan 7	H	Bournemouth	L	0-1		5,317

Apps
Sub Apps
Gls

League Cup

1	Aug 30	A	Carlisle Utd	D	1-1	Deary	2,396
	Sep 4	H	Carlisle Utd	W	3-0	Garner 2, Taylor	2,955
2	27	H	Sheffield Wed	W	2-0	Coughlin, Cunningham	5,492
	Oct 12	A	Sheffield Wed	L	1-3*	Morgan	12,237
3	Nov 1	A	Tranmere Rovers	L	0-1		9,454

* after extra-time. Blackpool won on away goals

Apps
Sub Apps
Gls

Siddall	Gore	Burgess	Deary	Methven	Elliot	Davies	Cunningham	Garner	Coughlin	Wright	Walwyn	Thompson	Morgan	Taylor	Walsh	Matthews	Madden	Kelly	O'Keefe	Rooney
1	2	3	4	5	6	7	8	9*	10	11	12									
1	2*	3	4	5	6	7	8	9#	10		14	12	11							
1		2	4	5*	6	7	8	9	10			12	3	11						
1		2	4	5	6	7	8	9	10*		14	12	3#	11						
1		2	4	5	6	7	8	9#	10*		14	12	3	11						
1		2	4	5	6	7	8	9	10		14	12	3*	11#						
1		2	4	5	6		8	9	10		7*		3	11		12				
1		2	4	5	6*		8	9	10	11#		12	3			7	14			
	6	2	4	5			8	9	10			11*	3			7	12	1		
	6	2	4	5			8	9	10		7	11*	3				12	1		
	14	2	4	5#	6		8	9	10			11	3			7*	12	1		
	11	2	4	12	6		8	9	10#			14	3			7*	5	1		
	7	2	4	5	6		8	9	10		12		3				11*	1		
1	7	2	4	5	6		8	9	10			11	3							
1	7	2	4	5	6		8	9	10		12	11*	3#	14						
1		2	4	5*	6	7	8	9	10	14	12		3	11#						
1		2	4*	5	6		8	9	10				3	11#	7	14	12			
1		2	4	5	6		8	9	10			14	3	11#	7*		12			
1		2	4	5	6	12	8	9	10			11	3*							
1		2	4	5	6	7	8	9	10		14		3*		12		11#			
1		2		5	6	7	8	9	10	11*	12		3		6					
1		2	14	5	6	7	8	9	10	11*	12		3		4#					
1	4	2		5	6	7	8	9	10		11		3							
1	4	2	10	5*	6	7	8	9			12#	14	3				11			
1	4	2	5		6	7	8	9				10	3				11			
1	4	2	5		6	7*	8	9	12			10	3				11			
1	4#	2	7	5			8	9	6		12	10	3		14		11#			
	4#	2	7	5		14	8	9	6		12	10	3				11*		1	
		2	7	5#	6	14	8	9	4		11	10*	3		12				1	
		2	7	5*	6	11	8	9	4		12	10	3						1	
		2	7	5*	6	11	8	9	4		12	10	3						1	
		2	7	5	6	11		9	4	12	8	10*	3						1	
		2	7	5	6	11		9	4		8	10	3						1	
1	7	2	4	5	6	11*		9	10			12	3				8			
1	8*	2	7	5	6	11			4			10	3			12	9			
1	7*	2		5	6	12		9	4	11		10	3				6			
1		2	4	5	6	7		9		11		10	3*				8			12
1		2	10	5	6	7		9	4	11		12	3*				8			
1	10	2	6	5	4	7		9	8		12					3*	11			
1	11	2			6	7		9	10	3	8	5*	12				4			
1		2		5	6	7		9	10	11#	8*	4	3			14	12			
1		2		5	6			9	10	11	8	4	3			7				
1	12	2	14	5	6*				10#	11	8	4	3			7	9			
1		2		5	6	12			10	11	8	4	3			7*	9			
1		2		5					10	11	8	4	3		6	7	9			
1		2			6			12	10	11	8*	4	3		5	7	9			
35	19	46	35	41	41	25	31	42	42	14	13	25	43	8	6	10	20	5	6	
	2		2	1		5		1	1	2	17	11	1	1	4	4	7			1
			5	1		2	8	11	5		3	8	3	3		1	4			

1		2	4	5	6	7	8	9	10				3	11						
1		2	4	5	6		8	9	10*			11	3		12		7			
1		2	4	5	6	7	8	9	10		12		3							11*
3		3	3	3	3	2	3	3	3			1	1	1			1			1
											1				1					
			1				2	2												

1	2	3	4	5	6	7	8	9	10	11*		12								
1		2	4#	5	6	7	8	9	10*			12	3	11			14			
1		2	4	5	6	7*	8	9	10		12		3	11						
1	12	2	4	5			8	9	10		11#		3		6*	7	14			
1	7	2	4*	5	6		8	9	10		11	12	3							
5	3	5	5	5	4	3	5	5	5	1	2		4	2	1	1				
	1										1	3					2			
			1				1	2	1				1	1						

League Table

	P	W	D	L	F	A	Pts
Wolverhampton W.	46	26	14	6	96	49	92
Sheffield United	46	25	9	12	93	54	84
Port Vale	46	24	12	10	78	48	84
Fulham	46	22	9	15	69	67	75
Bristol Rovers	46	19	17	10	67	51	74
Preston North End	46	19	15	12	79	60	72
Brentford	46	18	14	14	66	61	68
Chester City	46	19	11	16	64	61	68
Notts County	46	18	13	15	64	54	67
Bolton Wanderers	46	16	16	14	58	54	64
Bristol City	46	18	9	19	53	55	63
Swansea City	46	15	16	15	51	53	61
Bury	46	16	13	17	55	67	61
Huddersfield Town	46	17	9	20	63	73	60
Mansfield Town	46	14	17	15	48	52	59
Cardiff City	46	14	15	17	44	56	57
Wigan Athletic	46	14	14	18	55	53	56
Reading	46	15	11	20	68	72	56
Blackpool	46	14	13	19	56	59	55
Northampton Town	46	16	6	24	66	76	54
Southend United	46	13	15	18	56	75	54
Chesterfield	46	14	7	25	51	86	49
Gillingham	46	12	4	30	47	81	40
Aldershot	46	8	13	25	48	78	37

1989-90

Division Three

Manager: Jimmy Mullen

Did you know that?

Blackpool reached the Final of the Manx Cup for the first time, where they lost to Blackburn Rovers on 15 August at Bloomfield Road by one goal to nil.

Despite an impressive FA Cup run, which saw the team in the fifth round for the first time since 1959, the team were relegated and Jimmy Mullen was sacked after just 11 months in charge.

Match No.	Date	Venue	Opponents	Result		Scorers	Attendance
1	Aug 19	H	Wigan Athletic	D	0-0		4,561
2	26	A	Notts County	W	1-0	Burgess	4,852
3	Sep 2	H	Shrewsbury Town	L	0-1		4,109
4	9	A	Bristol City	L	0-2		7,172
5	16	H	Crewe Alexandra	L	1-3	Briggs	4,722
6	23	A	Mansfield Town	W	3-0	Gabbiadini 2, Diamond	2,629
7	26	A	Preston NE	L	1-2	Madden	8,920
8	30	H	Birmingham City	W	3-2	Own-goal, Garner (pen), Gabbiadini	5,737
9	Oct 6	H	Reading	D	0-0		3,321
10	14	A	Leyton Orient	L	0-2		4,126
11	17	A	Northampton Town	L	2-4	Briggs, Garner (pen)	3,098
12	21	H	Cardiff City	W	1-0	Owen	3,502
13	28	A	Rotherham Utd	D	1-1	Garner	5,570
14	31	H	Bury	L	0-1		4,184
15	Nov 4	A	Bristol Rovers	D	1-1	Madden	5,520
16	11	H	Brentford	W	4-0	Madden 2 (1 pen), Eyres, Morgan	2,512
17	25	H	Tranmere Rovers	L	0-3		4,106
18	Dec 2	A	Swansea City	D	0-0		4,029
19	16	H	Fulham	L	0-1		2,548
20	26	A	Bolton Wanderers	L	0-2		9,944
21	30	A	Chester City	L	0-2		2,405
22	Jan 1	H	Huddersfield Town	D	2-2	Methven, Garner (pen)	5,097
23	13	H	Notts County	D	0-0		3,146
24	20	A	Wigan Athletic	D	1-1	Garner	3,179
25	Feb 3	H	Mansfield Town	W	3-1	Owen, Garner (pen), Richards	4,402
26	10	A	Crewe Alexandra	L	0-2		3,978
27	13	A	Shrewsbury Town	D	1-1	Eyres	2,300
28	23	A	Tranmere Rovers	L	2-4	Garner (pen), Eyres	7,873
29	Mar 3	H	Walsall	W	4-3	Bradshaw, Eyres, Methven, Groves	3,174
30	6	A	Birmingham City	L	1-3	Richards	6,738
31	10	H	Preston NE	D	2-2	Brook, Garner (pen)	8,108
32	13	H	Bristol City	L	1-3	Brook	3,227
33	17	A	Reading	D	1-1	Owen	3,752
34	20	H	Leyton Orient	W	1-0	Richards	2,746
35	24	H	Northampton Town	W	1-0	Eyres	3,290
36	27	A	Walsall	D	1-1	Richards	3,134
37	31	A	Cardiff City	D	2-2	Eyres, Brook	2,850
38	Apr 7	H	Rotherham Utd	L	1-2	Brook	3,508
39	10	A	Bury	L	0-2		3,133
40	14	A	Huddersfield Town	D	2-2	Coughlin, Gouck	4,845
41	16	H	Bolton Wanderers	W	2-1	Brook, Eyres	5,438
42	21	A	Fulham	D	0-0		3,816
43	24	H	Chester City	L	1-3	Methven	3,724
44	28	A	Brentford	L	0-5		4,784
45	30	H	Swansea City	D	2-2	Owen, Brook	1,842
46	May 5	H	Bristol Rovers	L	0-3		6,776

Final League Position: 23rd in Division Three

Apps
Sub Apps
Gls

FA Cup

1	Nov 18	H	Bolton Wanderers	W	2-1	Eyres, Garner	7,309
2	Dec 9	H	Chester City	W	3-0	Brook, Burgess, Owen	4,099
3	Jan 6	H	Burnley	W	1-0	Methven	8,091
4	27	H	Torquay Utd	W	1-0	Owen	6,781
5	Feb 18	H	Queens Park Rangers	D	2-2	Groves, Eyres	9,641
5R	21	A	Queens Park Rangers	D	0-0*		15,323
5R2	26	A	Queens Park Rangers	L	0-3		12,775

* after extra-time

Apps
Sub Apps
Gls

League Cup

1	Aug 22	H	Burnley	D	2-2	Briggs, Garner	4,540
	29	A	Burnley	W	1-0	Bradshaw	6,083
2	Sep 19	A	Barnsley	D	1-1	Gabbiadini	7,515
	Oct 3	H	Barnsley	D	1-1*	Briggs	5,259
3	Oct 25	A	Exeter City	L	0-3		6,508

* after extra-time. Blackpool won 5-4 on penalties

Apps
Sub Apps
Gls

McIlhargey	Burgess	Morgan	Gore	Briggs	Matthews	Bradshaw	Sinclair	Garner	Coughlin	Wright	Madden	Methven	Owen	Eyres	Thompson	Elliott	Diamond	Gabbiadini	Bartram	Davies	Brook	Hawkins	Wood	Jones	Groves	Gouck	Richards	Gayle
1	2	3	4	5	6	7*	8	9#	10	11	12	14																
1	2	3	4	5		6		9*	10	11	8	7	12															
1	2	2	4#	5	14	11		10*	8	7	9	6			12													
1	2	3	4	5	10	11*		9		7		6			8	12												
1	2	3	4	5	14			10		12			7	11*		6#	8	9										
1	2	3	4	11				10				5	7			6	8	9										
1	2*	3	4	11		6#		10	14	12	8	5	7					9										
1	2	3	4	11				10	8			5	7			6		9										
1	2	3	4	11				10	8	12		5	7			6*		9										
1	2	3	4	11	6*		12	10	8			5	7	9														
1	2	3	4*	11			9	10	8	6		5	7	12														
1	2	3		6			9*	10	8	12		5	7	11	4													
	2			11				10	4	3	8	5	7			6			1			9						
	2			11				10	4	3	8	5	7*	12		6			1			9						
	2	3		11			12	10	4		8	5	7			6			1			9*						
	2	3		11				10#			8	5	7*	9		6			1	12		14						
1		3	2		7#			10	4*		8	5	12	11		6				14	9							
	7	3	2					10	4		8	5	9	11		6			1									
	2	3*	7					10	4			5	9	11		6			1	12	8							
	2*		7					10	4	3	14	5	9#	11		6			1	12	8							
		12	7		14			10	4	3		5		11		6			1	2#	9	8*						
		3	7					10	4	2		5	9	11		6			1		8							
1		3	7					10	4	2		5	9*	11		6					8	12						
1		3	7	11		8		10	4*	2		5	9#			6	14			12								
1		3	7			14		10#	4	2		5	9*	12		6									8		11	
1		3	7			14		10	4#	2		5		11*		6				12					8		9	
1		3	7			9		10	4	2		5		12		6*									8		11	
1		3	7			6#		10	4	2		5	14	12							9				8*		11	
1		3#	7			6		10	4*	2		5		9						14	12				8		11	
1		3	7			6#		10		2		5		9						14	8*	12			4		11	
1		3*	7			12		10		2		5		9						6	8				4		11	
		3	7					10		2*		5		9		6				12	8		1		4		11	
			2			3		10	7#			5	12	9*		6					8		1		4	14	11	
						3		10	7			5		9		6				2	8		1		4		11	
						3		10				5		9		6				7	8		1	2	4		11	
						3		10				5		9		6				7	8		1	2	4		11	
						3		10				5	12	9*		6				7	8		1	2	4		11	
		12	6			3	14	10	11*			5		9						7	8#		1	2	4			
		3	6					10	11			5		9						7	8		1	2	4			
		3	6					10	11*			5		9							8		1	2	12	4	11	
		3	6					10	7			5		9						2	8		1		4	12	11*	
		3	6		2			10	11			5		9						7	8		1			4		
		3	6		14			10	7#			5	12	9						2	8		1			4	11*	
		3			6		12	10	11			5	7	9						2	8*		1			4		
		3			6	11#	7	10*				5	12	9						2	14		1		8	4		
		3			6	14	7	12				8	11	9						2	8		1		10*	4		
22	19	36	34	17	8	17	5	45	33	20	9	44	21	30	2	25	2	5	9	14	23	4	15	6	18	6	16	
		2			4	4	4	1	1	4	2	1	7	5	1	1	1			9	2	3			1	2		
	1	1		2		1		8	1		4	3	4	7			1	3			6				1	1	4	

McIlhargey	Burgess	Morgan	Gore	Briggs	Matthews	Bradshaw	Sinclair	Garner	Coughlin	Wright	Madden	Methven	Owen	Eyres	Thompson	Elliott	Diamond	Gabbiadini	Bartram	Davies	Brook	Hawkins	Wood	Jones	Groves	Gouck	Richards	Gayle
1		3			7*			10	4		8	5		11		6				12	9					2		
1	2	3						10	4			5	9	11		6*				12	8					7		
1		3						10	4	2		5	9	11		6					8					7		
1		3				12		10	4*	2		5	9#	11		6				14					8	7		
1		3				6		10	4	2		5	12	11							9*				8	7		
1		3*				6		10		2		5	4#	11			14			12	9				8	7		
1		3#				6		10	4*	2		5	14	11						12	9				8	7		
7	1	7			1	3		7	6	5	1	7	4	7		4					6				4	7		
						1							2				1			5								
	1							1				1	2	2							1				1			

McIlhargey	Burgess	Morgan	Gore	Briggs	Matthews	Bradshaw	Sinclair	Garner	Coughlin	Wright	Madden	Methven	Owen	Eyres	Thompson	Elliott	Diamond	Gabbiadini	Bartram	Davies	Brook	Hawkins	Wood	Jones	Groves	Gouck	Richards	Gayle
1	2	3	4	5				9	10	11	8	7		6*	12													
1	2	3	4	5		11		10	8	7	9	6																
1	2	3*	4	11				10		12	14	5	7			6	8#	9										
1	2*	3	4#	11				10	8	12		5	7	14		6		9										
	2	3		11				10	8	6	12	5	7		4*							9						
4	5	5	4	5		1		5	4	3	2	5	3	1	1	2	1	2				1						
										2	2			1	1													
				2		1		1										1										

League Table

	P	W	D	L	F	A	Pts
Bristol Rovers	46	26	15	5	71	35	93
Bristol City	46	27	10	9	76	40	91
Notts County	46	25	12	9	73	53	87
Tranmere Rovers	46	23	11	12	86	49	80
Bury	46	21	11	14	70	49	74
Bolton Wanderers	46	18	15	13	59	48	69
Birmingham City	46	18	12	16	60	59	66
Huddersfield Town	46	17	14	15	61	62	65
Rotherham United	46	17	13	16	71	62	64
Reading	46	15	19	12	57	53	64
Shrewsbury Town	46	16	15	15	59	54	63
Crewe Alexandra	46	15	17	14	56	53	62
Brentford	46	18	7	21	66	66	61
Leyton Orient	46	16	10	20	52	56	58
Mansfield Town	46	16	7	23	50	65	55
Chester City	46	13	15	18	43	55	54
Swansea City	46	14	12	20	45	63	54
Wigan Athletic	46	13	14	19	48	64	53
Preston North End	46	14	10	22	65	79	52
Fulham	46	12	15	19	55	66	51
Cardiff City	46	12	14	20	51	70	50
Northampton Town	46	11	14	21	51	68	47
Blackpool	46	10	16	20	49	73	46
Walsall	46	9	14	23	40	72	41

1990-91

Division Four

Manager: Graham Carr/Billy Ayre

Did you know that?

Graham Carr became the shortest-serving manager in Blackpool's history when he was sacked after just four months in charge.

Billy Ayre took over and the team created two new home records. From November 1990 to November the following year, Blackpool were unbeaten in 24 home games and won 15 in a row.

On 22 May 1991 Stan Mortensen died, just a day after Blackpool had made the Play-off Final at Wembley

The penalty shoot out against Torquay United was the first time promotion would be decided that way.

Despite failing to gain promotion, Billy Ayre was rewarded with a new contract and a directorship of the club.

Match No.	Date	Venue	Opponents	Result		Scorers	Attendance
1	Aug 25	A	Scunthorpe Utd	L	0-2		3,024
2	Sep 1	H	Rochdale	D	0-0		3,357
3	8	A	Northampton Town	L	0-1		4,300
4	15	H	Wrexham	W	4-1	Stant, Eyres, Own-goal, Rodwell	3,497
5	18	H	Burnley	L	1-2	Stant	4,737
6	22	A	Chesterfield	D	2-2	Groves, Garner (pen)	3,549
7	29	H	Hartlepool Utd	W	2-0	Eyres, Groves	3,181
8	Oct 3	A	Scarborough	W	1-0	Groves	1,713
9	6	A	Torquay Utd	L	1-2	Stant	2,884
10	13	H	Darlington	L	1-2	Garner	4,092
11	20	H	Gillingham	W	2-0	Stant, Eyres	3,041
12	22	A	Stockport County	D	0-0		4,337
13	27	A	Halifax Town	L	3-5	Rodwell 2, Stant	1,945
14	Nov 3	H	Walsall	L	1-2	Groves	3,233
15	10	H	Aldershot	W	4-2	Sinclair, Taylor, Garner (pen), Lancaster	2,065
16	24	A	Doncaster Rovers	L	0-1		2,113
17	Dec 1	A	Hereford Utd	D	1-1	Bamber	2,588
18	15	H	Maidstone Utd	D	2-2	Garner, Bamber	2,341
19	23	A	Carlisle Utd	L	0-1		5,195
20	26	H	Peterborough Utd	D	1-1	Garner	3,658
21	29	H	Lincoln City	W	5-0	Groves 2 (1 pen), Bamber 2, Eyres	2,519
22	Jan 1	A	York City	W	1-0	Horner	3,115
23	12	A	Rochdale	L	1-2	Bamber	2,621
24	19	H	Scunthorpe Utd	W	3-1	Bamber 2, Garner	2,494
25	26	A	Wrexham	W	1-0	Garner (pen)	2,393
26	Feb 5	H	Chesterfield	W	3-0	Bamber, Horner, Garner	2,357
27	16	H	Doncaster Rovers	W	2-0	Taylor, Horner	3,533
28	23	A	Aldershot	W	4-1	Bamber 2, Garner 2	2,164
29	Mar 2	H	Hereford Utd	W	3-0	Bamber 2, Richards	3,636
30	9	A	Maidstone Utd	D	1-1	Richards	2,253
31	12	H	Scarborough	W	3-1	Richards, Taylor, Bamber	3,798
32	16	A	Hartlepool Utd	W	2-1	Horner, Rodwell	2,840
33	19	A	Darlington	D	1-1	Own-goal	4,108
34	23	H	Torquay Utd	W	1-0	Bamber	4,778
35	30	A	Peterborough Utd	L	0-2		7,721
36	Apr 2	H	Carlisle Utd	W	6-0	Bamber 2, Horner, Groves (pen), Rodwell, Richards	5,368
37	6	A	Lincoln City	W	1-0	Bamber	4,003
38	13	H	York City	W	1-0	Groves	5,086
39	17	H	Cardiff City	W	3-0	Groves, Horner, Rodwell	4,813
40	20	A	Gillingham	D	2-2	Davies, Horner	3,028
41	23	A	Burnley	L	0-2		18,398
42	27	H	Stockport County	W	3-2	Eyres, Groves 2	8,590
43	30	H	Halifax Town	W	2-0	Rodwell, Groves	5,883
44	May 2	A	Cardiff City	D	1-1	Garner (pen)	1,793
45	7	H	Northampton Town	W	2-1	Eyres, Groves	7,298
46	11	A	Walsall	L	0-2		8,051

Final League Position: 5th in Division Four

Apps
Sub Apps
Gls

Play Offs

SF	May 19	A	Scunthorpe Utd	D	1-1	Rodwell	6,536
	22	H	Scunthorpe Utd	W	2-1	Eyres 2	7,596
F	31	N	Torquay Utd	D	2-2*	Groves, Own-goal	21,615

* - after extra-time. Torquay won after penalties

App
Subs
Goals

FA CUP

1	Nov 17	H	Grimsby Town	W	2-0	Groves, Garner	4,175
2	Dec 10	H	Huddersfield Town	W	2-0	Groves, Own-goal	6,329
3	Jan 5	H	Tottenham Hotspur	L	0-1		9,563

Apps
Sub Apps
Gls

League Cup

1	Aug 28	A	Darlington	D	0-0		2,254
	Sep 4	H	Darlington	D	1-1*	Brook	1,696

* - after extra-time. Darlington won on away goals

Apps
Sub Apps
Gls

Mcllhargey	Gore	Bradshaw	Groves	Briggs	Wright M	Sinclair	Brook	Lancaster	Garner	Eyres	Taylor	Rodwell	Wright A	Stant	Davies	Hedworth	Horner	Gouck	Smalley	Owen	Barber	Bamber	Richards
1	2	3#	4	5	6	7	8*	9	10	11	12	14											
1	2		4	5	6	7	8	9*	10	11	12		7										
1	2		4	5*	6	7		9	10	11		14	3	8	12								
1	6		4			12		9#	10	11		7	3	8*	14	2	12						
1	6		4			12		9	10	11		7	3	8#	12	2*	14						
1	6		4			8			10	11		7	3	9	2		5						
1	6		4			8			10	11		7*	3	9	12	2	5						
1	6		4			8			10	11		7	3	9		2	5						
1			4			8			10*	11		7	3	9	12	2	5		9				
1			4	5		14	8#		10	11		7	3	9	12	2			6*				
1			4	5		8			10	11		7	3	9		2			6				
1			4	5		8			10	11		7	3	9		2			6				
1	12		4			8			10	11		7	3	9	14	2*	5		6#				
1			4			12		8*	10	11	14	7	3	9#	2		5		6				
1	6		4			9		8	10		11*	7	3		2		5			12			
1	6		4	5		9*			10	11	12	7	3			2	8						
	6		4	5		9			10			7	3			2	8				1	11	
1	6		4	5		9			10			7	3		2		8*					11	12
	6		4	5		9			10	11*		7	3		2		8				1		12
1	6		4	5		9			10*	14		7#	3		2		8					11	12
1	6		4	5		9				11		7	3		2		8					10	
1	6		4	5		9	12			11*		7	3		2		8					10	
1	6		4*	5		12			10	11		7	3		2		8					9	
1	6		4						10		11	7	3		2	5	8					9	
1	6		4						10		11	7	3		2	5	8					9	
1	6		4			14			10	12	11*	7#	3		2	5	8					9	
1	6		4			12			10		11	7*	3		2	5	8					9	
1	6		4						10		11	7	3		2	5	8					9*	12
1	6		4						10*		11	7	3		2	5	8					9	12
1	6		4	5						14	11	7#	3			2	8*	12				9	10
1	6		4	5							11	7	3		8	2						9	10
1	6		4	5						12	11*	7	3		2		8	14				9	10#
1	6		4	5							11	7	3		2		8					9	10
1	6		4	5						12	11#	7*	3		2		8	14				9	10
1	6		4	5						12	11*	7	3		2		8#	14				9	10
1	6		4							11	14	7	3		2	5*	8	12#				9	10
1	6		4	5		2				11		7	3				8					9	10
1	6		4	5					12	11		7	3		2		8					9	10*
1	6		4	5					12	11		7	3		2		8					9*	10
1	6		4	5		12			10*	11		7	3		2		8						9
1	6		4	5		12		14	10	11		7*	3		2		8						9#
1	6		4	5		12			10	11		7	3		2		8						9*
1	6		4	5					10	11		7	3		2		8					9*	12
1	6		4	5		12			10	11		7	3		2		8						9*
1	6		4	5					10	11		7	3		2		8						9
1	6		4	5#		12			10	11	14	7	3		2		8						9*
44	40	1	46	30	3	19	3	7	34	30	13	43	45	12	30	20	37		6		2	23	16
	1					12	1	1	2	6	6	2			7		2	5		1			6
			11			1		1	13	6	3	7		5	1		7					17	4

Mcllhargey	Gore	Bradshaw	Groves	Briggs	Wright M	Sinclair	Brook	Lancaster	Garner	Eyres	Taylor	Rodwell	Wright A	Stant	Davies	Hedworth	Horner	Gouck	Smalley	Owen	Barber	Bamber	Richards
1	6		4	5					10	11	9	7	3		2		8						
1	6		4	5*		12			10	11	9	7	3		2		8						
1	6		4			12			10	11	8	7	3		2*		5					9	
3	3		3	2					3	3	3	3	1		3		3					1	
						2																	
			1							2		1											

10

Mcllhargey	Gore	Bradshaw	Groves	Briggs	Wright M	Sinclair	Brook	Lancaster	Garner	Eyres	Taylor	Rodwell	Wright A	Stant	Davies	Hedworth	Horner	Gouck	Smalley	Owen	Barber	Bamber	Richards
1	6		4	5*		9			10			7	3		12	2	8						11
1	6		4	5		12			10	11*		7	3			2	8						9
1	6		4	5		9			10			7	3			2	8					11	
3	3		3	3		2			3	1		3				3	3					1	2
						1							2		1								
			2						1												1		

Mcllhargey	Gore	Bradshaw	Groves	Briggs	Wright M	Sinclair	Brook	Lancaster	Garner	Eyres	Taylor	Rodwell	Wright A	Stant	Davies	Hedworth	Horner	Gouck	Smalley	Owen	Barber	Bamber	Richards
1	6	3	4	5		7	8	9*	10	11			2										12
1	6	3#	4	5		7	8	9*	10	11	12	14	2										
2	2	2	2	2		2	2	2	2	2			2										
										2	1	1											1
							1																

League Table

	P	W	D	L	F	A	Pts
Darlington	46	22	17	7	68	38	83
Stockport County	46	23	13	10	84	47	82
Hartlepool United	46	24	10	12	67	48	82
Peterborough United	46	21	17	8	67	45	80
Blackpool	46	23	10	13	78	47	79
Burnley	46	23	10	13	70	51	79
Torquay United	46	18	18	10	64	47	72
Scunthorpe United	46	20	11	15	71	62	71
Scarborough	46	19	12	15	59	56	69
Northampton Town	46	18	13	15	57	58	67
Doncaster Rovers	46	17	14	15	56	46	65
Rochdale	46	15	17	14	50	53	62
Cardiff City	46	15	15	16	43	54	60
Lincoln City	46	14	17	15	50	61	59
Gillingham	46	12	18	16	57	60	54
Walsall	46	12	17	17	48	51	53
Hereford United	46	13	14	19	53	58	53
Chesterfield	46	13	14	19	47	62	53
Maidstone United	46	13	12	21	66	71	51
Carlisle United	46	13	9	24	47	89	48
York City	46	11	13	22	45	57	46
Halifax Town	46	12	10	24	59	79	46
Aldershot	46	10	11	25	61	101	41
Wrexham	46	10	10	26	48	74	40

1991-92

Division Four

Manager: Billy Ayre

Did you know that?

Aldershot went out of business, so the six goals that Blackpool had scored against them over two matches were expunged from the record books.

Alan Wright was sold to Blackburn Rovers for a then club record fee of £400,000.

When Blackpool were promoted, they became one of the founder members of the new Second Division after the formation of the Premier League.

Match No.	Date	Venue	Opponents	Result		Scorers	Attendance
1	Aug 17	H	Walsall	W	3-0	Horner, Eyres, Garner	4,141
2	24	A	Carlisle Utd	W	2-1	Rodwell, Bamber	4,399
3	31	H	Scunthorpe Utd	W	2-1	Groves, Own-goal	3,273
4	Sep 3	A	York City	L	0-1		2,686
5	7	A	Mansfield Town	D	1-1	Bamber	2,629
6	14	H	Cardiff City	D	1-1	Horner	3,931
7	17	H	Gillingham	W	2-0	Bamber 2	3,055
8	20	A	Doncaster Rovers	W	2-0	Bamber, Taylor	2,428
9	28	H	Rotherham Utd	W	3-0	Groves, Rodwell, Eyres	5,356
10	Oct 5	A	Northampton Town	D	1-1	Sinclair	3,355
11	13	H	Lincoln City	W	3-0	Groves (pen), Horner, Bamber	5,086
12	10	A	Barnet	L	0-3		5,085
13	Nov 2	H	Scarborough	D	1-1	Groves	3,057
14	5	A	Aldershot	W	5-2	Rodwell 3 (1 pen), Groves, Bamber	1,685
15	9	A	Chesterfield	D	1-1	Taylor	4,917
16	19	H	Wrexham	W	4-0	Sinclair 2, Bamber 2	2,842
17	23	H	Crewe Alexandra	L	0-2		4,434
18	30	H	Halifax Town	W	3-0	Bamber 2, Groves	3,118
19	Dec 14	A	Rochdale	L	2-4	Rodwell, Bamber	2,892
20	21	H	Carlisle Utd	W	1-0	Bamber	3,440
21	26	A	Walsall	L	2-4	Bamber, Eyres	4,675
22	28	A	Scunthorpe Utd	L	1-2	Groves	4,271
23	Jan 1	H	York City	W	3-1	Gouck, Bamber, Eyres	3,534
24	4	A	Maidstone Utd	D	0-0		1,774
25	11	H	Burnley	W	5-2	Rodwell 2, Kerr, Bamber, Garner	8,007
26	18	A	Hereford Utd	W	2-1	Bamber 2	3,008
27	Feb 8	A	Wrexham	D	1-1	Garner (pen)	4,053
28	12	A	Halifax Town	W	2-1	Rodwell, Bamber	2,158
29	15	H	Rochdale	W	3-0	Groves, Gouck, Eyres	4,652
30	18	H	Barnet	W	4-2	Groves, Rodwell, Bamber, Eyres	5,149
31	22	A	Burnley	D	1-1	Bamber	18,215
32	29	H	Maidstone Utd	D	1-1	Garner	4,136
33	Mar 3	H	Hereford Utd	W	2-0	Groves, Bamber	3,560
34	10	H	Aldershot	W	1-0	Eyres	3,728
35	14	A	Scarborough	W	2-1	Bamber, Eyres	1,965
36	21	H	Chesterfield	W	3-1	Rodwell, Davies, Bamber	4,447
37	28	A	Crewe Alexandra	L	0-1		4,913
38	31	A	Cardiff City	D	1-1	Bamber	8,430
39	Apr 4	H	Mansfield Town	W	2-1	Bamber 2	6,055
40	11	A	Gillingham	L	2-3	Horner, Eyres	3,684
41	14	H	Doncaster Rovers	W	1-0	Eyres (pen)	4,353
42	20	A	Rotherham Utd	L	0-2		8,992
43	25	H	Northampton Town	W	1-0	Bamber	5,915
44	May 2	A	Lincoln City	L	0-2		7,884
Final League Position: 4th in Division Four							Apps
							Sub Apps
							Gls

Play Offs

SF	May 10	A	Barnet	L	0-1		5,629
	13	H	Barnet	W	2-0	Groves, Garner (pen)	7,588
F	25	N	Scunthorpe Utd	D	1-1*	Bamber	22,741
							App
							Subs
							Goals

FA CUP

1	Nov 16	H	Grimsby Town	W	2-1	Groves, Bamber	4,074
2	Dec 7	H	Hull City	L	0-1		4,554
							Apps
							Sub Apps
							Gls

League Cup

1	Aug 20	A	Mansfield Town	W	3-0	Bamber 2, Own-goal	2,124
	27	H	Mansfield Town	W	4-2	Bamber 3, Groves	2,155
2	Sep 24	H	Barnsley	W	1-0	Bamber	4,123
	Oct 8	A	Barnsley	L	0-2*		6,315
*-after extra-time						Apps	4
							Sub Apps
							Gls

McIlhargey	Davies	Wright	Groves	Stoneman	Gore	Rodwell	Horner	Bamber	Garner	Eyres	Richards	Gouck	Hedworth	Sinclair	Taylor	Briggs	Brook	Burgess	Murray	Mitchell	Bonner	Howard	Kerr	Kearton	Leitch	Cook	Murphy
1	2#	3	4	5	6	7	8*	9	10	11	12	14															
1	2	3	4	5	6	7		9	10	11		8	14														
1	2	3	4		6	7	5	9	10	11	12	8*															
1	2	3	4	5#	6	7	8	9	10*	11	12	14															
1	2	3	4		6	7	8	9	10	11			5														
1	2	3	4		6	7	8	9	10#	11			5	14													
1	2	3	4		6	7	8	9#	12	11				14	10*	5											
1	2	3*	4		6	7	8	9	12	11				10		5											
1	2	3	4		6	7	8	9		11				10		5											
1	2	3	4		6	7	8	9		11				10		5											
1	2	3	4		6	7	8	9		11				10		5											
1	2*	3	4	12	6	7	8	9		11				10#	14	5											
1			4		6	7	8	9		11				14		5	10#	2	3*	12							
1			4	3	6	7	8*	9		11				10		5		2			12	14					
1			4	3	6	7		9		11				10	14	5#		2			8						
1	12		4	3	6	7	8#	9		11				10	14	5		2*									
1	12		4	3	6*	7	8#	9		11				10	14	5		2									
1	2		4	3		7		9	12	11			6	10*	14	5					8#						
1	2*		4	3	6	7		9	11			8#	5	10	14						12						
1			4	3	6	7		9		11		8		10		5		2									
1			4	3	6	7		9	12	11		8*		10#	14	5		2									
1			4	3	6	7		9	5	11		8			10			2									
1			4	3	6	7		9	10	11		8						2	3								
1			4	3	6	7		9	10	11		8						2					5				
			4	3	6	7		9	10	11		8						2					5	1			
	2		4		6	7		9	10	11		8				5							3	1			
	2*		4		6	7		9	10	11		8		12		5							3	1			
	2		4		6	7		9	10	11		8				5							3	1			
	2		4		6	7*	14	9	10	11		8#		12		5							3	1			
	2		4		6	7		9	10	11		8				5							3	1			
	2		4		6	7*		9	10	11		8		12		5							3	1			
	2		4		6		14	9	10	11		8#		7*		5							3	1	12		
	2		4		6		8	9#	10*	11		14		12		5							3	1	7		
	2#		4		6	7	8	9		11		14		12		5							3	1	10*		
	2		4		6	7	8	9	10*	11				12		5							3	1			
	2		4		6	7	8	9	10	11				12		5#							3	1	14*		
			4		6	7	8	9	10	11		5						2						1		3	
			4		6	7#	8	9	10	11		5		12				2						1		3	
	2		4		6	7*	8	9	10	11		5												1	12	3	
1	2*		4	14	6	7	8	9	10	11		5#													12	3	
1			4	5	6	7	8	9	10*	11				12				2								3	
1			4		6	7#	8	9	10	11		14		12		5		2								3*	
1	12		4	5	6	7#	8	9		11				10*				2							14	3	
1			4	5	6	7	8	9		11				10				2								3	
29	27	12	44	18	43	42	27	44	27	43		20	4	16	2	26	1	17	2		2		13	15	2	8	
	3			2			2		4		3	5		13	7					1	2	1			5		
	1		10			11	8	28	4	10		2		3	2								1				

McIlhargey	Davies	Wright	Groves	Stoneman	Gore	Rodwell	Horner	Bamber	Garner	Eyres	Richards	Gouck	Hedworth	Sinclair	Taylor	Briggs	Brook	Burgess	Murray	Mitchell	Bonner	Howard	Kerr	Kearton	Leitch	Cook	Murphy
1	7*		4		6	14	8	9		11		5#		10				2	12							3	
1	5		4		6	7	8	9	10	11			3					2								3	
1	5*		4		6	7	8#	9	10	11			3	14				2								3	12
3	3		3		3	2	3	3	2	3		1	1	1				3								3	
						1								1					1								1
			1					1	1																		

10

McIlhargey	Davies	Wright	Groves	Stoneman	Gore	Rodwell	Horner	Bamber	Garner	Eyres	Richards	Gouck	Hedworth	Sinclair	Taylor	Briggs	Brook	Burgess	Murray	Mitchell	Bonner	Howard	Kerr	Kearton	Leitch	Cook	Murphy
1			4	3	6	7	8	9		11			3	10		5		2									
1	2*		4	3		7		9	12				6	10*	11						8	14					3
2	1		2	2	1	2	1	2		1			1	2	1	1		1			1						
									1													1					
			1					1																			

McIlhargey	Davies	Wright	Groves	Stoneman	Gore	Rodwell	Horner	Bamber	Garner	Eyres	Richards	Gouck	Hedworth	Sinclair	Taylor	Briggs	Brook	Burgess	Murray	Mitchell	Bonner	Howard	Kerr	Kearton	Leitch	Cook	Murphy
1	2	3	4	5	6	7		9	10	11		8															
1	2	3	4*	5	6	7		9	10	11	12	8															
1	2*	3	4		6	7	8	9	12	11				10		5											
1	2	3	4	12	6	7*	8	9		11				10		5											
4	4	4	3	4	4	2	4	2	4		2		2		2												
				1					1		1																
			1					6																			

League Table

	P	W	D	L	F	A	Pts
Burnley	42	25	8	9	79	43	83
Rotherham United	42	22	11	9	70	37	77
Mansfield Town	42	23	8	11	75	53	77
Blackpool	42	22	10	10	71	45	76
Scunthorpe United	42	21	9	12	64	59	72
Crewe Alexandra	42	20	10	12	66	51	70
Barnet	42	21	6	15	81	61	69
Rochdale	42	18	13	11	57	53	67
Cardiff City	42	17	15	10	66	53	66
Lincoln City	42	17	11	14	50	44	62
Gillingham	42	15	12	15	63	53	57
Scarborough	42	15	12	15	64	68	57
Chesterfield	42	14	11	17	49	61	53
Wrexham	42	14	9	19	52	73	51
Walsall	42	12	13	17	48	58	49
Northampton Town	42	11	13	18	46	57	46
Hereford United	42	12	8	22	44	57	44
Maidstone United	42	8	18	16	45	56	42
York City	42	8	16	18	42	58	40
Halifax Town	42	10	8	24	34	75	38
Doncaster Rovers	42	9	8	25	40	65	35
Carlisle United	42	7	13	22	41	67	34

1992-93

Division Two

Manager: Billy Ayre

Did you know that?

Hartlepool United had gone a record 13 League games without a goal, until they came to Bloomfield Road.

The game against Rotherham United on 16 January was billed as a 'buy a player' League match. Money from the gate receipts would be given to manager Billy Ayre to purchase a new player. He bought Andy Watson who became a fans' favourite.

Blackpool only just avoided relegation, but took pleasure in seeing rivals Preston go down to the basement division.

Match No.	Date	Venue	Opponents	Result		Scorers	Attendance
1	Aug 15	A	West Brom Albion	L	1-3	Rodwell	16,527
2	22	H	Exeter City	W	2-0	Robinson, Sinclair	3,999
3	29	A	Leyton Orient	L	0-1		4,310
4	Sep 1	A	Bolton Wanderers	L	0-3		7,291
5	5	A	Mansfield Town	D	1-1	Duffield	4,322
6	12	A	Swansea City	L	0-3		3,861
7	15	H	Bournemouth	W	2-0	Eyres, Robinson	3,455
8	19	H	Brighton & Hove Albion	D	2-2	Stringfellow, Sinclair	4,618
9	26	A	Rotherham Utd	L	2-3	Horner, Sinclair	4,408
10	Oct 2	A	Hartlepool Utd	L	0-1		2,837
11	10	H	Preston NE	L	2-3	Sinclair, Briggs	7,631
12	16	A	Stockport County	D	0-0		5,680
13	24	H	Burnley	L	1-3	Gouck	7,942
14	31	A	Port Vale	L	1-2	Eyres	7,057
15	Nov 3	H	Huddersfield Town	D	2-2	Mitchell, Eyres	3,441
16	7	A	Reading	D	0-0		4,163
17	18	H	Stoke City	L	1-3	Ward	8,028
18	28	A	Hull City	L	2-3	Eyres, Horner	3,906
19	Dec 12	A	Wigan Athletic	L	1-2	Gouck	2,492
20	20	H	Fulham	D	1-1	Horner	3,802
21	26	H	Bradford City	D	3-3	Gouck 2, Eyres (pen)	5,448
22	28	A	Chester City	W	2-1	Sinclair, Eyres	3,787
23	Jan 5	H	Swansea City	D	0-0		3,417
24	9	A	Bournemouth	L	1-5	Bamber	3,807
25	16	H	Rotherham Utd	W	2-0	Bamber, Horner	6,144
26	26	H	Leyton Orient	W	3-1	Eyres, Bamber, Sinclair	3,164
27	30	A	Exeter City	W	1-0	Bamber	3,384
28	Feb 6	H	West Brom Albion	W	2-1	Horner 2	9,386
29	13	A	Mansfield Town	D	2-2	Eyres 2 (2 pen)	3,593
30	20	H	Bolton Wanderers	D	1-1	Eyres (pen)	8,054
31	27	A	Preston NE	D	3-3	Davies, Watson 2	10,403
32	Mar 6	H	Hartlepool Utd	D	1-1	Horner	4,926
33	9	A	Plymouth Argyle	L	1-2	Bamber	5,959
34	13	H	Reading	L	0-1		4,160
35	20	A	Huddersfield Town	L	2-5	Bamber 2	6,249
36	23	H	Hull City	W	5-1	Bamber 2, Sinclair, Eyres, Leitch	3,515
37	27	A	Stoke City	W	1-0	Sinclair	17,918
38	31	A	Brighton & Hove Albion	D	1-1	Sinclair	5,170
39	Apr 3	H	Plymouth Argyle	D	1-1	Eyres	4,397
40	6	H	Wigan Athletic	W	2-1	Eyres 2 (1 pen)	5,096
41	10	A	Bradford City	L	0-2		6,191
42	13	H	Chester City	W	2-0	Eyres (pen), Bamber	5,078
43	17	A	Fulham	L	0-1		4,633
44	24	H	Stockport County	W	2-0	Sinclair, Bamber	7,205
45	May 1	A	Burnley	D	2-2	Sinclair, Bamber	12,475
46	8	H	Port Vale	L	2-4	Eyres, Bamber	9,295

Final League Position: 18th in Division Two

Apps
Sub Apps
Gls

FA Cup

1	Nov 14	H	Rochdale	D	1-1	Mitchell	4,069
1R	25	A	Rochdale	L	0-1		

League Cup

1	Aug 19	A	Tranmere Rovers	L	0-3		
	25	H	Tranmere Rovers	W	4-0	Murphy, Robinson, Own-goal, Eyres	2,734
2	Sep 23	H	Portsmouth	L	0-4		
	Oct 6	A	Portsmouth	L	0-2		

McIlhargey	Davies	Murphy	Horner	Briggs	Gouck	Rodwell	Sinclair	Duffield	Garner	Eyres	Robinson	Bonner	Martin	Burgess	Thornber	Mitchell	Murray	Speak	Leitch	Stringfellow	Stoneman	Gore	Bond	Harvey	Ward	Bamber	Dickins	Spooner	Watson	Cook	Bailey	Beech
1	2	3	4	5	6*	7	8	9	10#	11	12	14																				
		3	4	5		7	8		10*	11#	9	14	1	2	6	12																
		3	4	5		7	8	12	10	11	9*		1	2	6																	
		3	4			7	8	12	10*	11	9		1	2	6		5															
	5	3	4			7	8	10*	12	11	9#		1	2	6	14																
	9	3	4	5		7		10#		11	12	8	1	2*	6			14														
	2	3	4	5		7	8#			11	9	14	1		6	12			10*													
	2	3	4	5		7	8			11	9		1						10	6												
	2*	12	4	5	10	7	8			11			1		6					9	3											
1		2	4	5	10	7	8			11	9				6						3											
1	2#	3	4	5	10	7	8			11		14								9*		6	12									
		3	4	5	10	7	8			11		9	1	2								6										
		2	4		10	7	8			11		9	1	3							5	6										
		5	4		10	12	8			11	9*	7	1	2								6		3								
		5	4		10	7	8			11		6	1	2		9								3								
			4	5	10	7	8			11		6	1	2		9								3								
		12	4	5	10	7	8#			11		14	1	2		9*								3	6							
		3*	4	5	10	7	8			11			1	2										12	9							
		3*	4	5	10	7	8			11			1	2		9																
	3	12	4	5	10	7#	8			11	9	6	1	2*		14																
	3*	7	4		10		8			11	9	6#	1	2					14		12	5										
	3	7	4		10		8			11	9*		1	2					12		5	6										
		3	4	5	10		8			11	7		1	2								6				9						
		3	4	5	10*		8			11		14	1	2		12					7#	6				9						
	2		4	5	10		8			11			1		3				7			6				9						
	2		4	5	10		8			11					3				7			6				9	1					
	2	10	4	5			8			11					3				7			6				9	1					
	2	10	4				8			11					3				7*			6				9	1	5	12			
	2	3	4		10		8			11												6				9	1	5	7			
	2		4		10		8			11					5							6				9	1		7			
	2		4	5	10		8			11												6				9	1		7	3		
	2		4	5	10		8			11					3	12						6				9	1		7*	3		
	2*	12	4	5	10#		8			11		14			3	7						6				9	1					
	2	10	4	5			8			11					3	7						6				9	1					
	2	10	4				8			11					3						5	6				9	1		7			
	2	10#	4	5			8			11					3				7			6				9	1		12		14	
		10	4	5			8			11					3*				7		12	6				9	1				2	
		10	4	5			8			11				3					7			6				9	1				2	
	2		4	5			8			11*				3					7			6				9	1		12		10	
	2		4	5	12		8			11									14			6				9	1		7#	3	10*	
	2		4	5	12		8			11									7*			6				9#	1		14	3	10	
	2		4	5	10		8			11					12				14			6				9#	1		7*	3		
	2		4	5#	10		8			11					12				14			6				9	1		7*	3		
	2		4	5	10*		8			11					12							6				9	1		7	3		
	2	12	4				8			11*			1		10				14			6				9			7#	3	5	
	2		4				8			11			1		10							6				9			12	3	5	7*
3	30	28	46	33	27	19	45	3	4	46	12	8	24	20	21	6	1		11	3	8	30		4	2	24	19	2	10	9	7	1
		5			2	1		2	1		2	7			3	6		1	6		2		1	1					5		1	
	1		7	1	4	1	11	1		16	2					1			1	1					1	13			2			

League Table

	P	W	D	L	F	A	Pts
Stoke City	46	27	12	7	73	34	93
Bolton Wanderers	46	27	9	10	80	41	90
Port Vale	46	26	11	9	79	44	89
West Bromwich Albion	46	25	10	11	88	54	85
Swansea City	46	20	13	13	65	47	73
Stockport County	46	19	15	12	81	57	72
Leyton Orient	46	21	9	16	69	53	72
Reading	46	18	15	13	66	51	69
Brighton & Hove Albion	46	20	9	17	63	59	69
Bradford City	46	18	14	14	69	67	68
Rotherham United	46	17	14	15	60	60	65
Fulham	46	16	17	13	57	55	65
Burnley	46	15	16	15	57	59	61
Plymouth Argyle	46	16	12	18	59	64	60
Huddersfield Town	46	17	9	20	54	61	60
Hartlepool United	46	14	12	20	42	60	54
Bournemouth	46	12	17	17	45	52	53
Blackpool	46	12	15	19	63	75	51
Exeter City	46	11	17	18	54	69	50
Hull City	46	13	11	22	46	69	50
Preston North End	46	13	8	25	65	94	47
Mansfield Town	46	11	11	24	52	80	44
Wigan Athletic	46	10	11	25	43	72	41
Chester City	46	8	5	33	49	102	29

1993-94

Division Two

Manager: Billy Ayre

Did you know that?

Blackpool ended a run of seven successive defeats with a home draw with Swansea City. The game saw free admission for the home supporters and a gate of over 7,000 was realised.

Trevor Sinclair was sold to Queen's Park Rangers for a club-record fee of £600,000.

Blackpool won the Lancashire Senior Cup for the first time since 1953. They beat Manchester United 1–0 at home in the Final.

The club announced a loss of only £6,999 in September proving that slowly they were becoming solvent again.

At the end of the season, chairman Owen Oyston took the unpopular decision to sack manager Billy Ayre.

Match No.	Date	Venue	Opponents	Result		Scorers	Attendance
1	Aug 14	A	Cambridge United	L	2-3	Quinn, Griffiths (pen)	4,903
2	21	H	Brentford	D	1-1	Watson	4,024
3	28	A	Wrexham	W	3-2	Sheedy, Beech, Bonner	4,957
4	31	H	Plymouth Argyle	W	2-1	Griffiths (pen), Watson	3,865
5	Sep 4	H	Barnet	W	3-1	Bonner, Griffiths, Bamber	4,328
6	11	A	Bradford City	L	1-2	Griffiths	6,869
7	14	A	Hartlepool United	L	0-2		2,114
8	18	H	Cardiff City	W	1-0	Griffiths	4,767
9	25	H	Bournemouth	W	2-1	Watson, Bonner	4,489
10	Oct 2	A	Rotherham United	W	2-0	Bonner, Watson	3,770
11	9	H	Swansea City	D	4-4	Mitchell 2, Griffiths, Watson	3,775
12	16	H	Port Vale	L	1-3	Griffiths	8,969
13	23	A	Exeter City	L	0-1		3,421
14	30	H	Brighton & Hove Albion	D	2-2	Watson, Griffiths	4,468
15	Nov 2	H	Hull City	W	6-2	Watson 2, Griffiths 2, Quinn, Beech	3,968
16	6	A	Reading	D	1-1	Griffiths	6,559
17	20	H	Huddersfield Town	W	2-1	Watson, Horner	4,704
18	27	A	Leyton Orient	L	0-2		3,369
19	Dec 4	H	Hartlepool United	W	2-0	Griffiths, Own-goal	3,130
20	11	A	Brentford	L	0-3		4,769
21	19	H	Cambridge United	L	2-3	Watson 2	4,576
22	28	H	York City	L	0-5		4,501
23	Jan 1	A	Burnley	L	1-3	Robinson	18,165
24	3	H	Bristol Rovers	L	0-1		3,311
25	8	H	Fulham	L	2-3	Bamber, Griffiths	3,374
26	15	A	Port Vale	L	0-2		7,915
27	22	H	Swansea City	D	1-1	Gouck	7,080
28	29	A	Brighton & Hove Albion	L	2-3	Robinson, Briggs	7,800
29	Feb 1	A	Stockport County	L	0-1		5,288
30	5	H	Exeter City	W	1-0	Bamber	3,747
31	12	A	Fulham	L	0-1		4,259
32	19	H	Wrexham	W	4-1	Watson 3, Bonner	4,069
33	22	A	Plymouth Argyle	L	1-2	Rodwell	7,102
34	26	A	Barnet	W	1-0	Watson	2,448
35	Mar 5	H	Bradford City	L	1-3	Gouck	5,276
36	12	A	Cardiff City	W	2-0	Watson, Griffiths	5,186
37	19	A	Bournemouth	L	0-1		3,335
38	26	H	Rotherham United	L	1-2	Mitchell	3,588
39	30	A	Bristol Rovers	L	0-1		4,231
40	Apr 2	H	Stockport County	W	2-0	Bonner, Watson	5,235
41	4	A	York City	L	1-2	Watson	5,470
42	9	H	Burnley	L	1-2	Griffiths	7,936
43	16	A	Hull City	D	0-0		6,211
44	23	H	Reading	L	0-4		4,529
45	30	A	Huddersfield Town	L	1-2	Watson	16,195
46	May 7	H	Leyton Orient	W	4-1	Bonner, Horner, Bamber, Watson	5,458

Final League Position: 20th in Division Two

Apps
Sub Apps
Gls

FA Cup

1	Nov 13	A	Port Vale	L	0-2		

League Cup

1	Aug 16	A	Doncaster Rovers	W	1-0	Watson	
	24	H	Doncaster Rovers	D	3-3	Quinn, Watson, Bamber	2,490
2	Sep 21	H	Sheffield Utd	W	3-0	Bamber 2, Watson	
	Oct 5	A	Sheffield Utd	L	0-2		
3	26	H	Peterborough Utd	D	2-2	Watson 2	4,863
3R	Nov 9	A	Peterborough Utd	L	1-2	Own-goal	

Martin	Davies	Cook	Horner	Stoneman	Gore	Watson	Leitch	Bamber	Bonner	Griffiths	Quinn	Beech	Briggs	Gouck	Sheedy	Mitchell	Robinson	Rodwell	McIlhargey	Bailey	Murphy	Whitworth	Symons	Thorpe
1	2	3	4	5	6	7	8	9	10*	11#	12	14												
1	2	3	4	6		7		9	8	11*	12	14	5	10#										
1	2	3			6	7		9	8	11		4	5		10									
1	2	3			6	7		9	8	11#	12	4	5*		10	14								
1	2	3		5	6	7*		9	8	11#	12	4			10	14								
1	2	3			6	7		9	8	11		4	5		10									
1	2	3		12	6	7			8	11#		4	5		10*	14	9							
1	2	3	4		6	7			8	11		9	5		10									
1	2	3	4			7		9	8	11		6	5		10									
1	2	3	4			7			8	11		6	5		10			9						
1	2	3	4			7			8	11			5	6	10*	12		9						
	2		4					9*	8	11	12	14	5	6		10		7	1	3#				
1	2	3	4			7			8	11			5	6	10			9						
1	2	3	4			7			8	11	12	14	5	6	10*			9#						
1	2	3	4			7			8	11	12	10	5	6*				9						
1	2	3	4			7			8	11	12	10*	5	6				9			9			
1	2	3	4			7			8*	11	12		5	6		10					2			
1		3	4		5	7			8	11	12			6	9	10*					2			
1		3	4	5		7	12		8	11	9*	6			10						2	5		
1		3	4		6	7			8	11	12				10	9*					9	5		
1	2	3	4		6	7			8*	11	14				10#	12					9	5*		
1	2	3	4			7				11	14	8		6	10#	12					6			
1	2	3	4			7		12		11		8	5	10			9*				6			
1	2	3	4			7#		12		11		8*	5	10		14	9				6			
1	2	3	4			7		8		11		12	5		10*		9							
1#	2	3	4		6			9		11			5		10	12	8*	7						
	2*	3	4		6			9		11			5	12	10		8	7						
1		3	4		6			9	8*	11		14	5	2	10#		12	7	14					
1		3	4		6			9	12	11#		2*	5	10		14	8	7	1					
1		3	4		6			9	2*	11#		12	5	10		14	8	7						
1		3	4	5	6	8		9	2	11#		14			10*		12	7						
1		3	4		6	8		9	2	11		10	5					7						
1		3	4		6	8		9	2			11	5	10				7						
1		3	4		6	8		9	2	11*		12	5	10				7						
1		3	4		6	8*		9	2	11			5	10			12	7						
1		3	4		6	8			2*	11#		12	5	10	9	14		7						
1		3	4		6*	8			2	11		12#	5	10	9	14		7						
1		3	4		6	8			2	11				10	9*	12		7			5			
1		3	4		6	8			2	11				10		9		7			5			
1		3	4	6		8			2	11		9		10				7			5			
1		3	4	6		8			2	11#		9*		10	12	14		7	1		5			
		3	4		6	8			2	12		9#	5	14	10*	11		7						
1		3	4		6	8			2	11		9	5#	10*		14		7			12			
1		3	4		6	8			2	11		9*	5			12		7			10			
1		3	4	5	6*	8			2			9				11	10	7					12	
1		3	4	5	6	8#		9*	2			10				11		7			12			14
43	24	45	41	9	29	40	1	20	39	42	1	24	32	25	25	8	9	28	3	1	14	3		
				1			1	2	1	1	13	11		2	1	16	3		1		2		1	1
			2			20		4	7	16	2	2	1	2	1	3	2	1						

League Table

	P	W	D	L	F	A	Pts
Reading	46	26	11	9	81	44	89
Port Vale	46	26	10	10	79	46	88
Plymouth Argyle	46	25	10	11	88	56	85
Stockport County	46	24	13	9	74	44	85
York City	46	21	12	13	64	40	75
Burnley	46	21	10	15	79	58	73
Bradford City	46	19	13	14	61	53	70
Bristol Rovers	46	20	10	16	60	59	70
Hull City	46	18	14	14	62	54	68
Cambridge United	46	19	9	18	79	73	66
Huddersfield Town	46	17	14	15	58	61	65
Wrexham	46	17	11	18	66	77	62
Swansea City	46	16	12	18	56	58	60
Brighton & Hove Albion	46	15	14	17	60	67	59
Rotherham United	46	15	13	18	63	60	58
Brentford	46	13	19	14	57	55	58
Bournemouth	46	14	15	17	51	59	57
Leyton Orient	46	14	14	18	57	71	56
Cardiff City	46	13	15	18	66	79	54
Blackpool	46	16	5	25	63	75	53
Fulham	46	14	10	22	50	63	52
Exeter City	46	11	12	23	52	83	45
Hartlepool United	46	9	9	28	41	87	36
Barnet	46	5	13	28	41	86	28

1994-95

Division Two

Manager: Sam Allardyce

Did you know that?

Sam Allardyce was appointed new manager, with Phil Brown as his assistant.

Mike Davies retired from playing after serving the club for 11 years.

The 7–1 defeat to Birmingham City was Blackpool's heaviest since a 1–10 reverse to Huddersfield Town in their first season in the top division back in 1929–30.

Match No.	Date	Venue	Opponents	Result		Scorers	Attendance
1	Aug 13	H	Huddersfield Town	L	1-4	Gouck	8,343
2	20	A	Bournemouth	W	2-1	Ellis 2	3,098
3	27	H	Shrewsbury Town	W	2-1	Horner, Ellis (pen)	4,248
4	31	A	Bristol Rovers	D	0-0		3,762
5	Sep 3	A	Crewe Alexandra	L	3-4	Griffiths (pen), Beech, Watson	4,915
6	10	H	Cardiff City	W	2-1	Brown, Ellis (pen)	4,189
7	13	H	Brighton & Hove Albion	D	2-2	Brown, Beech	3,438
8	17	A	Brentford	L	2-3	Quinn, Horner	4,157
9	24	H	Wrexham	W	2-1	Brown (pen) ??	5,105
10	Oct 1	A	Rotherham Utd	W	2-0	Quinn, Ellis	3,517
11	8	A	Hull City	L	0-1		3,829
12	15	H	Bradford City	W	2-0	Watson, Ellis	6,156
13	22	H	Swansea City	W	2-1	Ellis (pen), Watson	4,911
14	29	A	Plymouth Argyle	W	2-0	Watson, Ellis	6,285
15	Nov 1	A	Oxford Utd	L	2-3	Watson 2	5,610
16	5	H	Leyton Orient	W	2-1	Ellis, Watson	4,653
17	19	A	Chester City	L	0-2		3,114
18	26	H	Wycombe Wanderers	L	0-1		4,846
19	Dec 10	H	Bournemouth	W	3-1	Ellis 2, Mitchell	3,847
20	17	A	Huddersfield Town	D	1-1	Watson	11,536
21	26	A	York City	L	0-4		4,542
22	27	H	Stockport County	L	1-2	Mitchell	5,745
23	31	A	Birmingham City	L	1-7	Bradshaw	18,025
24	Jan 2	H	Peterborough Utd	W	4-0	Quinn 2, Ellis, Watson	3,692
25	7	A	Cardiff City	W	1-0	Watson	3,467
26	14	H	Cambridge Utd	L	2-3	Murphy, Mellon	4,076
27	28	H	Plymouth Argyle	W	5-2	Watson 2, Ellis, Mellon 2	3,599
28	Feb 4	A	Wycombe Wanderers	D	1-1	Quinn	6,380
29	7	A	Leyton Orient	W	1-0	Watson	3,301
30	11	H	Oxford Utd	W	2-0	Gouck, Quinn	5,206
31	18	A	Cambridge Utd	D	0-0		3,192
32	21	H	Chester City	W	3-1	Mitchell, Mellon (pen), Own-goal	4,649
33	25	H	Rotherham Utd	D	2-2	Mitchell, Ellis	5,043
34	28	A	Swansea City	L	0-1		2,308
35	Mar 4	A	Wrexham	W	1-0	Watson	4,251
36	7	H	Crewe Alexandra	D	0-0		5,859
37	11	A	Shrewsbury Town	D	0-0		4,261
38	18	H	Bristol Rovers	L	0-2		4,484
39	25	H	Brentford	L	1-2	Brown	4,663
40	Apr 1	A	Brighton & Hove Albion	D	2-2	Watson, Ellis	7,157
41	4	H	Birmingham City	D	1-1	Quinn	4,494
42	15	A	Stockport County	L	2-3	Quinn, ??	5,021
43	18	H	York City	L	0-5		3,517
44	22	A	Peterborough Utd	L	0-1		5,716
45	29	A	Bradford City	W	1-0	Ellis	5,036
46	May 5	H	Hull City	L	1-2	Ellis	4,251

Final League Position: 12th in Division Two

Apps

Sub Apps

One own-goal — Gls

FA Cup

1	Nov 14	A	Preston NE	L	0-1		

League Cup

1	Aug 16	H	Chesterfield	L	1-2	Quinn	2,570
	23	A	Chesterfield	L	2-4	Brown, Ellis	2,516

Sealey	Brown	Burke	Bonner	Horner	Gore	Rodwell	Gouck	Bamber	Ellis	Griffiths	Quinn	Gibson	Briggs	Beech	Stoneman	Watson	Cook	Thompson	Moore	Martin	Thorpe	Mitchell	Bradshaw	Capleton	Murphy	Mellon	Sunderland	Morrison	Davies	Rowett	Darton	Lydiate	Parkinson
1	2	3	4	5	6	7*	8#	9	10	11	12	14																					
1	2	3		4	6	12			10	11	9	8	5*	7																			
1	2	3		4		7*	11	9	10		8			6	5																		
1	2	3	4	6		7*	11		10	12	9*			8	5																		
1	2	3	14	4	6	7*	11#			12	9			8	5	10*																	
1	2			4		7*	11		10		9			8			3	5	6														
1	2		12	4		7*	11*			10	9			8			3	5	6														
	2		6*	4	12	7#	11			10	9			8			3		5	1	14												
	2			4					10	11*	9			8	7		3	5	6	1		12											
	2	3#		4		12	7		10		9			8			14	5	6	1		11*											
	2	3		4			7#			10	9			8		12	14	5	6	1		11*											
	2	3	12	5			4		10	11	9*			8		7			6	1													
	2	3		6			12		10	11	9*			8		7		5		1			4										
	2	3		6					10	11	12			8		9*		5		1		7	4										
	2	3		6					10	11				8		9		5		1		7	4										
	2	3		6					10	11				8		9		5		1		7	4										
	2	3	8	6			12		10	11*	14					9#		5		1#		7	4	15									
		3	11	6					10		9							5				7	8*	1	2	4	12						
		3	7	6			12		10		9#					14		5				11		1	2	8		4*					
		3	7	6					10		9*					12		5				11		1	2	8		4					
	12	3	7#	6			14		10					4		9		5				11		1	2*	8							
	2	3		6			7		10					4		9		5				11		1		8							
	2*	3		12			4		10		7					9						11	6	1	5	8							
	2	3					11		10		7			4		9				1			6			8		5					
	2	3		6			11		10		7			4		9*				1		12				8		5					
				6			11		10		7			4		9				1		12			3*	8		5	2				
				6			11		10		7					9				1			4			8		5		2	3		
				4			11		10		7					9				1			6			8		5		2	3		
				4			11		10		7*					9				1		12	6			8		5		2	3		
				4			11		10		7					9				1			6			8		5		2	3		
	12		14	4			11				7					9				1		10#	6			8		5*		2	3		
	6		12	4			11				7*					9		5		1		10				8				2	3		
	6*		12	4			11		10		7							5		1		9				8				2	3		
			12	4			11		10		7					9				1		5*	6			8				2	3		
			4				11		10		7					9				1			6			8				2	3	5	
			12				11		10		7#					9				1		14	6			8		4*		2	3	5	
							11		10		7*			12						1		9	6			8		4		2	3	5	
							11		10		7			12						1		9*	6			8		4		2	3	5	
	2			5			8		10		9			4#		12				1		11*	6							7	3		14
	2						8		10		9			4		12				1		11*	6							7	3	5	
	14						8		10		9*			4#		12				1		11	6					7		2	3	5	
							7		10		9					12				1		11	6			8		4		2	3*	5	
							7		10		9					12						11	6*	1		8		4		2	3	5	
	2						7		10		9#			12		14						11*	6	1		8		4			3	5	
	2	3					11*		10		12			7		9				1			6			8		4				5	
	2	3					11		10					4		9*				1		7#	6	15		8	12					5	
7	28	23	9	33	3	7	35	2	40	12	37	1	1	25	4	24	4	17	7	31		25	26	8	6	26		18	1	17	18	11	
	3		8	1	1	2	4			2	4	1		3		9	2				1	5		2			2						1
	5			2			2		17	1	9			2		15						4	1		1	4							

League Table

	P	W	D	L	F	A	Pts
Birmingham City	46	25	14	7	84	37	89
Brentford	46	25	10	11	81	39	85
Crewe Alexandra	46	25	8	13	80	68	83
Bristol Rovers	46	22	16	8	70	40	82
Huddersfield Town	46	22	15	9	79	49	81
Wycombe Wanderers	46	21	15	10	60	46	78
Oxford United	46	21	12	13	66	52	75
Hull City	46	21	11	14	70	57	74
York City	46	21	9	16	67	51	72
Swansea City	46	19	14	13	57	45	71
Stockport County	46	19	8	19	63	60	65
Blackpool	46	18	10	18	64	70	64
Wrexham	46	16	15	15	65	64	63
Bradford City	46	16	12	18	57	64	60
Peterborough United	46	14	18	14	54	69	60
Brighton & Hove Albion	46	14	17	15	54	53	59
Rotherham United	46	14	14	18	57	61	56
Shrewsbury Town	46	13	14	19	54	62	53
Bournemouth	46	13	11	22	49	69	50
Cambridge United	46	11	15	20	52	69	48
Plymouth Argyle	46	12	10	24	45	83	46
Cardiff City	46	9	11	26	46	74	38
Chester City	46	6	11	29	37	84	29
Leyton Orient	46	6	8	32	30	75	26

1995-96

Division Two

Manager: Sam Allardyce

Did you know that?

Owen Oyston was sentenced to six years in prison on 22 May for the rape of a schoolgirl. His wife, Vicky, took control of the club.

After beating Burnley on 12 March, Blackpool went to the top of the table, their highest position since 1978.

The disastrous late run in for promotion followed by the Play-off debacle meant the sack for manager Sam Alardyce. On the same day Terry Yorath, who had taken Hull City down, was given a new contract.

Match No.	Date	Venue	Opponents	Result		Scorers	Attendance
1	Aug 12	A	Bristol City	D	1–1	Quinn	7,734
2	19	H	Wrexham	W	2–0	Eliis 2	4,799
3	26	A	Hull City	L	1–2	Lydiate	4,755
4	29	H	Peterborough Utd	W	2–1	Preece, Quinn	3,902
5	Sep 2	A	Shrewsbury Town	W	2–0	Preece 2	3,182
6	9	H	Stockport County	L	0–1		6,602
7	12	H	Bournemouth	W	2–1	Preece, Morrison	3,884
8	16	A	Brighton & Hove Albion	W	2–1	Ellis, Mellon	6,158
9	23	H	Crewe Alexandra	W	2–1	Preece, Ellis	7,301
10	30	A	Bradford City	L	1–2	Preece	6,820
11	Oct 7	A	Brentford	W	2–1	Preece (pen), Ellis	5,313
12	14	H	Chesterfield	D	0–0		6,855
13	21	A	Rotherham Utd	L	1–2	Preece (pen)	3,663
14	28	H	Oxford Utd	D	1–1	Quinn	5,303
15	31	H	Bristol Rovers	W	3–0	Gouck, Quinn, Ellis	3,877
16	Nov 4	A	Swindon Town	D	1–1	Quinn (pen)	12,470
17	18	H	York City	L	1–3	Holden	4,514
18	25	A	Walsall	D	1–1	Mellon	4,459
19	Dec 9	A	Crewe Alexandra	W	2–1	Ellis, Watson	4,551
20	16	H	Bradford City	W	4–1	Watson 2, Ellis, Bonner	4,857
21	23	A	Notts County	D	1–1	Own goal	5,522
22	Jan 1	A	Carlisle Utd	W	2–1	Bryan, Linighan	7,532
23	13	A	Wrexham	D	1–1	Preece	5,479
24	20	H	Bristol City	W	3–0	Morrison, Ellis, Preece (pen)	4,838
25	23	H	Wycombe Wanderers	D	1–1	Preece	3,877
26	Feb 3	H	Hull City	D	1–1	Holden	4,713
27	10	A	Wycombe Wanderers	W	1–0	Watson	5,285
28	13	H	Swansea City	W	4–0	Watson, Preece, Ellis, Bonner	3,992
29	17	A	Bournemouth	L	0–1		4,157
30	20	H	Shrewsbury Town	W	2–1	Quinn, Own goal	4,210
31	24	H	Brighton & Hove Albion	W	2–1	Mellon 2	4,937
32	27	A	Stockport County	D	1–1	Ellis	7,711
33	Mar 2	A	Burnley	W	1–0	Preece	10,082
34	9	H	Notts County	W	1–0	Ellis	7,187
35	12	H	Burnley	W	3–1	Mellon, Bonner, Ellis	8,941
36	16	A	Swansea City	W	2–0	Ellis, Watson	4,478
37	23	H	Carlisle Utd	W	3–1	Linighan 2, Quinn (pen)	8,144
38	26	A	Peterborough Utd	D	0–0		4,425
39	30	H	Brentford	W	1–0	Quinn (pen)	5,899
40	Apr 2	A	Chesterfield	L	0–1		7,002
41	6	A	Oxford Utd	L	0–1		7,875
42	8	H	Rotherham Utd	L	1–2	Preece	6,850
43	13	A	Bristol Rovers	D	1–1	Linighan	5,626
44	20	H	Swindon Town	D	1–1	Barlow	9,175
45	27	H	Walsall	L	1–2	Quinn (pen)	9,148
46	May 4	A	York City	W	2–0	Morrison, Ellis	7,147

Final League Position: 3rd in Division Two

Apps

Sub Apps

Two own-goals — Gls

Play-Offs

SF	May 12	A	Bradford City	W	2-0	Bonner, Ellis	
	15	H	Bradford City	L	0-3		9,593

FA Cup

1	Nov 11	H	Chester City	W	2-1	Quinn, Lydiate	5,004
2	Dec 2	H	Colwyn Bay	W	2-0	Preece, Quinn	
3	Jan 6	A	Huddersfield Town	L	1-2	Quinn	12,424

League Cup

1	Aug 15	A	Bradford City	L	1-2	Ellis	3,670
	22	H	Bradford City	L	2-3	Ellis, Mellon	4,553

Capleton	Brown	Barlow	Lydiate	Mellon	Bradshaw	Quinn	Bonner	Gouck	Ellis	Preece	Bryan	Banks	Brown	Beech	Darton	Morrison	Holden	Watson	Yallop	Linigham	Barber	Allardyce	Nixon	Charnock	Philpott	Thorpe	Pascoe
1		3	4	5	6	7*	8	9	10	11	12		2														
		3	4	5	6	7*		9	10	11	12	1	2	8													
		3*	4	5	6	7	13	9#	10	11	2	1	12	8													
			4	5	6	7*	8		10	11	2	1		12	3	9											
			4	5	6	7	8		10	11	2	1		12	3	9*											
			4	5*	6	7	8		10	11	2	1			3	9	12										
		3	4	5	6	7*	8		10	11	2	1				9	12										
	12	3	4	5	6'	13	8*	14	10	11#	2	1				9	7										
		3	4	5		6*	8		10	11	2	1		12		9	7										
			4	5*		6#	8		10	11	2	1		12	3	9	7	13									
		3	4	5		6	8		10*	11	2	1		12		9	7										
		3	4	5		6#	8	12	10*	11	2	1				9	7	13									
			4	5		6	8			11	2	1		12	3	9	7	10*									
	3		4	5		6	8		10*	11#	2	1		12		9	7	13									
	3		4	5		6	8*	7	10	12	2	1			13	9#	11										
	12		4*	5	9	6	8	7	10		2	1					11		3								
				5		6	8#	7*	10		2	1		12		9	11	13	3	4							
				5	7	6	8*		10	12	2	1			13	9	11		3#	4							
		3	7	5		6	8		10		2	1		12			11	9*		4							
		3	7	5		6	8*		10		2			12	13		11#	9		4'	1	14					
		3	7	5		6	8		10		2	1				9		11		4							
		3	7	5		6*	8#		10	12	2	1			13	9		11		4							
	12	3*	7	5		6	8		10	13	2	1				9		11#		4							
	3		7	5		6#	8*	12	10	11	2	1				9		13		4							
	3		7	5*		6	8	12	10	11	2	1				9#	13'	14		4							
		3*		5	7	6	8	12	10	11	2	1					9#	13		4							
		3		5	7	6*	8			11	2						9	10		4			1	12			
		3	12	5	7	6	8#			11	2*						9	10		4			1	13			
		3'	13	5	7	6#	8		12	11	2						9*	10		4			1	14			
		3		5	7	6	8		10*	11	2			12			9			4			1				
		3		5	7	6	8	12	10	11	2						9*			4			1				
		3#		5	7	6	8		10	11*	2					9		12		4			1	13			
		3		5	7	6	8		10	11*	2					9		12		4			1				
		3		5	7	6*	8		10#	11	2			12		9		13		4			1				
		3		5	7	6	8*		10	11#	2			12		9		13		4			1				
	12	3*		5	7			8	10	11	2			6				9		4			1				
		3		5	7	6		8	10	11	2							9*		4			1		12		
	12	3		5	7*				10	11	2			13		9		6#		4			1		8		
		3	7			6	5		10	11	2			12		9				4			1		8*		
	12	3*	7	5		6	8		10	11#	2					9				4			1		13		
		3	7	5		6	8*		10	11	2					9				4			1		12		
	12	3	7'	5		6*	8		10	11	2					9		13		4#			1		14		
		3	7	5		6	8	12	10*	11	2							13		4			1		9#		
	12	3	7	5		6	8		13	11	2							10*		4			1		9#		
	9'	3	7	5	4	6#	8		10	11*	2												1		12	13	14
		3#		5	7	12	8	13	10	11'	2					9*		6		4			1		14		
1	5	34	30	45	25	42	41	8	41	37	44	24	2	3	5	29	19	14	3	29	1		20		4		
	8		2			2	1	8	2	4	2		1	15	4		3	13				1		4	6	1	1
		1	1	6		9	3	1	14	14	1					3	2	6		4							

League Table

	P	W	D	L	F	A	Pts
Swindon Town	46	25	17	4	71	34	92
Oxford United	46	24	11	11	76	39	83
Blackpool	46	23	13	10	67	40	82
Notts County	46	21	15	10	63	39	78
Crewe Alexandra	46	22	7	17	77	60	73
Bradford City	46	22	7	17	71	69	73
Chesterfield	46	20	12	14	56	51	72
Wrexham	46	18	16	12	76	55	70
Stockport County	46	19	13	14	61	47	70
Bristol Rovers	46	20	10	16	57	60	70
Walsall	46	19	12	15	60	45	69
Wycombe Wanderers	46	15	15	16	63	59	60
Bristol City	46	15	15	16	55	60	60
Bournemouth	46	16	10	20	51	70	58
Brentford	46	15	13	18	43	49	58
Rotherham United	46	14	14	18	54	62	56
Burnley	46	14	13	19	56	68	55
Shrewsbury Town	46	13	14	19	58	70	53
Peterborough United	46	13	13	20	59	66	52
York City	46	13	13	20	58	73	52
Carlisle United	46	12	13	21	57	72	49
Swansea City	46	11	14	21	43	79	47
Brighton & Hove Albion	46	10	10	26	46	69	40
Hull City	46	5	16	25	36	78	31

1996-97

Division Two

Manager: Gary Megson

Did you know that?

Blackpool's League Cup home game against Chelsea was the first time the club had featured on Sky Sports as a live match.

Gary Megson was appointed as new manager but left in controversial circumstances a year later.

5 September 1996 marked the 100th anniversary of Blackpool's first League match.

Match No.	Date	Venue	Opponents	Result		Scorers	Attendance
1	Aug 17	H	Chesterfield	L	0-1		6,014
2	24	A	Bristol City	W	1-0	Eliis	9,387
3	27	A	Rotherham United	W	2-1	Philpott, Preece	2,914
4	31	H	Wycombe Wanderers	D	0-0		4,856
5	Sep 7	H	Walsall	W	2-1	Philpott, Quinn (pen)	5,176
6	10	A	Burnley	L	0-2		13,599
7	14	A	Brentford	D	1-1	Quinn (pen)	5,908
8	21	H	Shrewsbury Town	D	1-1	Eliis	4,452
9	28	A	Luton Town	L	0-1		5,303
10	Oct 1	A	Crewe Alexandra	L	2-3	Brabin, Quinn	4,314
11	5	A	Bury	L	0-1		5,317
12	12	H	Gillingham	W	2-0	Ellis, Mellon	4,320
13	15	H	Wrexham	D	3-3	Preece 2, Mellon	4,014
14	19	A	Bristol Rovers	D	0-0		5,823
15	26	H	Watford	D	1-1	Quinn	6,072
16	30	A	Millwall	L	1-2	Malkin	7,179
17	Nov 2	A	Peterborough Utd	D	0-0		7,011
18	9	H	Bournemouth	D	1-1	Quinn	3,744
19	19	A	Stockport County	L	0-1		4,572
20	23	H	Notts County	W	1-0	Quinn (pen)	3,598
21	30	A	Watford	D	2-2	Malkin, Brabin	12,017
22	Dec 3	H	Plymouth Argyle	D	2-2	Philpott, Malkin	2,690
23	13	A	Preston NE	L	0-3		14,626
24	21	H	York City	W	3-0	Ellis, Quinn 2 (1 pen)	3,432
25	Jan 1	A	Shrewsbury Town	W	3-1	Preece 2, Mellon	2,787
26	18	H	Crewe Alexandra	L	1-2	Eliis	4,760
27	25	H	Millwall	W	3-0	Ellis, Quinn, Darton	4,523
28	Feb 1	A	Bournemouth	D	0-0		8,201
29	8	H	Peterborough Utd	W	5-1	Ellis 3, Preece, Bryan	4,001
30	15	A	Notts County	D	1-1	Quinn	5,281
31	22	H	Stockport County	W	2-1	Quinn, Ellis	5,772
32	25	H	Burnley	L	1-3	Quinn	7,331
33	Mar 1	A	Plymouth Argyle	W	1-0	Eliis	5,585
34	8	A	York City	L	0-1		3,693
35	15	H	Preston NE	W	2-1	Clarkson 2	8,017
36	18	A	Walsall	D	1-1	Clarkson	3,459
37	22	H	Bristol City	W	1-0	Preece	4,518
38	29	A	Chesterfield	D	0-0		4,974
39	31	H	Rotherham United	W	4-1	Linighan, Clarkson, Ellis, Barlow	5,524
40	Apr 5	A	Wycombe Wanderers	L	0-1		5,619
41	12	H	Bury	W	2-0	Ellis 2	6,812
42	15	H	Luton Town	D	0-0		4,382
43	19	A	Gillingham	W	3-2	Quinn, Mellon, Clarkson	5,151
44	22	H	Brentford	W	1-0	Preece	4,030
45	26	H	Bristol Rovers	W	3-2	Preece 2, Bonner	6,673
46	May 3	A	Wrexham	L	1-2	Eliis	5,664

Final League Position: 7th in Division Two

Apps
Sub Apps
Gls

FA Cup

1	H	Wigan Athletic	W	1-0	Quinn (pen)
2	H	Hednesford Town	W	0-1	

League Cup

1	A	Scunthorpe United	L	1–2
	H	Scunthorpe United	W	2-0
2	H	Chelsea	L	1-4
	A	Chelsea	W	3-1

Banks	Bryan	Barlow	Butler	Linighan	Thorpe	Bonner	Mellon	Quinn	Ellis	Philpott	Preece	Dixon	Brabin	Lydiate	Darton	Onwere	Woods	Malkin	Bradshaw	Brightwell	Carden	Clarkson	Ormerod	Russell
1	2	3	4	5	6#	7	8	9	10	11*	12	13												
1	2	3	4	5	14	7	8	9'	10*	11#	12	13	6											
1	2	3	4	5		7	8	9*	10	11#	12	13	6											
1	2	3	4	5#	12	7*	8		10	11	9		6	13										
1	2	3	4			7		9#	10	11*	8	12	6	5	13									
1	2	3#	4			12	8	9	10	11*	7	13	6	5										
1	2	3	4	5*		12	8	9	10	11#	7	13	6											
1	2	3*	4	5		7'	8	9	10	11#	12	13	6			14								
1	2#	12	13	5		7	8	9*	10		14	3	6	4		11'								
1		12	4	5		7	8	9	10			3*	6	2		11								
1		12	4	5	13	7*	8	9'	10#		14	3	6	2		11								
1		3	4	5			8	9	10	12	11		6	2			7*							
1		3	4	5	12		8	9*	10		11	13	6	2			7#							
1		3	4	5				9	10		11		6	2		7	8*	12						
1		3	4	5			8	9#	10	12	11		6	2		13		7*						
1		3	4	5	12		8	9#	10'	13	11		6*	2				7	14					
1		3	4	5			8	9	12	10*	11		6	2				7						
1		3	4	5			8	9	12	10#	11*		6'	2		13		7	14					
1	2	3	4	5		7	8	9	12	11			6					10*						
1	2	3	4	5		7	8	9	12	11			6					10*						
1	2	3	4			7	8	9	10				6*			12		11	5					
1	2	3	4		12	7			10	11*				5		8		9	6					
1		3		5*	2	7	8		10	9	11								4	6	12			
1	2	3	4	5		7	8	9	10	6	11													
1	2	3	4	5		7	8	9	10#	6*	11		12							13				
1	2	3	4	5*			8	9	10	7#	11		6	12	13									
1	2	3	4	5			8	9*	10		11		6		7			12						
1	2	3	4	5			8	9	10		11		6		7*			12						
1	2	3	4	5			8	9	10		11		6		7									
1	2	3	4	5			8	9	10		11				7							6		
1	2	3	4	5			8	9	10	7*	11#				12			13				6		
1	2#	3*	4	5			8	9	10	7	11				12			13				6		
1	2	3	4	5			8	9	10	7*	11				12							6		
1		3	4	5		12	8	9	10		11			2	7*							6		
1		3	4	5		7	8	9	10		11*			2					12			6		
1	2	3	4	5		7#	8	9*	10		11				12				13			6		
1	2	3	4	5		7	8	9	10*		11								12			6		
1	2	3	4	5		7	8		10		11				9*							6	12	
1	2	3	4	5*		7	8		10		11				9#				12			6		
1	2	3'		5		7*	8		10		11		12		9#				4			6	13	14
1	2	3		5	13	9*	8		10		11		6	4	12							7		
1	2	3		5		9#	8		10	12	11*		6	4								7	13	
1	2	3	9	5		12	8	13	10		11		6*	4#								7		
1	2	3	4	5			8	9	10*	13	11'		6#					12				7	14	
1	2	3	4	5		10	8	9			11		6									7		
1	2	3*	4	5			8	9	10	12	11		6#					13				7		
46	34	43	41	42	2	25	43	37	41	20	35	3	30	18	8	5	3	8	4	1		17		
		3	1		7	4		1	4	6	6	8	2	2	7	4		7	6	1	1		4	1
	1	1		1		1	4	13	15	3	10		2		1			3				5		

League Table

	P	W	D	L	F	A	Pts
Bury	46	24	12	10	62	38	84
Stockport County	46	23	13	10	59	41	82
Luton Town	46	21	15	10	71	45	78
Brentford	46	20	14	12	56	43	74
Bristol City	46	21	10	15	69	51	73
Crewe Alexandra	46	22	7	17	56	47	73
Blackpool	46	18	15	13	60	47	69
Wrexham	46	17	18	11	54	50	69
Burnley	46	19	11	16	71	55	68
Chesterfield	46	18	14	14	42	39	68
Gillingham	46	19	10	17	60	59	67
Walsall	46	19	10	17	54	53	67
Watford	46	16	19	11	45	38	67
Millwall	46	16	13	17	50	55	61
Preston North End	46	18	7	21	49	55	61
Bournemouth	46	15	15	16	43	45	60
Bristol Rovers	46	15	11	20	47	50	56
Wycombe Wanderers	46	15	10	21	51	56	55
Plymouth Argyle	46	12	18	16	47	58	54
York City	46	13	13	20	47	68	52
Peterborough United	46	11	14	21	55	73	47
Shrewsbury Town	46	11	13	22	49	74	46
Rotherham United	46	7	14	25	39	70	35
Notts County	46	7	14	25	33	59	35

1997-98

Division Two

Manager: Nigel Worthington

Did you know that?

Nigel Worthington took over as player-manager, and Blackpool were involved in a lengthy dispute with Megson's new club Stockport County.

Match No.	Date		Venue	Opponents	Result		Scorers	Attendance
1	Aug	9	H	Luton Town	W	1-0	Lydiate	6,547
2		16	A	Bristol City	L	0-2		9,043
3		23	H	Wycombe Wanderers	L	2-4	Quinn, Brabin	4,733
4		30	A	Bournemouth	L	0-2		4,196
5	Sep	2	A	Wrexham	W	4-3	Ellis 3, Bonner	3,763
6		7	H	Carlisle Utd	W	2-1	Ellis, Carlisle	7,259
7		13	A	Wigan Athletic	L	0-3		5,517
8		20	H	Oldham Athletic	D	2-2	Quinn, Philpott	7,714
9		27	H	Southend Utd	W	3-0	Bonner, Ellis, Clarkson	4,542
10	Oct	4	A	Millwall	L	1-2	Ellis	7,042
11		11	A	Fulham	L	0-1		7,760
12		18	H	Grimsby Town	D	2-2	Quinn, Ellis	5,234
13		21	H	Chesterfield	W	2-1	Clarkson, Quinn (pen)	3,682
14		25	A	Bristol Rovers	W	3-0	Bonner, Clarkson, Preece	6,183
15	Nov	1	A	Watford	L	1-4	Preece	9,723
16		4	H	Northampton Town	D	1-1	Clarkson	3,685
17		8	H	Burnley	W	2-1	Clarkson, Preece	7,429
18		18	A	Gillingham	D	1-1	Ellis	5,045
19		22	H	York City	W	1-0	Strong	4,508
20		29	A	Walsall	L	1-2	Clarkson	3,933
21	Dec	2	H	Plymouth Argyle	D	0-0		3,281
22		13	A	Brentford	L	1-3	Preece	3,725
23		20	H	Preston NE	W	2-1	Preece, Philpott	8,342
24		26	A	Carlisle Utd	D	1-1	Ormerod	8,010
25		28	H	Wrexham	L	1-2	Ormerod	5,424
26	Jan	10	A	Luton Town	L	0-3		5,574
27		17	H	Bournemouth	W	1-0	Clarkson	4,550
28		24	A	Wycombe Wanderers	L	1-2	Preece	5,073
29		31	H	Wigan Athletic	L	0-2		5,288
30	Feb	3	H	Bristol City	D	2-2	Preece, Bent	3,724
31		7	A	Oldham Athletic	W	1-0	Bent	6,576
32		14	H	Millwall	W	3-0	Bryan, Malkin, Preece	4,455
33		21	A	Southend Utd	L	1-2	Brabin	3,340
34		24	A	Grimsby Town	L	0-1		4,924
35		28	H	Fulham	W	2-1	Preece, Clarkson	5,183
36	Mar	7	H	Watford	D	1-1	Clarkson	5,237
37		14	A	Northampton Town	L	0-2		6,586
38		21	H	Gillingham	W	2-1	Malkin, Clarkson	4,165
39		28	A	York City	D	1-1	Preece	3,650
40	Apr	4	H	Walsall	W	1-0	Preece	4,451
41		7	A	Burnley	W	2-1	Clarkson, Bent	13,413
42		11	A	Plymouth Argyle	L	1-3	Own-goal	5,655
43		13	H	Brentford	L	1-2	Taylor	3,926
44		18	A	Preston NE	D	3-3	Clarkson 2, Hills	13,500
45		25	H	Bristol Rovers	W	1-0	Brabin	7,057
46	May	2	A	Chesterfield	D	1-1	Carlisle	4,462

Final League Position: 12th in Division Two

Apps
Sub Apps
Gls

FA Cup

1	Nov	15	H	Blyth Spartans	W	4-3	Preece, Linighan, Clarkson 2	4,814
2	Dec	6	A	Oldham Athletic	L	1-2	Ellis	6,590

Apps
Sub Apps
Gls

League Cup

1	Aug	12	H	Manchester City	W	1-0	Preece	8,084
		26	A	Manchester City	L	0-1*		12,563
2	Sep	16	H	Coventry City	W	1-0	Linighan	5,884
	Oct	1	A	Coventry City	L	1-3	Linighan	9,565

Apps
Sub Apps
Gls

Banks	Bryan	Bradshaw	Butler	Lydiate	Brabin	Bonner	Clarkson	Quinn	Philpott	Preece	Linighan	Malkin	Mellon	Rogan	Bent	Ellis	Worthington	Carlisle	King	Dixon	Strong	Ormerod	Hughes	Foster	Reid	Longworth	Hills	Haddow	Greenacre	Conroy	Taylor	Barnes	Thompson	Nowland
1	2	3	4	5	6	7	8	9	10	11																								
1	2*	3	4	5	6	7	8		10	11	12	9																						
1	2	3*	4	5	6	7#	8	9	10'	11	12	15	14																					
1	2		4	5	6	7#	8'			11		14	9	3	15	10																		
1	2		4		7		6*		12	11			8		9	10	3	5																
1	2		4#		12	7	6		14	11			8		9	10	3*	5																
1	2			3	4*	7	6	14	12	11			8		9#	10		5																
1	2*	3		4		7		9	6	11'	5		8		15	10		12																
1	2	3		4		7#	14	9'	11	15	5*		8		6	10	12																	
1	2	3*		4		7	6			11	5	9#	8		14	10	12																	
1	2			4		7	12	9	6*	11	5		8			10	3																	
1	2			4		7	14	9	6#	11	5		8		12	10	3*																	
1	2		4			7	8	9	6	11	5					10	12		3*															
1	2		4		15	7	8	9#	6	11'	5				14	10	12		3*															
1	2		4			7	8	9*	6	11	5				12	10			3															
1	2		4			7	8	9	6	11	5					10			3															
1	2		4		12	7	8	9	6	11	5					10			3*															
1			4	2	6	7	8		11	14	5#				9	10			3*	12														
1			4	2		7	8		11	6*					9	10				3	5	12												
1			4	2		7	8		11#	6*		12			9	10	14			3	5													
1	2		4		12	7	8		11			9#			6*	10				3	5	14												
1	2		4				8		11#	10		9			12					3	5		6	7*	14									
1*	2		4				8		11	10	12	9'			7#					3	5	14	6		15									
1	2		4				8		11	10		9*			7					3	5	12	6											
1	2		4			7	8		11	10*	5				12						3	9	6											
1	2		4	3		7	8		10	11	5*				14			12				9	6#											
1*			4	6		7#	8			11					10			5				9			14	12	3							
1	2			6	7*		8			11		14			10			4			5	9#					3	12						
1	2			6	12	7	8			11		14			10			4*			5	9#					3							
1	2		4			7	8		12	11	6	9*			10						5						3							
1	2		4			7	8			11	6	9*			10						5		12				3							
1	2		4		14	7	8	12		11	6	9*			10#								5				3							
1	2		4	6*	14	7#	8		12	11		9			10								5				3							
1	2		4	5*	10		8		12	11	6	9											7				3							
1	2*		4	5#	10		8		14	11	6	9'			15			12					7				3							
1	2		4	5*	10		8		6	11					9								7				3		12					
1	2		4	5*	10	7	8			11	6	14			12								3						9#					
1	2		4			7	8			11	6	12			10								5				3		9*					
1	2		4			7*	8			11	6				10								5				3		12	9				
1	2		4				8		7	11	6				10								5				3			9				
1	2		4		7		8			11	6				10								5				3			9*	12			
	2		4	12#	7		8		14	11	6				10								5*				3			9		1		
1	2*		4		12		8		7	11	6				10								5				3				9			
1	2		4		14		8		7	11	6				10#								5				3			12	9*			
1	2				10		8		7	11								5					6				3				9		4	
1	2		4		10		8		11			9#						6					5			14	3				7*			12
45	42	6	37	22	16	31	42	11	27	42	26	13	9	1	25	18	4	8	6	6	11	5	20	1			19		2	3	4	1	1	
				1	9		3	2	8	2	3	7	1		11		5	3		1		4	1		3	2		1	2	1	1			1
	1			1	3	3	13	4	2	11		2			3	8		2			1	2					1				1			

1			4	2		7	8		6	11	5				9*	10#				3		14				12								
1	2		4	5	6	7	8		11			12	3		9*	10				3														
2	1		2	2	1	2	2		2	1	1				2	2				2														
												1										1				1								
							2			1	1					1																		

1	2	3	4	5	6	7	8	9	10*	11		12																						
1	2		4	12	6	7	8	9#		11#	5*	14	10	3		14																		
1	2	3	4			7	8	9	6	11*	5	12				10																		
1	2	3	4			7	6		11	9	5		8			10																		
4	4	3	4	1	2	4	4	3	3	4	3		2	1		2																		
		1		1								3				1																		
										1	2																							

League Table

	P	W	D	L	F	A	Pts
Watford	46	24	16	6	67	41	88
Bristol City	46	25	10	11	69	39	85
Grimsby Town	46	19	15	12	55	37	72
Northampton Town	46	18	17	11	52	37	71
Bristol Rovers	46	20	10	16	70	64	70
Fulham	46	20	10	16	60	43	70
Wrexham	46	18	16	12	55	51	70
Gillingham	46	19	13	14	52	47	70
Bournemouth	46	18	12	16	57	52	66
Chesterfield	46	16	17	13	46	44	65
Wigan Athletic	46	17	11	18	64	66	62
Blackpool	46	17	11	18	59	67	62
Oldham Athletic	46	15	16	15	62	54	61
Wycombe Wanderers	46	14	18	14	51	53	60
Preston North End	46	15	14	17	56	56	59
York City	46	14	17	15	52	58	59
Luton Town	46	14	15	17	60	64	57
Millwall	46	14	13	19	43	54	55
Walsall	46	14	12	20	43	52	54
Burnley	46	13	13	20	55	65	52
Brentford	46	11	17	18	50	71	50
Plymouth Argyle	46	12	13	21	55	70	49
Carlisle United	46	12	8	26	57	73	44
Southend United	46	11	10	25	47	79	43

1998-99

Division Two

Manager: Nigel Worthington

Did you know that?

In December 1998, a Midland-based consortium made an £18 million offer for the club.

Vicky Oyston officially stood down as chairman on 3 April 1999, to be replaced by her son Karl.

A new stadium was in the offing at a Greenfield site called Whyndyke Farm just off the M55. Numerous disputes between the owner and the club followed, and the plan as never taken up.

On 10 April, the club was awarded half a million pounds by the Sport England lottery fund to help the youth development programme.

Also plans for the rebuilding of the dilapidated Bloomfield Road were now well in advance.

Match No.	Date	Venue	Opponents	Result		Scorers	Attendance
1	Aug 8	A	Manchester City	L	0-3		32,134
2	15	H	Oldham Athletic	W	3-0	Bent, Malkin, Bushell	5,258
3	22	A	Wigan Athletic	L	0-3		4,853
4	29	D	Gillingham	D	2-2	Thompson, Clarkson	3,994
5	Sep 1	A	Bournemouth	D	1-1	Clarkson	6,785
6	5	H	Northampton Town	W	2-1	Clarkson, Thompson	4,017
7	8	H	Notts County	W	1-0	Shuttleworth	3,849
8	12	A	Lincoln City	W	2-1	Clarkson, Aldridge	3,954
9	19	H	Luton Town	W	1-0	Nowland	5,695
10	26	A	Stoke City	W	3-1	Carlisle, Aldridge 2	15,002
11	Oct 3	H	York City	L	1-2	Bushell	5,633
12	10	H	Millwall	L	2-3	Aldridge 2	5,295
13	17	A	Walsall	L	0-1		4,728
14	21	A	Reading	D	1-1	Bryan	8,450
15	31	H	Fulham	L	2-3	Hills, Aldridge	5,904
16	Nov 7	A	Wrexham	D	1-1	Lawson	3,511
17	10	A	Bristol Rovers	W	2-0	Ormerod, Lawson	5,361
18	21	H	Preston NE	D	0-0		10,868
19	28	A	Burnley	L	0-1		11,925
20	Dec 5	H	Chesterfield	D	1-1	Lawson	3,278
21	12	H	Wycombe Wanderers	D	0-0		2,990
22	18	A	Colchester Utd	D	2-2	Ormerod, Hughes	3,228
23	26	H	Wigan Athletic	D	1-1	Garvey	5,147
24	28	A	Macclesfield Town	W	1-0	Own-goal	3,919
25	Jan 2	A	Gillingham	L	0-1		7,022
26	9	H	Manchester City	D	0-0		9,752
27	16	A	Oldham Athletic	L	0-3		5,353
28	30	H	Macclesfield Town	W	2-1	Ormerod, Clarkson	4,569
29	Feb 6	A	Northampton Town	D	0-0		5,592
30	13	A	Notts County	W	1-0	Bushell	4,778
31	20	H	Lincoln City	L	0-1		4,215
32	27	A	Luton Town	L	0-1		4,646
33	Mat 6	H	Stoke City	L	0-1		5,504
34	12	H	Wrexham	D	1-1	Ormerod (pen)	3,905
35	16	H	Bournemouth	D	0-0		3,186
36	20	A	Fulham	L	0-4		12,869
37	27	A	Chesterfield	W	2-1	Sturridge, Clarkson	4,027
38	Apr 3	H	Walsall	L	0-2		5,432
39	5	A	Millwall	L	0-1		6,672
40	10	H	Reading	W	2-0	Aldridge (pen), Clarkson	3,617
41	13	H	Burnley	L	0-2		5,658
42	17	A	Preston NE	W	2-1	Nowland,Ormerod	15,337
43	24	H	Bristol Rovers	L	1-2	Ormerod	5,033
44	27	A	York City	L	0-1		2,971
45	May 1	A	Wycombe Wanderers	D	2-2	Ormerod, Clarkson	5,286
46	8	H	Colchester Utd	W	2-1	Ormerod, Clarkson	4,866

Final League Position: 14th in Division Tow

Apps
Sub Apps
Gls

FA Cup

1	Nov 14	A	Wigan Athletic	L	3-4	Blunt, Ormerod, Aldridge	4,640

Apps
Sub Apps
Gls

League Cup

1	Aug 11	H	Scunthorpe Utd	W	1-0	Conroy	1,873
	18	A	Scunthorpe Utd	D	1-1	Bent	2,211
2	Sep 15	H	Tranmere Rovers	W	2-1	Aldridge 2	3,954
	22	A	Tranmere Rovers	L	1-3	Malkin	5,765

Apps
Sub Apps
Gls

Banks	Bryan	Hills	Butler	Hughes	Bardsley	Bent	Clarkson	Aldridge	Bushell	Blunt	Malkin	Conroy	Carlisle	Brabin	Ormerod	Thompson	Rogan	Shuttleworth	Robinson	Nowland	Rowe	Garvey	Lawson	Patterson	Barnes P	Jarrett	Peacock	Couzens	Barnes K	Sturridge	Caig	Watts
1	2	3	4	5	6	7*	8	9	10	11#	12	14																				
1		3	4	5*	2	7	8		10		11#	9	12	6	14																	
1		3			2	7	8		10		11	9	5	6		4																
1	2	3*			4		8	15	10		11	9'	5	6	14	7	12#															
1	2				4		8		10		11#	9	5		6	7		3*	12	14												
1*	2				4		8	6#	10		11	9'	5		15	7		3	12	14												
1	2				4		8	9*	10		11		5		6	7		3		14												
1	2			4			8	9	10		11#		5	14	6*	7		3		12												
1*	2			12	4	14	8	9#	10		11		5		6#	7		3		14												
1	2			7	4*	14	8	9	10		11#		5	12	6			3														
1*	2			7		15	8	9'	10		11		5	4	6#			3		14	12											
1	2			10'	4*	15	8	9			11		5	12	6#	7		3		14												
1	2	3				7#	8	9	10		11		5			4		6*		14		12										
1	2	3	4			7*	8		10		11		5		12	6			9#			14										
1	2	3	4			12	8	7	10			11#	5			6			9*	14												
1	2	3	4			12	8	9*	10		11#		5		14	6							9									
1	2	3	4			14	8	7#	10		11		5		12	6*			12				9#									
1	2	3	4	6			8	7*	10		11		5		12								9									
1	2	3	4	6		14	8		10				5	7*	11#					12			9									
1	2			6	4	14	8		10		11#		5		9*			3		12			9									
1	2	3		6	4	14	8		10		11		5		7*					12#				9								
		3	6	2	4	12	8		10*		11#		5		9					14				7	1							
1	2	3	4	5	6		8								11					9		7		10								
1	2	3	4	5	6	14	8				12				11#					9		7*		10								
1	2		4	5	12	14	8				11				9'	6*	3			15				10		7#						
1	2		4		6	7*	8		10		11'		5		15					12			9	3								
1	2				5*	6	9		7		11#		4		14	3	12						10	8								
1			4	5	6	12	8		10				14		11	2	3*			7#		15	9'									
1	2		5	3	4	12	8	14	7						11	6*				9			10#									
1	2		4	5	6	3	8	9	10						11					7												
1*	2	3	4	5	6	11#	8	9	10											7		14					12					
1	2	3		5	6*	14	8	9'	10			7	4		11	12#				15												
1	2	3	4	10		14	8	12					5		11					9								6*	7#			
1	12	3*	4	6		14	8		10				5		11					9'								2	15	7#		
1	12	5	3	8		11	6		7*				4		10					14								2		9#		
1	2	3		6		7	8						5		11					12								4	10*	9		
	12	3		6		7	8						5				14			10		11						2*		9#	1	4
	2	5		7		8					14		4		12		15			10'		11				6*				9#	1	3
	2	3*		6		7	8	9					5		10		12			14		11#									1	4
	2	10		6		8#	7	9'			15		4		11		5			14											1	3
	2	8*		6		9	7				10		4		11		5			12											1	3
	2				6	7	8						5		11	4*	3	12		9#		14						10			1	
		10'		2	4	7*	8						5		11	14	3	12		9#		15									1	6
	2	12		10	4#	7	8				14				11	5'	3*			9		15									1	6
	2*			10	4	7	8				9				11#		3	5		14		12									1	6
	12			5	2	8	9				10#				4		3*	6		14		15									1	7
36	37	27	20	32	27	21	45	18	30	1	25	7	34	5	30	19	9	12	2	13		5	9	7	1	2		6	2	5	10	9
	4	1		1	1	18		3			5	1	2	3	10	2	5	2	3	23	1	9					1		1			
	1	1		1		1	9	7	3		1		1		8	2		1		2		1	3							1		

Banks	Bryan	Hills	Butler	Hughes	Bardsley	Bent	Clarkson	Aldridge	Bushell	Blunt	Malkin	Conroy	Carlisle	Brabin	Ormerod	Thompson	Rogan	Shuttleworth	Robinson	Nowland	Rowe	Garvey	Lawson	Patterson	Barnes P	Jarrett	Peacock	Couzens	Barnes K	Sturridge	Caig	Watts
1	2	3	4			14	8	9	10	7#					11			6*	5							12						
1	1	1	1				1	1	1	1					1			1	1													
						1																				1						

Banks	Bryan	Hills	Butler	Hughes	Bardsley	Bent	Clarkson	Aldridge	Bushell	Blunt	Malkin	Conroy	Carlisle	Brabin	Ormerod	Thompson	Rogan	Shuttleworth	Robinson	Nowland	Rowe	Garvey	Lawson	Patterson	Barnes P	Jarrett	Peacock	Couzens	Barnes K	Sturridge	Caig	Watts
1		3	4	5	2	7	8	9*	10		12	11		6																		
1		3	4*	5	2	7	8		10		11	9	12	6																		
1	2		4				8	9	10		11#		5	14	6*	7		3		12												
1	2			9	4	12	8		10		11		5		6*	7#		3	14													1
4	2	2	3	3	3	2	4	2	4		3	2	2	2	2	2		2												0		
						1					1		1	1					1	1												
						1		2			1	1																				

League Table

	P	W	D	L	F	A	Pts
Fulham	46	31	8	7	79	32	101
Walsall	46	26	9	11	63	47	87
Manchester City	46	22	16	8	69	33	82
Gillingham	46	22	14	10	75	44	80
Preston North End	46	22	13	11	78	50	79
Wigan Athletic	46	22	10	14	75	48	76
Bournemouth	46	21	13	12	63	41	76
Stoke City	46	21	6	19	59	63	69
Chesterfield	46	17	13	16	46	44	64
Millwall	46	17	11	18	52	59	62
Reading	46	16	13	17	54	63	61
Luton Town	46	16	10	20	51	60	58
Bristol Rovers	46	13	17	16	65	56	56
Blackpool	46	14	14	18	44	54	56
Burnley	46	13	16	17	54	73	55
Notts County	46	14	12	20	52	61	54
Wrexham	46	13	14	19	43	62	53
Colchester United	46	12	16	18	52	70	52
Wycombe Wanderers	46	13	12	21	52	58	51
Oldham Athletic	46	14	9	23	48	66	51
York City	46	13	11	22	56	80	50
Northampton Town	46	10	18	18	43	57	48
Lincoln City	46	13	7	26	42	74	46
Macclesfield Town	46	11	10	25	43	63	43

1999-2000

Division Two

Manager: Nigel Worthington/Steve McMahon

Did you know that?

Manager Nigel Worthington resigned after a defeat to Preston North End to be replaced by Steve McMahon.

The home games on 15 and 29 January against Luton Town and Brentford respectively were titled 'break the gate'. It was scheme where revenue generated from a gate above 3,500 would be given to the manager for team strengthening.

After relegation back to the bottom tier, manager McMahon took the squad on a close season tour of the Caribbean, where they won the tournament.

Match No.	Date	Venue	Opponents	Result		Scorers	Attendance
1	Aug 7	H	Wrexham	W	2-1	Ormerod 2	5,008
2	14	A	Luton Town	L	2-3	Ormerod, Nowland	5,176
3	21	H	Gillingham	D	1-1	Murphy	4,203
4	28	A	Brentford	L	0-2		5,353
5	30	H	Oxford Utd	D	1-1	Carlisle	3,670
6	Sep 4	A	Bristol City	L	2-5	Ormerod, Murphy	8,439
7	11	A	Notts County	L	1-2	Carlisle	5,512
8	18	H	Bournemouth	D	0-0		4,471
9	25	H	Wycombe Wanderers	L	1-2	Ormerod	3,452
10	Oct 2	A	Bristol Rovers	L	1-3	Murphy	7,715
11	9	A	Chesterfield	D	0-0		2,804
12	16	H	Bury	L	0-5		5,270
13	19	H	Oldham Athletic	L	1-2	Murphy	3,845
14	23	A	Wycombe Wanderers	W	2-0	Nowland, Lee	5,021
15	Nov 2	A	Cardiff City	D	1-1	Murphy	4,523
16	6	H	Wigan Athletic	D	2-2	Murphy, Durnin	4,535
17	14	A	Burnley	L	0-1		12,898
18	23	H	Millwall	L	1-2	Murphy	2,819
19	27	H	Cambridge Utd	W	2-1	Murphy, Clarkson	4,040
20	Dec 4	A	Wrexham	D	1-1	Hills (pen)	2,668
21	18	A	Preston NE	L	0-3		16,821
22	26	H	Stoke City	L	1-2	Nowland	5,274
23	28	A	Scunthorpe Utd	L	0-1		5,147
24	Jan 3	H	Colchester Utd	D	1-1	Bent	3,462
25	8	A	Reading	D	1-1	Matthews	7,297
26	15	H	Luton Town	D	3-3	Ablett, Clarkson, Bushell	5,262
27	22	A	Gillingham	W	3-1	Richardson, Bushell, Matthews	6,805
28	29	H	Brentford	L	0-1		5,270
29	Feb 5	A	Oxford Utd	W	1-0	Murphy	5,179
30	8	H	Reading	L	0-2		4,291
31	12	H	Bristol City	L	1-2	Murphy	5,066
32	19	A	Cambridge Utd	W	2-0	Carlisle, Newell	4,636
33	26	A	Bournemouth	L	0-2		4,464
34	Mar 4	H	Notts County	W	2-1	Lumsden, Clarkson	4,277
35	7	A	Wigan Athletic	L	1-5	Gill	6,451
36	11	H	Cardiff City	D	2-2	Gill, Hills (pen)	5,015
37	18	A	Millwall	D	1-1	Gill	10,506
38	21	H	Burnley	D	1-1	Gill	8,029
39	25	A	Stoke City	L	0-3		10,002
40	Apr 1	H	Preston NE	D	0-0		9,042
41	8	A	Colchester Utd	D	1-1	Thomas	3,351
42	15	H	Scunthorpe Utd	L	0-2		5,542
43	22	A	Bury	L	2-3	Gill, Newell	3,857
44	24	H	Bristol Rovers	W	2-1	Gill, Thomas	5,635
45	29	A	Oldham Athletic	D	1-1	Carlisle	6,290
46	May 8	H	Chesterfield	D	2-2	Coid, Gill	3,860

Final League Position: 22nd in Division Two

Apps
Sub Apps
Gls

FA Cup

1	Oct 30	H	Stoke City	W	2-0	Carlisle, Nowland	4,721
2	Nov 20	H	Hendon	W	2-0	Clarkson, Durnin	2,975
3	Dec 13	A	Arsenal	L	1-3	Clarkson	34,143

Apps
Sub Apps
Gls

League Cup

1	Aug 10	H	Tranmere Rovers	W	2-1	Hughes, Clarkson	3,298
	24	A	Tranmere Rovers	L	1-3	Clarkson	4,800

Apps
Sub Apps
Gls

Barnes	Bryan	Hills	Bardsley	Carlisle	Couzens	Hughes	Bent	Clarkson	Ormerod	Murphy	Lambert	Nowland	Thompson	Caig	Whitley	Aldridge	Shuttleworth	Robinson	Forsyth	Connell	Bushell	Rachel	Garvey	Coid	Lee	Durnin	Beesley	Quailey	Matthews	Ablett	Richardson	Jaszczun	Lumsden	Newell	Gill	Byfield	Thomas	Wellens	Trees	Astafjevs	Jones
1	2	3	4	5	6*	7	8#	9	10	11	12	14																													
1	6*	9	2	3	5	7		8	10	11		14	4																												
		3*	4	5	2	8	7		11#	10		12	6	1	9	14																									
	15		4	3	2	5	7#	9	11	10		14		1	8'		6*	12																							
	2	5		3		4	9*	7	10#	11		14		1	6	14			8																						
	2	5		3	7	4*	6#	8	10	11		14		1				12	9																						
	5	2	3	4	8		9	6	11	7				1					10																						
	2	3	4	5		6	7*			11		14		1	9	12			10	8#																					
	2	3	4	5		6*	7#		9	10		15		1	11	14			8'		12																				
	2	5	6	3		4	12		11	10		9*			8				7			1																			
	2	5	8	3		4		7	10'	11		15		1					6				9*	12																	
	2	5	3	4		6	8*	11	9#	10		12		1					7					14																	
	12	5		3		4		7	8	10				1	6			2*						11	9																
	12	3		4		5		6	8#	11		14		1				2*	15		7			10'	9																
	2	5		3		4		7		10		11'		1				2*	12		6			8#	9	15															
	2	3		4		5	12	7	15	11'				1				7*	14		6			9#		10															
	5	2		3		4	12	7		10				1							7			8	9*	11															
	2	5		3*		4	12	6		10		14		1							7			11	9#	8*	12														
		2	3	4		5		6		10	14	12		1*							7				9#	11	8														
	7	2		3	12	4		5		10		14		1							6				9*		8	11#													
		3	4	5	2	6*	7	8				9#		1						14				12	11		10														
		2	3	4			11	6				9		1			8*				7		14	12	10#		5														
			2	6			9	5				11#		1			3			14	7			8			4		10												
			2	3			9*	8		10				1			5		7		6			12			4		11												
		9	2	3	14	4*		7		11				1			12		6#		8			15			5		10'												
			2	4			9	7		11*				1							6			12			3		10	5	8										
			2	3			7	8						1							9						4		11	5	10	6									
		2	3	4			10	7		11				1							8*								12	5	9	6									
		5	2	4	12		10	6		11				1							8*						3				7		9								
		4	2	3			8#	12		11				1							6*						14			5	7	10	9								
		4	2	5			12	7		11				1																3	6	8	9*	10							
		4	3	5				7		11				1																6	8	2	9	10							
		4		5		6		7		11				1																3	8	2	9	10							
		2	5	3		12	14	9		11				1																4	7	8	6*	10#							
		4	6	5		15	14	8		10#		12		1																3	7*	2			9	10'					
1		6	2	3	7*		12	11																			4			12	9	5			8	10					
1			3	5	2	4	12	6																							9	10		7	8	11*					
1*			3	5	2#	4	12	6													14										9	10		7	8		11				
1			2	3	6*	4		9		14																					9	5		10#	7		11	12			
1			2	3	5*	4				10											12			9							7#	8			6		11	14			
1			2	3		4				9														6*							7	8		12	5		11	10			
1			2*	3		4#				9														12			14				8	6		10	5		11	7			
1		2*	5'			3				14											15			7			4#				8	9		10	6		11	12			
1*			2#			3'				14											16			9			4				5@	6		10	7		11	8	12		
1			4	5						14											12			2			3				8*	6		10#	7		11	9			
						7				15	14		12	1							6#			2			4*					4		10	8		11'	9			3
12	15	33	36	44	12	31	18	34	13	34		5	2	33	7		4	4	10	1	17	1	1	13	9	4	15	1	5	9	20	19	6	12	12	3	9	5			1
	3				3	2	10	1	1	5	3	15	1			4	1	2	3	2	6		1	8		1	3		1	1				1				3	1	1	
		2		4			1	3	5	10		3									2			1	1	1			2	1	1		1	2	7		2				

	2	4		3		5	12	6		10		8		1*				9	14		7			11#			
	7	2		3		4	14	6		10		15	3	1					12		5			9#	8*	11'	
		9	2	3		4		8		10		11	3	1							7				6		5
	2	3	1	3		3		3		3		2		3				1			3			2	2	1	1
							2					1							2								
				1				2				1														1	

1	12	2*	3	4	8	5	9#	6	10	11		14	7				
			4	5	2	6	9	7	10			11*		1	8	12	3
2		1	2	2	2	2	2	2	2	1		1	1	1	1		1
	1											1				1	
						1		2									

League Table

	P	W	D	L	F	A	Pts
Preston North End	46	28	11	7	74	37	95
Burnley	46	25	13	8	69	47	88
Gillingham	46	25	10	11	79	48	85
Wigan Athletic	46	22	17	7	72	38	83
Millwall	46	23	13	10	76	50	82
Stoke City	46	23	13	10	68	42	82
Bristol Rovers	46	23	11	12	69	45	80
Notts County	46	18	11	17	61	55	65
Bristol City	46	15	19	12	59	57	64
Reading	46	16	14	16	57	63	62
Wrexham	46	17	11	18	52	61	62
Wycombe Wanderers	46	16	13	17	56	53	61
Luton Town	46	17	10	19	61	65	61
Oldham Athletic	46	16	12	18	50	55	60
Bury	46	13	18	15	61	64	57
Bournemouth	46	16	9	21	59	62	57
Brentford	46	13	13	20	47	61	52
Colchester United	46	14	10	22	59	82	52
Cambridge United	46	12	12	22	64	65	48
Oxford United	46	12	9	25	43	73	45
Cardiff City	46	9	17	20	45	67	44
Blackpool	46	8	17	21	49	77	41
Scunthorpe United	46	9	12	25	40	74	39
Chesterfield	46	7	15	24	34	63	36

2000-01

Division Three

Manager: Steve McMahon

Did you know that?

A new crest, which is still in use today, was adopted and matches that of the local town.

The Kop and West Stands of Bloomfield Road were dismantled and a new stadium started to be built during the close season.

Before the game at Kidderminster Harriers, Blackpool were in 91st position in the Football League.

Brett Ormerod scored in the Play-off Final at Cardiff. He would do the same 10 years later in the Championship Play-off Final at Wembley.

Match No.	Date	Venue	Opponents	Result		Scorers	Attendance
1	Aug 12	H	Hull City	W	3-1	Ormerod, Murphy J,Simpson	5,862
2	19	A	Cardiff City	D	1-1	Murphy J	11,019
3	26	H	Leyton Orient	D	2-2	Simpson, Coid	4,816
4	28	A	Torquay Utd	L	2-3	Ormerod, Wellens	2,384
5	Sep 2	A	Scunthorpe Utd	L	0-1		3,822
6	9	H	Hartlepool Utd	L	1-2	Morrison	4,562
7	12	H	Brighton @ HA	L	0-2		3,406
8	16	A	Lincoln City	D	1-1	Murphy J	2,753
9	23	H	Chesterfield	L	1-3	Bushell	3,970
10	29	A	Kidderminster Harriers	W	4-1	Simpson 2, Ormerod 2	3,891
11	Sep 8	H	Southend Utd	D	2-2	Murphy J, Ormerod	3,915
12	14	A	Plymouth Argyle	L	0-2		3,651
13	17	A	Mansfield Town	W	1-0	Wellens	2,328
14	21	H	Macclesfield Town	W	2-1	Hills, Coid	3,700
15	24	H	Carlisle Utd	W	3-2	Hills, Murphy J, Clarkson	4,744
16	28	A	Cheltenham Town	W	1-0	Murphy J	3,798
17	Oct 4	H	Shrewsbury Town	L	0-1		4,850
18	11	A	Barnet	L	0-7		2,520
19	25	H	Darlington	W	2-1	Ormerod, Simpson	3,683
20	Dec 2	A	Rochdale	L	0-1		4,186
21	16	H	Exeter City	W	3-0	Murphy J 2, Ormerod	2,907
22	22	A	York City	W	2-0	Ormerod, Hughes	2,705
23	26	H	Halifax Town	L	0-1		5,044
24	Jan 13	H	Torquay Utd	W	5-0	Ormerod, Simpson 2 (1 pen), Reid, Clarkson	3,549
25	16	A	Hull City	W	1-0	Murphy J	4,450
26	27	H	York City	W	1-0	Wellens	3,938
27	Feb 3	H	Scunthorpe Utd	W	6-0	Simpson (pen), Murphy J 2, Wellens, Reid, Milligan	4,161
28	10	A	Hartlepool Utd	L	1-3	Ormerod	3,973
29	13	H	Cardiff City	W	1-0	Ormerod	4,417
30	17	H	Lincoln City	W	2-0	Shittu, Murphy J	4,596
31	20	A	Brighton @ HA	L	0-1		6,756
32	24	A	Chesterfield	L	1-2	Wellens	4,812
33	Mar 3	H	Kidderminster Harriers	W	5-1	Murphy J 3 (1 pen), Wellens, Ormerod	4,624
34	6	H	Plymouth Argyle	W	1-0	Walker	4,570
35	10	A	Southend Utd	W	3-0	Wellens, Simpson, Walker	4,810
36	17	H	Mansfield Town	D	2-2	Murphy J, Ormerod	5,241
37	20	A	Leyton Orient	L	0-1		4,086
38	24	A	Macclesfield Town	L	1-2	Walker	3,045
39	31	A	Exeter City	L	0-2		3,836
40	Apr 10	A	Halifax Town	W	2-1	Simpson, Clarkson	3,311
41	14	A	Carlisle Utd	L	0-1		6,096
42	16	H	Cheltenham Town	D	2-2	Murphy J,Ormerod	5,192
43	21	A	Shrewsbury Town	L	0-1		3,129
44	26	H	Rochdale	W	3-1	Clarkson, Ormerod, Murphy J	5,470
45	28	H	Barnet	W	3-2	Ormerod, Simpson	5,289
46	May 5	A	Darlington	W	3-1	Ormerod, Shittu, Wellens	5,428

Final League Position: 7th in Division Three

Apps
Sub Apps
Gls

Play-Offs

SF	May 13	H	Hartlepool Utd	W	2-0	Ormerod 2	5,720
	16	A	Hartlepool Utd	W	3-1	Ormerod 2, Hills	5,836
F	26	N	Leyton Orient	W	4-2	Hughes, Reid, Simpson, Ormerod	23,600

N-played at Millenium Stadium, Cardiff

Apps
Sub Apps
Gls

FA Cup

1	Nov 18	H	Telford Utd	W	3-1	Murphy J, Ormerod 2	2,780
2	Dec 10	H	Yeovil Town	L	0-1		3,757

Apps
Sub Apps
Gls

League Cup

1	Aug 22	A	Stockport County	W	1-0	Nowland	3,014
	Sep 5	H	Stockport County	W	3-2	Murphy J 2, Newell	3,133
2	19	A	Norwich City	D	3-3	Murphy J 2, Ormerod	9,369
	Oct 2	H	Norwich City	L	0-5		4,038

App
Sub
Goals

Caig	Bushell	Hughes	Milligan J	Newell	Collins	Coid	Ormerod	Murphy N	Hawe	Simpson	Clarkson	Murphy J	Hawe	Jones	Jaszczun	Nowland	Wellens	Morrison	Barnes	Maley	Reid	Hills	Thompson	O'Connor	Kennedy	Brown	Walker	Shittu	Milligan M	Parkinson	Meecham
1	2	3	4*	5#	6	7	8	9	10	11	12	14																			
1	2	3	4*	5#		6	7	8		10	12	14	9'	15	11																
1	3	4	14			7	9	10		11#	5	6		8*	2	12															
1	3	4	5*			7	10#	15		11'	12	6		9	2	14	8														
1	3	4	6*	8		7				11		9			2	12	10	5													
	3	4	6*	8#		7	11	14			12	9			2		10	5	1												
	3	4				7	11			8	6	9			2	12	10*	5	1												
	3	4			7	8	10			11		6			2		9	5	1												
	4	3*			7#	6	11			8		10		12	2	14	9	5	1												
	3	4			7	8	10*			11		6		9	2	12		5	1												
	8	5*			7	6	10			9		11		12	2				1	3	4										
	3				6	7	9*			10	14	5		8	2	12#	15		1	11'	4										
1			4			7				10	5	6					8				3	2	9	11							
		12			6	7				10	4	5					8				3	2	9	11*	1						
		12			9	8				6	7	10			14		4				5	2*	11#	3	1						
		2			5	7	14			10#	6	11			12		8				3	9*		4	1						
		3			9	5	14			10	8	11			6		7				4			2#	1*	12					
		3			6	7	9			10		5					8				4	2		11	1						
		4*			7	2	11			9	12	10					8				5	3		6	1						
	6				7	2	11			9	8	10							1		4	3		5							
		4*			7	8	11			9	6	10			2				1		5	3	12								
		4			7	8	11			9	6	10			2				1		5	3									
	14'	4			7*	3	11			9	8	10			2	15	12		1		5	6#									
		4	8			3	11			9	12	10#			2	14	7		1		5	6*									
		4	8			3	11			9*	6	10			2		7		1		5		12								
		4*	6		12	8	11				14	9			2		7#		1		5	3	10								
		4	8'		15	3	11			9#	12	10			2	12	7		1		5	6*									
		4	8			3	11			9		10			2*		7		1		5		6#	12			14				
		2	4#		14	3	11			9	12	8					7		1*				6	5			11				
	12	2*	3#		14	5	11			9	14	8					7		1					10			4#	6			
	12		8		6	5	11			9		10			2		7#		1			3*					14	4			
	12	2	8#	14	6	3				9		10			5*		7		1								11	4			
	6		8			5	11#	12		9	14	10'			2*		7		1		3						15	4			
	3		5*		7	8	11			9		10			2				1		6						12	4			
	12		8*		6	5	11#			9		10			2		7		1		3						14	4			
	12		8#		6	3	11			9		10			2		7*		1		5						14	4			
	6*		8		7	4	11			9		10			2				1		3						12	4			
		14	8			6	11			9#		10			2*		7		1		3						12	4#	14	5	
		3	8			6#				9		10			2		7		1		4*						11	12	14	5	
		3				6	14			9*	8	10			12		7		1			5					11#	4		2	
		3	12			6	11#			9*	8	10					7		1			5					14	4		2	
		3			14	12	11			9#	8	10			6		7#		1			5					12	4		2*	
		3	12		8#	6	15			9		10					7		1		4	5*					11'	14		2	
						6	11#			9	8*	10			5		7		1		3						12	4	14	2	
	12					6	11			9		10			5*		7		1		3							4	8	2	
	12		8*			3	11			9		10#					7		1		5						14	4	6	2	
6	16	31	23	4	23	45	36	3	1	44	16	44	1	4	32		34	6	34	2	29	18	6	10	6		6	15	2	9	
	8	3	3	1	5	1	4	3			12	2		3	3	10	2						2	1		1	12	2	3		
	1	1				2	17			11	4	18					8	1			1	2					3	2			

Caig	Bushell	Hughes	Milligan J	Newell	Collins	Coid	Ormerod	Murphy N	Hawe	Simpson	Clarkson	Murphy J	Hawe	Jones	Jaszczun	Nowland	Wellens	Morrison	Barnes	Maley	Reid	Hills	Thompson	O'Connor	Kennedy	Brown	Walker	Shittu	Milligan M	Parkinson	Meecham
	12		14			6	11			9#	8	10			3		7*		1		5							4		2	
		12	14			9	11				8	10	3		3		7		1		5*	6#						4		2	
		4	12			6	11'			9#	8	10					7*		1		5	3	15						14	2	
		1				3	3			2	3	3			2		3		3		3	2						2		3	
	1	1	3																				1						1		
		1					5			1											1										

Caig	Bushell	Hughes	Milligan J	Newell	Collins	Coid	Ormerod	Murphy N	Hawe	Simpson	Clarkson	Murphy J	Hawe	Jones	Jaszczun	Nowland	Wellens	Morrison	Barnes	Maley	Reid	Hills	Thompson	O'Connor	Kennedy	Brown	Walker	Shittu	Milligan M	Parkinson	Meecham
	12	2		15	8	6	11'			9#	14	10					7*				5	4		3	1						
	7@	4			8	6'	11			9	16	10			14				1*		2	5	15	3#							12
	1	2			2	2	2			2		2					1		1		2	2		2	1					0	
	1			1							2				1								1								
							2					1																			

Caig	Bushell	Hughes	Milligan J	Newell	Collins	Coid	Ormerod	Murphy N	Hawe	Simpson	Clarkson	Murphy J	Hawe	Jones	Jaszczun	Nowland	Wellens	Morrison	Barnes	Maley	Reid	Hills	Thompson	O'Connor	Kennedy	Brown	Walker	Shittu	Milligan M	Parkinson	Meecham
1	3	4		7*		8	11			9	5	10		6	2	12															
	3	4		6		8				9	14	10		11	2	12	7		1*										5#		
	3	4			6	8	11			9		10		5	2		7		1												
	7	4			6	8	11	3		9#		10		5*	2	14	12		1												
1	4	4		2	2	4	3	1		4	1	4		4	4		2		3										1		
											1					3	1														
				1			1					4				1															

League Table

	P	W	D	L	F	A	Pts
Brighton & Hove Albion	46	28	8	10	73	35	92
Cardiff City	46	23	13	10	95	58	82
Chesterfield	46	25	14	7	79	42	80
Hartlepool United	46	21	14	11	71	54	77
Leyton Orient	46	20	15	11	59	51	75
Hull City	46	19	17	10	47	39	74
Blackpool	46	22	6	18	74	58	72
Rochdale	46	18	17	11	59	48	71
Cheltenham Town	46	18	14	14	59	52	68
Scunthorpe United	46	18	11	17	62	52	65
Southend United	46	15	18	13	55	53	63
Plymouth Argyle	46	15	13	18	54	61	58
Mansfield Town	46	15	13	18	64	72	58
Macclesfield Town	46	14	14	18	51	62	56
Shrewsbury Town	46	15	10	21	49	65	55
Kidderminster Harriers	46	13	14	19	47	61	53
York City	46	13	13	20	42	63	52
Lincoln City	46	12	15	19	58	66	51
Exeter City	46	12	14	20	40	58	50
Darlington	46	12	13	21	44	56	49
Torquay United	46	12	13	21	52	77	49
Carlisle United	46	11	15	20	42	65	48
Halifax Town	46	12	11	23	54	68	47
Barnet	46	12	9	25	67	81	45

2001-02

Division Two

Manager: Steve McMahon

Did you know that?

Brett Ormerod was sold to Southampton for a club record fee of £1.75 million.

The two new stands at Bloomfield Road were opened with the home match with Huddersfield Town, but sadly the fans saw a 2–1 defeat.

Blackpool returned to the Millenium stadium and were again victorious.

Match No.	Date	Venue	Opponents	Result		Scorers	Attendance
1	Aug 11	H	Reading	L	0-2		5,613
2	18	A	Bournemouth	W	1-0	Hills	3,709
3	25	H	Wycombe Wanderers	D	2-2	Ormerod, Thompson	5,010
4	27	A	Brighton @ HA	L	0-4		6,696
5	Sep 8	A	Oldham Athletic	L	1-2	Ormerod	6,650
6	15	A	Huddersfield Town	W	4-2	Collins, Ormerod 3	10,691
7	18	H	Queens Park Rangers	D	2-2	O'Kane, Fenton	5,774
8	22	H	Cambridge Utd	D	1-1	Ormerod	5,096
9	25	A	Northampton Town	W	3-1	Ormerod 2, Fenton	5,103
10	29	H	Wigan Athletic	W	3-1	Murphy J, Coid, Mackenzie	5,279
11	Oct 4	A	Tranmere Rovers	L	0-4		10,354
12	13	H	Colchester Utd	W	2-1	Ormerod 2	5,546
13	20	A	Peterborough Utd	L	2-3	O'Kane, Murphy J	3,500
14	23	A	Wrexham	D	1-1	Ormerod	5,640
15	27	H	Chesterfield	W	1-0	Fenton	5,395
16	Nov 3	A	Brentford	L	0-2		3,798
17	6	H	Stoke City	D	2-2	Ormerod 2	4,921
18	10	H	Swindon Town	W	1-0	Coid	5,018
19	20	H	Notts County	D	0-0		4,118
20	24	A	Bristol City	L	1-2	Simpson (pen)	9,876
21	Dec 1	A	Port Vale	D	1-1	Coid	5,390
22	15	H	Cardiff City	D	1-1	Hills	4,880
23	22	A	Bury	D	1-1	Payton	4,830
24	26	H	Oldham Athletic	L	0-2		5,772
25	29	H	Brighton @ HA	D	2-2	Hughes, Collins	5,419
26	Jan 1	A	Stoke City	L	0-2		16,615
27	12	H	Bournemouth	W	4-3	Own-goal, Walker, Hills (pen), Fenton	4,583
28	19	A	Reading	L	0-3		13,732
29	26	H	Bury	L	0-1		4,923
30	Feb 2	A	Wigan Athletic	W	1-0	Murphy J	7,357
31	9	H	Peterborough Utd	D	2-2	O'Kane, Hills	4,604
32	16	A	Colchester Utd	D	1-1	Walker	3,553
33	19	A	Wycombe Wanderers	W	4-1	Taylor, Walker 2, Murphy J	5,803
34	23	H	Huddersfield Town	L	1-2	Marshall	8,981
35	26	A	Cambridge Utd	W	3-0	Walker 2,O'Kane	2,986
36	Mar 2	A	Queens Park Rangers	L	0-2		10,203
37	5	H	Northampton Town	L	1-2	Fenton	4,924
38	9	A	Cardiff City	D	2-2	Murphy J 2	11,629
39	12	H	Tranmere Rovers	D	1-1	Murphy J	6,860
40	16	H	Port Vale	W	4-0	Murphy J 2, Walker, Bullock	7,811
41	19	H	Brentford	L	1-3	Taylor	4,865
42	30	A	Swindon Town	L	0-1		5,085
43	Apr 1	H	Wrexham	W	3-0	Own-goal, Murphy J, Wellens	7,066
44	6	A	Notts County	L	0-1		7,783
45	13	H	Bristol City	W	5-1	Walker, Murphy J 2, Bullock, Hills	9,333
46	20	A	Chesterfield	L	1-2	Murphy J	4,788

Final League Position: 16th in Division Two

Apps
Sub Apps
Gls

FA Cup

1	Nov 17	H	Newport County	D	2-2	Jazczun, Mackenzie (pen)	5,005
1R	28	A	Newport County	W	4-1*	Ormerod 2, Murphy J, Own-goal	3,721
2	Dec 8	H	Rochdale	W	2-0	Murphy J, Simpson	5,191
3	Jan 5	A	Charlton Athletic	L	1-2	Hills	17,525

*-after extra-time

Apps
Sub Apps
Gls

League Cup

1	Aug 23	H	Wigan Athletic	W	3-2	Ormerod 3	4,237
2	Sep 10	H	Leicester City	L	0-1		4,866

Apps
Sub Apps
Gls

Barnes	Parkinson	Jaszczun	O'Kane	Hughes	Reid	Wellens	Simpson	Hills	Ormerod	Murphy J	Collins	Bullock	Mackenzie	Thompson	Milligan J	Murphy N	Clarkson	Pullen	Coid	Fenton	Caldwell	Milligan M	Blinkhorn	Marshall	Payton	Walker	Day	Taylor	Clarke	Dunning
1	2	3	4	5	6*	7#	8	9	10	11	12	14	15																	
1	2	12	3	4		9'	8#	5*	10	11		15	7	6	14															
1		9	2	4*		6	8#	12	10	11		5	7	3	14															
1		3	2			6		5	10#	11	7	8	14		9*	4	12													
			2	4	3	8	14	5	10	11#	7	9	6*					1	12											
		2	4		3	8	14	5	10	11'	7*	9#	12					1	6	15										
		3	4		5	8#	12	6*	11	10	7	9						1	2	14										
		3			5		8*	9	11	10	7	6		4				1	2	12										
	12	3*	6		5		9		11	10'	8#	7	14	4				1	2	15										
		9	2		3		8'		11	10	7#	6*	12	4	14			1	5	15										
	12	3*	4				6		11	10'	7	9	8#	5	14			1	2	15										
	2		7		4		9		10	14		6*		12	8			1	3	11#	5									
	2		6		4*		9		11	10#		8	12	14	7			1	3		5#	14								
	2		7		4		11*		10			6		5	9			1	3			8	12							
	2*	12	8		3	14	9		10			6#			7			1	5	11	4									
	2	3	4		5	12	10	14	11			8			6*			1		7#	9									
		3	8		5*	14	9	12	10			6			7#			1	2		4			11						
		3	8			7*	9	5	10			6			12			1	2		4			11						
1		5	8	3		7	9*	14	11	10#	12	6							2					4						
1		5	8	12	3*	7	9#	14	11	10		6							2					4						
1			3		4	7*	9	5	10	8	12	6							2					11						
1	2	5	14	3			9	12		10	7	6	8*											4	11#					
1	2	5	7	3			9	12		10		6*	8											4	11#	14				
1	2*	5	4	3		12	9'	8#			7	6	14	15										11		10				
1		5#	2*	12		8	14	9			7	6		3										4	11	10				
1		2		3		8#	14	9			7	6	15	5*										4	11'	10	12			
1		5			3	8	14	9#		10'	7	6							2	14				4*		11	12			
1		5#	14	12	3*	8		9			7	6							2	10#				4		11	14			
1			14	2		7	8'	9		12	6#			3*	15				5							11	4	10		
1		5	14	12		7		9		11	8#	6							2					4*			3	10		
1		5	7#			8		9		11	14	6*							2					4		12	3	10		
1		5	3		2	6		9		11	7*	12												4		8		10		
1		5	3		2	6		9		11	7													4		8		10		
1		5	3		2	6		9		11	7	12												4		8*		10		
1			3		2*	6		9		11'	7	15								14				4		8#		10	12	
1		5#	2			8	15	9		14	7	6'												4*		11	12	10	3	
1		15		14		8	9'	5		11	7	6							2*	10			12				3#		4	
1		2		12		6	7			11		9*			8				5					3				10	4	
1		5		12		8		9		11	7	6#							2					3*		14		10	4	
1		14	12	3		8	9#	5		11	7	6							2*							15		10'	4	
	2*	5	8	3	4		9			14	12				6		7	1		10#						11'		15		
1	2	3		4*		6		9		11		7#								15						14	12	10'	5	8
	2	5			3	7		9		11'		6*			15			1					14			10		12	4	8#
1		5	2		3	7*		9		11	12	6														10#		14	4	8
1		5*	2		3	7'		9		11	15	6#							12							10		14	4	8
1		5*	2		3	12		6#		11	7				14				15							10		9'	4	8
30	13	35	33	13	26	31	25	30	21	33	25	37	6	10	9	1	1	16	24	6	6	1		21	4	16	4	13	10	
	2	4	5	7		5	7	7		4	7	4	8	3	8		1		3	9		1	3			5	5	4	1	5
			4	1		1	1	5	13	13	2	2	1	1					3	5				1	1	8		2		

Barnes	Parkinson	Jaszczun	O'Kane	Hughes	Reid	Wellens	Simpson	Hills	Ormerod	Murphy J	Collins	Bullock	Mackenzie	Thompson	Milligan J	Murphy N	Clarkson	Pullen	Coid	Fenton	Caldwell	Milligan M	Blinkhorn	Marshall	Payton	Walker	Day	Taylor	Clarke	Dunning
		4	8	3*			9	5	10	11		6	12		7			1	2											
1			8*	3	4	7	9#	5	10	11		6	14		12				2											
1		5		4	3*		9	10		11	7	6	8	12					2										14	2
1		3	12		4	10#	9*	5			7	8	14						2	11'				6			15			
3		3	2	3	3	2	4	4	2	3	2	4	1		1			1	4	1				1						1
			1										3	1	1												1		1	
		1					1	1	2	2			1																	

Barnes	Parkinson	Jaszczun	O'Kane	Hughes	Reid	Wellens	Simpson	Hills	Ormerod	Murphy J	Collins	Bullock	Mackenzie	Thompson	Milligan J	Murphy N	Clarkson	Pullen	Coid	Fenton	Caldwell	Milligan M	Blinkhorn	Marshall	Payton	Walker	Day	Taylor	Clarke	Dunning
1	5*	9	2	3		6	7#		11'	10		12	8	4	14					15										
		4	2		3	8	12	5*	11	10	9#	7	14					1	6											
1	1	2	2	1	1	2	1	1	2	2	1	1	1	1				1	1											0
							1				2	1	1		1					1										
									3																					

League Table

	P	W	D	L	F	A	Pts
Brighton & Hove Albion	46	25	15	6	66	42	90
Reading	46	23	15	8	70	43	84
Brentford	46	24	11	11	77	43	83
Cardiff City	46	23	14	9	75	50	83
Stoke City	46	23	11	12	67	40	80
Huddersfield Town	46	21	15	10	65	47	78
Bristol City	46	21	10	15	68	53	73
Queen's Park Rangers	46	19	14	13	60	49	71
Oldham Athletic	46	18	16	12	77	65	70
Wigan Athletic	46	16	16	14	66	51	64
Wycombe Wanderers	46	17	13	16	58	64	64
Tranmere Rovers	46	16	15	15	63	60	63
Swindon Town	46	15	14	17	46	56	59
Port Vale	46	16	10	20	51	62	58
Colchester United	46	15	12	19	65	76	57
Blackpool	46	14	14	18	66	69	56
Peterborough United	46	15	10	21	64	59	55
Chesterfield	46	13	13	20	53	65	52
Notts County	46	13	11	22	59	71	50
Northampton Town	46	14	7	25	54	79	49
Bournemouth	46	10	14	22	56	71	44
Bury	46	11	11	24	43	75	44
Wrexham	46	11	10	25	56	89	43
Cambridge United	46	7	13	26	47	93	34

2002-03

Division One

Manager: Steve McMahon

Did you know that?

On 18 January, Blackpool played their 4,000th League match. It was against Northampton Town at Bloomfield Road.

The South Stand was demolished and the pitch moved as Bloomfield Road continued its rebuild. Also the East Stand was taken down so nothing of the old ground was to remain.

Match No.	Date		Venue	Opponents	Result		Scorers	Attendance
1	Aug	10	A	Bristol City	L	0-2		11,891
2		13	H	Luton Town	W	5-2	Clarke P 2, Taylor 2, Dalglish	6,377
3		17	H	Swindon Town	D	0-0		6,404
4		23	A	Northampton Town	W	1-0	Murphy	5,556
5		25	H	Oldham Athletic	D	0-0		8,201
6		31	A	Huddersfield Town	D	0-0		9,506
7	Sep	7	H	Tranmere Rovers	W	3-0	Southern, Hills (pen), Taylor	6,834
8		14	A	Wycombe Wanderers	W	2-1	Hills 2 (1 pen)	5,815
9		17	A	Barnsley	L	1-2	Murphy	9,619
10		21	H	Port Vale	W	3-2	Murphy 2, Clarke P	7,756
11		28	A	Chesterfield	L	0-1		4,488
12	Oct	5	H	Cheltenham Town	W	3-1	Own-goal, Wellens, Walker	6,649
13		14	A	Queens Park Rangers	L	1-2	Taylor	11,335
14		19	H	Cardiff City	W	1-0	Hills	7,744
15		26	A	Plymouth Argyle	W	3-1	Taylor 2, Murphy	8,717
16		29	H	Stockport County	L	1-3	Milligan	7,047
17	Nov	2	A	Brentford	L	0-5		5,888
18		9	H	Wigan Athletic	L	0-2		7,676
19		23	A	Crewe Alexandra	L	0-3		7,019
20		30	H	Notts County	D	1-1	Clarke C	5,843
21	Dec	14	A	Mansfield Town	L	0-4		4,001
22		21	H	Peterborough Utd	W	3-0	Grayson, Bullock, Walker	5,068
23		26	A	Oldham Athletic	D	1-1	Murphy	9,415
24		28	H	Colchester Utd	W	3-1	Walker, Grayson, Murphy	6,040
25	Jan	1	H	Huddersfield Town	D	1-1	Hills (pen)	7,184
26		18	H	Northampton Town	W	2-1	Walker (pen), Murphy	5,646
27		22	A	Swindon Town	D	1-1	Taylor	4,787
28		25	A	Colchester Utd	W	2-0	Murphy, Coid	3,305
29	Feb	1	H	Bristol City	D	0-0		7,290
30		8	A	Wigan Athletic	D	1-1	Taylor	10,546
31		11	A	Luton Town	W	3-1	Murphy 3	6,563
32		15	H	Brentford	W	1-0	Murphy	6,203
33		22	A	Tranmere Rovers	L	1-2	Evans	9,111
34	Mar	1	H	Wycombe Wanderers	W	1-0	Murphy	7,266
35		4	H	Barnsley	L	1-2	Murphy	6,827
36		8	A	Port Vale	L	0-1		4,394
37		15	H	Plymouth Argyle	D	1-1	Taylor	8,772
38		18	A	Cardiff City	L	1-2	Taylor	11,788
39		22	A	Stockport County	D	2-2	Murphy, Grayson	6,599
40		29	H	Queens Park Rangers	L	1-3	Taylor	8,162
41	Apr	5	A	Notts County	L	1-3	Robinson	5,551
42		12	H	Crewe Alexandra	L	0-1		7,623
43		19	A	Peterborough Utd	L	0-1		4,587
44		21	H	Mansfield Town	D	3-3	Blinkhorn 2, Taylor	6,173
45		26	A	Cheltenham Town	L	0-3		5,150
46	May	3	H	Chesterfield	D	1-1	Taylor	7,999

Final League Position: 13th in Division Two

Apps
Sub Apps
Gls

FA Cup

1	Nov	16	A	Barnsley	W	4-1	Hills, Murphy, Dalglish, Taylor	6,857
2	Dec	7	H	Torquay Utd	W	3-1	Own-goal, Taylor, Murphy	5,014
3	Jan	4	H	Crystal Palace	L	1-2	Own-goal	9,062

Apps
Sub Apps
Gls

League Cup

1	Sep	10	A	Burnley	L	0-3		7,448

Apps
Sub Apps
Gls

Barnes	Grayson	Clarke C	Clarke P	Hills	Bullock	Southern	Collins	Wellens	Taylor	Walker	Hughes	Jaszczun	Dalglish	O'Kane	Coid	Murphy	Burns	Milligan	Thornton	McMahon	Theoklitos	Gulliver	Blinkhorn	Richardson	Hendry	Thornley	Flynn	Evans	Robinson	Doughty
1	2	3	4	5	6	7	8	9*	10#	11'	12	14	15																	
1	2	5	4	9	6	8		7	12	10*		3	11																	
1	2	4	3	9	6	7#	12	8	15	11'		5*	10	14																
1			3		6	7	12	8	14		4	5	11#	2	9*	10														
1	14	12	4			7*	12	8	11	10	3	5	9#	2*	6															
1	2		4			7	14	8#	12	10	3	5	11'	9	6*		15													
1	2	15	5	9		7		8	11	14	4'	3*	10		6	12#														
1	2		4	9	6	7		8	12			3	11*	5		10														
1	2		4	9	6	7		8#	15	14	12	5*	11'	3		10														
1	2		3	5	6*	7		8	9		4		11			10		12												
1	2		4	8				7	9	12	3		11*	6	5	10														
1	2		4	9		7		8	11*	12	3	5	6			10														
1	2	4		9*		7		8	11	12	3	5	6			10														
1	2	3	4	9*		7		8	6			5	11#	12	14	10														
1	2	3	4	9#	12	7		8	11			5	6*		14	10														
1	2	3	4		14	7			11'	15		5	6*	8#	9	10		12												
1	2	3	4	5	6*	7		8	11'	15		12	9#		14	10														
1	2	3		9	6	7#		8				5*	11		4	10			12	14										
1	2	3		5	6#	7		8	14		12		11'	15	4	10			9*											
	2	3			6	7*		8	11'	14			9#		4	10			15		1	5	12							
	2	3			6*	7	14	8	11	12			9'	15	5	10					1	4#								
1	2				6#	7		8	9'	11			12	14	5	10						15		3	4*					
1	2			12	6*	7		8	9#	11			14		5	10								3	4					
1	2			12	6#	7		8	9'	11	14			15	5	10								3	4*					
1	2			12	6#	7		8	9'	11			14		5*	10								3	4	15				
1	2*			5#	15	7		8	9'	11		14	12		4	10											3	6		
1	2				6	7		8*	12	11#					5	10								4		12	3	9		
1	2					6		7#	9	11		12	14		5*	10								3			4	8		
1	2				12	7		6	15	11'					14	10								3	4	9#	5	8*		
1	2				6	7		12	15	11'					14	10								3	4	9#	5	8*		
1	2	12			9	7			11						5	10								3	4*		6	8		
1	2				9	7			11						5	10								3	4		6	8		
1	2				9	7			11'	15		12			5#	10								3*	4	14	6	8		
1	2			5	9*	7#		14		11'		15				10								3	4	12	6	8		
1	2			5#	9	7		14	15	11'						10								3	4	12	6	8*		
1	2	15			9	7		8	14	11#					5	10'		12							4	3	6*			
1	2			14	9	7			11				12		5*	10								3	4	8#	6			
1	2				9	7		8	11						5	10								3	4		6			
1	2			12	9	7*		8	11	15	14				5	10'								3		9#	6			
1	2				9			8	7	11'					5		15	14					12	3			6*		10#	
1	2				9			8#	7	15		4*			5		12			14				3		10'	6		11	
1	2				9				6		4				5*		7	12		14			15	3		8#	6		10'	
1	2	12		8	9				7	11'	4*				5			12					15	3*			6		10	
1	2	3		14	9			8	15						5#		4	12		7*			11				6		10'	
1	2			12	9			8	14		4			3#	5		10*			7			11'				6		15	
1	2				9			8	11'	12	4				5	15	10*			7			11#				6		14	
44	44	13	16	19	34	38	1	36	30	19	12	15	20	8	31	33	4		1	3	2	2	3	20	14	7	21	10	5	
	1	5		7	4		5	3	14	13	5	6	7	6	5	2	3	7	2	3		1	4			5			2	
	3	1	3	5	1	1		1	13	4			1		1	16		1					2					1	1	

Barnes	Grayson	Clarke C	Clarke P	Hills	Bullock	Southern	Collins	Wellens	Taylor	Walker	Hughes	Jaszczun	Dalglish	O'Kane	Coid	Murphy	Burns	Milligan	Thornton	McMahon	Theoklitos	Gulliver	Blinkhorn	Richardson	Hendry	Thornley	Flynn	Evans	Robinson	Doughty
1	2	3		9*	6	7		8	15	14		4	11'	12	5	10#														
	2	3			6*		7	8	11'	12			9#	14	5	10					1	4								15
1	2	4*		9	14	7	15	8		11			8	12	5#	10								3		7'				
2	3	3		2	2	2	1	3	1	1		1	2		1	3					1	1		1		1				
					1		1		1	2				3																1
				1					2				1			2														

Barnes	Grayson	Clarke C	Clarke P	Hills	Bullock	Southern	Collins	Wellens	Taylor	Walker	Hughes	Jaszczun	Dalglish	O'Kane	Coid	Murphy	Burns	Milligan	Thornton	McMahon	Theoklitos	Gulliver	Blinkhorn	Richardson	Hendry	Thornley	Flynn	Evans	Robinson	Doughty
1	2			9	14	7	4#	8*	11	12		3	10'	6	5	15														
1	1			1		1	1	1	1			1	1	1	1															0
					1					1						1														

League Table

	P	W	D	L	F	A	Pts
Wigan Athletic	46	29	13	4	68	25	100
Crewe Alexandra	46	25	11	10	76	40	86
Bristol City	46	24	11	11	79	48	83
Queen's Park Rangers	46	24	11	11	69	45	83
Oldham Athletic	46	22	16	8	68	38	82
Cardiff City	46	23	12	11	68	43	81
Tranmere Rovers	46	23	11	12	66	57	80
Plymouth Argyle	46	17	14	15	63	52	65
Luton Town	46	17	14	15	67	62	65
Swindon Town	46	16	12	18	59	63	60
Peterborough United	46	14	16	16	51	54	58
Colchester United	46	14	16	16	52	56	58
Blackpool	46	15	13	18	56	64	58
Stockport County	46	15	10	21	65	70	55
Notts County	46	13	16	17	62	70	55
Brentford	46	14	12	20	47	56	54
Port Vale	46	14	11	21	54	70	53
Wycombe Wanderers	46	13	13	20	59	66	52
Barnsley	46	13	13	20	51	64	52
Chesterfield	46	14	8	24	43	73	50
Cheltenham Town	46	10	18	18	53	68	48
Huddersfield Town	46	11	12	23	39	61	45
Mansfield Town	46	12	8	26	66	97	44
Northampton Town	46	10	9	27	40	79	39

2003-04

Division Two

Manager: Steve McMahon

Did you know that?

Blackpool became the most successful team at Cardiff's Millenium stadium after another Football League Trophy victory.

After numerous disagreements with the chairman, including once resigning and then changing his mind, manager Steve McMahon left the club at the end of the season.

Match No.	Date	Venue	Opponents	Result		Scorers	Attendance
1	Aug 9	A	Queens Park Rangers	L	0-5		14,581
2	16	H	Wycombe Wanderers	W	3-2	Taylor 2, Hilton	5,960
3	23	A	Oldham Athletic	W	3-2	Danns, Douglas, Taylor	6,745
4	25	H	Barnsley	L	0-2		6,039
5	30	A	Swindon Town	D	2-2	Douglas, Taylor	6,219
6	Sep 13	H	Bournemouth	L	1-2	Wellens	5,607
7	16	A	Brentford	D	0-0		3,818
8	20	A	Stockport County	W	3-1	Grayson, Clarke, Murphy	5,420
9	27	H	Notts County	W	2-1	Southern, Danns	6,206
10	30	H	Grimsby Town	L	0-1		5,491
11	Oct 4	A	Brighton & HA	L	0-3		6,483
12	11	A	Colchester Utd	D	1-1	Taylor	3,265
13	18	H	Hartlepool Utd	W	4-0	Douglas, Taylor 3 (1 pen)	6,871
14	21	H	Rushden @ Diamonds	L	2-3	Murphy 2	5,234
15	25	A	Plymouth Argyle	L	0-1		12,372
16	Nov 1	A	Sheffield Wed	W	1-0	Taylor	21,450
17	11	H	Wrexham	L	0-1		4,864
18	15	H	Chesterfield	W	1-0	Taylor	5,252
19	22	A	Peterborough Utd	W	1-0	Taylor	4,411
20	29	H	Bristol City	W	1-0	Taylor	5,989
21	Dec 13	H	Luton Town	L	0-1		5,739
22	26	H	Tranmere Rovers	W	2-1	Murphy, Johnson	8,340
23	28	A	Wrexham	L	2-4	Taylor, Flynn	6,171
24	Jan 10	H	Queens Park Rangers	L	0-1		7,329
25	14	A	Port Vale	L	1-2	Sheron	4,523
26	17	A	Wycombe Wanderers	W	3-0	Coid, Taylor, Davis	4,834
27	24	H	Oldham Athletic	D	1-1	Coid	7,508
28	27	A	Barnsley	L	0-3		7,918
29	31	H	Swindon Town	D	2-2	Taylor, Dinning	6,463
30	Feb 7	A	Tranmere Rovers	D	1-1	Taylor	7,919
31	20	A	Hartlepool Utd	D	1-1	Sheron	5,497
32	28	H	Plymouth Argyle	L	0-1		6,203
33	Mar 2	A	Rushden @ Diamonds	D	0-0		3,764
34	6	H	Port Vale	W	2-1	Dinning (pen), Wellens	6,878
35	13	A	Luton Town	L	2-3	Dinning (pen), Blinkhorn	6,343
36	16	H	Brentford	D	1-1	Wellens	4,617
37	24	A	Bournemouth	W	2-1	Sheron, Murphy	6,436
38	27	H	Stockport County	D	1-1	Sheron	7,604
39	30	H	Colchester Utd	D	0-0		5,473
40	Apr 3	A	Notts County	L	1-4	Sheron	5,100
41	10	H	Brighton @ HA	W	3-1	Sheron, Matias, Murphy	6,194
42	12	A	Grimsby Town	W	2-0	Murphy, Coid	4,775
43	17	H	Sheffield Wed	W	4-1	Murphy 2, Sheron 2	7,388
44	24	H	Chesterfield	L	0-1		4,117
45	May 1	H	Peterborough Utd	L	1-4	Bullock	7,200
46	8	A	Bristol City	L	1-2	Southern (pen)	19,101

Final League Position: 14th in Division Two

Apps
Sub Apps
Gls

FA Cup

1	Nov 8	H	Boreham Wood	W	4-0	Taylor 2, Coid, Burns	3,969
2	Dec 6	A	Oldham Athletic	W	5-2	Taylor 3, Southern, Richardson	6,143
3	Jan 3	A	Portsmouth	L	1-2	Taylor	13,479

Apps
Sub Apps
Gls

League Cup

1	Aug 12	A	Barnsley	W	2-1	Taylor 2	5,378
2	Sep 23	H	Birmingham City	W	1-0	Taylor	7,370
3	Oct 28	H	Crystal Palace	L	1-3	Southern	6,010

Apps
Sub Apps
Gls

Barnes	Grayson	Hilton	Flynn	Davis	Coid	Bullock	Wellens	Danns	Sheron	Taylor	Richardson	Clarke	Douglas	Jones L	Walker	Evans	Southern	Murphy	Mansaram	Doherty	Jazsczun	Jones B	Elliott	Burns	Johnson	McMahon	Wiles	Dinning	Hessey	Blinkhorn	Donnelly	Matias	Clancy	Mangan	Edge
1	2*	3	4#	5	6'	7	8	9	10	11	12	14	15																						
		5	3	4	14	6*	7#	8	10'	11	2	12	9	1	15																				
	14	5	3*	4	9#	6		8	10	11'	2	12	7	1	15																				
	12	5	3#	4	6'		8	7	10	11	2*	12	9	1	15																				
	2	3*	4	5	7	14	8		10#	11	6	12	9	1																					
				3		9	7	8	10#	11	2	4	6*	1	14	5	12																		
	2			3		12	6#	7	10	11	5*	4	8	1		9	14																		
	2			3		15	6	7	10#	11'	5*	4	8	1		9	12	14																	
	2			3	12	14	7	8#	10	11'		4	6	1		5*	9	15																	
	2			3	5#	15	7	8	10'	11		4*	6	1*			9	14	12	14															
	2	9		3	5*	12	6		14	11		4	8	1			7#	10																	
	2	5		3	4	6	7*			11	12	14	8	1			9#	10																	
1	2	5		3	12	6*	7	8	14	11		4	9#			15		10'																	
1	2*	5		3	12	9#	7	8	14	11		4	6					10																	
1	2			3	5*	12	11	8		14		4	6			9	7#	10																	
1	2		15	3		8	6*		14	11'		4	9			5	7	10#			12														
	2*	14	3		8	6	15		10'	11	12	4					7	9			5#	1													
			4		8	6	7			11	2						9	10			5	1	3												
			3		8	6#	7	14		11	2					12	9	10			5*	1	4												
	14		3	12	8	6*	7#			11	2					5	9	10				1	4												
	2*		3	14	8	6#	7		10'	11						5						1	4	12	9	15									
	12		3	4	8	6	7*			11	2			1		5		10						14	9#										
	2*	14	3		8	6				11		12		1		5#		10					4	15	9'	7									
	2	9#		4	8	6*	7		14	11				1		5		10					3		12										
	2*	9		4	8	6	7		14	11				1		5#		10					3			12									
	2	5		4	8	6*	7#		15	11'				1				10					3	14		9	12								
1	2*		3		8	6#			10'	11	12				15	5							4			9	14	7							
1			3		8	6*			10	11	2					5							4	14		9#	12	7							
1	12		3		8	6	7		10#	11	2*					5	14						4					9							
	2		3		8	14	6		15	11#	7			1	10'	5	12						4			9*									
	2				8	6			14	11'	3			1	10#	5	14						4			9#		7	15						
1	2		3		8	6*	7		11							5	9	10					4							12					
1	2		3			14	7		11#		8				12	5	9						4					6		10*					
1	2		3	12		6	7		11							5	8						4					9		10*					
1	2			3		14	7		11'						10	5*					12		4			8#		9	3	14					
			3	14		6	7		15		2			1			12	10			8		4					9#	5*	11'					
			3	14	8	6#	7		11		2			1			12	10					4					9	5*						
			3		12	6	7		11		2			1				10			5*		4					9#			12	14			
1	2		3		5	6	7*		11'								12	10					4						14	15	8	9#			
1	2			3	5	6	7		11'								12	10					4	14						15	8*	9#			
1			3	12	5	6*	7		11'		2						14	10					4							15	8	9#			
1			3		6#		7		11		2						14	10'					4	12					5*	15	8	9			
1			3			6#	7'		11		2						14	10					4	5*		15					8	9	12		
1	2		3			14	6										7*	10					4	5		15				11'	8	9#		12	
1			5			6	7		11'		2							10					4	9		14	15			12	8#		3*		
			3		5*	6	7		11		2						9	10					4	12							8#			14	1
20	29	12	29	22	30	33	40	12	28	30	24	11	15	21	3	20	15	27	1		5	5	28	3	3	7		10	4	4	8	6	1		1
	5	2	1	6	5	11	1	1	10	1	4	7	1		6	2	13	3		1	2			8	1	5	4		2	7	1	1	1	2	
	1	1	1	1	3	1	3	2	8	16		1	3				2	9							1			3		1		1			

Barnes	Grayson	Hilton	Flynn	Davis	Coid	Bullock	Wellens	Danns	Sheron	Taylor	Richardson	Clarke	Douglas	Jones L	Walker	Evans	Southern	Murphy	Mansaram	Doherty	Jazsczun	Jones B	Elliott	Burns	Johnson	McMahon	Wiles	Dinning	Hessey	Blinkhorn	Donnelly	Matias	Clancy	Mangan	Edge
1	2		12	7*	8'	6			9#	11		3					4	10			5			14		15									
			3	4		6*	7		15	11'	2	12		1		5	8	10						9#		14									1
	2	9	3	4	8	6	7*			11#		12	8	1		5		10							14										
1	2	1	2	3	2	3	2		1	3	1	1		2		2	2	3			1			1											1
			1						1			2												1	1	2									
					1					6	1						1							1											1

Barnes	Grayson	Hilton	Flynn	Davis	Coid	Bullock	Wellens	Danns	Sheron	Taylor	Richardson	Clarke	Douglas	Jones L	Walker	Evans	Southern	Murphy	Mansaram	Doherty	Jazsczun	Jones B	Elliott	Burns	Johnson	McMahon	Wiles	Dinning	Hessey	Blinkhorn	Donnelly	Matias	Clancy	Mangan	Edge
	12	2	3	4		6	7*	8	10#	11	5	14	9	1																					
	2			4	14	12	7#	8	10'	11		3	9	1*		5	6	15															1		1
1	2			4	8	6*	7#		14	11		3	9			5	12	10													1				1
1	2	1	1	3	1	2	3	2	2	3	1	2	3	2		2	1	1												0			1	0	2
	1				1	1			1			1					1	1													1				
										3							1																1		

League Table

	P	W	D	L	F	A	Pts
Plymouth Argyle	46	26	12	8	85	41	90
Queen's Park Rangers	46	22	17	7	80	45	83
Bristol City	46	23	13	10	58	37	82
Brighton & Hove Albion	46	22	11	13	64	43	77
Swindon Town	46	20	13	13	76	58	73
Hartlepool United	46	20	13	13	76	61	73
Port Vale	46	21	10	15	73	63	73
Tranmere Rovers	46	17	16	13	59	56	67
Bournemouth	46	17	15	14	56	51	66
Luton Town	46	17	15	14	69	66	66
Colchester United	46	17	13	16	52	56	64
Barnsley	46	15	17	14	54	58	62
Wrexham	46	17	9	20	50	60	60
Blackpool	46	16	11	19	58	65	59
Oldham Athletic	46	12	21	13	66	60	57
Sheffield Wednesday	46	13	14	19	48	64	53
Brentford	46	14	11	21	52	69	53
Peterborough United	46	12	16	18	58	58	52
Stockport County	46	11	19	16	62	70	52
Chesterfield	46	12	15	19	49	71	51
Grimsby Town	46	13	11	22	55	81	50
Rushden & Diamonds	46	13	9	24	60	74	48
Notts County	46	10	12	24	50	78	42
Wycombe Wanderers	46	6	19	21	50	75	37

2004-05

Division One

Manager: Colin Hendry

Did you know that?

Colin Hendry was appointed manager after finishing his playing days at Bloomfield Road.

Scott Taylor was top scorer, yet was to leave the club within a year after complaining of the travelling. He joined Plymouth Argyle on the South Coast.

Match No.	Date		Venue	Opponents	Result		Scorers	Attendance
1	Aug	7	A	Doncaster Rovers	L	0-2		7,082
2		10	H	Sheffield Wed	L	1-2	Edwards R	6,713
3		14	H	Stockport County	L	0-4		6,745
4		21	A	Hartlepool Utd	D	1-1	Taylor	5,144
5		28	H	Luton Town	L	1-3	Taylor	5,793
6		30	A	Peterborough Utd	D	0-0		4,142
7	Sep	11	A	Hull City	L	1-2	Taylor	15,568
8		18	H	Swindon Town	D	1-1	Taylor	5,229
9		25	A	Port Vale	W	3-0	Taylor, Vernon 2	5,347
10	Oct	2	H	Bournemouth	D	3-3	Clarke, Vernon, Edwards P	5,525
11		10	A	Oldham Athletic	W	2-1	Murphy, Wellens	7,125
12		16	H	Colchester Utd	D	1-1	Murphy	6,464
13		19	A	Bradford City	L	1-2	Taylor (pen)	7,622
14		23	A	Brentford	W	3-0	Murphy 2, Taylor	6,722
15		30	H	Huddersfield Town	D	1-1	Murphy	7,676
16	Nov	6	A	Chesterfield	L	0-1		4,978
17		9	H	Wrexham	W	2-1	Clarke, Taylor (pen)	5,054
18		20	H	Tranmere Rovers	L	0-1		6,490
19		27	A	Barnsley	L	0-1		9,084
20	Dec	7	H	Torquay Utd	W	4-0	Taylor, Parker 3	4,179
21		11	H	Bristol City	D	1-1	Taylor (pen)	5,220
22		18	A	Walsall	L	2-3	Taylor, Parker	5,476
23		26	H	Hull City	L	0-2		8,774
24		28	A	MK Dons	L	1-3	Taylor (pen)	4,943
25	Jan	1	A	Wrexham	W	2-1	Murphy 2	5,601
26		3	H	Port Vale	L	0-2		4,834
27		15	A	Swindon Town	D	2-2	Parker, Clarke	5,526
28		22	H	MK Dons	W	1-0	Edwards P	5,798
29	Feb	5	A	Colchester Utd	W	1-0	Grayson	3,526
30		8	H	Oldham Athletic	W	2-0	Clarke, Edwards P	5,563
31		19	A	Huddersfield Town	L	0-1		10,614
32		22	H	Bradford City	W	2-1	Southern, Parker	4,805
33		26	A	Bristol City	D	1-1	Wellens	10,977
34	Mar	5	H	Walsall	W	2-0	Murphy, Southern	6,844
35		8	A	Bournemouth	W	3-2	Parker 2, Own-goal	5,390
36		12	A	Sheffield Wed	L	2-3	Southern, Wellens	21,539
37		19	H	Doncaster Rovers	D	1-1	Murphy	6,548
38		22	H	Brentford	W	2-1	Southern 2	5,478
39		28	H	Hartlepool Utd	D	2-2	Southern (pen), Clarke	6,853
40	Apr	2	A	Luton Town	L	0-1		7,816
41		9	H	Peterborough Utd	L	0-1		5,090
42		12	A	Stockport County	W	1-0	Parker	4,302
43		16	A	Tranmere Rovers	D	0-0		8,568
44		23	H	Chesterfield	W	1-0	Grayson	5,613
45		30	A	Torquay Utd	L	0-2		5,347
46	May	7	H	Barnsley	L	0-2		7,571

Final League Position: 16th in League One

Apps
Sub Apps
Gls

FA Cup

1	Nov	13	H	Tamworth	W	3-0	Wellens 2, Parker	4,796
2	Dec	4	H	Port Vale	W	1-0	Taylor	4,669
3	Jan	8	A	Leicester City	D	2-2	Clarke, Southern	16,750
3R		18	H	Leicester City	L	0-1		6,938

Apps
Sub Apps
Gls

League Cup

1	Aug	24	A	Crewe Alexandra	L	1-4	Taylor	2,994

Apps
Sub Apps
Gls

Ilic	Grayson	Flynn Mike	Livesey	Clare	Richardson	Wellens	Bullock	Edwards R	Taylor	Murphy	McGregor	Parker	Shaw	Barrowman	Burns	Jones L	Edwards P	Coid	Flynn Michael	Vernon	Clarke	Evans	Gorre	Blinkhorn	Jones B	Southern	Paterson	Lynch	Stuhr-Ellegaard	Eldershaw	Warhurst	Anderson	Grabovac	Butler	Donnelly	Daly	Boyack	Edge	Wright
1	2	3	4*	5	6#	7	8	9	10	11	12	14																											
1*		3		5	6	7	8	9	11	10	2	4#	12	14																									
1	12	3		5	6	7#	8	9	11'	10	2	4*		15	14																								
	4	9		5	2		8	6	10		7	11				1	3*	12																					
	8#	9		5	2*		4	6	10	11	7	12				1	3		14																				
		9		5			4	6	10	11	7					1	3	2	8																				
		3		5			4	6	10		7	12				1	9*	2	8	11																			
		8			12	7	6#		10		3					1	9	2*		11	4	5	14																
		3			6	7			10		8					1	9	2		11	4	5																	
	8				6	7			10	12	3					1	9	2		11*	4	5																	
	8				6	7			10	11	3					1	9	2			4	5																	
	8				6	7			10	11	3	12				1	9	2*			4	5																	
	8			12	6	7			10	11	3*					1	9	2			4	5																	
	8			3	6	7			10	11						1	9	2			4	5																	
	8			3	6	7			10	11					9	1		2			4	5																	
	8				6	7		12	10		3	15			14		9#	2			4	5*		11'	1														
	8			12	6*	7			10		3	15			14		9#	2			4	5		11'	1														
	8			5	6*	7		4	10	11#	3	12					9				4			14	1														
	8#			5*	6	7		9	10		3	11			2						4			14	1	12													
	8			2	14	7			10		3	11			9						4	5			1*	6#	12												
	8*			2		7			10		3	11			9			12			4	5			1	6													
	8*			2	6	7	14		10		3	11			9#							5			1	4		12											
	8			2*	12	7	6#		10		3				14	1					4	5				9		11											
	8'				6*	7	12		10	11	3	15			9#	1		2			4	5				14													
	7			6						11	3	12			9			2			4	5				8		10*	1										
	7			6#			15			11	3	10			9'			2			4	5				8		14	1*	12									
	7			6				5			3	10			9#			2			4				1			11			7*	12	14						
	7			12	6*			5		11#	3	10					9	2			4				1	8							14						
	8			2		7		3				6*					9				4	5			1	10		11			12								
	8					7		3				6					12	2			4	5			1	9		11#			14		10*						
	8#					12	15	10		11		6					9'	2			4	5			1	8					3*			14					
						7	6			11		10			9	1		2			4	5				8								3					
						7	6			11		10			9	1		2			4	5				8								3					
	14				5*	7	6			11	12	10'			9#	1	15	2			4					8								3					
	7						6			11	3	10			9	1	12	2*			4					8								5					
						7	6	4*		11	3	10	14		9#	1	12				4					8								5					
						7	6	14		11	3	10#			9*	1		2			4					8								5	12				
	14						6	5		11'	3	10	15		9	1*	12	2			4					8#									7				
	15			16			6	5			3	10	11@		9'	1*	14	2			4					8									7#	12			
	3						6	5		11		10	12		9*	1		2			4					8									7				
							6	5		11	3	10	14		9#	1		2			4					8						12			7*				
	7						6	5		11	3	10*	12			1	9	2			4					8													
	7*						6	5		11	3	10#	12			1	9	2			4					8									14				
	7*						6	5		11	3	10#	14			1	9	2			4					8								12					
	7						6*	5		11	3		12			1	9'	2			4					8						9#			14		15		
	7#						6*	5		11	3		10'			1	9	2			4					8	15					14			12				
3	32	9	1	19	20	27	24	24	24	30	36	26	2		19	29	22	33	2	4	38	22		2	12	25		5	2		2	1	1	6	4				
	4			4	3	1	4	2		1	2	9	9	2	4		6	2	1				1	2		2	2	2		1	2	3	2	2	4	1	1		
	2					3		1	12	9		9					3			3	5					6													

Ilic	Grayson	Flynn Mike	Livesey	Clare	Richardson	Wellens	Bullock	Edwards R	Taylor	Murphy	McGregor	Parker	Shaw	Barrowman	Burns	Jones L	Edwards P	Coid	Flynn Michael	Vernon	Clarke	Evans	Gorre	Blinkhorn	Jones B	Southern	Paterson	Lynch	Stuhr-Ellegaard	Eldershaw	Warhurst	Anderson	Grabovac	Butler	Donnelly	Daly	Boyack	Edge	Wright
	8'			6		7		12	10		3	11				1	9	2#			4	5*		15		14													
	8			6		7		5*	10		3	14			9	1		2			4	12		11#															
	8*			6		12		5		11	3	10	8		14			2			4					8		9#	1										
	8'			6		15	6#	5			3	10	14					2			4					8		11@			16							1*	12
	4			4		2	1	3	2	1	4	3			1	1	1	4			4	1		1		2		2	1									1	
						2		1				1	1		1							1		1		1					1								1
						2			1			1									1					1													

Ilic	Grayson	Flynn Mike	Livesey	Clare	Richardson	Wellens	Bullock	Edwards R	Taylor	Murphy	McGregor	Parker	Shaw	Barrowman	Burns	Jones L	Edwards P	Coid	Flynn Michael	Vernon	Clarke	Evans	Gorre	Blinkhorn	Jones B	Southern	Paterson	Lynch	Stuhr-Ellegaard	Eldershaw	Warhurst	Anderson	Grabovac	Butler	Donnelly	Daly	Boyack	Edge	Wright
	7	9		4	6		8	5	10		3	11				1		2																					
	1	1		1	1		1	1	1		1	1				1		1																					
									1																														

League Table

	P	W	D	L	F	A	Pts
Luton Town	46	29	11	6	87	48	98
Hull City	46	26	8	12	80	53	86
Tranmere Rovers	46	22	13	11	73	55	79
Brentford	46	22	9	15	57	60	75
Sheffield Wednesday	46	19	15	12	77	59	72
Hartlepool United	46	21	8	17	76	66	71
Bristol City	46	18	16	12	74	57	70
Bournemouth	46	20	10	16	77	64	70
Huddersfield Town	46	20	10	16	74	65	70
Doncaster Rovers	46	16	18	12	65	60	66
Bradford City	46	17	14	15	64	62	65
Swindon Town	46	17	12	17	66	68	63
Barnsley	46	14	19	13	69	64	61
Walsall	46	16	12	18	65	69	60
Colchester United	46	14	17	15	60	50	59
Blackpool	46	15	12	19	54	59	57
Chesterfield	46	14	15	17	55	62	57
Port Vale	46	17	5	24	49	59	56
Oldham Athletic	46	14	10	22	60	73	52
Milton Keynes Dons	46	12	15	19	54	68	51
Torquay United	46	12	15	19	55	79	51
Wrexham	46	13	14	19	62	80	43
Peterborough United	46	9	12	25	49	73	39
Stockport County	46	6	8	32	49	98	26

2005-06

League One

Manager: Colin Hendry/Simon Grayson

Did you know that?

Colin Hendry was put on 'gardening leave' midway through the season and eventually dismissed.

Simon Grayson was made new manager on a temporary basis, but was given the full-time position at the end of the season.

Blackpool only officially avoided relegation on the final day of the season, but a fans pitch invasion brought concerns that the club would be deducted points. No action was taken by the FA.

On 19 May, Latvian businessman Valeri Belokon invested £5 million in the club with a promise of a higher stake in the future. He declared that he would like to see Blackpool play in the Premier League within five years. He got his wish one year early.

Match No.	Date	Venue	Opponents	Result		Scorers	Attendance
1	Aug 6	H	Chesterfield	L	1-3	Parker	6,469
2	9	A	Tranmere Rovers	D	2-2	Vernon, Murphy	7,509
3	13	A	Yeovil Town	D	1-1	Murphy	5,698
4	20	H	Swindon Town	D	0-0		5,144
5	27	A	Rotherham Utd	L	0-4		4,384
6	29	H	Bradford City	W	1-0	Wiles	6,468
7	Sep 2	A	Doncaster Rovers	W	1-0	Donnelly	5,484
8	10	H	Hartlepool Utd	L	1-2	Wright	5,494
9	17	A	Bristol City	D	1-1	Blinkhorn	9,576
10	24	H	MK Dons	W	3-2	Clarke (pen), Own-goal, Burns	4,723
11	27	A	Nottm Forest	D	1-1	Parker	17,071
12	Oct 1	A	Swansea City	L	2-3	Parker, Donnelly	13,911
13	9	H	Colchester Utd	L	1-2	Wright	4,793
14	15	A	Barnsley	D	2-2	Wiles, Wright	7,945
15	22	H	Brentford	D	0-0		5,041
16	29	A	Gillingham	L	1-2	Parker	6,300
17	Nov 13	H	Scunthorpe Utd	W	5-2	Murphy 2, Morris 2, Wright	6,016
18	19	A	Colchester Utd	L	2-3	Murphy, Wright	3,031
19	26	A	Chesterfield	D	1-1	Harkins	4,585
20	Dec 6	H	Bournemouth	L	1-3	Wright	4,326
21	10	H	Tranmere Rovers	D	1-1	Clarke	5,069
22	17	A	Swindon Town	D	0-0		5,766
23	26	A	Port Vale	W	2-1	Wiles, Parker	5,666
24	31	A	Walsall	L	0-2		5,046
25	Jan 2	H	Southend Utd	L	1-2	Parker	5,271
26	10	H	Oldham Athletic	W	1-0	Gobern	5,977
27	14	A	Huddersfield Town	L	0-2		11,977
28	21	H	Bristol City	D	1-1	Murphy	4,842
29	24	H	Doncaster Rovers	W	4-2	Butler, Morris, Parker, Clarke	4,836
30	28	A	Hartlepool Utd	W	3-0	Clarke 2 (2 pens), Parker	4,421
31	Feb 4	H	Nottm Forest	D	2-2	Bean, Fox	8,399
32	11	A	MK Dons	L	0-3		5,691
33	14	H	Huddersfield Town	L	0-1		6,004
34	18	A	Bournemouth	D	1-1	Murphy	5,349
35	25	H	Yeovil Town	W	2-0	Own-goal, Murphy	5,747
36	Mar 11	H	Rotherham Utd	D	0-0		5,934
37	18	H	Port Vale	W	1-0	Williams	5,494
38	21	A	Bradford City	L	0-1		7,192
39	25	A	Oldham Athletic	L	1-3	Southern	6,480
40	Apr 1	H	Walsall	W	2-0	Williams, Southern	6,129
41	8	A	Southend Utd	L	1-2	Williams	8,180
42	15	H	Swansea City	W	1-0	Parker	6,709
43	17	A	Brentford	D	1-1	Clarke	7,339
44	22	H	Barnsley	D	1-1	Parker	6,912
45	29	A	Scunthorpe Utd	L	0-1		5,917
46	May 6	H	Gillingham	D	3-3	Blinkhorn, Parker 2	8,541

Final League Position: 19th in League One

Apps
Sub Apps
Gls

FA Cup

1	Nov 6	A	Doncaster Rovers	L	1-4	Clarke (pen)	4,332

Apps
Sub Apps
Gls

League Cup

1	Aug 23	H	Hull City	W	2-1	Clarke (pen), Grayson	3,819
2	Sep 20	A	Leicester City	L	1-2	Parker	7,386

Apps
Sub Apps
Gls

Jones	McGregor	Edwards	Clarke	Coid	Parker	Doolan	Southern	Prendergast	Murphy	Vernon	Blinkhorn	Grayson	Wiles	Donnelly	Edge	Pogliacomi	Butler	Burns	Wright	Morris	Garcia	Armstrong	Warrender	May	Harkins	Gobern	Wilcox	Joseph	Gordon	Wood	Fox	Bean	Kuqi	Taylor S	Lasley	Taylor A	Stockley	Williams	Anderson
1	2*	3	4	5	6	7#	8	9	10	11'	12	14	15																										
1	2	3	4	5	6	7*	8	9	10	11#		12		14																									
1*	2	3	4	5	6	7#	8	9	10	11'		14		15	12																								
	2	3	4	5	6	7*	8	9	10	11#		12	14			1																							
	2	3	4	5	11	7	12	9#	10'	15		8*	14	6		1																							
	12	3	4	2	11	7#	14		10'	15		8	6*	9		1	5																						
	12		4	2*	11	7	8		15	10'		3	6#	9		1	5	14																					
	12	3	4		11'	7*	8		14	10#		3	6	9		1	5		15																				
	2	3	4		11#		8	12			14	7	6*	9		1	5		10																				
		3	4	2	14		8			12	11#	7	6*	15		1	5	9	10'																				
	2	3	4	5	6	12	8						8*	9		1		11#	10	14																			
	2	3*	4		11		8			15		7	14	9		1	5	12	10'	6#																			
	2	3#	4			15	8			11'	14	7#	6			1*	5	9	10	14	12																		
	2		4	3	11	7	8				12		6			1		9*	10			5																	
	2	14	4			7	8	9*	12		11#		6			1			10			5	3																
	2	3	4		11	7#	8		10		15		6			1				14		5	9'																
		3	4			7	8	14	10	15			6#			1*			11'	9		5	2	12															
		3	4			14	8	14	10				6#			1	12		11	9		5*	2		7'														
1	12	3	4	5	14				10					6						9			2*		7	8#	11												
1	14	3	4	5	12		8		10				15						11'	9*					7	2#	9												
1		3	4	5*	11		8		10'				14				12		15	7			2		6		9#												
1	3		4		11	7	8		10								5			6			2				9												
1	3		4		11	7*	8		10#				6'	12			5		14				2			15	9												
1	3		4		11	7	8		15	10'			12	6*			5						2			14	9#												
1	3*		4		11		8		15	10'			6#	7			5			12			2			14	9												
1			4		11	15	8		10				14	7			5			6#			2*			6'	9	12											
1			4		11		8		10	14				15			5*			7'			12			6#	9	2	11										
1			4		11'		8		10	15			12	6*			5			7							9	2		3#	14								
1			4		11'			8	10								5			7#			12			14	9	2*		3		6	15						
1			4*		11'		12	8	10								5			7							9#	2		3		6	15	14					
1		12	4		11			8	10								5			7								2*			3	6		9					
1		14	4					8	10		15						5			7#							9				3*	6	2'	10	12				
1		3	4				5	8#	10		11									7			2*				9					6	14		12				
1		3#	4		14		8		10								14			7										11#		6		5*	9	2			
1		3	4		11		14		10				12							7							9			5#		6			9*	2			
1			4		11'		8	14	10		15		12				5			7*			2				9			5#						3			
1			4		11		15	8'	10					5			12			7							9	2*				6					3	14	
1			4		11		8#		10					12			14			7'							9	2			3*	6					3	15	
1		12	4		11		8	15	10#											7'							9*	2			5	6					3	14	
1		3	4		11		8*	7#	10'					14						12							9	2			12	6						5	
1		3	4		11		8*				15			5*						12#							9	2			14	6			7			10'	
1		3	4		11		8	7#			14			5#						15							9	2				6					12	10'	
1		3*	4		11		8	7			15									12							9	2				6					14	10'	
1		3	4		11		8	7			14			5*													9	2				6			12			10#	
1		3	4		11		8	7#			15			5*													9	2				6			12		14	10'	
1		3*	4		11			7'			10		14							15							9	2		5		6			7#		12		
31	16	28	46	13	36	15	36	18	29	9	4	8	14	17		15	19	4	10	21		5	13		4	4	26	15	1	7	4	17	1	3	4	3	3	6	
	5	4			4	4	5	5	5	7	12	4	12	7	1		4	2	3	9	1		2	1		4		1			3		3	1	4		4	3	
			6		12		2		8	1	2		3	2			1	1	6	3					1	1					1	1						3	

	2	3	4			7#	8	12	10	14	11	9	6			1							5*																
	1	1	1			1	1		1		1	1	1			1							1																
								1		1																													
			1																																				

	2	3	4	5	11	7	12	9	10			8*		6		1																							
	2		4		15	7		10#		11'	14	8*	6	9		1	5	3																					12
	2	1	2	1	1	2		2	1	1		2	1	2		1	1	1																					
					1		1				1																												1
			1		1							1																											

League Table

	P	W	D	L	F	A	Pts
Southend United	46	23	13	10	72	43	82
Colchester United	46	22	13	11	58	40	79
Brentford	46	20	16	10	72	52	76
Huddersfield Town	46	19	16	11	72	59	73
Barnsley	46	18	18	10	62	44	72
Swansea City	46	18	17	11	78	55	71
Nottingham Forest	46	19	12	15	67	52	69
Doncaster Rovers	46	20	9	17	55	51	69
Bristol City	46	18	11	17	66	62	65
Oldham Athletic	46	18	11	17	58	60	65
Bradford City	46	14	19	13	51	49	61
Scunthorpe United	46	15	15	16	68	73	60
Port Vale	46	16	12	18	49	54	60
Gillingham	46	16	12	18	50	64	60
Yeovil Town	46	15	11	20	54	62	56
Chesterfield	46	14	14	18	63	73	56
Bournemouth	46	12	19	15	49	53	55
Tranmere Rovers	46	13	15	18	50	52	54
Blackpool	46	12	17	17	56	64	53
Rotherham United	46	12	16	18	52	62	52
Hartlepool United	46	11	17	18	44	59	50
Milton Keynes Dons	46	12	14	20	45	66	50
Swindon Town	46	11	15	20	46	65	48
Walsall	46	11	14	21	47	70	47

2006-07

League One

Manager: Simon Grayson

Did you know that?

Mr Belokon increased his stake in the club to 20 per cent.

Blackpool's famous 'perfect 10' resulted in promotion to the Championship for the first time since 1978.

The 31,000 Blackpool fans at Wembley was the biggest number to travel to watch the team in their history.

This was their 100th season overall in the Football League.

Match No.	Date	Venue	Opponents	Result		Scorers	Attendance
1	Aug 5	A	Brentford	L	0-1		6,048
2	8	H	Nottm Forest	L	0-2		7,635
3	12	H	Rotherham Utd	L	0-1		5,677
4	19	A	Bristol City	W	4-2	Vernon, Jackson, Parker, Graham	10,630
5	26	H	Gillingham	D	1-1	Vernon	5,056
6	Sep 2	A	Millwall	D	0-0		7,692
7	9	A	Port Vale	L	1-2	Southern	5,171
8	12	H	Chesterfield	D	1-1	Gillett	4,600
9	16	H	Oldham Athletic	D	2-2	Vernon, Morrell	6,794
10	23	A	Doncaster Rovers	D	0-0		5,424
11	26	A	Carlisle Utd	L	0-2		8,401
12	30	H	Leyton Orient	W	3-0	Morrell, Hoolahan (pen), Parker	5,298
13	Oct 8	A	Brighton@HA	W	3-0	Southern, Vernon 2	5,146
14	14	H	Yeovil Town	D	1-1	Vernon	6,812
15	21	A	Crewe Alexandra	W	2-1	Morrell, Barker	5,765
16	28	H	Bradford City	W	4-1	Fox, Hoolahan (pen), Parker 2	6,300
17	Nov 4	A	Northampton Town	D	1-1	Morrell	5,762
18	18	H	Huddersfield Town	W	3-1	Parker, Southern, Morrell	7,414
19	24	A	Tranmere Rovers	L	0-2		4,585
20	Dec 5	H	Cheltenham Town	W	2-1	Morrell, Hoolahan	4,851
21	9	H	Swansea City	D	1-1	Vernon	6,216
22	15	A	Scunthorpe Utd	W	3-1	Morrell, Hoolahan (pen), Parker	4,527
23	23	A	Bournemouth	W	3-1	Parker 2, Fox	5,758
24	26	H	Carlisle Utd	W	2-1	Own-goal, Parker	9,473
25	30	H	Doncaster Rovers	W	3-1	Vernon 2, Barker	7,952
26	Jan 1	A	Chesterfield	L	0-2		4,351
27	13	H	Port Vale	W	2-1	Morrell, Fox	6,661
28	20	A	Leyton Orient	W	1-0	Southern	5,217
29	Feb 3	H	Brentford	L	1-3	Vernon	6,086
30	17	H	Bristol City	L	0-1		6,696
31	20	A	Nottm Forest	D	1-1	Hoolahan (pen)	16,849
32	24	H	Millwall	L	0-1		6,547
33	27	A	Oldham Athletic	W	1-0	Morrell	6,956
34	Mar 3	A	Gillingham	D	2-2	Burgess, Fox	5,949
35	6	H	Bournemouth	W	2-0	Forbes, Burgess	6,184
36	10	H	Brighton@HA	D	0-0		8,164
37	17	A	Yeovil Town	W	1-0	Morrell	6,012
38	24	A	Bradford City	W	3-1	Williams, Morrell, Vernon	8,984
39	27	A	Rotherham Utd	L	0-1		4,025
40	31	H	Crewe Alexandra	W	2-1	Hoolahan, Williams	7,203
41	Apr 7	H	Tranmere Rovers	W	3-2	Parker, Hoolahan, Morrell	8,091
42	9	A	Huddersfield Town	W	2-0	Jorgensen, Williams	11,432
43	14	H	Northampton Town	W	4-1	Brandon 2, Hoolahan (pen), Own-goal	7,334
44	21	A	Cheltenham Town	W	2-1	Williams, Southern	5,093
45	28	H	Scunthorpe Utd	W	3-1	Jorgensen, Barker, Parker	9,482
46	May 5	A	Swansea City	W	6-3	Morrell 4, Parker 2	18,903

Final League Position: 3rd in League One

Apps
Sub Apps
Goals

Play-Offs

SF	May 13	A	Oldham Athletic	W	2-1	Barker, Hoolahan	12,154
	19	H	Oldham Athletic	W	3-1	Southern, Morrell, Parker	9,453
F	27	N	Yeovil Town	W	2-0	Williams, Parker	59,313

N-played at Wembley stadium

Apps
Sub Apps
Goals

FA Cup

1	Nov 11	A	Huddersfield Town	W	1-0	Hoolahan (pen)	6,597
2	Dec 2	A	MK Dons	W	2-0	Parker, Morrell	3,837
3	Jan 6	H	Aldershot	W	4-2	Vernon, Morrell 2, Burgess (pen)	6,355
4	27	H	Norwich City	D	1-0	Evatt	9,491
4R	Feb 13	A	Norwich City	L	2-3*	Jackson, Barker	19,120

Apps
Subs
Goals

League Cup

1	Aug 22	H	Barnsley	D	2-2*	Vernon 2	3,938

*-Barnsley won 4-2 on pens

Apps
Sub Apps
Goals

Evans	Joseph	Barker	Jackson	Tierney	Forbes	Southern	Fox	Prendergast	Vernon	Parker	Coid	Hoolahan	Graham	Weir-Daley	Evatt		Gillett	Morrell	Bean	Burgess	Jorgensen	Dickinson	Blinkhorn	Wilkinson	Farrelly	Fernandez	Gorkss	Rachubka	Williams	Brandon	Edge	Hart
1	2	3	4	5*	6	7	8	9#	10	11	12	14	15																			
1*	2	3	4#	5'	6	7	8	9	10	11		14	16	12	15																	
1		3	4	5*	6	7		9#	10'	14	2	15	11		12		8															
1	15	3	4	5'	6*	7	8		10	12			14		2		11	9#														
1	14	3	4*		6	7			10	15	5	11#			2		8	9'	12													
1	12	3	4*	5		7			10#	11					2		8	9	6	14												
1	2	3		5*		7			10'	14	12	11			4		8	9		15	6#											
1		3	4			7		14	10'	12	5	11#			2		8*	15		9	6											
1		3	4			7#	14		10'	15	5	11			2		8*	12		9	6											
1		3	4			7	12		10	14	5	11*			2		8			9#	6											
1		3	4			7	6*		10#	12	5	11			2		8	14		9												
1	12	3	4			7	6'			14	5	11			2*		8#	10		9	15											
1		3	4			7	6		14	15	5	11			2		8*	10'		9#	12											
1	12	3	4			7	6		10	15	5*	11			2		8#	11'			14											
1		3	4			7	6*		10#	15		11			2		8	11'			12	5	14									
1		3	4		8*	7	6	14		10'		11#			2			11			12	5	15									
1		3	4		8*	7	6			10		11			2		12	9#		14		5										
1		3	4		8*	7	6#		15	10'		11			2			9		12	14	5										
1		3	4		8	7	6#		14	10'		11			2*			9		15		5		12								
1		3	4		8*	7	6		14	10'		11			2			9#		12		5		15								
1		3	4*		8	7	6		12	10		11			2			9#		14		5										
1		3	4		8*	7	6#		12	10		11			2			9'			15	5			14							
1		3	4	12	8*		6		15	10'					2			9	11	14	7#	5										
1		3	4		8#	7	6			10		11			2			9'		15	14	5*				12						
1		3	4			7	6*		15	10#		11			2			9'	12	14	8	5										
1		3	4	12	14	7	6			10		11			2			15		9'	8#	5*										
1		3	4	5	8	7	6		10#	12								9		14	8*						11					
1		3	4		8	7	6		10#	14		11*			2			9'		15	12						11					
1		3*	4		8#		6		15	10		11			2		12	14		9	7'						11					
1		3	4	5*	8#	7	6'		9	10		11			2		15			14	12											
1		3	4		12	7*	6		9#	10		11			2		8			14							5					
1		3	4		14	7#	6		12	10'		11			2		8	15		9							5*					
		3	4		12	7	6			14	5	11*			2		8	9#		10								1				
		3	4		12	7#	6		15	14	5	11'			2		8*	9		10								1				
		3			11#		6		15	14	5	12			2		8*	9		10'	7						4	1				
		3			11*		6		15	12	5	14			2		8	9#		10'	7						4	1				
		3	14		8*		6		10'	15	5	11#			2		12	9			7						4	1				
		3			8*		6#		10	12	5	11'			2		14	9	15		7							1	7			
		3	4		8*				10#	14		11			2		8	9	12		7							1	5			
		3	4			12	6#		15	10		11			2		14	9'			7							1	5	8*		
		3	4*		12	15	6'		14	10		11			2			9			7								5	8#	1	
		3	4		8#	6			15	10		11*			2		14	9'			7						12		5			1
		3	4		8#	6				10	12	11'			2		15	9			7								5*	14		1
		3	4		15	6				10'		11#			2		12	9			7						14		5	8*		1
		3	4		12	6	15			10'		11			2		14	9#			7*								5	8		1
		3	4		8*	6	12		14	10		11#			2		15	9'			7								5			1
32	3	46	41	8	26	37	35	3	20	25	15	37	1		42		20	34	2	13	21	12					8	8	9	4	1	5
	5		1	2	8	2	4	2	17	21	3	5	3	1	2		11	6	4	14	10		2	2	1	1	2			1		
		3	1		1	5	4		11	13		8	1				1	16		2	2								4	2		

		3	4		8	6				10		11			2			9			7							1	5			
		3	4		8*	6#	14			10		11'			2		15	9		12	7							1	5			
		3	4		8*	6	12		14	10'		11#	8		2		15	9			7							1	5			
		3	3		3	3				3		3			3			3			3							3	3			
							2		1								2			1												
		1				1				2		1						1											1			

1		3	4		8		6*		14	10#		11			2			9			7	5										
1		3	4		8	7	6*			10					2			9#	12		7	5				14						
1		3	4	5	8	7	6'		10						2			9	15	12					11#		14					
1		3	4		8*	7	6#		10'	15		11			2			9		12	14						6					
1		3	4	5*	8#	7	6		10'	11		11			2					15	14						12					
5		5	5	2	5	4	5		3	3		3			5			4			2	2			1		1					
									1	1									2	3	2					1	2					
		1	1						1	1		1			1			3		1												

1		3	4	5		7	6#	9'	10	15	12	11*			2			9	14													
1		1	1	1		1	1	1	1			1			1			1														
										1	1								1												-	
									2																							

League Table

	P	W	D	L	F	A	Pts
Scunthorpe United	46	26	13	7	73	35	91
Bristol City	46	25	10	11	63	39	85
Blackpool	46	24	11	11	76	49	83
Nottingham Forest	46	23	13	10	65	41	82
Yeovil Town	46	23	10	13	55	39	79
Oldham Athletic	46	21	12	13	69	47	75
Swansea	46	20	12	14	69	53	72
Carlisle United	46	19	11	16	54	55	68
Tranmere Rovers	46	18	13	15	58	53	67
Millwall	46	19	9	18	59	62	66
Doncaster Rovers	46	16	15	15	52	47	63
Port Vale	46	18	6	22	64	65	60
Crewe Alexandra	46	17	9	20	66	72	60
Northampton Town	46	15	14	17	48	51	59
Huddersfield Town	46	14	17	15	60	69	59
Gillingham	46	17	8	21	56	77	59
Cheltenham Town	46	15	9	22	49	61	54
Brighton & Hove Albion	46	14	11	21	49	58	53
Bournemouth	46	13	13	20	50	64	52
Leyton Orient	46	12	15	19	61	77	51
Chesterfield	46	12	11	23	45	53	47
Bradford City	46	11	14	21	47	65	47
Rotherham United	46	13	9	24	58	75	38
Brentford	46	8	13	25	40	79	37

2007-08

The Championship

Manager: Simon Grayson

Did you know that?

A new club record of 12 consecutive victories (carried over from last season) was created with the opening games of the season.

Blackpool avoided relegation back to the third tier on the last day of the season. Ian Holloway's Leicester City was one of the teams who dropped down.

Simon Grayson released 11 players at the end of the season as part of a major rebuild.

Match No.	Date		Venue	Opponents	Result		Scorers	Attendance
1	Aug	11	A	Leicester City	W	1-0	Southern	26,650
2		18	H	Bristol City	D	1-1	Morrell	8,983
3		25	A	Wolves	L	1-2	Taylor-Fletcher	24,294
4	Sep	3	H	Hull City	W	2-1	Taylor-Fletcher, Burgess	7,902
5		15	A	Burnley	D	2-2	Hoolahan (pen), Morrell	16,843
6		18	H	Sheffield Utd	D	2-2	Crainey, Burgess	9,512
7		22	H	Colchester Utd	D	2-2	Morrell, Barker	7,959
8		29	A	Watford	D	1-1	Hoolahan (pen)	16,580
9	Oct	2	A	Coventry City	L	1-3	Morrell	15,803
10		6	H	Plymouth Argyle	D	0-0		8,784
11		20	H	Crystal Palace	D	1-1	Fox	9,037
12		23	A	West Brom Albion	L	1-2	Vernon	22,030
13		27	A	Sheffield Wed	L	1-2	Hoolahan	19,238
14	Nov	5	A	Barnsley	L	1-2	Southern	8,531
15		10	H	Scunthorpe Utd	W	1-0	Gorkss	8,051
16		24	A	Southampton	L	0-1		21,075
17		27	H	Norwich City	L	1-3	Slusarski	7,759
18	Dec	1	H	Queens Park Rangers	W	1-0	Burgess	8,527
19		3	A	Scunthorpe Utd	D	1-1	Flynn	4,407
20		8	A	Preston North End	W	1-0	Hoolahan (pen)	17,807
21		11	H	Cardiff City	L	0-1		7,214
22		15	H	Stoke City	L	2-3	Flynn, Barker	9,123
23		27	H	Coventry City	W	4-0	Hoolahan (pen), Flynn, Gorkss, Vernon	8,690
24		26	A	Sheffield Utd	D	1-1	Jorgensen	26,409
25		29	A	Colchester Utd	W	2-0	Vernon 2	5,160
26	Jan	1	H	Burnley	W	3-0	Gorkss, Burgess, Jorgensen	9,599
27		12	A	Charlton Athletic	L	1-4	Burgess	21,412
28		19	H	Ipswich Town	D	1-1	Jorgensen	9,154
29		26	A	Bristol City	L	0-1		15,465
30	Feb	2	H	Leicester City	W	2-1	Taylor-Fletcher, Dickov	9,298
31		9	A	Hull City	D	2-2	Dickov 2	18,407
32		12	H	Wolves	D	0-0		9,413
33		16	A	Ipswich Town	L	1-2	Dickov	21,059
34		23	H	Charlton Athletic	W	5-3	McPhee, Gorkss, Taylor-Fletcher 2, Dickov	9,134
35	Mar	1	A	Norwich City	W	2-1	McPhee 2	24,531
36		4	H	Barnsley	D	1-1	Taylor-Fletcher	8,080
37		8	H	Southampton	D	2-2	Southern, Gorkss	9,050
38		11	A	Queens Park Rangers	L	2-3	Burgess, Gorkss	11,538
39		15	H	Preston North End	D	0-0		9,629
40		22	A	Stoke City	D	1-1	Burgess	20,019
41		29	A	Crystal Palace	D	0-0		16,028
42	Apr	8	H	West Brom Albion	L	1-3	Burgess	9,628
43		12	A	Cardiff City	L	1-3	Morrell	14,715
44		19	H	Sheffield Wed	W	2-1	Jorgensen, Dickov	9,633
45		26	A	Plymouth Argyle	L	0-3		12,911
46	May	4	H	Watford	D	1-1	Burgess	9,640

Final League Position: 19th in the Championship

Apps
Sub Apps
Gls

FA Cup

3	Jan	5	A	Barnsley	L	1-2	Fox	8,276

Apps
Sub Apps
Gls

League Cup

2	Aug	28	A	Derby County	D	2-2*	Gorkks	8,658
3	Sep	25	H	Southend Utd	W	2-1#	Hoolahan,Jackson	5,022
4	Oct	31	A	Tottenham Hotspur	L	0-2		32,196

*-after extra-time - Blackpool won 7-6 on penalties
#-after extra-time

Apps
Sub Apps
Gls

Rachubka	Barker	Jackson	Evatt	Crainey	Taylor-Fletcher	Southern	Fox	Hoolahan	Parker	Morrell	Jorgensen	Hills	Gorkss	Burgess	Vernon	Forbes	Flynn	Welsh	Coid	Jackson	McMahon	Slusarski	McPhee	Dickov	Green	Holt	Marriappa	Martin	Evans
1	2	3	4	5	6*	7	8	9#	10	11	12	14																	
1	2	3		5	6*	7	8	9	14	11#	12		4	10'	15														
1	2	3		5	6*	7	8	9	14	11#	12		4	10'	15														
1	2	3	4	12	6#	7	8	9	10	11'			5*	14		15													
1	2	3	4	5	6#	7*	8	9	10'	11				15			12	14											
1	2	3	4	5	6*	7	8	9	14	11#				10				12											
1	2	3	4*	6	6#	7	8	9	15	11'			12	10				14											
1	2	3			6	7	8	9*	14	11'	15	12	4				10#		5										
1	2	3			6*	7#	8	9	15	11'			4		12		10	14	5										
1	2	3		5	6*	7#	8	9	10	11'	14				15			12		4									
1	2	3		5	6*	7	8#	9	10	11			4				14	12											
1	2	3*		5	14	7	8'	9	10				4		11		15		6#	12									
1	2	3		5		7#	8'	9	10		15		4		11		14	12	6*										
1	2	3			6'	7	8*	9	10	11#	12	14	4		15				5										
1	2			14	6*	7		9#	10	11'	8		4		15			12	5		3								
1	2			12	6	7	14	15		11	8#		4					9'	5		3*	10							
1	2			3	6#	7		9	15	11	8		4		12			14	5*			10'							
1	2	3		5	12	7#	14	9		15	8		4	11				6*				10'							
1	2	3*		5	6		8#	9	14	11'	7		4	10			15	12											
1	2	3*	12	5	6'			9#	15	11	7		4	10			8	14											
1*	2	3	12	5	6#				10	15	7		4	11		14	8	9'											
1	2		3	5	6*		14	9		15	7#		4	11			8	12				10'							
1	2		3	5	6*		12	9		11'	7		4	10	15		8#	14											
1	2	15	3	5	6*		14	9#		11'	7		4	10			8	12											
1	2	3		5	6		12	9*		11'	7		4	15	10#		8					14							
1	2	3		5	6*		12	9		14	7		4	11'	10#		8					15							
1	2	3		5	6		12	9		14	7*		4	11	10#		8						14						
1	2		3	5	6*		14	9		15	7		4	11			8#	12					10'						
1	2		3	5			9	15		11'	7#		4	11	12		8	14					10'						
1	2		3	5	6			9*		12	7		4	11'			8	15					10#	14					
1	2	14	3	5	6			9#		15	7		4	11			8*							10'	12				
1	2	3	4	5	6	8*		9			7			11									14	10#	12				
1	2	3	4*		6	8		9			7	5		11#					12				14	10					
1	2		3	5	6*	8		9#		15	7		4	14									11	10'	12				
1	2		3	5	6*	8		9		11'	7		4	14			15		12				10#						
1	2		3	5	6*	8		9		11'	7#		4	15			14	12					10						
1	2		3	5	6*	8		9		12	7#		4	15			14						10	11'					
1	2		3	5	6*	7#	14	9	12	11'			4	15			8						10						
1	2		3	5	6*			9	12	14	7		4	11			8						10#						
1	2		3	5	6*			9			7		4	11			8						10			12			
1	2		3	5	6*			9			7		4	11'			8		14				10#	12		15			
1	2		3	5	6	12		9			7		4	11'			8*						10#	14		15			
1	2		3	5	6	7	15	9		12			4	11'			8#						10*	14					
1	2		3	5	6*	8		9		15	7		4	14									10'	11#	12				
1	2	5*	3			8		9		12	7		4	14					15				10	11'	6#				
1*	2		3			8		9		14	7		4	11@			15		5				10'			16	12	6#	
46	46	24	27	37	40	30	16	44	10	24	30	1	39	25	5		20	3	9	1	2	4	16	7	1			1	
		2	2	3	2	1	11	1	11	15	7	3	1	10	9	2	9	17	4	1		2	3	4	4	4	1		
	2			1	6	3	1	5		5	4		6	9	4		3					1	3	6					

Rachubka	Barker	Jackson	Evatt	Crainey	Taylor-Fletcher	Southern	Fox	Hoolahan	Parker	Morrell	Jorgensen	Hills	Gorkss	Burgess	Vernon	Forbes	Flynn	Welsh	Coid	Jackson	McMahon	Slusarski	McPhee	Dickov	Green	Holt	Marriappa	Martin	Evans
1		3	4	5	6'		8	12		14	15	2		10	11#		7	9*											
1		1	1	1	1		1					1		1	1		1	1											
								1		1	1																		
							1																						

Rachubka	Barker	Jackson	Evatt	Crainey	Taylor-Fletcher	Southern	Fox	Hoolahan	Parker	Morrell	Jorgensen	Hills	Gorkss	Burgess	Vernon	Forbes	Flynn	Welsh	Coid	Jackson	McMahon	Slusarski	McPhee	Dickov	Green	Holt	Marriappa	Martin	Evans
	2	3	5			15	8	14	10	12		7#	4		11'	6	9*												1
	2	14			6#		8	15	10'	12		7*	4		11		9	3	5										1
1	2	3*		5	6		8	9	10	15			4		11'		7#	14	12										
1	3	2	1	1	2		3	1	3			2	3		3	1	3	1	1										2
		1				1		2		3								1	1										
		1						1					2																

League Table

	P	W	D	L	F	A	Pts
West Bromwich Albion	46	23	12	11	88	55	81
Stoke City	46	21	16	9	69	55	79
Hull City	46	21	12	13	65	47	75
Bristol City	46	20	14	12	54	53	74
Crystal Palace	46	18	17	11	58	42	71
Watford	46	18	16	12	62	56	70
Wolverhampton	46	18	16	12	53	48	70
Ipswich Town	46	18	15	13	65	56	69
Sheffield United	46	17	15	14	56	51	66
Plymouth Argyle	46	17	13	16	60	50	64
Charlton Athletic	46	17	13	16	63	58	64
Cardiff City	46	16	16	14	59	55	64
Burnley	46	16	14	16	60	67	62
Queens Park Rangers	46	14	16	16	60	66	58
Preston North End	46	15	11	20	50	56	56
Sheffield Wednesday	46	14	13	19	54	55	55
Norwich City	46	15	10	21	49	59	55
Barnsley	46	14	13	19	52	65	55
Blackpool	46	12	18	16	59	64	54
Southampton	46	13	15	18	56	72	54
Coventry City	46	14	11	21	52	64	53
Leicester City	46	12	16	18	42	45	52
Scunthorpe United	46	11	13	22	46	69	46
Colchester United	46	7	17	22	62	86	38

2008-09

The Championship

Manager: Simon Grayson

Did you know that?

Simon Grayson resigned on Christmas Eve and took over at League One side Leeds United.

Blackpool were knocked out of the FA Cup by non-League opposition for the first time since Yeovil Town in 2000.

Tony Parkes was expected to be named as full-time manager after steering the team clear of relegation, but left immediately after a meeting with the chairman Karl Oyston.

It was the seventh time in his career that Parkes had taken over as a temporary manager.

Match No.	Date	Venue	Opponents	Result		Scorers	Attendance
1	Aug 9	H	Bristol City	L	0-1		8,244
2	16	A	Norwich City	D	1-1	Burgess (pen)	23,727
3	23	H	Sheffield Utd	L	1-3	Kabba	8,611
4	30	A	Southampton	W	1-0	Burgess (pen)	15,629
5	Sep 13	H	Barnsley	W	1-0	Kabba	8,363
6	16	A	Burnley	L	0-2		13,752
7	20	A	Birmingham City	W	1-0	Taylor-Fletcher	20,983
8	27	H	Coventry City	D	1-1	Burgess	8,462
9	30	A	Queens Park Rangers	D	1-1	Taylor-Fletcher	12,500
10	Oct 4	H	Cardiff City	D	1-1	Gow	7,328
11	18	A	Doncaster Rovers	D	0-0		11,342
12	21	H	Derby County	W	3-2	Gow, Taylor-Fletcher, Burgess	7,267
13	25	H	Crystal Palace	D	2-2	Burgess, Evatt	7,597
14	28	A	Cardiff City	L	0-2		17,570
15	Nov 1	A	Watford	W	4-3	Southern, Burgess, Taylor-Fletcher, Gow	13,517
16	8	H	Ipswich Town	L	0-1		7,349
17	16	H	Preston North End	L	1-3	Hammil	9,643
18	22	A	Wolves	L	0-2		22,044
19	25	H	Sheffield Wed	L	0-2		7,054
20	29	A	Plymouth Argyle	W	2-1	Dickinson 2	9,969
21	Dec 2	H	Charlton Athletic	W	2-0	Dickinson 2	6,648
22	9	A	Reading	L	0-1		16,514
23	13	A	Nottm Forest	D	0-0		19,103
24	20	H	Swansea City	D	1-1	Gow	7,007
25	26	A	Sheffield Wed	D	1-1	Gow (pen)	25,044
26	29	H	Wolves	D	2-2	Taylor-Fletcher, Edwards	8,906
27	Jan 17	A	Coventry City	L	1-2	Campbell	15,551
28	24	H	Birmingham City	W	2-0	Campbell, Southern	8,105
29	27	H	Queens Park Rangers	L	0-3		6,656
30	31	A	Crystal Palace	W	1-0	Campbell (pen)	13,810
31	Feb 7	H	Doncaster Rovers	L	2-3	Vaughan, Campbell	7,452
32	14	A	Ipswich Town	D	1-1	Baptiste	19,299
33	18	A	Derby County	L	1-4	Edwards	26,834
34	21	H	Watford	L	0-2		7,451
35	28	A	Bristol City	D	0-0		16,855
36	Mar 3	H	Burnley	L	0-1		7,679
37	7	H	Norwich City	W	2-0	Ormerod, Adam	7,505
38	10	A	Sheffield Utd	D	2-2	Blackman, Campbell	25,273
39	14	A	Barnsley	W	1-0	Small	12,228
40	21	H	Southampton	D	1-1	Campbell (pen)	7,947
41	Apr 4	H	Plymouth Argyle	L	0-1		8,103
42	11	A	Preston North End	W	1-0	Adam	21,273
43	13	H	Reading	D	2-2	Southern, Campbell	7,722
44	18	A	Charlton Athletic	D	2-2	Campbell (pen),Hughes	19,615
45	25	H	Nottm Forest	D	1-1	Ormerod	9,279
46	May 3	A	Swansea City	W	1-0	Campbell	16,316

Final League Position: 16th in the Championship

Apps
Sub Apps
Gls

FA Cup

3	Jan 3	A	Torquay Utd	L	0-1		8,276

Apps
Sub Apps
Gls

League Cup

2	Aug 12	A	Macclesfield Town	L	0-2		1,631

Apps
Sub Apps
Gls

Rachubka	Coid	Edwards	Evatt	Hammill	Taylor-Fletcher	Southern	Jorgensen	Camara	Burgess	Wright	Vaughan	Aluko	Rehman	Fox	Kabba	Barker	Nardiello	Martin	Gow	Broomes	McPhee	Mitchley	Hendrie	Baptiste	Dickinson	Reid	Harte	Owens	O'Donovan	Campbell	Crainey	Nemeth	Marshall	Gilks	Ormerod	Adam	Blackman	Small	Mahon	Hughes	Walton	Green	Merella	
1	2	3	4	5	6*	7	8#	9	10	11	12	14																																
1	2*	3	4	5'	6			9	10	11	15		12	7#	14																													
1	12	3	4	5	6#		8	9*	10	11'	15			14	7	2																												
1	12	3	4	5	6*		8'	9	10		15		14	7#	11	2																												
1		3	4	5'	6	14	8#	9	10		12			7*	11	2	15																											
1		3	4	5	6#	7	8'	9*	10		11					2	14	12	15																									
1		3	4		6*	7	8	9	10		11#		12		5	2			14																									
1		3	4	12	6	7*	8	9	10		11				5	2																												
1		3	4		6	7	8	9	10		11*				5	2				12																								
1		3	4	5	6	7		9	10#		11				11*	2			12		14																							
1		3	4	12	6	7	8	9	10#		11*				11	2			14																									
1	5	3	4	12	6*	7	8		10		11#					2		14	9																									
1	5	3	4	14	6*	7#	8		10		11					2			9			12																						
1	5	3	4	12	6	7	8*		10		11					2			9#			14																						
1	5	3	4	12	6	7	8		10		11*					2			9																									
1		3	4	15	6	7	8#	5*	10		11'			12	14	2			9																									
1		3	4	11	6*	7#	8	5	10						15	2			9'		12		14																					
1		3	4	11	6	7*		5	12					14	10#				9'		15		8	2																				
1		3	4	11	6*	7			14						10	12		5	9		12#		8	2*																				
1		3	4	11	6*	7			10					12		2		5	9'				8#		14	9																		
1		3	4	11*	12	7			10'						14	2		5	15				8		9#	6																		
1		3	4	11*	15	7			10'					12		2		5	9#				8		14	6																		
1	12	3*		11#	15	7			10'					9		2		5	14					4	8	6																		
1			4	11	12	7			10#					9	15	2		5	14					3	8'	6*																		
1		3	4		11	7								10		2		5	9						8	6																		
1		3	4		11#	7			15		14			10		2		12	9						8'	6	5*																	
1		3	4		11	7*			10#		14			6		2											5	12	8	9														
1		3	4		11	7#	14							6		2		10'									5	12	8*	9	15													
1		3	4		11						7			6		2		10'									5*	15	8#	9	12	14												
1	5		4		11						7#			6		2		15						3					8	9'			7*	12	14									
	5		4		11						10			7#		2								3					8*	9			12	1	14	6								
		3			11		8				10			7		2								5					8	9	4			1										
		3			11		8				10*			7		2								5					8	9	4			1	12									
		3			11		8				10			7#		2								5				12	8*	9	4			1	14									
1	12		4*		11#		8				10			15		2								5				14		9	3				7#	6								
1	5				11*		8				10					2								3				14	12	9	4				7'	6#	15							
1	5				11	7	12				10*					2								3						9#	4				8	6	14							
1	5				11	7	12									2		14						3				8*		9	4					6	10#							
1	5*	12				7	14						4			2		11						3						9	4				15	6	10'	8#						
1		3				7	12									2								4				14		9					10'	6*	15	8	5#					
1		3				7*	14		15		11					2					12			5						9#	4				10	6				8'				
1		3				7	15		10		11					2								5*					8#	9'	4				14	6					12			
1		3				7	12				11					2								5					8*	9	4				14	6				10#				
1			4			7	15		10'		11#					2								5						9	3				12	6		8*		14				
1	12		4			7	14				11					2								5						9	3				10#	6		8*						
1	4					7	12				11					2								5					8	9	3				10*	6								
42	13	35	33	15	34	34	20	14	25	3	26			15	10	42		10	12				5	21	5	7	4	1	11	20	14		1	4	7	13	2	4	1	2				
	5	1		7	4	1	11		4		7	1	3	6	5	1	2	5	7	1	5	2	1		2			7	1		2	1	1	1	8		3			1	1			
		2	1	1	5	3			6		1				2				5					1	4					9					2	2	1	1		1				

Rachubka	Coid	Edwards	Evatt	Hammill	Taylor-Fletcher	Southern	Jorgensen	Camara	Burgess	Wright	Vaughan	Aluko	Rehman	Fox	Kabba	Barker	Nardiello	Martin	Gow	Broomes	McPhee	Mitchley	Hendrie	Baptiste	Dickinson	Reid	Harte	Owens	O'Donovan	Campbell	Crainey	Nemeth	Marshall	Gilks	Ormerod	Adam	Blackman	Small	Mahon	Hughes	Walton	Green	Merella	
1	5		4			7	12		10		11			9		2	8#										5															6*		14
1	1		1			1			1		1			1		1	1										1															1	1	
							1																												-		-							

Rachubka	Coid	Edwards	Evatt	Hammill	Taylor-Fletcher	Southern	Jorgensen	Camara	Burgess	Wright	Vaughan	Aluko	Rehman	Fox	Kabba	Barker	Nardiello	Martin	Gow	Broomes	McPhee	Mitchley	Hendrie	Baptiste	Dickinson	Reid	Harte	Owens	O'Donovan	Campbell	Crainey	Nemeth	Marshall	Gilks	Ormerod	Adam	Blackman	Small	Mahon	Hughes	Walton	Green	Merella	
	2*	3	4	5	6	7			10	11#	12	9'	14					5																1								15		
	1	1	1	1	1	1			1	1		1						1																1										
											1		1																													1		

League Table

	P	W	D	L	F	A	Pts
Wolverhampton	46	27	9	10	80	52	90
Birmingham City	46	23	14	9	54	37	83
Sheffield United	46	22	14	10	64	39	80
Reading	46	21	14	11	72	40	77
Burnley	46	21	13	12	72	60	76
Preston North End	46	21	11	14	66	54	74
Cardiff City	46	19	17	10	65	53	74
Swansea	46	16	20	10	63	50	68
Ipswich Town	46	17	15	14	62	53	66
Bristol City	46	15	16	15	54	54	61
Queens Park Rangers	46	15	16	15	42	44	61
Sheffield Wednesday	46	16	13	17	51	58	61
Watford	46	16	10	20	68	72	58
Doncaster Rovers	46	17	7	22	42	53	58
Crystal Palace	46	15	12	19	52	55	56
Blackpool	46	13	17	16	47	58	17
Coventry City	46	13	15	18	47	58	54
Derby County	46	14	12	20	55	67	54
Nottingham Forest	46	13	14	19	50	65	53
Barnsley	46	13	13	20	45	58	52
Plymouth Argyle	46	13	12	21	44	57	51
Norwich City	46	12	10	24	57	70	46
Southampton	46	10	15	21	46	69	45
Charlton Athletic	46	8	15	23	52	74	39

2009-10

The Championship

Manager: Ian Holloway

Did you know that?

The South Stand was finally completed by the end of the season, meaning Blackpool had a five-figure crowd for the first time at Bloomfield Road since the visit of Preston North End a decade earlier.

Ian Holloway was appointed as the new manager.

The 37,000 fans at Wembley was a new record for the number of people travelling to watch the team.

Over 60,000 cheered their heroes on the promenade the next day as Blackpool celebrated promotion to the Premier League.

Blackpool won nine of their last 11 games to win promotion.

Blackpool were back in the top flight for the first time since 1971.

Match No.	Date	Venue	Opponents	Result		Scorers	Attendance
1	Aug 8	A	Queens Park Rangers	D	1-1	Burgess	14,013
2	15	H	Cardiff City	D	1-1	Evatt	7,698
3	18	H	Derby County	D	0-0		8,056
4	22	A	Watford	D	2-2	Baptiste, Taylor-Fletcher	12,745
5	29	H	Coventry City	W	3-0	Adam(pen), Burgess, Taylor-Fletcher	8,239
6	Sep 12	A	Leicester City	L	1-2	Adam	22,827
7	16	H	Newcastle Utd	W	2-1	Ormerod, Euell	9,647
8	19	A	Nottm Forest	W	1-0	Adam	23,487
9	26	H	Peterborough Utd	W	2-0	Euell, Bouazza	7,728
10	29	A	Bristol City	L	0-2		13,673
11	Oct 3	A	Crystal Palace	L	1-4	Baptiste	15,749
12	17	H	Plymouth Argyle	W	2-0	Seip, Vaughan	7,765
13	20	H	Sheffield Utd	W	3-0	Seip, Euell, Southern	8,042
14	24	A	Swansea City	D	0-0		14,724
15	31	A	Doncaster Rovers	D	3-3	Ormerod, Emmanuel-Thomas, Burgess	10,312
16	Nov 7	H	Scunthorpe Utd	W	4-1	Evatt, Adam, Burgess, Baptiste	7,727
17	21	A	Reading	L	1-2	Ormerod	15,945
18	30	H	Preston North End	D	1-1	Clarke	9,861
19	Dec 5	H	Barnsley	L	1-2	Adam (pen)	8,108
20	8	A	Middlesbrough	W	3-0	Taylor-Fletcher 2, Adam	18,089
21	12	A	Ipswich Town	L	1-3	Evatt	19,831
22	26	A	Derby County	W	2-0	Own-goal, Ormerod	30,313
23	9	A	Cardiff City	D	1-1	Adam	19,147
24	16	H	Queens Park Rangers	D	2-2	Adam, Taylor-Fletcher	7,600
25	19	H	Sheffield Wed	L	1-2	Adam	8,007
26	23	H	Watford	W	3-2	Adam, Southern, Ormerod	6,855
27	30	A	Coventry City	D	1-1	Bannan	16,019
28	Feb 3	H	West Brom Albion	L	2-3	Southern, Dobbie	8,510
29	6	H	Leicester City	L	1-2	Dobbie	8,484
30	9	A	Sheffield Wed	L	0-2		19,058
31	13	A	Preston North End	D	0-0		19,840
32	16	H	Middlesbrough	W	2-0	Ormerod, Campbell	7,936
33	20	H	Reading	W	2-0	Campbell, Adam	7,147
34	27	A	Barnsley	L	0-1		12,347
35	Mar 6	H	Ipswich Town	W	1-0	Euell	8,635
36	13	A	West Brom Albion	L	2-3	Adam, Ormerod	21,592
37	16	A	Sheffield Utd	L	0-3		22,555
38	20	H	Crystal Palace	D	2-2	Adam, Burgess	9,702
39	23	H	Swansea City	W	5-1	Ormerod 2, Evatt, Burgess, Taylor-Fletcher	9,149
40	27	A	Plymouth Argyle	W	2-0	Adam, Dobbie	10,614
41	Apr 2	A	Scunthorpe Utd	W	4-2	Own-goal, Coleman, Campbell 2	7,508
42	5	H	Doncaster Rovers	W	2-0	Campbell, Dobbie	9,701
43	10	A	Newcastle Utd	L	1-4	Ormerod	47,010
44	17	H	Nottm Forest	W	3-1	Adam (pen), Campbell 2	11,164
45	24	A	Peterborough Utd	W	1-0	Campbell	7,812
46	May 2	H	Bristol City	D	1-1	Ormerod	12,296

Final League Position: 6th in the Championship

Apps
Sub Apps
Gls

Play-Offs

SF	May 8	H	Nottm Forest	W	2-1	Southern, Adam (pen)	11,805
	11	A	Nottm Forest	W	4-3	Campbell 3, Dobbie	28,358
F	22	N	Cardiff City	W	3-2	Adam, Taylor-Fletcher, Ormerod	82,244

N-played at Wembley Stadium

Apps
Sub Apps
Gls

FA Cup

3	Jan 2	H	Ipswich Town	L	1-2	Ormerod	7,332

App
Sub
Goals

League Cup

2	Aug 11	A	Crewe Alexandra	W	2-1	Nowland, Nardiello	2,991
3	26	H	Wigan Athletic	W	4-1	Demontagnac, Burgess, Adam, Taylor-Fletcher	8,089
4	Sep 22	A	Stoke City	L	3-4	Vaughan, Clarke, Burgess	13,957

Apps
Sub Apps
Gls

Rachubka	Crainey	Evatt	Baptiste	Edwards	Adam	Taylor-Fletcher	Southern	Euell	Burgess	Vaughan	Clarke	Ormerod	Demontagnac	Nardiello	Eardley	Emmanuel-Thomas	Bangura	Bouazza	Eastham	Gilks	Seip	Martin	Bannan	Butler	Coid	Campbell	Dobbie	Husband	Coleman	Nowland	Hudson	Almond
1	2	3	4	5	6	7	8	9	10	11*	12	14																				
1	2	3	4	5	6	7*	8	9		11		10#	12	14																		
1		3	4	5	6#	7*	8			11'	12		14		2	15																
1	2	3	4		6	7*	8	9#	14	11	12	15			5	10'																
1	2	3		5	6#	7*	8	9	10'	12		11			4	15	14															
1	2	3		5	6	12	8*	9#	10		15	7'			4	11		14														
1	2	3	4		6#	11	8	9				7			5	14	12	10*														
1	2	3*	4	12	6	11	8	9			15	7'			5	14		10#														
1	2		4	5	6#		8	9	15	11		7'			3*		14	10	12													
1	2		4	5	6#		8	9	10'	11	15	12			3	14		7*														
1	2		4	5	6		8	9	14	11	15	10'			3*	7#		12														
	2*	3	4		6		8	14	10'	11	9#		15		12			7		1	5											
	2		4		15	6'		9		12		10	7#		3	8	11*	14		1	5											
	2	12	4		6'		8	9	15	11	10				3*		14	7#		1	5											
	2	3	4			12	8	9	10	11		7*				7				1	5											
	2	3	4		6#		8	14	10		7'	15				9	12	11*		1	5											
	2*	3	4		6	15	8#	9	10	11	14	7'								1	5	12										
	2	3	4		6*		8	15	10'	11	7#	14						9		1	5		12									
	2		4	5	6	12	8	15	10'	11	7#				3			9*		1			14									
1	2	3	4	5*	6	10'	8	14		11		7			12		15						9#									
	2	3		5	15	10	14	9		11		12			4		8#	9*		1			6'									
1	2	3	4*	12	6#	10	8	9	11			7	14		5			15														
1			4		6	10#	8		11	12		7'		14	5							9*	15	2								
1	2	3	4		6	10'	8	14	12	11#		7		15	5								9*									
1	2	3	4		6	14	15	9'	10	11*		7		10#	5								12									
1	2	3*	4		6	10'	8		15	11		7	14	12	5								9#									
1	2	3	4	5	6*	10	8		15	11		7	12										9'									
1	2	3		5	6	14	8		10'	11													4#	12	7*	9	15					
	2	3*	4		6	10	8		14	11			12		5					1			8#				9					
1	2		4	5		10	8*	6	14	11#							14						3		9	7'	12				
	2	3	4	5		6	8		10	11		7								1						9						
	2	3	4	5	6	10#	8			11*		7'						12		1				14		9	15					
	2	3	4		6	10*	8		15	11		7'						12		1				5		9#	14					
	2	3	4		6		8	15	10'	11		7#						14		1				5		9*	12					
			4	5	6		8	7	12	11	14				2					1		3*				9	10#					
			4	5	6		8	7'	15	11		14			2					1		3*	12			9	10#					
	2		4	5	6		8#	10'	14	11		7			3*					1		15		12		9						
	2	3	4		6	14	8		12		7'	15	4							1			7#				9	10*	5			
	2	3	4		6*	10	8	15	10'		7#	11								1			15					12	5			
	2*	3	4		6	10	8	9'	11		7#									1		12	14				15		5			
		3	4		6	10#	8		11	15	7'							12		1		2				14	9*		5			
	2	3	4		6	10	8			11									7*		1						9	12		5			
	2	3	4		6	10#	8		7'	11*		15								1			12			9	14		5			
	2	3	4		6	10#	8	15		11*		7'								1			14			9	12		5			
	2	3	4		6	10*	8	14		11		7'								1			12			9#	15		5			
	2	3	4		6	10#	8		14	11*		7								1			12			9'	15		5			
20	41	35	42	19	41	28	43	22	20	34	9	26	1	1	22	6	2	11		26	7	4	8	4	1	14	6	1	9			
		1		2	2	7	2	10	15	4	9	9	7	4	2	5	7	8	1			3	11	3		1	10	2				
		4	3		15	6	3	4	6	1	1	11				1		1			2		1			8	4		1			

	2	3	4		6	10*	8		12	11		7								1			15			9#	14		5			
	2	3	4	12	6*	10#	8		14	11		7'								1						9	15		5			
	2	3	4		6	10#	8		14	11*		7'	8							1			12			9	15		5			
	3	3	3		3	3	3			3		3								3						3			3			
				1				3														2				3					
					2	1	1					1														3	1					

1	2	3	4	12	6	10#	8	9'		11*		7	15		5																	
1	1	1	1		1	1	1	1		1		1			1																	
				1								1								1										
												1																				

		3	4	5		10'					7	11#	14	6						1		6								8	9	14
	2		4	5	6	14	15	12	10'	8		11	7#		3		9*			1												
			4	5	6				10	11	7				12	7#	9	14	3*	1		6										
	1	1	3	3	2	1			2	2	2	2	1	1	1	1	2		1	3		2								1	1	
						1	1	1					1		1			1														1
					1	1			2	1	1		1	1																1		

League Table

	P	W	D	L	F	A	Pts
Newcastle United	46	30	12	4	90	35	102
West Bromwich Albion	46	26	13	7	89	48	91
Nottingham Forest	46	22	13	11	65	40	79
Cardiff City	46	22	10	14	73	54	76
Leicester City	46	21	13	12	61	45	76
Blackpool	46	19	13	14	74	58	70
Swansea	46	17	18	11	40	37	69
Sheffield United	46	17	14	15	62	55	65
Reading	46	17	12	17	68	63	63
Bristol City	46	15	18	13	56	65	63
Middlesbrough	46	16	14	16	58	50	62
Doncaster Rovers	46	15	15	16	59	58	60
Queens Park Rangers	46	14	15	17	58	65	57
Derby County	46	15	11	20	53	63	56
Ipswich Town	46	12	20	14	50	61	56
Watford	46	14	12	20	61	68	54
Preston North End	46	13	15	18	58	73	54
Barnsley	46	14	12	20	53	69	54
Coventry City	46	13	15	18	47	64	54
Scunthorpe United	46	14	10	22	62	84	52
Crystal Palace	46	14	17	15	50	53	49
Sheffield Wednesday	46	11	14	21	49	69	47
Plymouth Argyle	46	11	8	27	43	68	41
Peterborough United	46	8	10	28	46	80	34

2010-11

The Premiership

Manager: Ian Holloway

:

Did you know that?

This was Blackpool's 100th consecutive season in the Football League.

Blackpool led the Premier League for two hours, the first time since 1957.

Blackpool fans were voted the fifth loudest in the PL home and away.

39 points would have given Blackpool safety in nine out of the last 10 seasons.

Match No.	Date	Venue	Opponents	Result		Scorers	Attendance
1	Aug 14	A	Wigan Athletic	W	4-0	Taylor-Fletcher, Harewood 2, Baptiste	16,152
2	21	A	Arsenal	L	0-6		60,032
3	28	H	Fulham	D	2-2	Own-goal, Varney	15,529
4	Sep 11	A	Newcastle Utd	W	2-0	Adam (pen), Campbell	49,597
5	19	A	Chelsea	L	0-4		41,761
6	25	H	Blackburn Rovers	L	1-2	Phillips	15,901
7	Oct 3	A	Liverpool	W	2-1	Adam (pen), Varney	43,156
8	17	H	Man City	L	2-3	Harewood, Taylor-Fletcher	16,116
9	23	A	Birmingham City	L	0-2		26,850
10	Nov 1	H	West Brom Albion	W	2-1	Adam (pen), Varney	15,210
11	5	H	Everton	D	2-2	Eardley, Vaughan	16,094
12	10	A	Aston Villa	L	2-3	Harewood, Campbell	34,330
13	13	A	West Ham Utd	D	0-0		31,194
14	20	H	Wolves	W	2-1	Varney, Harewood	15,922
15	27	A	Bolton Wanderers	D	2-2	Evatt, Varney	25,851
16	Dec 11	A	Stoke City	W	1-0	Campbell	26,879
17	28	A	Sunderland	W	2-0	Campbell 2	42,892
18	Jan 1	A	Man City	L	0-1		47,296
19	4	H	Birmingham City	L	1-2	Campbell	14,550
20	12	H	Liverpool	W	2-1	Taylor-Fletcher, Campbell	16,089
21	15	A	West Brom Albion	L	2-3	Vaughan, Taylor-Fletcher	25,316
22	22	H	Sunderland	L	1-2	Adam (pen)	16,037
23	25	H	Man Utd	L	2-3	Cathcart, Campbell	15,574
24	Feb 2	H	West Ham Utd	L	1-3	Adam	15,095
25	5	A	Everton	L	3-5	Baptiste, Puncheon, Adam	38,202
26	12	H	Aston Villa	D	1-1	Grandin	16,000
27	22	H	Tottenham Hotspur	W	3-1	Adam (pen), Campbell, Ormerod	16,069
28	26	A	Wolves	L	0-4		29,086
29	Mar 7	H	Chelsea	L	1-3	Puncheon	15,584
30	19	A	Blackburn Rovers	D	2-2	Adam 2 (1 pen)	27,209
31	Apr 3	A	Fulham	L	0-3		25,692
32	10	H	Arsenal	L	1-3	Taylor-Fletcher	16,030
33	16	H	Wigan Athletic	L	1-3	Campbell	16,030
34	23	H	Newcastle Utd	D	1-1	Campbell	16,003
35	30	H	Stoke City	D	0-0		16,003
36	May 7	A	Tottenham Hotspur	D	1-1	Adam (pen)	35,585
37	14	H	Bolton Wanderers	W	4-3	Campbell 2, Puncheon, Adam	15,979
38	22	A	Man Utd	L	2-4	Adam, Taylor-Fletcher	75,400

Final League Position: 19th in the Premier League

Apps
Sub Apps
Gls

FA Cup

3	Jan 8	A	Southampton	L	0-2		21,464

Apps
Sub Apps
Gls

League Cup

2	Aug 24	A	MK Dons	L	3-4*	Ormerod, Sylvestre, Adam	7,458

* after extra-time

Apps
Sub Apps
Gls

Gilks	Baptiste	Cathcart	Crainey	Evatt	Adam	Grandin	Harewood	Taylor-Fletcher	Ormerod	Vaughan	Basham	Euell	Sylvestre	Keinan	Demontagnac	Eardley	Varney	Southern	Campbell	Carney	Phillips	Kingson	Edwards	Rachubka	Reid	Beattie	Puncheon	Kornilenko	Halstead	Francis-Reynolds	Thomsett	Barkhuizen	Roberts	Coid	Husband
1	2	3	4	5	6	7	8*	9#	10'	11	12	14	15																						
1	2	3	4	5	6	7	9#	10'	14	11			8*	12	15																				
1	2	3	4	5*	6	7		9	10	11						12	8																		
1			4	5	6	7'	14		10#	11				2		3	8*	12	9	15															
1	10		4	5	6	7'	15	12	14	11				2		3*	8#		9																
1		3	4	5	6	14	8#	7	10'	11						2*	15		9		12														
1		3#	4	5	6	7'		10		11				14		2*	8	15	9		12														
1		3	4	5	6	7#	14	10		11						2*	8		9		12														
1		3	4	5	6*		7#	10	15	11						2	8'	12	9		14														
1		3#	4	5	6	7		10		11				15		2*	8'		9	12	14														
1		3	4	5	6	15	14	10'		11						2	8#	7*	9		12														
				12	15		9#		10		5	11'	8	2*				6	14	4	7	1	3												
1*		3	4	5	6	7'	14	10		11						2	8		9#		15	12													
		3	4*	5	6		7'	14		11			15			2	8		9	12	10#	1													
		3	4	5	6	7'		10#	14	11						2	8*	12	9	15		1													
		3	4	5	6	7*		10		11						2	8		9		12	1													
		3	4	5		7'		10#		11			6*			2	8	12	9	14	15	1													
		3	4	5	6			10#	14	11			7*			2	8		9		12	1													
		3	4	5	6			10'	12	11		15				2	8#	14	9		7*	1													
	14	3	4	5	6	7'		10#		11						2	8*	12	9		15	1													
	14	3	4	5	6	7'		10	12	11						2*	8#		9		15	1													
		3	4#	5	6	7'	15	10	14	11						2	8				9	1*		12											
	4	3		5	6	7	14	10#		11						2	8*		9		12	1													
	4	3*		12	6		14	10		11						2	8'		9	5		1			7#	15									
	4			5	6	7	14			11						2		15	9'	5			12	1		10#	3*								
	4	3		5	6	7'	10*			11							8#		9	5	12	1			14		15								
	4	3		5	6				15	11			7*			2		12	9		14	1				10#		7'							
	4	3		5					12	11			8*			2	15	6	9		14	1				10#		7'							
	4		3	5					15	11						2		6		5#	14	1*			9'	10	7		12						
	2	3	4	5	6*	7'		10		11							8#	12			15	1			14		9								
	2	3	4	5	6	7'		10	8#	11										15		1				9*	12	14							
	2	3	4	5	6			10									8'	11*	9		12	1			15		7#	14							
1		3	4	5	6	7'		10#								2	8*	11	9		14					15	12								
1	3		4	5	6			10#		11						2	12	8	9		7*						15								
1	3		4	5	6			10#		11						2	14	8	9		7*							12							
1	3	14	4	5	6			10#		11						2*		8	9							12	15	7'							
1	3	14	4	5	6#			10'	12	11						2		8	9							15	7*								
1	3		4	5	6			10'	12	11						2	15	8*	9		14						7#								
18	19	28	31	36	34	21	7	29	6	35	1	1	6	3		30	24	11	30	5	6	19	1	1	2	5	6	3							
	2	2		2	1	2	9	2	13		1	2	2	3	1	1	5	10	1	7	21	1	1	1	3	4	5	3	1						
	2	1		1	12	1	5	6	1	2						1	5		13		1						3								

Gilks	Baptiste	Cathcart	Crainey	Evatt	Adam	Grandin	Harewood	Taylor-Fletcher	Ormerod	Vaughan	Basham	Euell	Sylvestre	Keinan	Demontagnac	Eardley	Varney	Southern	Campbell	Carney	Phillips	Kingson	Edwards	Rachubka	Reid	Beattie	Puncheon	Kornilenko	Halstead	Francis-Reynolds	Thomsett	Barkhuizen	Roberts	Coid	Husband
	4								10			9'	8	5		2*		6			7		3	1						12	6#	14	15		
	1								1			1	1	1		1		1			1		1	1							1				
																														1		1	1		

Gilks	Baptiste	Cathcart	Crainey	Evatt	Adam	Grandin	Harewood	Taylor-Fletcher	Ormerod	Vaughan	Basham	Euell	Sylvestre	Keinan	Demontagnac	Eardley	Varney	Southern	Campbell	Carney	Phillips	Kingson	Edwards	Rachubka	Reid	Beattie	Puncheon	Kornilenko	Halstead	Francis-Reynolds	Thomsett	Barkhuizen	Roberts	Coid	Husband
					14	12		15	10		7		6*	5	9	2							3						1			11#		4	8#
									1		1		1	1	1	1							1						1			1		1	1
					1	1		1																											
					1				1				1																						

League Table

	P	W	D	L	F	A	Pts
Manchester United	38	23	11	4	78	37	80
Chelsea	38	21	8	9	69	33	71
Manchester City	38	21	8	9	60	33	71
Arsenal	38	19	11	8	72	43	68
Tottenham Hotspur	38	16	14	8	55	46	62
Liverpool	38	17	7	14	59	44	58
Everton	38	13	15	10	51	45	54
Fulham	38	11	16	11	49	43	49
Aston Villa	38	12	12	14	48	59	48
Sunderland	38	12	11	15	45	56	47
West Bromwich Albion	38	12	11	15	56	71	47
Newcastle United	38	11	13	14	56	57	46
Stoke City	38	13	7	18	46	48	46
Bolton	38	12	10	16	52	56	46
Blackburn Rovers	38	11	10	17	46	59	43
Wigan Athletic	38	9	15	14	40	61	42
Wolverhampton	38	11	7	20	46	66	40
Birmingham City	38	8	15	15	37	58	39
Blackpool	38	10	9	19	55	78	39
West Ham United	38	7	12	19	43	70	33

Blackpool FC Statistics

Finishing positions:

Highest: 2nd in Division One (1956)
Lowest: 21st in Division Four (1983)

Largest victory: 10–0 (v Lanerossi Vicenza, Anglo-Italian Cup on 10 June 1972)

Largest defeat: 1–10 (v Small Heath, Division Two, on 2 March 1901 and v Huddersfield Town, Division One, on 13 December 1930)

Consecutive victories: 12 (between 31 March 2007 and 14 August 2007)

Consecutive defeats: 8 (between 26 November 1898 and 7 January 1899 and between 28 November 1964 and 16 January 1965)

Largest transfer fee paid: £1.25 million (DJ Campbell from Leicester City 2010)

Largest transfer fee received: £1,750,000 (Brett Ormerod, from Southampton, 2001)

Most Football League appearances: Jimmy Armfield (569, between 27 December 1954 and 1 May 1971)

Most consecutive League appearances: Georgie Mee (195, between 25 December 1920 and 12 September 1925)

Most goals in total: Jimmy Hampson (252, between 15 October 1927 and 25 December 1938)

Most Football League goals: Jimmy Hampson (248)

Most League goals in one season: Jimmy Hampson (45, 1929–30)

Most goals in one game: 5 (Jimmy Hampson; v Reading on 10 November 1928 and Jimmy McIntosh; v Preston North End on 1 May 1948)

Fastest goal: 11 seconds: Bill Slater (v Stoke City on 10 December 1949) and James Quinn (v Bristol City on 12 August 1995)

Most capped player: Jimmy Armfield (43; for England)

Longest-serving manager: Joe Smith (22 years, 9 months; from 1 August 1935 to 30 April 1958)

Largest attendance – Pre-2002: 38,098; v Wolverhampton Wanderers on 17 September 1955.

Largest attendance – 2002 onwards: 16,116 (99.48 per cent of capacity; v Manchester City on 17 October 2010)

INTERNATIONALS

England		Years	App	Goals
Harry	Bedford	1922–24	2	1
Jimmy	Hampson	1930–32	3	5
Harry	Johnston	1946–53	10	0
Stan	Mortensen	1946–54	25	23
Stan	Matthews	1946–57	36	3
Eddie	Shimwell	1949	1	0
Tommy	Garrett	1951–54	3	0
Ernie	Taylor	1953–54	1	0
Bill	Perry	1955–56	3	2
Jimmy	Armfield	1958–66	43	0
Ray	Charnley	1962–63	1	0
Tony	Waiters	1963–65	5	0
Alan	Ball	1964–66	14	1

Scotland				
Phil	Watson	1933	1	0
Alex	Munro	1938	1	0
Frank	O'Donnell	1938	2	0
Jimmy	Blair	1946	1	0
Allan	Brown	1951–54	11	3
George	Farm	1952–59	10	0
Hugh	Kelly	1952	1	0
Jackie	Mudie	1956–58	17	9
Tony	Green	1971	4	0
Charlie	Adam	2009–present	7	0
Stephen	Crainey	2010–present	2	0

Wales				
Fred	Griffiths	1899–00	2	0
Dai	Astley	1938–39	1	1
Glyn	James	1965–71	9	0
Wyn	Davies	1973	1	0
David	Vaughan	2008–present	8	1
Neil	Eardley	2009–present	4	0

Northern Ireland		Years	App	Goals
Sammy	Jones	1933–34	1	1
Peter	Doherty	1934–36	4	0
Malcolm	Butler	1938–39	1	0
Derek	Spence	1976–80	15	3
James	Quinn	1996–98	10	1
Craig	Cathcart	2010–present	2	0

Rep Ireland				
Mickey	Walsh	1975–77	4	1
Wes	Hoolahan	2008	1	0

Latvia				
Kaspers	Gorkss	2006–08	14	1

Algeria				
Hameur	Bouazza	2009–10	6	1

Australia				
David	Carney	2010	7	2

Ghana				
Richard	Kingson	2010	3	0

Player Records

Player	Seasons	League		FA Cup		League Cup		Total	
		App	Goals	App	Goals	App	Goals	App	Goals
Ablett G	1999-00	9	1	0	0	0	0	10	1
Adam C	2008-11	91+3	31	1	0	2+1	2	94+4	33
Adams R	1948-51	14	1	2	0	0	0	16	1
Ainscough J	1950-54	6	0	0	0	0	0	6	0
Ainscow A	1971-78	178+14	28	5+2	0	10	0	193+16	28
Alcock T	1967-76	184+6	21	4	1	15+1	0	203+7	22
Aldridge M	1998-00	18+7	7	1	0	2+1	2	21+8	9
Allardyce C	1995-96	0+1	0						
Allen W	1901-02	6	0	0	0	0	0	6	0
Aluko S	2008-09	0+1	0	0	0	0	0	0+1	0
Anderson G	1900-04	78	29	0	0	0	0	78	29
Anderson S	2004-05	1+3	0	0	0	0	0	1+3	0
Anderson T	1903-04	2	0	0	0	0	0	2	0
Anderton W	1901-07	102	10	0	0	0	0	102	10
Appleton L	1914-20	33	3	0	0	0	0	33	3
Armes S	1933-34	4	0	0	0	0	0	4	0
Armfield J	1954-71	569	6	33	0	25	0	627	6
Armstrong C	2005-06	5	0	0	0	0	0	5	0
Armstrong D	1958-59	1	0	0	0	0	0	1	0
Ashurst J	1979-81	53	3	4	0	2	1	59	4
Ashworth JF	1938-39	4	0	0	0	0	0	4	0
Astley D	1938-40	20	6	0	0	0	0	20	6
Atherton W	1898-99	13	0	0	0	0	0	13	0
Ayres G	1926-28	33	4	1	0	0	0	34	4
Baddeley A	1908-09	32	3	2	0	0	0	34	3
Bailey I	1984-85	3	0	0	0	0	0	3	0
Bailey N	1992-94	8	1						
Bainbridge J	1910-21	114	11	4	0	0	0	118	11
Baker LH	1919-23	21	0	0	0	0	0	21	0
Ball A	1962-66								
	1980-81	146	45	7	1	8	3	161	40
Bamber D	1979-83								
	1990-92	152+5	75	10+1	3	11	11	173+6	89
Banks J	1897-99	11	0	0	0	0	0	11	0
Banks S	1995-99								
Bangura A	2009-10	2+7	0	0	0	2	0	4+7	0
Bannan B	2009-10	8+11	1	0+2	0	0	0	8+13	1
Baptiste A	2008-11	85+5	3	2	0	3	0	90+5	3
Barber F	1990-91								
	1995-96	3	0	0	0	0	0	3	0
Barcroft AT	1901-02	1	0	0	0	0	0	1	0
Bardsley D	1981-84								
	1998-00	108+1	0	1	0	5	0	114+1	0
Barker S	2006-09	137+1	6	6	1	4	0	147+1	7
Barkhuizen T	2010-11	0	0	0+1	0	1	0	1+1	0
Barlow A	1995-97	77+3	2						
Barnes K	1998-99	2+1	0	0	0	0	0	2+1	0
Barnes P	1997-04	149	0	7	0	7	0	163	0
Barnes R	1956-59	9	0	0	0	0	0	9	0

Player	Seasons	League App	League Goals	FA Cup App	FA Cup Goals	League Cup App	League Cup Goals	Total App	Total Goals
Barrowman A	2004-05	0+2	0	0	0	0	0	0+2	0
Barnett LH	1926-29	46	0	2	0	0	0	48	0
Barrass M	1919-25	168	53	12	1	0	0	180	54
Barton F	1972-73	18	1	0	0	5	2	23	3
Bartram V	1989-90	9	0	0	0	0	0	9	0
Basham C	2010-11	1+1	0	0	0	1	0	2+1	0
Bate T	1905-06	24	1	1	0	0	0	25	1
Baverstock H	1921-23	18	0	0	0	0	0	18	0
Baxendale J	1900-01	11	0	0	0	0	0	11	0
Bean M	2005-07	19+4	1	0+2	0	0+1	0	19+7	1
Beare H	1920-26	169	112	11	6	0	0	180	118
Beattie J	2010-11	5+4	0	0	0	0	0	5+4	0
Beech C	1992-98	53+29	4						
Beesley P	1999-00	15+3	0	1	0	0	0	16+3	0
Bennett L	1903-06	42	13	0	0	0	0	42	13
Bent J	1997-00	64+39	5	2+3	0	4+1	1	70+43	6
Bentley W	1968-77	289+7	11	10+1	1	19	2	318+8	14
Benton W	1920-31	353	24	18	0	0	0	371	24
Berry E	1919-20	5	1	0	0	0	0	5	1
Best GA	1925-27	27	0	1	0	0	0	28	0
Betts M	1975-76	4+3	0	0	0	0	0	4+3	0
Billington S	1901-02	1	0	0	0	0	0	1	0
Binks S	1925-27	55	9	2	0	0	0	61	9
Birch W	1907-08	13	0	0	0	0	0	13	0
Birchall J	1900-03	86	3	0	0	0	0	86	3
Birkett B	1896-07	215	44	4	0	0	0	219	44
Bisell S	1978-79	1	0	0	0	0	0	1	0
Blacklaw A	1970-71	1	0	0	0	0	0	1	0
Blackman N	2008-09	2+3	1	0	0	0	0	2+3	1
Blair D	1936-39	121	0	5	0	0	0	126	0
Blair JA	1937-47	50	8	1	0	0	0	51	8
Blair R	1981-82	36+1	3	5	0	2	0	43+1	3
Blinkhorn M	2001-07	13+5	5	1+2	0	0+1	0	14+8	5
Blunt J	1998-99	1	0	1	0	0	0	2	0
Bond R	1992-93	0+1	0						
Bonner M	1991-98	155+23	14						
Bokas F	1935-36	6	0	2	0	0	0	8	0
Booth D	1971-72	12	0	0	0	3	0	15	0
Booth K	1956-57	1	1	0	0	0	0	1	1
Booth R	1912-20	96	5	4	0	0	0	100	5
Boulton A	1900-02	56	1	0	0	0	0	56	1
Bouazza H	2009-10	11+8	1	0	0	0+1	0	11+9	0
Bowey K	1979-80	3	1	0	0	0	0	3	1
Boyack S	2004-05	0+1	0	0	0	0	0	0+1	0
Bowl HT	1936-37	2	1	0	0	0	0	2	1
Bowman T	1896-98	38	2	0	0	0	0	38	2
Bradshaw G	1924-27	43	0	0	0	0	0	43	0
Bradshaw D	1994-98	61+6	1						
Bradshaw M	1986-91	34+9	1	5+1	0	3	1	42+10	2
Bradshaw R	1908-12	29	0	4	0	0	0	33	0
Bradshaw TD	1896-97	17	5	0	0	0	0	17	5
Brabin G	1996-99	51+14	5						
Brallisford A	1933-36	17	8	0	0	0	0	17	8

Player	Seasons	League App	League Goals	FA Cup App	FA Cup Goals	League Cup App	League Cup Goals	Total App	Total Goals
Bramhall N	1982-83	0+3	0	0	0	0	0	0+3	0
Brand D	1983-84	3	0	0	0	0	0	3	0
Brandon C	2006-07	4+1	2	0	0	0	0	4+1	2
Bridge A	1932-33	7	0	0	0	0	0	7	0
Briggs G	1989-95	139	4						
Brightwell D	1996-97	0+1	0	0	0	0	0	0+1	0
Brindley H	1907-08	19	2	1	0	0	0	20	2
Britton I	1983-86	100+6	15	7	0	6	1	113+6	16
Broadhurst C	1929-31	18	6	0	0	0	0	18	6
Brockbank A	1979-83	32+4	1	0+1	1	3	0	35+5	2
Brook G	1989-92	27+3	6	6	1	2	1	35+3	8
Brookes S	1927-32	26	4	0	0	0	0	26	4
Brooks JS	1901-02	3	1	0	0	0	0	3	1
Brooks L	1014-15	2	0	0	0	0	0	2	0
Broomes M	2008-09	0+1	0	0	0	0	0	0+1	0
Browell T	1926-30	67	27	4	2	0	0	71	29
Brown A	1905-06	3	0	0	0	0	0	3	0
Brown A	1950-57	163	68	22	6	0	0	185	74
Brown F	1920-23	10	0	3	0	0	0	13	0
Brown N	1913-14	13	2	0	0	0	0	13	2
Brown P	1994-96	33+11	5						
Brown R	1965-71	54+7	13	1	1	5+2	0	60+9	14
Brown R	1995-96	2+1	0						
Bryan M	1995-00	172+9	4						
Buchan T	1913-14	24	2	0	0	0	0	24	2
Buchan T	1946-47	9	0	0	0	0	0	9	0
Buchan W	1937-48	100	35	4	0	0	0	104	35
Bullock M	2001-05	128+23	4	10+1	0	4+3	0	142+27	4
Burder MJ	1900-02	35	0	0	0	0	0	35	0
Burgess B	2006-10	83+47	23	0+5	1	3	2	86+52	26
Burgess D	1988-93	85	1	5	1	10	0	100	2
Burke D	1994-95	23	0						
Burke P	1913-21	18	0	0	0	0	0	18	0
Burke R	1938-39	1	0	0	0	0	0	1	0
Burns M	1969-74	174+7	53	7	1	15	8	196+7	62
Burns J	2002-06	30+17	1	2+2	1	1	0	33+19	2
Burridge J	1970-76	134	0	4	0	10	0	148	0
Burrows A	1959-60	1	0	0	0	0	0	1	0
Bushell S	1998-01	63+15	6	5+1	0	8	0	76+16	6
Butler A	2009-10	4+3	0	0	0	0	0	4+3	0
Burt J	1909-11	7	2	0	0	0	0	7	2
Bussey W	1933-34	25	8	2	1	0	0	27	9
Butcher WRM	1937-38	4	0	0	0	0	0	4	0
Butler B	1985-88	48+16	5	2+2	0	3+1	0	53+19	5
Butler H	1923-27	45	14	0	0	0	0	45	14
Butler J	1981-83	4+1	0	1	0	2	0	7+1	0
Butler M	1935-40	25	0	1	0	0	0	26	0
Butler T	1996-99								
	2004-06	123+7	1						
Byfield D	1999-00	3	0	0	0	0	0	3	0
Butterworth A	1932-34	22	5	0	0	0	0	22	5
Cahill R	1911-12	21	0	0	0	0	0	21	0
Caig T	1998-01	49	0	3	0	0	0	52	0

Player	Seasons	League App	League Goals	FA Cup App	FA Cup Goals	League Cup App	League Cup Goals	Total App	Total Goals
Caine B	1957-58	1	0	0	0	0	0	1	0
Caldwell S	2001-02	6	0	0	0	0	0	6	0
Camara M	2008-09	14	0	0	0	0	0	14	0
Campbell DJ	2008-11	67+2	33	0	0	0	0	67+2	33
Campbell H	1960-61	11	0	0	0	2	0	13	0
Campbell G	1897-98	6	0	0	0	0	0	6	0
Capleton M	1994-95	8	2						
Carden P	1996-97	1	0	0	0	0	0	1	0
Cardwell L	1930-38	132	6	11	0	0	0	143	6
Carlisle C	1997-00	86+4	7	3	1	4+1	0	93+5	8
Carney D	2010-11	5+7	0	0	0	0	0	5+7	0
Carr S	1930-31	14	2	0	0	0	0	14	2
Carruthers SL	1923-24	2	0	0	0	0	0	2	0
Carthell S	1898-99	4	1	0	0	0	0	4	1
Carthy S	1903-04	16	1	0	0	0	0	16	1
Cathcart C	2010-11	28+2	1	0	0	0	0	28+2	1
Cegielski C	1984-85	5+1	1	0	0	0	0	5+1	1
Chadwick E	1904-05	34	8	1	0	0	0	35	8
Chandler J	1977-80	31+6	6	1+1	1	3	0	35+7	7
Chandler W	1935-36	15	2	0	0	0	0	15	2
Chapman R	1912-13	2	0	0	0	0	0	2	0
Charles J	1912-24	228	30	13	3	0	0	241	33
Charlton T	1913-14	22	3	1	0	0	0	23	3
Charnley R	1957-68	363	193	21	10	23	19	407	222
Charnock P	1995-96	4	0	0	0	0	0	4	0
Chi Doy C	1960-62	2	1	0	0	0	0	2	1
Clancy S	2003-04	1+1	0	0	0	0	0	1+1	0
Clare R	2004-05	19+4	0	4	0	1	0	24+4	0
Clarke C	2001-04	34+13	2	4+3	0	2+1	0	40+17	2
Clarke P	2002-03 2004-06	100	14	5	2	2	1	107	17
Clarkson P	1996-02	155+17	34	9	4	10+2	2	174+19	40
Clarke J	1896-97	13	6	0	0	0	0	13	6
Clarke T	1906-12	141	0	6	1	0	0	147	1
Clarke W	1911-12	6	1	4	0	0	0	10	1
Clarkin J	1896-98	54	11	0	0	0	0	54	11
Clennel S	1910-11	32	18	1	1	0	0	33	19
Clough A	1921-22	1	0	0	0	0	0	1	0
Coid D	1999-11	230+36	9	18	1	11+3	0	259+39	10
Coleman A	1970-71	17	0	2	0	2	1	21	1
Coleman S	2009-10	12	1	0	0	0	0	12	1
Collier J	1906-07	2	0	0	0	0	0	2	0
Collins L	2000-03	49+17	2	5+1	0	4+2	0	58+20	2
Colville G	1896-97	5	0	0	0	0	0	5	0
Conn D	1980-81	3	0	0	0	0	0	3	0
Connell D	1999-00	1+2	0	0	0	0	0	1+2	0
Connor J	1905-15	282	13	17	0	0	0	299	13
Connor P	1896-97	4	1	0	0	0	0	4	1
Conroy M	1984-86	66	2	1	0	6	0	73	2
Conroy M	1997-99	11+2	0	0	0	2	1	13+2	1
Conway A	1965-66	0	0	0	0	1	0	1	0
Cook L	1904-05	7	0	1	0	0	0	8	0
Cook M	1991-95	66+2	0						

Player	Seasons	League App	League Goals	FA Cup App	FA Cup Goals	League Cup App	League Cup Goals	Total App	Total Goals
Cook W	1936-37	19	1	0	0	0	0	19	1
Cookson WS	1902-03	33	8	0	0	0	0	33	8
Cooper JE	1963-64	4	0	0	0	0	0	4	0
Copestake L	1905-07	19	1	0	0	0	0	19	1
Coughlin R	1987-90	99+2	8	13	0	9	1	121+2	9
Couzens A	1998-00	18+3	0	0	0	2	0	20+3	0
Crainie D	1984-85	6	0	0	0	0	0	6	0
Cowan W	1927-28	1	0	0	0	0	0	1	0
Cowie S	1911-12	3	0	0	0	0	0	3	0
Cox J	1897-98								
	1909-12	85	18	1	0	0	0	86	18
Crainey S	2007-11	124+5	1	2	0	2	0	128+5	1
Cranston W	1961-65	33	0	2	0	3	0	38	0
Craven J	1965-72	154+11	24	7+1	1	13	2	174+12	27
Crawford B	1932-34	55	5	3	0	0	0	58	5
Crawford B	1959-65	98	11	3	0	12	0	113	11
Crewdson R	1904-13	209	0	11	0	0	0	220	0
Crompton L	1924-28	87	0	9	0	0	0	96	0
Crook MS	1925-29	51	12	1	0	0	0	52	12
Crosland J	1946-54	64	0	10	0	0	0	74	0
Crosswaithe H	1906-07	1	0	0	0	0	0	1	0
Cunningham A	1987-89	71	18	5	2	8	3	84	23
Curran A	1921-27	98	3	11	0	0	0	109	3
Curtis J	1973-77	96+6	0	4	0	3	0	103+6	0
Dale G	1909-13	40	0	3	1	0	0	43	1
Dalglish P	2002-03	20+7	1	2	1	1	0	23+7	2
Danns N	2003-04	12+1	2	0	0	2	0	14+1	2
Darlington E	1905-06	4	0	0	0	0	0	4	0
Darton S	1994-97	31+11	1						
Davidson D	1948-50	16	0	0	0	0	0	16	0
Davidson V	1978-79	23+2	3	0+1	0	5	3	28+3	6
Davies J	1903-04	1	0	0	0	0	0	1	0
Davies M	1983-95	186+20	13						
Davies S	1912-13	3	0	0	0	0	0	3	0
Davies W	1973-75	34+2	5	1	0	2	0	37+2	5
Davis S	2003-04	22+6	1	3	0	3	0	28+6	1
Dawson E	1938-39	12	1	0	0	0	0	12	1
Dawson H	1908-11	26	4	2	0	0	0	28	4
Day R	2001-02	4+5	0	0+1	0	0	0	4+6	0
Dean B	1967-68	0+1	0	0	0	0	0	0+1	0
Deary J	1980-89	285+17	43	17+2	5	20	5	322+19	53
Demongtanac I	2009-11	1+8	0	0+1	0	2+1	1	3+10	1
Dewhurst WA	1898-99	2	0	0	0	0	0	2	0
Diamond A	1989-90	2+1	1	0+1	0	1	0	3+2	1
Dick G	1946-48	47	13	7	1	0	0	54	14
Dickins M	1992-93	19							
Dickinson C	2006-07	12	0	2	0	0	0	14	0
Dickinson L	2008-09	5+2	4	0	0	0	0	5+2	4
Dickson J	1898-99	1	0	0	0	0	0	1	0
Dickov P	2007-08	7+4	6	0	0	0	0	7+4	6
Didymus E	1909-10	3	0	0	0	0	0	3	0
Dinning T	2003-04	10	3	0	0	0	0	10	3
Dixon B	1996-98	9+8	0	2	0	2+1	0	13+9	0

		League		FA Cup		League Cup		Total	
Player	Seasons	App	Goals	App	Goals	App	Goals	App	Goals
Dodds E	1938-40	15	13	0	0	0	0	15	13
Dobbie S	2009-10	6+13	5	0	0	0	0	6+13	5
Doherty P	1933-36	83	28	5	1	0	0	88	29
Doherty S	2003-04	0+1	0	0	0	0	0	0+1	0
Dollins J	1911-13	18	1	4	1	0	0	22	1
Donachie J	1920-21	19	1	0	0	0	0	19	1
Donovan T	1984-85	2	0	0	0	0	0	2	0
Donnelly C	2003-05	12+5	0	0	0	0	0	12+5	0
Donnelly S	1896-97	14	5	0	0	0	0	14	5
Doolan J	2005-06	15+4	0	1	0	2	0	18+4	0
Dorrington J	1900-05	78	0	0	0	0	0	78	0
Dougall R	1933-36	74	2	2	0	0	0	76	2
Douglas J	2003-04	15+1	3	0	0	3	0	18+1	3
Douglas T	1931-34	60	15	5	1	0	0	65	16
Douglas W	1896-98	60	0	0	0	0	0	60	0
Dowes A	1978-79	1	0	0	0	0	0	1	0
Downes P	1925-31	152	32	6	1	0	0	158	33
Downes R	1982-84	24+1	3	3	0	4	1	31+1	4
Downhall J	1911-12	1	0	0	0	0	0	1	0
Doyle R	1979-81	47+2	2	3	0	4	1	58+2	2
Drain T	1909-10	4	0	0	0	0	0	4	0
Drummy D	1979-80	4+1	0	0	0	0	0	4+1	0
Duckworth TC	1902-06	34	5	4	0	0	0	38	5
Duffield P	1992-93	3+2	1						
Dumper J	1920-21	19	1	0	0	0	0	19	1
Dunckley A	1906-07	15	3	1	0	0	0	16	3
Dunning D	2001-02	0+5	0	1	0	0	0	1+5	0
Durie D	1952-64	296	84	19	7	15	2	330	93
Durnin J	1999-00	4+1	1	1	1	0	0	5+1	2
Dyer A	1983-87	101+7	19	3+1	0	8+1	1	112+9	20
Dyke AS	1921-22	1	0	0	0	0	0	1	0
Dyson K	1971-76	91+3	30	3	1	7	1	101+3	32
Eardley N	2009-11	52+3	1	2	0	2+1	0	56+4	1
Eastham G	1938-47	44	9	1	0	0	0	45	9
Edge L	2003-07	2+1	0	1	0	0	0	3+1	0
Edge T	1922-23	5	0	0	0	0	0	5	0
Edwards P	2004-05	22+6	3	1	0	0	0	23+6	3
Edwards R	2004-11	107+11	3	5+2	0	7	0	119+13	3
Ellegaaard K	2004-05	2	0	1	0	0	0	3	0
Elliot S	1988-90	66+1	0	7	0	6	0	79+1	0
Elliot S	2003-04	28	0	0	0	0	0	28	0
Ellis T	1994-98	140+6	54						
Elmore G	1909-10	34	6	0	0	0	0	34	6
Elston H	1898-99	10	0	0	0	0	0	10	0
Emmanuel J	2009-10	6+5	1	0	0	1	0	7+5	1
Entwistle W	1980-82	27+5	6	2+1	2	0	0	29+6	8
Euell J	2009-11	23+12	4	2	0	0+1	0	25+13	4
Evans A	1909-12	39	0	4	0	0	0	43	0
Evans A	1974-75	4+2	0	0	0	0	0	4+2	0
Evans G	2003-05	20+2	0	2	0	2	0	24+2	0
Evans P	2002-03	10	1	0	0	0	0	10	1
Evans L	1898-03	56	6	0	0	0	0	56	6
Evans R	2006-07	32	0	5	0	1	0	38	0

Player	Seasons	League App	League Goals	FA Cup App	FA Cup Goals	League Cup App	League Cup Goals	Total App	Total Goals
Evanson J	1973-76	63+4	0	3	0	1	0	67+4	0
Evatt I	2006-11	179+7	6	8	1	4	0	191+7	7
Everest J	1931-34	42	1	5	0	0	0	47	1
Exton E	1898-99	1	0	0	0	0	0	1	0
Eyres D	1989-93	119+5	33						
Fairhurst H	1919-21	47	0	3	0	0	0	50	0
Falconer G	1949-50	4	0	0	0	0	0	4	0
Farley J	1976-77	1	0	0	0	0	0	1	0
Farm G	1948-60	465	1	47	0	0	0	512	1
Farrelly G	2006-07	0+1	0	1	0	0	0	1+1	0
Farrow G	1936-48	148	15	6	0	0	0	154	15
Fawcett R	1955-60	4	0	0	0	0	0	4	0
Fenton E	1948-59	195	20	19	0	0	0	214	20
Fenton G	2001-02	6+9	5	1	0	0+1	0	7+10	5
Fernandez V	2006-07	0+1	0	0+1	0	0	0	0+2	0
Ferns P	1983-85	43+3	0	3	0	3+1	0	49+4	0
Finan R	1933-40	173	85	7	4	0	0	180	89
Finningan T	1976-78	13+3	3	0	0	2	0	15+3	3
Fisher H	1963-69	52+3	1	3	0	7+1	0	62+4	1
Fisher L	1968-69	1	0	0	0	0	0	1	0
Fishick A	1925-28	59	36	0	0	0	0	59	36
Fiske W	1907-14	217	0	7	0	0	0	224	0
Fletcher FA	1898-99	32	0	0	0	0	0	32	0
Fletcher P	1979-82	19+1	7	0	0	2	1	21+1	8
Flynn M	2004-05 2007-08	22+10	3	1	0	3	0	26+10	3
Flynn M	2002-05	59+1	1	2+1	0	2	0	63+2	1
Forbes A	2006-08	29+10	1	5	0	1	0	35+10	1
Forbes J	1923-24	19	0	0	0	0	0	19	0
Ford J	1921-22	1	0	0	0	0	0	1	0
Forsyth R	1999-00	10+3	0	0+2	0	0	0	10+5	0
Foster J	1901-02	28	6	0	0	0	0	28	6
Foster M	1997-98	1	0	0	0	0	0	1	0
Fox D	2005-09	70+26	6	7	1	4	0	81+26	7
Francis E	1905-07	37	11	6	1	0	0	43	12
Francis-Reynolds	2010-11	0	0	0+1	0	0	0	0+1	0
Frith D	1952-57	30	0	5	0	0	0	35	0
Fuschillo P	1971-74	8+3	0	0	0	0+1	0	8+4	0
Gabbiadini R	1989-90	5	3	0	0	2	1	7	4
Gadsden E	1923-25	8	0	0	0	0	0	8	0
Gamble GF	1898-99	9	3	0	0	0	0	9	3
Gardner P	1976-82	149+3	1	5	0	14	0	168+3	1
Garner A	1988-93	76+6	12						
Garrett T	1947-61	306	3	28	1	0	0	334	4
Garvey S	1998-00	6+10	1	0	0	0	0	6+10	1
Gattins A	1904-05	1	0	0	0	0	0	1	0
Gavin P	1920-22	48	0	4	0	0	0	52	0
Gayle M	1989-90	0	0	0	0	1	0	1	0
Gibson C	1994-95	1+1	0						
Gibson W	1928-30	14	0	1	0	0	0	15	0
Gilks M	2008-11	51+1	0	3	0	1	0	55+1	0
Gill J	1925-26	15	4	1	0	0	0	16	4
Gill W	1999-00	12	7	0	0	0	0	12	7

		League		FA Cup		League Cup		Total	
Player	Seasons	App	Goals	App	Goals	App	Goals	App	Goals
Gillett N	1896-02	5	0	0	0	0	0	5	0
Gillett S	2006-07	20+13	1	0	0	0	0	20+13	1
Gillow WB	1912-14	25	2	2	0	0	0	27	2
Gladwin C	1908-13	89	0	6	0	0	0	95	0
Gobern L	2005-06	4+4	1	0	0	0	0	4+4	1
Goddard P	1981-82	4	2	0	0	0	0	4	2
Gordon D	2005-06	1	0	0	0	0	0	1	0
Gore I	1988-95	188+4	0						
Gorkss K	2006-08	47+3	6	1+2	0	3	2	51+5	8
Gorre D	2004-05	0+1	0	0	0	0	0	0	0
Gosling G	1898-99	1	0	0	0	0	0	1	0
Gouck A	1989-96	121+28	12						
Goulding PA	1909-11	15	0	1	0	0	0	16	0
Gow A	2008-09	12+7	5	0	0	0	0	12+7	5
Gow J	1904-08	61	4	6	0	0	0	67	4
Grabovac Z	2004-05	1+2	0	0	0	0	0	1+2	0
Graham D	2006-07	1+3	1	0	0	0	0	1+3	1
Grandin E	2010-11	21+2	1	0	0	0+1	0	21+3	1
Grant W	1927-35	220	0	8	0	0	0	228	0
Gratrix R	1953-65	400	0	23	0	13	0	436	0
Grayson S	2002-06	114+14	6	10	0	6+1	1	130+15	7
Green A	1966-72	121+1	13	5	3	10	3	136+1	19
Green J	1959-67	135	9	4	0	8	2	147	11
Green R	1913-15	31	4	2	0	0	0	33	4
Green S	2007-08	1+4	0	0	0	0	0	1+4	0
Greenacre C	1997-98	2+2	0	0	0	0	0	2+2	0
Greenall C	1980-87	179+4	9	9	0	12	2	200+4	11
Gregson CWS	1914-15	3	0	0	0	0	0	3	0
Gregson J	1957-59	4	1	0	0	0	0	4	1
Griffiths B	1993-95	54+3	17						
Grimwood J	1927-28	9	0	0	0	0	0	9	0
Groves A	1977-78	11+4	1	1	0	0	0	12+4	1
Groves P	1989-92	114+1	24	9	4	6	1	129+1	29
Grundy WA	1906-09	63	26	2	1	0	0	65	27
Gulliver P	2002-03	2+1	0	1	0	0	0	3+1	0
Hacking J	1921-25	33	0	0	0	0	0	33	0
Haddow P	1997-98	0+1	0	0	0	0	0	0+1	0
Hall A	1933-39	42	10	3	1	0	0	45	11
Hall J	1978-79	1	0	0	0	0	0	1	0
Hall T	1952-53	2	0	0	0	0	0	2	0
Hall W	1929-31	23	3	0	0	0	0	23	3
Halsall L	1897-98	5	1	0	0	0	0	5	1
Halsall S	1961-62	2	0	0	0	0	0	2	0
Halstead FD	1920-21	1	0	0	0	0	0	1	0
Halstead M	2010-11	0+1	0	0	0	1	0	1+1	0
Hamilton J	1928-30	28	0	0	0	0	0	28	0
Hamilton SE	1924-26	2	0	0	0	0	0	2	0
Hammill A	2008-09	15+7	1	0	0	1	0	16+7	1
Hampson J	1927-38	361	248	12	4	0	0	373	252
Hancock H	1905-06	27	6	5	3	0	0	32	9
Harewood M	2010-11	7+9	5	0	0	0	0	7+9	5
Hardcastle P	1971-74	29+6	0	0	0	3+2	0	32+8	0
Hardman PH	1900-03	71	10	0	0	0	0	71	10

Player	Seasons	League App	League Goals	FA Cup App	FA Cup Goals	League Cup App	League Cup Goals	Total App	Total Goals
Hargreaves H	1926-27	3	0	0	0	0	0	3	0
Harkins G	2005-06	4	1	0	0	0	0	4	1
Harris S	1953-58	15	4	0	0	0	0	15	4
Harrison F	1898-99	2	0	0	0	0	0	2	0
Harrison G	1931-32	16	1	2	0	0	0	18	1
Harrison S	1971-78	140+6	2	5	0	8+1	2	153+7	4
Harrison W	1898-99	1	0	0	0	0	0	1	0
Harrison W	1979-82	78+5	6	7	2	5	0	90+5	8
Hart J	2006-07	5	0	0	0	0	0	5	0
Hart N	1981-83	35+1	0	3	0	4+1	0	42+2	0
Hart P	1973-78	143	15	6	0	7	1	156	16
Harte I	2008-09	4	0	1	0	0	0	5	0
Harvey A	1961-64	11	0	0	0	4	0	15	0
Harvey R	1992-93	4+1	0						
Hateley A	1898-99	4	1	0	0	0	0	4	1
Hatton D	1969-76	250+1	7	9	0	14	1	273+1	8
Hatton R	1976-78	75	32	3	1	6	2	84	35
Hauser P	1957-62	83	10	10	1	4	0	97	11
Hawe S	2000-01	1	0	0	0	0	0	1	0
Hawkins N	1989-90	4+3	0	0	0	1	0	5+3	0
Hayward E	1937-52	275	0	22	0	0	0	297	0
Heathcote J	1919-22	89	33	4	0	0	0	93	33
Hedworth C	1990-92	24	0	4	0	0	0	28	0
Hendrie L	2008-09	5+1	0	0	0	0	0	5+1	0
Hendry C	2002-03	14	0	0	0	0	0	14	0
Hepton S	1952-55	6	3	0	0	0	0	6	3
Hesford I	1977-83	202	0	13	0	15	0	230	0
Heslop T	1912-13	29	4	2	0	0	0	31	4
Hessey S	2003-04	4+2	0	0	0	0	0	4+2	0
Hetzke S	1982-86	140	18	10	0	10	1	160	19
Heywood F	1902-05	34	4	0	0	0	0	34	4
Higginson W	1901-02	3	0	0	0	0	0	3	0
Hill F	1936-38	45	8	2	0	0	0	47	8
Hill S	1959-64	71	1	4	0	9	0	84	1
Hills J	1997-03 2007-08	148+18	17	13	2	7	0	168+18	19
Hilton K	2003-04	12+2	1	1	0	1	0	14+2	1
Hird H	1922-23	4	0	0	0	0	0	4	0
Hoade SJ	1909-11	25	3	3	0	0	0	28	3
Hobbs FW	1927-28	24	0	0	0	0	0	24	0
Hobson A	1947-54	60	3	2	0	0	0	62	3
Hockaday D	1976-83	131+16	24	10+2	2	19+1	0	160+19	26
Hodgson J	1903-04	2	0	0	0	0	0	2	0
Holden M	1978-79	2+1	0	0	0	1+1	0	3+2	0
Hogg R	1904-05	27	4	0	0	0	0	27	4
Holden R	1995-96	19+3	2						
Hollingworth J	1905-06	10	0	1	0	0	0	11	0
Holt G	2007-08	0+4	0	0	0	0	0	0+4	0
Hoolahan W	2006-08	84+6	14	3+1	1	2+2	1	89+9	16
Horne D	1960-66	117+1	17	6	0	13	4	136+1	21
Horner P	1990-95	184+5	26						
Howard A	1991-92	0+1	0	0+1	0	0	0	0+2	0
Howard J	1911-12	1	0	0	0	0	0	1	0

Player	Seasons	League App	League Goals	FA Cup App	FA Cup Goals	League Cup App	League Cup Goals	Total App	Total Goals
Howard S	1919-21	9	0	0	0	0	0	9	0
Howson EW	1898-01	22	0	0	0	0	0	22	0
Hoyle T	1898-99	21	1	0	0	0	0	21	1
Hughes D	1903-04	1	0	0	0	0	0	1	0
Hughes E	1965-67	27+1	0	1	0	5	0	33+1	0
Hughes J	1969-71	5+3	0	0	0	1	0	6+3	0
Hughes I	1997-03	140+15	4	8	0	10	1	158+15	5
Hughes RA	1927-28	2	0	0	0	0	0	2	0
Hull A	1902-06	116	0	6	0	0	0	122	0
Hunter T	1919-21	13	4	0	0	0	0	13	4
Husband S	2009-11	1+2	0	0	0	1	0	2+2	0
Hutchison A	1930-31	6	2	0	0	0	0	6	2
Hutchison T	1967-73	162+2	10	6	2	17	3	185+2	15
Ingram G	1966-68	33+1	17	1	0	1	0	35+1	17
Ilic S	2004-05	3	0	0	0	0	0	3	0
Jacklin W	1919-20	1	0	0	0	0	0	1	0
Jackson M	2007-08	1+1	0	0	0	0	0	1+1	0
Jackson M	2006-08	68+3	1	6	1	3+1	1	77+4	3
James EG	1960-75	395+6	22	14	1	31	2	440+6	25
Jarrett J	1998-99	2	0	0+1	0	0	0	2+1	0
Jaszczun T	1999-04	108+15	0	5	1	7	0	120+15	1
Jeffrey W	1982-83	12+2	1	1+1	0	1	0	14+3	1
Jennings P	1925-30	7	0	0	0	0	0	7	0
Johnson S	1905-07	34	1	5	0	0	0	39	1
Johnson S	2003-04	3+1	1	0+1	0	0	0	3+2	1
Johnston H	1937-55	398	11	40	3	0	0	438	14
Johnston J	1968-72	20+6	2	2	0	4	1	26+6	3
Jolly A	1904-05	5	0	0	0	0	0	5	0
Jones B	2003-05	17	0	0	0	0	0	17	0
Jones E	1999-01	5+3	0	0	0	0	0	5+3	0
Jones G	1978-80	18+8	5	1	0	0	0	19+8	5
Jones H	1922-26	96	0	9	0	0	0	105	0
Jones J	1898-99	3	0	0	0	0	0	3	0
Jones J	1903-06	19	0	0	0	0	0	19	0
Jones J	1912-20	113	0	3	0	0	0	116	0
Jones L	2003-06	81	0	4	0	3	0	88	0
Jones P	1986-88	30+5	0	6	0	2	0	38+5	0
Jones P	1989-90	6	0	0	0	0	0	6	0
Jones S	1933-39	165	6	5	0	0	0	170	6
Jones T	1933-38	153	38	8	2	0	0	161	40
Jorgensen C	2006-09	74+28	6	2+4	0	0	0	76+32	6
Joseph M	2005-07	18+6	0	0	0	0	0	18+6	0
Kabba S	2008-09	10+5	2	0	0	0	0	10+5	2
Kay M	2005-06	0+1	0	0	0	0	0	0+1	0
Kaye A	1959-61	48	9	3	1	1	0	52	10
Keach W	1897-98	16	0	0	0	0	0	16	0
Kearns A	1904-05	15	3	0	0	0	0	15	3
Kearton J	1991-92	15	0	0	0	0	0	15	0
Keenan H	1912-23	101	3	8	0	0	0	109	3
Keinan D	2010-11	3+3	0	1	0	1	0	5+3	0
Kellow A	1978-80	57	23	3	1	4	0	64	24
Kelly G	1988-89	5	0	0	0	0	0	5	0
Kelly H	1946-60	428	8	40	1	0	0	468	9

Player	Seasons	League App	League Goals	FA Cup App	FA Cup Goals	League Cup App	League Cup Goals	Total App	Total Goals
Kelly J	1954-61	200	9	9	0	0	0	211	9
Kemp F	1970-72	19+2	1	2	0	1	0	22+2	1
Kennedy G	1946-50	9	0	2	0	0	0	11	0
Kennedy J	2000-01	6	0	0	0	1	0	7	0
Kerr PW	1919-20	5	0	0	0	0	0	5	0
Kerr D	1991-92	13	1	0	0	0	0	13	1
Kerr R	1978-80	18+4	2	0	0	4	0	22+4	2
Kidd J	1910-15	61	0	7	0	0	0	68	0
Killean E	1903-04	5	0	0	0	0	0	5	0
King H	1907-08	10	1	0	0	0	0	10	1
King P	1997-98	6	0	0	0	0	0	6	0
Kingson R	2010-11	19+1	0	0	0	0	0	19+1	0
Kirkham J	1898-99	3	0	0	0	0	0	3	0
Kornilenko S	2010-11	3+3	0	0	0	0	0	3+3	0
Kuqi N	2005-06	1+3	0	0	0	0	0	1+3	0
Lambert R	1999-00	0+3	0	0	0	0	0	0+3	0
Lancashire G	1987-88	2+5	0	0	0	0+1	0	2+6	0
Lancashire D	1990-91	7+1	1	0	0	2	0	9+1	1
Lane J	1913-20	94	65	5	2	0	0	99	67
Lasley K	2005-06	4+4	0	0	0	0	0	4+4	0
Latheron E	1908-09	1	0	0	0	0	0	1	0
Lauderdale J	1929-31	19	6	2	0	0	0	21	6
Lavery J	1906-07	16	0	0	0	0	0	16	0
Law N	1985-87	64+2	1	2	0	0	0	66+2	1
Lawson I	1998-99	9	3	0	0	0	0	9	3
Lax W	1931-33	25	0	0	0	0	0	25	0
Lea L	1960-68	158+2	13	6	0	13	3	177+2	16
Leadbetter J	1897-01	65	10	0	0	0	0	65	10
Leaver J	1920-26	106	4	11	0	0	0	117	4
Lee D	1999-00	9	1	2	0	0	0	11	1
Leitch G	1991-94	14+12	1						
Lennard D	1971-73	42+3	9	2	0	4+1	0	48+4	9
Lester M	1987-88	24	2	4	0	0	0	28	2
Lewis T	1938-39	12	3	1	1	0	0	13	4
Lewis W	1946-50	42	0	0	0	0	0	42	0
Linighan D	1995-98	97+3	5						
Livesey D	2004-05	1	0	0	0	0	0	1	0
Longden E	1930-33	61	7	2	0	0	0	63	7
Longworth S	1997-98	0+2	0	0+1	0	0	0	0+3	0
Lovett W	1920-21	2	0	0	0	0	0	2	0
Lowe W	1904-08	11	0	0	0	0	0	11	0
Lowson E	1921-23	5	0	0	0	0	0	5	0
Loydon E	1964-65	2	0	0	0	0	0	2	0
Lumsden C	1999-00	6	1	0	0	0	0	6	1
Lydiate J	1994-98	70+6	2						
Lynch S	2004-05	5+2	0	2	0	0	0	7+2	0
Lyon H	1908-09	8	2	1	0	0	0	9	2
Lyon TK	1936-38	6	0	1	0	0	0	7	0
Lythgoe D	1955-56	3	1	0	0	0	0	3	1
McAllister T	1979-80	16	0	0	0	4	0	20	0
McAteer A	1986-88	35+6	0	3	0	2	0	40+6	0
McCall A	1947-51	86	15	2	0	0	0	88	15
McCulloch J	1912-13	1	0	0	0	0	0	1	0

		League		FA Cup		League Cup		Total	
Player	**Seasons**	**App**	**Goals**	**App**	**Goals**	**App**	**Goals**	**App**	**Goals**
McCormack M	1947-48	12	3	0	0	0	0	12	3
McDonough FJB	1931-34	82	0	4	0	0	0	86	0
McDougall E	1979-81	11+2	0	0	0	2	0	13+2	0
McEvoy A	1981-82	6	0	0	0	0	0	6	0
McEwan B	1973-74	4	0	0	0	2	0	6	0
McEwan M	1903-05	44	1	1	0	0	0	45	1
McEwan S	1974-82	198+9	24	13	2	14	6	225+9	32
McGinley P	1986-87	2+9	1	1	0	0	0	3+9	1
McGinn A	1919-25	132	2	10	1	0	0	142	3
McGregor M	2004-06	52+7	0	5	0	3	0	60+7	0
McGrotty W	1970-72	2+2	1	0	0	0	0	2+2	1
McHardie D	1897-98	24	0	0	0	0	0	24	0
McIlhargey S	1989-94	101+1							
McIntosh J	1935-38								
	1946-49	79	22	8	5	0	0	87	27
McIntosh W	1924-25	1	0	0	0	0	0	1	0
McIntosh W	1948-52	51	15	5	1	0	0	56	16
McIntyre S	1927-28	6	2	0	0	0	0	6	2
McIvenney J	1922-23	16	4	1	0	0	0	17	4
McKenna J	1954-57	25	2	0	0	0	0	25	2
MacKenzie A	1923-24	6	1	0	0	0	0	6	1
MacKenzie N	2001-02	6+8	1	1+3	1	1+1	0	8+12	2
McKnight G	1946-54	32	9	5	1	0	0	37	10
McLaren M	1938-39	2	0	0	0	0	0	2	0
McLelland J	1930-33	66	25	3	2	0	0	69	27
McMahon S	2002-04	10+8	0	0+2	0	0	0	10+10	0
McMahon A	2007-08	2	0	0	0	0	0	2	0
McNicholas J	1970-71	0+1	0	0	0	0+1	0	0+2	0
McNiven D	1982-84	45+4	11	5	2	1+1	1	51+5	14
McPhee J	1962-70	249+10	15	13	1	19	2	281+10	18
McPhee S	2007-09	16+8	3	0	0	0	0	16+8	3
Madden C	1986-90	73+17	24	6+1	3	6+4	0	85+22	27
Maggs P	1931-32	24	0	2	0	0	0	26	0
Mahon A	2008-09	1	0	0	0	0	0	1	0
Maley M	2000-01	2	0	0	0	0	0	2	0
Malkin C	1996-99	46+19	6						
Malone R	1978-80	48+1	1	2	0	0	0	50+1	1
Malpas A	1927-28	1	0	0	0	0	0	1	0
Manigan A	2003-04	0+2	0	0	0	0	0	0+2	0
Mann A	1971-72	3	0	0	0	1	0	4	0
Marsden A	1967-69	4+1	0	0	0	2	0	6+1	0
Marsh C	1919-21	5	0	0	0	0	0	5	0
Marshall I	2001-02	21	1	1	0	0	0	22	1
Marshall P	2008-09	1+1	0	0	0	0	0	1+1	0
Martin A	1922-29	25	2	0	0	0	0	25	2
Martin B	1957-64	187	1	9	0	13	0	209	1
Martin J	1896-98	52	17	0	0	0	0	52	17
Martin J	2007-10	15+8	0	0+1	0	3	0	18+9	0
Martin L	1992-93	24	0						
Matias P	2003-04	6+1	1	0	0	0	0	6+1	0
Matthews N	1985-90	67+9	1	1	0	7	0	75+9	1
Matthews R	1999-00	5+1	2	0	0	0	0	5+1	2
Matthews S	1947-62	391	17	49	1	1	0	440	18

Player	Seasons	League App	League Goals	FA Cup App	FA Cup Goals	League Cup App	League Cup Goals	Total App	Total Goals
Mauchline R	1938-39	4	0	0	0	0	0	4	0
May S	1978-79	4	0	0	0	0	0	4	0
Mayes A	1986-87	12+1	6	1	0	0	0	13+1	6
Mayo J	1982-83	5	1	0	0	0	0	5	1
Mayor F	1898-99	2	0	0	0	0	0	2	0
Mee GW	1920-26	216	21	14	0	0	0	230	21
Mellon M	1994-98	123+1	14						
Mercer K	1983-84	31	9	5	3	2	0	38	12
Mercer W	1925-29	20	0	0	0	0	0	20	0
Meredith J	1923-28	190	27	10	3	0	0	200	30
Metcalfe RS	1911-12	3	0	1	0	0	0	4	0
Methven C	1986-90	168+7	11	12+1	1	14	1	194+8	13
Middleton J	1935-37	10	3	2	1	0	0	12	4
Miller P	1903-04	3	0	0	0	0	0	3	0
Miller PE	1908-11	41	13	2	0	0	0	43	13
Miller W	1910-11	6	0	0	0	0	0	6	0
Millership H	1912-15	30	0	0	0	0	0	30	0
Milligan J	2000-03	32+21	1	1+1	0	0+1	0	33+23	1
Milligan L	1976-79	19	0	1	0	2+1	0	22+1	0
Milligan M	2000-02	3+5	0	0	0	0	0	3+5	0
Milne G	1967-70	60+4	4	2+1	0	4+2	1	66+7	5
Milne W	1911-12	21	6	2	1	0	0	23	7
Mingay H	1919-24	155	0	7	0	0	0	162	0
Mitchell FJ	1914-15	5	0	0	0	0	0	5	0
Mitchell N	1991-95	39+28	8						
Mitchell T	1911-12	3	0	0	0	0	0	3	0
Mitchley D	2008-09	0+2	0	0	0	0	0	0+2	0
Moir I	1964-67	61	12	0	0	5	2	66	14
Moore D	1983-87	115+1	1	6+1	0	6	0	127+2	1
Moore K	1974-77	33+5	3	2+1	0	2	0	37+6	3
Moore N	1994-95	7	0						
Morfitt JW	1931-32	1	0	0	0	0	0	1	0
Morgan H	1904-05	25	4	1	1	0	0	26	5
Morgan S	1985-90	135+9	10	16	0	13	2	164+9	12
Morgan W	1980-82	41	4	1	0	0	0	42	4
Morley F	1909-12	80	22	1	0	0	0	81	22
Morrell A	2006-08	61+21	22	4+1	3	1+3	0	66+25	25
Morris C	1979-82	87	26	7	3	6	3	100	32
Morris I	2005-06	21+9	3	0	0	0	0	21+9	3
Morris JJ	1906-07	17	4	0	0	0	0	17	4
Morrison A	1994-98 2000-01	53	4						
Mortensen S	1946-56	325	197	29	25	0	0	354	222
Mount C	1896-97	9	5	0	0	0	0	9	5
Mowbray H	1967-71	88+3	0	4+1	1	8	0	100+4	1
Mudie J	1949-61	324	144	31	11	1	0	356	155
Muggleton C	1987-88	2	0	0	0	0	0	2	0
Munro A	1936-49	136	17	10	1	0	0	146	18
Murphy A	1984-85	1+7	0	0+1	0	0	0	1+8	0
Murphy J	1991-95	48+7	1						
Murphy J	1999-06	233+22	83	16	5	9+2	4	258+24	92
Murphy N	2000-02	4+3	0	0	0	1	0	5+3	0
Murray J	1969-71	6+3	1	0	0	0	0	6+3	1

Player	Seasons	League App	League Goals	FA Cup App	FA Cup Goals	League Cup App	League Cup Goals	Total App	Total Goals
Murray M	1991-93	3	0						
Murray R	1937-38	2	0	0	0	0	0	2	0
Musgrove C	1905-06	4	0	0	0	0	0	4	0
Napier P	1961-63	2	0	0	0	1	0	3	0
Nardiello D	2008-10	1+6	0	1	0	1	1	3+6	1
Neal R	1925-31	85	17	2	1	0	0	87	18
Nelson S	1946-48	10	0	0	0	0	0	10	0
Nemeth K	2008-09	0+1	0	0	0	0	0	0+1	0
Nesbitt B	1911-12	12	4	0	0	0	0	12	4
Newell M	1999-01	16+2	2	0+1	0	2	1	18+3	3
Nicholson P	1970-71	3+3	0	0	0	1+1	0	4+4	0
Nightingale A	1898-99	5	0	0	0	0	0	5	0
Nixon E	1995-96	20	0						
Noble P	1979-83	92+5	14	7	0	4	0	103+5	14
Norris R	1896-99	58	5	0	0	0	0	58	5
Nowland A	1997-01	18+49	5	2+2	1	1+5	1	21+56	7
Oates G	1961-69	119+3	26	1	0	7	2	127+3	28
O'Connor J	2000-01	10+1	0	2	0	0	0	12+1	0
O'Doherty E	1919-23	2	0	0	0	0	0	2	0
O'Donnell F	1937-47	30	17	1	0	0	0	31	17
O'Donnell H	1938-47	14	2	1	0	0	0	15	2
O'Donnell J	1930-32	55	0	4	0	0	0	59	0
O'Donovan R	2008-09	11+1	0	0	0	0	0	11+1	0
O'Kane J	2001-03	41+11	4	2+4	0	3	0	46+15	4
O'Keefe E	1984-87	33+3	23	0	0	2	0	35+3	23
O'Keefe V	1986-89	7	0	0	0	0	0	7	0
O'Neil T	1972-73	7	0	0	0	0	0	7	0
Oram D	1934-36	28	9	2	0	0	0	30	9
O'Rourke W	1983-86	98	0	3	0	8	0	109	0
Onwere U	1996-97	5+4	0						
Ormerod B	1996-02								
	2009-11	144+50	59						
Owen A	1911-12	2	0	1	0	0	0	3	0
Owen G	1989-91	21+8	4	4+2	2	3	0	28+10	6
Owens G	2008-09	1+7	0	0	0	0	0	1+7	0
Owers EH	1907-08	9	3	0	0	0	0	9	3
Oxberry J	1927-32	74	20	1	0	0	0	75	20
Pagnan F	1912-14	23	1	0	0	0	0	23	1
Park W	1938-39	2	0	0	0	0	0	2	0
Parker K	2004-08	100+45	36	6+2	2	5+2	1	111+49	39
Parker S	1972-75	10+6	2	0	0	2	1	12+6	3
Parkinson G	2000-02	25+2	0	0	0	1	0	26+2	0
Parkinson J	1896-09	365	52	10	1	0	0	375	53
Parkinson R	1896-97	8	1	0	0	0	0	8	1
Parkinson S	1994-95	0+1	0						
Parr H	1896-99	85	2	0	0	0	0	85	2
Parr WW	1935-39	15	1	0	0	0	0	15	1
Parry R	1960-65	128	27	7	0	11	5	146	32
Pascoe C	1995-96	0+1	0						
Pashley T	1978-83	201	7	13	1	15	2	229	10
Patterson S	2004-05	0+2	0	0	0	0	0	0+2	0
Patterson M	1998-99	7	0	0	0	0	0	7	0
Payton A	2001-02	4	1	0	0	0	0	4	1

Player	Seasons	League App	League Goals	FA Cup App	FA Cup Goals	League Cup App	League Cup Goals	Total App	Total Goals
Pearson A	1906-07	4	0	0	0	0	0	4	0
Pearson H	1929-31	55	0	2	0	0	0	57	0
Pentland F	1903-04	8	5	0	0	0	0	8	5
Perry W	1949-62	394	119	40	10	2	0	436	129
Peterson B	1956-62	101	16	3	0	5	1	109	17
Phillips M	2010-11	6+21	1	1	0	0	0	7+21	1
Philpott L	1995-98	66+14	14						
Pickering F	1969-71	49+1	24	4	1	3	0	56+1	25
Pickford P	1903-04	1	0	0	0	0	0	1	0
Pierce G	1983-84	27	0	5	0	0	0	32	0
Pogliacomi L	2005-06	15	0	1	0	2	0	18	0
Pollard S	1981-82	0+1	0	0	0	0	0	0+1	0
Popplewell S	1920-21	1	0	0	0	0	0	1	0
Powell R	1986-88	14	0	0	0	0	0	14	0
Power J	1921-22	18	6	1	0	0	0	19	6
Pratt T	1904-05	8	2	0	0	0	0	8	2
Preece A	1995-98	114+12	35						
Prendergast R	2005-07	21+7	0	0+1	0	3	0	24+8	0
Prentis J	1962-66	6	0	0	0	2	0	8	0
Price N	1984-85	13	0	0	0	0	0	13	0
Priest P	1986-87	1	0	0	0	0	0	1	0
Pritchett K	1982-84	36+1	1	1	0	2	0	39+1	1
Pullen J	2001-02	16	0	1	0	1	0	18	0
Puncheon J	2010-11	6+5	3	0	0	0	0	6+5	3
Purdy A	1927-29	31	0	1	0	0	0	32	0
Quailey B	1999-00	1	0	0	0	0	0	1	0
Quinn C	1929-32	37	6	2	0	0	0	39	6
Quinn J	1993-98	128+22	37						
Quinn P	1910-20	152	16	5	1	0	0	157	17
Quinn P	1962-64	34	9	2	1	0	0	39	6
Rachel A	1999-00	1	0	0	0	0	0	1	0
Rachubka P	2006-11	120+1	0	4	0	1	0	125+1	0
Rafferty W	1972-74	35+1	9	0	0	0	0	35+1	9
Raisbeck L	1905-06	15	0	0	0	0	0	15	0
Ramsay S	1927-32	105	2	2	0	0	0	107	2
Ramsbottom N	1970-72	12	0	0	0	1	0	13	0
Ratcliffe A	1920-21	13	2	2	2	0	0	15	4
Rattray C	1929-34	52	9	3	0	0	0	55	9
Reece HJ	1931-33	4	0	0	0	0	0	4	0
Reed J	1997-98	0+3	0	0	0	0	0	0+3	0
Reeves G	1912-13	4	0	0	0	0	0	4	0
Rehman Z	2008-09	0+3	0	0	0	0+1	0	0+4	0
Reid A	1932-33	13	1	1	0	0	0	14	1
Reid A	2010-11	2+3	0	0	0	0	0	2+3	0
Reid B	2000-02	58	2	5	0	1	0	64	2
Reid GH	1920-21	3	2	0	0	0	0	3	2
Reid K	2008-09	7	0	0	0	0	0	7	0
Reid WH	1907-09	32	3	1	0	0	0	33	3
Reilly J	1904-06	2	0	0	0	0	0	2	0
Richards C	1989-92	32+9	8	2	0	0+2	0	34+11	8
Richardson I	1982-83	4+1	2	0	0	0	0	4+2	0
Richardson JE	1920-22	32	0	3	0	0	0	35	0
Richardson K	1999-00	20	1	0	0	0	0	20	1

Player	Seasons	League App	League Goals	FA Cup App	FA Cup Goals	League Cup App	League Cup Goals	Total App	Total Goals
Richardson L	2002-05	64+7	0	2	1	2	0	68+7	1
Richardson P	1982-83	4	0	0	0	0	0	4	0
Rickett W	1947-50	44	7	5	0	0	0	49	7
Rimmer H	1906-08	20	0	0	0	0	0	20	0
Ritchie A	1928-30	31	5	2	0	0	0	33	5
Roberts J	2010-11	0	0	0+1	0	0	0	0+1	0
Robinson C	1928-29	5	0	0	0	0	0	5	0
Robinson C	1951-55	21	2	3	0	0	0	24	2
Robinson D	1992-94	21+5	4						
Robinson J	1947-49	25	0	6	0	0	0	31	0
Robinson P	2002-03	5+2	1	0	0	0	0	5+2	1
Robinson P	1998-00	6+5	0	2	0	0+1	0	8+6	0
Robinson TE	1933-34	2	0	0	0	0	0	2	0
Robson J	1964-68	60+4	14	1	0	4	2	65+4	16
Robson W	1913-15	46	0	1	0	0	0	47	0
Rodaway W	1983-84	41	0	4	0	2	0	47	0
Rodwell A	1990-95	139+5	20						
Rogan A	1997-99	10+5	0	0	0	1	0	11+5	0
Rookes J	1903-04	23	5	0	0	0	0	23	5
Rookes W	1913-22	98	4	7	0	0	0	105	4
Rooney S	1987-89	4+5	0	2+1	0	0	0	6+6	0
Ronson W	1974-79 1985-86	127+4	12	4	0	10	1	141+4	13
Rose F	1907-08	6	0	0	0	0	0	6	0
Rosebroom F	1921-23	20	2	0	0	0	0	20	2
Rowe G	1963-71	101+4	12	4	0	7	2	112+4	14
Rowett G	1994-95	17							
Roxburgh A	1932-29	57	0	3	0	0	0	60	0
Rush P	1980-82	11	0	0	0	0	0	11	0
Rushton F	1913-14	1	0	0	0	0	0	1	0
Russell K	1996-97	1	0	0	0	0	0	1	0
Salt S	1960-61	18	0	1	0	2	0	21	0
Sanderson C	1905-06	2	1	0	0	0	0	2	1
Sbragia R	1980-82	24+2	1	0	0	1	0	25+2	1
Scarr JG	1896-99	10	0	0	0	0	0	10	0
Scott J	1898-09	309	15	10	0	0	0	319	15
Scott L	1982-83	2	0	0	0	0	0	2	0
Sealey S	1994-95	7							
Seip M	2009-10	7	2	0	0	0	0	7	2
Sendall R	1985-88	6+5	0	0+1	1	2	0	8+6	1
Serella D	1982-84	34+1	3	5	0	5	2	44+1	5
Sermani L	1978-79	1	0	0	0	0	0	1	0
Seward P	1979-80	0+1	0	0	0	0	0	0+1	0
Shankley J	1930-31	5	0	0	0	0	0	5	0
Sharat H	1952-53	1	0	0	0	0	0	1	0
Sharp C	1913-14	3	0	0	0	0	0	3	0
Shaw G	1909-11	6	0	0	0	0	0	6	0
Shaw G	1987-88	4+2	0	0	0	0	0	4+2	0
Shaw M	2004-05	2+9	0	0+1	0	0	0	2+10	0
Shimwell E	1946-57	288	5	36	2	0	0	324	7
Sheedy K	1993-94	25+1	1						
Sheron M	2003-04	28+10	8	1+1	0	2+1	0	31+12	8
Shipman T	1933-37	36	0	0	0	0	0	36	0

Player	Seasons	League App	League Goals	FA Cup App	FA Cup Goals	League Cup App	League Cup Goals	Total App	Total Goals
Shittu D	2000-01	17+2	2	0	0	0	0	17+2	2
Shuttleworth B	1998-00	16+3	1	1	0	3	0	20+3	0
Sibbald J	1914-22	74	15	3	2	0	0	77	17
Sibley E	1937-47	74	0	1	0	0	0	75	0
Siddall B	1983-87								
	1988-89	117	0	10	0	11	0	138	0
Simmonite G	1980-83	63	1	4	0	6	0	73	1
Simpkin C	1971-73	31+3	1	2	0	2	0	35+3	1
Simpson P	2000-02	71+7	13	6	1	5+1	0	82+8	14
Sinclair B	1977-78	0+2	0	0	0	0+1	0	0+3	0
Sinclair T	1989-93	85+29	15						
Singleton T	1960-61	0	0	0	0	2	1	2	1
Skirton A	1966-69	76+1	25	2	1	8	2	86+1	28
Slater WJ	1949-52	32	9	3	3	0	0	35	12
Smailes J	1932-35	92	25	6	0	0	0	98	25
Smalley A	1929-33	25	1	0	0	0	0	25	1
Sluzarski B	2007-08	4+2	1	0	0	0	0	4+2	1
Smalley P	1990-91	6	0	0	0	0	0	6	0
Small W	2008-09	4	1	0	0	0	0	4	1
Smethurst P	1959-60	1	0	0	0	0	0	1	0
Smith B	1979-80	18+1	1	0	0	2	0	20+1	1
Smith K	1954-58	4	4	0	0	0	0	4	4
Smith M	1975-76	8	5	0	0	0	0	8	5
Smith P	1979-80	1	0	0	0	0	0	1	0
Smith W	1932-33	1	0	0	0	0	0	1	0
Snowdon B	1955-60	18	1	0	0	0	0	18	1
Southern K	2002-11	274+39	27	13+1	2	4+4	1	291+44	30
Speak C	1992-93	0+1	0						
Speight T	1900-01	5	0	0	0	0	0	5	0
Spence D	1976-77								
	1979-80	82+3	21	6	1	7	2	95+3	24
Spencer J	1911-12	1	0	0	0	0	0	1	0
Spencer S	1903-04	1	1	-0	0	0	0	1	1
Spooner S	1992-93	2	0						
Stant P	1990-91	12	5	0	0	0	0	12	5
Starkey H	1956-59	2	0	0	0	0	0	2	0
Steele S	1983-84	3	0	0	0	0	0	3	0
Stephenson C	1908-09	1	0	0	0	0	0	1	0
Stephenson L	1950-55	23	10	4	1	0	0	27	11
Sterling RL	1908-09	1	0	0	0	0	0	1	0
Stewart P	1981-87	188+13	56	7	2	10	3	205+13	61
Stirzaker H	1896-03	154	13	0	0	0	0	154	13
Stockley S	2005-06	3+4	0	0	0	0	0	3+4	0
Stonehouse K	1983-86	53+3	19	3	0	1+2	0	57+5	19
Stoneman P	1991-95	39+5	0						
Streets S	1924-26	14	2	4	2	0	0	18	4
Stringfellow I	1992-93	3	1						
Strong G	1997-98	11	1	0	0	0	0	11	1
Stroud W	1921-22	2	0	0	0	0	0	2	0
Sturridge S	1998-99	5	1	0	0	0	0	5	1
Stuart A	1896-99	44	1	0	0	0	0	44	1
Suart R	1946-50	103	0	9	0	0	0	112	0
Suddaby P	1970-80	330+1	10	10	0	30	0	370+1	10

Player	Seasons	League App	League Goals	FA Cup App	FA Cup Goals	League Cup App	League Cup Goals	Total App	Total Goals
Suddick A	1966-77	305+5	65	10+1	2	26+1	9	341+7	76
Summerbee M	1976-77	3	0	0	0	0	0	3	0
Sunderland J	1994-95	0+2	0						
Swan A	1906-09	26	1	1	0	0	0	27	1
Swarbrick L	1903-04	1	0	0	0	0	0	1	0
Swift F	1928-30	3	0	0	0	0	0	3	0
Sylvestre L	2010-11	6+2	0	1	0	1	0	8+2	1
Symons P	1993-94	1	0	0	0	0	0	1	0
Taylor A	1965-71	94	0	4	0	8	0	106	0
Taylor A	2005-06	3	0	0	0	0	0	3	0
Taylor E	1951-58	222	53	20	2	0	0	242	55
Taylor J	1928-29	4	1	0	0	0	0	4	1
Taylor M	1986-92	107+14	43	8	2	6+2	1	121+16	46
Taylor S	2005-06	3+1	0	0	0	0	0	3+1	0
Taylor S	1997-98 2001-05	91+20	44	6+1	9	5+1	4	102+22	57
Taylor T	1900-01	4	0	0	0	0	0	4	0
Taylor-Fletcher G	2007-11	134+15	24	2	0	4+2	1	140+17	25
Teasdale J	1984-85	1+6	1	0	0	0	0	1+6	1
Theoklitos M	2002-03	2	0	1	0	0	0	3	0
Thomas P	1969-70	12+1	0	1	0	0	0	13+1	0
Thomas J	1999-00	9	2	0	0	0	0	9	2
Thomas R	1934-35	6	2	0	0	0	0	6	2
Thompson C	1988-90	27+12	8	1	0	1+4	0	29+16	8
Thompson D	1994-95	17	0						
Thompson F	1896-97	6	0	0	0	0	0	6	0
Thompson F	1914-15	3	0	0	0	0	0	3	0
Thompson H	1977-81	92+7	7	3	0	7	0	102+7	7
Thompson J	1923-24	6	1	0	0	0	0	6	1
Thompson T	1961-69	155+1	2	7	0	11	0	173+1	2
Thompson P	1997-02	38+7	3	0+2	0	4	0	42+9	3
Thomson B	1985-87	50+2	6	1	0	2	0	53+2	6
Thomson H	1969-71	60	0	3	0	5	0	68	0
Thomson R	1933-34	24	1	1	0	0	0	25	1
Thornber S	1992-93	21+3	0						
Thornley B	2002-03	7+5	0	1	0	0	0	8+5	0
Thornton S	2002-03	1+2	0	0	0	0	0	1+2	0
Thorpe L	1910-14	92	1	6	0	0	0	98	1
Thorpe L	1993-97	3+10	0						
Thorpe P	1924-28	113	5	2	0	0	0	115	5
Threlfall E	1900-11	320	10	11	2	0	0	331	12
Tierney P	2006-07	8+2	0	2	0	1	0	11+2	0
Tilbrook C	1925-26	1	0	0	0	0	0	1	0
Tilford A	1926-29	53	0	1	0	0	0	54	0
Tilotson S	1907-09	18	0	0	0	0	0	18	0
Tong D	1974-79	71+8	7	0+2	0	5+3	0	76+13	7
Tongue B	1908-09	4	0	0	0	0	0	4	0
Topping R	1905-06	3	0	0	0	0	0	3	0
Tremelling L	1919-20	7	0	0	0	0	0	7	0
Tremelling W	1924-31	114	43	5	1	0	0	119	44
Tufnell S	1927-33	90	4	6	0	0	0	96	4
Tulloch B	1914-24	178	0	8	0	0	0	186	0
Tully K	1972-74	10+1	0	0	0	1	0	11+1	0

Player	Seasons	League App	League Goals	FA Cup App	FA Cup Goals	League Cup App	League Cup Goals	Total App	Total Goals
Turley H	1913-15	11	0	0	0	0	0	11	0
Turner P	1962-67	10+1	3	1	0	2	0	13+1	3
Upton WS	1928-34	74	25	4	1	0	0	78	26
Varney L	2010-11	24+5	5	0	0	0	0	24+5	5
Varty WC	1933-34	2	0	0	0	0	0	2	0
Vaughan D	2008-11	98+11	4	2	0	2+1	1	102+12	5
Vernon S	2004-08	38+34	19	4+2	1	5	2	47+36	22
Waddell R	1964-67	28	5	1	0	1	1	30	6
Waddington J	1904-08	32	6	1	0	0	0	33	6
Wagstaffe D	1978-79	16+2	1	1	0	2+1	0	19+2	1
Waiters A	1959-67	258	0	10	0	18	0	286	0
Wake B	1906-07	3	0	0	0	0	0	3	0
Waldron A	1977-79	22+1	1	0	0	0	0	22+1	0
Walker C	1983-84	8+1	3	0	0	0	0	8+1	3
Walker R	2000-04	44+36	15	1+2	0	0+1	0	45+39	15
Walker T	1908-09	7	2	0	0	0	0	7	2
Wallace J	1933-48	243	0	7	0	0	0	250	0
Walters CE	1910-11	6	0	0	0	0	0	6	0
Walsh M	1973-78	172+8	72	6	1	8	3	186+8	76
Walsh M	1983-89	145+8	5	8+1	0	10	0	163+9	5
Walton S	2008-09	0+1	0	0	0	0	0	0+1	0
Walwyn K	1987-89	51+18	17	4+1	1	6+1	0	61+20	18
Wann D	1969-72								
	1981-82	24+12	0	4	1	1+1	0	29+13	1
Ward A	1992-93								
Ward R	1977-79	41	0	1	0	3	0	45	0
Wardle W	1948-51	60	1	3	0	0	0	63	1
Warhurst P	2004-05	2+2	0	0+1	0	0	0	2+3	0
Warren H	1924-27	5	0	0	0	0	0	5	0
Warrender D	2005-06	13+2	0	1	0	0	0	14+2	0
Wassell G	1932-36	97	0	5	0	0	0	102	0
Watkinson A	1921-23	10	1	0	0	0	0	10	1
Watmough R	1934-38	100	32	5	3	0	0	105	35
Watson A	1922-36	373	22	17	0	0	0	390	22
Watson A	1992-96	88+27	43						
Watson P	1931-38	171	11	7	1	0	0	178	12
Watt J	1962-63	5	0	0	0	2	1	7	1
Watts J	1998-99	9	0	0	0	0	0	9	0
Wellens R	1999-05	176+15	16	10+2	2	8+1	0	194+18	19
Wellock M	1923-27	26	7	0	0	0	0	26	7
Welsh A	1980-81	1	0	0	0	1+1	0	2+1	0
Welsh A	2007-08	3+17	0	1	0	1+1	0	5+18	0
West G	1960-62	30	0	1	0	2	0	33	0
Weston J	1975-80	97+8	8	5	0	5	0	107+8	0
Weston W	1907-09	42	5	1	0	0	0	43	5
Whalley A	1908-09	5	2	1	1	0	0	6	3
White H	1922-25	70	18	6	1	0	0	76	19
White T	1967-70	34	9	1	0	2	2	37	11
Whiteside F	1908-09	6	0	0	0	0	0	6	0
Whitley J	1999-00	7	0	0	0	1	0	8	0
Whittingham R	1907-09	53	28	0	0	0	0	53	28
Whittingham S	1908-10	48	0	3	0	0	0	51	0
Whittle W	1903-04	4	0	0	0	0	0	4	0

		League		FA Cup		League Cup		Total	
Player	**Seasons**	**App**	**Goals**	**App**	**Goals**	**App**	**Goals**	**App**	**Goals**
Whitworth N	1993-94	3	0						
Wilcox J	2005-06	26	0	0	0	0	0	26	0
Wilcox T	1906-07	37	0	1	0	0	0	38	0
Wiles S	2003-06	14+16	3	1	0	1	0	16+16	3
Wilkinson A	1924-25	5	0	0	0	0	0	5	0
Wilkinson F	1912-13	15	1	0	0	0	0	15	1
Wilkinson A	2006-07	0+2	0	0	0	0	0	0+2	0
Wilkinson J	1931-33	60	16	4	0	0	0	64	16
Williams EL	1898-99	22	1	0	0	0	0	22	1
Williams G	1980-81	30+1	2	2	1	3	0	35+1	3
Williams R	2005-07	18+3	8	0	0	0	0	18+3	8
Williams WD	1924-28	26	13	1	0	0	0	27	13
Wilson B	1976-80	21+10	6	0	0	5+1	0	26+11	6
Wilson F	1897-98	23	1	0	0	0	0	23	1
Wilson G	1911-20	83	14	7	0	9	0	90	14
Wilson H	1928-32	50	1	4	0	0	0	54	1
Windridge D	1983-87	87+12	18	6	0	5	1	98+12	19
Winstanley G	1896-97	2	0	0	0	0	0	2	0
Witham R	1933-38	149	0	7	0	0	0	156	0
Withers A	1950-55	15	6	0	0	0	0	15	6
Wolfe G	1929-31	28	0	2	0	0	0	30	0
Wolstenholme A	1909-12	76	14	5	1	0	0	81	15
Wolstenholme T	1902-05	91	0	1	0	0	0	92	0
Wood G	1971-77								
	1989-90	132	0	4	0	8	0	144	0
Wood N	2005-06	7	0	0	0	0	0	7	0
Wood JW	1922-26	58	0	1	0	0	0	59	0
Woods W	1996-97	3	0						
Worthington N	1997-98	4+5	0	0	0	0	0	4+5	0
Wright A	1987-92	94+7	0	8	0	10+2	0	112+9	0
Wright J	1948-59	157	1	10	0	0	0	167	1
Wright JW	1902-03	7	0	0	0	0	0	7	0
Wright M	1990-91	3	0	0	0	0	0	3	0
Wright R	1925-28	30	1	1	0	0	0	31	1
Wright W	1951-55	14	2	1	0	0	0	15	2
Wright T	2005-06	10+3	6	0	0	0	0	10+3	6
Wylie R	1953-55	11	0	0	0	0	0	11	0
Yallop F	1995-96	3+3	0						
Yarnall HG	1914-15	9	1	0	0	0	0	9	1

Roll of Honour

John D. Cross
Ade Nunnerley
Pete Moore
Mark Chandler
Andrew Lunan
Tom Hellon
Seamus Slowey
Andrew Cogan
Martin & Bill Broadley
Jason Butterworth
Darren Butterworth
Malcolm Andrew
Michael Smith
Richard Walmsley
Tony Butcher
Oliver Verity
Paul & Nikki Eliffe
J. K. Lane
Robert Brown
Samuel Brown
Robert Bolsom
Gaz Cook
Dave Horn
Darren Horn
Derek Parkinson
Simon Fielding
Bryan Bolton
Trevor Hatton
Barry Ward
Cliff Smith
Steve Hutcheon
Peter Duerden
Andy Taylor
Tim Collister
Bob Collister
Phil Corbett
Graham Holgate
Stanley John Gibson
Elgar Williams
Bethan Williams
Rhydian Williams
John Jenkinson
Chris Compton
Chris Pritchard
Dave Booth
Ken Worley 1929-2009
Paul Palgrave
Duncan Cowburn
Mark Cowburn
Nathan Cowburn
Phil Moore
Jim, Gill & Stephen Pyper
Paul Willis
Graham Melling
Clifford Collier (1928-2003)
Rory Monaghan
Alan Greaves
Jim Warwick
Stephen Jenkinson
John Hawkings
Richard Hawkings
Jake Hawkings
Paul Hawkings
Steve Yarwood
Steve Moore
Jamie Trotter
Andrew Day
Mick Turner
Barry Gunston
George Snowden-Pears
Jack Penswick - True Tangerine
David J. Turner
Steven Vincent Armitage
Michael Forrest
David Forrest
Richard Gardner
Carl Hiltunen
Mark Hillary

Chris Bluck
Peter Parr
David Kenneth Allan
Sophie Jayne Allan
Simon Shane
Neal Horrocks
Stephen Bennett
Richard Morton
Lee Morton
Stanley Morton
Steve Brassington
Shane Brassington
Carl T. Goode
Joe Gradwell
Marcus Wilde
Colin McGown
Dave Tomlinson
David & John Akhurst
Francis Alexander Hemsworth
Marco Vidoretti
Dave Hart
Douglas Hanson
David Thompson
Dave Maddox
Danilo "Dan" Ronzani (Bologna)
Bevan Ridehalgh
Nicholas Griffith
Chris Battersby
Alan McGhee (Ayr)
David Pickering
Tony Armstrong
Tony Matthews
Pete Bowley
Robert Cronshaw
Russell Pinfold
Tony Balaam
Steve Haynes
The Whelan Tracy Family
Keith Jenkinson
Patrick Jenkinson
Matthew Jenkinson
Les Smith
Craig Harrop
Ian & Susan Hall
George Gray
Evie Hindle
Graham Hindle
Roy Atkinson
Brian Rayner
Jonathan Parker
Rennie Parker
Graham Cope
Mark Greene
Andy Higgins
Stewart Coleman
Andrew David Coleman
Geoff Birch
John Driver
Paul Latham
Roy James Gilpin
Peter M. Farrow
Daniel South
Harry & Allan Sumner
Sean Doherty
Scott & Derek Greer
Ian Carden
Jonathan Westhead
Stu Williams
Malcolm Evans
Sean, Debbie & Sophie Newbury
Peter James
Wilf Brooks
Rob Stuart
Yorkshire Seasiders
Martin O'Malley
Paul Antony Williams
Andrew Bennett
Billy Lewis
Vincent Howcroft
Harry Curwood
Stewart Meggs
Mark A. Harrison
Paul S. Harrison
Bernard Harrison
David Moy
Ernest Roy Ward
Tim Wilson
Steve Caron

James Caron
Matthew Caron
Daniel Caron
Glenn Bowley
Paul Bowley
Gail Bowley
Jack Bowley
Neil Hunter
Frank Kirby
Graham John Butterworth
Steve Brodie
Chris Oleksy
Gary Douglas Wareing
Gareth Lougher
David Haythornthwaite
Andrew Dickman
Philip Walsh
Peter Capper

ND - #0162 - 090625 - C0 - 234/156/33 - PB - 9781780913803 - Gloss Lamination